Predicting Malicious Behavior

Predicting Malicious Behavior

Tools and Techniques for Ensuring Global Security

Gary M. Jackson, PhD

John Wiley & Sons, Inc.

Predicting Malicious Behavior: Tools and Techniques for Ensuring Global Security

Published by
John Wiley & Sons, Inc.
10475 Crosspoint Boulevard
Indianapolis, IN 46256
www.wiley.com

ISBN: 978-1-118-16613-0
ISBN: 978-1-118-22625-4 (ebk)
ISBN: 978-1-118-23956-8 (ebk)
ISBN: 978-1-118-26418-8 (ebk)

Manufactured in the United States of America

10 9 8 7 6 5 4 3 2 1

For general information on our other products and services please contact our Customer Care Department within the United States at (877) 762-2974, outside the United States at (317) 572-3993 or fax (317) 572-4002.

Wiley publishes in a variety of print and electronic formats and by print-on-demand. Some material included with standard print versions of this book may not be included in e-books or in print-on-demand. If this book refers to media such as a CD or DVD that is not included in the version you purchased, you may download this material at http://booksupport.wiley.com. For more information about Wiley products, visit www.wiley.com.

Library of Congress Control Number: 2012933633

I dedicate this book to the Reverend Manuel Lee Jackson and Linnie Mae Jackson, my loving parents, recently deceased, and my sister, Reita (DeDe) Carringer, and brother, Kevin Lee Jackson.

About the Author

Dr. Gary M. Jackson is an Assistant Vice President and Technical Lead within the CyberSecurity Business Unit at Science Applications International Corporation (SAIC). A behavioral psychologist with specialties in artificial intelligence and automated assessment, Dr. Jackson has designed and developed scores of advanced applications across both corporate and U.S. Government settings. Dr. Jackson's career has spanned academia as Assistant and Associate Professor (University of South Florida), Director of R&D and Treatment Development in various clinical settings, Research Psychologist within the U.S. Secret Service Intelligence Division, Intelligence Officer and Chief of three advanced technology branches within the Central Intelligence Agency, Vice President and Director of Research and Development for Psychological Assessment Resources (PAR), Director of the Center for the Advancement of Intelligent Systems (CAIS) for the American Institutes for Research, and, until recently, the Founder, President, and CEO of Psynapse Technologies in Washington, D.C. Dr. Jackson has extensive R&D and field experience in counterterrorism, counterintelligence, and asymmetric warfare prediction. He was a former President of the Florida Association for Behavior Analysis (FABA). He holds B.A. and Ph.D. degrees from Southern Illinois University–Carbondale and an M.A. degree from University of Illinois. He has completed additional postdoctoral training in neurophysiology at the University of South Florida Medical School. Fusing the behavioral and computer sciences, Dr. Jackson is the inventor of the patented automated behavioral assessment (AuBA) technology, CheckMate intrusion protection system, InMate misuse detection system for insider threat, and automated prediction of human behavior technology.

Credits

Executive Editor
Carol Long

Senior Project Editor
Kevin Kent

Technical Editor
Dr. Eric Cole

Production Editor
Kathleen Wisor

Copy Editors
Caroline Johnson
Gayle Johnson

Editorial Manager
Mary Beth Wakefield

Freelancer Editorial Manager
Rosemarie Graham

Associate Director of Marketing
David Mayhew

Marketing Manager
Ashley Zurcher

Business Manager
Amy Knies

Production Manager
Tim Tate

Vice President and Executive Group Publisher
Richard Swadley

Vice President and Executive Publisher
Neil Edde

Associate Publisher
Jim Minatel

Project Coordinator, Cover
Katie Crocker

Proofreader
Nicole Hirschman

Indexer
Johnna VanHoose Dinse

Cover Designer
Ryan Sneed

Media Project Manager 1
Laura Moss-Hollister

Media Associate Producer
Josh Frank

Media Quality Assurance
Doug Kuhn

Acknowledgments

Although I conceptualized, designed, and led the development of AuBA over the past three decades, it takes very talented developers to pursue, develop, and validate new technology in such a radical area as prediction of human behavior. Skeptics abound, and traditional statisticians loom large. It takes a village to pursue radical new approaches and methodologies. For these reasons, I have many to thank for their dedication, contributions, and effort to make AuBA a reality.

Beginning in the early clinical days, my colleague and lifelong friend Charles Antonelli and I developed methods to alter institutional environments to provide antecedents and consequences to support adaptive behavior and suppress highly inappropriate and maladaptive behavior. The precursors to AuBA were born in those early clinical days, and thoughts started focusing on prediction and not just behavior change. At the time, Lincoln State School in Lincoln, Illinois, was the largest institution for the developmentally disabled in the world. Indeed a challenge; we made a difference.

Carrying what was known as contingency management to Florida at Sunland Center of Miami working with such colleagues as Melinda S. Gentile and then Florida Mental Health Institute (FMHI) at the University of South Florida, I continued in research and treatment development, leading several programs for different populations with serious mental illness. At USF such talented colleagues as Dr. Roger Patterson, Dr. Lawrence Schonfeld, Dr. Louis Penner, Dr. Carla Kelly, David Eberly, and I developed new behavior methods to significantly impact the downward slide of the elderly, and developed methods to reverse the occurrence of serious behavior associated with aging. We found that creating the right environment and providing appropriate behavioral treatment could enhance the lives of many elderly patients. The clinical methods I developed were direct precursors to AuBA.

In 1985, I left academia for the government. Many individuals were key in continuing to pursue significant changes in altering a statistical view of prediction to one with a strong science of human behavior foundation that incorporated proven principles of behavior analysis. At the top of the list of individuals to thank is a very talented developer who after hearing my brief on how we could pursue a new technology for prediction of human behavior stopped what he was doing and joined my team as lead developer within the U.S. Secret Service. Marion Georgieff was a loyal and dedicated professional, and our ideas and concepts starting taking shape in advanced pattern classification and software supported by Special Agents David Bressett, Kenneth Baker, and Phil Leadroot.

Then the missing years — the CIA. During this period of time very special recognition is given to those who must remain nameless. They made those years possible for me and were contributors to, as well as supporters of, the new anticipatory vision. Leaving the CIA, I took a position as Vice President and Director of Research and Development for Psychological Assessment Resources in Lutz, Florida. Working closely with Dr. R. Bob Smith, Cathy Smith, and later Justin Smith as part of the AuBA team, the PAR psychological team helped me to fuse ideas of commercial psychological assessment practices into the developing predictive methodology. The development of interpretive reports was especially important, as well as the insistence on quality development of software that is psychologically based. Coming back to Washington to the American Institutes for Research (AIR), I created the Center for the Advancement for Intelligent Systems (CAIS), which morphed into my own spin-off, Psynapse Technologies, to market the developing AuBA technology. This was a time of exuberant growth in the technology thanks to government funding and the strong support from Mr. Larry Willis, the Defense Advanced Research Projects Agency (DARPA) Program Manager. Larry realized the vision and spearheaded support that made AuBA actually possible. Without Larry's vision and directed support, there would not be the AuBA of today. Other key support from DARPA included Dr. Sean O'Brien and Dr. Robert Hummel. Dr. Ruth Willis at the Naval Research Laboratory (NRL) added significantly to support provided. Special appreciation is expressed to the Office of Naval Research support provided by William Krebs and Anita Berger, as well as the former Deputy Chief of Naval Operations, Former Vice Admiral John Morgan.

Of special note is Byron Raines, who has remained part of the AuBA approach for over 11 years now, and, until taking a new position recently, Joan Wang, who has been a faithful AuBA developer for over 11 years. In addition for the past 22 years, Rosemarie Hesterberg has provided undying support and loyalty and was responsible for suggesting that I use AuBA for network protection. While dedicated staff may come and go, the contributions of these dedicated colleagues rank very high and their fingerprints are all over AuBA. I truly appreciate their dedication not only to the technology but also to supporting the AuBA vision. There are also other notables who contributed to development at this time. Mona Habib lent her Arabic expertise. Helene Mullaney was a key staff member who quickly grasped the concepts and mentored/trained others in the rapidly developing methodology and automation. A born leader as smart as they come, she helped move the technology forward. Bob McMahon was a key contributor to CheckMate and InMate as cyber applications constructed from AuBA technology. AIR Company support provided by Dr. Michael Kane and Sol Pelavin, the talented AIR CEO, was always appreciated and necessary for continued growth.

Spinning off Psynapse Technologies, my wife, Dr. Stephanie Jackson, my Deputy at the time, demonstrated her considerable talent as a professional and former school principal. She provided superb support for all company operations, and for that, I am appreciative. Dr. Terry Gudaitis, Julian Kamil, and Jeff Hall assisted in moving the technology forward on the application side, as well as Byron Raines and Joan Wang. Of special mention is a world-class expert who has supported AuBA since beginning with the CIA. A computer scientist and network intrusion expert, Dr. Eric B. Cole was there at the beginning when we worked out the first cyber network protection prototype for government funding and is still contributing today. Dr. Cole graciously consented to be technical editor for this book and wrote the foreword. Eric is actually a part of the vision of providing a paradigm shift in security. AuBA offers a new approach, and his support as one of the best has been truly appreciated, as have his contributions.

At SAIC, who acquired AuBA intellectual property, special appreciation is expressed to supporters Clay Stewart, Richard Shipman, and Dennis Andersh, as well as Hawaii staff Roger Medd and Brian Banks. Dr. Mary M. Quinn's support as a behavioral colleague has been invaluable. Current support by Roger Tjarks as a Chief Scientist and Julie Taylor as Director of our Cyber operations is especially appreciated. Although many teams have worked on the development of AuBA over the years, the current Columbia, Maryland, team of Byron Raines, Ricky Smith, Garrett Henderson-Tjarks, Gary Cruttenden, Jonathon Conti-Vock, Erin Britz, Kyle Kubin, William Pollock, Kyle Mann, June Liu, and James (Don) Bowers led by the very talented development team leader Paul McAllister, and the Arlington, Virginia, team of Carl Symborski, Marguerite Barton, Geoffrey Cranmer, Jasmine Pettiford, and Kathleen Wipf are at the top. Paul McAllister, as a true collaborator, has made more recent developments a reality through new and improved software application. On a personal note, much appreciation is expressed to my family: Dr. Stephanie Jackson, daughter Ashley Henley and her husband Jason, daughter Kary Borden, and grandchildren Kayla and Jared Borden for supporting me over the decades and tolerating many hours of work above and beyond the norm that was necessary to develop AuBA.

Last, but certainly not least, I would like to acknowledge John Wiley & Sons. Writing the content of a book is the purview of the author, but publishing a book is a collaboration and ongoing interaction between an author and publications staff. From the early collaboration of the book with Carol Long, Acquisition Editor, to the very talented editorial leadership and personal work of Senior Project Editor Kevin Kent supported by content editors Maureen Spears, Rebekah Worthman, and Rayna Erlick, and Technical Editor Dr. Eric B. Cole, I express great appreciation for their talent and patience. I also want to thank all of the staff members who worked on the evolutionary development of AuBA with names just too high in number to list individually, but your many contributions are deeply appreciated. Most important, thank you reader for taking the time to read and study what this village of professionals has done for the future of security.

Contents at a Glance

Contents

Foreword

The ancient Chinese proverb states, "May you live in interesting times." When it comes to cyber security, this statement is definitely true. We cannot go a day without hearing about another organization being compromised. No one is spared. Government, commercial organizations, universities, and non-profits are all being compromised. For many organizations it is a very frightening, frustrating, and scary time because the old tools and methodology that we have used in the past to properly defend our networks no longer work. Organizations are spending tremendous amounts of money, energy, and effort on security, and they are still getting compromised. One executive pulled me aside during a consultant engagement and said, "Be honest with me. Is trying to secure an organization helpless? Should we just give up?" The good news is things are not hopeless and we can get ahead of the curve, but we have to change our way of thinking. As Albert Einstein stated, "We cannot solve our problems with the same thinking we used when we created them."

The threat has changed dramatically over the past 3 years, but our approach to security has not changed. Traditional threats were treated by using reactive security. An organization would wait for an attacker to break in and cause harm, and then it would react to the threat and improve its security. With today's threats increasing and becoming stealthier, targeted, and data focused, reactive security no longer works. Predictive, proactive security is the answer. We need to stop looking for signs of an attack, get inside the mind of the adversary, and understand how it thinks and operates. We need to combine computer science with psychology to get at the root of the problem, not just treat the symptom.

Many years ago while I was working with Dr. Gary M. Jackson, one of the most brilliant scientists and technology visionaries, he briefed me on a concept called CheckMate. The concept was simple. Computers do not attack, people do.

People ultimately write the code, create the malware, and control what is behind any attack. If people are ultimately behind the attack and people are creatures of habit, why not predict human behavior via a computer resulting in more robust defensive measures of prediction? The technology was amazing, but the problem was the world was not ready for it. Ten years ago the idea was way ahead of its time. Gary created technology that would effectively deal with the APT (advanced persistent threat); the only issue was he needed to wait 7 years for the term to be created. In essence, CheckMate needed to wait for the adversary's sophistication to catch up to prove the uniqueness of this technology.

While many people today are talking about the concept and starting to perform research in the area, this book is based on 20 years of validated research on how to catch an adversary. The concepts presented in this book are not things that *might* work; they are proven technologies that *have* worked over and over again.

In reading through this book, the world is now given the details straight from the developer for dealing with sophisticated attacks. Detecting attacks through signatures is old school. Predicting attacks by understanding malicious behavior is the future. If you understand the concepts that are covered in this book, Gary provides a step-by-step detailed handbook of how to get inside the mind of the adversary and provide proper defensive measures to protect an organization today and in the future.

While very few people will have the distinct honor and privilege to learn from the master directly, this book allows everyone to gain the insight and knowledge of what is required to defend a network that will scale from the person who created the fundamental technology for predicting behavior.

— Dr. Eric Cole

Introduction

When we think of, or discuss, human behavior, we are focusing on behavior in the past, present, or future — there are no other options. The past is irrevocable and can be described accurately with hindsight and facts. The present is intriguing, and we can describe it as news. In comparison, the future is elusive, there are no facts, and we are constantly surprised by behavior that could not be anticipated. The fall of the Berlin Wall, the collapse of a major power such as the Soviet Union, and the terrorist attack on September 11, 2001, within the United States were unanticipated. The future, it appears, is exceedingly difficult to predict accurately and in a consistent manner. History teaches us how to describe the past, journalism teaches us how to describe the present, and this book describes how we can accurately predict future human behavior.

I wrote *Predicting Malicious Behavior: Tools and Techniques for Ensuring Global Security* to highlight a new technology that fuses the behavioral and computer sciences to predict future human behavior. The presented technology is based on tested scientific methods, not hopes or guesses as to how future events will unfold. The book presents solid methods that began with a solid foundation of applied behavior analysis (ABA) and describes the current computer science/ artificial intelligence extensions presented in as automated behavior analysis (AuBA). The similarity in acronyms is by design. I wanted to pay homage to ABA as the basic scientific foundation. However, the many extensions, inventions, patents, and automation have demonstrated how clinically based ABA principles can be extended to the accurate prediction of malicious behavior on a global scale.

What is ABA? Applied behavior analysis has its roots in operant psychology and behavior modification fueled by a desire to help others. Basically clinical in nature, this field in psychology focuses on suppressing maladaptive and inappropriate behavior and reinforcing the occurrence of appropriate behavior. There are dedicated practitioners in every state. ABA is known and used internationally. It is a method of behavior change. It's basic tenet is that behavior does not occur in a vacuum but occurs in response to preceding events and situations we call antecedents and is encouraged to occur or not occur by the consequences of the behavior that immediately follow. Clinically, by establishing a baseline of behavior, one can work to modify antecedents or consequences, or both, that are associated with inappropriate behavior to encourage appropriate behavior instead. Any change in behavior can be compared to baseline measures to determine the degree of improvement of the target behavior.

What is AuBA? I developed automated behavior analysis with the assistance of many teams across three decades. The basic principles outlined in ABA of behavior being preceded by antecedents and followed by consequences have been maintained in AuBA. However, AuBA is not a clinical method. It is a new technology for *predicting* human behavior. In contrast, ABA is a behavior change methodology, not a prediction methodology. AuBA is also a new technology that moves away from the classroom or institutional setting where antecedents are confined to an immediate space to a global expansion of worldwide events and situations and how this affects the behavior of adversarial groups and even collective behavior of a country. This is a different ball game! To accurately predict malicious human behavior that serves as a threat to our national security requires technology and science, and it requires invention and discovery.

I started as an ABA clinician being heavily influenced by such pioneers of operant psychology as Dr. B. F. Skinner, researcher and innovator; Dr. Nathan Azrin; and the practical application skills of Dr. Jon Bailey. I developed AuBA by standing on the shoulders of ABA giants. I developed new clinical treatments and, in the process, developed a specialty that focused on severely aggressive and even self-injurious behavior. In 1985 I left the world of clinical treatment development and academia for a position as a Research Psychologist within the Intelligence Division of the U.S. Secret Service. Threat was the focus, and ABA was a start but artificial intelligence and computer science extensions were necessary. But ABA was not designed for such expansive threat faced by our country. Eventually recruited into the Central Intelligence Agency (CIA) as an Intelligence Officer, my respect for global problems grew exponentially, and I was humbled. It was apparent that the advantages of ABA were relevant, but it was just as clear that this venue was not a classroom or institutional environment; this was a global environment and prediction was much more important than clinical intervention.

Although thoughts of prediction started during my clinical days as a licensed Psychologist within the state of Florida and a past President of the Florida Association of Behavior Analysis (FABA), it was very clear that a new methodology and even technology would have to be developed to narrow that immense and daunting number of preceding events on a global basis to just those few that set the stage for an adversary's behavior to occur. However, thanks to scientific methodology, my knowledge of computer science and artificial intelligence, necessity, government funding, and my persistent desire to make a difference in the world of threat to national security, AuBA was born. It now has grown and has been refined to a new emerging science of human behavior on a global scale. It represents a paradigm shift in security. To date, security for the most part means putting into place methods to prevent attacks in the future based on past attacks. Counterterrorism, network security, battlefield strategy, counterinsurgency, and many other forms of security to protect national security are reactive. They are based on past behavior only. They do not anticipate future behavior. AuBA represents a predictive and proactive approach to security. Instead of building defenses based on past attacks only, it can anticipate future malicious behavior so that security can extend to protecting against future attacks. This is a significant expansion of not only behavior principles but also security practices and methods.

Overview of the Book and Technology

The purpose of *Predicting Malicious Behavior*: *Tools and Techniques for Ensuring Global Security* is not just to present AuBA as a new technology but to show you how to view globally based threat with a new predictive perspective and how to use the AuBA tools to predict future malicious and adversarial behavior. It is an extensive presentation of expanded principles of human behavior prediction. If you read the book in its entirety, global threat will be more understandable, and much of the mystery of how to predict future behavior will be removed.

What is new? AuBA has been developed based on a number of discoveries. They are highlighted in the following:

- The antecedent-behavior-consequences (ABC) sequence of ABA holds for AuBA.
- The ABC sequence had to be adjusted drastically to account for global threat (antecedents and consequences are global in nature).
- The complexities of prediction require rather sophisticated pattern classification technology and artificial intelligence to handle the many impending antecedents that surpasses human cognitive ability to identify.
- Specific computer science tools had to be developed to emulate the human process of identifying antecedents and relevant consequences that result in specific behaviors that threaten national security.
- The incorporation of best practices computer science validation methodology is essential for developing automated predictive engines that may be used in real-time prediction of adversarial behavior.
- Tools had to be developed that could extract antecedents from past text accounts of malicious behavior across languages.

- Automated pattern classification required incorporating many heuristics into automation that were acquired over 25 years of experience in predicting malicious human behavior.

- AuBA variants had to be developed that could take as input network packets, physical sensor output, and past text accounts of malicious behavior to build predictive applications across network security, malicious intent from movement patterns, and predictive models from past accounts of behavior.

- With or without the use of technology, the principles and techniques provide a much improved perspective on future malicious behavior.

The increasing threat epitomized by 9/11, serious and increasing cyber threat, domestic and foreign threat, threat of weapons of mass destruction, and insidious insider threat have fueled my development activity and the activity of my research teams over three decades. There simply had to be a better way to protect ourselves than waiting to see what happens and then building defenses based on what has already happened. The current security approach of developing signatures to recognize attacks that have occurred in the past is in many ways an act of desperation. It is an act that says there is no other way. This book presents a different way. Let's anticipate so that we can be better prepared.

Who Should Read This Book

I wrote the book to be useful first and foremost to anyone interested in a new perspective on how future malicious behavior may be predicted accurately and consistently over time. It stands in marked contrast to many works that suggest that prediction of future behavior is not possible. I wrote the book to present evidence that future behavior may be predicted and then proceed to provide examples of future prediction and how to do it.

Following this general statement, the book has a strong leaning toward security personnel, both in counter threat to national security and in network security. We need a paradigm shift to move us away from a reactive, signature detection–based security approach to a more proactive and predictive approach. The principles I present not only make it clear that a proactive shift is necessary but also outline what principles we should shift to.

I highly recommend that every student and practitioner in behavioral psychology and applied behavior analysis read this book. It presents how their field has been extended to extremely difficult global security applications. It is ABA-based as a foundation, and specific methods and innovations are presented to show how advancement can occur in different threat domains. I have worked for three decades to develop this technology. I am very supportive of students wishing to move into this new arena, and there are many theses and dissertations waiting to extend the methods in this book even further. This is the way of science. I will maintain a website (prethreat.com) in which students, their professors, and I can interact and highlight continued advances exerted by continuing research and development. It will be a central place where ideas for expansion and substantive national security issues may be discussed.

Government officials, analysts, and officers are faced with the need to anticipate threat on a daily basis. Having been an intelligence officer faced with the same, often high-pressure, need to be accurate in anticipating threat, I present you with a new approach to help improve accuracy across time. It is up to you to learn it and use it. However, I have provided the detail for you to get started.

Although this book focuses on the prediction of malicious behavior, the principles and techniques hold true for non-malicious behavior, as well. For those readers who want to focus on increasing the occurrence of appropriate behavior and not just on predicting threat, the principles and tools presented are equally as relevant. If this is your interest, you will gain expertise by absorbing the content.

Law enforcement is a critical area of concern. AuBA is relevant for predicting criminal behavior. We are currently in proprietary arrangements with those working in law enforcement, and for that reason I could not provide details. However, we have learned the prediction of criminal behavior or success/nonsuccess in such areas as probation can be determined early so that earlier intervention can take place to help ensure success and prevent recidivism.

Traditional ABA areas are also of great interest. In addition, the book presents how AuBA may be used to understand such individuals as serial murderers like Ted Bundy and Jeffrey Dahmer; Ted Kaczynski, the Unabomber; Timothy McVeigh, the Oklahoma City bomber; the shoe bomber Richard Reid; and the underwear bomber Umar Farouk Abdulmutallab. The book shows how to assess both the individual and the group.

This is basically a start-to-finish book, meaning that it is best read in its entirety from the start. I have endeavored to present principles, move to technology, present the tools, and provide examples, culminating in a walkthrough DVD of the tools and applications and how they may be used.

How This Book and DVD Are Organized

I organized this book into 20 chapters and an accompanying DVD. First, the DVD. It was decided early on in the careful planning of this book between Carol Long, the acquisition editor, and me that the book should include a practical *how-to* DVD. The book would present the new predictive analytics, and the DVD would show how the AuBA tools work and how you can use them. The DVD does just that. It is divided into two major sections:

- The AuBA tools, ThemeMate and AutoAnalyzer, used for developing predictive human behavior assessment/predictive engines
- Specific applications developed from the predictive engines such as the CheckMate Network Intrusion protection system

The book is divided into 20 chapters in four sections. A description of each section follows.

Part I: Understanding the Dark Side: Malicious Intent

This section focuses on malicious behavior and malicious intent from a behavioral perspective. A behavioral approach focuses on the context in which behavior occurs. For example, behavior is preceded by specific events or situations we label as antecedents and are followed by events or situations resulting from the occurrence of the behavior. These are consequences. The antecedent-behavior-consequence sequence is the foundation of applied behavior analysis (ABA) in psychology. ABA is a clinical methodology that is used internationally to basically alter behavior of clients to discourage inappropriate behavior and encourage appropriate behavior. However, global threat and the prediction of specific adversary behavior do not follow from basic ABA methodology, although the antecedent-behavior-consequence sequence is essential. Using this sequence and adding artificial intelligence methods and computer science, I invented automated behavior analysis (AuBA). This section provides the basics of AuBA as applied to such examples as terrorism, serial murder, cyber threat, and other forms of individual and group malicious and threatening behavior. This section provides the basics of AuBA as a new technology to predict future malicious behavior accurately and consistently. Although this serves as an introduction to the diversity of the adversary from an AuBA perspective, AuBA tools and techniques are also introduced.

This part includes the following chapters:

Chapter 1: "Analyzing the Malicious Individual"

Chapter 2: "Analyzing the Malicious Group"

Chapter 3: "Analyzing Country-Level Threats"

Chapter 4: "Threats and Security Nightmares: Our Current Reactive State of Security"

Chapter 5: "Current Network Security"

Chapter 6: "Future Threats to Our National Security"

Part II: Dissecting Malicious Behavior

This second section of the book provides a drill down into the specific and powerful principles of human behavior that form the foundation of AuBA. The principles are provided with real-world examples of significant threat to our well-being and national security. The section provides details on initial methods to analyze the behavior of the malicious individual and malicious group, as well as the national threat directed toward our security. Real-world examples are provided. The section emphasizes the notion that current security across cyber and warfare domains is primarily reactive. The call for a paradigm shift from reactive to proactive and from signatures to prediction is made using AuBA as a technology and a set of methods supporting that paradigm shift. The section highlights cyber threat and network security, as well as asymmetric warfare (imbalance of forces), where a small group can present such a major threat as witnessed during the infamous September 11, 2001, attack within our nation's borders by al-Qaeda. The section ends with a focus on global threat and the relevance of AuBA on that scale.

Part II includes the following chapters:

Chapter 7: "Applying Behavior Principles: Predicting Individual Malicious Behavior"

Chapter 8: "Applying Behavior Principles: Predicting Group Malicious Behavior"

Chapter 9: "Applying a Predictive Methodology: From Principles to Practice"

Chapter 10: "Predicting Domestic Threat"

Chapter 11: "Computer Networks: Protection from External Threat"

Chapter 12: "Computer Networks: Protection from Internal Threat"

Chapter 13: "Predicting Global Threat"

Part III: Applying Tools and Methods

This section provides details on how to model malicious behavior of individuals and groups for the purpose of predicting adversary behavior in the future. It presents the hybrid manual/automated forerunner of AuBA that is still relevant today, as well as the more fully automated AuBA. The use of behavior principles that serve as the foundation to AuBA is demonstrated with such tools as Microsoft Excel to empower those without the AuBA tools to explore the concepts. Following tool-assisted modeling, the AuBA tools, ThemeMate and AutoAnalyzer, are presented. The mastery of the tools is highlighted, with an emphasis on preparing for the analysis of future terrorism.

Part III includes the following chapters:

Chapter 14: "Predictive Capability in Software: Tools for a New Approach"

Chapter 15: "Predictive Behavioral Modeling: Automated Tools of the Trade"

Chapter 16: "Developing AuBA Applications"

Chapter 17: "Mastering AuBA Tools for Real-World Use"

Chapter 18: "Analyzing Future Malicious Behavior"

Part IV: Predicting Malicious Behavior: Tools and Methods to Support a Paradigm Shift in Security

This final section of the book is to prepare you for the details in using AuBA to actually predict future malicious behavior and intent. Specific methodological steps are presented. The chapters emphasize the need for AuBA as a new approach to accurately predict human behavior and how it may be used to develop models to support security applications across cyber and other security-related areas. The section focuses on practical application of models once developed, how to develop predictive models, and the need for such models in today's rising threat on a global level. Keys to how to use the technology are presented to the reader to assist in understanding malicious behavior from an AuBA perspective.

Part IV includes the following chapters:

Chapter 19: "AuBA Future Extensions Today"

Chapter 20: "How to Predict Malicious Behavior: A Walkthrough"

The Accompanying DVD

The DVD for the book is divided into two sections: (1) details in the use of the AuBA tools, ThemeMate and AutoAnalyzer, and (2) demonstrations of CheckMate and InMate, two cyber-based, network protection tools designed to protect networks from external and internal threat, respectively. By observing the instructional DVD, you will be presented with the details of how to conduct AuBA predictive modeling for the prediction of human behavior and with a walkthrough of new technology for network protection that is not signature based or anomaly based. These two applications convert packet-level activity in real time to assessments of human behavior threat and presence of malicious intent.

With Chapter 20 taking you completely through both the manual method and AuBA step-by-step with examples and with the DVD content taking you through all the software and showing you how it works, you have a complete walkthrough of how to predict malicious behavior.

Automated Behavior Analysis: A True Paradigm Shift

This book presents the culmination of 30 years of work to develop and refine a new technology for accurately and consistently predicting malicious human behavior. Although effective as a new approach to not only predicting malicious behavior on a local or global scale, it remains a work in progress. We desperately need a paradigm shift in security. We can no longer afford to wait for a damaging event to happen so that we can prepare signatures to recognize it should the exact attack occur again. We need technology that can anticipate the first-time attack and in time so that mitigation can occur. AuBA is a giant step in that direction. I view the technology presented in *Predicting Malicious Behavior*: *Tools and Techniques for Ensuring Global Security* as a road map for the future — a future that embraces technology that is proactive instead of reactive and predictive instead of a historical documentation as to how we were harmed. The work presented is a beginning dialogue for those interested in prediction of human behavior, enhancements in security, or a better understanding of the dark side that threatens us and our national security. To support this view, I present my contact information below. I intend to be accessible to support research and application.

Thank you.

Gary M. Jackson, PhD

www.pre-threat.com

Reading this book may raise questions of implementation. I am operating a website in support of AuBA predictive modeling. You can access this site at www.pre-threat.com. You can also reach me at gmjack@comcast.net or telephone 443-510-8904.

Understanding the Dark Side: Malicious Intent

In This Part

Analyzing the Malicious Individual

We are all as unique as our fingerprints. No two of us are alike. Even identical twins exhibit different behavior under different circumstances. We are born with a genetic design that dictates our eye and hair color, height, weight, temperament, musical ability, and an immense number of other attributes. However, through life's experiences we are molded by a combination of biology and environment to be who we are and to behave the way we do.

We all respond continuously to events and situations in our environment that precede our behavior. We continually respond to any environmental context in which we find ourselves. As stated in the Introduction, a behavioral perspective considers these preceding events and situations to be *antecedents*. When we do exhibit behavior in the presence of precursor events, our behavior has *consequences*. Antecedents prompt behavior to occur, and consequences maintain it, increase it, or decrease it in the future, based on the desirability of the consequences. I refer to the antecedent-behavior-consequence sequence as *ABC* simply to use a less wordy term. In this chapter, you will learn to use ABC principles to help analyze malicious behavior. In later chapters you will learn how to use the concepts along with new methods to accurately anticipate malicious behavior.

Analyzing the Unique Individual

The method of behavior analysis presented in this book may be used to analyze and anticipate the behavior of an individual or group. When you compare the two, perhaps surprisingly, the individual often exhibits more behavioral variety than a group. Members of a group typically share common beliefs or are united for a common cause. The commonality among the members means that the group may act as a single entity, at least in some ways. They may respond to similar antecedent conditions with similar behaviors and are reinforced by similar consequences of their actions. Street gang members may dress alike, use the same slang, target the same individuals for harm, and remain in the gang because of bonded similarities. Although there are individual differences even within the members of a group, the commonalities simplify group analysis.

To ensure adequate analysis of the individual, the following are two of the most important principles to follow:

- First, we need to ensure that we have adequate and multiple observations of behavior under various conditions.
- Second, observations must include adequate descriptions so that we can identify the who, what, when, where, and how of past behaviors.

In the absence of observation we can use subject matter expert (SME) descriptions, but it is essential that the SMEs are knowledgeable.

DEFINITION A *subject matter expert* is someone who maintains knowledge and details of a specific topic at a level that is more extensive than that of others. For example, a cardiologist attains and maintains knowledge of the functioning of the heart that is much deeper than that possessed by other individuals.

We want to identify the antecedents, behavior, and consequences of past behavior (see Chapter 7 for details). Therefore, we seek to identify what environmental conditions serve as antecedents that precede the behavior of interest, as well as what follows the behavior — the consequences. Multiple examples of all three components — antecedents, behavior, and consequences, in that order — allow us to predict the person's future behavior when similar antecedents and the promise of similar consequences are present.

As a simple example to demonstrate the concepts, if we observe pedestrians crossing a busy intersection, we know that the crosswalk light will flash that it is okay to cross. The antecedents in this case are the flashing crosswalk light, followed immediately by the behavior of interest — pedestrians crossing the intersection. The consequence is that pedestrians cross successfully without injury and with minimal risk. If the crossing light is not on and cross traffic is occurring, we can predict that pedestrians will not try to cross the intersection. Not crossing when the flashing crosswalk sign is not on with oncoming traffic again ensures safety at the intersection as a consequence. Therefore, we can predict with a high probability of success that when there is oncoming traffic, pedestrians will cross when the flashing crosswalk signal is on and will not cross when the signal is off. The antecedent controls the behavior.

However, with continued observation we are likely to determine that if the crosswalk light is not on and there is no oncoming traffic, pedestrians will likely cross quickly. This is a more complex and more accurate analysis. The behavior of crossing the intersection can be predicted accurately under two antecedent conditions: (1) the flashing crosswalk signal is on and traffic is stopped, and (2) the crosswalk signal is flashing or not flashing, but there is no oncoming traffic. Therefore, the two methods of crossing are likely to occur in the future because both lead to successful consequences — a safe crossing of the intersection.

Malicious behavior is very similar to this oversimplified example. Such behavior does not just happen. It occurs in response to environmental antecedents and is reinforced by the consequences of the behavior. For example, the presence of an abortion clinic and the comings and goings of the staff serve as antecedents (A) to an abortion clinic bomber. Committing a bombing is the behavior (B) that we are interested in predicting. The consequences (C) of the bombing, such as disruption of abortions stemming from physical damage, injury, or even death of the workers, reinforces the act of bombing. This ABC sequence forms the basis of behavioral modeling that has been shown to be predictive. The ability to predict future behavior is not based on a specific type of statistical method or detailed study of the behavior of interest. Prediction of behavior is based on the underlying antecedents and consequences associated with past behavior.

NOTE The ability to predict future behavior is not based on a specific type of statistical method or calculation. Accurate anticipation of behavior is based on the underlying model and the components of behavior used to develop the predictive model.

Interestingly, the ability to predict behavior does not rely on the individual to be rational or sane. In many of our past clinical cases, we used applied behavior analysis to help treat psychotic episodes, hallucinations, delusional talk, and other forms of abnormal behavior. Even in cases where a person is considered mentally ill or deficient, his or her behavior may still be predicted accurately if ABC behavior principles are applied diligently. In short, everyone responds to the environment from their own perspective, regardless of whether the antecedent conditions are present, or valid, from their perspective. Whether the target of the analysis is a world leader, a terrorist, or the criminally insane, the ABC components help us analyze and predict their behavior.

> **NOTE** We don't have to thoroughly understand *why* a person commits
> a specific type of malicious act to predict its occurrence in the future. We
> do, however, need to identify the precipitating antecedent events and the
> desired consequences that followed each occasion of the malicious behavior
> in the past.

As a real example, Jeffrey Dahmer was a serial killer who targeted young males. Therefore, young males, their activities, and the locations they frequented became antecedents to Dahmer's behavior of visiting these same locations. Once a victim was targeted in one of these locations, the victim himself became an antecedent that prompted Dahmer's next step, which was to approach the victim. During Dahmer's interaction with the potential victim, that person's responses served as antecedents to Dahmer's approach of inviting the victim to his home, where subsequent molestation and death were waiting. If the sequence of behaviors was successful, we can predict with some certainty that the murders would continue.

Dahmer murdered 17 males over 13 years, one at a time. The antecedents to the multiple attacks, the actual behavior of murder, and the sexual molestation after death were all highly similar to each other. Dahmer's actions were an example of how malicious, fatalistic behavior may be patterned. His serial murders were also examples of behavior increasing in frequency because of the consequences (his not being apprehended and his ability to engage in sexual molestation). Until he was caught, he was free to continue his murders at an increasing pace. Finally, he was apprehended after a victim narrowly escaped and brought police to Dahmer's house. When the police arrived, they discovered pictures of young murdered men, a head in the refrigerator, and disintegrating bodies in a container of flesh-eating and bone-dissolving chemicals.

An analysis of the behavior across many individuals indicates that antecedents, behavior, and consequences are specific to the individual. The more bizarre the case example, the more assured we can be that the individual is responding to conditions in ways that are very different from our normal behavior.

The following sections present analyses of three persons with malicious intent as examples of the many and varied malicious cases:

- Richard Reid, the infamous shoe bomber
- Ted Bundy, the infamous serial killer
- The general, anonymous individual cyber attacker

These examples are purposely very different — for example, in the case of Ted Bundy, the subject could be considered to be mentally disturbed. Still, in each case the behaviors described in the examples, however repulsive, can be analyzed for predictive patterns using the methods presented in this book. The latter case, the cyber attacker, is meant to be unidentifiable to demonstrate that the identity of an individual is not a requirement to conduct a behavior-based analysis.

Richard Reid: The Shoe Bomber

On December 22, 2001, Richard Reid boarded American Airlines flight 63 bound for Miami, Florida, from Paris, France. It was less than 14 weeks after the devastating al-Qaeda 9/11 attacks against the World Trade Center in New York City and the Pentagon and an aborted airliner attack downed in the fields of Pennsylvania when passengers intervened. En route, Reid took his seat like all the other passengers, but he wasn't like the other passengers. He was reportedly intent on killing everyone aboard the flight before the plane would reach Miami. Perhaps encouraged by the events just 14 weeks earlier (the infamous al-Qaeda 9/11 attack) and his self-proclaimed identification with al-Qaeda, Reid was serious, was prepared, and would kill himself along with the other passengers in the attempt. His chosen weapon was 10 ounces of pentaerythritol tetranitrate (PETN), a powerful explosive that, if detonated, would bring down the plane into the depths of the Atlantic Ocean.

Reid had received terrorist and explosives training in Pakistan and Afghanistan. He considered the United States the enemy, and he was on a quest to attack the evil country. Consistent with past terrorist attacks, the plan was to commit a horrific attack that would cause shock and despair.

The Event

The actual event that transpired was apparently different from what was planned. On the day before the incident, Reid attempted to board the same American Airlines flight but was prevented from doing so. His appearance was unkempt, and he had no luggage. This was enough to raise suspicion among cautious security personnel. Questioned but not held, Reid missed the flight. He successfully boarded the same flight the next day, December 22. During the flight, Reid attempted to light a fuse with a match. The short fuse led to explosives hidden in his shoe. Alert passengers smelled the match and reported it. Confronted by an alert flight attendant, Reid tried twice to light the fuse in his shoe, and it did not start. Restrained and then arrested, he eventually pleaded guilty to all eight counts brought against him, including attempted murder and attempted use of a weapon of mass destruction. Reportedly defiant and displaying no remorse, Reid proclaimed during his trial that he was the enemy of the United States and expressed allegiance to al-Qaeda. He was sentenced to life imprisonment with no chance of parole.

The Motivation

Using applied behavior analysis, motivation is seen as identified antecedents and consequences of specific behavior. We can't see inside the person, but we can see what antecedents he responds to and what follows the behavior that is desirable to him. We can only infer inner motivation, but we can actually measure the observable ABC components. For example, antecedents can include reported U.S. actions and past terrorist events, as well as receiving training, being provided with a bomb, having a plan for using the bomb, arranging a flight, and boarding the plane. These events can be counted, measured in length of time, and, as such, form the basis of a scientific analysis.

Reid's bombing attempt can be viewed as a behavioral chain. Such a chain occurs as a series of antecedents (A), behavior (B), and consequences (C). In a behavioral chain, consequences of the first behavior, if successful, serve as antecedents to the second behavior, which then has consequences, as shown in Figure 1-1. These consequences then serve as antecedents to the third behavior in the sequence, followed by consequences of the third behavior, and so on, until the final behavior is completed. In this way, complex behavior can occur as a sequence of events. If an ABC sequence fails during one of the steps, the chain breaks down, and the ultimate event, even if planned, does not occur, unless there is a second behavior chain to follow if the first fails. If there is, the second plan occurs when failure at a step serves as an antecedent for initiating the second plan.

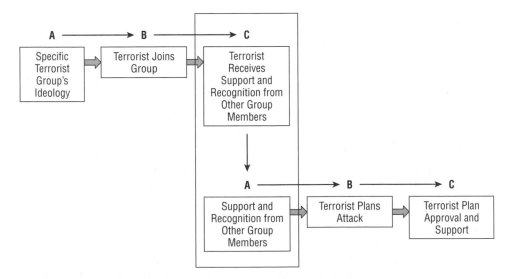

Figure 1-1: A behavioral chain in which a complex sequence of events may be described as consequences of one behavior becoming antecedents to a second behavior and so on until the entire chain is completed.

Reid either did not have a backup plan or was prevented from initiating it. The disruption of the plan came in the form of flight attendants who attempted to stop him from lighting a fuse on two occasions. Eventually, after the struggles with the flight attendants, Reid was subdued with the assistance of fellow passengers. For Reid, a series of chained events leading to the attempt was clear. Reid had planned the event for some time, had received training, was provided with bomb materials, and identified with al-Qaeda. He had followed a sequence of events that led to the end goal — attempting to light the fuse to explosives that, if detonated, would have brought down the flight.

Causes

The causes of terrorism are as varied as terrorist groups. However, Reid identified with al-Qaeda and, as such, incorporated the group's motivations, goals, and objectives. Targeting may be complex. Although primarily civilian, the World Trade center symbolized *towering* success and Western greatness and might. The vehicle for Reid's planned act was American Airlines containing civilians, bound for the United States. Combining this fact with the 9/11 attacks and the motivation, goals, and objectives of al-Qaeda, Reid's selection of the target and his subsequent actions are clear in retrospect. This was his chance to achieve infamy and to make his mark against a proclaimed enemy — the United States.

A Behavior Analysis

Analyzing Reid's behavior raises questions about his true purpose. On the day before the incident, Reid had tried boarding the same flight but with no luggage, and his appearance was sloppy enough to raise suspicion. Those intent on committing malicious behavior in public typically either attack immediately or attempt deceptive behavior by hiding in plain sight while they prepare for a malicious attack. It would be unusual for a terrorist with past training to attempt to board a flight with insufficient preparation, no backup plan, and an appearance so unusual as to raise suspicion. Terrorists often commit acts by blending in with the crowd. Reid did not blend.

During the flight, Reid attempted to light a fuse leading to the shoe that was then in his lap while passengers sat around him. It was obvious that the smell of a match would be noticed. For example, a lighter that would not have the sulfur odor of a match could have been used. The lighting of the shoe fuse could have been completed in the restroom, away from the passengers, with a gas lighter or an electric igniter so that Reid would not have been detected as easily. Last, the consequences of the detonation would likely have been the loss of a plane and lives in the Atlantic Ocean. Given the depth of the Atlantic, it may have never been retrieved properly and, therefore, difficult to determine the cause of the crash.

Given the *apparent* ineptness of the act, it is quite possible that the incident actually occurred as planned. When Reid was apprehended, the media produced a flurry of articles and television and radio reports about the incident. Media attention was heavy. Many articles dubbed Reid "the shoe bomber," and, as a result, we are still taking off our shoes at airport security lines 11 years later. The impact of the incident has been remarkable and exists only because Reid was apprehended and prevented from carrying out an actual bombing.

In my opinion, the Richard Reid incident was a success. He did not die in the process, and because of the detection of his overly obvious behavior, security practices have been affected at great cost for the past 11 years — with no end in sight. The media coverage of the incident provided consequences. Reid was allowed to make statements about his cause in court. His picture has been widely disseminated. His cause has been publicized. The incident has likely had more of an impact without bringing the plane down than if the explosion had actually occurred.

Because he was jailed, we will never know if Reid would have made another attempt. However, behavior principles also include modeling. We can review the extensive work of practitioners such as Albert Bandura to explore this interesting area in detail. Modeling basically refers to the process of one person's imitating the behavior of another. For example, if a person with malicious intent observes (including reading detailed accounts of) another's behavior that appeared to be successful, the second person may repeat the behavior. We typically call this *copycat* behavior, and we see its occurrence in criminal behavior.

To point to the possible reasoning that the Richard Reid incident was successful, a close repeat occurred 8 years later on Christmas Day. Umar Farouk Abdulmutallab boarded Northwest Airlines flight 253 from Amsterdam to Detroit — another flight leaving Europe for a destination in the United States. Abdulmutallab had the same chemicals in his underwear that Reid had in his shoe. No doubt they were in his underwear because of the potential to have shoes checked by security because of the Reid incident. Reportedly, Abdulmutallab returned from the restroom, placed a blanket over his lap, and lighted his pants. Again, there was no explosion, although the terrorist received burns. He too was apprehended. The incident received widespread media coverage, which contained the perpetrator's message.

Even if the underwear bombing was modeled after the shoe bombing, it is our experience that modeled behavior is just that — only the behavior is copied. The second person commits similar terrorist behavior but in reaction to antecedents that fit his cause and context. The consequences may be very different. In this way we can see similar terrorist attacks from different groups in response to different antecedents.

The direct and obvious success of both Reid and Abdulmutallab's *attempted* airliner bombings was that both terrorists evaded airport security and spawned widespread media attention as a result of being apprehended. The latter incident raised considerable concern and new scrutiny of airport security. As is obvious with the Reid incident, the primary, typically reactive, security practice resulting from the attempt was inspection of shoes. This provided some cause for concern and fuel for late-night comedians when the underwear bombing attempt was reported. Would we be required to remove our underwear? Obviously not. However, because we can't remove our underwear, we have seen an increase in the use of body scanners.

What is the next step? Many security lines at airports now check belts and shoes and use scanners. The result will be that terrorists may simply alter their approach. Our security posture is not only reactive but also literal. In the examples given, the explosives simply moved from the shoe to the underwear. Given that terrorists alter their tactics based on our security policies, we may be approaching a body cavity bombing attempt if airliners remain a vehicle to support the incident. Because of the location of a body cavity bomb, it is not likely to be accidentally discovered. If the intent is truly to bring down an airliner full of innocent civilians, we are more likely to witness a suicide-bombing explosion in an airliner.

> **NOTE** *Automated behavior analysis* **(AuBA) is the automation and extension of applied behavior analysis for the purpose of predicting malicious behavior. Patented tools assist in automating the formerly manual process to achieve rapid and accurate behavioral modeling on a global security basis. The accompanying DVD demonstrates how the AuBA tools and applications can work in real time.**

Ted Bundy: The Infamous Serial Murderer

Theodore ("Ted") Robert Bundy was one of the most brutal serial murderers in U.S. history. Bundy shattered many views of the serial murderer. He was a law student, was described as handsome and well mannered, and was interested in politics. Yet he was a cold-blooded killer who targeted attractive young women. He became an expert at attracting women, convincing them to go to a remote location, and then killing them, often violently. Although he admitted to 30 murders, new evidence has surfaced to indicate that he may have committed many more.

Bundy developed a skill for convincing selected targets to accompany him to remote locations, where he could kill them without being seen. He would have sex with the corpses. On occasion, he would behead the victim and keep the head in his house. He was a self-described despicable human being who would use a faked injury or need for assistance to lure his victims. He would wear a cast, use crutches, and even fake police identification as a means to weaken the chosen victim's defenses and to allay her suspicions.

Bundy was brutal, often beyond words. He often bludgeoned his victims using a crowbar. His behavior occurred in three stages:

1. He would select and attract a victim.

2. He would transport and then kill her.

3. He would engage in sex with and desecrate the corpse.

Each stage was honed as a set of skills strengthened by continued success (desirable consequences for the perpetrator). On occasion he would alter the pattern, but the killings were notable more for their strong similarities than for their differences.

Similarities of Targets

Bundy selected his targets based on similarities. All the victims have been described as attractive young females. They all had long dark hair; the hair was parted down the middle; and many were associated with college. His selection of targets for his attacks was highly specific.

The Motivation

Motivations are complex and often difficult to identify. Richard Reid committed a public act that was highlighted by his apprehension. In contrast, Ted Bundy committed private acts with the objective of not being detected or apprehended. More similar to a Jeffrey Dahmer, serial murderers must plan carefully and hone their skills to separate a victim from others, isolate the person, and kill him or her while remaining undetected. Because the acts are committed by these individuals in private, it is fair to say that public attention, media exposure, and detection are not contributing factors to the cause of the repeated behaviors. It is clear that when such heinous crimes are committed, the person is deranged, with motivations that are likely never to be discovered. It is even possible that the perpetrator himself could not describe the reasons for his actions. The causes are complex and deeply seated.

However, a behavior analysis can provide insight in such serious cases of flagrant abuse against humanity. Although we don't know why Bundy committed such acts, we can determine observable antecedents for him that included young, attractive women. Antecedents for Jeffrey Dahmer included young males. Consequences were similar to some extent. The consequences of killing the victim in both cases were that sexual molestation and dismemberment could occur.

Behavior analysis can provide the types of insights that would otherwise be lost. Behavior analysis is crucial in cases where there is not the possibility to observe the behavior we are trying to predict or influence. By studying past behaviors, we can gain a better understanding of how serial murderers operate. When we compare Dahmer and Bundy, we see the behaviors of luring a target to a private location and the brutal, sexually oriented behavior of the perpetrators are similar. In one case, the targets were exclusively male, and in the other case, they were exclusively female.

Today, we face many adversaries that target the United States, its citizens, and our national infrastructure. These adversaries, whether terrorists, insurgents, or cyber hackers, are usually not known to us until after the fact and, in many cases, never known. Often, all we have are examples of their behaviors. The examples may be in the form of reports, news articles describing past attacks, or SMEs who know extreme details about past behaviors. The lack of direct observation of behaviors poses problems for many forms of analysis. However, applied behavior analysis and automated behavior analysis, with their reliance on identifying preceding antecedents and following consequences, provide a means to better understanding not only adversary behavior but also in the case of the latter, a mechanism and set of tools to predict it.

Examples of past cases provide a mechanism by which we can learn and practice behavior analysis concepts and methods and not worry about passing along sensitive information from a current security-sensitive case.

Determining the Complexities Underlying Individual Malicious Behavior: A Behavior Analysis

The stages in the process in which Bundy started with victim selection and ended with post-death behavior had similarities to other cases, for example, Jeffrey Dahmer, as noted earlier in the chapter. In both cases the length of time between murders decreased over time; the killings started to occur more frequently. The ultimate consequence that ended the chain of events for each victim was the interaction with the corpse after death. In both serial cases, the process started with target selection and acquisition. In both cases, the victim had to have enough trust to join the killer and move to a location less likely to result in detection. In a recent documentary on serial killers, a former FBI profiler indicated that these different locations are referred to as *scenes*. Typically, the more scenes, the more complex the thinking of the perpetrator and the more careful the methods of selecting the target, of attracting the target, and of committing the murder. For Bundy, the stages described can be analyzed with the antecedents and consequences of the behavior defining each stage.

Table 1-1 is a high-level overview of an analysis of Bundy's serial killer behavior. The analysis depicts three sequential stages, leading from selection of the victim through corpse manipulation and sexual activity. Each stage is defined as a major behavior (target selection, transporting/killing the victim, and post-death corpse desecration/sex). Each stage of behavior is associated with common antecedents and consequences.

Table 1-1: Dissecting Ted Bundy's Murders

STAGE	ANTECEDENTS	BEHAVIORS	CONSEQUENCES
Isolating the target as the victim	Age (youth), attractive, female, long hair, dark hair, straight hair	Approach target, fake injury or identity, wear cast, use crutches, request assistance	Victim in car
Transporting and killing the victim	Volkswagen Beetle, victim in passenger seat	Handcuff victim, hit victim with blunt-force object, render victim unconscious	Victim incapacitation complete
Post-death sex/corpse mutilation	Victim is dead, corpse	Sex with corpse, decapitation, mutilation, return to victim and repeat behaviors	Control over corpse, completion of sexual activity, corpse desecrated or decapitated

Each depicted stage in the behavioral chain was reinforced by the consequences of the behavior of that stage. Stage 1 began with selecting a target victim. Antecedents to the selection were age (young), gender (female), long dark straight hair, and attractiveness. The presence of these antecedents under the right conditions would prompt Bundy to fake an injury to attract the victim. Once the victim responded, Bundy would request assistance or otherwise try to get the target into his Volkswagen Beetle. (In one case he impersonated a police officer and asked the victim to go the station with him.) The act of the victim getting into his car reinforced Bundy's behaviors up to this point. The objective was to select the target and get her into his domain, where he had control and would be less likely to be identified.

Once the victim — not knowing that this would be her last voluntary act on Earth — accompanied Bundy in his car, Bundy moved to the next stage. This stage was to incapacitate the victim so that he could carry out his ultimate objectives. The form of incapacitation typically was violent and painful if the young lady was not rendered unconscious. It could include being handcuffed, being hit in the head with a crowbar, or suffering any other form of blunt-force trauma. What is important to realize in the Bundy cases is that victim's death was not the final objective. It was an interim objective to leave the victim in the ultimate state of submission. After the victim's death, Bundy could initiate his final objective. This included sex with the corpse, mutilation, and often repeated visits to the site to engage in the same behaviors until the disintegration of the body no longer supported the sexual degradation.

It is likely that if this chain of behaviors had been prevented from occurring at any stage, the behavior would have ceased for that time period and that target. It is more likely that Bundy would have waited for a new situation with a new victim. However, Bundy was successful in his repetition of behaviors. He had honed his skills to the point where he could rely on obtaining the assistance of an attractive and trusting young lady who fit his target profile.

Removing Subjectivity and Bias from the Behavior Analysis

Perhaps the most surprising fact of the Bundy case is that he received marriage proposals from young women while on death row. He orchestrated his own defense and even received positive comments from the judge upon his sentencing to death. The judge said that Bundy would have made a good attorney and that he had no animosity against him. This event is surprising given the path of destruction and devastation Bundy left, affecting not only his victims but also their families. It does demonstrate that Bundy was charismatic and used this trait as a tool to win over others.

Behavior analysis provides a method to remove subjectivity and bias. It provides a scientific set of methods that can identify key elements of behavior to help us understand better how behaviors occur over time. This is precisely why we need behavior analysis and its unbiased assessment of behavior. Again, the methods do not depend on a rational world.

We need behavior analysis to objectively analyze antecedents, behavior, and consequences of malicious intent so that we can avoid the seductions that Bundy was able to orchestrate all the way to the electric chair. Whether we are examining Jeffrey Dahmer, Ted Bundy, or anyone else who exhibits severe malicious intent, it is clear that behaviors are complex and must be dissected for us to understand them fully. Identifying antecedents and consequences does not depend on psychological, psychiatric, sociological, or family background — it focuses on the objective identification of key environmental events and situations that support the continued occurrence of the behavior. Last, the methods provide a mechanism to both predict and influence the occurrence of future behavior.

The Individual Cyber Attacker

The Internet is one of the most impressive technological advances of our lifetime. Humans exist by communicating, and the Internet provided a new, instantaneous method of doing so. It led to an evolution of communication that now includes intranets, social media sites, websites to meet anyone's needs and desires, webcams placed literally all over the globe, instant financial transactions, and instant news. But the new technology has also attracted malicious intent and behavior that is moving as fast as, if not faster than, the actual technologies. More important, the Internet is rife with malicious intent, and we do not know the perpetrators. Again, this is a primary reason for using behavior analysis methods to better anticipate future cyber attacks.

The lone hacker has evolved from what is known as an ankle biter, script kiddie, or nuisance hacker to a sophisticated hacker capable of wide-ranging damage or theft. The situation is worsening, and both ankle biters and more sophisticated hackers remain. In total, their numbers and sophistication have increased. However, behavior principles can be used to understand how such behavior occurs. With such understanding, new technology can follow to intervene and prevent damage and theft.

Identifying the Threat from the Lone Cyber Attacker

In the early days of the Internet, the public simply did not understand the technology. Therefore, hackers of that era were granted the aura of *genius*, even though they could have been skipping school and avoiding education at the time. They typically were young, members of the hacker community, and learning by doing, sharing code, and seeking vulnerabilities to exploit. Hackers were divided into two groups: those who stated they were doing good, and *crackers*, who had malicious intent. However, a hacker who claims to do good by entering networks or applications uninvited to find their security vulnerabilities and then notify the owners is much like a stranger breaking into your house to check your security system. It is often a bogus justification. I don't want anyone getting into my computer network or any of my applications uninvited, no more than I want someone breaking into my house or car.

NOTE For simplicity, this book uses the term *hacker* to describe anyone who enters networks and applications uninvited.

As time passed from the 1980s and 1990s into a new century, it was clear that hacking had more rewards than simply recognition from peers. Money could be made by damaging or stealing information residing within protected networks; money could be made by stealing proprietary information and selling it to a competitor; and money could be made by stealing classified information and selling it to a foreign government. An organization might also pay a hacker to shut down a competitor's network with something as simple as a denial-of-service (DOS) attack. (Such an attack simply directs a waterfall of information or requests at a network so quickly and in such large amounts that the network cannot function.) More recently, credit card numbers, identities, and banks are being targeted at an increasing rate.

The individual attacker can show malicious behavior in a variety of ways. He or she has vast latitude with time, freedom of action, available code, and the high probability of not being caught. A new hacker might carry out his or her first attacks with some apprehension. The fear of being detected fades away as the individual learns how to be deceptive and realizes how difficult it is to be detected.

As stated, behavior principles indicate that if behavior is successful, it will continue. It may even increase in frequency. In short, it may escalate. There are many cases of beginning hackers becoming very good at what they do very quickly. Repeated acts followed by success as a consequence increases the behavior's occurrence over time. Success takes many forms for a hacker. Success in maliciously affecting sites, evading capture, or even avoiding detection, and perhaps identifying with the many movies and TV shows that depict hackers as the elite, work to bolster future hacking behavior. With practice come greater skill and greater knowledge.

NOTE The more a hacker hacks, the better he or she becomes. Practice, and available hacking code, makes perfect.

Catching a hacker takes excellent forensics, expensive investigation resources, and a solid reason to prosecute. As a result, until protection technology improves, effective hacking is here to stay and grow.

Hacking has become more sophisticated. In recent years, it has become apparent that advanced persistent threats (APTs) may be one of our most serious concerns. APTs can come from a foreign state-sponsored intelligence service that is always present and waiting to gain access. As pointed out by my SANS instructor friend and colleague, Dr. Eric B. Cole, when an unsuspecting user clicks a seemingly harmless link, the damage may already be done. One of many APT-vigilant programs may be installed on the user's hard drive by means of the innocent click and immediately begin monitoring the user's actions to capture user IDs and passwords. Of course, as soon as the hacker has the user ID and password, he or she can access the network at will as an approved user and can cause significant harm or steal restricted information.

In the past, we associated malicious intent with the person causing the damage. We now have to broaden this concept. The malicious intent may be part of an APT organized threat, but the innocent individual inside an organization may be the unwitting participant who unlocks the security doors for the malicious service. Malicious intent and behavior must now be broadened to include the behaviors of the inside innocent employee who simply does not know about or practice good security policy.

Recognizing the Power of Being Anonymous

It is easier to be malicious if the probability of being caught is small to nonexistent. Certain events and situations in the environment actually suppress behavior. For example, a yellow traffic light turning red as you approach suppresses your driving through the intersection. When the light turns green, the color serves as an antecedent to driving through the intersection. If you follow the antecedent rules, you may continue to drive through intersections with a low probability of an accident (successful consequences). The individual hacker encounters very few situations in which hacking behavior must be suppressed. Because hacking activity may be bounced through different servers (relays), it is difficult to impossible to conduct an actual traceback under normal circumstances. A person can remain anonymous in the midst of a flurry of hacking activity. Anonymity spawns the courage to attack. After all, the victim doesn't know who you are. This is even more true if networks or sites are attacked at random. The hacker simply continues attacking different sites until he or she is successful.

Although there is only a slight chance that a hacker will be identified, precautions can still be taken. As the individual attempts to hack into sites, he acquires deceptive practices to maintain his anonymity. In studying hacking in detail, I have reduced the many factors that are associated with hacking to just two significant variables if we are concerned with external threats only. To be a successful hacker and be a significant threat, one needs only:

- To have the *expertise* to conduct effective hacking
- To be *deceptive* to ensure not being caught

Chapter 17 discusses in detail my patented CheckMate and InMate applications, produced by SAIC:

- **CheckMate** converts samples of network packets into the behavioral measures of the degree of *expertise* and *deception* present at any one time for every external user entering a network.
- **InMate**, similar in construction, converts users' network activities into *intent to engage in misuse* and *deception* for all insiders (employees, contractors, interns, and so on).

The hypothesis in conceptualizing CheckMate was that if expertise (E) and deception (D) are simultaneously higher than preset thresholds, malicious behavior is occurring or will occur in the very near future (in seconds). If high E and D occur at the same time and the option is set, CheckMate can intervene and block the potential offender's connection. InMate works in a similar manner, except that if an insider threat is identified, an alert is immediately forwarded to security. Most important, CheckMate (working to protect against external threats) and InMate (working to protect against internal threats) provide a combined approach that is unparalleled. The dual external and internal threat protection that concentrates on true human behavior, as opposed to network activity, is a totally new security methodology.

CROSS-REFERENCE AuBA applications to address both external and internal computer network threats are discussed in Chapters 11, 12, and 17 (CheckMate and InMate products). The DVD contains demonstrations of the applications working.

CheckMate and InMate are constructed from automated behavior analysis (AuBA) technology. They are good examples of new, proactive security technology that is not based on signatures or anomaly detection. The differences between this new technology and signature and anomaly detection are explained in detail in Chapters 5 and 12. The new technology works on the basis of real-time behavior assessment methods presented in this book. By applying behavior principles and techniques and focusing on human malicious behavior, as opposed to network behavior, new proactive protection technology is surfacing. This new technology presents the case and the foundation for a new approach to security practices.

Recognizing When a Hacker Is Detached from the Target

Human behavior has suppressors. If suppressors are present, malicious behavior may not occur. But if the suppressors are removed, malicious behavior occurs. For example, criminal behavior is unlikely to occur to any great extent within one or two blocks of a police station. The risk of getting caught is just too high, and there are too many other places to commit a crime where the chances of detection are slim. In this example, the police station acts as an ever-present stimulus to suppress malicious behavior in that immediate vicinity. However, if the police station moved 5 miles away, crime levels would probably return to normal for the region after the suppressor stimuli are gone. Likewise, if you place a security system warning sticker in your front window, the potential breaking-and-entering criminal may pass your house in favor of one that doesn't appear to be protected. There are too many other houses to break into where there is less chance of setting off an alarm.

Although these are simple examples, they illustrate to some extent why hacking occurs at such a high rate and appears to be increasing. There are few suppressors. In other words, it is well known among hackers that if a known attack is modified using typical hacker evasion tactics, the new attack is not likely to be picked up by typical signature detection designed to catch only past attacks. Therefore, to the sophisticated hacker, signature detection is simply not a suppressor. Just change a known attack and send it back through, and it is likely not to be detected. This is our primary network security flaw in existence today.

Being a hacker who approaches target networks remotely, and maybe even at random, means that the hacker has little or no investment in the target and may not even know anything about it. When one has malicious intent, it helps to not know the target if an act will be committed against that target. Being detached lessens guilt, remorse, and all the other psychological factors that can work to suppress the hacking behavior against that target. Certainly, a hacker does not attack targets who are friends or members of the accepted hacking culture. We don't see hacking wars to speak of, although there are a few exceptions between warring groups/countries. Even if the target is well known, such as a Fortune 500 company or a major financial institution, it is relatively easy to remain detached. After all, the hacker's perception is that the Fortune 500 companies are filthy rich and can absorb loss. At least, that is the reasoning to maintain the detachment.

At the time of writing this book, the *Occupy Wall Street* movement and its many derivatives show that Americans are protesting the corruption and unfairness that exists between mammoth-sized companies with rich staffs and the more common Americans. As the slogan goes, "We are the 99%." This means that 1% hold the wealth, while 99% do not. Therefore, there is likely little guilt in attacking these super-rich companies/organizations.

The detachment from a selected target, the potential for recognition from other hackers, and the sense of acting in a covert manner fuel the ankle biter/script kiddie, as well as more sophisticated hackers. Whether under the guise of helping by discovering security holes or pure intent to be a nuisance, the ankle biter is of concern, although mild. It is when we add significant motivation to inflict significant harm that the degree of malicious intent is of much greater concern.

Recognizing Motivation

Motivation for committing any individual malicious network attack is of serious concern because the perpetrator wants to inflict harm on others. The number of malicious acts that can be committed is limited only by the hacker's imagination. Severity of the behavior ranges from mild malicious behavior that creates a nuisance to significant theft or sabotage. Regardless of the number of malicious acts that can be directed at a network, there are only two ways to inflict harm on others.

1. The perpetrator can do something harmful to a person or group (for example, denial-of-service attack to disrupt the organization's normal business operations).

2. The perpetrator can take away something pleasant or something that a person or group owns (for example, classified or proprietary information).

Although we cannot determine someone's motivation with certainty, analyzing components of behavior can help us infer malicious intent.

It is important to realize that APT from a sponsor such as the Chinese is very important. As reported by many open source news articles, one of China's primary goals is to be the world's leader in technology within a decade. There are two ways to accomplish this: (1) to develop new technology that is superior to all other technology developed worldwide (not likely), and (2) to steal proprietary technology secrets from top private, commercial, and government sites. In my opinion, the primary reason for the many attacks and thefts of information we are experiencing that point to the Chinese clearly fit the latter category. If they enter a network and make copies of proprietary information, leaving the original information, they have engaged in theft that increases their technology and makes them more competitive. Let's not fool ourselves. This is happening. It doesn't matter that it is a copy — the secrets are gone and continue to leave. We desperately need new technology to stop this U.S. brain drain to coordinated and state-supported hacking, or we should take all proprietary and sensitive information off the networks!

Because no specific personality type commits malicious network attacks, and because profiles of individuals are as varied as the number of profilers, behavior analysis presented in this book provides a structure for studying the significant malicious behaviors in question. The structure provides us with reliable and valid ways to anticipate adversary behavior.

A set of antecedents serves as signals indicating that it is time for a specific behavior to occur. In a sense, the presence of a set of antecedents is like removing the safety on a gun; it is now ready to shoot. It is clear that we all act in response to the presence of antecedents. If you want to cross a busy street, the oncoming cars or a lack thereof serve as an antecedent for signaling when you can cross the street safely. You may stand on the corner with the motivation to cross, but you cross only when the antecedent conditions say the coast is clear. Regardless of the motivation, the conditions must be right for a specific behavior to occur. That is a key point — regardless of the internal motivation, the hacker's behavior is moderated by environmental antecedents and consequences of the hacking behavior.

Identifying the Power of Disruption

The focus of security practices is to maintain order and the presence of non-malicious behavior, or to minimize damage if it should occur. Therefore, security has to be concerned with all forms of malicious activity. If we observe a protest on television, we notice the presence of law enforcement and security forces. Security personnel are often thrust into disruptive environments where either active malicious behavior is occurring or great potential for disruption is accelerating quickly into harmful conditions. This is also true of computer networks, except that it is not quite so obvious as a public disruption on the street. Hackers embrace being anonymous to all but their friends. Disruption and the nature of how it plays out depend on the context.

Disruption by an individual in public is intended to cause a public effect. Recently I saw on the evening news the apprehension of an overweight man running and frolicking through a parking lot naked. You may wonder why someone would do this. You may also assume that this would not be considered normal behavior — something that most people observe frequently. It would be a very interesting world indeed if this were the norm, based on who decided to be the perpetrator! However, it is clear that such behavior resulted in a public disruption. The behavior literally stopped traffic, the smartphones were out in a second, and the behavior was recorded for posterity. The person committing the act responded to public antecedents. Many people were present to ensure an audience, and his being subdued by security was public and recorded. We may not know his inner reason for the behavior, but it occurred in public, and he succeeded in his objective of disrupting events and saying, "Look at me."

This is an example of disruption on one end of the spectrum. It is an example of being public, in public, to gain public attention, perhaps at all costs. Being apprehended and cuffed while on his stomach on the hot blacktop may have been an undesired consequence. Being apprehended and handcuffed this way should, according to behavioral principles, decrease the probability of the same behavior occurring under the same circumstances in the future. Perhaps joining a nudist colony would be a sound backup plan.

On the other end of the spectrum is computer network hacking. This extreme includes behavior that is not public, and the hacker does not necessarily want to be known, discovered, or apprehended. The hacker embraces anonymity, except for seeking the adoration of the select few with whom he or she may share the exploit. The key to many hacking attacks may simply be profit from theft of credit card information, financial data, or other personal information, such as social security numbers that can be sold. To a lesser extent, disruption may be the goal. This objective is simple: interfere with the normal operations of a specific organization by disrupting network operations. Why? Disruption is easy — very easy! It requires far less expertise than covertly entering a network and stealing and actually achieving financial gain. Disruption can be caused by almost anyone and, with a minimum of planning, can be conducted with little worry about being caught.

There has been expressed concern about a dual terrorist attack — one that is conventional with multiple coordinated bombings but backed up by disrupting all networks to stop first responder communication. This is a nightmare scenario that has not happened yet. However, we should be aware that it is relatively easy to shut down network communication at the time of a coordinated but conventional terrorist attack.

To seriously disrupt an organization, the hacker may use any number of possible denial-of-service (DOS) activities. A relatively simple DOS attack is fueled by malicious intent to cause harm. The objective is to disrupt an organization's activities by paralyzing its network. The basic DOS attack may result in a total loss of normal communication within the network temporarily. Hackers learn quickly that a DOS attack can be fairly simple to initiate. Protection from DOS attacks has improved, and today's high-speed networks are more difficult to clog. However, a disruptive DOS attack remains a serious threat from a hacker who targets that organization or from a hacker who simply wants to disrupt the operation of any network.

It's sad, but true. A large set of hackers is content to simply be mischievous and cause disruption. This type of hacker achieves desirable consequences by sharing the success with peers. He or she also feels a sense of success simply from achieving his or her disruption objective. If the hacker fails, he or she is off to the next network. The second type of disruption is when hackers target an organization for a specific purpose. In this case they have a reason why they want to hurt the organization. If at first they don't succeed, they may try again until they do succeed. Regardless of the motivation, the acts of both types of hackers have the same effect. However, the random act of DOS versus the repeated attempts represents different levels of threat. The hacker who targets an organization is often a more serious threat, because he or she might keep trying until he or she succeeds, and his or her success begets even more attempts.

Recognizing the Need for Theft

Theft is an act fueled by motivation as old as humankind itself. Theft has been around as long as humans have recognized and valued possessions. Someone gains a possession, and someone else wants to take it.

NOTE For a hacker, theft on a network can bring the thrill of achieving financial gain with little effort and little concern for getting caught.

Theft using a computer network of multiple servers joining multiple bank branches as targets is much like robbing multiple banks. The interconnected target with an accumulation of assets or valuable objects is a significant target. It is one-stop shopping. Penetrating a physical bank or network of banks that hold great wealth and the possibility of achieving gains financially by stealing some of that wealth is an increasing objective. However, today, stealing credit card numbers, committing identity theft, and selling stolen restricted information may be just as valuable.

Theft is perceived as being easy. The criminal looks at theft as a means to an end. It is a way to obtain money for whatever reason money is desired. In the field of applied behavior analysis, money is a powerful conditioned, or secondary, reinforcer. This is a fancy way of saying that money has secondary value because it can obtain an almost infinite number of primary desired objects and services in our world. Instead of obtaining a flat-screen television as a reinforcer, obtaining money means that you can purchase anything you want. This feature is what makes money so attractive. Secondary, or conditioned, reinforcers are extremely powerful. By stealing credit card numbers or identities, a person only needs to sell them quickly to obtain money. There is a large market for credit card numbers and identities. If someone can steal numerous numbers or identities at one time from within a network and sell them to a bidder who wants such information, significant financial gain is ensured.

Information is also a conditioned reinforcer. It is a two-step process, much like selling credit card numbers or social security numbers. Aldrich Ames and Robert Hanssen were notorious and very damaging spies working against the U.S. government from inside. They stole classified information of great value to Russia, their customer. Ames worked for the CIA in an impressive position of trust. He then violated that trust and sold classified information to the Russians. Hanssen, a key counterintelligence head at the FBI, sold trusted inside and strictly held information to the Russians as well. Although their motivations for conducting espionage against their own country occurred as the result of a complicated set of internal motivations, a behavior analysis simplifies what they did over the years they operated as spies for a U.S. adversary. Obtaining classified information and then selling it is the same two-step process as obtaining and selling proprietary information. However, their disgruntled feelings toward the CIA and FBI added to their reasons for committing espionage against our country, not just their chances of financial gain.

Regardless of the target — obtaining classified or restricted proprietary information, identities in the form of social security numbers, or credit card numbers — the objective is to obtain valuable information. The theft then can be converted into money by selling it to a customer who seeks such information. Theft can be complicated because of a number of motivations fueling the theft. However, a behavior analysis makes such theft more understandable and predictable. If a constellation of indicators suggests extreme disgruntlement, a need for revenge against supervisors, or a need for recognition, even if from a foreign government, the stage may be set for insider theft. And if the individual is in debt and needs money, and he or she has a low sense of ethics and loyalty to his or her country, the probability of theft rises sharply for that individual.

A Behavior Analysis

The behavior analysis of theft and disruption depends on the specific perpetrator and the context in which he or she operates. To conduct a predictive analysis, we would need to isolate the specific examples of theft or disruption and capture/identify the precursor antecedents that preceded the behaviors of concern and the consequences that followed. It is important to first define exactly the behavior of concern. For example, is it the act of stealing information or the act of selling information to an adversary that marks the behavior of concern? Is it the act of breaking into a network or the behavior of stealing information? Once the behavior has been defined, antecedents that precede that specific behavior and the consequences that follow are more clear. We then repeat this process across examples. Last, we try to find the common antecedents across all the examples. These common antecedents can then become predictors if we use them with the procedures outlined in this book and the DVD walkthrough.

Modeling the Individual: Advantages and Disadvantages

As noted earlier in the chapter, it is my experience that modeling the behavior of a group is easier than modeling an individual. All members of the group are individuals, but if we were to model an individual of that group, the antecedents and consequences would be remarkably similar across members. The individual represents the freedom to be different. Therefore, we focus on specific environmental influences affecting only the individual.

Table 1-2 shows the advantages and disadvantages of predictive modeling of the individual (such as a foreign leader) compared to predictive modeling of a group (such as a terrorist group). This table is the result of operational lessons learned across numerous models developed from clinical cases and cases across foreign adversaries. Furthermore, the table displays true advantages and disadvantages of behavior modeling of individuals using manual applied behavior analysis and patented automated behavior analysis modeling.

NOTE I was awarded one of my patents on *methods and tools to automate the process of predicting human behavior*. This was the foundation of automated behavior analysis, or AuBA, described in this book for behavior-based predictive modeling of malicious behavior.

Table 1-2: Advantages and Disadvantages of Modeling Individual Malicious Behavior

ADVANTAGES	DISADVANTAGES
The specific antecedents and consequences for one person allow prediction of specific behaviors.	The unique set of antecedents and consequences must be identified for each person modeled — one person, one model.
Data collection often takes less time than data collection for a group, because only the antecedents, behaviors, and consequences for that person are required.	It is more challenging to identify antecedents and consequences for the individual as compared to a group.
Unusual behavior of a person can be modeled.	You must be sure that a sufficient number and variety of behaviors for the person are captured.
Uncommon combinations of antecedents can be used to predict behavior under new conditions.	The predictive model for one individual is unlikely to generalize to another individual. We all are different.
If the person modeled has been covered sufficiently by the press, news articles may be used to extract antecedents, behaviors, and consequences.	Sufficient and multiple examples of behaviors under a variety of conditions are required.

The automated behavior analysis described in this book consists of a set of patented tools and methods proven to predict malicious adversarial behavior. AuBA automates much of the manual process required to conduct predictive modeling using elements of applied behavior analysis and adds numerous enhancements. Lessons learned have been incorporated into the new technology.

How Individuals May Vary

We are individuals. Like fingerprints, we are unique. Even if we observe identical twins, differences in behavior are readily apparent. These individual differences are developed from birth and maintained throughout life. The experiences within our environment tend to shape what we react to and how we react. The effects of our actions encourage us either to act the same way in the future when followed by desirable consequences or to change if the behavior is followed by undesirable consequences. Each experience is associated with a unique set of antecedents for the behavior we exhibit, and each behavior is followed by the effects of that behavior within the environment.

Our behavior within any context will receive immediate feedback from other individuals or from the physical environment itself. This ongoing and continuous environmental interaction adds to our innate biological and genetic design to make us who we are. The analysis of malicious behavior at the individual level must take this into consideration. Identifying different behaviors of individuals to the same or similar antecedents indicates that the antecedent-behavior-consequence sequence across individuals is specific to the individual. For example, two children may grow up in the same neighborhood under similar family conditions. One attends college, and the other becomes a drug addict and becomes a murderer. The environments and family situations were highly similar, but the behaviors were entirely different. Why? If you read this book in its entirety, you will know the answer.

To highlight how individuals can be so different, the following types are presented as examples of malicious behaviors that are familiar to everyone. In these cases, something went wrong. More than likely the person's complex inner motivations interacted with the environment. However, we can understand the behavior and even predict it without knowing the inner mechanisms operating.

The Loner

Theodore ("Ted") John Kaczynski, known as the Unabomber, was a brilliant PhD mathematician. He was the youngest faculty member ever hired by the prestigious Berkeley University after skipping grades, starting Harvard at age 16, and earning his master's and PhD degrees in mathematics from the University of Michigan. It was obvious that Kaczynski was different very early in his life. First, he was brilliant, with a talent for math. Second, he did not socialize well, preferred not to interact with others, and appeared to prefer math to people. Both characteristics continued throughout his life; he excelled in mathematics and became increasingly focused on being alone. After teaching only a few years at Berkeley, with less than stellar performance, he resigned. At 29 years of age, he moved to a 10-by-12-foot one-room cabin in Montana, about the size of two queen-size beds put together. With no amenities, he lived an austere life as a recluse.

While a recluse, Kaczynski sent a total of 16 bombs over 17 years that killed 3 people and injured 23. Antecedents to his attacks included individuals associated with technology — universities and airlines in particular. In fact, the term *Unabomber* is derived from the terms *un*iversity and *a*irlines. The primary consequence of his bombing behavior was success. For many years he evaded detection and capture — at least until his suspicious brother notified the FBI. Needless to say, Kaczynski has not acknowledged his brother David's attempts to communicate with him since his imprisonment.

The Chameleon

As described earlier in this chapter, Ted Bundy was one of the most violent serial killers in American history. Bundy was, by all accounts, a brilliant law student with a long-term girlfriend. He obscured his serial-murder lifestyle by posing as a socially acceptable person liked by many. Bundy was a chameleon. He drastically altered his behavior to match the existing conditions, much like a chameleon lizard changes its color to match the background so that it will not be detected. He existed as a nice young man in public and was one of the worst serial murderers in our country's history in private. Interestingly, both sets of behavior, public and private, were associated with their own sets of antecedents and consequences. Ted Bundy is a good example of how a person can live a double life.

The Social Misfit

On April 26, 2007, Seung-Hui Cho shot and killed 27 fellow students and 5 faculty members and injured 25 others at Virginia Tech University. Cho committed his shootings in two attacks separated by only a few hours. The threat exhibited by the first set of killings was not communicated throughout the campus. Cho then came back and continued killing and injuring staff and students.

Cho had a mental-health-troubled youth that included a series of psychiatric diagnoses. The details of this troubled past were withheld from the university. Cho simply did not fit in. His behavior was tainted with violent overtones, stalking, and handguns. As a child he was occasionally bullied at school, which was an unpleasant, painful experience for him. Monday morning quarterbacking suggests this was a key to his later attacks. The antecedents to these two attacks were clear — students and faculty. Likely representing Cho's school problems over many years, the unfortunate victims may have been stand-ins for all his past problems.

As part of the violent theme that plagued Cho, he chose hollow-point rounds for his shootings. As part of my orientation to the U.S. Secret Service as a research psychologist, I observed a special agent demonstrate the power of a hollow-point round at the firing range. Using a typical pointed round, he first shot a gallon jug of water at a distance of about 75 feet with his 9-millimeter pistol. The bullet cleanly went in the front of the jug, traveled through, and exited the back. Water streamed out of the entrance and exit holes. It was obvious that this type of bullet could go through a body. Then, using the same type of bullet but with a hollow-point head, the agent shot another water-filled jug. This jug literally exploded, with water spewing in every direction, like a water balloon dropped from a tall building onto the pavement. It was a chilling exercise. Given the same firepower and an identical shell, the simple fact that the bullet's head had an indentation made the projectile much more deadly. The only reason to shoot someone with a hollow-point round is to minimize the victim's chances of survival.

Cho was a social misfit with a great deal of internal rage. Unfortunately, he did not surface as a concern even in the midst of many danger signals. He had exhibited severe mental issue since childhood, as recognized by school staff from elementary school and high school. His choice of the type of bullet used is significant. A hollow-point bullet is meant to kill, not to wound. Armed with extremely lethal firepower, he clearly meant to kill. In addition, not only did he engage in a shooting, he came back a second time to complete more lethal acts. Combining Cho's very troubled background with the selection of firepower with hollow-point ammunition indicates that he was deadly serious.

The Individual versus the Group

This chapter has focused on the behavior analysis of the individual versus the group. In summary, the group is often easier to model than the individual. The primary considerations in predicting the behavior of the individual versus the group are identifying the following:

- The antecedents leading to the defined behavior of interest that are specific to the individual
- The consequences of malicious behavior, the desirable consequences that maintain or increase the frequency of occurrence of the behavior, or the undesirable consequences that result in a decrease in the occurrence of the behavior in the future

The next chapter focuses on the group versus the individual. The methods are similar, but the differences are significant. The focus will be on these differences. The group works to keep members similar in terms of beliefs and behaviors to maintain the group's integrity and identity. Because a group acts more as one entity, in some ways analyzing the group is easier than analyzing an individual. It is true that the individual is loosely tied to usual ways of behaving and can change behavior quickly. However, individuals are still creatures of habit. As humans, we all exhibit patterned behavior, and that makes our behavior predictable.

NOTE AuBA exists as the only patented automation and extension of applied behavior analysis. Compared with manual modeling methods, the AuBA methodologies and tools have numerous advantages. At the end of each chapter a key advantage of this new technology will be presented.

Advantages of AuBA #1: Automated Summarization

This chapter describes basic behavioral principles for analyzing individual behavior. These principles are very important because they provide a way to analyze behavior when the perpetrator is or is not known. Many psychological methods depend heavily on direct observation of the person being analyzed. Over the course of two decades, my teams and I have moved the basic applied behavior analysis approach to the use of text accounts of past behavior as a corpus to replace direct observation. This is important because in comparison to clinical settings, where the person is available for observations and environments are constrained, text accounts of past behaviors may be used to replace direct observation. Figure 1-2 shows the basic AuBA process. Basically, text-based documents are presented to the first automated tool, ThemeMate. The output of ThemeMate is then forwarded to AutoAnalyzer, and the completed predictive engine is then embedded in the predictive application.

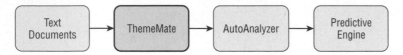

Figure 1-2: The AuBA process that processes textual accounts of past behavior to produce a predictive engine using two automated tools, ThemeMate and AutoAnalyzer

There are many advantages to AuBA. At the end of each chapter, a specific feature of the technology will be described. This chapter highlights one of the primary features of ThemeMate, and the following list highlights some of the primary features of ThemeMate that will be presented across chapters.

- The AuBA methodology includes automated methods to accurately identify antecedents and consequences of past behaviors in text-based reports and news articles describing past behaviors.

- ThemeMate summarizes large numbers of documents describing past behavior, identifies the most important features across all the documents, and presents salient features.

- ThemeMate automatically extracts antecedents associated with behaviors and constructs a data array, which is processed by AutoAnalyzer.

- AutoAnalyzer automatically conducts advanced behavior analytics to develop and validate predictive engines that may be used to accurately predict future behavior.

Although the accompanying DVD demonstrates these model-building tools, I will provide details in each chapter that demonstrate different advantages of AuBA. This chapter highlights a very useful feature — the automated identification of key points across all documents submitted for processing. This is a specific feature of ThemeMate. The feature enables us to submit a single document or collection of documents to ThemeMate to obtain the x number of key points embedded in the text. The user can specify how many key points are to be returned. This automated *CliffsNotes*-like feature is very valuable in summarizing all content very rapidly. Currently, ThemeMate provides this summarization in English or Arabic, but it can be readied to work with any new language in approximately two weeks. When I designed ThemeMate, it was based on the cognitive process we use to extract key points and to extract antecedents associated with behavior. Comparing the automated ThemeMate extraction to human extraction of key points returns highly similar or the same summarization points.

To demonstrate this ThemeMate feature, I collected more than 150 separate open source documents of Osama bin Laden's statements, speeches, interviews, fatwas (declarations of war), and threats. I submitted all these text documents to ThemeMate and set the option to summarize all documents by providing the six most important points across all documents. There are two reasons for using ThemeMate to do this: (1) Such a summary has been shown to be highly similar to an analysis completed manually by a SME, and (2) ThemeMate can conduct the extraction and summarization across languages (for example, English and Arabic) and can provide key motivation points for an individual or group if it contains statements made by the individual or group, interviews, and authoritative articles about the individual or group. The primary difference between this AuBA automation and a manual analysis is that it took ThemeMate 90 seconds to complete its analysis for this demonstration, whereas it can take an SME many weeks to study and extract key features. Thus, the actual use of this feature is simply left to the imagination of the user.

Figure 1-3 presents the unedited results of the ThemeMate analysis of the more than 150 documents. As a manual comparison, it is followed with an expert assessment of Osama bin Laden's motivations. This assessment was produced by Michael Scheuer and extracted from a transcript video of an interview of Scheuer conducted by Alan Bock. This interview may be viewed at www.youtube .com/watch?v=bYZizO0f0lk&feature=player_embedded#!.

Bin Ladin: Our duty -- and we carried it out -- is to rouse the nation for jihad against the United States, Israel, and their supporters for the sake of God.

Bin Ladin believed US military bases in Saudi Arabia were on holy land, and he believed they were there to help support Israel.

Is there any clearer sponsorship of Zionist terrorism in Palestine, Lebanon, and elsewhere than the US sponsorship?"

Usama Bin Ladin pledged to fight against the alliance of the United States and Israel.

Bin Ladin: The United States will not even dream of enjoying security if we do not experience security as a living reality in Palestine, the land of the two holy mosques, and all Muslim countries, God willing.

Bin Ladin stressed that what the United States wants from Afghanistan with regard to combating "Islamic extremism" is to "prevent the Taliban government from implementing the Islamic Shari'ah and to cooperate with it against the threat that the Arab mujahidin pose to the United States."

Figure 1-3: The output of ThemeMate when set to return the five most important points contained in the more than 150 Osama bin Laden–focused documents presented for analysis.

As background, Scheuer headed the Osama bin Laden–focus team at the CIA from 1996 to 1999, as reported in open source reviews of his books and this taped interview. I was familiar with his work from inside the CIA, as well as his books, which were completed more recently. Scheuer is perhaps the world's authority on the motivations of Osama bin Laden and al-Qaeda. His assessment in the taped interview is the result of many years of studying Osama bin Laden's actual words in speeches, warnings, and so forth. His controversial views are the results of actually analyzing the content of bin Laden's words. Scheuer has drawn different conclusions based on actual study of bin Laden's words. Therefore, ThemeMate and Scheuer should agree, to some extent, as both are processing actual speeches, interviews, and so forth. We would not expect an exact match, because the documents are not identical, but we should see a strong similarity.

Scheuer's analysis of the true motivations of bin Laden presented in the recorded interview provided four key motivational points for Osama bin Laden. These points as presented in the interview were:

- The United States actively supports Israel.
- The United States occupies lands in the Arab peninsula.
- The United States supports tyrannies that govern most of the Arab world.
- The primary goal is to evict the United States from their lands.

A comparison between the careful analysis that Scheuer completed after years of study and the 90-second ThemeMate processing of documents reveals the close comparison between the separate analyses. Scheuer should be complimented on his objective analysis drawn from content analysis, not bias. ThemeMate automatically provides a rapid, nonbiased assessment that cannot be influenced by external or political pressures.

In Summary

This is an important introductory chapter on the topic of predicting individual adversarial threatening behavior that can impact our national security. The work, methods, and procedures I have discussed are a unique application and automation of applied behavior analysis — a field in psychology that emphasizes influencing and predicting individuals' behavior. AuBA is the SAIC-owned, author-invented, new set of tools and methods for security to help ensure our protection as a nation. AuBA is proactive, not reactive. Behavioral methods applied to terrorism, insurgency, war, network hacking attacks, and insider threats represent a paradigm shift in human predictive technology. They move from current reactive approaches to proactive methods that have been proven to predict threatening behavior in real time.

The methods described in this chapter have proven that antecedents to adversary behavior can be extended to the following:

- Network packets for computer network prediction
- Physical sensor output to serve as antecedents that convert sensor-based tracked movement of individuals into predictions of malicious intent
- Test extraction from past text accounts of adversarial behavior
- A unique way of capturing antecedent, behavior, and consequence information from SMEs when data is sparse or missing

Remember these key points:

- Adversarial behaviors on a global basis are associated with predictive antecedents and identifiable consequences.
- Behavior analysis principles can reliably predict adversary behavior.
- Following the principles and methods described in this book can allow us to move from a reactive security policy to a more proactive stance in which we can anticipate attacks before they happen.
- If you absorb and use the methods and procedures presented in this book, you can effectively predict future occurrences of malicious behavior.

Analyzing the Malicious Group

This chapter focuses on an introduction to the analysis of group behavior and presents findings from an automated behavior analysis (AuBA) of documents about groups presented. Although methods and procedures used for analyzing groups are highly similar to those used for analyzing and predicting the behavior of the individual, the group represents a cohesiveness that works to make behavior similar in response to common antecedents. A group is bound together by common beliefs and either stated or unstated operating principles. Conducting a complete analysis of the individual or group takes an understanding of behavior principles and the use of analytical tools. Groups of concern tend to fall into three major areas: terrorism, cyber, and criminal. Although a group's targeting, motivations, and methods are quite different across these three areas, all groups respond to external antecedents and consequences.

Perhaps it is counterintuitive, but we can't predict behavior accurately by studying past accounts of behavior alone; instead, we must identify the antecedents and consequences associated with past behaviors and how they interact with a group's motivation, guiding principles, and leadership. Once we know the context of past behaviors of groups, we can anticipate future behavior by determining the presence and absence of the identified antecedents and potential consequences in the future. I explore these areas in this chapter with groups. In later chapters and the accompanying DVD, I will go through the steps to actually produce predictive results.

Understanding the Group Adversary

I offer the following definition of *group* to use for predictive modeling of malicious behavior:

DEFINITION A *group* comprises of two or more individuals who are united by and actively share common beliefs, ideology, or concerns.

This definition ensures that a collection of individuals choose to form a type of community of interest. Members of the group tend to act as a single entity on the basis of the unifying factor or factors because they choose to be identified by common interests. It is important to note that malicious behavior does not come from the group structure itself; instead, malicious intent and behavior comes from the motivation and objectives of the group.

Al-Qaeda members are collectively a group, albeit a loosely defined group. However, even if spread across the world as a sort of franchise, all al-Qaeda members subscribe to the basic tenents outlined by Osama bin Laden. They:

- loathe the U.S.–Israel alliance
- are strongly pro-Palestinian
- want to eliminate U.S. and Western occupation in foreign countries

These are the foundational principles for al-Qaeda, as discovered by the type of AuBA completed at the end of Chapter 1. They are the factors that serve as the glue that maintains the function and focus of the group.

Although there are many different ways to model all types of groups, the group definition I present here is extremely useful for predictive modeling of malicious behavior. In individual modeling we must identify that set of antecedents serving as precursors to the behavior of the one individual being analyzed. In group modeling of malicious behavior, we focus on identifying that set of antecedents serving as precursors for malicious behavior of the group as a whole. In fact, we are much less interested in the behavior of the group members in favor of the group actions in total.

Both the malicious group and the malicious individual can be extremely damaging, hurtful, and even fatal to others. They have that in common. However, it is usually not as difficult to predict group behavior accurately as compared to the lone individual because of the interactive and supportive nature of a group and the fact that there is pressure to *keep in line* as a member. The individual, on the other hand, has no restrictions on his or her behavior and no group foundation to which he or she must adhere. The group exists as a means to unite those with common beliefs and objectives, and we can use that to our advantage as we seek to discover the antecedents and consequences associated with specific behaviors of interest of potentially malicious groups.

Analyzing al-Qaeda

It is important to note that the following report was made possible by submitting more than 300 documents describing the 9/11 al-Qaeda attack to automated ThemeMate analysis. All facts presented were surfaced by ThemeMate. Although ThemeMate is the first tool used to provide a predictive capability, I have used it often to provide a rapid analysis for report preparation. When we consider that the capability exists to conduct this analysis in other languages, the utility of the tool becomes even clearer. The narrative is provided as an example of the beginning stages of malicious group analysis. Although we can refine the data array that is presented with this analysis to AutoAnalyzer to construct a predictive engine, I prefer extracting the incidental facts first to obtain an objective view of the incident and potential causes.

In the early morning of September 11, 2001, it had been nearly 70 years since a foreign attack occurred on U.S. soil. On December 7, 1941, the emperor of Japan authorized 353 fighter planes to attack Pearl Harbor, Hawaii. Using a vast mobile support infrastructure that had moved covertly across the Pacific to its target, the Japanese caught the United States totally by surprise. By the end of the fighter plane attack, more than 2,400 Americans had been killed and many ships and aircraft had been destroyed or crippled. After the attack, President Franklin Delano Roosevelt declared that the date of the attack would live on in infamy. During the mid morning of September 11, 2001, al-Qaeda launched the second foreign surprise attack against Americans on U.S. soil. 9/11 is the second date to live on in infamy.

> **NOTE** Al-Qaeda is somewhat of a hybrid. An analysis of the group demonstrates that a group exhibiting malicious behavior, including terrorist groups, does not have to be strictly organized.

Automated Behavior Analysis Summary

At the end of Chapter 1, the first advantage of ThemeMate, one of the two AuBA tools that produce predictive models, was presented. This summary feature is very important in that when we process documents describing past attacks, background, reviews, and the results of considered opinions by those who have studied the group extensively, we derive an objective analysis of leadership, what motivates the group, malicious behaviors engaged in, and the antecedents–behavior associations necessary to construct the data array that is passed to AutoAnalyzer to construct a predictive engine.

The user has control over the extraction process by submitting subsets of the overall documents that emphasize only one area. For example, if we want a detailed objective analysis of leadership, we would submit a subset of documents that focused only on leadership. We also can instruct ThemeMate to focus only on leadership by adding keywords to narrow analysis only to this area if the whole corpus is processed at one time. In other words, we have two methods to focus ThemeMate. We can submit documents that concentrate only on the one area in which we are interested, or we can submit the entire corpus and instruct ThemeMate, through the use of *focus words*, to concentrate on only one area. As an example of the latter, if we want to concentrate on the group's leadership principles, we might enter the following words into the focus words section before running ThemeMate: *leader, leaders, leadership, laden, guidelines, guide, principle, principles*. By operating ThemeMate with these focus words, we will see themes developed only in these areas. Inevitably, an initial run will turn up new themes and new words to add to the focus words. Typically, several quick runs with this tool provide us with a detailed and objective analysis of the topic.

Figure 2-1 shows the conceptual use of focus words. We begin by developing a large corpus of documents describing the group incidents (World Trade Center [WTC] North Tower, WTC South Tower, Pentagon, and the airliner crash in Pennsylvania). Documents were selected from those prepared the same day of the attack to 3 months after the attack to ensure coverage of key principles. We then enter keywords into the focus words section and run ThemeMate. The results are key themes and summary sentences identifying key points in the text across all documents.

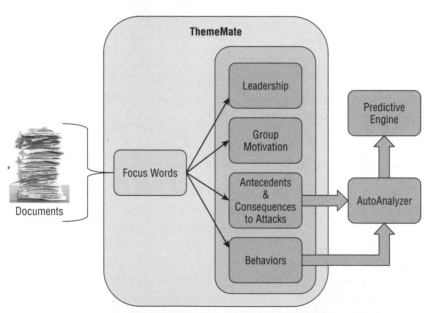

Figure 2-1: The AuBA process whereby several topics may be pursued from the same overall corpus of documents using the focus words feature to guide automated summarization.

The following describes al-Qaeda from a group analysis perspective that resulted from a ThemeMate analysis of accumulated documents describing the 9/11 attack.

On September 11, 2001, 19 al-Qaeda terrorists hijacked four airliners and used them in surprise attack, suicide missions against the United States within its borders. First, an airliner crashed into the North Tower of the World Trade Center (Figure 2-2), followed by a second airliner crashing into the South Tower. A third plane crashed into the Pentagon, a building I had been on my way to and a staff member had just exited. A fourth airliner crashed into a Pennsylvania field as a result of brave passengers trying to wrest control of the plane from the terrorists.

Figure 2-2: The surprise attack against the World Trade Center North Tower was the beginning of the 9/11 attack.
© Kentannenbaum | Dreamstime.com

The World Trade Center towers struck by the airliners collapsed amidst opaque, inferno-like clouds of toxic ash with those on the ground running not only for cover but for their lives. Within just a few hours, nearly 3,000 victims had lost their lives and 6,000 had been injured. As some sense of what was happening started to surface from bewilderment and fear, we slowly were able to put the pieces together. In the midst of one of the more surreal and devastating events in our country's history, details about the towering bravery of those passengers who tried valiantly but failed to wrest control of the airliner away from the terrorists in Pennsylvania surfaced. We saw images of unfortunate souls jumping from the inferno occurring within the World Trade Center towers where they were trapped. We have heard about the many first responders who died in the towers trying to save others, and we admire their dedication to place the lives of others before their own lives. The planned terror to accompany an attack was there to an unprecedented degree.

Al-Qaeda, the group that perpetrated this attack, is presented here because the attack was the most devastating that our country has yet experienced within its borders. Although the December 7, 1941, Japanese attack on Pearl Harbor was devastating and drew the United States into World War II, 9/11 was perpetrated by a small contingent of 19 terrorists armed with nothing more than box cutters and resulted in a global war on terrorism. This example indicates that we must take group malicious behavior seriously. An advantage of AuBA is that we receive an objective view of the behavior, and the process extracts associated antecedents and consequences without bias. The capability to predict future behavior accurately depends on an objective analysis of the behavior, motivations and leadership, and the external associated antecedents and consequences. The objective extraction is important because it helps prevent us from adopting popular or political views of events. Instead, AuBA tools such as ThemeMate provide key themes embedded in the documents.

NOTE ThemeMate identified themes associated with both the 1941 Pearl Harbor attack and the 9/11 attack. Specifically, the comparison focuses on the attacks as the two most significant foreign adversary attacks within our country's borders in our country's history.

Formed by Osama bin Laden, al-Qaeda remained under his guidance until May 2, 2011, when a U.S. Navy SEALs team and CIA forces invaded his protected hiding compound and killed him. Because Islamic spiritual guidance stresses burying a body within 24 hours, and there was no clear taker for his body within that short time frame, he was buried at sea. At the time of writing this chapter, 60-year-old Ayman al-Zawahiri, bin Laden's longtime lieutenant, has taken his predecessor's spot as the leader of the al-Qaeda organization. This was not a surprise. Exceedingly loyal al-Zawahiri had been waiting faithfully in the wings for a long time.

On the basis of the automated analysis of documents describing numerous facets of al-Qaeda, the organization is a loosely structured group intent on global domination. The organization maintains centralized leadership that grants the right to be associated in subgroups across the globe. The concept is similar to a franchise such as McDonald's or KFC. The CEO of McDonald's does not make the day-to-day decisions of a McDonald's in Annapolis, Maryland. However, the McDonald's in Annapolis, Maryland, looks and behaves in a manner that is very similar to that of all other McDonald's restaurants, and the food meets common standards of the organization. You can go to any McDonald's and the food will almost be identical because of these common standards. The organization sets the structure and ground rules, and the leadership sets general rules to live by.

The Organization

Al-Qaeda is a Sunni Islam group bound together by the strictly held belief that leadership is by a Caliph. A *Caliph* is a leader who is elected by Shura, a process of selecting a successor as stipulated by Sharia, or religious, law. Unlike Shia Muslims, who believe leadership should be passed through family, the Sunni underpinnings of al-Qaeda and its founder, Osama bin Laden, start with this common foundation of elected leadership.

The structure of al-Qaeda has evolved into two major paths:

- First, al-Qaeda is a very strict religious entity with a strongly held Sunni foundation. A behavior analysis indicates that Osama bin Laden's released communications to the masses referenced God more frequently than any other concept as a conceptual set of themes. The Islamic Sunni religious foundation is extremely strong and forms the common glue that keeps the organization intact.

- Second, the structure supports an army of militants who operate globally. In total, the entire organization forms a worldwide base capable of launching attacks against enemies identified in its declared war, or jihad, against its enemies. Its members are totally intolerant of the smaller Shia worldwide community, whom they have targeted for attacks, and al-Qaeda abhors the U.S.–Israel alliance and maintains an active disregard for Jews, Israel, the United States, and Western allies.

Group Dynamics

Al-Qaeda is unlike the U.S. military, a top-down hierarchy whereby strategic direction begins at the top and filters down through layers of leadership to tactical forces on a daily basis. Rather, Osama bin Laden provided a general level of leadership and guidance, while al-Qaeda cells could carry out tactical attacks with some measure of autonomy. Bin Laden offered repeated announcements to the world to explain his position on a number of topics.

Targets of the attacks have varied. Part of the reason for the variation is that there are two pressures within al-Qaeda with regard to targeting. One force comes from religious militants within the organization, and the other force comes from the more military-focused forces within al-Qaeda. These different views, combined with almost autonomous selection of targeting at the local level, result in different targeting and methods from within the same organization. From various embassies to the *USS Cole* naval ship to the World Trade Center and the Pentagon, the targets of attacks have been significant and often symbolic. It is important to note that global domination continues as a likely underlying al-Qaeda goal even though bin Laden is no longer its leader.

Focused on ridding foreign lands of U.S. and Western ally influence and occupation, al-Qaeda has attacked allies to discourage association with the United States. The decentralized structure of the group has provided maximum flexibility to conduct such attacks worldwide. This type of flexibility was exceedingly important for the group during the years 2001–2011 when bin Laden was pressed into hiding by U.S. forces. Even in hiding bin Laden could provide general guidance, while the local operational cells could exhibit successful attacks in their respective regions.

The Motivation

Group structure is not a cause of malicious behavior. Instead, group structure assists in successfully conducting malicious behavior. Rather than structure, motivation of the group is the key to malice. We could have two groups with almost identical structure; however, one group may engage in malicious attacks with intent to cause harm, injury, or death, while the other group could work to gather donations for cancer treatment. The underlying motivation of the group results in the obvious differences between the two groups.

There is not a specific type of organizational structure that defines a malicious group, no more than there is a specific personality type that defines a spy, terrorist, or leader. The underlying motivation and ideology of a group serves as the glue that binds members together. Al-Qaeda has clearly stated distaste for the United States, its Western allies, and Israel/Jews. All members share these common dislikes. Not only do these commonalities provide a strong bond that energizes the group, they serve to guide targeting.

Declarations of War

As a direct response to the 9/11 attack, the United States declared a global war on terrorism. The purpose of the declaration was to defeat terrorism. By moving from a more reactive stance to one where we would proactively pursue terrorists, we would increase the chances that future terrorist acts could be prevented. Approximately 5 years earlier, bin Laden had basically declared war against the United States by issuing a fatwa. Years later, a second fatwa was issued in a similar manner. The purpose of the fatwas was to authorize the targeting of Americans and associated allies anywhere in the world.

DEFINITION A *fatwa* in Islamic terms is an order or religious ruling established by knowledgeable leadership. Sunni-based fatwas such as those issued by Osama bin Laden to kill Americans worldwide would be considered as strong guidance for followers.

The overt declarations of war removed any doubt concerning the intent and objectives of al-Qaeda toward the United States, and vice versa. The struggle, or war, ended for Osama bin Laden on May 2, 2011, when U.S. Navy SEALs and CIA forces invaded a fortified compound in Pakistan and killed bin Laden. However, the struggle continues under Osama bin Laden's successor, Ayman al-Zawahiri.

A Behavior Analysis

Applying behavior principles of group analysis to al-Qaeda helps to provide insight into targeting and how attacks are orchestrated. Technically, attacks against the United States by al-Qaeda have had clear antecedent conditions serving as environmental cues suggesting the timing of the attacks. Certainly, the consequences of such attacks have maintained the occurrence of the attacks over time — they have been successful in achieving planned death and destruction.

Figure 2-3 depicts the typical antecedent-behavior-consequence sequence. However, it is important to note that the sequence is not automatic. In other words, if antecedents associated with past malicious behavior occur again in the future, there is no guarantee that behavior associated with these antecedents in the past will occur again. There is an increased probability that the behavior will occur, but there exists a complex interaction among antecedents and a group's behavior. A group's training, guidelines, and teachings interact with the antecedents to result in the behavior. In the case of al-Qaeda, the past bin Laden fatwas, the Islamic teachings adhered to by members, and past training all combine to structure the behavior when it occurs.

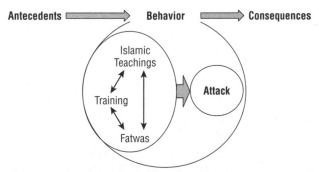

Figure 2-3: A conceptual view of how antecedents, behavior, and consequences interact in contributing to the occurrence of group behavior.

On the basis of fatwas and released statements from Osama bin Laden, stated enemies in al-Qaeda's declared war include the United States, Israel, and Western allies. The group is motivated by the desire to rid foreign lands of U.S. and ally occupation. All members fully embrace this basic tenet; therefore, the activities of their enemies take on a special emphasis and interest. At any given time, there is literally a world of events and situations occurring. However, the ideology and motivations of al-Qaeda focus its attention to the activities of the United States and Western allies. Like al-Qaeda members are wearing blinders, other events and situations are not as important and may simply be ignored. For example, particular interest is focused on Iraq and Afghanistan because of the presence of foreign troops in these countries.

Targets in the future will also have the same attributes. Osama bin Laden is dead, but through his successor the targeting and attacks will continue. Al-Qaeda will continue to catch us off guard because of its careful planning and surveillance. Too often intelligence becomes a detailed study of past events. This is not intelligence; it is a form of Monday morning quarterbacking. All seems to make sense in retrospect, and when that attack occurs that was one of hundreds of scenarios we thought of prior to the attack, we have the false sense that we anticipated it. We tend to forget it was just one scenario of hundreds we had conjured up before the fact. This still leaves us with a reactive stance to al-Qaeda. It doesn't repeat the same specific targeting, and it doesn't exhibit that same attack behavior twice. A detailed study of focusing only on past behavior does not help significantly in anticipating future actions; rather it requires a detailed study of past behaviors as the specific behaviors relate to associated antecedents and consequences. A behavior analysis approach that emphasizes the antecedents-behavior-consequences associations, as opposed to studying only past behaviors, allows us to better understand the group in terms of what it responds to (antecedents) and what works to reinforce its behavior over time (consequences) can be more effective in anticipating future attacks.

We need a proactive shift with proactive behavior analysis methods to develop more accurate anticipation of future al-Qaeda attack behavior. The bottom line, based on our ThemeMate analysis and included report, in my opinion (based on fact) is that we will see additional serious attacks with mass casualties characterized by an increasing variety of tactics. Motivations have not changed; there is a new leader who served at Osama bin Laden's side for many years; fatwas have not changed; and the United States is still supportive of Israel. The U.S. and Western allies militaries maintain their presence in foreign countries of concern to al-Qaeda. Persons and installations that fit within the al-Qaeda motivational radar will continue to be targeted. This is a long-term struggle that will not go away with tit-for-tat military victories.

Analyzing Hezbollah

As with the preceding ThemeMate analysis of al-Qaeda, I also submitted a corpus of more than 300 documents to ThemeMate to extract the basics of the group, motivational factors, targeting principles, and common antecedents and consequences across documents. The following report illustrates the degree of detail of malicious group behavior that can be extracted. It took approximately 5 minutes for the automated extraction to reveal key themes and summarization principles for both al-Qaeda and Hezbollah. The articles selected spanned a decade of terrorist activity to ensure they were representative.

In contrast to Islamic Sunni formed and run al-Qaeda, Hezbollah is an Islamic Shia group. Supported financially by Iran, Hezbollah has been in existence for almost 30 years. Hezbollah, meaning *Party of God*, has been engaged in a long-term struggle with Israel since the group's inception. Known as the group that was instrumental in driving Israeli forces out of Lebanon, the group has also gained recognition for supporting the development of schools and hospitals. The comparison of Hezbollah and al-Qaeda is of special interest. The conflict between Sunni and Shia forms of religion, based primarily on succession of leaders being voted in by knowledgeable leaders (Sunni) versus following family lines (Shia), is real and, as they say, palpable. There is an ongoing Sunni versus Shia conflict that is likely to continue for as long as both groups are present. The long-term dislike and struggle is a testament to the basic strength of the religious and ideological underpinnings of some adversarial groups.

A very old and familiar proverb passed down for centuries states *the enemy of my enemy is my friend*. Israel is the common enemy of both al-Qaeda and Hezbollah. The degree of common distaste for Israel may be greater than the conflict between Shia and Sunni roots. Although both organizations would like to eradicate Israel, Hezbollah has been involved much more with the daily struggle on the ground. Hezbollah clearly became more powerful and gained recognition when it was successful at driving Israeli forces out of Lebanon. Like al-Qaeda, Hezbollah uses the perceived occupation of regional land by U.S., Israeli, or allied military as a basic tenet supporting its resistance and existence.

That Hezbollah is Iranian born and financed is an important fact. The Ayatollah Khomeini in Iran was a very strong influence over Hezbollah, from both religious and financial perspectives. The Iranian ties and influences remain today.

The Organization

The larger conflict between Iran and Israel is well known and describes the same struggle between Hezbollah and Israel. Being formed and supported by Iran with strong religious origins, Hezbollah can be viewed as locally transplanted

Iranian distaste for Israel. The radical Shia nature that forms the foundation of Hezbollah highlights Israeli activities as antecedents to Hezbollah attacks. Sayyed Hasan Nasrallah, as the leader of the organization, has grown in status as Hezbollah has gained strength. Nasrallah assumed leadership when the former leader, Abbas Musawi, was assassinated by the Israelis in 1992.

Under Nasrallah's leadership, Hezbollah has proven to be much more structured than the previously described al-Qaeda. Nasrallah has publicly stated and supported the total destruction of Israel, so we have to be concerned about the continued carryover effects to the United States because of the historically strong ties between Israel and the United States.

As an organization, Hezbollah exists in two forms:

- A strong and feared guerrilla force capable of fending off strong Israeli forces

- A more global international terrorist method of operation, known as *modus operandi*

Hezbollah has executed many hundreds of attacks against Israeli, U.S., and Western targets. For example, in the name of the Islamic jihad, its suicide truck bombing of the U.S. marine and French military barracks in Lebanon in 1983 resulted in 299 deaths and is still considered to be one of the deadliest terrorist attacks.

DEFINITION *Modus operandi*, as a term, means a specific repeatable method of responding or behaving. As terrorist tactics, if a terrorist group repeats similar methods of operation, we describe the commonalities as a *modus operandi* (MO).

Consistency of Behavior

Hezbollah engages in consistent attacks — assassinations, assaults, hijackings, and bombings — with common distinguishing characteristics. The term *modus operandi*, basically used for habitual commitment of crimes, is appropriate for Hezbollah. The manner and style of attacks are similar across incidents, and targeting is consistent across both of its MO styles: international terrorism and guerrilla warfare.

NOTE Terrorist groups vary considerably in consistency of operation. Hezbollah is one of the more consistent in actions and targeting, whereas al-Qaeda varies considerably in its type of target and MO.

Predictability to a minor extent is aided by consistency of targeting and repeatable MO. However, when we consider that accurate prediction is a result of identifying antecedents to adversary malicious behaviors, prediction can occur accurately whether the group is consistent in actions or not. Who, where, what, when, and sometimes why depends on the antecedent-behavior-consequence dynamics and not that groups repeat the same attacks in the same way at the same time. Although Hezbollah is consistent across targeting its victims and in attack behavior MO, this is not the primary reason for the ability to accurately anticipate its behavior. Knowing that specific actions of Israel, the United States, or allies set into motion an increased chance for Hezbollah retaliation is more useful. In short, consistency of behavior in analyzing a group's behavior is useful but not necessary when analyzing its behavior and in anticipating future actions.

The Motivation

To determine the motivation that underlies Hezbollah's adversarial behavior, ThemeMate identifies several key points:

- Hezbollah was formed with strong Iranian Islamic Shia ideology, including support from Ayatollah Khomeini's supporters.

- Israel, the United States, and Western allies form the primary targets for terrorist attacks.

- Any form of perceived regional Israeli occupation of a country other than Israel, especially Lebanon, raises anger and desire for retaliation.

- Ongoing funding from Iran continues to solidify Hezbollah's focus on the enemies of Iran.

Motivation of a group is very important because it tends to solidify environmental antecedents for terrorist attacks. For example, if we study targets for past attacks as compared to motivational characteristics listed, the striking correspondence between the two is apparent. Motivation provides a guide to targeting and specific antecedents to terrorist attacks.

Consequences for terrorist group activity are very important as well. If terrorist attacks against a designated target that is consistent with the group's motivational foundation result in success, similar attacks will occur in the future. If an attack results in failure, such as perpetrators being apprehended and jailed, that MO is likely to be modified. Humans do not tend to repeat behaviors that have unsuccessful consequences. In analyzing malicious behavior, careful attention paid to identifying antecedents and successful or unsuccessful consequences are extremely useful for anticipating future behavior.

Targeting Consistency

The importance of considering motivation as related to antecedents and consequences of past behaviors of interest assists greatly in determining targets of future attacks. In many cases, such as with Hezbollah, identifying targeting is not a surprise. For example, Israel will be a target, of course. We can accompany many broad pronouncements with a great deal of certainty. Technically, we can even provide a very high confidence interval that such targeting will occur. However, if we want to become more detailed in our pronouncements, if we want to take our predications to the next level, such as specifying if the next target will be military or civilian, then the appropriate type of detailed analysis of past behavior, motivation, antecedents, and consequences is required. Again, a simple study of past behaviors alone is not sufficient for a predictive analysis.

Consistency of targeting across groups varies considerably. Hezbollah is fairly straightforward because of consistency. Certainly, Hezbollah would not be surprised if we provided a pronouncement that Israeli military forces will be a target for its future guerrilla warfare activity. Such general pronouncements are not surprising, nor are they particularly useful. Detailed anticipation of adversary malicious behavior is different. It will always be a goal, and if the methods provided in the walkthrough on the DVD and in the latter chapters of this book are followed, determining specifics is possible.

A Behavior Analysis

In 1988, Hezbollah published its ideology in *The Jerusalem Quarterly* (Fall, 1988). The official *program* included several key points: rid Americans, French, and other allies from Lebanon; seek revenge against the Phalange (ultra right political party in Lebanon); and encourage its youth to choose an Islamic government. Listed in a section of its own was a call for the destruction of Israel. To the present, much has remained the same.

Hezbollah has been credited with attacks against Americans, such as the U.S. embassy in Beirut (killing 17 Americans and 46 others) and 6 months later the dual truck bombings directed at the U.S. marine and French barracks in Beirut (killing 241 Americans and 58 French), as well as numerous other attacks around the world. True to form of published ideology, those targeted tend to match the stated words.

Table 2-1 presents a top-level analysis of Hezbollah. Although deep analyses will be demonstrated in the walkthrough and DVD in this book, a broad overview from a behavior analysis perspective is helpful, because this type of analysis forces us to consider antecedents and consequences of attack behavior that suggest when conditions are right for attacks to occur and helps us move away from a single focus on the attacks themselves.

It should be noted that the conflict between Hezbollah and Israel has resulted in many hundreds if not thousands of significant altercations, depending on the definition of *significant*. Hezbollah, for example, has peppered Israel over the years with Katyusha rockets. These relatively small rockets have the effect of harassment and have generated fear among Israeli citizens. Hezbollah gained in strength under Nasrallah's leadership when Israel had to eventually withdraw all military within the country. The withdrawal also increased recognition of the group within the region and caught worldwide attention. The consequence of Israel withdrawing was to essentially reinforce Hezbollah's determination to push back against Israel.

Table 2-1: A Top-Level Analysis of Hezbollah Antecedents and Consequences

ANTECEDENTS	BEHAVIOR	CONSEQUENCES
Attempt by Israel to move forces into Lebanon U.S. support of foreign or Israeli movement into Lebanon Movement of U.S., French, or other Western allies into Lebanese region Open and active Phalange opposition to Hezbollah Israeli attack against Palestinian person(s) Foreign attempt to support strengthening of Israel Foreign attempt to support Israel in Palestinian struggle	Primarily assault, bombing, kidnapping, and rocket bombardment (historically Katyusha rockets)	Death, injury, property damage, harassment, media attention to highlight the Hezbollah cause, prevention of Israeli movement into Lebanon, ongoing reinforcement of Hezbollah stated ideology, leverage, political and financial support (Iran/ Syria), fear, withdrawal of Israeli troops

Table 2-1 presents only a high-level view of antecedents prompting Hezbollah resistance and attacks. A detailed analysis points to over 100 antecedents. Some combination of these antecedents occurs on a daily basis, and the promise of desired consequences is ever-present. Both Israel and Hezbollah exhibit offensive and defensive behavior. The result is back and forth reactions. In other words, the Hezbollah activities serve as antecedents for Israeli retaliation behavior, and the Israeli retaliation behaviors serve as antecedents for Hezbollah attacks against Israel. It is not difficult to see that this is a formula for a long-term struggle.

This is a characteristic pattern of behavior. The eye for an eye principle has its roots in religion. It has existed over thousands of years as a way to moderate conflict. It basically means that we should not overreact to an assault or attack; rather we should meet malicious behavior directed at us with a measured response that is equal to the initial assault. Because of this overriding principle in the Mideast, there has not been an overwhelming response to defeat the adversary. Instead, one assault begets a response in kind. That response is viewed as an attack and begets a response from the adversary, and so on and so on. For this reason, at least from a behavioral perspective, there is no end in sight to this back and forth, action-reaction pattern.

ThemeMate provided us with the facts to prepare the report to this point. Synthesizing the facts of the report, including the identification of the cyclic, back and forth, eye for an eye tactics, allows us to make a conclusion.

Conclusions: A behavior analysis perspective views the ongoing struggle between Israel and Hezbollah as a chain of behavior on both sides. It will take an agreement to stop at some jointly determined date with both sides adhering to a long-term cease-fire regardless of what happened just before the beginning of the cease-fire. Antecedent conditions on both sides will have to be addressed. Israel will likely never give on its right to exist, and Hezbollah will never give on its ideology, supported by Iran and its refusal to recognize Israel. If both sides agree to not retaliate on an eye for an eye basis at some date, then the first step is completed. It may be possible to then work out the differences based on antecedent conditions as grievances through negotiation instead of loss of life.

Analyzing the Coordinated Group Cyber Threat

Chapter 1 focused on individual threat. When thinking about cyber threat, we tend to think of the lone hacker attacking networks either at random until damage is done or by diligently going after a specific target until successful. As time has progressed over the past decade, it has become obvious that the financial element has entered the picture as an additional motivator, as well as the availability of classified or proprietary information/data. The media has been prolific in covering the *suspected* coordinated People's Republic of China (PRC) attempts and successes in intruding into a variety of sensitive networks worldwide to extract sensitive information. Unlike the analysis of group malicious behavior, such as al-Qaeda and Hezbollah, a study of group cyber attack behavior is much more difficult because the perpetrators are more likely to be anonymous.

To conduct an analysis, we collected and submitted more than 200 open source media articles describing attacks against U.S. proprietary targets to ThemeMate. These articles consisted of persistent and ongoing threat associated with a multitude of ongoing attacks and fit the definition of advanced persistent threat (APT). This type of threat is represented by a relatively new term. APT means nation-state supported and advanced threat. Because of the significance of this type of advanced threat that has the resources to remain persistent as directed against a specific target, it is covered here. However, if we wanted to focus on a decentralized group that at least has an identity, we could focus on the international hacktivist organization known as *Anonymous*. Although not nearly as serious of a group in terms of threat to the United States, the loosely defined group is an organization tied together by a common community of interests.

> **NOTE** McAfee defined advanced persistent threat (APT) as a "targeted cyberespionage or cybersabotage attack that is carried out under the sponsorship or direction of a nation-state for something other than a pure financial/criminal reason or political protest." (*Network World*, http://www.networkworld.com/news/2011/020111-advanced-persistent-threat.html)

A behavior analysis perspective, as applied to suspected Chinese APT, focuses not only on what has occurred in the past but also on the targeting, the motivations fueling such intrusions, why the behavior is reoccurring, and the antecedents prompting the incursions into privacy of U.S. networks/organizations and the suspected consequences of maintaining the intrusive behaviors.

According to a U.S. House of Representatives report prepared by the Subcommittee on Oversight and Investigations of the Committee on Foreign Affairs dated April 15, 2011, we have been labeled as the enemy by the PRC, and we have been the target of massive cyber theft of sensitive and restricted information. The report, titled *Communist Chinese Cyber-Attacks, Cyber-Espionage and Theft of American Technology*, states that China has focused its efforts to obtain U.S. technology secrets for many years. To quote Dana Rohrabacher, the chairperson of the subcommittee preparing the report, "The United States is under attack."

This is a profound statement and has shades of the horror of the 9/11 al-Qaeda attack on the United States. The fact that we are under serious cyber attack resulting in theft of our technology is critical. We need to learn to fear the effects of cyber intrusions into our borders just as we fear a terrorist bombing, hijacking, or 9/11 attack. Losing defense information on weapons systems through cyber theft could essentially result in our defense technology not being able to save lives when we count on it. This is serious. American citizens are accustomed to seeing threat and seeing the effects of an attack. Cyber attacks are different. They are more difficult to see, and the results may not always be determined.

Unlike the individual hacker as described in Chapter 1, a coordinated group hacking effort will provide additional manpower to direct toward a target, and if an attack is organized properly, results can be almost guaranteed.

The report indicates that China does approach hacking U.S. and other countries' networks as a well-organized effort. This organization includes China's research facilities, businesses, defense agencies, and computer network operations as a cohesive force tasked with targeting technology secrets. What fuels this very large effort? Part of China's official national policy is to be self-sufficient and become the lead in technology during the next 40 years. Stealing vital information that took years to develop is an obvious shortcut.

Stealing ideas and methods can save many years of development and, perhaps more important, steer development efforts away from technological blind alleys and wrong turns. The path to significant research findings is not like boarding a train in Washington and traveling a well-known path on the designated track to New York City. Instead, it is more like navigating across open water without navigation aids or a map. Stealing vital technology secrets is like stealing those missing navigation aids and the map showing how to get there. This is a primary reason that motivates corporate espionage within industry. Time to full productization isn't really fueled by the desire to improve technology as an end in itself. It is about business. To be competitive, one must reach the market quickly. To take the market lead requires speed of development, competitive pricing, insight into exactly what is needed and what will sell, and hardened products.

If the technology desired is within the defense area, then speed of development may be even more important. To protect one's country from the perceived threat of attack requires not only understanding an adversary's technology but also understanding the countermeasures, as well. China appears to have embraced this perspective and is actively engaged in an organized effort to acquire technological advances by theft as part of its national research and development program.

Although China has officially declared the United States as an enemy, the need to protect proprietary and classified information from all countries is essential unless part of a sharing program with clear goals and objectives. As we say in intelligence, *there are no allies*. Research and development (R&D) is extremely expensive; there is no reason to give away competitive advantage. So, does this mean we must have excessive controls on our proprietary development secrets? No!

We tend to be a trusting country in that much of our R&D has few safeguards. Part of science and engineering historically has been to share methods and results. As researchers we go to conferences and present our latest research, emphasizing both our methods and our findings. We publish detailed methodological steps not only in scientific journals but also in the popular press. Many technology-focused publications, such as *Jane's Defence Weekly*, provides key information of defense technologies. Successful fiction writers in our country such as Tom Clancy need only to read press releases, journals, and defense-related publications and watch science documentaries to abstract the knowledge to write extremely enjoyable and accurate books. We simply give much of our technology away.

Given that a foreign country such as China could actually learn much about our technology by simply having teams to scour publications releases, and surely they do, how much better is it to have a cohesive network hacking capability to steal those secrets that don't make it to the press? It is invaluable. In the case of proprietary and classified information theft, a national policy that condones stealing must exclude a policy emphasizing ethics and being a member of the global community.

Although theft of proprietary and classified information appears to be first and foremost, China has other reasons for hacking into other countries' networks. In early 2010, Google released to the media that its had discovered Chinese incursions into its network. One of the reasons was to use a phishing attack to access Gmail (Google's popular e-mail account system that anyone can use) accounts of Chinese human rights activists. A phishing attack consists of spoofing (faking) a real site. When you receive an e-mail with a link to this site, it automatically inserts malicious code that may be capable of stealing your user ID and password, or maybe even credit card or other personal information. By using this type of attack, the Chinese were identifying Chinese human rights activists — their enemy — by accessing their Google Gmail accounts.

The mounting evidence is overwhelming. The Chinese are using an organized hacking group, or sets of groups, to combine skills to be effective in achieving their national goals and objectives.

The Group Structure

It is believed that the primary cyber hacking force comes from the People's Liberation Army (PLA) within China. The PLA, the world's largest military, is a significant force. To place it in perspective, the PLA has as many individuals in its ranks as we do with all women, men, and children in the United States combined. Access to such a large pool of individuals means that the cream of the crop may be chosen for specialized purposes. Also, if we consider that others may be used outside of the military, we are facing an awesome and likely growing force of a cyber army. Reviewing the Chinese press also points to a patriotic appeal to all citizens. If you couple the guidelines of a national policy to surge ahead in technological advances with a patriotic appeal, you realize that citizens may be convinced that by helping gather proprietary and classified information, they are helping the country.

It is not for certain what the structure of the cyber hacking group(s) is. If it is contained within the PLA, we can assume a military-like structure that is especially regimented. As a military group, we would expect strategic leadership at the top that serves as the guide for tactical hacking among the cyber soldiers.

For the most part, U.S. security policies take a defensive approach. The purpose from a cyber perspective is to protect networks from invasion, theft, and damage. We can expect that because China appears to be behind many cyber invasions of our trusted networks that it more than likely has offensive and defensive elements.

Invading networks to extract information requires stealth and expertise. China does not wish to be identified as cyber soldiers working diligently to steal the world's technology secrets. Therefore, it must exercise its duties with the dual characteristics mentioned in the previous chapter: expertise and deception. As mentioned, my work on malicious cyber attack narrowed characteristics to these two behavioral dimensions. They are likely especially relevant for coordinated group hacks at our protected networks.

It is logical that if foreign groups are to be effective in entering our specialized and targeted networks to steal the type of information they want, they need great skill. This degree of expertise is greater than the skill if they were just required to inflict damage — for example, a denial-of-service attack to shut down a network temporarily does not require a great deal of expertise. To steal targeted information, navigation through a network is necessary to locate the material needed. Likewise, the incursion must be conducted with a great deal of deception and stealth to not be discovered. The ability to keep going back to the site to gather information, as well as new updated information, means that they need to avoid discovery, because any detected attempts to steal information can result in the rapid dissemination of offending IP addresses for broad-based network protection across organizations, or multiple networks within an organization.

DEFINITION A *whitelist* is typically a list of IP addresses allowed to enter a network while all others are blocked. In this way, only known, trusted individuals or organizations may have access. Conversely, a *blacklist* is a set of IP addresses that are known to engage in malicious behaviors and that may be denied access.

Using a combination of whitelists and blacklists as a rapid course of action could be effective in preventing the proliferation of an attack. However, the process would have to occur in real-time because a smart perpetrator is not going to keep using the same IP address. Given relatively slow forensics, if an attack is discovered days or even hours after the fact, blocking IP addresses may not be that effective if the perpetrator has been back repeatedly using different source IPs. Speed is the key, and its one that we must conquer to become truly proactive within the cyber threat space.

Surprisingly, an analysis of malicious behavior in general shows that there are only two ways malicious offensive behavior may be directed toward another person, group, or organization.

- The first way is to inflict harm or damage of some type. In other words, the perpetrator presents something undesired or painful to the target.

- The second way is to take away something pleasant or desired.

As an analogy, if a foreign group inflicts a denial of service at one of our networks to flood and overwhelm it, it is using the first type of malicious behavior. If the same group were to enter a site surreptitiously and steal restricted, proprietary, or classified information, it would be exhibiting the second type of malicious behavior. Methods used for both approaches may overlap, but they require entirely different skill sets.

Conclusions: ThemeMate analysis provided as many facts as possible given the anonymity of the perpetrators. However, the degree of information obtained by processing a corpus of open source documents allows us to provide a synthesis of findings and draw conclusions. The following is an example of the type of conclusions that can be drawn, even if the perpetrator and structure of the coordinating group are not known with certainty.

During the spring and summer of 2011, the news began to report on the Chinese establishment of what essentially equates to cyber commands to protect against informational warfare within the PLA. So, by China's official admission, the PLA is in the cyber informational warfare business, albeit with a stated defensive purpose. Therefore, given the importance that China places on becoming the leader in technology, the rather apparent attempts to steal information from the United States and other countries, the importance of the effort by placing it within the PLA, and the anticipated huge scale of the operation, we have to assume the effort has the following structure:

- Typical military structure with strategic guidance at the top and tactical hacking among the cyber soldiers

- Extensive assessment of skill levels and potential for selection of individuals to participate as cyber soldiers

- Extensive training to prepare individuals for incursions into foreign networks with high skill and high deception

- Levels of military supervision to span strategic planning down to tactical daily hacking

- Attempts to reinforce cyber soldiers for success in achieving objectives

- A collection of state-of-the-art hacker tools and methods

- Attendance at worldwide conferences to keep abreast of the latest methods and procedures (both defensive network intrusion courses and Black Hat–related meetings)

- Directed tasks and targeting in which specific targeting occurs based on the type of technology desired

DEFINITION A *Black Hat meeting* brings together hackers (crackers) to share hacking techniques and scripts to gain access into networks for the purpose of inflicting damage or achieving theft of proprietary or classified material.

According to the *Communist Chinese Cyber-Attacks, Cyber-Espionage and Theft of American Technology* report, the U.S. patent office receives approximately 500,000 patent applications a year from around the world with about half of these being from the United States. Despite this massive volume, the report indicates that the U.S. patent office has the oldest computers in the federal government. Again, we may simply not be placing enough emphasis on proprietary information. Old technology does not provide much protection against incursions into the inner workings and protected information. Given that some unknown fraction of the patent applications should not be shared, we may have to assume that access to these applications may have already been gained. There is obviously a difficult balance to strike between having an open and free society that shares scientific and engineering advances in the name of a type of technological academic freedom and making it more difficult to steal U.S. technology advances from foreign powers.

Furthermore, we tend to act as though a U.S. patent is enough. A U.S. patent is important, but to have full protection, we must file for international patents. It is simply too easy to go outside of the United States and pursue the same basic idea under a foreign patent. Some choose trade secret protection, although trade secrets are effective only to the degree that they stay secret. It is very difficult to prevent loss of trade secret information. Therefore, if patents are going to be filed to protect proprietary information, foreign patents should be filed at the same time.

The Motivation

On April 29, 2009, the *Wall Street Journal* reported that the 300 billion dollar F-35 fighter plane network was breeched and hackers were able to steal several terabytes of detailed information, including design data. Obviously, this is an immense amount of information when perhaps a single document or two of the right kind could be too much.

NOTE A terabyte of information is equivalent to all of the information in a small technical library, while 2 terabytes is all of the textual information available in a midsized technical library.

Given that the current cyber warfare elements are in the PLA, it is apparent that military-related technology would be high on the list for theft. Much R&D work is expended on developing new fighter aircraft, and loss of proprietary information can be devastating. The F-35 represents a new breed of aircraft that is versatile, comes in different variants for different purposes, and has stealth capability. No doubt a target for espionage and theft, the F-35 is representative of the type of technology targeted.

China represents a formidable opponent in the cyber domain. To give perspective to China's versatility and to demonstrate the power of the Chinese focus on acquiring proprietary information, on April 8, 2010, the Chinese were able to route approximately 15 percent of all Internet traffic through its servers. This is a significant feat, and it's one that is difficult to achieve without detection. Of particular note is that the U.S. government/military flow of traffic was part of this traffic rerouting for the 18 minutes that it occurred. Of course, once information is on their servers, that information can be stored and examined.

The motivation of the Chinese appears to be fairly clear. First, given the patriotic policy to surge ahead and be world leaders in technology, shortcuts are needed. Intellectual theft is definitely a shortcut. Theft of intellectual and classified information using cyber methods and tools can occur at the speed of light, or close to it, with minimal risk. Hackers working in concert can work effectively to target numerous U.S. sites for proprietary or classified information theft. Large numbers of cyber soldiers can work relentlessly until success is achieved.

The Chinese are dedicated to making continued rapid advances in technology and to continue growing their cyber capability. The desire to shortcut the development process and to acquire sensitive information from other countries is considered fair game. The result is very strong motivation to continue the type of group effort observed and to use cyber methods to obtain their goals. Earlier in this chapter, I presented two forms of malicious behavior: unpleasant or undesirable stimuli presented to a target or pleasant or desirable objects taken away from a target. The Chinese approach in the cyber area is definitely the latter. Their motivation does not seem to be the delivery of unpleasant stimuli such as disruption, denial of service, and so on. Instead, they seek to remove information, technology, data, and perhaps clues to our current technological avenues.

A Behavior Analysis

Chapters 19 and 20 and the DVD will present in detail how to use the principles in this book to predict malicious behavior. To do that requires the background presented in these initial chapters. A major part of the predictive method is a clear understanding of the three components: antecedents, behavior, and consequences. This sequence not only is important in prediction but also provides a structure for gaining insight into the who, where, when, why, what, and how of malicious behavior. Too often, an analysis of malicious group behavior is based on an analysis of the behaviors only. For example, by counting the types of past tactics of a group such as Hezbollah or al-Qaeda, you can discover the base rate of behavior, which is simply the percentage that certain tactics such as assault, bombing, hijacking, and so on have occurred in all past attacks. This approach tells us the preferred methods from the most frequent to the least frequent. However, it is not sufficient for true prediction of future behavior.

Using a behavior analysis to identify antecedents and consequences of behavior begins the process of identifying the key components for a deeper predictive analysis. These components combined with motivation, ideology, group guidelines, and recent adversary behavior all interact to provide a basis for anticipating a group's next actions.

You must keep in the forefront that analysis and prediction of human malicious behavior does not depend on a particular statistical approach. The secret sauce does not lie in the statistical methods used. Humans don't react statistically; they react to the environment. Base rates simply state what the probability of the next act may be, not when, who will be targeted, how, where the event will occur, or the specifics of targeting. Basically, base rates are informative but not predictive. The key to accurate analysis and anticipation of future malicious behavior depends on the underlying model used to determine patterns of behavior that will repeat in the future.

Analyzing China's cyber activities to gain access to proprietary technological information or to identify and track Chinese human rights activists in the Google e-mail system depends on understanding the motivations and ideology that focuses the Chinese on specific antecedent conditions in the environment that signal that it is time to conduct a cyber event. The successful consequences will reinforce the same methods. However, we can expect to see a shift in methods because not all methods used have been successful.

Success in hacking to the degree that China has exhibited depends on two forms of success.

- First, the information desired has been acquired. From this perspective, the Chinese have had success. Because of the success, we can expect cyber-based theft to continue.

- The second form of success is deception — if they are going to engage in the high frequency and volume of cyber theft we have observed, then they will need to do so with increased successful deception. They will have to be stealthier.

The United States now understands the policy of surging forward to be a lead in technology, the use of cyber methods to steal classified and proprietary information, and the growth of China's military information warfare component.

We can add to this the Chinese desire not to be discovered engaging in cyber theft. They typically deny that they have engaged in this activity when accused. Because of this, we can expect extended development in the deception area if China's efforts are to become more covert.

The lack of success that follows behavior will typically mean that the group will shift its behavior slightly. Whether behaving as an individual or as a group, humans do not tend to repeat behavior that ends in lack of success. As the old saying goes, which has been attributed to Albert Einstein, "Insanity is doing the same thing, over and over again, but expecting different results." As a general rule, we do not keep repeating the same behavior over and over again unless it leads to success. If we repeat behavior, then it is because it is followed by the same expected results.

At this stage it is safe to say that they do not admit to or claim any incidents of cyber theft. Perhaps one of the key concepts of a behavior analysis on this topic is the definition of success, as it is so critical to considering if behavior observed will continue as-is or shift based on something less than success. Being caught at what equates to significant espionage can be very embarrassing culturally. Given the complex economic relationship between China and the United States and the competition for top spots in technology, it is essential that better methods of deception be developed and incorporated into the Chinese cyber methodology. This makes it much more challenging for U.S. security practices.

It is very clear that a reactive, signature-detection-based network intrusion methodology will not detect alterations in deception. As mentioned in the previous chapter with individual analysis, we need to also be proactive with malicious group analysis. It is possible to anticipate shifts in behavior if the Chinese are caught in the act. The question becomes, "Can we anticipate how the behavior will change?" The Chinese cyber threat is growing rapidly.

Advantages of AuBA #2: Theme-Guided Smart Searches

Submitting a text corpus to AuBA-automated tools is key for the creation of both significant theme-based reports and the development and validation of predictive engines. Typically, an analyst collects documents of interest until there is a sufficient number to submit to ThemeMate. Rather than simply collecting text articles of interest for a specific set of topics, ThemeMate provides an additional method for building the all-important text corpus that will lead to behavior-based theme identification. I call the feature *theme-guided smart search*. The basic principle is that for every unique theme identified within the initial corpus, ThemeMate selects a set of keywords that support the development of any given theme. Each theme identified across all documents may have a set of 10–50 words, depending on the ThemeMate-determined significance of the theme.

These sets of words are found under Theme Components in ThemeMate. If you happen to be particularly interested in Theme #16 (T16) and you go to Theme Components and click on the theme components for that theme, the ThemeMate tools automatically use these words as search words for a Google search. The results are almost immediate. The exact same documents often are returned from these seemingly unrelated words. More important, highly similar documents will be identified. These new documents may be added to the corpus to augment that specific theme with more detailed background information.

For example, we developed a new phishing module for the CheckMate application. This application processes external traffic coming into a network to assess the presence of threat. To develop the module, we collected a set of documents that showed examples of phishing attacks. ThemeMate identified more than 100 conceptual themes. Theme 16 (T16) was identified as *Copy-Paste*. This theme, stated as two keywords we call a pair, was generated and associated with the many examples of phishing, which included an e-mail that had a copy and paste request. Of course, if you click on copy and paste in an e-mail, malicious code will be installed on your hard drive. A ThemeMate "pair" is a shorthand method of identifying a theme using the least number of words possible.

Figure 2-4 shows a screenshot of the keywords ThemeMate selected for the copy-paste theme. The words are probably not the typical words we would use for a search. If the user clicks on this set of words, a Google search uses the terms and returns results of the search, as shown in the screenshot of the actual search results (Figure 2-5). The results are typical in that document links returned are very relevant to the topic. These additional documents may then be added to the corpus to augment information on copy and paste methods associated with phishing attacks.

T16	copy paste accept adds get list somebody tell virus because called everyone

Figure 2-4: The keywords ThemeMate saved for a copy-paste feature of some phishing attacks.

Figure 2-5: A Google search that occurs when a user clicks on the theme components shown in Figure 2-4.

In Summary

This chapter presents an introduction to how group analysis using behavior-based methods can work. It is not a step-by-step treatise on how to conduct the analysis — that will come throughout the book and in the accompanying DVD. There are a variety of group efforts to conduct malicious threats resulting in causing damage, harm, and death and in the theft of proprietary and classified information. The types of groups that demand our concern include terrorist groups, organized criminal group activity, and those groups engaged in coordinated cyber attacks. However, there are many types of malicious groups. Such groups include:

- Foreign terrorist groups
- Domestic terrorist groups

- Domestic hate groups
- Coordinated cyber attack groups
- Domestic gangs
- Criminal groups
- Outlaw groups (for example, motorcycle gangs)

These groups may all be analyzed and future behavior anticipated using the methods presented in this book.

Why is group behavior so feared? It is an interesting fact that with the exception of 9/11 when approximately 1 terrorist-related citizen death occurred for each 15 auto accident fatalities in the United States, there is approximately 1 terrorist-related citizen death for each 900 to 1,000 auto accident fatalities for any given year. Yet, it is fair to say that we as a society fear terrorism more than auto fatalities. Although the numbers killed in auto accidents far outweigh the numbers lost to terrorism, there is one very large difference. Psychologically, when we enter a car we have direct control of the vehicle. Our hands are on the steering wheel, our foot is on the accelerator and brake, our eyes are on the road, we are aware of the traffic conditions, we view the mirror, and our ears are tuned to sounds of driving and warnings from others in the car. If we are unfortunate enough to be at the wrong place at the wrong time and are victims of terrorism, or other group violence, there is no control. The inability to have control is fearful to us as humans. With control comes reduction in fear.

Analysis of group malicious behavior can result in a better understanding of that group's behavior and, as will be demonstrated at the completion of this book, the ability to anticipate group behavior accurately. Understanding is like control; it helps in removing fear. Although there are many reasons to develop and improve methods to predict malicious behavior, reducing the elements of surprise and reducing fear as a result of surprise rank among the top reasons.

To analyze malicious group behavior, we must determine the ideology and motivation of the group, as well as any guidelines for operating as a group member. These *rules* interact with environmental influences to focus a group in targeting victims and also contribute to the definition of success or lack of success that is so important to maintaining the behavior of the group.

This chapter laid out the basics of analysis by showing examples of group malicious behavior. Terrorism in the form of al-Qaeda and Hezbollah poses a threat to U.S. citizens. This threat is growing. Cyber threats are a relatively new form of fear for U.S. citizens. We need to learn to realize just how serious cyber attack and theft are as threats to our national and economic security. More important, this book demonstrates how we can improve our safety through the use of behavior analysis to make our security policies more proactive.

CHAPTER 3

Analyzing Country-Level Threats

In the days of muskets, clipper ships, and gunpowder poured from a powder horn, the physical location of North America, with the vast Atlantic Ocean to the east and the Pacific Ocean to the west, provided natural barriers to attack. This changed when the British invaded the colonies from across the Atlantic during the Revolutionary War and again during the War of 1812. Then, in the mid-1860s, Mexico attacked across land borders during the Mexican American War. On December 7, 1941, 353 Japanese fighter planes attacked Pearl Harbor in Hawaii, drawing the United States into World War II — a new era of warfare had surfaced.

Compared to the basic soldier-to-soldier warfare of the past, Pearl Harbor ushered in the use of modern-day technology as a tool to support attacks against the United States. Technology had effectively removed what protection was left of the vast distance the ocean had provided to that time.

Technology today has significantly reduced the protection afforded by natural barriers. Cyber attacks launched from foreign entities can reach a computer holding sensitive data inside the Department of Defense in Virginia within seconds with little to no probability that the attacker will be identified. Boundaries are still there, just different. Instead of an ocean, we have firewalls and network intrusion detection applications. However, these boundaries are simply diminishing in effectiveness. We are now facing a new threat profile. This chapter addresses the concerns of the new world of threat made possible with modern-day technology.

Threats to Our National Infrastructure

Threats to the United States have evolved parallel with advancements in technology. When this country was formed, communication between two people with one in Great Britain and one in the colonies would occur via letter or from an acquaintance carried by ship across the expanse of the Atlantic Ocean. If there was an answer, the return trip occurred in the same way and in the same time frame. The interchange could take many months.

Communication via e-mail, Twitter, or a text message can leave one person in Great Britain and is received by a person in the United States within a second, with a return response occurring in an additional second. The time it takes to convey a message and get a response across the two countries now occurs approximately 6-8 million times faster than in colonial times. In addition, we can now have real-time video teleconferences and speak with and see the other person instantly literally anywhere in the world.

When the captains of those early ships crossed the Atlantic Ocean to arrive in America, they navigated with a compass, a few crude instruments, and incomplete charts. Now, at a push of a button, we know our exact location anywhere on Earth within a few feet. In fact, if we hook the GPS device to the steering mechanism of a missile, it can guide itself to the actual destination target with unparalleled accuracy.

The firepower in colonial days amounted to a muzzle-loaded handgun, rifle, or cannon. It could take 30 seconds to a minute for a real speed demon to reload after a single shot. Today, a Mac machine pistol found on the streets can fire from 18 to 20 rounds per second, meaning 1 minute of continuous fire is equivalent to over 1,000 colonialists shooting their handheld weapon once in 1 minute.

Then add flight. On December 17, 1903, Wilbur and Orville Wright made the first powered flight at Kitty Hawk, North Carolina. The plane was in the air 12 seconds and traveled 120 feet. In 2011, a little more than 100 years later, the Defense Advanced Research Projects Agency (DARPA), a frequent funder of my work, test flew the fastest plane in the world, which was designed to travel 13,000 miles per hour and could travel 43.3 miles in those same 12 seconds.

In 1946, the United States dropped an atomic bomb on Hiroshima and 3 days later another massive atomic bomb on Nagasaki in Japan, effectively ending World War II. These single weapons carried the firepower of approximately 15,000 tons of TNT explosive. Approximately 70,000 people lost their lives immediately in Hiroshima alone with at least as many buildings destroyed. The world was in awe. Today, a single hydrogen bomb may be thousands of times more powerful than the atomic bombs dropped on Japan in WWII.

Many countries now maintain nuclear warheads. Figure 3-1 shows an estimate of current active warheads maintained by nine countries, not including stockpiled weapons. Threats have increased on a global basis with each warhead developed. One needs only to examine the Cuban Missile Crisis of October 1962 to realize just how close the United States and Russia came to mutual annihilation, taking much of the world with them.

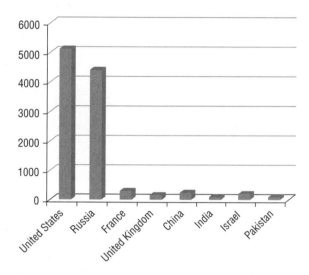

Figure 3-1: The approximate number of nuclear warheads maintained by country

The amount of nuclear weapons firepower has escalated over the years, moving from the United States being the sole holder of the technology in World War II to a growing number of countries holding these weapons today. Although there has been a concerted effort to decrease the number of weapons actively maintained, the numbers and combined destructive power remains exceedingly high.

There have been many other technological advances that have changed our world. We have witnessed manned space travel, and now our unmanned flights reach the outer planets of the solar system and send back images, technically allowing our eyes to travel in outer space. Television allows us to go along for the ride and lets us witness worldwide events in real time.

Complete encyclopedias could be written that simply list the technological advances occurring since the founding of America. It is fair to say that there have been many more technological advances in this period of time than in all of the combined years of recorded history prior. With all the tremendous benefits of technology in such areas as science, medicine, communication, education, security, flight, and so on, technology has also aided those who intend harm to the United States and its citizens.

Traditionally, war between two countries, or among multiple countries, was fought more or less along the lines of one country's military being pitted against another country's military. As time continued, technology has helped to change the face of warfare. Strategy and tactics have changed. *Asymmetric warfare* was invented. This type of warfare occurs when an imbalance of forces is present and the more disadvantaged side from a force perspective can balance the struggle with the element of surprise and by not following centuries of warfare strategy and tactics.

This is our country's new threat. Because numerous countries are now capable of annihilating one another with nuclear weapons of almost unimaginable proportions, warfare has changed. The increase in the effectiveness of terrorism and the advent of significant and damaging cyber attacks are examples of the new threat. Enemies of the United States who could not even dream of a traditional war with us can engage in asymmetric warfare tactics and inflict considerable damage capitalizing on the elements of surprise.

Although asymmetric warfare tactics can be carried out in a more cost-effective manner than traditional warfare, it is still expensive and requires support. For this reason, many terrorist groups of today are state-supported — that is, they receive direct financial support, training, intelligence, and weapons from countries that view the United States as the enemy. Because it can be difficult to prove that a country has supported a specific terrorist group in a specific act, it is difficult for the United States to retaliate against the supporting country, even if the group claims responsibility.

There are exceptions, and occasionally state support is determined. For example, Iranian support for the Hezbollah organization is well known. The support helps focus attacks on Israel as part of its stated "annihilate Israel" objective. Perhaps two of the best examples of direct support and complicity were the determinations that Libya directly supported the April 5, 1981, bombing of a German nightclub and the December 21, 1988, bombing of the in-flight Pan American flight 103 jumbo jet over Lockerbie, Scotland. In the former incident, 3 were killed and hundreds injured. In the Pan Am flight 103 bombing, 270 individuals were killed, including victims on the ground when the plane crashed in Lockerbie from a height of more than 30,000 feet.

Because of the rising asymmetric warfare threats to our country, with an increased emphasis after the 9/11 al-Qaeda attack, the Department of Homeland Security (DHS) was formed to protect our country's infrastructure.

NOTE The Department of Homeland Security has a vital mission: to secure the nation from the many threats we face. This requires the dedication of more than 230,000 employees in jobs that range from aviation and border

security to emergency response, from cyber security analyst to chemical facility inspector. Our duties are wide-ranging, but our goal is clear — keeping America safe. See `www.dhs.gov/xabout` **for more information.**

Although DHS also includes protection and recovery from natural disasters, this chapter focuses on a primary concern: foreign country threat to the United States. Any form of attack within our borders must be and will remain a major concern of DHS, as well as all citizens of our country. State support is very difficult to prove. Given terrorist tactics and the expense to maintain active operations, it is advisable to assume support from adversary countries until proven otherwise. For example, it was a time-consuming process to determine if Libyan leaders had supported the German discotheque and Pan Am 103 bombings. It is well known that Iranian-founded Hezbollah is actively supported by Iran today with potential political support from Syria. It is also likely that Pakistan supports a variety of terrorist elements within Pakistan. In the case of the latter, Ramzi Yousef, the mastermind of the first World Trade Center bombing, and Mir Aimal Kansi (Kasi), the CIA headquarters killer, were captured in Islamabad, Pakistan. More recently, Osama bin Laden, the most infamous of all terrorists in history, was killed by U.S. Special Forces and the CIA in Pakistan within line of site from the primary Pakistani military academy, where he had hidden for years.

The world of terrorism and foreign country complicity is covert — it is not advertised, and much is conducted as intelligence operations. Table 3-1 lists sample threats to the United States, its citizens worldwide, and allies that could require foreign state support. These threats require constant vigilance on the parts of our military and intelligence, as well as our foreign allies. The seriousness of the types of attacks listed underscores our need to be better able to anticipate threats as they surface.

Table 3-1: Threats Facing the United States and Allies with High Potential of Adversarial Nation-State Support

TYPE OF THREAT	INFRASTRUCTURE TARGET AND TACTIC	TECHNOLOGY
Cyber attack	Inflict damage — for example, denial-of-service (DOS) attacks during conventional attacks to disrupt first responders	Advanced knowledge of cyber attack tactics to disrupt communication
Cyber theft	Cyber theft of classified information or proprietary technology — network intrusion, phishing, spear phishing	Advanced knowledge and skills in deceptive intrusion and theft of desired restricted material

Continued

Table 3-1 (continued)

TYPE OF THREAT	INFRASTRUCTURE TARGET AND TACTIC	TECHNOLOGY
Chemical	Potential weapon of mass destruction against Americans on U.S. soil	Knowledge of toxic chemicals and chemical weapons construction
Biological	Potential weapon of mass destruction against Americans on U.S. soil	Knowledge of fatal biological agents and biological agent weapons construction
Radiological	Potential dirty bomb to contaminate symbolic and real government/military targets in dense U.S. gatherings	Knowledge of radiological materials, safe handling, and unique bomb construction using conventional explosives spreading radioactive material
Nuclear	Detonated stolen or purchased nuclear weapon to cause massive numbers of American casualties	Low probability event but maximum devastation and loss of life, potential nuclear *suitcase bomb*, densely populated major cities
Explosives (suicide bombing)	Military/government-hardened targets such as military bases, seats of government facilities, mass transit in United States (metro, train, airliner)	Advanced explosives knowledge and bomb-making skills — potential massive amounts of explosive or personal device
IED explosives (remote or timed detonation)	Massive U.S. civilian or military gatherings and extensive damage, mass transit in United States (metro, train, airliner)	Advanced high-yield explosives knowledge and bomb-making skills for leave-behind bomb
Suicide attacks outside of the United States	Symbolic attacks focused on American citizens and allies to show lack of ability to remain safe worldwide	Assault or bombing skills, surveillance knowledge of gatherings of multiple Americans or allies, or U.S. military in groups
Assault	Gatherings of U.S. military, allies, or U.S. citizens, airports, cafes/restaurants, foreign markets	Knowledge and skills in using handheld assault weapons and close assault tactics

For proactive security planning, we must realize that significant terrorist groups enjoy support in the form of funds, training, and even planning. The groups operate covertly, depend on the element of surprise, and operate within the United States. However, it has become more difficult to operate within the boundaries of the United States after 9/11. All U.S. citizens are more aware and more likely to report suspicious activity and suspicious individuals. This means that terrorists and foreign states targeting the United States must be even more deceptive than in the past and maintain more expertise. Attacks have to be smarter and result in even greater numbers of casualties. It is important for them to exceed the destructiveness and shock value of the infamous 9/11 attack.

At the same time as we increase our awareness of smart attacks within our borders by foreign elements, to be proactive we must understand the following:

- The United States is an adversary to many and maintains the most powerful military in the world armed with advanced technology and unprecedented firepower.

- A foreign country is not likely to attack the United States directly because of superior U.S. retaliation capability. The retaliation would be swift, effective, and devastating from a symbolic and actual surgical strike perspective to that country.

- A foreign country targeting the United States is likely to support a proxy group to attack within our borders or to target citizens and allies on a global basis.

- For the most part, our borders are secure, with perhaps the exception of the U.S./Mexican border, and attacking entities are more likely to use advanced technology to support their operations against the United States.

- We must realize that cyber attack is the *new* method of warfare whereby a foreign country can use specialized cyber attack groups trained to inflict damage or to steal classified/proprietary secrets with a current very low probability of being caught.

It is a new world. Technology has evolved to the degree that explosives are more advanced, pack more destructive power, and are more difficult to detect by conventional means. With the surfacing of enhanced cyber attack capabilities, we must be more advanced than the adversary if we are to move to a proactive stance. We must be able to anticipate attacks before they occur so that we can be ready to either prevent or mitigate any damage when the attempts do occur — attempts that currently occur on a daily basis and will most certainly be a part of our future.

Analyzing the Specific Threat of Terrorist Attacks

Terrorism has changed over the years to a current state where we must take a more proactive and predictive stance if we are to prevent significant damage and loss in the future. The 9/11 al-Qaeda attack demonstrated to the United States and the world how effective a surprise terrorist attack can be within our own borders. Beyond the loss of almost 3,000 individuals and property, the symbolic damage was immense. From a symbolic perspective, 19 terrorists had attacked a major economic and public target, as well as our strategic military headquarters. The coordinated attack highlighted gaping holes in our defenses and occurred while we watched helplessly in horror.

As a result of the 9/11 attack, the DHS was formed to coordinate all agencies and services that focus on infrastructure protection. However, it is essential that we not just take a stance that we will have superior reactive stances and heightened first responder effectiveness. These are essential but do not go far enough. We need improved methods of anticipating foreign-born attacks, whether that attack comes from a decentralized terrorist organization like al-Qaeda, state-supported terrorism, or the unlikely foreign state direct attack.

Current Terrorist Threats to the United States

The events of the infamous 9/11 al-Qaeda attack first had the immediate dual effect of shocking our country and forcing a sense of despair. Everyone old enough to realize what was happening during the 9/11 attack remembers precisely what he or she was doing at the time of the attack. As President George W. Bush visited a Florida elementary school class, the then White House Chief of Staff, Andrew Card, bent over and whispered into the President's ear, "America is under attack." The statement may have been softly whispered, but it was the whisper that was heard around the world. Reactions were varied. To the radical Islamic militant world, the reaction was gloating and rejoicing. To the vast majority of American citizens, shock would quickly turn to anger to accompany the severe sense of loss. On that day, emotions were rampant, but the plan for retaliation was already forming.

9/11 may have changed our view of terrorism forever. Prior to 9/11, terrorism was feared as an almost random, low-frequency event. Victims were considered to have been at the wrong place at the wrong time, usually somewhere around the world, not within the boundaries of the United States. As I noted at the end of Chapter 2, the risk of being killed while driving our car is far greater than the possibility of being killed in a terrorist attack, yet we are more likely to fear a terrorist attack than driving. The reason: Any threat that is accompanied by lack of control is highly feared. Flying in an airliner is so fearful for some that they simply do not fly, the decision to fly or not being the only form of control possible with flying. However, on that infamous day in our country's history, terrorism took on a new perspective. In one day, we realized that 19 terrorists could rival or surpass the Japanese attack on Pearl Harbor in 1941 that launched us into World War II. The events of 9/11 launched us into a true war against terrorism. Ironically, both attacks were by air. The Japanese Imperial Navy's attack on Pearl Harbor consisted of 353 fighter aircraft and 6 aircraft carriers and supporting firepower. 9/11 likely surpassed the damage of Pearl Harbor and consisted of only 19 terrorists and 4 hijacked commercial airliners. More important, we learned definitively that such a devastating attack could occur within the United States. Targets were carefully selected, and victims were not simply targets of opportunity.

Fear of terrorism now includes concern over weapons of mass destruction (chemical, biological, radiological, and nuclear weapons). Like our view of crime, which we do not expect to go away, our view of terrorism is it's a threat that is not going to go away. Furthermore, we realize that the incentive is there for adversaries to inflict even greater loss of property and life in carefully selected targets within the United States.

Al-Qaeda remains the top terrorist threat to the United States. Although the top leadership of the organization has been decimated, the organization remains intact and has the strength of being decentralized. The killing of Osama bin Laden on May 2, 2011, may have had the effect on the radical militant Islamic world that the 9/11 attack itself had on Americans. We experienced extreme pain, but out of the pain came a resolve that has resulted in the partial destruction of the al-Qaeda organization. Furthermore, on August 22, 2011, just 3 months after bin Laden was killed, Atiyah Abd al-Rahman, the designated number two leader of al-Qaeda, was killed. Al-Qaeda has been dealt two very powerful blows. Still, although the historical leadership is dead, al-Qaeda is very much alive. In any war, complacency and a false sense of victory are not options. We must remember that this organization can accomplish much with very little.

The United States is currently engaged in a war in Afghanistan, having just ended the 9-year war in Iraq, and supported NATO in the midst of the collapse of the Muammar Gadaffi regime in Libya. At the same time, the United States continues to be a strong ally and supporter of Israel and maintains allies with like-minded Western and Latin American countries. The effect is to continue to alienate both the Arab and the Islamic radical militants. These entities, and the various militant groups spawned to wage war against the United States, continue with goals and objectives to expel the U.S. presence from foreign lands, eradicate the State of Israel, and drain the United States of its financial resources. These militant groups seek to not only destroy the United States and its citizens around the world but seek financial and political support as well.

Analyzing threats from other countries by applying the extended form of applied behavior analysis and automated behavior analysis presented in this book using textual accounts of past events in the media results in the following as key antecedents to anti-U.S. attacks and anti-U.S. sentiment from foreign states and terrorist organizations:

- U.S. past and current presence in foreign lands.
- U.S. wars against countries such as Iraq and Afghanistan.
- U.S. support for the State of Israel.

- U.S. attacks and support of attacks against radical militant organizations that oppose the United States.

- Financial and political support to radical militant organizations from state benefactors (for example, Iran, Syria, Libya, and so on).

- The United States develops and maintains much of the top technology in the world.

- The United States is a holder of classified information that would betray the long-term and short-term strategic and tactical plans of the country.

- The United States is fueled by its economy with the economy remaining a foundation of the global economic structure.

- The U.S. association with and perceived influence over NATO and the United Nations.

- Militant- and state-perceived U.S. leadership on a global basis.

- Desecrating two holy Islamic lands with U.S. and Israeli presence within Saudi Arabia (Mecca, Medina, and the Prophet's Mosque) and Jerusalem (al-Aqsa Mosque and Dome of the Rock).

As a true behavior analysis highlights, antecedent conditions, combined with group motivations, provide the impetus for targeting and for militant action. Different entities respond to different antecedents in this presented set of conditions. Whereas China may react to the United States being the developer and holder of technological advances and work to acquire such secrets through advanced cyber theft (covered later in this chapter), foreign states and Islamic militant terrorist organizations are likely to respond to the remaining antecedents.

Malicious intent and behavior can occur when a targeted enemy such as the United States or Israel exhibits behavior in one or more of the listed antecedent areas. For example, the current Saudi Arabian leadership may be rejected by Islamic radical militants such as al-Qaeda if they are supportive of any U.S. or Israeli presence at selected holy sites within both Saudi Arabia and Jerusalem. The presence alone desecrates the pure religious sanctity of the sites. Saudi Arabia's tolerance of U.S. or Israeli presence within these sites is viewed in much the same way as the actual presence of the foreign impure trespassers.

An attack against the United States with nation-state support can fit both that nation's strategic plans and the need to support a terrorist organization. It is expensive to keep a strong terrorist organization thriving and in operational readiness. Such organizations are not businesses. They exist primarily to inflict damage and, as such, require external funding. What better funding organization could there be than a foreign state that shares grievances against the United States that is capable of providing some quiet combination of weapons, training, money, direction/guidance, intelligence, and military/asymmetric warfare guidance?

Table 3-1 (earlier in the chapter) made it clear that terrorist organizations can attack using a wide variety of tactics against a wide variety of targets. In considering a likely form of attack, we need to determine the likelihood of a more traditional form of attack versus a new form of attack. The latter increases the element of surprise in both the timing of the attack and the nature of the attack itself.

■ More traditional attacks would include remote or timed detonation of a bomb or a suicide bombing against more traditional targets. Because of the conflict in Iraq and Afghanistan, terrorist organizations have had many years to practice their skills in developing improvised explosive devices (IEDs) and suicide bombing technology. Devices, types of explosive materials used, and tactics have evolved to a state where IEDs and suicide bombings can be especially effective.

SUICIDE BOMBINGS: A SPECIAL CASE

Why are suicide bombings a special case as compared to other terrorist tactics? When an adversary believes strongly in giving his or her life as a delivery vehicle for a suicide bombing, the tactic has a high probability of success. A human-guided suicide bombing mission can home in on a very specific target, recognize potential detection, and use logic to avoid detection. I specialize in the design and construction of smart applications to detect malicious behavior and to react accordingly. During my many years in developing this automated behavior analysis (AuBA) specialty, my ongoing review of *smart systems* revealed to me that, as amazing as it all is, modern-day technology still cannot come close to the decision-making capability of the human brain. Given that a suicide bomber has been well trained in surveillance, deception, and bomb delivery, he or she will be able to cognitively avoid unanticipated obstacles and detection as the target is approached. However, it is also likely that a new form of attack could occur in contrast to a well-homed and tested tactic such as suicide bombing.

■ New attacks have the advantage of no signature, making it more difficult to determine the identity of the perpetrator, at least for a significant period of time. A new form of attack can result in confusion that can delay a retaliatory response. Furthermore, a new form of attack is less likely to be met with an existing defense. From a terrorist group's perspective, it is not known whether the United States has a countermeasure for new tactics. However, it is logical that the United States is not likely to have a defense against an attack never before witnessed because we tend to be reactive. Once an attack occurs, we will look for that type of attack in the future.

The 9/11 al-Qaeda attack within the United States is an example of a first-time attack. Prior to that time, we had not witnessed the simultaneous hijacking of fully fueled airliners as suicide bombing vehicles to be flown by terrorists into designated high-profile symbolic, economic, and military targets within the borders of the United States. The hybrid hijacking-suicide bombing mission encountered no countermeasures except for the impromptu resistance from a group of passengers on the airliner forced down into a field in Pennsylvania. To those passengers' well-deserved credit, they provided a countermeasure on the spot to a new attack.

There are distinct advantages to an attack within the United States not resembling past attacks. It is simply more likely that a second 9/11 type of attack would be a new form of attack. This assumption is based on the following:

- All terrorist attacks take planning and require specific orderly steps through completion. Such steps increase the probability of detection and mitigation before the attack can occur.

- Safe exit from a massive attack back out of the country is not likely; therefore, such an attack is likely to be a suicide operation.

- Because of 9/11, the awareness of U.S. security and law enforcement has been heightened as witnessed by active security measures in our airports.

- Measures used by U.S. security/law enforcement and the nature of technological countermeasure and detection devices tend to be reactive based on past attacks, making it more difficult to repeat the same or highly similar attack (for example, a repeat of the 9/11 method of operation is not likely).

- It is important not to fail, making a new form of attack with no countermeasures a likely approach.

- The 9/11 al-Qaeda attack set the bar for destructiveness and loss of life. The next terrorist attack would likely have to exceed the effects of 9/11.

It is also important to note that terrorist organizations can cooperate and share training and expertise. For example, open source searching (searching unrestricted media reports such as newspaper articles) shows some cooperation between al-Qaeda and Hezbollah. This is unusual given that al-Qaeda is Sunni and Hezbollah is Shia. In the Muslim world, the Shia and Sunni are violently opposed to one another, and there is evidence of cross-organization targeting of one another. However, as the old saying goes, "the enemy of my enemy is my friend." It is likely that violently opposed terrorist organizations such as Sunni-based al-Qaeda and Shia-based Hezbollah could cooperate in an attack against a common hated target — the United States.

The 9/11 incident changed the world in many ways. However, from a U.S. concern, it set the bar in terms of destructiveness and loss of life. Therefore, I think we should anticipate a new form of attack. In the next section, prevention of terrorist attacks within the United States will be explored.

Preventing Terrorist Attacks on U.S. Soil

Behavior analysis of past malicious behavior across a wide variety of topics indicates commonalities, or findings, that should be highlighted. These commonalities appear to be universal and serve as a foundation for understanding and predicting malicious behavior. More important, the findings can support a paradigm shift in security measures that could result in a move from a current reactive stance to more of a proactive and predictive stance. By being proactive with an improved ability to determine the who, where, when, what, and how of malicious behavior directed at the United States, we can develop more informed security measures to increase prevention instead of merely heightening our reactions.

The following lists some of the significant findings I've come to after conducting different studies and modeling malicious behavior on a global basis:

- In the antecedent-behavior-consequence (ABC) sequence in which malicious behavior is preceded by antecedent conditions that set the stage for threatening behavior to occur and desired consequences (death, property damage, or obtaining desired secrets), antecedents and the promise of desired consequences remain stable over time, and only the malicious behavior is modified.

- Terrorist groups are formed with a stable foundation of beliefs that remains the same over time, with the foundation stressing why the organization exists and giving a clear description of who is the enemy.

- Repeat perpetrators endeavor to change their behavior over time to avoid establishing signatures that would make detection of planned attacks easier; however, generally speaking, U.S. defenses remain signature based.

- The who, where, when, what, and how that underscores the prediction of malicious behavior relies on the identification of general and specific antecedents that contribute to future behavior, not in the study of past behavior alone.

- Contrary to popular belief, the best predictor of future behavior is *not* past behavior. The best predictor of future behavior *is* the past ABC associations that form patterns whereby future behavior will likely occur under the same or highly similar antecedent and consequence conditions.

- Malicious behavior rarely occurs in response to a single antecedent; malicious behavior is more likely to occur when a set of antecedents occur simultaneously or in close proximity in time.
- The ABC sequences that form the foundation of human behavior predictive patterns are identifiable through tested methodology using text-based accounts of past malicious events.

This book outlines methods to extract antecedents that set the stage for malicious behavior to occur. Once you identify such antecedents are identified and establish patterns either manually or automatically, you can expect that future malicious behavior will occur when the same or highly similar environmental conditions are present.

> **NOTE** It is essential to realize that the exact constellation of antecedent events does not have to occur; the antecendent events just have to be highly similar. For example, the visit of the President of the United States to the Mideast may set the stage for local terrorist activity. At a later date, the visit of the Secretary of State from the United States may have the same effect without the presence of the President.

The implications for security are far-reaching. Security exists to reduce the occurrence of malicious behavior. To reduce malicious behavior, security can do only three things:

1. During the course of malicious behavior occurring, *stop* the behavior from continuing using measured force (match force with force).

   A radical anti-abortion group is demonstrating in front of an abortion clinic. A pro-abortion group enters the site of the demonstration. Soon, members of both groups begin to shout and taunt members of the opposing group. One member hits a member of the opposing group with a placard he is carrying, injuring the struck person. It is apparent that at any second violence is going to escalate. Available security steps in actively and separates the two groups, ordering that any sign of violence will result in law enforcement arrests. The person striking the other person is removed by law enforcement, and the protest continues without additional signs of violence other than the expected occasional cross-group taunts.

2. Provide a deterrent to the occurrence of malicious behavior by being present at a location where the malicious behavior could occur to *suppress* the actual occurrence of the behavior when it does occur.

   The President is starting a speech on the steps of the Springfield, Illinois, capitol building while campaigning for reelection. The President is surrounded by U.S. Secret Service special agents. They are dressed in suits and are easily identifiable with similar sunglasses and mannerisms. Their presence suppresses malicious behavior and outbursts from the few in the crowd who are not pro-President.

3. Detect, apprehend, and incarcerate a perpetrator to prevent future occurrences of malicious behavior.

On repeated occasions, a cyber attacker had successfully intruded into a sensitive network of a major bank. As a result, credit card numbers were stolen. Security had been tracking network intrusions using the CheckMate intrusion-protection system and, with forensics tools, identified specific features of the attacker. Working with law enforcement and with the cooperation of network administrators, network security personnel assisted in the process of identifying the perpetrator, a former bank employee. The perpetrator was apprehended, tried, and found guilty and is currently incarcerated, serving an extended sentence.

However, by changing to a predictive security model, we would find that preventing occurrences of terrorist attacks can occur in five primary ways:

1. Accurately anticipate the occurrence of a terrorist attack so that the attack may be prevented from occurring using improved predictive methods or by cultivating and correlating tips.

2. By analyzing key environmental characteristics of past attacks, develop a profile indicating likely approach and tactic to be used and, as a result, determine where security resources would best be placed to serve as a deterrent or to be ready when the attack occurs.

3. Using behavior-based tracking and locating technology, identify the likely location of perpetrator(s) and apprehend to prevent imminent attack.

4. Harden security in predicted high-probability locations for attack to present proactive increased security where resources can best be located to be maximally effective.

5. Using identified predictors as influence points, modify the environment to change antecedents to attack to minimize antecedent conditions that are likely to lead to an attack.

Taken together as a whole, the presented information, if realized, would represent a shift in security preparedness with increased vigilance to thwart attacks. It is clear that prediction of malicious behavior such as terrorist attacks is complicated and requires incorporating the details I discuss throughout this entire book. However, based on technology I am presenting, the preceding five objectives are, indeed, possible.

Improving Network Security

There are dire consequences for a country that attacks the United States openly and in a conventional manner. As a country, the United States is resilient and maintains a culture that supports swift and harsh retaliation to those who have attempted to harm or who have succeeded in harming citizens. One needs only to remember the manner in which World War II in the Pacific theatre was ended. Japan attacked the United States, and ultimately, the United States dropped the atomic bombs on Hiroshima and Nagasaki within 3 days of one another, definitively ending the war. The bombing marked the only time in history that nuclear weapons have been used. Consequently, reason dictates that direct attack against the United States by a foreign country is not likely.

But the fact that a country would be foolhardy in orchestrating and carrying out an attack within the borders of the United States does not mean that a country would not support covert operations against the United States. One method described earlier in this chapter is for a country to use a proxy or stand-in. Libyan support for past terrorist attacks from likely established groups is an example. However, there is a second method. Cyber attack or cyber theft is a strong alternative that affords anonymity. It is exceedingly difficult and time-consuming to:

- Identify a sophisticated and possible first-time attack or theft
- Trace back malicious network behavior to the actual perpetrator
- Protect against attacks, especially new, creative attacks
- Identify the perpetrator beyond a shadow of doubt
- Prosecute a perpetrator, even if suspected

We are accustomed to thinking of an attack from country to country or terrorist group to country. This thinking includes weapons, explosives, airliners being flown into buildings, and numerous terrorists coordinating their activities in a single or simultaneous attack. It is difficult to imagine a network attack that could match or exceed the damage caused by a well-planted bomb. Such an attack can be covert and may not be noticed until after the perpetrators have caused damage, covered their tracks, and vacated the network.

What are the objectives of a well-planned cyber attack? Table 3-2 presents just a sample of motivations that would encourage a country to attack the United States through covert cyber mechanisms.

Table 3-2: Objectives of Significant and Sophisticated Cyber Attacks against the United States

MOTIVATION	PLANNED ATTACK AND EFFECT
Disrupt business practices	Denial-of-service attack to harm business of an organization
Disrupt first responder communication	Combined with conventional terrorist attack heightens damage and loss of life
Obtain sensitive proprietary or classified information	Theft takes many forms, but a phishing or spear phishing attack may be used to entice an employee to click on a harmless link that results in downloading a Trojan to steal the user ID and password, allowing attackers full access to sensitive files
Inflict property damage and loss of life	Gain access to a portion of the power grid or flood gates of a major dam to gain control and create a blackout or create flooding
Steal identities/ credit cards	Using various well-known cyber methods, acquire identities that may be sold to acquire additional capital to fund terrorism and to provide identities for entry and exit within the United States
Initiate a cyber-economic bomb	Attack Wall Street to shut down trading or disrupt ports for shipping to create chaos and significant economic loss

Table 3-2 presents samples of cyber attack that are not just ideas. All listed motivations and examples can happen. The exact nature of a cyber attack is limited only by the imagination of the perpetrator. Although there are some technical limits on being malicious, and a hacker must have the expertise and practice deception to avoid detection, there remains a very large number of ways attacks can be generated as new, first-time attacks, or old attacks can be combined to form new attacks. Because of the wide variety of ways a hacker can be malicious, we must rely on defenses to try to keep hackers out of our networks. To counter serious attack attempts, we rely on network security and network security specialists.

Current Network Security

For the most part network security relies on three tools:

1. Signature detection technology
2. Anomaly detection technology
3. Human expertise (human expert knowledge)

Signature detection exists as rules created to detect attacks that have occurred in the past. Although effective to some extent, the technology cannot anticipate new attacks because new malicious cyber activity has no rules generated for detection. Consequently, the approach is rife with what are called false negatives. A false negative occurs when a network security tool processes network traffic and passes the traffic as non-malicious when it is, in fact, malicious. However, because misses are extremely difficult to determine, especially with new attacks, it is very difficult to obtain accurate false-negative numbers. In fact, such systems are so overtuned that they often are seen as having high false positives (calling non-malicious traffic malicious). In short, signature detection is characterized by many errors in detection.

Anomaly detection relies on developing statistical norms, or averages, of network behavior and then flagging activity that is significantly different than the norm. The Achilles' heel for anomaly detection is false positives, the other type of network intrusion detection error. A false positive occurs when a detection device indicates that activity is malicious when it is not malicious. Because human behavior is characterized by variety, simply being different than the norm does not mean the person is malicious. In other words, anomaly detection cannot reliably differentiate between *anomaly good* and *anomaly bad*.

To be as effective as possible, *human expertise* is required to adjust anomaly detection and to write signatures on an ongoing basis for signature detection. Often, a serious attack gets by the existing technologies, and human knowledge in forensics is required to track down the attack through voluminous and mixed network traffic. Unfortunately, network intrusion detection is difficult, often ineffective, and reactive.

Of course, there are those who would disagree with me that current network intrusion technology is inadequate, particularly vendors. However, working closely with network administrators and security staff entrusted with the responsibility of keeping our networks safe has made the lack of capability of current tools to provide adequate protection painfully obvious to me. In fact, there seems to be a new principle at work that serves as an indictment against the effectiveness of current network intrusion detection tools. I label this principle as the *surrender principle* and define it in the following manner:

The surrender *principle of network detection describes the phenomenon by which high-frequency and obvious attempts to intrude into networks with malicious intent or to determine vulnerabilities of a network as a precursor to imminent cyber attack are labeled as* normal *and therefore are ignored.*

The labeling of malicious network activity as *normal* is a means to justify the inability of the technology available today to stop surveillance of networks for vulnerabilities and imminent attack. The labeling of such activity as normal is meant to communicate that the network staff should not be concerned with the high volume of attempts to intrude. Of course, such activity is malicious and should be labeled as such. But, because current technology cannot serve as a deterrent to hackers exploring a network for attack points, it is easier to list it as an annoyance and normal nuisance activity. This is a failure of network intrusion to adequately handle precursor activity to serious attacks. It is not the fault of the overstressed network security staff; it is the result of inadequate network protection technology.

Today, the current state of network security is reactive. We must observe an attack after damage may have been done and then design a signature as rules to detect the attack if it occurs again. Actually such a scenario happens daily. The unskilled hacker may continue the same attack repeatedly across different networks because that is what he or she knows with a limited repertoire. However, the professional hacker or the hacker working for a foreign intelligence service or military is highly skilled and not likely to repeat activity that could be identified by rules defining past attacks. Again, this is an indictment of technology, not the human effort to protect our networks. It is much like a security guard at a professional football game constantly scanning 70,000 attendees looking for any sign of threat — just too overwhelming of a task to be maximally effective. The network security staff is simply being overpowered.

What of major vendors? How much of the proceeds go into R&D to improve technology? I overheard one CEO indicate his company didn't need tons of R&D because it was selling product.

Network attack detection technology needs to move from time-consuming, after-the-fact forensics on the part of extremely dedicated network intrusion experts. The detection of new, creative network attacks and intrusions must occur in milliseconds versus weeks to months if the security stance is to make a paradigm shift from a reactive stance to a more proactive and preventative stance. Humans plan cyber attacks and execute them against targets. Yet, we tend to think of attacks as entities themselves. We must be able to better anticipate human behavior and the intent behind network attacks that could harm our infrastructure. We need to assess human behavior behind the attacks, not just network behavior.

Why is this important? We now know that a hacker or group of dedicated hackers could shut down the controls of a dam that holds back millions of tons of water. They could shut down the power grid or significant portions. This would be critical at the time of a conventional and massive terrorist attack like 9/11. First responders and recovery personnel may not be able to communicate, worsening the effects of such an attack. In addition, we know that a foreign power can enter our restricted networks and basically steal classified or sensitive proprietary technology data and information.

Cyber attack is a special case. It is relatively new, and it affords the perpetrator anonymity. There is no need to use a terrorist group cutout or proxy. The foreign country can simply support the development of a group of cyber specialists trained to attack or invade covertly to steal secrets or, in conflict, tie up networks in such a way that the networks become nonfunctional. This explains the situation in which we currently find ourselves in the cyber field.

AuBA network tools, as presented in this book, represent a significant departure from signature detection and anomaly detection. When designing the patented network application, I wanted to ensure that the application would be proactive, as opposed to reactive, and capable of predicting an imminent attack and provide rapid assessments based on human behavior instead of network behavior. Using human behavior assessment technology, the tools can detect new forms of attacks without the high false-positive error rates of anomaly detection and can catch first-time attacks to avoid the high false-negative rates of signature detection. The effect is to provide a more proactive set of tools. If we can be more proactive and accurately anticipate attacks before they occur, then blocking the attack before damage occurs becomes a real option.

Current Foreign Threats to Network Security

To this point, we have discussed external threat coming into a network from country-supported intrusion methodologies. However, we have not yet emphasized perhaps the major problem — insider threat and espionage. Historically, the trusted insider gone bad has resulted in a tremendous loss of both proprietary information, as in the case of corporate espionage, and classified information, as in the case of Americans being corrupted by foreign powers to provide classified secrets. The number of industrial espionage cases is astounding, requiring extensive databases just to list the incidents. We are all familiar to some extent with traditional spies such as Robert Hansen from the FBI, Aldrich Ames from the CIA, Jonathan Pollard from the NSA, and Ana Montes from the DIA, all American spies working for foreign governments to turn over U.S. secrets. No agency is immune to the corrupt insider. As a former intelligence officer, I am particularly sensitive to espionage. I know that many of us who have dedicated ourselves to the protection of our country find it is especially hurtful when one of our own turns bad.

Insider threat occurs in a variety of ways. This topic is covered in more detail in Chapters 10 and 12 of this book. However, as a major point, there is no set personality type of an American trusted to protect national secrets who gives them away for ideology or for pay. Because of the rapid expanse of digital technology, the Internet, network communications, and speed-of-light transactions across the globe, insider theft of restricted information is easier than ever. The relatively recent release of hundreds of thousands of classified documents by WikiLeaks has ushered in a new age; that is, the use of modern-day technology to aid the traitor who works as an insider for foreign governments. It is not enough that all countries engage in spying to obtain state secrets, but now we have the Internet to distribute or send such documents.

There are several forms of insider threat:

- The insider working alone to gather restricted information (proprietary or classified) to sell to the highest bidder

- The insider who seeks a partner external to the organization to assist in delivery and distribution of restricted material

- An insider recruited by a foreign intelligence service or an insider in advanced technology recruited by a competitor

Regardless of the situation, the loss of internal restricted information can be devastating. In fact, depending on the types of information stolen, lives have been lost as a result. Proprietary and classified material theft stolen by insiders is a dangerous business that can be more damaging than we can accurately estimate. Although there is a damage assessment each time a spy is caught, it is very difficult to determine the extent of the damage caused by the release of classified data/information. How does one measure the violation of trust?

Based on CheckMate technology, the InMate application will also be presented in the walkthrough DVD accompanying this book. Similar to CheckMate, InMate was designed to focus on detecting new insider threat activity not defined by signature detection or anomaly detection technologies. The application of AuBA to security-related problems is revealing the advantages of analyzing human behavior as opposed to network behavior. Technologies such as CheckMate and InMate offer a more proactive approach to identifying both insider and external threat. CheckMate is a patented AuBA-based application that converts network activity from each user/IP in a network to human behavior assessments every 100 milliseconds (1/10th of a second) to identify threats in the form of high expertise and deception. InMate is a sister application that focuses on insiders (employees, contractors, students, and so forth), with assessments made every 100 milliseconds to determine the degree of deception and intent to engage in misuse that are present at any one time. The accompanying DVD demonstrates these applications in use.

Understanding Current Technology for Protecting Our Networks

As I stated earlier in the chapter, we currently have two network intrusion detection technologies: signature detection and anomaly detection. To be honest, anomaly detection has not yet lived up to its potential. Although a good idea, it is plagued by very high, if not intolerable, false-positive errors (saying that sampled activities are malicious when they are not). Yet, signature detection is plagued by the other type of network intrusion detection error, false negatives, and, if over tuned, very high false positives. Perhaps more serious than the false positives of anomaly detection, false negatives label activity that is damaging as non-malicious and lets it pass. This is a serious indictment against current technology. We simply must do better to get ahead of what is a growing number of adversaries on a global basis.

> **WARNING**   There can be no debate. Current signature and anomaly detection technologies are simply inadequate to meet today's network security needs. Successful intrusions are frequent, and damage is continuous and escalating. It is the human who attacks; the network is simply an enabler. Adequate mitigation of damage and loss will depend on the introduction of human behavior–based predictive technology that will anticipate the behavior of the person behind the attack so that preventative blocking can occur to stop imminent damage. AuBA is a move in that direction.

Facing Chemical, Biological, Radiological, and Nuclear (CBRN) Threats

It is actually difficult to top the 9/11 al-Qaeda attack in terms of destruction, loss of life, and the sheer shock and terror generated as a consequence. However, if a terrorist organization is to top the devastation of 9/11, then a chemical, biological, radiological, or nuclear (CBRN) attack is a likely approach.

> **WARNING**   Always remember: The objective of terrorism is to invoke intense despair and fear resulting from a single attack or coordinated multiple attacks against unaware victims who have little to no chance for a defense.

To clarify the nature of a CBRN attack, I offer the following descriptions:

- **Chemical:** A chemical attack would likely be in the form of poisonous gas. Although a wide variety of poisonous gasses have been used in warfare with devastating effects against humans, a nerve agent such as sarin would be a logical choice of terrorists. Death can come within minutes as the colorless and tasteless nerve agent attacks the nervous and muscular systems. On March 20, 1995, the Aum Shinrikyo Japanese terrorist group released sarin gas in a coordinated attack across multiple subway trains in Tokyo. Despite the imperfect delivery of the chemical agent, 12 victims were still killed and hundreds to thousands injured. It is known that terrorist groups have experimented with chemical delivery systems such as crop dusters, an ideal method of dispersion.

- **Biological:** A biological agent for use in a terrorist act would be a naturally occurring virus, fungus, or type of bacteria that can be cultivated and released on massive numbers of innocent individuals to result in mass casualties. Compared to chemical dispersion, the cultivation and release of lethal biological agents is much easier, and such agents require relatively little biological knowledge to weaponize. Almost immediately after the 9/11 al-Qaeda attack, anthrax was delivered by the U.S. mail system in envelopes. During the multiple events, five people were killed. As an example, the anthrax events revealed the ease with which biological agents may be delivered. Because of the nature of the agents, they also may be spread from human to human.

- **Radiological:** A radiological terrorist weapon is basically synonymous with the term *dirty bomb*. First, a radiological weapon is NOT a nuclear bomb. Instead, it is the spread of radioactive material in the environment by means of conventional explosion. The victim, if fortunate enough to escape the blast effects, would likely exhibit radiation sickness and perhaps long-term cancer. Given explosion and dispersal in a densely populated area, the long-term effects for many could result from one dirty bomb.

- **Nuclear:** The detonation of a nuclear weapon within a densely populated municipal area within the United States would define the ultimate and maximally effective terrorist attack weapon. Such a weapon is not likely to be a homegrown device, and the development of nuclear weapons is very complex. However, there are numerous open source media reports/articles about unaccounted-for portable *suitcase bomb* nuclear weapons developed by the former Soviet Union. Although small yield as compared to conventional nuclear weapons, these missing weapons are many times more powerful than conventional explosives of the same size. Detonation of any type of nuclear weapon within the borders of the United States would result in nothing short of public panic.

Understanding the Threat of a Biological Attack

This discussion has led to the most devastating potential terrorist weapons. Although there are those who have claimed that some weapon types may be too devastating for terrorists to use, we would do well to study the motivations and potential targeting antecedents presented in this chapter. It is important to note that the United States has decimated much of the al-Qaeda leadership, including killing the leader, Osama bin Laden, and the current number two leader, Atiyah Abd al-Rahman. Given motivations listed in this chapter for foreign states and terrorist groups that could do their bidding, losses on the side of major countries and terrorist organizations could justify the use of weapons of mass destruction. A state willing to engage in revenge for war or to satisfy long-term anti-U.S. doctrine may be able to make a transaction for a current missing nuclear or other CBRN weapon and make it available to a willing terrorist group.

The threat of a terrorist attack using tactics that could top the 9/11 attack is real. Terrorist organizations have time on their side, and they can savor a 9/11 attack for a long time. However, once memorials are erected and more confederate lives are lost within their organization or within a supporting country, the probability of a massive attack within U.S. borders increases. Given decimation of much of the al-Qaeda leadership by U.S. forces, it is also important for al-Qaeda to demonstrate that the organization is alive and well and still a force to be considered.

Currently the United States is exhibiting antecedents associated with terrorist attacks. Looking back at the key motivations that form a foundation of anti-U.S. sentiment, it should be clear that the United States remains a target and will for some time.

Anticipating the Dirty Bomb

A dirty bomb is a likely weapon to be used against the United States. Again, it is not a true nuclear weapon. The detonation of a nuclear bomb is controversial even in the Islamic radical militant world. However, the dirty bomb, which can create grave concern if detonated in Washington, D.C., or New York City, is far easier to acquire, build, and use when compared to a nuclear weapon. To clarify, a nuclear weapon results in a true nuclear, mushroom cloud explosion that is equivalent to very large amounts of explosive material. The bombs dropped on Japan by the United States were true nuclear bombs. A dirty bomb, or radiological weapon, is a conventional explosive but has radioactive material packed with the bomb. It is a dispersal device whose purpose is to contaminate an area or people with radioactive material. When a typical bomb explodes, it spreads the radioactive material across a wide area. Although a conventional explosive serves as the bomb, the terms "radiological" and "radiation" are associated with contamination, cancer, and radiation sickness. It has both the immediate explosive effects of the conventional explosive and the contamination effects created by radioactive material being spread over a designated area, keeping all clear of that site until decontamination can occur. A dirty bomb detonation would be a first and generate immense media attention, highlighting the cause of the perpetrator. In many ways, a dirty bomb epitomizes the horror attached to the release of any CBRN weapon, but it is easy to construct, is easy to detonate, and can be portable.

If a conventional explosive device will suit the purpose of an incident, then a dirty bomb is not likely to be used. For example, a conventional explosive device made of TNT, PETN, or C4 would be all that is needed to bring down an airliner, as we saw with the Pan Am 103 incident over Scotland. A dirty bomb would be more useful to contaminate an area that would ensure long-term media coverage for the cause of the organization claiming responsibility. The use of a dirty bomb also does not fit the profile of a suicide bombing. Instead, the dirty bomb is more likely to be used with a timed or remote detonation at the site of a symbolic target because of the contamination effects of dispersed radioactive material.

This discussion of where a dirty bomb might or might not be used highlights how we must be aware of the antecedent conditions that would favor the use of one type of CBRN weapon over another, which is only one of the many uses of a carefully completed behavior analysis. After the completion of this book, you should find such an analysis easier.

Advantages of AuBA #3: Reducing Errors and Inefficiencies of Manual Predictive Modeling

AuBA not only presents new technology to conduct behavioral modeling for the purpose of developing predictive engines but also adds automation to much of the process. This automation results in the construction and validation of predictive models 400 times faster than the time it used to take our manual teams and processes. However, speed was not the sole criterion for developing AuBA; accuracy is just as important as speed. We have found that the AuBA automation removes many opportunities for human error. This reduction in error has a corresponding increase in accuracy of developed and validated models.

AuBA started as a manual process based on basic applied behavior analysis. However, additions such as advanced pattern classification; artificial neural network technology; automated extraction of antecedents, consequences, and motivational factors; automated validation; and the ability to associate global antecedents to malicious behavior have resulted in a new technology with applied behavior analysis roots. This new technology includes different and unique hybrid behavior and computer science applications designed for AuBA working in concert as one set of tools.

Prior to automation, I used behavior analysis methods in clinical settings. The basic ABC sequence was especially useful in identifying key contextual factors in the environment that were associated with behaviors to be changed. However, there were many challenges to overcome to move this manual clinical process to automation. For the methodology to be predictive, many computer science features would have to be married with behavioral features.

Although new features would have to be added to move behavioral methodologies to a state of accurate prediction, the basic manual process was followed in the design of automation. Figure 3-2 illustrates these basic steps.

The horizontal steps at the top of the figure illustrate the key steps we would take in clinical work. Of course, much of the work was cognitive on the part of the clinician. The human brain is especially good at finding patterns. However, if the process was to be automated, this part would have to be duplicated. The horizontal steps at the bottom illustrate that the same steps were followed in designing automation. However, two tools would have to be invented: ThemeMate and AutoAnalyzer. These tools were designed to process key information, much like we do when conducting an analysis manually, as shown in the top steps of the figure.

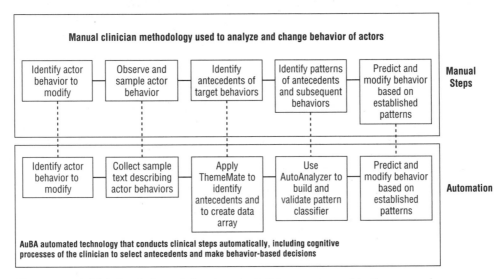

Figure 3-2: A high-level view of the steps in AuBA as compared to the manual clinical steps

ThemeMate is a software application designed to process text accounts of past behavior either in a database or as free text, such as news articles. Because of its unique patented features, it can process text in different languages and extract the key information we need for predictive or influence modeling. After ThemeMate has extracted key information, it automatically constructs a data array that contains extracted antecedent themes as columns and the text examples (for example, articles) as distinct rows. It then completes the array by placing a 1 in a cell if that theme exists for that example, or a 0 if it does not. This process, which used to take weeks, now can occur in minutes with no errors. It takes 2 weeks to prepare ThemeMate to read a new language. Once modified for a new language, ThemeMate can construct a model using that language in the exact same manner and time it takes to construct a validated model in English.

AutoAnalyzer is a pattern classification speed demon. It takes as input the data array output of ThemeMate and constructs artificial neural network pattern classifiers, reduces the antecedent themes to the most predictive set, validates the models using best practices validation methods, calculates accuracy, and presents the optimal model for use. We have made comparisons of the automated process to our standard manual method; however, it is an intimidating comparison. The automation is many times faster, can identify many more antecedent themes, and can work across languages. Most important, the technology now frees up our time so that we can spend it preparing needed reports, conducting other types of analyses, and developing new applications.

Many details of the process will be discussed throughout this book, and demonstrations of ThemeMate and AutoAnalyzer are provided on the accompanying DVD.

In Summary

This chapter presented the results of multiple behavior analyses of country-level threats, as well as country-level threats carried out by proxy. A country with a very strong grievance against the United States is likely to use a stand-in, or proxy, to conduct an actual attack because of the might of the U.S. military and our country's willingness to strike back swiftly and convincingly. In this way, blame may be diverted, and the terrorist organization receives the credit.

In any behavior analysis of an adversary, it is essential first to determine the foundational motivations that form the underlying basis for the anti-U.S. sentiment. Targeting and attack antecedents are associated with these basic motivations. Furthermore, AuBA analysis of targeting and attack antecedents and considering consequences that would likely be desirable for the terrorist group lead to the prediction of likely terrorist attacks. This is how study of the ABC sequence can help lead us to predictive conclusions.

A single exception to the use of a terrorist organization proxy is the use of cyber attacks against the United States either to inflict damage or to acquire technological, sensitive, or classified materials. Such acts may be conducted by the actual country without the use of a proxy attacker because of the extreme difficulty in proving the source of the attack, lending the attacker anonymity.

In this chapter I also made the case that we need a paradigm shift in network intrusion technology. With unmistakable evidence of frequent and successful attacks against networks, it is apparent that traditional signature and anomaly detection technologies are not effective in stopping cyber attacks. We need to augment current technologies focusing on network behavior with AuBA-like technologies that emphasize the human behind the attack. The next chapter emphasizes and delves deeper into the reactive stance of current network intrusion technologies.

Threats and Security Nightmares: Our Current Reactive State of Security

This chapter focuses on the current threats we face within the United States and the difficulty facing security on a daily basis in ensuring our safety. As a country, we face a relatively high degree of threat from a wide variety of sources. Such threat emanates from a massive amount of violent crime, gangs, murders, and shootings. We see killings in the streets, schools, malls, and workplaces. However, not all threat is violent. We now face an unprecedented threat from cyber assault. We are now a computer-based society, and we are no stranger to viruses, identity theft, cyber stalking, and stolen credit card numbers. Our businesses are attacked daily, and there are diligent and successful efforts to invade our government, military, and corporate computers to steal classified and proprietary information. Threat is everywhere, and we have to learn better how to move beyond a reactive stance to proactive protection.

The threat we face is not random. It occurs for a reason. Using behavior analysis methods as presented in this book, whether manual or automated, we may be able to accurately anticipate events born from current threat. Such anticipation is absolutely necessary if security resources and policies are to be more effective. Security, as a discipline, cannot be everywhere and do everything. By accurately anticipating threatening events of concern, security resources may be more efficiently used and in a more proactive manner. In this chapter I explore just how an improved understanding of malicious behavior can prepare the way for a more proactive security stance.

Analyzing Mall, School, Workplace, and Other Seemingly Random Public Violence

On April 19, 1995, a Ryder truck parked in front of the Alfred P. Murrah Federal Building in Oklahoma City, Oklahoma, and within minutes exploded with such force that 168 people were killed, including children in a day care center within the building. Hundreds of others were seriously injured. The person who led the plan of attack and who parked the truck in the spot where the deadly blast took place was Timothy McVeigh. He and his coconspirators were apprehended, and McVeigh was executed by lethal injection a little over 6 years after the bombing. Not only was McVeigh born and raised in the United States, he had served in the army, fought in the First Gulf War, received a Bronze Star, and was honorably discharged. On April 20, 1999, in Columbine, Colorado, two Columbine High School seniors, Eric Harris and Dylan Klebold, entered the school after their primary plan to shoot fleeing victims from a bombing failed. They were heavily armed. As they walked through the school, they began shooting and targeted fellow students and faculty almost indiscriminately. Being a victim was a product of being at the wrong place at the wrong time. Although pent up grudges fueled the attack, the focus was to simply kill. For nearly an hour, they meandered about the school shooting and attempting to set off fire bombs. At the conclusion of the hour of pure mayhem, they turned their guns on themselves and committed suicide, leaving 13 others dead (12 students and 1 teacher) and 21 injured.

Robert Hawkins entered the Westroads shopping mall in Omaha, Nebraska, on December 5, 2007. Robert, not yet 20 years old, was armed with a semiautomatic rifle. At no particular time or as a result of no particular event that is known, Hawkins pulled out the concealed rifle and began shooting indiscriminately. In less than 10 minutes, he had killed 8 shoppers and wounded 4 others and then killed himself.

These acts of deadly violence are just a sample of the many similar acts that have occurred within our country's borders perpetrated by our own citizens. Not counting serial and mass murderers covered in Chapter 1, which typically includes some form of victim targeting, the acts of deadly violence we see in malls and schools are basically targets of convenience. Victims, for the most part, just happened to be within range of the weapons used during the killing sprees or bombings. In the case of McVeigh, he had targeted a federal building, having been distressed over federal law enforcement raids against specific groups in the past. However, he basically stated that he did not care who was inside the building and later confessed that he was not aware that there was a day care center in the building. He had not bothered to determine who his victims were going to be. In the many school and mall shootings we have seen in our country, the victims were specifically targeted not because of who they were but for simply being within range of the firepower brought into the facilities.

A conclusion may be drawn from the types of attacks presented — the focus of the attacks is more on the attack itself and not on specific individuals. The world events and situations occurring at any one time represent potential antecedents to an immense number of individuals and variety of behaviors. For some individuals, malicious behavior is the result. For other individuals, the current constellation of factors serves as triggers for non-malicious behavior. What is it about the perpetrators of these massive attacks that preceding events and situations prompt malicious, deadly behavior while the same events and situations have totally different effects on others? The answer to this important question may provide valuable insight into why massive public killings are occurring.

As I discussed earlier in the book, applied behavior analysis as a discipline depends heavily on the antecedent-behavior-consequence (ABC) sequence. The approach is not 100 percent external to the individual, but little consideration is provided to the internal state of the individual in analyzing behavior of a specific type. The internal state is typically the domain of other areas of psychology or psychiatry. However, in developing the automated behavior analysis approach presented in this book, I have found that extensions and expansions have been absolutely necessary. For example, to explain how such behaviors as the Oklahoma City bombing, the Columbine high school setting, and the Westroads shopping mall in Omaha can occur, you must also consider a much deeper understanding of the history, motivations, and ideology of the perpetrator. In short, unlike Pavlov's dogs, which salivated immediately and automatically at the site of meat or the conditioned bell when presented (classical conditioning), the conditioning associated with applied behavior analysis emphasizes that certain behaviors simply increase in probability of occurrence when a certain pattern of antecedents occur. The person's history, ideology, and motivations intervene between external antecedents and the actual occurrence of behavior and can either suppress or encourage the occurrence of the malicious behavior.

In the case of Timothy McVeigh, he became increasingly upset with the federal government, beginning with his time in the army. Although honorably discharged, a sense of disgruntlement was forming. He was also upset when federal law enforcement moved on groups, who he perceived were defending their Second Amendment rights to bear arms. In particular, in 1995 the Bureau of Alcohol, Tobacco, Firearms, and Explosives (ATF) moved on the Branch Davidians, a religious group in Waco, Texas, headed by David Koresh. The religious sect refused to cooperate with the agency, and a siege that lasted for almost two months ended in a fire that destroyed the Branch Davidian compound, killing Koresh and 80 of his followers, including women and children. McVeigh was incensed. Over time he began to associate with others who shared his radical views of militancy. Several in this company would eventually be coconspirators of the Oklahoma City bombing.

A behavior analysis perspective focusing on malicious behavior and extreme threat within our country is based on the nuances of behavior associated with specific antecedents for a specific individual or group. The two-month siege between ATF and the Branch Davidians at Waco, Texas, included ongoing and intense conflict and was covered by the media with enormous national interest. Many millions witnessing the television images and newspaper and weekly news magazines were exposed to the same images. However, McVeigh was affected to the degree that he drove to Waco and protested. It is clear that the siege affected McVeigh deeply. This incident, along with other incidents associated with the federal government, resulted in McVeigh's targeting of a federal government building. By studying his history in detail and his clear distaste for the Waco incident in which the buildings housing the Branch Davidians were destroyed by the government, you can see how antecedents for a massive attack would include a government building in an eye-for-an-eye manner. In fact, both the Branch Davidian's buildings and the government building contained women and children.

The events and situations associated with Waco and other similar events are processed by each of the millions of individuals who witness them through filters of history, motivation, ideology, worldview, political leanings, religion, and other factors. Although there is absolutely no way of determining individual effects and views of the incident across all who were exposed to the incident, the presence of the Oklahoma City National Memorial (Figure 4-1) obviously shows public identification with the many victims of McVeigh's bombing, not with McVeigh and his cause — he was executed. Terrorists, whether foreign or domestic, believe strongly in their causes and often commit acts to bring attention to these causes. However, few are sympathetic.

The interaction of external events with the internal makeup of each individual results in different effects for each individual. For McVeigh, the Waco siege had a powerful negative impact on him. Therefore, the Waco siege events were antecedents to an internal state of anger that fueled McVeigh's active planning of a revenge event directed at the federal government.

Table 4-1 provides a top-level view of how the same incident serves as an antecedent event resulting in entirely different behaviors from various individuals based on the individual's role, history, sympathies, ideology, and other associated internal psychological states and traits. As you can see, the Waco siege spurred Timothy McVeigh into action as evidenced by actually traveling to the site of the siege. Once he was at the site, he protested the government's role and advocated for the right to bear arms. The typical ATF agent who was present and experienced the same antecedent situation and events exhibited totally different behavior. The agent's behavior was focused on stopping the siege.

Figure 4-1: The Oklahoma City National Memorial — a testament to the victims of the worst terrorist attack by a U.S. citizen within the United States.
© Refocus | Dreamstime.com

Table 4-1: Different Behaviors and Perceptions Occurring as a Result of the Same Single Event

INDIVIDUAL	ANTECEDENT	BEHAVIOR	CONSEQUENCE
Timothy McVeigh	Federal government assault on Branch Davidians' and Second Amendment rights	Traveled to Waco and demonstrated for pro-gun rights	Increased anger, which served as antecedent for planning revenge
ATF agent	Branch Davidians' resistance to initial attempt to deliver a search warrant and killing of ATF agents	Maintained standoff and insisted on bringing Branch Davidians to justice	Agents ended standoff by raiding the facility; in the process, a massive fire resulted in mass casualties

Continued

Table 4-1 (continued)

INDIVIDUAL	ANTECEDENT	BEHAVIOR	CONSEQUENCE
Pro-government media observer	Witnesses two-month standoff caused by Branch Davidians' resistance to reasonable search	Continued to monitor media (TV and read articles) about Branch Davidians' resistance	General sympathy for agents initially killed trying to serve warrant and then for total loss of life on both sides
Anti-government media observer	Witnesses two-month standoff caused by ATF interference in Branch Davidians' rights	Continued to monitor media (watch TV and read articles) about ATF's insistence on invading Branch Davidians' space and rights	General sympathy for loss of Branch Davidians' innocent lives

It is important to realize that McVeigh and a typical ATF agent were not acting differently simply because they are different. Their different behaviors were the result of the same antecedents acting on individuals with different roles, histories, and so on. Members of the public had different reactions to the same event as well. The general public is composed of individuals with diverse ideologies, political leanings, and views of the world. As discussion occurred over the evening news, those individual differences led to those individuals processing the same information very differently. McVeigh, as a growing militant, found others who shared his views. He gravitated toward like-minded individuals, with some eventually becoming coconspirators.

Figure 4-2 describes a key characteristic of human behavior that works to the benefit of those with malicious intent. On the left side of the diagram two types of individuals are depicted: anti-government (Anti G) and pro-government (Pro G). Similar to the north and the south poles of two magnets pulling toward one another, individuals with similar views and histories tend to be attracted to one another. By flocking together, individuals with anti-government views may express views and find agreement and acceptance that otherwise would not be found if they associated with those in the pro-government group. In a sense, the human characteristic of basically associating with those who are like us and repelling those who are not can result in very strong support systems for radical views, given that others can be located who share or are tolerant of the same views. The feelings that work to tie an anti-government radical militant group together can be very strong. In the case of McVeigh, the group of similar minded individuals provided support for action.

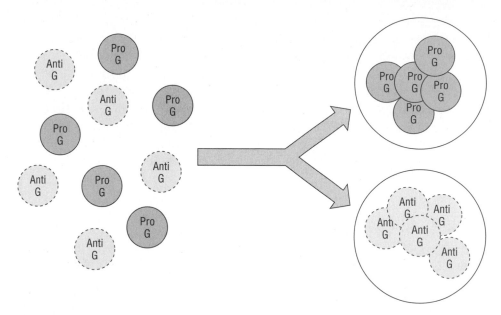

Figure 4-2: A depiction of individuals grouping by common ideology, motivations, worldview, and interests. Anti G is anti-government, and Pro G is pro-government.

Unlike many individuals who can share opposing views, radical militants can move to action to make a statement, actions that may include assaults or deadly attacks against not only those who hold opposing views but also those perceived as causing the problem. In McVeigh's militant world, he believed he was moved to action to correct the injustices caused by the federal government, in general. It may have been no accident that the Oklahoma City bombing included children because the end of the Waco siege resulted in children losing their lives.

As Figure 4-2 shows, individuals tend to group themselves according to internal views, psychological similarities, and worldviews. These internal states can take meaning in politics, wars, or any other significant factor. Clubs and associations are the result of like-minded individuals forming groups with non-malicious intent. Sailors form yacht clubs to gather and share sailing experiences. Bowling advocates form bowling leagues and clubs where they can share the love of their sport. The examples are endless. However, it may be more difficult to find others who share radical or militant views for the simple reason that there are just fewer radicals and people who hold such views. A militant individual may be less inclined to let others know of his or her controversial views.

The individual child pornographer very carefully probes others in an attempt to find similar views. Perhaps, surprisingly, they often find one another. Serial murderers, such as Ted Bundy or Jeffrey Dahmer, are not likely to share views for fear of discovery and go to extremes to present a life to the public that is different from their inner views and desires. Therefore, the more radical the view or the more distance between the individual and the norm, the less likely the perpetrator will associate with others. Without a support system, the typical loner that we read about simply feeds on his or her own thoughts. Opposing views or feedback may simply not exist. Isolation of self can allow a perpetrator to obsess over past bullying, difficult times in school, or strong disgruntlement in the workplace for not getting a promotion. Those with opposing views tend to become the enemy. In the world of the person with malicious intent stemming from past experiences, it is okay to retaliate.

Making Sense of Seemingly Senseless Public Attacks

What makes someone conceal a semiautomatic weapon, enter a mall or school, and start shooting at the first targets of opportunity encountered? Obviously the shooter did not stalk a specific individual into the mall to shoot that one person in public; such killings are committed in as private a manner as possible to avoid detection. We can assume that such violent, aggressive, and public acts are expressions of anger. As an emotion, anger fuels drastic acts.

It is my experience, after decades of modeling/profiling experience, that acts of anger often block suppressors, clear thought, and hesitancy.

Acts of anger are committed quickly, are deadly, and may make use of surrogate targets. As an example of a surrogate target, if a shooter has been bullied over the years and the acts have led to extreme anger, the target could become generalized. This means that if a specific group of high school students bullied a student and the student enters the school with a semiautomatic weapon, targets of opportunity, not necessarily the specific students who bullied him, may satisfy the need to get back at the school and its students.

A more recent phenomenon is the increase in teen suicide as a result of being bullied in school. In one case a student who has been bullied comes to school with an automatic weapon and kills fellow students, almost indiscriminately, and another student who has been bullied commits suicide. Both situations are sad and scream out the need for increased security training and early intervention in the schools.

However, there are clear environmental and person-specific indicators that such incidents may be imminent. The DVD describes a behavior analysis methodology that shows how to analyze these difficult cases to determine the indicators. If security has indicators, then perhaps early intervention can occur. Most certainly, we as a society and especially school personnel need to deal with the problem of bullying in our schools. We need to identify bullies, and we need to identify the early indications that a student is being adversely affected.

Security for schools and public places like shopping malls is difficult. First, a school may not even have security personnel, or if there is security in the mall or school, they may not be properly trained. What are the indicators that an event may be building in the school? Where would a shooter most likely enter in a mall to start shooting the innocent victims? By analyzing past accounts of these incidents, we can extract the antecedents to such attacks that can lead to an improved awareness.

First, it helps to know why we are witnessing killings conducted by a single person, or maybe two if there is an accomplice (as in Columbine). Just a few decades ago such acts did not occur at a high rate. Why are they happening now? This is a very important question. The following is provided as an experience-based hypothesis as to why we are seeing the problems we are seeing, and then we will explore how to analyze the behaviors to derive indicator answers.

Why Are We Violent?

We do not live in a safe country. Generally speaking, Switzerland is safe. Canada is safe. The United States is not. What is it about the United States that seems to attract attacks, assaults, killings, assassinations, and extremely high levels of violent crime? Why is the daily loss of life to malicious behavior so extraordinarily high?

Our country was founded on a struggle against the elements in a new world, which included Native Americans who did not want to be displaced. Throughout our country's history, we have been involved in almost constant conflict with others. The current "personality" of our country is assertive, if not aggressive. We work to help maintain peace across the globe. However, to others, we appear to be encroaching on the territory of others. Why are we viewed as aggressors, and what effect has our history had on us currently? We can take a brief, non-judgmental look. The key to behavior analysis is to simply identify antecedents, behaviors, and consequences in a non-biased manner, although it can be difficult.

Maybe current views of the United States are a result of our wrestling free of Great Britain to be our own country during a bloody revolutionary war. Certainly we cannot forget the fight resulting from almost eradicating Native Americans as we pushed from the Atlantic Ocean all the way to the Pacific, clearing the land not only of trees but of humanity as well. We also fought Mexico on repeated occasions, which resulted in wresting away Texas, California, and much of the southwestern territory. Then again, we had a repeat fight with Great Britain during the war of 1812. We also have to consider when we picked up arms in the North and South and fought one another, neighbor against neighbor, and brother against brother, in our bloodiest of all wars — the Civil War.

We also had the gun slinging days of the Wild West, where laws were often seen as guidelines, at best. We also had our foreign wars, such as World War I, World War II, Korea, Vietnam, Granada, Iraq, and Afghanistan, which represents only a partial list of wars/skirmishes in foreign lands. Our Cold War with Russia was as intense as if we were physically fighting — likely because a mutual nuclear attack between the United States and Russia could have destroyed the world as we know it. We realize just how close we came to annihilation during the U.S.–Russia conflict over the Cuban Missile Crisis. We also ended World War II by dropping the first nuclear bombs on Hiroshima and Nagasaki, instantly vaporizing hundreds of thousands of individuals. Of course, our intense days of racial strife, played out in the streets or massive protests of Vietnam, formed a foundation of violence. Regardless, as a country of assertive, if not aggressive, people, we certainly do not shy away from conflict.

Don't Tread on Me was one of our country's first mottos. Being armed was so important that our forefathers placed it in the Constitution, and we reaffirmed it as the Second Amendment — the inalienable right to bear arms. Our country was born within a wilderness to which our ancestors were not accustomed. From the very beginning there was a struggle against the elements and Native Americans who did not want our encroachment. We fought, aggressed, and took the land we believed to be part of our destiny. We have fought since those early days with a bravado that attracts attention, commands respect — if not fear — and has spawned violence internally.

Our country is one that seeks peace primarily on our terms and seems focused on solving its problems quickly and effectively, using force if necessary. As a result, we have evolved as a society that proudly fights to protect its rights and the rights of our allies. However, in the process of being a proud country that will not let others tread on us under any circumstances and that honors the many dead who have fought to maintain our rights and way of life, we have also spawned individuals ready to right injustices from their own radical perceptions that are different from the societal norm. The mall and school shooters are seeking revenge and perpetrate mass killings to get back at the public or fellow students who have rejected or bullied them. Bullying in school has been around for as long as there have been schools. So, what is different?

The scientific answers to these questions are very difficult to determine. We don't do experiments whereby one group of students is treated one way and the others are treated a second way to determine which group does better in the long run. Correlational studies simply tell us that factors are associated, but they do not show causation. Therefore, we have to speculate to some degree. However, a properly applied analysis of malicious and violent behavior can not only help us in predicting its occurrence in the future but also help assist security planning. Such planning can include where best to place resources to improve prevention and provide insights into the immediate precursors to public violence.

If we submit reports of past school and mall shootings to a behavior analysis, we observe similarities. As an example, the following is a set of principles that have surfaced from the type of analysis presented in this book:

- Selecting a target for an attack is a direct function of past painful experiences.

- Attacks often end in suicide or *death by cop* as the ultimate consequence of the act to end the emotional pain.

- Targets of school and mall shootings are often symbolic, with attacks directed at society in general as opposed to the specific individuals causing the pain.

- Targets of workplace violence are specific, with the focus of shootings directed at coworkers or supervisors associated with past painful experiences.

- A significant number of cases include notes or other forms of textual or verbal communication prior to the incident indicating the perpetrator will be famous.

- Surrendering once the act begins does not appear to be an objective.

DEFINITION *Death by cop* **is a law enforcement slang term to indicate when one commits suicide by committing an act whereby law enforcement or security is forced to kill the individual.**

The preceding principles extracted from past reports help us to start determining antecedents to attacks that can serve as indicators prior to their occurrence. First, the tactics used depend on the type of violence. Workplace shootings are very specific and different from mall and school shootings. However, it is clear that the disgruntled, sometimes expelled or bullied student may be at risk of moving toward an act of revenge. The disgruntled employee who has lost his job or who has lost the self-perceived deserved promotion is also at risk.

Not all students who are not doing well or employees who are disgruntled go on to commit acts of violence. Because past incidents show a lack of support system for perpetrators, it is highly likely that the presence of family, friends, or even school administrators showing support may be effective in suppressing acts of violence. Certainly the disgruntled without a visible support system can be viewed as a potential threat.

Violent shooting acts (or planned bombings) of the type on which we are focusing are planned to occur once. They are suicide missions undertaken by those with the intent to take others with them. The emotional pain is often so high that suicide can stop the pain, but the satisfaction of harming the society that has rejected them is an objective. The pattern is distinctive: Go to a public place or the school, kill others, kill self. We need to change this to add what to look for as warning signs prior to the individual going to the public place to commit the act. A behavior analysis of past incidents suggests the following as danger signals:

- The person is withdrawn and does not socialize well with others as an apparent result of perceived ostracism or bullying.

- The person is failing in the workplace and expresses anger at an increasing rate.

- Any individual in the workplace that becomes a repeated target of angry outbursts of a disgruntled employee without an active support system is at risk of being targeted by the disgruntled employee in the future.

- The potential shooter may communicate warnings or threats to others through notes, texting, e-mails, or verbal communication prior to an act.

- The person has the means to carry out an attack (has acquired weapons, bomb-making materials, or so on).

- The person has a fascination with semiautomatic or automatic weapons and handguns.

- The person has expressed an unusual desire to be famous or known by society.

Also, of special note as it relates to school bullying, there appears to be a gender issue. A female student mercilessly bullied is more likely to commit suicide to stop the emotional pain. The male student may decide to take others with him. Parents, other family members, school administrators, and teachers need to take special note of any student or youth who appears to be heavily bullied. Parents simply need to make themselves aware of the types of e-mails received and the content. Frequent and open discussions with the child can circumvent a major disaster. Temporary depressive states caused by bullying do not tend to be a topic a child volunteers to discuss. It is embarrassing for a child to complain of not being popular or being the target of bullying. Typically, the child wants parents to be proud of him or her, and bullying is perceived as a lack of self-worth. The result is self-inflicted withdrawal and ultimately a violent act directed at the self or at the self and others.

NOTE A behavior analysis of workplace, shopping mall, and school shootings indicates that suicide by means of a violent act is a preferred and easier route than asking for help and to admit to self-perceived ostracism or bullying.

We are losing some of our youth. Although it is difficult to conjure up sympathy for a person who walks into school and kills others and then himself, we must be more aware of warning signs for the sake of those individual and potential victims. Developing patterns through behavior analysis of past incidents allows us to start forming the picture of desperation that fuels much of the violence we are witnessing within the schools, malls, and the workplace.

WARNING Every human being desires to be wanted and acknowledged. Parents and school officials cannot depend on a student to volunteer that he or she may not be popular and is the object of serious bullying. Only through having open and frequent communication and being alert to signs of withdrawal and depression/sadness will the one at risk be identified. Likewise, a spouse cannot depend on his or her partner volunteering that he or she is failing in the workplace. Again, open communication is essential to ferret out difficulties. A climate of family love, communication, and support is the best preventative we have at the moment.

It is important to make one more essential point. Bullying is not something new, but we have had a significant addition to our lives over the past 60 years that has, perhaps, contributed to violent acts. First, we had the addition of television in our lives. It started mildly, and depictions of a person being killed were not actually shown but more implied. Then it moved to showing people being killed. Perhaps the television show depicted a bank robber being shot, but there was no blood or splattering of body tissue that can accompany being shot at close range. Eventually came graphic movies and more graphic television.

To skip to the present, our youth are pounded with graphic depictions of people being killed violently with automatic weapons, bombs, and other creative ways. Heads and limbs are blown off, blood is splattered — often back on the shooter — and it is obvious that the person with weapons wields tremendous killing power. On top of this, we have extremely realistic video games and virtual worlds to explore where we can kill others or be killed and jump up again ready to fight. Current-day movies, television, video games, and virtual worlds expose our children to an amazing number of violent incidents without realistic outcomes.

NOTE It has been estimated that 61 percent of TV programming contains violence, with children's programming being the most violent.[1]

There are two significant concerns here. First, there is much research to show how we acquire behavior through the modeling of behavior of others. The groundbreaking work of Dr. Albert Bandura and initial modeling research still stands as a hallmark of psychological research. Many researchers have

---

[1]*Violence as Entertainment*, Crime Prevention Resource Center, Fort Worth, Texas (http://user1722603.sites.myregisteredsite.com/sitebuildercontent/sitebuilderfiles/vaereport.pdf)

continued his initial research. From this research we understand children watching violent acts committed by famous stars they may hold in high esteem may be significantly impacted. Second, repeated exposures to violence on a daily basis in video games, virtual world combat, television, and movies can desensitize those exposed to the effects of violence. In other words, brandishing a semiautomatic or automatic weapon to kill others may not be shocking to those who are exposed to video depictions on a daily basis.

It is beyond the scope of this chapter to describe the details of a behavior analysis method to identify indicators that will allow us to detect an imminent incident of violence. This chapter was designed to introduce the topic and to provide some initial findings. Chapter 20 and the DVD will provide a walkthrough of a manual method to identify antecedents and how to use the identification to predict future behavior. In addition, a description of available automated tools and examples of their use with video clips showing their operation and results will be presented. However, you are encouraged to read the entire book prior to going to the walkthrough. The basic understanding of all components to a behavior analysis with either manual or the SAIC automated methods is essential for success in predictive modeling.

Unanticipated Terrorist Network Attacks

Past incidents reveal that our schools, shopping malls, and workplaces are at risk of lethal attack. Behavior analysis indicates that the reasons for such attacks may be desperation, and there is hope that we can learn warning signs and intervene before such incidents occur.

The behavior analysis of past incidents, particularly with previous media text reports, present the who, what, where, when, and how of past incidents. These past accounts contain potential antecedents, descriptions of the behavior, and consequences of the acts. By using methods presented in this book, you can convert these factors to a predictive model. Given the premise that we can develop effective predictive behavior models, of increasing concern is the terrorist move toward cyber attack. An analysis of the infamous al-Qaeda 9/11 attacks revealed that the targets represented military and economic targets. Today, both types of targets can be attacked with cyber tactics without the difficulties associated with learning to fly airliners, tactical planning, movement of operatives into the United States, the extreme costs associated with maintaining operatives in the United States, and risks of Americanization associated with operative exposure to American society.

There are two basic reasons for protecting against a terrorist cyber attack:

- The risk of encountering a dual traditional terrorist attack whereby a terrorist organization repeats a major, mass casualty attack combined with a cyber attack to disrupt first responder communication and to induce confusion

- The risk of a concerted and coordinated terrorist organization cyber attack against the power grid, economic, or communications infrastructure

As opposed to foreign countries attacking U.S. networks to steal proprietary and classified technology secrets, terrorist attacks would be less concerned with acquiring technology secrets unless they were interested as a means to a destructive end. The planned terrorist attack would be more likely conducted to disrupt and to cripple national infrastructure. Although we understand the basic motivation that may fuel a terrorist organization attack against the United States, the devil is in the details — when, where, what, who, and how. This is where a detailed behavior analysis comes in to play and new technology to disrupt surprise, first-time attacks.

Understanding the Element of Surprise

Within the cyber world we have two basic methodologies to detect external attack to a network: signature detection and anomaly detection. Signature detection relies on identifying a past attack and characterizing it with a rule so that if it occurs again, it can be readily detected. Anomaly detection depends on creating a statistical norm of a network and then flagging anything that fits outside of the norm as suspicious. A variant of anomaly detection, protocol anomaly detection, was designed to get around the many problems that plague the normalizing of a network for anomaly detection. Protocol anomaly detection depends on building anomaly detectors that include models of TCP/IP protocols using particular specifications associated with specific protocols. Basically, protocol anomaly detection does get around many problems of normalizing a network for traditional anomaly detection, but it is not without its own problems. The bottom line is that neither method is capable of anticipating new and creative terrorist cyber attacks.

Terrorists are resourceful and creative. They rarely replay an attack methodology against the United States because they know we are a formidable opponent with vast resources. Terrorists do not like failure, and the first way to achieve failure is to repeat past attacks that signature detection or some form of anomaly detection (or both) can identify.

It is to the terrorist's advantage to design a new attack or set of coordinated attacks not known to signature detection rules or developed anomaly patterns. It is essential that attacks occur without precursor probing, which can be detected as indicators of imminent attack. The element of surprise is extremely important. The Japanese attack on Pearl Harbor and the 9/11 al-Qaeda attack on the United States still stand as the worst foreign attacks on U.S. soil. Timothy McVeigh's surprise Oklahoma City bombing remains the worst attack of its type in U.S. history. Surprise is as important as the weapons used, if not more important.

Terrorists embrace the concept of *asymmetric warfare*. Unlike a typical war between two major powers, where the balance of power may be more equal, asymmetric warfare is warfare between a major power and a separate entity that clearly is not matched in strength and firepower. Therefore, the weaker entity uses different tactics. The 9/11 al-Qaeda attack is a prime example of asymmetric warfare. The 19 terrorists armed, only with sharp implements, were able to hijack four airliners to use as guided missiles wrapped within the element of surprise.

DEFINITION *Asymmetric warfare* **is warfare between two entities with an imbalance of forces whereby the entity that has less capability may be capable of gaining the upper hand through the elements of surprise and unconventional tactics.**

Because of the element of surprise and the extreme advantages of anonymity and destructiveness capable with a cyber attack, we must be ready for such a terrorist attack. One can only speculate on an all-out attack against our economic or power grid structures. This is not science fiction. It has already been shown that the power systems may be brought down by a cyber attack and that major banks may suffer losses due to smart cyber theft. The new AuBA technologies CheckMate and InMate (discussed in detail in Chapter 17 and demonstrated in the DVD walkthrough) are designed to detect new, first-time cyber attacks and are not based on signature detection or anomaly detection. Instead, the technology assesses packet-level activity for suspicious human cyber behavior that is attack-oriented, although it may not have been identified in the past. Like the Department of Pre-Crime in the Tom Cruise movie *Minority Report*, CheckMate and InMate can predict and anticipate first-time cyber attacks. As such, this new approach represents a more proactive security approach to cyber attack prevention.

Anticipating the Unknown

Often, prediction in the physical sciences is offered as being superior to prediction in the behavioral sciences. For example, in the area of astronomy it is usual to predict celestial events many decades away. Case in point, Halley's Comet returns every 75 years to be seen in the heavens. As soon as it appears, we know we can see it again in 75 years. This is the ultimate in predictability. However, these are static events, not dynamic and ever changing. If we examine such physical dynamic events as hurricanes, tsunamis, earthquakes, volcanic eruptions, floods, and other natural disasters, the physical sciences are not reliable in predicting events more than a few days in the future. For this reason, weather forecasts are accurate only for 5–6 days, even with the multiple supercomputer models used to predict the weather. So, I want to compare the physical science methods of prediction with the behavioral sciences methods of prediction presented in this book.

Our AuBA methods used for predicting adversary behavior do as least as good as the physical sciences prediction of natural dynamic phenomenon (for example, weather). In essence, dynamic, changeable variables are difficult for any science, and we are proud to say that our behavioral predictions of malicious behavior can match the time frames of the best physical sciences predictions. In addition, the best physical sciences weather predictions are typically based on supercomputer models, especially hurricane tracking and prediction. It is, in fact, rare that the weather bureau can provide an accurate path of a hurricane more than 24 hours in advance.

The basic AuBA methodology extends prediction of adversary behavior for longer periods of time as evidenced by independent validation of predictions. Furthermore, the methods developed work on a typical PC or laptop and do not require a supercomputer. As stated, human behavior is not statistical. Therefore, a solid foundation in behavior analysis is more likely to result in accurate anticipation of human behavior than sophisticated statistical modeling of the behavior itself.

Can Technology Detect First-Time Attacks?

The quick answer to this question is: *Yes*. The AuBA and manual methods we have developed have been shown to be effective in independent and government-supported validation tests to predict adversary behavior accurately. This includes first-time attacks. AuBA is a set of patented and, therefore, unique behavior analysis predictive methodologies. Applied behavior analysis is a field within psychology that concentrates on analyzing behavior based on environmental influences. The approach is used worldwide. A form of the methodology known as functional analysis of behavior is federally mandated to use in all school systems in the country. The basic applied behavior analysis methods can help us to understand and influence specific behaviors. However, the extensions to the methods presented in this book allow us to analyze behavior on a more global basis with increased confidence that we can predict specific forms of malicious behavior.

Applied behavior analysis used in school systems, prisons, and so on is constrained by the environment. Although there are exceptions, applied behavior analysis is typically used within a facility. In this case, antecedents and consequences are part of the constrained environment. When I left the clinical and academic settings to join the U.S. Secret Service, it was clear that applied behavior analysis could be of benefit, although at the time in 1985 it was not used in the government. However, after initial tries at analyzing threats, we found it obvious that antecedents and consequences for those who threaten from a worldwide basis were not limited to a facility. Instead, they were global. When we expanded to threats of terrorism to protectees of the service, it was even more obvious that extensions and modification were in order.

Over the course of many years, the AuBA methods have been refined to extend applied behavior analysis to the prediction of adversary behavior accurately. It is fair to say that extensions had to be added for the behavioral methods to be predictive of adversary behavior that threatens U.S. national security. We are now capable of anticipating new adversary and cyber threats as a result of the patented automation known as automated behavior analysis (AuBA). This book helps prepares the analyst for technology that before now did not exist. Designed for global use and the identification of antecedents and consequences of adversary behavior on a worldwide scale, the methods represent the only extension and automation of applied behavior analysis in this area.

Detecting the New Attack

The government authorized a well-known testing laboratory to test the capability of CheckMate to identify unknown, first-time attacks. To check this capability, they compared CheckMate to the two leading signature detection products of the day. The test began by presenting cyber attacks that both leading products and the CheckMate application could detect. Then, using hacker evasion tactics, testers altered the attacks in such a way that all attacks would be new. They then presented these new attacks to all three products. CheckMate identified the new attacks with much greater accuracy than the leading products. Because CheckMate does not use signature or anomaly detection, and anticipates attack threat based on assessment of human characteristics, it represents a more proactive approach that does not have to be present to identify a new attack.

In the cyber world, there are two major types of new attacks:

- First, there is a zero-day attack. This type of attack is characterized as a new attack designed to exploit a specific, previously unknown vulnerability in a network/system. The term *zero day* refers to the fact that there are no days of awareness of the vulnerability prior to the attack.

- Second, there is a modification of a known attack to result in a variation that will not be detected by current signatures written to find the original attack. The emphasis is on the modification, not the discovery of a specific unknown vulnerability, as with a true zero-day attack.

There is often confusion between new attacks and zero-day attacks. Both are new attacks, but zero-day attacks not only must be new but also must be designed to exploit a specific unknown vulnerability. A new attack that is not zero day can simply be a modification of an existing attack to evade current signatures. For example, in 2008 the Conficker worm was released as a true zero day attack designed to exploit previously unknown Windows operating system vulnerabilities. It reportedly took more than 6 months to fully understand and contain this threat. In the meantime, the worm infiltrated more than 7 million government and private computers. This is in marked contrast to simple modifications of known attacks to have the new modification slip by existing signatures in a signature detection application such as Snort.

Because CheckMate technology was designed as a human behavior assessment technology, as opposed to a network behavior tool, it has the capability to detect threatening human behavior behind the attack, even when a new attack is presented the first time.

Advantages of AuBA #4: Building Predictive Applications

AuBA does not rely on trying to discover what makes a terrorist or a malicious hacker or why a Ted Bundy becomes a serial killer. We leave that to other areas of psychology, psychiatry, and other social and behavioral sciences. Instead, AuBA begins with malicious behavior already present and predicts its occurrence so that it may be prevented. The approach, based on the antecedent-behavior-consequence (ABC) sequence, gives us a mechanism that clearly states that malicious behavior occurs in response to environmental antecedents that interact with internal motivation that is already present. If behaviors occur in the presence of antecedents and are followed by consequences of the behavior that are desired, then the probability of future occurrences of the behavior is increased in the presence of those antecedents. This means that if the antecedents associated with past malicious behavior occur in the future, we are likely to see the same or highly similar behavior occur in response.

In addition to this framework of understanding malicious behavior across a variety of threat domains (for example, terrorism, hacking, malicious intent, insider threat, and so forth), AuBA also consists of the methodologies and tools to actually identify the antecedents associated with past events and to construct the predictive engines to anticipate future occurrences of the behavior.

The construction of the predictive application occurs in two major steps. The first step is to develop and validate a predictive engine, or engines; the second step is the construction of the actual application by embedding the predictive engine(s) as the smart or decision-making component. The construction of the predictive engine makes use of the ThemeMate and AutoAnalyzer tools, as described in "Advantages of AuBA" section in Chapter 3. These tools, in sequence, identify the antecedents associated with past behaviors (ThemeMate) and then construct and validate the optimal predictive engine (AutoAnalyzer).

Figure 4-3 depicts the second stage. In this stage, the trained and validated predictive engine is placed within the application that we are constructing. To date, applications have been developed using sensor output, network packets, and text-based news articles of world events. Usually, our applications have consisted of several different such predictive engines, each focusing on a specific area of the problem to predict.

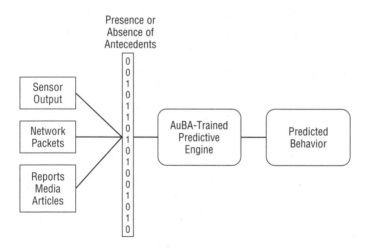

Figure 4-3: Once an AuBA predictive engine is completed, it is designed to process antecedents from sensors, text, or network packets and then is embedded into an application.

One predictive engine may focus on predicting the *what* of the projected behavior, whereas another engine may focus on the *when*, and so forth. Basically, a predictive engine is a validated pattern classifier that has been trained to provide a predictive output such as *attack* or *no attack* when presented with a vector of 1s and 0s. If the process of developing a predictive engine resulted in 40 antecedents, then the vector has 40 spaces for the 1s and 0s — one space for each of the 40 antecedents. Basically, we either manually or automatically determine whether or not each antecedent is present now. If present, that antecedent gets a 1; if absent, it gets a 0. Once we determine if each antecedent is present or absent, we will have a vector of 1s and 0s. This becomes the input to the predictive engine.

The predictive engine processes the presence or absence of each antecedent and provides as output the closest match of behaviors trained to be associated with antecedents in the pattern classification process. This is our prediction. The purpose of the application is to provide an interface to the user. This interface provides a means to enter the presence or absence of the antecedents, a method to present the vector to the predictive engine(s), and a means to present a report of the results back to the user.

The predictive engines take as input the presence or absence of each antecedent as a vector of 1s and 0s. The predictive engines are either a statistical process or an artificial neural network.

In Summary

This chapter has emphasized current threats facing our country every day. There has been an increase in shootings in public places, such as schools, malls, and workplaces. In addition, we have had major attacks committed by U.S. citizens against U.S. citizens. Although it is beyond the scope of the current chapter to show the details of a behavior analysis methodology, the types of conclusions we can derive based on a behavior analysis of past incidents was presented. In future chapters procedural details will be presented. However, I strongly urge you to read the book in its entirety to assimilate all the details necessary to conduct effective predictive modeling.

This chapter emphasized that it is possible to predict adversary behavior accurately. I contend that when they are applied to human behavior, which is dynamic and ever changing, the predictive capabilities of methods presented in this book surpass the physical science's ability to predict dynamic physical events such as weather, volcanic eruptions, tsunamis, hurricanes, earthquakes, and so forth. In addition to predicting malicious behavior, the methods presented may be useful in gaining an understanding of why specific forms of malicious behavior occur. Proactive prevention of the types of malicious behaviors presented in this chapter depends on the improved understanding of the contextual dynamics of antecedents and consequences of past behaviors and how they contribute to predictions of future behaviors.

Current security approaches are primarily reactive and based on defining signatures of past attacks so that if an attack occurs again in the future, the signatures can detect the same attack when it occurs. The automated behavior analysis methods and tools presented in this book are very different and proactive. By emphasizing the antecedents and consequences of past behaviors, we can predict accurately that a specific behavior will likely occur in the future in response to past antecedents and consequences. In other words, instead of expecting the same behavior to occur and describing it with signatures or rules, we identify the precursors (antecedents) that set the stage for the behavior to occur and the consequences that encourage the behavior to occur based on analysis of past behaviors. Then, when specific constellations of antecedents and promised consequences that were associated with past behaviors are identified, the same or highly similar behavior tends to follow. This proactive methodology enables us to develop more anticipatory and less reactive security methods.

Current Network Security

In a recent National Geographic Channel video presentation titled *On Board Air Force One*, Colonel Mark Tillman, who flew Air Force One with the President on board on September 11, 2001, was interviewed. In that interview, Colonel Tillman said of 9/11:

> *Sadly they beat us. The terrorists beat us. I am ready to admit it hands down, they beat us. So, we had to change everything to make sure they wouldn't beat us again.*

As a result of 9/11, much has been done. Among the many changes: The Department of Homeland Security (DHS) was formed, we have decimated much of the al-Qaeda leadership, and we are fighting a global war against the terrorism that led to 9/11. However, we as a nation truly remain under serious cyber attack. Far less has been accomplished in forming an improved and proactive cyber attack defense. Continued attacks are swift, effective, and in some cases crippling. The attacks are originating from malicious attackers inside our country, as well as from foreign sources and adversaries, and our defense simply is not getting better. Losses as measured by effects of actual disruption of network operations or the loss of classified or proprietary information are obvious and fly in the face of promised protection.

This chapter is focused on the truthful evaluation of the effectiveness with which current network intrusion detection technologies protect our networks and prevent unauthorized access and damage. Basic network protection concepts and technology have not changed appreciably in decades, while attacks continue to grow more advanced and effective on a daily basis. Primarily reactive, current detection methods must be augmented with more proactive human behavior analysis technology capable of anticipating new attacks, as opposed to simply waiting for past attacks to reoccur.

Hacking and National Network Security

The severity and frequency of cyber attacks directed against government, private, and public sectors continue to increase at an alarming rate. At the same time, current intrusion detection and protection methodologies struggle to provide effective countermeasures. The expansion of hacker intrusion knowledge by means of the Internet, Black Hat conferences, publications, and personal intercommunication contribute greatly to the rising damage and threat to our protected networks. Even the unsophisticated hacker who does his or her homework and downloads easily accessible hacking instructions or scripts can inflict serious and costly damage. Furthermore, the nature of attacks has changed. In past years, network and systems were the target; more recently, the user is considered as a high-priority entry point.

Our national security depends on the protection of classified government, strategic, and tactical military secrets, as well as the protection of our national infrastructure. However, national security also depends on the protection of our advanced technology and economic viability. The very network interconnectivity that we have struggled to protect is the very interconnectedness that has helped to place the United States in the spotlight on a global stage. We have arguably the most powerful military force on Earth, possess advanced intelligence methods, and exert global leadership. However, this worldwide presence creates antecedent conditions that attract adversary threat. Because of the overt power of the United States, the safest way for adversaries to attack our infrastructure and to escape detection is through intrusion into networks. This is where the United States is most vulnerable.

Just two to three decades ago when networks, Internet, and global interconnectivity were new, everyone was in a learning phase. This was universal. There was much to learn. It was all very exciting. I constructed my own computer from a kit, and once the basic computer was working, I was excited by the realization that communication within a new cyber world could occur at almost instantaneous speeds, different sites within the cyber world could be visited, and documents could be shared in an instant. Almost as immediately, those with malicious intent also entered the scene. As most of us were learning the newest of technology and realizing the enormous implications, the advances were not lost on the individual hacker or the organized adversary. The Internet presented a new frontier for malicious intent — a frontier that could support an almost infinite variety of adversarial attack behavior.

Basically, when the inventors of the precursors to the Internet, known as ARPANET (DARPA), presented the new capability, the implications were recognized immediately by the technologically aware. At the time, I rode to work to the U.S. Secret Service in Washington, DC, in a carpool. It was an interesting carpool composed of members from the Secret Service, National Science Foundation (NSF), World Bank, and FDIC — all technologically astute. The NSF member of the group, Fred, mentioned he was testing a new network application. It appeared that the NSF was the first to test this DARPA-invented network interconnectivity, and Fred was fortunate enough to have a connection.

Here I was as a psychologist with a bent for invention and all things technical listening to an NSF expert describe this new interconnectivity that could allow him and his colleagues instant communication — and it wasn't the telephone. This was remarkable, and it underscored the value of the possibility of almost-instant sharing of document attachments, extended text sharing, and the possibility of instant collaboration using intellectual and proprietary secrets to facilitate scientific advancement. Now we almost take it for granted.

> **NOTE** It is time to stop the myth that all malicious hackers are geniuses, as depicted in the movies and on television. Although there are some very talented individuals who are astute at hacking, the malicious hacker has the element of surprise, scripts, code shared with others, and sometimes insider information on his or her side. The real heroes work on the side of preventing damage from hackers, They must be well rounded, be alert on an ongoing basis, be knowledgeable of all varieties of attacks, know all forms of vulnerabilities, and be prepared for new classes of attacks. Malicious hackers are akin to break-in artists. They hit and run and do not want to face the target directly.

Shortly thereafter, it was apparent that those with malicious intent who could not make a contribution to the actual science would try to disrupt it, which was far easier, and lacked imagination. Malicious hackers were born. There are still hackers but there are now specializations. Not only do we have the basic hacker who finds it entertaining to disrupt and attack, but also on the other end of the continuum, we have the professional hacker who steals secrets or causes disruption for a price, perhaps for a foreign government.

Yes, there are different categories — hackers, crackers, and so on. However, just like the protection of my home with an advanced perimeter security system, I don't want someone in my house checking my security without my permission. That would be unwanted intrusion and trespassing. A certain number of hackers use the excuse that they are hacking to check security so that they can let the targeted organization know of their vulnerabilities. No thanks. Hackers are not welcome without invitation.

Hacking is malicious intent. The hacker is invading the property of another person; he or she is being malicious and likely harbors serious malicious intent. Invading a network does not really require talent. It just requires persistence and, for the most part, using available destructive methods developed by others.

Unless a professional, the typical hacker attempts to be a big fish in a small pond. Recognition is important, even if it comes from a very small group of fellow hackers. Is it difficult to be a hacker and disrupt network operations or steal proprietary secrets? No, not really. The vast majority of hackers are not the geniuses of movies. Hackers who would invade a network to cause damage of one sort or another, including loss of desired information or data, are criminals engaging in theft or vandalism. Almost anyone with a PC and Internet can download attack scripts, determine intrusion techniques, and create new attacks from old attacks using hacker evasion tactics to evade current signature detection network intrusion technologies. Contrary to what the movies may portray, this is not genius; this is simply an indictment of our current technology not being able to stop these network penetrations more effectively.

However, like any normal bell-shaped curve, the abilities and talents of hackers vary, from the novice hacker (often referred to as a script kiddie or ankle biter) to the APT skilled intrusion expert. The professional may be working for a nation-state and pose significant and creative risk to our country's security and national infrastructure. We do not want to be lulled into a false sense of security because we have neophytes attacking. We must remember that there are hackers who can disrupt our most sensitive sites and steal information without us knowing it is missing until much later. For the beginners with low expertise and little knowledge of how to be truly deceptive, typical signature detection is effective because they simply keep repeating the same small number of attacks against various sites until successful. There are signatures for such activities. Again, on the other end of the continuum of expertise and deception, the professional either picks or is assigned a specific target and persists with creative attacks to obtain what is desired from the benefactor. It is this latter category of hacking with which we must be very concerned.

NOTE Hackers vary considerably along the dimensions of expertise and deception. Even beginners can cause damage with something like a denial of service. Armed with a PC, access to the Internet, and scripts and other hacker tools, even the low-skilled hacker can pose a threat. The professional hacker definitely poses a serious threat, and we have to contend with these serious threats on an ongoing basis.

The inadequacies of current signature-based and anomaly detection methodologies in preventing serious misuse, combined with the inordinate number of highly skilled and costly staff required to operate and maintain these types of systems, dictate the need for a new and effective technology. Without adequate countermeasures to network attacks, loss is going to continue to occur and worsen.

Currently, the effectiveness we do have with current technologies is a testament to the constant care and feeding of such systems by our network intrusion experts. In some situations, when multiple hackers attack a single site, perhaps even without knowledge of one another's efforts, it is that forensics or network intrusion expert who makes sense of the malicious attacks. The intrusion experts, the humans behind the technology, are the ones who make the current technology, signature detection and the less often used anomaly detection, look as good as those limited technologies can look. Basically, without the network intrusion expert using the available tools (and enhancing them with invaluable skill and knowledge), the tools would fail because of their inability to be adaptive.

However, I must admit that there is a talented group of extremely talented adversaries who are very good at what they do. These paid professionals are dedicated to exploit our network vulnerabilities, create damage, or steal secrets. They are equivalent to our best network intrusion specialists except that they also have either malicious intent toward the United States or are paid to inflict loss or damage directed toward their adversary. We must remember that a typical hacker needs only to know a few methods to be effective. He or she can use the same methods repeatedly against a very large number of networks until success is achieved. On the other hand, a professional adversary may be directed to a single target and must have many skills in his or her arsenal. To create a new zero-day exploit or engage in theft without being detected is an adversary skill set that begs for better U.S. network intrusion defenses.

Growing Damage and Threat

We are witnessing increased damage and loss through the process of network intrusion. The growing damage and threat depends strongly on three major forms of attack:

- The external threat from a hacker or group of hackers intent on causing damage or stealing restricted information
- The trusted insider who goes bad as a result of disgruntlement, or the promise of compensation for stealing inside secrets (insider with intent)
- The insider working in collusion with or being duped by an outsider to facilitate damage and loss (insider without intent)

The insider threat has grown steadily. Although insider threat will be covered in multiple chapters in this book, it will be covered in detail in Chapter 12.

PRIVATE BRADLEY MANNING AND WIKILEAKS

A recent alleged incident serves as a prime example of the insider threat. Bradley Manning, a U.S. Army soldier, has been accused of sending 250,000 sensitive and classified documents to WikiLeaks for distribution. WikiLeaks was founded in 2006, supported by multiple countries and groups around the world. Its purpose was to disseminate and publish classified and sensitive documents that were forwarded to the organization. This purpose was established when the organization was founded and remains the primary purpose today. Obviously controversial, it has worked blatantly to make U.S. secrets public.

Specifically, according to *World News* with Diane Sawyer, in a news report on July 29, 2010, U.S. Army Private Bradley Manning, stationed in Iraq at the time, was arrested for passing classified documents to WikiLeaks. The estimate of the total number of documents passed to WikiLeaks has ranged from 90,000 to 250,000. In confidence, Manning had sought advice from Adrian Lamo, featured in a *Wired* magazine article on hacking. Manning thought Lamo would be sympathetic to his disgruntled feelings about U.S. policies in Iraq. However, after his concern over the activities of Manning increased over time, Lamo eventually tipped off the FBI. Manning allegedly used Lady Gaga CDs as a vehicle to download volumes of classified documents and remove from the classified site where he was working. The alleged release of documents by Manning was preceded by Manning releasing two classified videos showing U.S. fighter plane attacks in Iraq.

More recently, while Manning has been kept in solitary confinement, WikiLeaks has released many hundreds of thousands of sensitive and classified documents that could endanger persons and U.S. security policy. Also, it has been noted in the news that WikiLeaks was actually under cyber attack itself. The cyber war wages on. Again, it does not take exceptional expertise for an insider to steal classified information; it often just requires motivation.

The fact that U.S. citizens commit treason and spy for foreign governments is not new. Infamous cases include FBI's Robert Hanssen, CIA's Aldrich Ames, NSA's Jonathan Pollard, and DIA's Ana Belen Montes. All had violated the confidence entrusted to them by the U.S. government by stealing secrets and passing them to foreign governments. No U.S. intelligence service or military branch has been immune. We will always have those individuals who seek to cause damage or to steal to seek revenge or to gain additional income; so it is with the flawed nature of human character.

I predict that within the current decade, protective and proactive technology will advance to the degree that a cyber attacker will be traced back to the actual machine used, and that with geolocation technology assistance, we will pinpoint the actual location, or source, of the attack. Through new AuBA technology that emphasizes the development and identification of *behaviorprints*, identities will be determined at the source end of an attack. All humans have distinct behavior and methods of operation in cyber attack just as they have unique fingerprints. We will see new detection capability surface and mature over the current decade.

NOTE The unsung, truly gifted individuals in the growing cyber war are the network intrusion subject matter experts (SMEs). These SMEs fight against network intrusions and must know a vast number of hacker methods and techniques. A hacker simply needs to be an automaton and master only a very limited handful of attacks that can be repeated across networks, hiding behind the anonymity that the Internet affords.

The real cyber super heroes are the certified and other knowledgeable network specialist teams mastering a vast number of methods to protect our classified and proprietary secrets. Current expert teams such as the SANS Internet Storm Center (ISC) or the CERT team work tirelessly to protect our networks. Although a dedicated hacker needs to know only a few effective techniques, these security professionals must acquire an almost encyclopedic knowledge of intrusion methods to muster a defense to the degree that technology can provide. It is a difficult task given the number of U.S. targets that have surfaced. Why should we be so concerned about cyber attack? The following is a brief list of known U.S. targets:

- Water treatment systems
- Energy and nuclear power plants
- Oil and gas facilities
- Business
- Proprietary technology advances
- Patents
- Government sensitive information
- Government classified information
- Personally identifiable information (PII)
- Commercial and government websites (for defacement)
- Internal theft of proprietary commercial and government secrets
- Internal disruption and sabotage

It is very clear that our national infrastructure and economic viability results in a large variety of targets for adversaries. We must work to prevent additional damage, and we must extend our perception of threat to include the insider and not just external threat to our country.

The damage caused by cyber attack to the U.S. government and corporate America would take multiple chapters just to describe. In the late 1980s and early

1990s, networks were introduced on a large scale. The growth of the technology, including the massive advances in communications technologies, may be unprecedented. All with a cell phone, smartphone, iPad, PC, Mac, and so on fully realize the impact that such technologies have had on our lives. We are also very much aware of network attacks and the need for security practices and applications to help keep our computers and networks productive and working efficiently both at home and at work. We have become more interconnected than ever, and now we have the *cloud*. There has been increasing opportunity to inflict malicious intent using network intrusion as a window into organizational secrets and daily functions.

Our interconnected nation is under attack. It is difficult to keep track of malicious network activity, and it is getting worse. The basic network security signature detection and anomaly detection technologies have changed little in concept since their inception and introduction. Unfortunately, cyber attacks have become more sophisticated, resulting in mounting damage and increased risk of future serious attacks.

Assessing Current Technology

The severity and frequency of cyber attacks directed against government, private, commercial, and public sectors continues to increase at an alarming rate. The spread of hacker intrusion knowledge via the Internet, conferences, publications, and personal communication contributes greatly to the escalation in sophistication of network intrusions. Even the unsophisticated hacker who does his homework and downloads easily accessible hacking instructions or scripts can inflict serious and costly damage. Meanwhile, current intrusion detection and protection methodologies are not providing effective countermeasures. We need a new and more effective technology.

Effective network intrusion detection has been an industry goal for over two decades, yet only two basic approaches have surfaced to offer a modicum of protection: rule-based detection (signature detection) and anomaly detection.

Signature Detection

Signature detection is the primary approach used, and it is, by definition, designed to be reactive. The methodology is designed to specify rules to define an attack that has already occurred so that the attacks may be identified when they reoccur.

In the world of networks, the smallest entity that can be processed from a source to a destination is a byte. Of course, significant information cannot be relayed in a single character, so a collection of bytes is gathered as a packet. A packet contains from 1,000 to 1,500 bytes, or characters. Much like atoms and molecules, where a molecule comprises atoms, information is passed from source to destination in packets and within each packet are bytes. When you complete an e-mail and send it to another person, the e-mail will be divided into packets that will travel to the intended destination and be reassembled in order to recreate the exact message. Networks are designed to process and move packets from a source to a destination.

The genius of ARPANET, the DARPA forerunner to the Internet, was that a small message generated from one computer could travel to a second computer to determine if the message could be received and, if so, send back a message to the source indicating that it could receive the message. When this *handshake* occurred as an indicator that all was well, then the message, as individual packets, could be forwarded. Each of these packets had a header that contained such information as the sending and receiving address (IP address) to ensure proper delivery, as well as an offset to be used to reassemble the packets at the destination site, if the packet was fragmented. Each packet would also have a payload section, in addition to a header. The header would be used for addressing, and the payload would consist of content expressed in bytes.

However, packets would not have to travel through the Internet the same way each time. If a hop from server to server was busy, then the packets could simply travel through a less busy, separate route with the least resistance. This design was important at the time, so that if an adversary somehow destroyed part of the world's Internet, packets could just be re-routed using a different route, and the desired message would still be received.

Whether information is generated for an e-mail by keyboard presses, scripts, and so on, the packet-based foundation always works the same with a *packet switching network* like the Internet. Packets may contain non-malicious activity or evidence of malicious activity because of the immense number of ways activities can be generated and transferred to a destination site. It is the job of signature detection to identify the presence of malicious activity by using rules established to detect certain types of activities present that are cause for concern. Signature detection products vary considerably, with some products allowing more freedom to develop new signatures.

A signature detection product can be partially effective if tuned properly and the product contains a rich repertoire of known attacks with rules to process network traffic. However, network protection effectiveness is dependent on staff knowledgeable in attack signatures and tuning methods. Unfortunately, because of the deep specialties required across forensics, network intrusion, and rule generation, there are not enough experts of the required caliber to meet the escalating industry needs. Of course, signature detection is ineffective against new forms of attack not in the system's attack repertoire. Hackers are resourceful; therefore, they frequently modify attacks to avoid detection. Signature detection can only report on reconnaissance, scanning, or cyber attack signatures if the rules are within the application. No rule, no detection. It is as simple as that.

More important, given that a signature detection product contains a specific set of rules to detect a known activity of concern, hackers can defeat the application. If attackers are aware of the existence of the rule(s), they can simply use typical hacker evasion tactics to alter the nature of the attack just enough to make the former activity different enough to escape existing rules. In other words, the rule(s) generated will still detect the former attack but not the variation.

Forensics: The Key to Defining New Signatures for Detection

Network forensics is an essential part of signature detection. Maximizing the use of a signature detection application such as open source Snort requires updating signatures when new forms of attack or threatening activity are identified. Network forensics is the process of analyzing network activity for the purpose of identifying evidence of threatening activity associated with cyber attacks against a network. It is also used for reconnaissance, surveillance, probes, or scans to detect vulnerabilities.

DEFINITION   *Network forensics* is the process of analyzing network activity for the purpose of identifying threatening activity associated with cyber attacks against a network or for reconnaissance, surveillance, probes, or scans to identify vulnerabilities.

Signature detection is static and non-adaptive. Once a rule is written, it will forever do the same thing it was constructed to do. If the objective is to identify known attacks and attacks recently found by means of network forensics, then signature detection can be effective. However, it will require constant forensics and traffic analysis to identify the types of new attacks that surface daily and, of course, the talent and time to continually write new rules to detect the latest threatening activities.

The signature detection rules can range from very simple rules that perhaps look only at the header of a packet to very complex rules that consider *state*, or memory of activities over time, to establish a time-based rule. The rules must not only be designed but also be written in a precise manner and tested for accuracy. It is not at all unusual to construct a rule only to find that it is not performing as planned. Complex rules can be difficult to construct, and a fair degree of testing may be required to determine if a rule is doing what it should be doing.

Perhaps the most difficult part of forensics is the process of searching through massive volumes of network traffic. Even if an attack is known to occur, identifying the nuances of the attack across mountains of traffic is daunting, at best. Once remnants of an attack have been identified, reconstructing the entire attack is difficult. If you have worked in intrusion detection for any time at all, you know that forensics experts are worth their weight in gold.

False Negative: Missing the New Attack

Network intrusion and forensics experts develop impressive repertoires over time. Experience helps refine the process of identifying classes and specific cyber attack tactics. However, if identifying attack behavior and scanning and surveillance precursors were not enough, hackers often modify their past attacks using evasion tactics to create *new* attacks. In this way, there is always a supply of new attacks that have a high probability of being effective and, because they are new attacks, are not likely to be detected. Unfortunately, for signature detection this means we must wait until the attack occurs and then gather the characteristics to construct a rule or set of rules to detect the attack if it occurs again.

The primary problem with signature detection is that it is prone to false negatives. A false negative means that the product falsely determines that activity that is truly malicious is not malicious. Of the two types of detection error, false positives and false negatives, false negatives are the more serious of the two. A false-negative error means that an attack was able to get through the signature detection defenses without detection and was able to inflict damage, or engage in theft of user IDs, passwords, or actual proprietary information. A false positive is non-malicious activity that gets flagged as malicious.

Although we currently rely heavily on signature detection for what it does well, it simply is not enough. The adversaries targeting U.S. infrastructure today are resourceful and creative. They are very capable of modifying past attacks with hacker evasions tactics to create new attacks, creating new attacks or classes of new attacks not observed in the past, or creating true zero-day attacks. In all cases, signature detection is likely to not catch the attack.

As discussed briefly in the previous chapter, a *zero-day* attack is a special case of a new attack but is not simply a modification of an existing attack or just a new form of attack. Basically, if an attacker is aware of a specific vulnerability in our network, operating system, or protective mechanisms and designs a new attack before the vulnerability is made public, then there are literally *zero days* between the discovery of the vulnerability and the creation of a defensive signature to defend against attacks exploiting that newly discovered vulnerability.

Signature detection is purely reactive technology that does not have the capability to detect new attacks through evasions tactics, new classes of attacks never before observed, or true zero-day attacks designed to exploit a just-discovered vulnerability. However, signature detection is very necessary at this time. Why? Because proactive detection with low error rates has not yet surfaced to accurately anticipate new attacks. The AuBA technology in this book is presented as a new behavior-analysis-based technology to meet this need. Not designed to replace current technology, it is presented as a third technology to specifically decrease the false-negative error rates associated with signature detection and to decrease the false-positive rates associated with anomaly detection.

Anomaly detection was developed as a separate and hopefully new approach that would be capable of detecting new forms of attack because of the inability of signature detection to detect new forms of attacks. As we will see in the next section, it too has a serious weakness.

Anomaly Detection

Anomaly detection is designed to characterize "normal" activity within a given network so that future "non-normal" activity may be flagged. The assumption is that non-normal activity equates to misuse or malicious intent. Furthermore, anomaly detection programs must be trained on the normal activity of a given network — not an easy task, particularly if the network contains malicious intent at the time of training. In other words, because our networks tend to have malicious scanning, probes, and attempts to attack across the weeks that it may take to train the anomaly detection application, the trained system is likely to include malicious activities trained as normal. Obviously, such activities will not be flagged as non-normal in the future.

Because the anomaly detection application must be trained on the specific network for which it will be used, there is likely no effective generalization of the training of the *norm* to other networks. Therefore, training must be repeated for any network using the technology — a costly and not entirely effective approach. As presented, signature detection suffers from false-negative errors (malicious activity not part of existing signatures get through by being falsely labeled as non-malicious). Since malicious activity is likely to be present during the process of determining the statistical average of the network, that malicious activity will be considered to be normal, or non-malicious, when it occurs in the future (false negative). However, anomaly detection is much more likely to suffer from false-positive errors — that is, labeling non-malicious activity as malicious.

Anomaly detection flags as malicious any activity that is not within the trained norm. Non-normal is not the same as malicious. For example, an employee who works late and accesses the network remotely from home at 2:00 A.M. gets flagged as malicious when in fact it is just non-malicious work — this is clearly a false positive. It is flagged as malicious when it is not.

On the other hand, signature detection has signatures for former attacks only. Therefore, any new attack not fitting a signature will be allowed through; a truly malicious activity that has no signature and is not detected is clearly a false negative.

This is the problem with signature detection today. It is not catching all the new activity coming through because it does not recognize the activity with existing signatures (clearly false negatives). If it is pinging away at noise, then that is a tuning issue — a separate issue altogether.

To clarify even further, signature detection in these cases is falsely letting activity through that is malicious, labeling it as negative or non-malicious (false negative). This happens because anomaly detection considers activity different from the established average as being malicious. The flaw: Activity that is not average does not equate to being malicious. Totally appropriate and non-malicious behavior can occur that is not average. This is the nature of human behavior.

More recently, protocol anomaly detection was developed as an extension of the more traditional form of network anomaly detection, although quite different as an approach. This new non-statistical development surfaced as an attempt to solve drawbacks associated with typical anomaly detection. Instead of establishing "normal" activity of a given network, protocol anomaly detection relies on learning specific TCP/IP protocols.

Since the more traditional form of anomaly detection has difficulty capturing normal network activity, training a system on protocols that are well established may be an improvement. In short, activity associated with the correct use of specific protocols is modeled and forms the basis for activity comparisons. However, false positives can still be very high in that inadequate protocol specifications result in less-than-accurate models of the protocols used.

Why is it so difficult to assess packet-level activity? Why not simply construct a system that requires only rules to identify activities belonging exclusively to hackers and block any visitor exhibiting any of the identified activities? Although signature detection methodologies have attempted to do just that for two decades, there is an overlap in packet-level activity between legitimate visitors and hackers that creates confusion. Figure 5-1 depicts a conceptual depiction of packet-level activity associated with malicious behavior and packet-level activity associated with non-malicious behavior. Conceptually, at any given time, it is more likely that there are activities associated with both malicious and non-malicious activities operating at the same time, even if activity is associated with an attack.

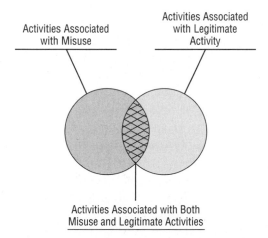

Figure 5-1: A conceptual depiction of activities associated with malicious intent and non-malicious intent — both occur at the same time, even if malicious behavior is occurring.

Even an attacker coming into a network must first establish the totally normal *handshake*, that is, a brief call to the destination to see if it can receive packets and a return indicating that the destination server can receive. (The exception is UDP, which does not have the handshake.) Because activity at specific time slices contain both legitimate and non-legitimate activities, it is exceedingly difficult for signature detection or anomaly detection to make pure calls of legitimate or non-legitimate activities.

Although there are activities and combinations of activities associated only with legitimate use and misuse, many activities and combinations are associated with both. Again, a hallmark of human behavior is the degree to which humans naturally adapt and normally exhibit non-normal behavior. In other words, the legitimate employee who changes patterns of network use may, in fact, be flagged by anomaly detection as a person of concern. Regardless of how well we construct the anomaly detection system, anomalous behavior can never equate exclusively to misuse or lack of legitimacy — legitimate human behavior is just too rife with anomalous behavior.

Defining the Norm

The term *normal* is a loaded term. For a psychologist like me, *normal* means something entirely different than what the term means to the anomaly detection specialist. The psychological meaning carries with it a connotation that normal behavior is acceptable behavior within society, while abnormal behavior is inappropriate behavior. In psychology, therefore, *normal* means more than just average behavior. In anomaly detection, the term *normal* is simply defined as a statistical type of average whereby a statistically significant difference from the average is considered to be non-normal. In short, much more complexity is required to determine psychological normal from non-normal than is needed to calculate an average. However, an anomaly detection approach does something similar to extract meaning from statistical averages. From a statistical perspective, anomaly detection makes a huge conceptual leap from the rather simple concept of determining differences from the established averages for network behavior to labeling such differences as malicious. However, malicious behavior is much more than simply a deviation from the norm. In fact, a true professional intent on damage or theft is likely to hide within concepts of what is typical or average behavior.

If a process of determining average behavior on a network is used to establish a standard across different forms of activity, this process captures activities that include both malicious and non-malicious activity (refer to Figure 5-1). Training on any network cannot be assumed to be capturing only non-malicious activity. If so, network intrusion would not be needed — the network would already free of malicious activity! Therefore, determining the average, which we will call the norm, is not a non-malicious standard to which deviations can be compared to determine non-normal. All that anomaly norming can do under the circumstances of training on a specific live network is to determine a base rate of malicious and non-malicious activity. Deviations from this base rate can only tell us if malicious or non-malicious activity is better or worse as a whole than the base rate.

Certainly, deviation from the "norm" cannot be used to indicate malice. If we could be assured that the target network was 100 percent clear of scans, probes, creative surveillance, and reconnaissance, and free from all forms of attack for the weeks of norming, then the approach would have more merit. Even then, it could not be highly accurate. The reason — human behavior is simply rampant with non-average but acceptable behavior.

I call deviations from the statistical average *anomaly-good* and *anomaly-bad*. Deviations will include anomaly-good whereby unusual and infrequent behavior may be exhibited that is totally non-malicious in character and is just different. They may also include deviations from the norm that flag malicious behavior that gets by signature detection; this is the reason why the approach persists today. However, the approach does not include methods to differentiate between anomaly-good and anomaly-bad. All significant deviations of a certain type are flagged as malicious because of this inability. The result is that anomaly detection is associated with alarmingly high false-positive rates (labeling non-malicious activity as malicious). Truly malicious behavior is the result of malicious intent of the individual, not statistical differences from the network average. Anomaly detection does nothing to attempt to measure true human malicious intent.

Currently anomaly detection is the research method of choice for detecting insider threat. The reasoning is that the insider such as an employee, contractor, or intern who exhibits behavior outside of the statistical average on a network is exhibiting malicious behavior. However, this is simply faulty reasoning. To repeat, malicious behavior, including that perpetuated by insiders, stems from malicious intent. It comes from being disgruntled or from promise of receiving pay for selling internal secrets. In fact, in studying many individuals with malicious intent such as true spies and true corporate espionage perpetrators, the individuals who escape detection for many years do so by appearing to be like the other employees. They seek to stay within the norm and may be too smart to go outside the norm.

Later in this book in detailed descriptions of AuBA-related CheckMate and InMate technologies, I demonstrate how behavior analysis of the individual behind the network activity can be assessed to more accurately determine malicious intent. Anomaly detection is basically a good idea from the perspective that it is not locked into signatures of past events. If new or zero-day attacks occur, it is actually possible that anomaly detection could identify the attack as new. However, the inability to determine malicious from non-malicious activity results in very high false-positive rates and is equivalent to *crying wolf*. If it flags activity as non-normal, the probability is higher that it is non-malicious. Through a description of AuBA technologies as related to network intrusion detection, you will see how this technology can actually work as an additional step to anomaly detection to process flagged cases to determine further anomaly-good from anomaly-bad. This is an example of why new human behavior–based technology may augment existing technologies.

Unanticipated Network Attacks: The Bane of Network Security

Hackers of all skill levels now know that there is an advantage in generating new malicious activity. By designing new attacks or intrusions into networks, hackers increase the probability that they will be successful. Why? First, new activity is not likely to be detected by signature detection — there are no rules to detect never before seen activity. Furthermore, an anomaly detection system may be throwing so many false positives that there may be too many flagged activities to identify the new activity as *anomaly-bad* until it is too late.

The modern-day hacker knows that there are several ways to generate new attacks.

- First, existing attacks can be modified using available techniques to result in modifications that can slip by signature detection.

- Second, hackers with exceptional skill know that it is actually relatively easy to derive new attacks from scratch given knowledge of contemporary detection methods and existing rules.

- Finally, if the knowledge is present to thoroughly target a specific organization and determine vulnerabilities, the discovery of a new vulnerability previously not known is an invitation for a zero-day attack.

For those who would dispute the ease with which current-day networks may be successfully breached, I would point out the many, almost daily, reports of successful intrusions into major organizations and government networks.

The unknown attack is an objective of the serious cyber attacker. We have much work left to do to significantly change our security posture. It bears repeating — our current inability to stop network intrusions that result in damage to major organizations in our country is not a failure of security personnel. Current damage points to the need for new and improved network protection technologies and even a better conceptualization of the problem facing us.

Moving Toward Fixing Current Ineffective Network Protection

One of our primary problems in network security is that we are using decades-old conceptualizations of the types of technology required to stop network intrusions to protect our national infrastructure. Simply continuing to rely on signature detection and anomaly detection to stop network intrusions, or even to reduce successful intrusions, by doing the same thing over and over again will not work. The results are going to be the same. True, we may have no alternative at the moment. However, a major shift is needed in network protection technology as soon as possible. We are facing a rise in the frequency and severity of network attacks, including insider threats. The evidence speaks for itself. Our effectiveness is decreasing as threat increases.

Attending the GFIRST conference in 2010, I observed a CIO of one of our major companies in our country giving a speech. To paraphrase, in that speech, he admitted defeat. He stated that we can't stop hackers with technology, so we should concentrate on policy. It is clear that a new approach is needed.

Winning or Losing?

If I answer this question honestly, I have to say to date that we are losing. Our adversaries are winning by being successful at infiltrating our organizations through our networks and basically having their way with us. First, we are losing because the networks used to protect our organizations are getting slammed with attacks. These attacks cause disruption, and we have witnessed embarrassing losses in classified information and sensitive proprietary data, as well as strategic and tactical information and plans. If there were any winning on our parts, it would be a product of our excellent network forensic and investigatory personnel who can point the finger at Chinese intelligence and other state-support of cyber activities directed against the United States. We have apprehended such alleged criminals as Bradley Manning, mentioned earlier in the chapter.

Certainly, detecting attacks after damage is done is better than not detecting attacks or damage at all, but that is a small consolation. It is not enough to detect after the fact. We must become more proactive with our technology. After decades of network protection experience, it is difficult to believe we are still using signature detection as our primary means of protecting networks. Being reactive by definition and designing signatures after we have been attacked is much like waiting to be bombed so that we can determine the size of the bomb. Proactive technology was needed a decade ago; it's absolutely vital now.

Adjusting Our Approach: The Need for a Paradigm Shift

Here is the big question: How do we become proactive? Currently we have signature detection that must rely on an attack occurring before we can characterize it with rules to look for it in the future, and we have anomaly detection that can detect something unusual but can't tell the difference between something that is unusual and non-malicious from something that is unusual and malicious. It is clear why the technology is less than totally effective. There is nothing wrong with signature and anomaly detection — they just need to be updated conceptually to be proactive with a corresponding decrease in false-negative and false-positive error rates. However, we also need to realize that a third type of technology is needed.

Currently we focus on network behavior as a method to infer malicious intent of the individuals behind the network activity. We study network behavior to predict behavior in the future. However, as pointed out throughout this book, the accurate prediction of malicious behavior depends on the identification of antecedent conditions that precede the malicious behavior. What is needed is a human behavior–based technology to augment the current network behavior signature detection and anomaly detection approaches.

Until we can better anticipate attacks and design defenses to protect against them before they can occur, it will be difficult, if not impossible, to win against the cyber adversary. However, the behavior analysis methods presented in this book show promise in moving toward a security-based paradigm shift. As the book progresses, I will show how the new technology relates to anticipation as opposed to reaction. I will also show effectiveness in anticipating network and organization attacks from external means and from insiders.

Augmenting the Concept of Network Behavior with Human Behavior

If a true proactive intrusion protection system is to be developed, it must have several salient characteristics not currently available with existing signature-based and anomaly detection technologies. Such systems should:

- Determine intent immediately and accurately (low false positives and false negatives) to prevent damage before it occurs

- Determine if a visitor being assessed when entering a site is legitimate or more than likely will create damage or attempt theft

- Implement immediate assessment of behavior and not just compare packet-level activities to sets of rules

- Identify unique, first-time attack modifications, in addition to traditional attacks, and have the capability to act immediately on such information

- Simultaneously and continuously track and assess all visitors of concern as they enter and navigate through the network

It is clear that the next generation of intrusion technology must focus on prevention. The systems of the future must operate earlier in real time and identify at least some form of attack not yet experienced without high error rates. As it states in the 2009 report prepared for the Chairman and Ranking Member of the U.S. Senate Committee on Homeland Security and Governmental Affairs titled *National Cyber Security: Research and Development Challenges Related to Economics, Physical Infrastructure and Human Behavior — An Industry, Academic and Government Perspective*:

> Technologists and policymakers must consider the human element carefully when developing security solutions. No culture can be made secure without understanding human behavior and motivation. Moreover, people — given the right level of understanding and awareness — can be engaged as a positive force in the quest for improved security.

This book seeks to meet that goal.

Identifying Human Intent by Analyzing Packets

The SAIC AuBA technologies I invented convert packet-level and application-level activities, as well as combinations of these activities, into meaningful interpretations of malicious and non-malicious behaviors. On the basis of a behavioral model developed over decades for the prediction of malicious behavior, you must first identify and detect antecedents to actual behavior.

CROSS-REFERENCE Chapter 17 is devoted to a drill down of the AuBA-based CheckMate and InMate applications, their functioning, and their validation as human behavior–based applications that can provide a more proactive stance to network security.

Within the area of network intrusion, specific activities generated by a visitor to a network produce an amazing number of measurable activities. If assessment is to be accurate, all packets must be captured and organized by a visitor in real time. This first stage, on the surface, may appear to be similar to signature detection in that AuBA network applications are continually scanning for specific types of activities, or behaviors. However, AuBA technology is actually searching for antecedents associated with both legitimate use and misuse of defined human behavior (not network behavior), including the inordinate number of antecedent combinations that can occur.

To accomplish real-time assessment, AuBA analyzes all relevant packet-level activity by reassembling and processing packets to present *bundles* of activities. It is important to note that although AuBA network applications such as CheckMate and InMate use an assessment interval to determine the size of the bundle across all visitors, the applications do not actually sample. Rather, CheckMate divides the continuous stream of traffic from a visitor into discrete bundles in sequence. All packets generated by a visitor are included in the behavior assessments. The heart of the assessment engine is a unique form of pattern classification. Each assessment engine uses a dedicated classifier trained to identify atomic-level activities that, in combination, form behavioral indicators of misuse or legitimate network behaviors (as the case may be).

External Threat Assessment: CheckMate

CheckMate is an AuBA real-time behavior assessment application that converts network traffic to validated behavioral measures of the human characteristics *expertise* and *deception*. The assessment process consists of real-time conversion of sequential, 100 millisecond collections of activity for each IP/user on a network with proprietary assessment engines. The CheckMate appliance is rack mountable and may be configured and operational in less than 30 minutes, requires no tuning, and has been validated in external testing to detect both known attacks and unknown or modifications of attacks that are not detected by typical signature detection products.

CheckMate does not work inline but, rather, assesses a copy of traffic in real time to avoid the possibility of slowing traffic processing and to present a stealthy deployment. If a blocking option is selected and an IP's behavior is assessed to be within a blocking region, CheckMate communicates a command to the firewall to block the connection. CheckMate may be placed on the DMZ to protect property residing on the DMZ, such as web and mail servers, or behind the firewall for securing intranets and private networks, as well as other property that may reside outside of the DMZ.

It has been demonstrated by independent, third-party testing that CheckMate exhibits the following characteristics:

- Real-time behavioral assessment of intent
- Capability to detect unique or new forms of attack
- Automated tracking and blocking
- Automated profile development to aid forensic analysis
- Scheduled and on-demand report creation
- User-friendly graphical user interface
- Cross-platform interoperability

Internal Threat Assessment: InMate

The InMate Insider Network Misuse Protection System (InMate) was developed as a derivative product of the CheckMate external network threat behavior assessment application. It was determined that different applications were required for external and internal threats because external and internal threats are driven by very different motivators and antecedents. The objective of both applications was to interject true human behavior assessment of intent into network protection technology dominated by reactive signature detection and false-positive-prone anomaly detection. I hypothesized that typical false-positive and false-negative errors could be decreased significantly by including human behavior assessment to overcome weaknesses inherent in anomaly detection and signature detection technologies.

InMate is capable of providing real-time behavioral assessment of internal network users for the purpose of identifying those individuals who are engaging in misuse. Behavioral assessment occurs by means of two unique pattern classifier assessment engines that convert network activity of an inside user into validated behavioral measures of Intent (I) and Deception (D).

- **Intent:** The assessed intent to engage in misuse
- **Deception:** The attempt to use methods that would make it more difficult to identify an inside user engaging in misuse

InMate represents a new behavioral assessment technology for internal network misuse identification. The InMate assessment paradigm is a dramatic departure from signature detection and anomaly detection methodologies. Currently, InMate collects network activity of each inside user and conducts multiple assessments per second for the duration the inside user is logged on to the network. The results of assessment modules are aggregated into a determination of assessed activity as legitimate, suspicious, or critical from an insider threat perspective.

Blind validation tests indicate that the proprietary pattern classification-based InMate assessment engines perform in an almost identical manner as nationally recognized network intrusion experts who have been trained in providing activity-specific Intent and Deception ratings. The InMate prototype exists as a self-tending, rack-mountable appliance. Typically, within 30 minutes of placing InMate in a rack, experts can configure the application and have it be totally operational with no additional tuning required. Because of the unique behavioral assessment technology, the incidence of false positives is minimized, while the true positive identification rate is enhanced, particularly for unique forms of internal misuse.

Envisioning an Effective Future Network Protection Technology

The purpose of this book is to demonstrate how current technology may be augmented with true behavior assessment methods and technology to increase the probability of accurate anticipation of adversary behavior. I have been extensively involved with developing behavior assessment technology capable of the accurate prediction of adversary behavior since 1985 when coming to the government from clinical and academic settings. During that time, the technologies presented in this book have evolved to the point where independent validation has shown that the current behavior analysis technologies presented extend applied behavior analysis and are capable of accurate prediction of adversary behavior across multiple domains.

Enhancing Current Technology with Behavior Analysis

There are many who believe that prediction of human behavior is not possible. The objective of this book is to demonstrate that such skepticism is not warranted. As I have noted, the methods and technologies I present predict malicious behavior with an accuracy that exceeds or equals predictions in physical science domains such as weather or dynamic natural disaster forecasting — and without brute-force super computer models.

We could not even cross the street unless we could predict the current traffic flow to judge when we can cross safely without getting hit. We predict threat to our careers and react accordingly. A physician predicts that a course of human disease will take a specific course unless treatment is provided to change the projected course. Likewise, a behavior therapist faced with a client who has a phobia of flying and simply cannot get on an airliner projects that the condition will continue and treats the individual with systematic desensitization, usually successfully, to assist in eradicating the phobia. Prediction of human behavior is used daily across a wide variety of domains. We have simply formalized it, developed specific technology to complete prediction of malicious intent, and validated methods to scientific standards. As applied to network intrusion, the methods presented certainly can assist signature detection and anomaly detection. It is clear that we are not currently winning. Until we adopt new behavior–based technology, we may fall farther behind.

Extracting Human Behavior from Digital Data

The key to adopting human behavior–based technology rests on the capability of technology to extract human behavior from digital data. If human behavior–based technology is to be successful in augmenting signature and anomaly detection, it is our job to show that human behavior–based technology can convert packet-level activity to measures of *expertise* and *deception* (CheckMate) and *intent to engage in misuse* and *deception* (InMate). As you progress through the book, you will be presented with validation and reliability data. To date, AuBA applications have converted digital data in the form of electronic media reports of past events of interest, sensor-based outputs showing movement of individuals, avatar behavioral measurement in virtual worlds, and packet-level activity in networks to predict adversary behavior and to determine the presence or absence of malicious behavior and intent.

Advantages of AuBA #5: Conducting a Human Behavior Assessment of Threats from Network Packets

At the end of Chapter 4, the AuBA advantage focused on embedding a trained predictive engine into an application. Because this chapter focuses on networks, I presented two AuBA-based cyber applications. CheckMate processes incoming traffic and converts 100 millisecond samples of packets by IP into the degree of expertise and deception present for that IP. The initial hypothesis I stated to obtain funding for CheckMate development stated that if both expertise and deception exceeded high thresholds at the same time for the same sample, then malicious intent was present and an attack was imminent. Testing demonstrated that this was true. Not being a signature or anomaly detection application, the AuBA-based application converts packet-level activity into human behavior assessment dimensions. Specifically, behavior monitors seek out certain behaviors as inputs and send them to the predictive engine. The predictive engine converts the information to the degree of expertise and deception present. Both CheckMate and Inmate (insider threat) were presented briefly earlier in this chapter.

Because CheckMate is human behavior–based and has no signatures, it is more proactive and capable of identifying harmful precursor behavior leading to an attack. If the option is set, the IP can be blocked when the expertise and deception exceed a critical threshold. Figure 5-2 shows the conceptualization of the assessment visualization whereby the degree of expertise is on the y axis (vertical axis) and the degree of deception is on the x axis (horizontal axis), from low to high in each case. This creates an area in the upper-right quadrant (critical region) that is high expertise and high deception. If tracked activity moves into this critical region, CheckMate has determined that malicious intent and behavior is present.

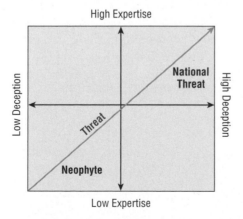

Figure 5-2: The CheckMate real-time assessment for a single IP.

The dimensions of expertise and deception were determined from extensive studies of individuals with malicious intent. In order to be malicious and be successful by not being caught, the person needs to have the expertise to complete the act and be deceptive to avoid being caught. CheckMate assesses both behavior dimensions on a continuous basis.

The key to this highlight is that the artificial neural network predictive engines in CheckMate were developed using the AuBA methodology. As such, they have been validated to operate in real time, be predictive, and provide a predictive decision within 50 microseconds of receiving input. Therefore, CheckMate can monitor and assess 1,000 IPs simultaneously 10 times a second with four assessment engines. If more is needed, copies can be made of the assessment engines.

Embedding smart, predictive engines into cyber applications represents a proactive approach to augment the much more reactive signature detection products. Furthermore, since anomaly detection is notorious for identifying non-malicious but different behavior as malicious (false positive), we have suggested that CheckMate process flagged anomalies to reduce false positives by determining threat from non-threat as determined by behavior assessment dimensions.

In Summary

We are experiencing a continued rise in the frequency and severity of network attacks from both insiders and external attackers, including coordinated state-supported targeting of the United States. It is clear that decades-old technology in the form of signature detection and anomaly detection can be augmented by human behavior–based predictive technology. This chapter has focused on both the threat and the introduction of human behavior–based prediction capability.

In the remaining chapters, examples of how behavior-based technology can be used to augment current network protection technology to decrease false-positive and false-negative error rates will be presented. We are under cyber attack. Unless we adopt human behavior–based predictive methods, it is my contention that we will forever be the prisoners of a reactive approach to network protection. It is time to infuse current technology with a shot of new, effective methods to help move us to a true proactive stance in network security.

Future Threats
to Our National Security

It is clear that the future is not a repeat of the past. Since 9/11, technology has increased at an astounding pace, our economy is in trouble, our resources have been stretched across wars in Iraq and Afghanistan, and we have had political crises and on occasion stalemates in Congress. Adversary behavior is a result of context, and the context in which we find ourselves today is unique. If we are simply looking for a repeat of the past, we won't be prepared for the new threats that we've never witnessed before.

Most agree that risk equals threat plus vulnerability. The rapidly expanding world of technology has assisted global interdependencies and interconnectedness in many positive ways. New vulnerabilities have been generated as a result of the increased capability to share information almost instantly. If we add the multitude of adversary attacks directed against the United States using technology as an assist, threat has increased as well. This places us within a new risk category — high. We must assume that planned attacks against the United States are based on the duality of both vulnerabilities we possess and threat of credible adversary attacks.

The best way to view threat is to process successful attacks in the past. Adversaries tend to repeat what has worked in the past — but with variation. It is the anticipation of variation that is the challenge.

This chapter reports on the results of numerous behavior analyses completed across multiple threat domains to provide informed data-driven projections of threats we, as a nation, will encounter in the future. In the following sections of this chapter, these high risk threats are explored.

Our Growing National Security Dependency on Computers and Networks

We are interconnected with one another and those across other nations on a global basis. Through the use of cell phones, smartphones, tweeting, texting, the Internet, the cloud, extranets, intranets, and such devices as iPads, PCs, Macs, and notebooks, we conduct business, meet people and arrange dates, maintain social relationships, watch movies and YouTube, listen to music, and generally keep track of one another in real time. This is the epitome of being connected. In addition, such interconnectedness provides the ability to process global information many times faster than in the past, with events broadcasted around the world in real time as they occur. However, technology has become a double-edged sword:

- It provides us with new and enhanced global surveillance and reconnaissance capability.
- The very technology that gives us this new capability also provides our adversaries with new avenues of attack.

Whether technology is a double-edged sword or not, we are dependent on the technologies that we have developed and fully embrace. The United States is an interconnected and technologically dependent nation, but the very technology we cherish also creates an immense number of vulnerabilities. External intrusion into our personal and business networks and organizations can result in theft of secrets, identities, and private information shared among individuals. The Internet and restricted networks provide targets for foreign exploitation. We have already witnessed an intelligence drain stemming from insider passing of classified documents to WikiLeaks and rampant theft of technology secrets. Decades ago, it is likely that few, if any, even dreamed of terrorists hijacking multiple, fully loaded airliners as suicide mission vehicles to successfully attack the United States from within its borders. However, if we use technology properly, we can ensure a more proactive protective approach that will enhance our defense of our national infrastructure.

Perhaps one of the greatest risks we face is in the area of cyber attack. Given that risk = threat + vulnerability, we are at the highest levels of cyber attack risk. We have witnessed repeated cyber attacks from hackers, both independent and state supported. We certainly have vulnerabilities, in that current signature and anomaly detection technologies do not provide totally adequate protection against such attacks on our networks, and even our personal devices are subject to invasion.

We, as a nation, represent a seductive cyber target for adversaries. The following is just a brief list as to why we are perhaps the leading cyber target in the world:

- The United States possesses and maintains technological superiority in many different areas. Other nations want this, and for some, theft is a shortcut.

- Cyber attack is a method that may be used to disrupt business, communications, and even first responder effectiveness.

- Cyber theft and cyber attack represent methods by which loss or damage may be achieved against the U.S. target with almost complete anonymity associated with little chance of being apprehended.

We have reached the point where we are not just dependent on computers and networks, but they are an essential way of doing business. Computers have perfect memory, and a single processor has the speed of thousands of individuals all working at the same time. We have made the transition from paper, typing, whiteout, and the mail to full digital transactions and communication. We can never go back. Industry, the government, military, universities, large business, small business, and personal work are all connected in one form or another with technology superglue that will not let go.

The other world of threat composed of conventional explosives, terrorist assaults with AK-47s against innocent victims, and suicide missions has also been aided significantly with new technology. The right technology tools can allow an adversary to absorb our communications, see any spot on Earth with real images and with exact coordinates, allow electronic surveillance and reconnaissance, and actually improve the destructive yield of the compact explosives used.

A first line of defense is to thoroughly understand how technology can be used against us. Our adversaries are smart, capable, perhaps educated in many of our finest schools in this country, and insistent on reducing our standing in the world, and they are achieving revenge for many perceived wrongs. Because of the widespread opportunities to exploit our country's vulnerabilities, it is essential that we develop improved methods for anticipating attacks to increase protection of our national infrastructure from adversary and insider threat attacks.

Increasing Threat on a Global Basis

As proof of our global interconnectedness and dependencies, we need only to observe our global economy. Being a student of the stock market, I predict daily how the U.S. stock market will fare that day by how the Asian and European markets unfold prior to the U.S. market opening each morning. These earlier market activities serve as antecedents that set the stage for how the U.S. stock market will perform. An astute investor placing real money in the stock market knows premarket indicators, or *antecedents* — in the form of Asian and European market performance — foretell the results of our stock market before it actually opens. As time has passed over the past decade, this global interdependency across global stock markets has become unquestionable.

It is important to realize that computers operating in networks control much of our national infrastructure. And those familiar with network operations, network security intrusion detection effectiveness, and network forensics are very familiar with the number of daily network scans for vulnerabilities. These networks serve as communication and data storage doorways into a large variety of organizations, many of which are financially based, but some represent other areas in our national infrastructure.

Computer and network dependencies are now a hallmark of our national infrastructure. The 2009 National Infrastructure Protection Plan stated:

The use of innovative technology and interconnected networks in operations improves productivity and efficiency, but also increases the Nation's vulnerability to cyber threats if cybersecurity is not addressed and integrated appropriately.

The report goes on to say:

A spectrum of malicious actors routinely conducts attacks against the cyber infrastructure using cyber attack tools. Because of the interconnected nature of the cyber infrastructure, these attacks could spread quickly and have a debilitating effect.

The question then becomes: How do we flag antecedents to predict future attacks against our national infrastructure? As way of example, the horror of 9/11 was a very different form of attack, but its MO (*modus operandi*) was a variant of a suicide mission rather than an attack involving improvised explosive devices (IEDs) targeting military, or the theft of proprietary technologies via network intrusions. Attacks vary in targeting, methods, and motivations, so to bring analytical order to what may appear to be seemingly random requires solid human behavior methodology; for any given adversary, we need to analyze the threat, determine key methods they used in the past, and determine the antecedents that preceded the specific type of attack.

As you progress through this book, you'll look at the adversary and how it operates, the appropriate method of behavior analysis for that adversary, and then an actual walkthrough exercise demonstrating how to anticipate future adversary behavior.

From a behavior analysis perspective, we know that identified antecedents of past attacks can foretell future attack behavior and that the degree of success achieved by past attacks determines if the same type of attack will occur in the future when identified antecedents are present. This type of analysis indicates that the most likely MO of future attacks at our infrastructure will be:

- Increased frequency and severity of cyber theft of restricted, sensitive, identity, and classified information through malware, phishing, and new variants of cyber theft
- Increased and enhanced advanced persistent threat emanating from foreign states

- Conventional and coordinated massive suicide bombings
- New emergent weapons (NEW)

NOTE There is an unacceptable probability of the use of a *new emergent weapon* (*NEW*) within the current decade. A NEW could consist of two categories of weapons with entirely different massive effects: category 1 is a chemical, biological, radiological, or nuclear weapon (CBRN) detonated to result in maximum loss of life, and category 2 is a massively coordinated cyber attack to target and totally disrupt the U.S. economy or communications.

Note that we do not expect to see carbon copy attacks in the future. To be successful within an increasingly security-aware country like the United States, adversaries must necessarily use variants of past attacks to escape signature detection. In this context, *signature detection* means more than in the cyber context (which is still relevant). We also have signatures of past terrorist attacks. For example, over time, Hezbollah attacks are very similar — the targets change but method of operation remains highly similar. Al-Qaeda, on the other hand, alters method as well as target (*USS Cole*, embassies, Pentagon, World Trade Center, etc.). By employing variants of past attacks, the signature detection mentality that underlies our security preparedness is easier to defeat.

Analysis from a targeting perspective has led to the following probable activity in the future:

- Cyber (highest probability)
  - Cyber theft targets
    - Commercial sites housing advanced technology
    - Government/military contractor sites containing sensitive and classified data
    - Government/military technology sites such as DARPA etc.
  - Cyber disruption targets
    - Power grid
    - Communications sites
    - First responder communications
    - Military attack vehicles (drones, fighters)
    - Economic targets (stock market, U.S. economy)
- Conventional suicide/timed bombings (within the United States)
  - Dense population (for example, mass transit, tunnel, hotel, or office building)

- Military/government (for example, Pentagon, White House, or Capitol)
- Symbolic (for example, World Trade Center memorial, historic site, economic site — Wall Street)

- Conventional suicide/timed bombings (external to the United States)
  - U.S. targets worldwide will include military/government personnel/ installations with occasional tourists.
  - U.S. allies would be targeted if apparent they are aiding the United States in wars or conflicts, including targeting of Islamic militants or in support of Israel against Palestinians.

The highest probability targeting is cyber theft as specified. The probability of such cyber activity is frequent, perhaps daily. Adversaries will include state-sponsored entities and foreign intelligence dedicated to U.S. cyber attack and intelligence gathering, as well as insiders in our own country. It is anticipated that full-out cyber attacks to totally disrupt operations, such as a portion of the power grid, is likely, but with a low probability of occurrence. A conventional massive suicide or timed detonation is also expected to be a low probability/ low frequency event, but likely to happen as a solitary event with massive loss of life and extensive damage. Such low frequency events would be expected to occur perhaps once in several years as opposed to cyber theft occurring almost on a continual basis. Allies of the United States are expected to be long-term targets of attack because of active support against Islamic militants or as a result of U.S./Israeli actions perceived to be anti-Palestinian.

The Ever-Increasing Sophistication of the Adversary

Most of the 23 James Bond movies have a villain, bent on world domination, who exploits vulnerabilities with sophisticated weaponry. The good guys, Q and the British intelligence service, work to develop the latest in technical gadgetry to help counter adversary threat. As time has advanced since the series began, most measures remain fanciful, but the plots are more plausible, as al-Qaeda leader Osama bin Laden became the villain who wished to impose Islamic domination while diminishing the role of the United States on a global stage. Sounds like fiction, but unfortunately it is nonfiction.

"THE VILLAIN WITH TECHNOLOGY" MOVIE GENRE

Hollywood and its equivalent in other countries use technology as a backdrop for many adventure and drama genres. Surprisingly, *The Net* presented technology that was actually available at the time. Sandra Bullock's character was tracked and had her identity stolen, which made her attempts to escape from evil exceedingly difficult. *Enemy of the State* provided a glimpse of Hollywood's elaboration of NSA technology, as again Will Smith's character was tracked nonstop by advanced technology. This genre dates back to what is considered to be the first spy novel written in 1903 — Erskine Childers' *Riddle of the Sands*, which generated a 1979 movie by the same name. The formula that Childers used was as follows: A villain attacks or attempts to attack the good guy, and the good guy has to stop the evil. The villain sometimes has the upper hand with technology and deception, which must be successfully countered before the last page of the book or the end of the movie.

The movie and novel depictions of the threat facing us today may for the first time not surpass the actual threat. It is likely that the typical citizen does not realize the extent to which identity theft can occur, how movement can be tracked using his or her cell phone, and how relatively easy it is for the computer and the network supporting its use can be compromised. For example, a phishing attack may be forwarded from deep within a state-supported foreign adversary and come as an e-mail on the person's computer. The e-mail may indicate that the user has exceeded the size limit of the e-mail mailbox and by clicking on the presented link more space will be added to avoid losing mail. The user clicks on the link and malware is immediately inserted into the computer's hard drive, where it is immediately ready to capture all user IDs and passwords to send back to the adversary. The adversary now has access. This all can happen in less than a minute, or as fast as the e-mail is read and the link is clicked.

You may think, "I would never click a link like that!" Enter spear phishing. Now an e-mail is received from the CEO of the company asking the user to read the latest network security attachment to help keep the company safe from network attacks from the outside. The e-mail is from the CEO after all, and it is about how to keep the company's computers and networks safe, so without thought, the user downloads the attachment. Of course, the attachment is malware and damage is done as soon as the user clicks *download*. Differentiating between real e-mail and phishing or spear phishing attacks is becoming exceedingly difficult, if not impossible without sophisticated examination of all e-mails.

WARNING   We must be very concerned about the increasing sophistication of the adversary and cannot underestimate the intelligence, creativity, and skills of those who would do harm to our national security and well-being. Our networks are being attacked daily with serious and sophisticated advanced persistent threat. We are losing proprietary information. Too often, we don't know damage has been done until after the fact.

How does the adversary become more sophisticated? This is a question with many answers, including the following:

- The adversary as a student may attend some of the best technical schools in the world, including within the United States.

- Adversary warriors train other adversary warriors — there are many accounts of terrorist groups colluding in training and sharing tactical know-how.

- There is state support for terrorist groups, which may include money, training, advanced weaponry, and intelligence.

- Some of the best technology in the world can be purchased, complete with operational manuals — they just buy it on the open market.

- There are black markets whereby advanced and portable weapons may be purchased.

- Terrorists learn by doing — experience is one of the best teachers.

- As a free society, the United States publishes technology in journals, popular technical magazines, books, etc.

- States engage in espionage and learn from technological leaks from other countries.

- Technological secrets are passed to an adversary for a price by unscrupulous and treasonous U.S. citizens working as insiders in some of our most advanced technology companies or government organizations.

This list is not comprehensive; however, it contains the more serious methods of acquiring advanced technology.

ACCESS TO MORE SOPHISTICATED WEAPONS

There is an alarming amount of missing nuclear material of all types. Perhaps one of the strongest fears is that a terrorist group intent on mass destruction acquires a nuclear weapon from a state in transition or by other nefarious means and detonates it within the United States. There are many variants of this most horrific of scenarios. For example, the same thing could occur with a massive biological agent, chemical attack, or radiological attack with a dirty bomb (spreading radioactive material with a conventional explosive). Weapons, and in particular a weapon of mass destruction, are products of technology. The number of deaths that can be achieved increases roughly with the sophistication of the weapon.

Anticipating Additional Asymmetric Warfare Attacks in the Future — Another 9/11?

The events of September 11, 2001, perpetrated by al-Qaeda on U.S. soil were a successful surprise attack against the United States that rivaled and perhaps exceeded the December 7, 1941, surprise attack by the Japanese on Pearl Harbor. Several years ago, I boarded a U.S. destroyer that departed Pearl Harbor for a day of naval exercises. It was a true experience. As we departed in a state-of-the-art destroyer with a seasoned and exceptional commander, I saw the monument to the Pearl Harbor attack off to the side. The humble thoughts of those who lost their lives on that immortal day flooded my consciousness. Here we were, a modern-day destroyer, with all the bells and whistles and advanced technology, leaving dock from a site that had witnessed horror and launched us into World War II.

This is a war. Make no mistake about it. It may be different, but that is the point. We need to recognize that this is a new war, and we need to recognize that it may not be fought on a physical battleground. We need to wake up and realize the new technological threat. Whether the enemy uses high-yield explosives or creative attacks with coordinated hijacked planes on suicide missions to kill thousands of innocent civilians, it is a new age of asymmetric warfare. Long gone are the days of one enemy facing another enemy on the battleground and taking turns shooting one another. Today, it is covert war where the less endowed enemy may have the advantage. There is no macho edict that says one enemy has to be face-to-face with the other enemy on a physical battleground to see who wins. This is a covert war where one individual has the capability to attack us using cyber technology and take out the East Coast power grid.

9/11 marked a change in our world as we know it. We have worked through the shock, and although still grieving, we are beginning to realize that this is war and how we must fight it was changed on 9/11.

We are not new to asymmetric warfare. During the Revolutionary War our minutemen learned that it was more effective to shoot the enemy from behind a tree than to stand in line with two opposing lines and take turns shooting and killing one another. True, it took considerable time for this new form of fighting war to take hold. In our Civil War, we still saw our North facing the South in lines, resulting in more than 600,000 deaths of Americans against Americans. But, asymmetric warfare did catch on. Our very talented and dedicated Special Forces stand as an excellent example of this new warfare; Osama bin Laden was not killed with a massive bomb — he was killed when U.S. asymmetric forces, using excellent intelligence, located and invaded his residence and surgically struck back for all the events and pain that 9/11 brought to us as a country.

The adversary has embraced asymmetric warfare, which basically means that a small group can use the element of surprise and covert methods to conduct a devastating attack on the most powerful of nations — successfully. If you are a movie buff, it is the epitome of the effectiveness of the Dirty Dozen. The enemy is hiding behind a virtual tree and attacking us daily using cyber warfare. In addition, we have to know that the next surprise attack is being refined now to result in a future attack to result in maximum loss of U.S. lives.

Al-Qaeda will need to exceed the devastating effects of 9/11. Although it is possible that the effects of 9/11 may have actually exceeded the organization's hopes for destruction, anything less than the same level of destruction on a future attack would make the organization appear weaker or less capable. The fact that the U.S. war effort against terrorism since 9/11 has resulted in severe damage to al-Qaeda, including loss of the significant spiritual, conceptual, and operational leader, Osama bin Laden, may have strengthened resolve to return with more devastating effects.

Al-Qaeda does not need thousands among thousands of warriors — it just needs the element of surprise motivated by its members' desire to lose their lives to honor God against what they consider to be a vile enemy. Although a cyber attack of massive proportions may be high on the list for some, it is not al-Qaeda's style. Instead, past incidents have been noted by violent physical explosions and obvious devastation and loss of life — it has worked well in the past, and there is no reason to expect a shift to a totally new form of attack. However, as always, we can expect significant variation in a coordinated and massive suicide attack within the nation's borders. Cyber attack is more likely to exist quietly as advanced persistent threat supported by foreign states.

Unanticipated Terrorist Attacks

Using and capitalizing on the element of surprise is likely the single most important tactical strategy for war ever invented. This tactic allows an imbalance of forces to more closely approximate balance, with the weaker side of two sides gaining strength far beyond its numbers or firepower. An analysis of 9/11 shows that part of the psychological effects of shock and surprise that many experienced was a direct result of the surprise of events unfolding before their eyes.

The advantage of surprise when used by the more disadvantaged force is an imbalance of lost lives. In the case of 9/11 almost 3,000 lives were lost, while only 19 terrorists were killed. If an attack is expected, the potential victims can prepare for the attack, not be bewildered when it hits, and minimize loss.

In the cyber world, we expect attacks on an ongoing basis. However, it is safe to say that the vast majority of cyber assaults are more minor or composed of scans and searches for vulnerabilities. However, if a major significant attack occurs that is new, then it is highly likely that the attack may be successful. In this case, typical signature detection is not likely to detect the new attack, unless the attack parameters are very close to an existing rule, or set of rules.

To maximize the effects of a cyber attack, it is important that the attack be:

- A surprise
- A new form of attack to avoid signatures
- Harmful
- Deceptive to avoid detection

Not all cyber attacks include all four characteristics; therefore, for an attack to be maximally effective, a high level of cyber skill is required. As mentioned, the AuBA CheckMate application is designed to convert packet-level activity into measures of *expertise* and *deception* and has been validated to identify new cyber attacks. The element of surprise is minimized because of the capability to detect new attacks. For this reason, the new form of cyber protection offered by AuBA technology moves from reactive to proactive protection (more about this in the section "The Dire Need for New Proactive Methods"). As you'll see in the walkthrough of AuBA technology on the DVD that accompanies this book and in the Chapter 17 drill down of CheckMate and InMate, it is possible to be better prepared for future cyber attacks.

Weapons of Mass Destruction

Weapons of mass destruction (WMD) include non-traditional weapons capable of large-scale loss of life or extensive physical damage. An important categorization of weaponry, it was the primary reason stated for the U.S. and British joint invasion of Iraq in 2003. Intelligence had reported the existence of WMD weapons and development under the Saddam Hussein regime. President George Bush and British Prime Minister Tony Blair had collaborated on the joint invasion to rid Iraq of WMD to ensure that such weapons would not be used. The reports of Saddam Hussein, the leader of Iraq, having used gas to kill the Kurdish people in Iraq in the past only heightened concerns. Although WMD were not located, the war brought to a close the reign of Hussein, who was captured, tried, and hanged.

Most place chemical, biological, radiological, and nuclear (CBRN) weapons within the realm of WMD. However, these types of weapons are very different. Although CBRN weapons are indeed in theory capable of massive loss of life, and nuclear is additionally clearly capable of extensive and widespread physical destruction, a radiological weapon such as a *dirty bomb,* or radiological material released in an area by means of a dispersal device, is less damaging. The purpose of this weapon is to spread radiological material by means of a conventional explosion — it is *not* a nuclear weapon, which results in a true, devastatingly powerful nuclear detonation. A radiological dirty bomb can result in the contamination of an area in which the material is dispersed. However, its main purpose would be to incite fear.

A chemical, biological, or nuclear weapon carries with it not only likely massive loss of life but significant fear as well. All three types of weapons have been used — they are not theoretical. Chemical weapons have been used throughout history, with such examples as World War I with the use of several forms of gas, including tear and mustard gas, among others. More recently, sarin gas was used in 1995 by the Aum Shinrikyo group on five subway trains in Tokyo. Also, of significance, was the reported use of gas in Iraq to target the Kurdish people, killing thousands. Of course, the only use of nuclear weapons was during World War II, when the United States effectively ended the war by dropping an atomic bomb on Hiroshima and Nagasaki within three days of one another, resulting in unparalleled death and physical destruction within the two Japanese cities. Surprising to most, biological weapons have been used extensively throughout history. However, again, more recently, most will remember the use of anthrax mailed in envelopes in the Washington, D.C., area beginning just a month after 9/11, resulting in the death of postal workers.

Considering the use of CBRN, it is likely that we will witness a terrorist use of one of these forms of weapons in the future. Radiological would probably be the least damaging, given its conventional explosive base if surfacing as a dirty bomb. A biological agent weapon could be particularly damaging because of the ability to use biological agents that cause diseases with no cure. Missing nuclear materials highlight global concern over the detonation of a true nuclear device — the most damaging of all weapons.

Water and Food Resources

We can live for only a matter of several days without water. Although we can live longer without food, extreme hunger and death from starvation is one of the most unpleasant diminishing conditions a person can experience. There is mounting concern that terrorists could contaminate specific water or food supplies as a means to cause extensive death and suffering. A terrorist attack hitting water and/or food would be targeting basic survival needs.

DEFINITION   *Food terrorism* is defined as an act or threat of deliberate contamination of food for human consumption with biological, chemical, and physical agents or radionuclear materials for the purpose of causing injury or death to civilian populations and/or disrupting social, economic, or political stability.[1]

---

[1]Terrorist Threats to Food, Department of Food Safety, Zoonoses and Foodborne Disease, Cluster on Health Security and Environment, World Health Organization, 2008.

THE HIERARCHY OF HUMAN NEEDS

Abraham Maslow was a psychologist trained in New York schools who formed a humanistic school of thought in psychology. He was best known for his conceptualization of the hierarchy of needs.[2] Figure 6-1 depicts Maslow's hierarchy. It is shaped like a pyramid; basic needs are at the bottom. When basic needs, like food, water, shelter, etc., are met, a person can move up the levels. Self-actualization is the highest level, which means the individual has advanced to the point of total introspection and self-improvement.

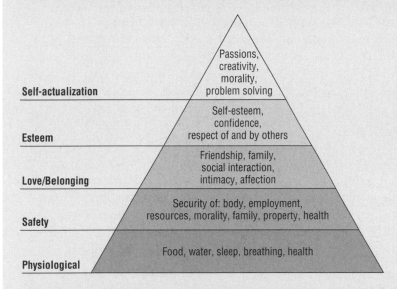

Figure 6-1: Abraham Maslow's hierarchy of needs. The most basic needs are at the bottom and the ultimate state of self-actualization is at the top of the pyramid.
© Icefields | Dreamstime.com

Unfortunately, millions of starving and shelter-less individuals around the world are striving to meet the basic foundation of needs. These inherent needs are ones that the readers of this book do not have to worry about. For those who struggle, it is the ultimate fear and panic — not knowing if the next drink of water or the next morsel of food will be there.

Terrorist threat to water and food supplies would cause the inherent panic that comes with failing to meet the most basic of physiological needs. It is also possible to contaminate supplies so that sickness and death result. The severity of this problem dictates the need for proactive understanding of terrorist characteristics and conditions under which contamination could occur. The use of behavior-based analytics to project highly probable scenarios can highlight specific targeting so that protective measures can be put in place for adequate prevention. It is

[2]Maslow, A. H., (1943) A Theory of Human Motivation, *Psychological Review* 50(4) pp. 370–96.

essential that likely targeting be clearly understood because of the immensity of land mass devoted to agriculture and water supply. This way, limited protective resources can be allocated where they can be maximally effective.

Diminishing Effectiveness of Network Security

The severity, sophistication, and frequency of cyber attacks and cyber theft are increasing at an alarming rate. However, current network protection technology is limited and is not preventing these attacks. *Advanced persistent threat* (APT) is a growing reality and can represent foreign nation-state support. At the basic level, APT represents foreign nation-state threat directed at a specific target. In marked contrast to some hacking attempts to use favorite techniques across a wide variety of sites until successful, APT exists for a very specific goal and very specific target. As a general rule, it's beneficial for a foreign nation-state to maintain the highest level skills possible because this is required to avoid detection. Detection means an increased chance of the activity being attributed to the nation, which can result in international conflict.

The increase in sophistication of cyber attacks and cyber theft and the significant APT targeting and recent successes are evidence of diminished network protection effectiveness. Although signature detection and anomaly detection are useful, necessary, and as effective as ever, they do not offset new cyber threat. To effectively catch up with these increased threats, the following additional characteristics would provide the necessary protection needed:

- **Proactive:** Protection from classes of attack and APT variants not identified with current detection technology
- **Predictive:** Anticipation of specific types of attack
- **Future threat:** Identification of new and zero-day attacks not observed in the past

Given that signature and anomaly detection remain stable while threat and sophistication continue to increase, the difference between threat and overall effectiveness is going to grow even wider, resulting in current technology diminishing in effectives. Figure 6-2 depicts this relative difference between current network protection effectiveness and growing sophistication of cyber threat. Notice the conceptual jump in threat when APT started.

Decreasing Safety for Americans Worldwide Post Osama bin Laden

On May 2, 2011, U.S. Navy SEALs conducted a surprise invasion of Osama bin Laden's residence and killed him, burying his body at sea shortly thereafter. On August 27, 2001, just 15 weeks later, a drone carried out an attack in Pakistan that killed Atiyah Abd al-Rahman, the then number 2 person of al-Qaeda. The death of al-Rahman was significant in that he headed operations for the organization.

The combination of both deaths, including the many other deaths of al-Qaeda members at the hands of the U.S. military, has a dual effect. First, it weakens the organization by removing key figures intimately familiar with all aspects of the organization's structure, goals, planning, and execution of plans. Second, the threat for U.S. citizens and allies worldwide has increased and has intensified.

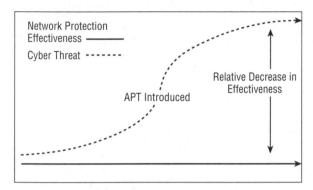

Figure 6-2: The growing difference between increased cyber threat and sophistication of attack and the relatively stable effectiveness of network protection

We should never underestimate the destructive capability and the resolve of a seriously wounded al-Qaeda. The organization does not function like a group of mercenaries for hire — its members are the truest of believers. They will give their lives to their cause without hesitation, which in large part is focused on dealing massive death and destruction to U.S. government, military, and symbolic/public targets, worldwide and within our U.S. borders.

Chapter 3 provided a list of antecedents, or precursor conditions, to terrorist and foreign state-sponsored attacks against U.S. targets. Although Osama bin Laden and Atiyah Abd al-Rahman were killed within four months of one another in 2011, antecedents to attacks have not changed, nor has the motivation and resolve to attack U.S. targets diminished. In fact, a case can be made that the risk of a massive attack is now higher. A wounded al-Qaeda must demonstrate to the world that it remains a viable and deadly threat to U.S. infidels.

The certain desire to seek revenge for killing bin Laden was felt on August 7, 2011, when 31 special operations personnel, including 22 Navy SEALs, were shot down and lost their lives in Afghanistan. Some of the warriors belonged to the SEAL team that killed bin Laden. Twenty days later, Atiyah Abd al-Rahman was killed in the drone attack.

This is war. Terrorism has changed. When I started in the field in 1985, terrorism consisted of more isolated attacks against small groups of individuals, perhaps at airline ticket counters, an airliner such as Pan Am 103, or the massive suicide vehicle-borne bombings of the U.S. and French barracks in 1983 in Beirut. As horrific as these past events have been, terrorism has taken on a more global face with attacks such as 9/11 that has elevated attacks to a new level of death and destruction. We see new weapons emerging such as the U.S. guided drones that fly in terrorist infested areas armed with missiles to take out specific targets such as Atiyah Abd al-Rahman. We see evidence of planning for mass casualty attacks against the United States.

There is no reason to expect that al-Qaeda threat has diminished because a significant number of al-Qaeda members have been killed. One need only to remember the death and destruction wielded by the single Timothy McVeigh, the perpetrator of the 1995 Oklahoma City bombing, to consider what one person can do. He may have had limited support, but this was a McVeigh directed and driven terrorist event. McVeigh's truck bomb killed 168 individuals, including children, and wounded many hundreds. True believers have been known to fight to the last person standing, particularly if the belief system raises status in the eyes of God for targeting the enemy of Islam.

Because the United States wielded successful attacks against the al-Qaeda organization, it is highly likely that we will witness additional significant attacks against U.S. targets worldwide. Given the need to show resolve and continued strength, we should expect these incidents to be significant with massive casualties.

Threats to Our Fragile Financial Markets

Our financial markets and trading are extremely sensitive and reactive to world antecedent events. Much like a single human, the stock market reacts as an organism when specific antecedent events occur. On 9/11, the New York Stock Exchange delayed opening because of the first airliner crash into the World Trade Center North Tower and closed all trading for the following week when the South Tower was struck by the second airliner just 17 minutes later. If there was confusion and indecision as to whether the first crash was an accident or not, all doubt was removed when the South Tower was struck by the second airliner. Other multiple and interconnected immediate economic effects also resulted from the attack.

It is not really possible to calculate the financial losses resulting from the 9/11 attacks. Costs associated with the loss of the airliners themselves, closing of airports and flights, defensive military flights to ensure no additional attacks, stock market closures, cost of rebuilding, days of work lost, and the incalculable loss of almost 3,000 lives makes it difficult to conduct an accurate damage assessment.

As it relates to the use of aircraft as terrorist weapons, a report issued under DHS support by the Center for Risk and Economic Analysis of Terrorism Events (CREATE) in 2005, the authors, T. Balvanyos and L. B. Lave, state:

> We think it likely that terrorists will target aircraft and that they will mount a visible attack, possibly succeeding in downing an aircraft. The vast majority of the resulting cost to the economy would be avoided if the public does not panic and if the government does not require costly actions designed to reassure the public, but which have little efficacy in preventing further loss.

The report goes on to present an impressive calculation of economic loss stemming from the terrorist destruction of one airliner with an associated shut down of airline traffic for 2.5 days. The estimated loss was calculated to be $6.3 billion for the 2.5 days. This cost can provide some perspective as to an incentive for terrorists to strike airliners in the future. The many unique features of 9/11 included this devastating financial impact across innumerable organizations (businesses and the airline industry among others), the stock market trading closures, the loss of lives, the extensive real and symbolic physical destruction, and the generated sense of damage to our country.

The *rules* of a behavior analysis indicate that the future occurrence of a specific behavior is a function of its consequences in the past. Certainly, given the devastating effects of 9/11 and outright success for al-Qaeda, we will see a repeat in the future, or a variant such as the targeting of other forms of mass transit.

The 9/11 attack also revealed that severe economic loss can result from a terrorist attack not directly targeting economic entities such as the stock market. The incident had an immediate and dramatic effect on the reactive markets. Economic loss for the nation is often a reaction to a dramatic change in conditions. The economic nature of our country is not proactive; it definitely is a reaction, whether increasing as gains or dropping as losses. This suggests a bonus for terrorists. By engaging in massive attacks directed at desired U.S. targets, they can adversely affect our economy indirectly. This is not to say that economic targets would not be hit directly. When one visits Ground Zero in New York City, it is painfully obvious that the World Trade Center was immediately adjacent to Wall Street.

Additional events have demonstrated the frailty of the U.S. trading market, which is a strong foundation of our economy. On May 6, 2010, the growing practice of automated trading, in which stocks are bought and sold electronically within fractions of a second, went haywire. A single, automated transaction initiated a chain reaction of trading that dropped the Dow Jones Industrial Average 600 points within just a few minutes. One company, Accenture, experienced stock dropping from $41 per share to one cent in just a short couple of minutes, creating panic. Fortunately, automated measures took control, and eventually losses were rectified. However, the incident demonstrated that the market was far more vulnerable to electronic manipulation in ways not totally understood.

Of course, an entire book could be written on the topic of targeting of the U.S. economy. It is vulnerable, and there is considerable threat, as we have seen. This places risk very high for continued assaults to our economy. Placing everything into perspective and cutting to the chase, we are likely to witness one or some combination of the following scenarios to cause economic damage:

- A repeat of a 9/11-type surprise attack but as a variant with a different target, which could have massive economic repercussions

- A direct attack with conventional explosives or a massive coordinated cyber attack directed against specific economic targets

- Continued efforts to keep the United States engaged in war, which has the effect of draining economic and financial resources

The Dire Need for New Proactive Methods

It is essential that our security posture move more toward a proactive stance. Since 9/11, we have been making strides in that direction, but more movement is needed. Reactive methods such as signature detection approaches require attacks to first occur before rules can be generated. We know that the most serious of hackers do not repeat known attacks against a single target, as with APT. The risk of repetition is detection and ineffectiveness. We must realize that we will constantly be faced with new variations of former attacks, whether in the cyber field or with terrorist targeting directed at the United States.

A key way to become more proactive is to clearly understand how methods of operation can and will change. Taking al-Qaeda as an example, on October 12, 2000, it bombed the *USS Cole*, a U.S. Navy destroyer in Aden. A year later, on September 11, 2001, al-Qaeda committed the infamous act with which we are so familiar. Targeting was very different across these two incidents. On one level, both included U.S. military targets (*USS Cole* and the Pentagon). On another level, a destroyer and the Pentagon are very different. Therefore, to be proactive, we need to define the level of granularity we wish to achieve. We must also realize that the primary terrorist threat organization to the United States, al-Qaeda, is decentralized, and targeting may be a function of local franchises. Regardless, a detailed functional analysis of antecedents to such attacks may lead to a clearer understanding of the nature of future attacks. Certainly, waiting for tips from informers, although vastly important, is not an acceptable proactive methodology.

To form a proactive stance at a granularity that mitigation (active methods to stop attacks) can occur will require the addition of behavioral sciences to understand the motivations-antecedent combinations that can point to possible attacks. Al-Qaeda does not repeat the same attack twice; therefore, a statistical baseline to show the most likely attack in the future is not useful. We already know that al-Qaeda is likely to engage in suicide bombings — but where, how, what type of target, and when? Behavior analysis is likely to be more useful in these types of analyses because of the identification of antecedents associated with specific features of an attack.

Moving from Reactive to Proactive Methodology

A reactive approach is entirely necessary; it is just not enough. It is essential to analyze past attacks regardless of the adversary, the nature of the behavior, and the effectiveness of the malicious behavior when directed against U.S. targets. However, there are entirely different methods to analyzing past behavior. A typical signature detection approach concentrates on describing the behavior of a past attack in enough detail that a signature may be written to recognize the behavior if it occurs again in the future. AuBA analyzes past attack behavior with three components: what were the antecedent conditions that preceded the attack behavior, the attack behavior itself, and the consequences of the attack (success, non-success, degree of success, etc.).

The signature detection approach must remain reactive because it is only describing the attack behavior itself. It is important because if the rule is accurate, the attack may be recognized again if it occurs. The AuBA approach, however, is predictive. Human behavior responds to antecedent conditions in the environment in such a way that if the same or highly similar antecedent conditions occur again, then we can predict with some certainty that the behavior will follow. This has been shown to be true across a wide variety of adversary behavior, including cyber attacks. This is especially true if the consequences of the malicious behavior paid off for the attacker. Humans tend to repeat what works and do not repeat what does not work.

An AuBA analysis leads to a more proactive approach in that recognition of combinations of antecedents can predict likely attacks. In addition, as will be demonstrated in later chapters, the approach can detect new attacks because they occur in response to highly similar antecedents conditions. The key, then, is to augment existing technology with more predictive behavior analysis methods.

Interjecting Behavior Analysis

AuBA methods will be presented in detail in Chapters 7–9 and 14–18. In addition, the walkthrough presented on the DVD provides a step-by-step process whereby you can learn to extract and use antecedents, behavior, and consequences for predictive and, therefore, more proactive modeling. The DVD also demonstrates the use of SAIC-automated AuBA tools that reduce manual error, produce predictive models an order of magnitude faster, and provide predictive engines that may be placed in predictive applications for use.

The single most important way of augmenting reactive approaches is to apply methods of human behavior analysis. The SAIC tools that will be presented consist of ThemeMate and AutoAnalyzer. Using both tools together emulates the human cognitive process of conducting manual behavioral modeling. The tools were developed to ensure accuracy, speed, perfect memory associated with computerization, and validated predictive results.

Informed Security: Removing the Element of Surprise

The beginning of this chapter emphasized that the element of surprise has been, perhaps, the single most important tactical warfare invention in history. By using the element of surprise combined with asymmetric warfare, 19 al-Qaeda terrorists hijacked four airliners and used them as suicide bombers to kill just shy of 3,000 people.

In my opinion, the best single countermeasure for surprise is the prediction of malicious behavior. If, in fact, we prove that methods such as those presented in this book predict serious adversary behavior and our enhanced security methods are lying in wait, then the element of surprise is gone. This is an exceedingly important concept.

An examination of the infamous 9/11 al-Qaeda attack shows that we were taken totally by surprise. We also missed the collapse of the Soviet Union, the technology sham of that same country, Pearl Harbor, the Oklahoma City bombing, etc. The element of surprise was present for each of these attacks or events. This was noted in the 9/11 Commission Report as a failure of the then security apparatus and, specifically, the lack of imagination within the CIA and FBI. The commission found that both agencies were still focused on Cold War strategies. Congress also received blame. According to the report, Congress should have provided much better oversight of the CIA and FBI.

On the basis of decades of experience working in the area of anticipating human behavior, I can attest to the need for imagination. We need the types of analyses that do not just project the past into the future but actually project how the past morphs into the future.

Imagination is not a gift usually associated with bureaucracies.

—9/11 Commission Report, July 2004

Imagination is more important than Knowledge.

—Albert Einstein

Advantages of AuBA #6: Automated Pattern Classification

One of the discoveries made along the way in the development of AuBA was that pattern classification was a necessity to accurately predict future human behavior. Pattern classification and pattern recognition represent a field of study of its own. Specific methods used can include statistical pattern recognition (SPR), artificial neural networks (ANNs), statistics, and machine learning. The design of ThemeMate, as described in previous chapters, was purposefully planned for pattern classification. During the development of AuBA, all these methods listed were tested.

The output of ThemeMate is a data array that has extracted antecedent candidates (called *themes*) as columns and examples of behaviors being modeled as rows. Each cell in the array is an intersection of one antecedent theme and one behavior example. Each cell is populated with 1s and 0s in which a 1 indicates that a specific antecedent in a column was present for that one behavior example and a 0 indicates that the one antecedent was not present for that specific behavior example.

To complete the array we add outcome columns at the end of the array. Outcomes are what we want to predict. Once that is complete, we have a classic pattern classification problem to solve. The basic idea: discover the patterns that exist among antecedents and specific outcomes across all behavior examples provided. Once the patterns are discovered, then the presence of specific antecedents in the future will be associated with the occurrence of specific behavior, such as threat or no threat, attack or no attack, and so on.

The pattern classification used in AuBA consists primarily of two basic methodologies:

- **Back propagation network (BPN):** The BPN is an artificial neural network that learns from examples. Once trained, the BPN takes input in the form of presence or absence of antecedents and outputs a prediction of human behavior.

- **Statistical pattern recognition:** The predictive engine in some cases is statistical in nature such as discriminant analysis or logistical regression working the identical way as a BPN. The only difference is the predictive algorithm.

During the process of developing AuBA, the pattern classification process was very lengthy, particularly as it related to the construction of a data array and the training of the predictive engines. The AuBA process has automated both.

The use of ANNs has been controversial in the past. Learning within the human brain was the inspiration that led to the development of neural network technology. There are literally hundreds of types of neural network algorithms. However, the BPN is the workhorse of neural networks. Although many neural networks are very esoteric and highly complex, the BPN is well understood. In fact, many introductory classes in artificial intelligence in computer science include the requirement that each student construct a BPN. Dr. Charles Butler, an expert in neural network technology, now deceased, studied neural network technology for decades. His assessment was that the BPN was responsible for about 85 percent of all successful neural network applications.

The accurate prediction of human behavior has not been demonstrated scientifically by focusing only on expert opinion or statistics alone. Our contribution is that basic principles of applied behavior analysis, when modified to make use of globally based antecedents processed with advanced pattern classification technologies such as a BPN, can result in accurate prediction. Basically, the notion that past behavior is the best predictor of future behavior has been discounted by AuBA. Instead, a much more accurate statement is that past antecedent-behavior associations are the best predictor of future antecedent-behavior associations. This book represents validated examples of the capability of AuBA pattern classification across multiple domains using network packets, text, and physical sensor outputs to predict future behavior accurately.

I admit that pattern classification can be a very complex undertaking, especially when using scientifically acceptable methods of validation. Not all application areas include a PhD in computer science as an available staff member to assist in this area. For this reason we automated the entire pattern classification process. Simply by providing a ThemeMate data array to AutoAnalyzer and clicking on *run*, we receive as the end product the optimized predictive engine that has been validated with blind cases. One of the primary advantages of the BPN when used in this form of pattern classification is that the engine can make *educated guesses*. Because we know that behaviors do not repeat themselves perfectly under the same antecedent conditions in the future, the predictive engine has to determine what behavior is most likely to occur when the antecedent conditions are close but not identical. The BPN has proven to be very difficult to surpass in this area. After two decades of work with the BPN, we have learned how to precisely train it for use in predicting malicious behavior. These discovered principles are embedded in the AuBA technology.

In short, the automated pattern classification capability of AuBA provides:

- Rapid and accurate behavioral modeling
- The ability to determine the most likely behavior that will occur when antecedent conditions do not repeat exactly the way they occurred in the past
- Predictive engines that are forgiving and capable of making educated guesses of what is likely to occur under unique antecedent conditions
- Fully automated AuBA pattern classification, reducing the need for highly specialized and difficult-to-find staff

As related to anticipating future threats, AuBA provides a rapid behavior modeling capability that can be threat based simply by submitting a corpus of text that includes past threat incidents or highly likely threat scenarios. Because of the rapid modeling, we can know within one day if a predictive model is possible and the effectiveness of that model by means of best practices validation.

In Summary

Much has transpired in the decade since 9/11. Certainly the world is more interconnected, and technology continues to expand seemingly at an exponential rate. Threat to our national infrastructure has also increased as we face daily cyber attacks and cyber threat. From a cyber perspective, advanced persistent threat support by foreign states has emerged and evolved to the degree that we have witnessed the loss of hundreds of thousands of sensitive and classified documents. Osama bin Laden was killed, as well as his chief operations deputy. It appears that more than ever terrorist groups such as al-Qaeda have reconfirmed their resolve to attack the United States, and foreign states represent a blatant threat to national security. An AuBA-based behavior analysis of trends and targeting indicates that for the remainder of the decade we are likely to see the following:

- **High probability:** Continued APT cyber threat supported by foreign states to target technology and restricted materials to assist in their assuming a technology lead on a global basis (for example, China).

- **High probability:** Expanding insider threat in which U.S. citizens employed by government, military, and business steal classified and sensitive documents to distribute and to sell — both as single individuals and in collusion with external individuals.

- **Moderate probability:** Threat of conventional high-explosive suicide missions within the U.S. borders will persist as we are likely see another attempt to rival 9/11 in which mass casualties and destruction would occur.

- **Moderate probability:** A coordinated attack directed at harming the U.S. economy, either indirectly as a result of massive loss of life and destruction or as a coordinated cyber attack specifically targeting financial or economic targets.

- **Low probability:** A terrorist use of a chemical, biological, radiological, or nuclear weapon as a weapon of mass destruction within U.S. borders.

To prepare for the future, our security must accelerate the movement from a reactive security stance to a proactive stance. By incorporating predictive methods, we can reduce the number one advantage that asymmetric warfare adversaries have — the element of surprise.

Part

II

Dissecting Malicious Behavior

In This Part

Applying Behavior Principles: Predicting Individual Malicious Behavior

The only thing we can do about the past is to learn from it. We can't go back and change the course of events leading to the present. We live in the present, adjusting our behavior to best meet existing conditions thrust upon us, often without warning. Perhaps life would be easier if we knew what future conditions would be before they occurred, but we usually don't. We are creatures of the present and are poorly prepared to anticipate the future.

How can we better prepare ourselves for the future? This chapter provides more details on how you can analyze and better anticipate malicious behavior. It also highlights the methods by which predicting human behavior helps us in preventing its occurrence.

Using a Behavior Analysis Methodology That Works

In our constantly changing world, we first take care of basic needs that currently have an impact on our personal lives, such as food and shelter. As psychologist Abraham Maslow so eloquently described in his theory of a hierarchy of needs in 1943,[1] once these basic needs are met, we can advance to taking care of social and complex psychological needs. Establishing and maintaining friendships, job satisfaction, love, and all manner of other objectives combine with meeting our most basic needs to absorb our attention and focus; life is a full-time job. Even if we construct a plan that guides us toward the future, we find that conditions are constantly changing, and our plan must be adjusted accordingly. Sometimes we modify our plan in minor ways. Other times unforeseen events are so drastic that we must modify our plan in major, life-altering ways. Mostly, however, we simply adjust to existing conditions of the day.

Why must we be so dynamic and ever changing? Our environment is complex, with an untold number and mix of factors that affect us every second, minute, and hour of every day. As noted by Charles Darwin, the impact of the environment on all organisms has been to shape the physical nature of the organisms over time. Successful adaptation to changing environmental conditions leads to survival, and less-than-successful adaptation leads to lack of survival, or even extinction of a species. Behaviorist B. F. Skinner's career was dedicated to showing that this powerful influence — the environment — also has a tremendous effect on our behavior and not just the physical evolutionary makeup of our species. To live successfully is to adjust successfully to our environment.

What is it in the environment that affects us to such a great degree? The answer is deceptively simple. Everything we face has meaning to us. The environment could be a person who walks up to you and starts a conversation. It could be a supervisor who acknowledges what an outstanding job you have done or tells you about a mistake you made. It could be the traffic as you commute home from work. It could be your spouse, your children, the news, the lack of news, being accepted (or not accepted) to the school you so desperately wanted, a competitor's getting the upper hand, the outside temperature, or an impending wedding. In short, there is potential for all factors we encounter to affect us. From this perspective, the past takes on greater importance. True, we cannot change it. But our past and the experiences we have had, shaped by the presence or absence of certain factors when these events occurred, make these factors more important than others. They become antecedents to our future behavior. Therefore, similar behaviors will occur in the future in the presence of the same or highly similar antecedents. We encounter the environment by encountering antecedents to behaviors we exhibited in the past.

How do we adapt to and interact with the environment? Again the answer is deceptively simple: We respond; we exhibit behavior. We exhibit all forms of behavior on a moment-to-moment basis. We talk, listen, smell, touch, move, sleep, drive, and interact with others. In short, we respond. We react to the many environmental conditions facing us by exhibiting behavior — and these behaviors are typically observable. These behaviors can be counted, timed, and

---

[1] Maslow, A. H., (1943) A Theory of Human Motivation, *Psychological Review* 50(4) pp. 370–96.

recorded. This means our behavior can be studied using scientific methods. We have established a dynamic interaction between the environment in the form of antecedents and our behavior as reactions or responses. Our behavior does not occur in a vacuum; instead, it is always associated with precursor antecedents.

Knowing that antecedents precede behavior would seem to be enough to predict behavior. We simply look for antecedents to known behavior and then predict the behavior when those antecedents occur again. Unfortunately, this is not enough information to allow us to study malicious behavior and accurately predict its future occurrence. We have all heard of Ivan Pavlov's groundbreaking experiments in the early 1900s. He showed dogs meat powder, which would make them salivate. Pavlov then rang a small bell every time he showed the dogs the meat powder. After many pairings of the meat and the bell, the dogs would salivate at the sound of the bell alone. This classical conditioning is important and shows how an environmental factor can affect a subsequent behavior, but it does not explain all the complexities involved in human behavior — particularly malicious behavior. In other words, complex human behavior is not simply composed of a series of automatic reactions to stimuli occurring in the environment.

To complete the basic foundation of studying and predicting complex malicious behavior accurately, we need to add consequences of behavior to our established connection between environmental stimuli and subsequent behavior. This three-fold approach of antecedents leading to behavior followed by consequences is extremely powerful. Consequences of our behavior strengthen that behavior in the presence of antecedents if the behavior was successful, or weaken our behavior in the presence of antecedents if the behavior was unsuccessful. This relationship and how it works was the genius of B. F. Skinner and the army of researchers and practitioners who followed him. By using all three components, antecedents-behavior-consequences, we can now restate the relationship in the following way:

> *If behavior occurring in the presence of specific antecedents is followed by consequences that are favorable to the person, the probability of future occurrence of that behavior in the presence of the same or highly similar antecedents is increased.*

> *Likewise, if behavior occurring in the presence of specific antecedents is followed by consequences that are unfavorable to the person, the probability of future occurrence of that behavior in the presence of the same or highly similar antecedents is decreased.*

In the first case, we would expect behavior to occur if antecedents associated with the behavior in the past occur again. In a sense, these antecedents encourage or prompt the behavior to occur. In the latter case, antecedents serve as a suppressor of the behavior.

The probability of future occurrence is about the future, not the past or the present. This is an obvious key to identifying future behavior. If we gather examples of an individual's behavior and record the antecedents and consequences associated with that behavior, we have the beginnings of a method to analyze, influence, and predict the behavior's future occurrence. This is the basis for applied behavior analysis, a field in psychology that focuses on the effects of the environment on behavior. Applied behavior analysis is the basic foundation from which I developed automated behavior analysis (AuBA) — a patented set of methods and tools used successfully to predict complex malicious behavior.

Using Behavior Principles to Analyze Behavior

It is necessary to place the basic foundation of applied behavior analysis into perspective. Skinner's pioneering work began in the 1930s; his operant conditioning approach was then extended from the laboratory to the real world. This work, conducted by countless numbers of practitioners, dramatically changed the lives of those who were institutionalized. It is one of the primary reasons why we see far fewer very large institutions for the developmentally disabled and mentally ill.

Through decades of work applying operant principles, the field of applied behavior analysis surfaced and has been successful. Severely disabled individuals with few to no basic daily living skills now had skills. Inappropriate and often self-injurious and aggressive behavior that separated the infirm from the public diminished, or even disappeared. Structuring the environment by altering antecedent conditions and by providing new favorable consequences resulted in significant behavior change. This behavior analysis environmental engineering approach emphasized the antecedents and consequences of behavior. Prediction had not yet surfaced to the degree presented in this book, but the approach actually made the future happen for the better for many disadvantaged individuals. The foundation for predictive work was laid by many professionals dedicated to bettering the lives of the disabled and disadvantaged.

Over the decades, the numbers of individuals in hard-core institutions decreased and the number living successfully in the community increased. Followed by successful application in educational settings, the work of these pioneers in applying behavioral principles has benefitted many people. Furthermore, this beginning science of human behavior gained knowledge, and as a result, we have a much better idea of how the environment affects behavior. We now have a clear view of how we can alter the environment to change behavior.

Today the clinical/scientific methods of applied behavior analysis and associated behavioral psychology approaches are being applied to many different domains. The work in this book represents long-standing efforts in the areas of defense, intelligence, and the automation of predictive principles as applied to malicious behavior, including the complex world of current cyber threats and cyber attacks. Because of the increased ability to anticipate behavior of an individual in the future, we are learning how to improve prevention and early mitigation. Consequently, we are rapidly approaching how we can change security from being reactive to being proactive and anticipatory.

We can now describe how new and emergent malicious behavior may be identified before it occurs and how we can prevent its occurrence. This will result in inevitable changes in how we approach security. It is past time for such a change. As the world becomes more threatening, as evidenced by the devastating September 11, 2001, al-Qaeda attack on the World Trade Center and the Pentagon, it is time to anticipate and not just react. Facing the possibility of a chemical or biological attack, a nuclear explosion, the consequences of a nuclear dirty bomb, or a forced network attack that results in a financial meltdown, we can no longer afford to simply wait and react. We need preemptive proactive security warriors, not just first responders.

Because applied behavior analysis is an approach used to influence behavior, we must modify the approach used to predict behavior. Furthermore, the concept of environment changes when we use behavior principles on a global basis. Clinically, I used a behavior analysis form to record data that would form the basis of a clinical intervention. Simple in structure, this form was divided into three sections: antecedents, behavior, and consequences. The form's purpose was to record examples of behavior of interest. First, you observe the behavior and describe it in the middle section. In the first section, you record all possible preceding events or situations (antecedents). These conditions can be the recorded time the antecedents occurred, people in the vicinity, location specifics, or activities occurring at the time. Last, any events occurring after the behavior and as a result of the behavior are listed. Each example of behavior exists as a complete and separate antecedent-behavior-consequence listing. For clarity, the following definitions are offered for the three components:

- An **antecedent** is any event or situation occurring immediately before the behavior of interest that is logically related to the behavior's occurrence.

- **Behavior** is the overt and observable action of an individual that is of interest to predict or influence.

- A **consequence** is any event or situation occurring immediately after the behavior of interest that is logically related to the behavior's occurrence.

Once a proper number of examples of behavior have been recorded, the information may be analyzed to find common antecedents and consequences associated with the occurrences of specific behavior. Environmental antecedents and consequence conditions are factors that support the behavior's occurrence. Knowing this, we can anticipate the behavior in the future in the presence of the same or highly similar conditions. In fact, this concept has been validated to be true across a wide variety of behaviors. Although the approach is not complicated, you are encouraged to go through the demonstrations of the AuBA technology tools and processes on the accompanying DVD. The DVD will show how to complete an AuBA predictive analysis with real-world data.

It is important to note that for some behavior classes of interest, such as network hacking, terrorism, theft, and fraud, observation is not likely. In these cases we may gather news articles or prepared reports about past examples. We can complete all three sections of a behavior analysis form from recorded observations or news articles about past events. Because reporting of past events tends to include the journalistic who, what, where, when, why, and how of past behavior, these components of reporting fall neatly within the antecedents, behavior, and consequences sections of a behavior analysis form.

A basic example can demonstrate how this type of analysis is useful in analyzing malicious behavior. It is an approach to analysis that can explain why network hacking is such a serious problem and why it is getting worse. First, a network's specific vulnerabilities are antecedents to specific attacks. For this reason, we see numerous scans directed against a network to identify vulnerabilities. The presence of unknown vulnerabilities serves as an antecedent to network exploration via scanning behavior. Second, hacking is associated with few negative consequences. One can engage in hacking with little concern about being caught.

Therefore, with identified antecedent vulnerabilities that invite network attack behavior and with minimal negative consequences to hacking, we observe high levels of network attacks. If we consider the same antecedent conditions (antecedent vulnerabilities) but add the potential consequence of financial gain to consequences, we can explain the increases in specific types of attacks against financial targets. In this case, we observe specific types of network attacks resulting in financial gain with little to no probability of identifying the perpetrator. Because of the dual consequences of potential for financial gain combined with little fear of being apprehended, the probability of future occurrence of the behavior is increased. In short, we expect to see such behavior maintained and even increase over time.

Using the previous example, we fight financial loss through the use of current network intrusion methods such as signature detection with limited success at best. Signature detection based solely on the past (which we cannot change) represents a reactive security approach. Basically, a network is assaulted successfully, leading to designing a signature that will identify that same attack so that it may be detected if it occurs again. However, that signature would have to be distributed to all networks to be successful, and, most important, it assumes that the same behavior will occur again. It is possible, but a talented hacker intent on achieving financial gain will already be using new attacks not known to current signature detection. Of course, if the hacker isn't that talented, a denial-of-service attack can just disrupt an organization if disruption and not financial gain is the goal.

NOTE Signature detection was developed to identify those consistent attacks that would just be repeated against new victims until success was achieved. For a while this worked. However, as the expertise of attackers increased and specific vulnerabilities could be detected, the advent of zero-day attacks that could not be detected with old signatures began to be the norm. Now it is best to think of signature detection as just one tool in the cyber protection arsenal, but it can no longer provide the protection it once afforded us. The method simply cannot protect against new attacks.

The approach of identifying past successful attacks for constructing signatures can never catch up with the serious, creative, talented hacker. Certainly, signature detection cannot prevent new, creative attacks. The approach is weak, and it is continuing in the future. Taking an AuBA approach, it is clear that even if the antecedents stay the same (presence of vulnerabilities) but the consequences change drastically, we could observe decreases in hacking overnight. For example, suppose we change the current consequence of not being identified and apprehended to a consequence that includes effective technology that can immediately trace back to an attacker and to the actual machine used for the attack. We would likely see a dramatic and almost immediate decrease in hacking as we know it. Unfortunately, we do not have traceback capability with a high degree of accuracy, so we would have to predict a continued increase in attacks because of little to no chance of being caught.

CROSS-REFERENCE This problem from a security perspective is addressed in Chapters 11 and 12 with new AuBA cyber assessment technology (the CheckMate and InMate products).

Environmental Variables

Applied behavior analysis and other behavioral psychology approaches often draw criticism because the approaches do not delve into the mind of the adversary. Instead, the behavioral approach focuses on identifying environmental variables associated with the occurrence of behavior so that we can predict the behavior's occurrence in the future when the same or highly similar antecedents are present. The criticism often continues by indicating that the person can do anything he or she wants; therefore, behavior is not controlled by the environment. Predicting malicious behavior is about probabilities, not 100 percent confidence that a specific behavior will occur. Also, although it is true that a person can exhibit almost any behavior without considering antecedents, he or she does not do that. The world would be chaos if all humans responded spontaneously without considering such antecedents as culture, laws, rules, convention, and patterns of past behavior. We are creatures of habit, and we develop patterns.

These patterns of behavior are formed as combinations of antecedents, behavior, and consequences.

As a simple example, suppose someone driving a car approaches an intersection. As he or she approaches, the traffic light provides antecedents such as traffic light color that exhibit total control over the driving behavior. If the light is green, the driver moves through the intersection. If the light is red, the driver slows to a stop. Technically, he or she could drive through under any color, but typically he or she doesn't because of the consequences of doing so if the light is red. In essence, the antecedent (light color) combined with consequences (presence of law enforcement or potential for a ticket, an accident, injury, or even death) results in control of the behavior. Interestingly, the same traffic light serves as antecedents for driving through the intersection and stopping, depending on another antecedent — direction of travel. Yes, someone could drive a car off a cliff if he or she wanted, but unless the car contains Thelma and Louise and we are viewing a movie, it just doesn't happen.

Currently, the reasoning behind such approaches as signature detection involves following the almost universally accepted lore: The best predictor of future behavior is past behavior. This belief is true to some degree. It's true enough to be believed by many. However, it is only partially correct. Over the past three decades, we have studied the prediction of malicious intent and behavior to develop the automated methods and tools presented in this book. This work has resulted in the following essential principles:

- The key to predicting behavior is not studying the behavior itself but identifying antecedents associated with the behavior of interest in the past.

- The best predictor of future behavior is not past behavior. The best predictor of future behavior is identifying antecedents and consequences associated with past behavior.

- If antecedents of past behavior are identified when those behaviors led to favorable consequences, there is an increased probability that the behavior will occur in the future if the same or highly similar antecedents occur.

- To predict future behavior from antecedents associated with the behavior in the past, a form of pattern classification is required to identify predictive patterns among antecedents and the following behavior.

- The accurate prediction of behavior rarely relies on the presence of a single antecedent. Complex human behavior typically occurs in association with repeatable constellations of identified antecedents.

Given that antecedents do establish control over behavior, identifying antecedent variables helps us understand behavior and anticipate the occurrence of that behavior in the future.

Different Environments, Different Antecedents

Identifying the appropriate antecedents for a specific type of behavior is based on the environmental context that contains the behavior. The AuBA technology, although based on applied behavior analysis, required numerous extensions so that such behavioral areas as terrorism, network hacking, criminal behavior, and tracking/locating could occur accurately. One of the primary reasons for these extensions was that different behaviors occur in different environments. These different environments affect the accurate selection of antecedents. Context must be taken into consideration.

The behavior analyst historically has worked within the classroom, an institution, or an organization of one type or another. The behaviors of interest occurred within these constrained environments. For example, if third-grader Johnny simply did not stay in his seat, a behavior analyst would have identified antecedents in the classroom that were associated with his out-of-seat behavior. The identification of consequences that occurred when he was out of his seat typically demonstrated what was reinforcing and maintaining his behavior. A teacher or behavior analyst would then alter the environment to change the behavior for the better (such as moving Johnny away from Billy).

Our studies and work have focused on those who threaten government and public officials — terrorists, worldwide network hackers, and other global adversary threats. Early in this work it was clear that methods were being moved from the classroom to the globe. This was a dramatic shift in focus. The fact that a peace conference would be held in the Middle East, or that a top U.S. official would visit a specific country, could serve as one of the primary antecedents associated with a terrorist attack. Once you leave the confines of a classroom or an institution, the antecedents could conceivably be significant activities occurring on a worldwide scale instead of within the confines of an organization or a room with four walls.

This realization led to the development of additional principles that have aided our predictions of malicious behavior on a global basis. The following principles are examples of additional findings.

- Antecedents occur within the target individual's or group's area of influence (organization, city, region, country, group of countries, or across the globe).

  - Example: The announcement of a peace conference to be held in the Middle East may be relevant as an antecedent for a Middle Eastern terrorist group. A peace conference to be held in Europe is not a relevant antecedent for the same group.

- To be completely effective, antecedents associated with the behavior of interest occur within days of the behavior, whereas relevant consequences are immediate.

  - Example: Relevant antecedents having an effect on imminent behavior precede the behavior by only days. The resultant behavior, such as a terrorist attack, has immediate consequences (damage, death, media attention). If there is a perceived attack against Palestinians by Israel, then the antecedent stage is set for retaliation by Hezbollah. The attack might not occur immediately, but it is likely to occur in close timing to the initial event.

- Identified antecedents to behavior are stable across time, although the nature of the behavior may vary.

  - Example: A cyber attacker intent on damaging an organization may alter his or her attack behavior by using a variety of attacks. He or she might add variation by using evasion tactics (such as fragroute), but always in response to the same antecedents that attracted him or her to that organization.

- The stability of antecedents associated with specific behaviors of interest provides a strong basis for a methodology to accurately predict behavior.

To predict behavior accurately is to understand the complex interaction of the person with the environment. This interaction is observable and measurable and is used to identify the patterns that exist among antecedents and subsequent behavior. The good news is that such data is available and that you can identify predictive patterns by using proper analytical methods. The bad news is that the individual, group, or country responds to antecedents in an idiosyncratic manner. Antecedents are not universal. They are highly specific to the individual, because we all have our own history of past antecedent-behavior-consequence associations. This individual history of associations explains why we all respond differently in the presence of the same antecedents. If we study the behavior of an adversary to predict the future occurrence of his or her behavior, we must identify the specific antecedents to which he or she responds.

Antecedents, Behavior, and Consequences

The basic antecedent-behavior-consequence method of analyzing behavior as expanded to adversarial malicious behavior on a global basis provides the foundation for new security perspectives. As noted earlier in the book, current security practices are primarily reactive. Much like signature detection, we develop security practices based on past identified threats. If a terrorist threat is detected in an El Al airport security line, security is increased at airport lines. Shortly after the massive al-Qaeda attack on U.S. soil, Richard Reid attempted to explode in flight explosives that were in his shoe. As a result, 11 years later we are still removing our shoes to go through security lines at airports. Security, for the most part, relies on signatures, although we tend to think of signature detection as cyber only.

Serious hacking attacks are identified forensically after the fact, and signatures are developed and implemented to identify that same attack if it occurs again. In short, a primary security stance is to identify what has happened in the past and to protect against it in the future. However, this concept needs updating to be useful for predictive analysis. Given an increase in predictive methods, mitigation can move toward preventing first-time malicious events.

In planning the design of the AuBA-based CheckMate and InMate applications, the capability to detect cyber threat without signatures and without anomaly detection was a primary feature. By converting packet-level activity to measures of the degree of expertise and deception present, threat can be detected from a human behavior perspective, as opposed to network-based signatures. In other words, when we speak of behavior on a network with AuBA applications, we are speaking of human behavior. Anomaly detection also focuses on behavior, but it is network behavior, not human behavior. This is a strong distinction between AuBA-related applications and others.

Because the CheckMate and InMate applications have the capability to detect threat from the perspective of human behavior versus network behavior and can identify levels of threat as precursor antecedents, it is possible to identify threat earlier in the attack process. As an attacker moves from initial activity to a threatening demeanor prior to an actual attack, it is possible to identify the threat earlier, as shown in Figure 7-1. As the illustration depicts, CheckMate, an intent-based technology, is designed to identify threat earlier than a network-based intrusion detection system (IDS) or a host-based application. CheckMate identifies the level of *expertise* (E) and *deception* (D) present in sequential 100 millisecond samples of activity. If the E/D measures exceed a critical threshold at the same time, then malicious intent is present. This intent can precede an actual attack, as compared to network and host-based applications.

Applying a behavior analysis approach to security methods and procedures lets us anticipate adversary behavior more accurately than simply relying on repetition of past behaviors. Also, as will be demonstrated with AuBA, tools can help us identify new and emergent malicious behavior occurring for the first time. Because of the detailed work completed on the antecedent-behavior associations and the AuBA tools that focus on this interaction, analysis has been aided by automation. Finally, the consideration of consequences in studying and analyzing past events is important. For example, in our early studies of terrorism, our prediction accuracy increased dramatically when we excluded examples of terrorist behavior that ended in failure (the perpetrator was apprehended). Applied behavior analysis has demonstrated convincingly that humans simply do not repeat behaviors that result in unpleasant or undesirable consequences. Therefore, such examples should be excluded from consideration when analyzing behavior for predictive purposes.

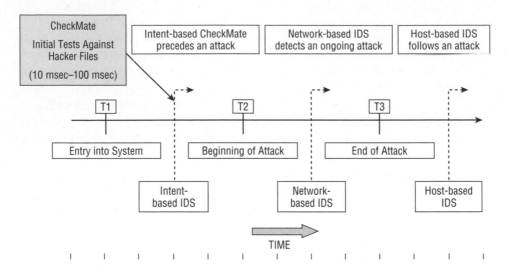

Figure 7-1: CheckMate was designed to identify threat earlier than current network and host-based applications.

So, it is important to analyze malicious behaviors of a group or individual that ended in success. Because behavior examples followed by favorable consequences are more likely to lead to predictive patterns (because those behaviors are more likely to be repeated), we need to study examples consisting of behaviors leading to success for the adversary. And further, success must be considered from the adversary's perspective and not from ours. For example, a suicide terrorist is successful if the explosion occurs and he or she is obliterated. This is a foreign concept to many in our country because of our cultural fear of dying. We tend to believe that suicide terrorists are forced into their roles. In fact, the vast majority are true believers, and the opportunity to be a successful suicide bomber is happily pursued because of the consequences. A Middle Eastern terrorist believes he will ascend to a paradise with 71 virgins. That is a big consequence to follow the simple act of pushing a button if one is a true believer. Of course, if one is not a true believer, the perceived consequence may seem a little shaky, and some reluctance may be present.

Cultural perspective is important, because it is essential to determine what is reinforcing (pleasant consequences) to the adversary from his or her perspective and not our own.

NOTE Culture does not have to be about another country. Culture can be shared beliefs and behaviors of a group with which one identifies.

For example, one of the major reasons for hacking is cultural. The early hacking culture was about showing other hackers how skilled you were. You would use a handle, such as "mad dog," and collect hacking exploits like notches on a gun. Your power came from acknowledgment from your peers about how good you were. If you were good enough, the government might even hire you! This was the stuff of movies, which only increased the favorable consequences of hacking. The hacking culture reinforced its own people, and the general public helped by making and watching movies and (incorrectly) believing hackers were geniuses. Our wonderment and, at times, adulation have helped feed the problem. However, to security professionals, many of these geniuses were simply ankle biters — a real nuisance.

Cyber war has started, and we are seeing cyber skirmishes as precursors. Early hackers wanted an audience, but criminals focused on financial gain or a country's intelligence service do not. Therefore, we expect to see behavior that is associated with significant deception and dramatic increases in expertise. To become more proactive, we must understand the evolution of behavior and the cultural contexts of modern-day hacking. Culture can create antecedents for hacking, shape hacking behavior, or provide the consequences to reinforce the new age of hacking we are entering. The same is true of terrorism. The nature of terrorism is changing. Mass casualties are now the goal, not just media attention, as in the past. Malicious behavior is becoming more serious as it morphs into more serious forms. Security needs a paradigm shift, and predictive behavior may be the answer. It is time to change from just studying network behavior to understanding human behavior.

Behavior Modeling

Behavior modeling consists of constructing a representation of a person, group, organization, or some collection of individuals bound by common causes and beliefs. The purpose of having a model is that the model behaves like the real thing. We can probe it to see how the real entity might act under different circumstances. This is especially important if the group is adversarial and no clear opportunities to observe the group exist.

In predictive modeling, we can predict the entity's next behaviors. It is apparent almost immediately that a model can help us learn how an adversary might behave, or what malicious behavior we might experience next. It is also apparent that if we are to trust the model that is constructed, it had better be accurate. It should be a valid representation of the person or group, and it must be reliable by providing the same results every time it processes the same factors.

Behavioral modeling using the antecedent-behavior-consequence approach is effective at identifying key environmental influences of specific types of behavior. AuBA and its extensions have been validated to predict adversarial behavior as future events. The basic scientific foundation remains the same whether we are conducting clinical modeling or modeling of a terrorist group or determining the future actions of terrorists to design a new security policy. The primary differences are in the information describing past events so that we can accurately extract the key factors associated with the behavior of interest.

News articles serve as our time machine. As examples, if we want to model domestic terrorism or abortion clinic bombings, we search for past events of the type we want to model as our beginning corpus. Then, using methods outlined in the DVD that comes with this book, we extract antecedents, behavior, and consequences for each event. When we are done, we have an accurate representation of the entity being modeled. We then add our pattern classification. After validation, the model reacts and behaves like the real thing, or as close as we can get.

To use the predictive model, we present a specific set of antecedents that describe recent events and enter them into the model as input. If we have done our work properly, the model will behave as the modeled entity would in the presence of that set of conditions. Because the adversary has not had time to act when presented with the current set of antecedents, the model's answer becomes the actual prediction of the adversary's behavior.

Automated Behavior Analysis (AuBA)

I invented AuBA, and my research teams developed it as software, for the following reasons:

- Applied behavior analysis using primarily a clinical methodology even when applied in different areas required extensions to move from influence to accurate prediction of future behavior.

- After developing a manual methodology that extended influence and clinical methods to real-world adversary prediction, it was determined that the process, although accurate, was too time-consuming for real-world use.

- The fusion of the computer and behavioral sciences promised to eliminate bias in modeling resulting from manual methods, to add the ability to model rapidly, and to automate both the input of data and the reporting of results.

- The process of modeling to the degree that accurate prediction can occur is not difficult, but it is involved. Automation simply makes it easier.

- Total automation meant that a model could operate automatically. Antecedent events on a global basis could be identified and processed by the predictive engines, and the automated analysis could be acted on.

This book presents several examples of AuBA in action. CheckMate is an automated behavior assessment application that protects a network from external attack by automatically converting network packets into behavior assessment measures. InMate uses the same behavioral assessment technology to identify insider threats. The technology represents a new security paradigm — one that is proactive instead of reactive. These examples used antecedents identified in network packet activity, whereas other applications use physical sensor data as input or antecedents present in news account of world events. These examples are covered in this book.

Using Tools to Assist Our Understanding

A number of AuBA applications have been developed to automatically identify malicious threats and predict imminent malicious behavior. To construct these applications, we used a common set of AuBA tools to conduct the actual modeling and to construct the predictive engines. These two SAIC tools I invented are ThemeMate and AutoAnalyzer:

- **ThemeMate** is a statistically based theme and predictor extraction tool that processes text such as news articles of past events to derive antecedent themes associated with past behaviors. If text examples of an adversary's behavior are gathered and presented to ThemeMate, it extracts the most relevant themes present across all the documents. These themes can be converted into antecedents, behavior, or consequences. Because of the statistical nature of the theme extraction, the technology may be applied across languages. After antecedent themes, or antecedent candidates, have been extracted and subjected to analyst validation, a data array is automatically created. It may be used to immediately correlate associations among antecedents and behaviors added to the data array and presented to AutoAnalyzer for predictive modeling.

- **AutoAnalyzer**, a behavioral application, is an automated pattern classification model builder. It takes as input the data array presented by ThemeMate and reduces the set of antecedent candidates to the most relevant events and situations serving as antecedent predictors. The application then constructs back propagation network (BPN) pattern classifiers and validates each model using the leaving-one-out (L-1) method of validation. For each developed model, the true-positive, true-negative, false-positive, and false-negative rates are presented. In addition, a Fisher's exact statistical significance test is automatically calculated on the blind testing results. A Fisher's exact test presents the probability that results obtained could have been the result of chance. For this reason, the lower the statistic, the better. For example, the highest we would want to see is a 0.05 level, or 5 chances in a 100 that results could have been obtained by chance. Developed models have been validated across terrorist groups, specific behavior of individuals, corporate espionage, and network hacker behavior, among others, with Fisher's exact results of typically less than 1 in 1,000,000.

Predicting Adversarial Behavior

Using AuBA tools, we collect documents such as news articles about past events and submit them to the AuBA process. We also can conduct the analyses manually using Excel, correlational analysis, and pattern classification. However, the process takes much longer and requires additional knowledge on the part of the analyst. The models we have developed usually are about 80 percent accurate. After decades of work in this area, it does not appear to be possible to predict future human behavior with complete accuracy, for a wide variety of reasons touched on throughout this book. However, it is safe to say that we never have complete knowledge, and data is often missing or sparse. Compared to guesses about adversary behavior in the future, our typical predictive accuracy in some areas is unprecedented.

In Chapter 18 the topic of sparse or missing data will be addressed. This is a special case of predictive behavioral modeling. However, we have found that models may be developed with the same accuracy using subject matter experts (SMEs) to describe scenarios and associated likely antecedents and consequences without actual examples of past behaviors. This has been especially useful in constructing new behavior-based network protection applications.

We have reports of past behavior; SMEs available so that we can extract antecedents, behavior, and consequences of future malicious behavior; or past behavior with no data but SME knowledge that can provide the who, what, when, where, and how. These items will help us develop accurate behavioral models.

Influencing and Preventing Adversarial Behavior

The AuBA products CheckMate and InMate are examples of preventing malicious behavior by predicting malicious behavior. I invented these technologies to predict external threats to a network (CheckMate) and threats from those working inside an organization (InMate). Although CheckMate and InMate will be explained in detail in Chapters 11 and 12, brief descriptions are provided here:

- **CheckMate** is a behavior-based AuBA application designed to protect networks from external attacks. Because insider threats and external threats are entirely different, with different motivations, CheckMate focuses on external individuals accessing a network. Converting samples of packets from each individual into the degree of *expertise* (E) and *deception* (D) present, the application provides alerts or can block the IP address if expertise and deception both exceed preset thresholds. Threat is defined as high E and D. An alert can warn of malicious behavior as it occurs, or predict that an attack is ready to occur, and then block the activity before damage can occur.

- **InMate** was designed to use the same behavior assessment technology as CheckMate. However, the insider already has access, so expertise is not required. In this case the two dimensions being tracked are *intent to engage* *in misuse* (I) and *deception* (D). InMate can detect an insider engaging in activity on the network that represents malicious intent and imminent malicious behavior. When such activity occurs, the alert is forwarded to security as opposed to a network administrator. Classifying an insider worker as potentially malicious can be damaging. Therefore, alerts are processed by security personnel trained in investigating suspicious insider behavior.

Figure 7-2 shows the conceptual assessment process whereby CheckMate converts samples of network packets into measures of E and D. One of the keys is to plot both dimensions simultaneously to create a region of high E and high D. When both happen at the same time, a threat is already occurring or is about to.

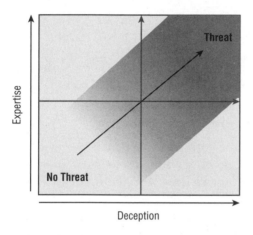

Figure 7-2: The assessment of human expertise (E) and deception (D) from samples of packet-level activity

Both CheckMate and InMate represent new technology that is different from the existing signature detection and anomaly detection approaches to network protection. As previously discussed, signature detection is a purely reactive approach that defines a past attack with a rule that can detect that specific attack if it occurs in the future. Typical antivirus software on your computer is an example. The problem is that humans are excellent generators of new attack behaviors or variations that can't be detected with these past signatures. In marked contrast, anomaly detection is based on determining normal behavior patterns on a network and then identifying any significant departure from the norm. There are no signatures, just deviations from the norm. However, if anomaly detection identifies activity that is significantly different from the norm, this does not mean the behavior is malicious. It is much more likely to be non-malicious. Deviations from a norm can simply be variations of non-malicious behavior.

Because CheckMate and InMate depend on assessment based on human behavior dimensions (E/D and I/D), the applications are not locked into signatures or differences from the norm. Instead, CheckMate and InMate detect truly suspicious or threatening behavior, even if it wasn't previously defined. Both applications have been proven to be capable of detecting new malicious activity not observed before with a low error rate.

As will be pointed out in later chapters, using AuBA even allows us to cross that fine line between predicting and influencing malicious behavior. Using principles of applied behavior analysis, AuBA-identified antecedents may be manipulated to influence subsequent behavior. This is an important point for security. Using AuBA for specific malicious behavior areas of focus gives you two options:

- Use improved methods to predict the behavior of the individual adversary
- Use AuBA methods to influence and change your adversary's behavior

Advantages of AuBA #7: Incorporating, Refining, and Expanding Behavior Principles for Global Security

AuBA is a unique, patented technology that incorporates new tools and methods to predict human behavior. Decades of unrelenting work to achieve accurate and validated predictive results on a consistent basis have resulted in the tools and methods presented in this book. Though AuBA is based on the basic sequence of antecedent-behavior-consequence that underscores the field of applied behavior analysis, we recognized early that many modifications and expansions would be required. However, after reviewing numerous methodologies in use, we found it was clear that the key to accurate prediction of future behavior was not embedded in the type of statistic used, any single method of machine learning or artificial intelligence applied, or the application of expert opinion captured through rules. Instead, the key was this basic antecedent-behavior-consequence sequence. In other words, *behavior in the past occurring in the presence of specific antecedent conditions that led to desired successful consequences would occur in the future in the presence of the same or highly similar antecedent conditions.*

As we have demonstrated and presented in AuBA-based patents, any number of pattern classification engines can be used to establish the patterns among identified antecedents associated with specific behaviors and the behaviors themselves. However, we have discovered that some methods work better than others. This dependency on classic behavior principles is what sets AuBA apart from other predictive methods that rely on computational methods alone. Even then, the behavior foundations of applied behavior analysis and the appropriate pattern classification methods are not enough. We still need to be able to identify specific antecedents that are associated with behavior in a global sea of potential antecedent conditions. Identifying antecedents to unruly behavior in the classroom has a primary focus in the classroom and maybe the home only. Terrorism, cyber threat, domestic bombings, and a whole set of other asymmetric warfare topics rely on global-based events that serve as antecedents. AuBA-based technology is required to identify relevant from non-relevant events and situations as likely antecedents in the midst of many thousands of variables that could be associated simply by chance.

Given this basic background, AuBA has extended applied behavior analysis in the following key ways:

- Introduced a methodology that moves the basic influence approach of applied behavior analysis to the prediction of future behavior

- Introduced a new automated tool (ThemeMate) for identifying key antecedents from numerous possible variables that preceded past events (behaviors) of interest

- Demonstrated that specific data arrays constructed by ThemeMate prepare basic data for prediction in 1/400th the time it takes manually

- Demonstrated that a back propagation network, an artificial neural network, works best in prediction as a general rule

- Demonstrated that because of the expansion to a global scale, advanced algorithms are necessary to identify subtle nuances that tie together antecedents, behavior, and consequences for prediction

- Demonstrated the special circumstances when approaches such as discriminant analysis, logistic regression, and multiple linear regressions should be used

- Introduced a fully automated application that constructs, optimizes, and validates predictive engines using ThemeMate output as input

- Demonstrated that the combination of ThemeMate and AutoAnalyzer results in expanding the antecedent-behavior-consequence sequence to levels appropriate for predicting malicious behavior on a global scale in as little as hours to one day, as opposed to many months

In homage to applied behavior analysis, I have labeled this new technology automated behavior analysis, or AuBA. This is similar to the acronym that could be used for applied behavior analysis, ABA. I intentionally planned this similarity because it is the scientific foundation of antecedent-behavior-consequence that separates AuBA from all other predictive methods. AuBA has expanded this basic concept and invented and integrated elements of the behavioral and computer sciences in such a way that accurate prediction can be achieved.

The tools developed that are capable of working across languages, automatically identify antecedents when they appear to be needles in a global haystack of variables, apply advanced pattern classification, and use automated best practices validation are absolutely necessary. Many decades have been spent reviewing and comparing other methods. In many cases, comparisons were truly independent and conducted by a third party. The results have demonstrated that the decision to keep AuBA as an extension of applied behavior analysis was sound and warranted. Developed for improving behavior in clinical, educational, and, more recently, business and other societal concerns as traffic and littering, AuBA has moved this basic behavioral approach to anticipating malicious behavior of adversaries.

Because of the expansion that now includes a global perspective, I hope that others, through research, theses, and dissertations, can continue to build on our discoveries and developments. Because of its reliance on basic behavior principles of applied behavior analysis, AuBA continues with a very strong and resilient scientific foundation.

Because AuBA is anticipatory in nature and has been designed to predict malicious intent and behavior, it is a natural next step to continue applying the technology in areas of security. From physical security to cyber security, our methods remain primarily reactive. We have to be hit with a new attack before security can react. Even if the attack is a known attack, security springs into action at the time of the attack. AuBA offers a technology that can begin the process of moving to a proactive approach, rather than a reactive approach. The accompanying DVD shows AuBA-based applications that are clearly anticipatory and proactive. It is my hope that the demonstrated applications may serve as a blueprint to start a more proactive security stance across the board.

In Summary

Mastering the behavior principles in this book will allow you to predict malicious behavior. At the same time, you will learn how to use the same behavior principles used for prediction to influence the individual adversary who creates the malicious behavior. AuBA automates and refines applied behavior analysis to improve the use of behavior principles to predict and influence behavior. AuBA tools increase accuracy and the speed with which you can build predictive models.

The individual is very different from a group and presents special challenges. However, much work has been completed with both individuals and groups to show how effective behavior principles are at predicting and influencing malicious behavior. This chapter introduces the major concepts. Later chapters and the analytical walkthrough on the DVD provide the details necessary for you to complete a thorough analysis of your own. Of prime importance is the difference between individuals and groups. The next chapter looks at groups in detail.

CHAPTER 8

Applying Behavior Principles: Predicting Group Malicious Behavior

During the process of developing AuBA, one of the significant discoveries made is that human behavior, whether generated by an individual or a group, may be studied and analyzed using similar behavioral methods. Because a group's individual members are bound together by common objectives, motivations, and sense of purpose, they will have a collective response to a set of antecedents, which working in combination prompt a specific malicious behavior. Over time, the realization of desired consequences to a group's acts reinforces and maintains the behavior while undesired consequences decrease the probability of future occurrence of the behavior.

In many ways, group behavior is more consistent than that generated by the individual; the adherence to the commonalties that forms the foundation of the group provides a common core that guides how all individuals respond within specific contexts. Often, the group may dress alike, have common nuances of language, and behave as one. In fact, the stated and unstated rules that guide adherence to the group core principles can lead to death if violated (for example, terrorist group, mafia, and so on). This chapter delves more deeply into analysis of malicious group behavior. The basic steps to conduct advanced behavior analytics are also introduced in this chapter.

Analyzing Threat

A consistent characteristic of a group engaging in malicious behavior is threat. *Threat* is perceived future harm. Basically, to a potential victim, harm may be realized in just two ways:

- The recipient perceives a high probability of physical or emotional pain or death that will be inflicted by the malicious person or group.

- The recipient perceives a high probability of loss of desired possessions or desired psychological state as a result of malicious actions of the person or group.

If a group has exhibited harmful, malicious behavior in the past, then the natural assumption is that the group could exhibit the behavior again. This keeps the potential for harm real.

The potential for harm is often realized as an event that confirms fear. Potential victims experience psychological effects of fear and may engage in steps to avoid being a victim. The avoidance of being a victim is one of the foundations of security. Protective measures may be put into place by security to protect others from harm.

WHEN HARM STRIKES

Al-Qaeda's past terrorist actions have been designed to inflict both pain and loss. The events of 9/11 resulted in thousands of lives lost and billions of dollars in damage, as well as significant disruption of national activities. As a result, protective measures were put into place at great expense to help decrease the probability of future significant malicious acts. For example, the cost and effort of combining many U.S. government agencies into the Department of Homeland Security (DHS) was a protective measure on the grandest of scales. The threat remains, and the DHS is better organized to deal with the ever-present threat from adversarial groups.

From an AuBA perspective, by submitting past accounts of malicious behavior to behavior analysis methodology, we can extract the components (antecedents, behavior, and consequences) that can lead to identifying predictive patterns. This analysis allows us to convert the potential for harm, or perceived threat, to a more precise likelihood of malicious actions in the future. Although protective measures have been taken since 9/11 and, in my opinion, security has increased in effectiveness, we still need a major shift from a more reactive to a more proactive stance. Predictive methods such as AuBA can help to achieve that transition.

Group Attempts to Inflict Harm and Damage

Malicious behavior that is harmful to others can be exhibited by an individual or a group. Earlier in this book, the obviously destructive behaviors of such individuals as Jeffrey Dahmer and Ted Bundy, among others, were presented. When we think of malicious groups, we tend to think of those groups that instill strong fear, such as street gangs, terrorist groups, advanced persistent threat (APT) hacking efforts, mafia, and Hell's Angels. The fear instilled by these groups is an amazing phenomenon; most people have not been direct victim of group actions, yet the perceived potential instills fear that makes all who experience the fear a psychological victim.

Al-Qaeda and other terrorist groups depend on and use fear as a means to achieve their goals. Terrorism is based on terror, and technology has assisted in spreading the behavior and message by means of televised images, immediate news reports, and images and reports beamed around the world as an event happens. As technology has advanced, we can now observe such events on our smartphones, iPads, and other devices. The ongoing events and the ability to actually observe effects in detail work to make terrorist behavior real to more people and help to instill and maintain fear.

So, the objective of malicious groups, such as a terrorist group, is to instill fear as a result of their actions. Maintaining fear keeps attention on the group's cause. However, if fear is going to be generated in others and maintained, then occasional malicious behavior must be exhibited. Therefore, malicious groups exhibit behavior as events across time. For example, the effects of 9/11 are still being felt a decade after the event.

> **NOTE** For a terrorist group who endeavors to instill fear in others, such as al-Qaeda, the more horrific the act exhibited, the less often malicious events have to occur to maintain that fear.

When Threats Turn into Actions

How does a malicious group convert threat to an actual malicious act? Reasons for any specific act include some combination of group motivation, guiding principles that form the foundation of the group, the presence of antecedents that set the stage for the malicious behavior to be exhibited, and the high probability that the behavior exhibited will result in desired consequences. When a specific combination of factors occurs, then a threshold is exceeded whereby a group acts.

Using al-Qaeda as an example, it is clear that U.S. presence on foreign lands and support for Israel in the struggle with the Palestinians are two of the major reasons for al-Qaeda terrorist-related actions. We might not like those reasons and prefer to believe that al-Qaeda simply cannot tolerate our love for freedom and rights of the individual, which is a better political reason for al-Qaeda's motivations, but it is not what guides actual terrorist actions. From a behavior analysis perspective, we must remain with facts and data. If a more proactive security approach is to surface, we must understand precisely the antecedent triggers that initiate action on the part of the adversary.

One of the advantages of a scientific methodology in analyzing adversary behavior is that it follows a scientific method. This method, described in detail in the DVD walkthrough, is based on sound methods of observation in which adversary behavior is defined, counted, and measured along with its associated antecedents and consequences. This method works to minimize bias and interpretations best left to politics. If we are going to predict adversary behavior accurately, then science must be the standard, not speculation or political expediency.

Terrorist groups tend to emphasize the foundation motivations of the group and externally related antecedent conditions until there is a match. For example, if the United States suddenly supports Israel in a new struggle with the Palestinians, then that context matches with the al-Qaeda's stated support of the Palestinian cause. We now have a combination of the group's often stated motivation with matching antecedent conditions. The stage is now set for retaliation.

Depending on the adversary, there is a typical *modus operandi* (method of operation) that follows. For all groups, there exists a common set of methods. This is a direct result of training in specific ways, specific skills within a group, and the desire to achieve specific types of effects. For example, Hezbollah follows two specific and distinct methods of operation. It exhibits either an international form of terrorism that consists of massive bombings or a more local assault method with AK-47s and other handheld weapons as an assault. From a cyber perspective, we see a common APT method that often consists of very deceptive phishing e-mails that invite you to respond in some way. The response invites the immediate transfer of malicious code to your hard drive. You may believe that you are responding to an e-mail from a bank, overloaded mailbox warning, or e-mail from human resources, but it is not real, and you are simply providing an avenue for an adversary to have access to your hard drive.

For groups such as Hezbollah and Hamas, their incidents are highly similar over time and occur at a high rate. For example, shelling, firing rockets, and exchanging sporadic firepower along with bombings fit the methods of operation. However, with a group like al-Qaeda, the events are more horrific and farther apart in time. The rate of terrorist activity appears to be related to the degree of devastation caused by the event. Groups will attempt to inflict harm at a rate that seems related to the wake of destruction left behind. If massive destruction was realized, then the next attacks would occur less often. It is as if massive attacks and the destruction that follows must be savored before the next attack occurs.

Attempts to Steal and Deceive

As stated before, adversary groups, whether state supported, terrorist groups, or cyber criminals, do not focus only on inflicting pain. They also cause their adversary to suffer the loss of something desired, which can be as devastating as inflicted pain. Using computers and networks as vehicles for theft is increasing at an alarming rate. Whether the objective is identity theft, theft of proprietary or highly technical trade secrets, passwords, user IDs, business information, or classified strategies, these relatively new forms of theft are extremely effective and felt deeply by the victims. As mentioned in Chapter 6, the alleged posting of more than a quarter million classified documents to WikiLeaks represents an entirely new form of theft, as well as motivation for conducting the theft.

Adversary groups are well trained in the art of deception. To successfully steal and not get caught requires considerable expertise, but that's still not enough; you must also be effective in hiding stolen property. To hide is to deceive. For this reason, when we analyze adversary behavior we focus not only on the behavior itself but also on the attempts to be deceptive.

When we typically think of an adversary, we think of attacks and inflicted pain and harm. However, we can expand the behaviors to analyze and gain additional insight into an adversary's behavior by studying how it deceives, how it hides, and how it escapes from committing an act against us if it is not a suicide mission.

Recently, we developed a phishing module for our CheckMate application (described in later chapters) to protect organizations from network phishing attacks. Using a very deceptive set of methods, the attacker works to make the recipient of an e-mail truly believe it is real and not suspect it as a simple cover to use methods to get the reader to click an attachment or a link. Of course, malware is inserted to the hard drive as soon as the link is clicked.

To develop the new human behavior–based phishing module, we studied examples of actual phishing attacks, and, using AuBA predictive tools, we extracted the common antecedents for this form of cyber attack. Although detectors are not used in favor of *behavior monitors* and must remain proprietary to prevent workarounds, it is fair to say that such behaviors as word choice in phishing versus non-phishing e-mails are very important. Remember, the AuBA ThemeMate tool is a very powerful text analysis and extraction tool. It is useful in many AuBA-related applications that are designed to differentiate between malicious and non-malicious behavior. Of course, the module will be updated on an ongoing basis to meet the challenges of creative and new attacks.

Obtaining Data to Assist in Understanding Adversary Behavior

As discussed briefly in Chapter 6, speculation as to the cause of adversary behavior is often after the fact and has the advantage of hindsight. By simply providing an explanation of past malicious behavior bolstered by a simple percentage of past incidents, the impression of prediction of human behavior is formed — but this approach does not result in accurate prediction of human adversarial behavior when subjected to scientific scrutiny. Speculation may lead to description, but not prediction under controlled conditions.

> **NOTE** AuBA represents the scientific method as it relates to the quantitative observation, analysis, understanding, and prediction of human behavior, as opposed to simple speculation.

As an example, consider Billy, whom the teacher has identified as disrupting the class by leaving his seat frequently. Frequently, speculation leads to unofficial determinations of attention deficit disorder (ADD) or attention deficit disorder with hyperactivity (ADHD), and it is far too easy to have medication prescribed for such behavior when, in fact, the causes may be more environmental and not medical. Of course, the appropriate approach in the classroom is to have a physical examination to rule out such problems as ADD or ADHD. The ideal combination is when the physician works closely with behavior analysts, teachers, aides, and school psychologists. In many cases, it is entirely possible that modification, often called *contingency management*, within the classroom can resolve behavior problems without resorting to medication. However, on occasion it is important to use behavior intervention in combination with medication.

Many scientific studies have demonstrated the power of contingency management in the classroom with such disruptive activity as frequent out-of-seat behavior both with and without the aid of medication. However, a solid behavior intervention program depends heavily on a true analysis of the behavior as it relates to the environment. This approach is federally mandated for all schools in the Individuals with Disabilities Education Act (IDEA). Currently, over 6 million special needs children receive services in the classroom through the federal IDEA law, and elements of behavior analysis are part of that law.

To conduct a behavior analysis, you need to conduct adequate observation. Although there are variations in how such behavior may be documented, a sound behavior-based program would use a variant of the following approach.

1. **Create an operational definition of the inappropriate behavior that you are interested in modifying.** For the trained behavior analyst working in the classroom, this is analyzing the high-frequency and very distracting out-of-seat behavior of Billy in the classroom. So, the definition could be: *Out-of-seat behavior is defined as any occasion of leaving a teacher-assigned seat without authorization during active classroom instruction.*

2. **Observe and measure the defined behavior under real-world conditions.** To ensure that our definition works, you need a minimum of two observers to watch Billy under real classroom conditions and count each occasion of

out-of-seat behavior. This is usually completed by sampling. For example, a time interval is defined and Billy is one of the students observed with the behavior counted for a segment, then another student and so on and back again to Billy, and the process of sampling continues. At the end of a classroom session, you have accurate counts of Billy's and other students' out-of-seat behavior.

3. **Repeat your observation over time.** Repeat your observation over multiple days. This will result in a baseline of counts across the days. A baseline is an indication of how frequent a behavior occurs before intervention is attempted. In this way, the behavior under intervention can be compared to the baseline to determine if there is a change when intervention started and if the change is in the right direction (for example, a drop in the frequency of out-of-seat behavior).

4. **Calculate the rate and refine the definition.** The counts of the separate observers are compared to determine inter-rater agreement. Typically, the counts conducted independently have to match at a minimum of 80 percent for each behavior recorded. If not, you make the definition clearer and repeat until the 80 percent requirement is met. Accurate inter-rater agreement ensures that the operational definitions are sound and will result in accurate counts. Once achieved, the definition works and one person can conduct the counts.

5. **Determine antecedents and modify behavior.** As you'll see later in the book, baseline counts form the basis for you to then introduce an intervention to modify Billy's behavior. Interventions can be found in the many classroom interventions texts that exist. However, if the observer has been careful to record the antecedents that preceded the out-of-seat behavior, then that is the clue as to what to modify. For example, if not assigned to a specific task for the entire class session, Billy tends to get out of his seat without permission and wander. An easy intervention is to ensure that his classroom time is complete with sufficient tasking that will last the entire classroom session. The other approach is to reinforce his "in-seat" behavior. For example, for every 5 minutes that Billy stays in his seat, the teacher simply walks by, checks the work, and acknowledges his working on the task. Later, the teacher may go to every 10 minutes, and then alter the time. In this way, Billy doesn't know when reinforcement is to occur, so must stay on task to get the attention.

The example provided focused on the individual, and generally, from an applied behavior analysis perspective, most intervention is on an individual basis. If one considers a classroom roughly to be a group, then intervention is often a series of individual programs with a distinctly different program for each child. This plan, under circumstances for children for special needs, is called the *individualized education plan* (IEP). To move from the very effective applied behavior analysis approach, which may go by many different names, to a global basis and adversaries that mean to place Americans in harm's way requires a significant alteration in methodology. However, it must be stated that the very powerful antecedent-behavior-consequence sequence that forms the basic foundation for applied behavior analysis forms the foundation for AuBA with all the refinements, extensions, computer science fusion, pattern classification, and consideration of antecedents on a worldwide basis made possible with the tools invented for AuBA. AuBA is basically applied behavior analysis on steroids!

> **NOTE** In the DVD walkthrough and in Chapter 20, the details and the nuances for this type of recording are presented. Chapter 20 provides a walk-through of the step-by-step methodology, while the DVD follows these steps but with a modeling example.

Moving from Applied Behavior Analysis and the Classroom to Global Adversary Behavior with AuBA

Although AuBA is relevant for analyzing any malicious, inappropriate, or distracting behavior, the intention is to go from the relatively constrained classroom situation, where applied behavior analysis is very effective, to such malicious behavior as terrorism, cyber threat, cyber attack, and state-supported cyber theft on a global basis. For these latter areas of focus, the AuBA extensions, refinements, and automation are required. Although the walkthrough on the DVD will show how these tough global behavior challenges can be conducted manually, it is extremely time-consuming, and AuBA is required to make true behavior analysis tractable. When you move to a global realm, you must modify the basic applied behavior analysis methodology specifically for global adversary behavior. Perhaps the biggest difference is that we do not have a terrorism equivalent to real-world classroom behavior from an observational perspective. We don't observe and count terrorist behaviors under real-world conditions, or we would stop it before it happened.

So, how do you observe, count, and record terrorist behavior? You use media accounts of past events. As described in Chapter 7, news articles are time machines. By gathering articles on past adversarial events of a certain type and group, you can extract the who, what, when, where, and how of past events because these common journalistic questions are answered in past articles. From these accounts you can define adversary behavior, extract antecedents and consequences, and count behaviors. By using AuBA methodology, we can predict the future occurrence of adversary behavior with acceptable accuracy.

The gathering of past articles includes using different search services. For example, my teams and I have used Google News, Nexis, Reuters, breaking CNN news, MSN, Yahoo! News, and so forth. The source is not as important as the ability of the search engines to retrieve specific news articles on past adversary events of interest. Just remember, some services are not free, but for a fee, they provide extensive and advanced search features. However, if these advanced features are not needed for retrieval, a service such as Google News is excellent.

Determining Who, What, Where, When, and How from Historical Data

You should observe several important guidelines for retrieving past accounts of adversary behavior for analysis using computerized search. These include:

1. **Use multiple sources:** When conducting searches, ensure that multiple accounts of the same event are retrieved from different news sources.

2. **Collect information on at least 30 events:** It is preferable to obtain news articles on more than 30 incidents of each type to be analyzed — for example, for Hezbollah, more than 30 examples of assaults and more than 30 examples of bombings.

NOTE If a group has not committed the basic 30+ examples per type of incident we prefer, use AuBASME (an approach presented in Chapter 9, which includes using subject matter expertise in lieu of missing data or presence of sparse data).

3. **Organize:** Place multiple examples of the same incident into the same file.

4. **Use unique file names:** Save each incident by a unique file name.

5. **Continue to build your data:** Once a corpus of examples of adversary behaviors is formed, it is essential to add to this corpus examples of adversary behavior not specifically associated with malicious behavior. For example, it is well known that Hezbollah engages in activities to build schools and hospitals. We call these examples *nons*, or non-malicious examples. We discovered decades ago that if our intent is to predict adversary behavior then we needed antecedents associated with both malicious and non-malicious behaviors. Then we can assess any daily context for an adversary as the presence or absence of antecedents associated with both malicious and non-malicious behavior. This is the real world, and the presence of both on any given day is a reality for all individuals and groups. Basically, if antecedents for malicious behavior far outweigh antecedents for non-malicious behavior, we would expect the occurrence of imminent malicious behavior. In reality, it takes the advanced pattern classification of AuBA to make that determination, but that is basically what occurs when a projection of malicious behavior is made by the technology.

NOTE The details of how to extract the basic who, what, where, when, and how will be presented in the walkthrough components of this book. However, at this point in the book it is important to realize that there are two basic ways of extracting and analyzing all the articles of past events. These methods are:

- **Manual:** A two-decade-long developed and tested methodology of extracting all relevant data manually will be presented.
- **Automated:** Use of patented AuBA tools will be presented with video clips of the use of these tools.

It is not the intent of this book to market the SAIC-acquired AuBA tools I invented. Rather, these tools are presented because of the order of magnitude decrease in modeling speed and significant reduction in human error that can be achieved using automation. Throughout the development of AuBA, I have worked to minimize the complexities involved in predicting future malicious behavior. It is not easy, but the process is characterized more by the need to follow simple steps as directed than by complexity. Whether you use the manual or automated methodologies presented, the result should be approximately the same. In direct comparison, the automation of AuBA outperforms the manual method. However, in comparison of the manual method to other statistical methods, the manual method is far superior because of the underlying behavioral foundation. It simply takes more than statistics to accurately predict future malicious behavior.

Behavior-Based Analytics

As you continue with the process of developing a corpus of articles of past events exhibited by an adversary and the process of analysis continues, you want to finalize the initial stage of data gathering and measurement (counting behaviors of interest) extracted from all raw news accounts in the corpus. This process is designed to capture the process whereby an analyst reviews past documentation of an adversary to draw out indicators, or antecedents. The end result in the patented behavior analysis process is a data array consisting of antecedents extracted as columns, examples as rows, and individual cells of the arrays scored with a 0 or a 1.

NOTE As you may (or may not) know, computerization basically equates to 0s and 1s. A bit in computer science is the basic unit of communication. Bits (binary digit) can be a specific most-basic state in computer science.

In AuBA design, I wanted to describe the presence or absence of a specific antecedent for each example used in the behavior analysis with the binary process that underlies all computer science. This would convert the world of indicators and examples to a format useful for advanced analytics.

The data array that results from our detailed analysis will be populated with 0s and 1s, whereby a 1 indicates the presence of an antecedent in that column being present for that behavior example as represented by a row. If the indicator in that column is not present for the example represented by that row, then the cell receives a 0. Figure 8-1 provides a view of a segment of a data array that includes extracted antecedents as columns; specific incidents, or behavior examples, as rows; and the completed 1s and 0s indicating the presence (1) of an antecedent for that behavior example or the absence (0).

	A1	A2	A3	● ● ●	An
Example1	0	0	1	1	1
Example2	1	0	1	1	0
Example3	1	0	1	0	0
Example4	0	0	1	0	0
Example5	1	1	0	1	1
Example6	0	1	0	0	1
● ●	1	0	0	1	0
Example n	1	0	1	0	1

Figure 8-1: A depiction of a portion of a data array for AuBA that includes antecedents, behavior examples, and presence (1) or absence (0) of an antecedent (columns) for any one example (rows).

The data array is an essential mechanism of the behavior analysis I described to convert the world of behavioral observation and measurement to the world of computer science and advanced behavior analytics. To those readers familiar with advanced statistics or pattern classification, this type of array should appear familiar. The array is essential because of the recent capability to conduct correlations and pattern classification with this type of behavioral data for the express purpose of prediction of human behavior. This data array provides the basis for extracting patterns that exist among antecedents and behaviors. To make the basic pattern discovery analysis complete, we must add outcome classes. For the data array, each row is an example of a specific adversary behavior, such as attack or no attack. This should be reflected in new columns added to the array at the end. For example, if we are going to predict attack or no attack, we would add two columns. The first could be "attack" and the second "no attack." For each behavior example (each row), we would add a "1" in the relevant column that described the behavior in that row. For example, if row 1 was a bombing, then we would enter a "1" in the attack column for that row and a "0" in the other column.

There is a very important point to be made for the reader. The key to the prediction of human adversary behavior has little to do with the statistical technique. Over the course of 25 years, I have worked with and compared notes with colleagues using Bayesian analysis, multiple linear regression, nearest neighbor processes, logit and probit models, discriminant analysis, and advanced applications of artificial neural networks to reach this conclusion: It is the basic behavior model that is responsible for prediction success — *not* the method of analysis.

As I pointed out in the patent process, it is apparent that you can substitute any pattern classification process. However, you must embrace the concept of antecedents, behavior, consequences, methods of antecedent extraction, and precise use of whatever pattern classification process to achieve accurate prediction.

Moving from Analysis to Prediction of Malicious Behavior

Prediction of adversary behavior requires high-quality data gathering, data extraction, appropriate pattern classification, and adequate validation. Shortcuts will lead to erroneous results and failure. Just like with weather prediction, many methods of predicting human behavior have surfaced — many as fanciful creations. However, when held to strict, independent party evaluation, few methods have shown true capability to predict repeatedly and accurately. I do not know of a single study that has demonstrated validation of predictive capability of humans in determining by speculation what may happen next. It is possible to get lucky and project that something will happen and the actual event and projection matches. But, if we check predictions weekly for six months and then determine accuracy in predictions as determined by a third party, then tested methods fail.

AuBA has been subjected to such scrutiny and has been shown to be over 80 percent accurate in determining if a specific group will attack or not, whether the target is going to be civilian or military, the general location, and the general approach that would be taken. Under DARPA funding, I was requested to train an application using AuBA to predict terrorist behavior of a specific terrorist group. Using the developed methods of AuBA, our team developed an application to process media and the AuBA analytic team produced weekly predictions. Once a week (Monday), weekly events in the media were processed, the application run, and predictions gathered. These predictions were forwarded to DARPA, which, in turn, forwarded them to a specific military intelligence group to determine accuracy across event, target, method of operation, and general location. After 24 weeks of weekly predictions, overall analyses of AuBA results revealed that the application was nearly 85 percent accurate on attack/no attack and almost 90 percent accurate on the remaining categories (that is, target, and so on).

To avoid criticism that our team could "just say attack and you would always be right," results were calculated using a confusion matrix approach. This means that true-positive, true-negative, false-positive, and false-negative rates were calculated. This covers all the bases. Within the 24 weeks of strict evaluation, there were actually 7 weeks in which there was no attack; AuBA predicted that for 6 of the 7 weeks the group would not attack, and it didn't.

NOTE To understand the meaning of what we've just covered, note the definitions for the following terms:

■ **True Positive (hit):** The application predicts a specific malicious behavior will occur, and it actually occurs.

■ **True Negative (hit):** The application predicts a specific malicious behavior will not occur, and it does not occur.

■ **False Positive (miss):** The application predicts a behavior will occur, but it does not occur.

■ **False Negative (miss):** The application predicts a behavior will not occur, but it does occur.

Figure 8-2 displays these definitions in table form. In the table, the predicted event occurs and the actual event follows. If there is a match, then it is a hit and the prediction was accurate. If it was a miss, then it was an error. There are only four ways to predict hits and errors using this approach, as the definitions and table show.

	Prediction	Actual Event	Result
True Positive	Malicious Behavior Will Occur	Malicious Behavior Occurred	Hit (Correct)
True Negative	Malicious Behavior Will Not Occur	Malicious Behavior Did Not Occur	Hit (Correct)
False Negative	Malicious Behavior Will Not Occur	Malicious Behavior Did Occur	Miss (Error)
False Positive	Malicious Behavior Will Occur	Malicious Behavior Did Not Occur	Miss (Error)

Figure 8-2: One of the primary ways in which accuracy is determined for predictive applications.

It is apparent that if a group attacks weekly, one could just predict attack every week and be 100 percent accurate. However, some groups may attack only once or twice a year (for example, al-Qaeda). Therefore, it is as important to predict no attack as (True Negative) accurately as actual attack (True Positive). In fact, a predictive application will perform at its best if it can predict both extremes.

The key to accurate prediction of adversary malicious behavior is to follow a designated, validated, and reliable methodology, such as AuBA or the manual version. Each point is relevant, depending on the objectives of the analysis. The following are the steps required to achieve accurate prediction:

1. Define the behavior of interest to predict.

2. Determine sources of past articles/documents describing past events of interest.

3. Search for and gather multiple electronic documents for each event and file by each incident, giving each file a unique identifier.

4. Extract antecedents.

5. Construct data array of antecedents by example and populate array with 1s and 0s in the precise manner described.

6. Conduct correlations to eliminate autocorrelation.

7. Determine outcomes to be predicted (for example, attack and no attack) and attach them to the array as the final columns. Remember, each row is an example of an actual event. Therefore, for this example, one of the columns will have a 1 and the other column will have a 0. If the incident in the row is an attack, the Attack column cell for that row would receive a 1 and the No Attack column would receive a 0.

8. Conduct correlations with output classes for analytical reports. By correlating each antecedent (columns) with output classes (Attack and No Attack), it is possible to determine which antecedents correlate highly with Attack and which antecedents correlate with No Attack.

9. Conduct pattern classification.

10. Validate using specific Leaving-One-Out cross-validation methodology using confusion matrix and Fisher's exact statistical significance; and once trained to accuracy criteria, use to predict adversary behavior by inserting into application and entering the presence or absence of antecedents.

NOTE You'll learn and follow the previous steps in greater detail in the walkthrough of this book. The steps have been validated to be effective. Step 8 is a special step you add to provide a descriptive, analytical report of a group that emphasizes the antecedent conditions to which they respond with attack/assault behavior or cyber attack or cyber theft. This type of analysis is useful when you want to consider a group's influences and motivations. For example, if you know that a specific mideastern terrorist group reacts to overt U.S. support of Israel's actions, which place Palestinians at a disadvantage, you can assume (with sufficient data) that the group is motivated to thwart the U.S. support of Israel under these conditions.

What Is Prediction?

Taking a behavior analysis perspective, a *prediction* about human behavior is a description of what behavior will be like in the future for a specific person or group. A scientific foundation means that behavior analysis prediction does not incorporate speculation or informed or educated guesses. It is certainly not prophecy, fortune-telling, or guessing. Prediction within the context of this book is also not a simple description of the past reoccurring in the future. Prediction must include how behavior may change in the future, although there may be similarities with the past.

AuBA and the manual version presented in this book result in reliable and valid prediction of specific human behavior. In this context, *reliability* is equated to reproducibility of results, or consistency. *Validity* refers to the ability of a method to measure what it is supposed to measure.

NOTE Human behavior changes on an ongoing basis, and a reliance on the past to predict future behavior is simply not reliable. If science could predict human behavior accurately, the highest priority would likely be warnings of malicious behavior that could harm us, including new forms of malicious behavior not previously witnessed or even detected. The inability to predict future behavior leaves us only with the past to know and the future to fear. From a security perspective, this places us in a reactive world where a defensive posture is the norm, and fear of future behavior is fueled by not knowing with some certainty what will happen next.

As previous chapters stressed, we desperately need a paradigm shift, moving from a primarily defensive and reactive stance to proactive protection. To become truly proactive is to become predictive. We currently face a variety of threats to our national infrastructure from a multitude of sources. Cyber threat, terrorist threat, and state-supported threat remain very high, and without the capability to predict future occurrences, we will remain reactive.

Information in this book is designed specifically to present a new approach to prediction of malicious behavior. This new approach improves proactive protective measures for threat based on a more solid and scientific foundation for reliable and valid predictive methods. To have a true paradigm shift, we must prove the accuracy, validation, and reliability of methods chosen. Following in the path of the validated, accurate prediction of terrorist group attack behavior with DARPA support presented in this chapter, methods and tools now exist for rapid predictive modeling.

EMPHASIZING METHODOLOGY AND NOT STATISTICS

The research and development path that ended with the validated predictive methods presented in this book was a long one littered with abandoned methods (statistical and otherwise) and procedures. The work completed using any combination of methods and statistical routines simply could not match the antecedent-behavior-consequence formulation of applied behavior analysis when combined with the appropriate additions, enhancements, and pattern classification.

Developing the methodology and validating applications existed as a true fusion of computer and behavioral sciences. Perhaps that is one reason why progress was lacking in the area of prediction of malicious behavior — few have worked diligently to marry these two sciences to result in desired effects. Both sciences are required, and neither alone can achieve the accuracy required to support a new proactive security approach.

Predicting Events before They Happen

There is a variety of types of prediction. For example, work has been completed to identify predictors that lead to college success. High school GPA and college entrance examinations do serve as predictors of college GPA and are used as college entrance requirements. It has been well established that children who have exhibited cruelty to animals have serious adjustment and behavior problems later in life (for example, Jeffrey Dahmer). Childhood cruelty to animals has surfaced as one of the primary indicators when compared to all other indicators researched. However, the search for predictors to be associated with attributes of success/failure in college is very different than the prediction of specific dynamic malicious behavior.

In the physical sciences, it is relatively easy to predict the occurrence of a celestial event. Astronomers are extremely accurate in predicting the return of Halley's Comet every 78 years or a lunar or solar eclipse. These scheduled and repeated events require only math and baseline movement of the celestial objects to project the new future path with high certainty. The events are not as dynamic as other physical phenomena such as earthquakes, volcano eruptions, tsunamis, or exact paths of hurricanes. Predicting human adversarial behavior is more like predicting the weather because such behavior is complex and depends on the complex interaction of group motivation, possible bylaws, stated targets, and antecedents to which the group will respond, and the consequences of terrorist group acts that are desired if the terrorist group behavior is to continue.

We don't need more experience with observations of complex human behaviors to be predictive. We just need a strong fusion of computer and behavioral sciences to form a methodological path suited for increased predictive accuracy and improved validation for complex human behavior. It is logical — if we are to predict human behavior more accurately, then we must start with a model of human behavior.

Examples of Real-World Event Prediction

Although there have been a variety of real-world AuBA predictive applications, one of the more dramatic is the development of the CheckMate and InMate network protection applications.

- **CheckMate:** Focuses on the identification of external threat to an organization by means of network protection.
- **InMate:** Focuses on the detection of insider threat on a network from within the organization.

Both are highlighted here for their ability to predict new, first-time attacks — a hallmark of the predictive applications and methodology emphasized in this book. Both will be covered in detail in Chapter 20 and in the walkthrough on the DVD.

Other applications emphasized in this book include:

- Prediction of real-world characteristics of those who operate avatars in virtual world games by measuring behavior of the avatar only (see Chapter 12)

- Monitoring of global cyber threat (Chapter 16)

- Identification of malicious intent from movement tracked by multiple physical sensor types, terrorism (see Chapter 9)

- As of late, specific cyber phishing attacks (see Chapter 2)

Of particular interest is the capability of the technology to anticipate behavior of both the malicious individual and the malicious group.

Predicting from Historical Information

The predictive methodologies to follow in detail fall into two general classes: (1) malicious behavior predictive models constructed from past accounts of malicious behavior, and (2) malicious behavior predictive models constructed in the absence of historical data or with significant missing data.

Following the basic steps provided in the previous section, "Moving from Analysis to Prediction of Malicious Behavior," the development of predictive models has worked equally well with individuals and groups. If the approach were to model based on historical events, then a representative sample of accounts of these past events would be gathered and the process started. If data were just too sparse or were missing, we would augment data with subject matter expertise using the AuBASME methodology.

One key to developing predictive models is selecting historical accounts prior to starting the process of antecedent extraction. By selecting the appropriate text accounts, you have total control on the front end. If you're using AuBA automation, then you submit these gathered text documents to ThemeMate, and the first-cut antecedents will be extracted when the corpus is processed. For this reason, you want to make sure examples provide a representative sample of group activity. For example, if a terrorist group exhibits 20 percent assault, 40 percent bombing, and 40 percent shelling, then a similar breakdown of incidents should be gathered. As always, the more incidents used in the analysis, the better. However, because typically you'll have a low number of incidents in asymmetric warfare, the technology presented is designed for what is called *small-n applications* — that is, designed for groups exhibiting a statistically small number of cases. This cutoff is approximately 30 cases in each category.

Predicting When Historical Data Is Rare or Missing

Often, asymmetric warfare groups have exhibited very few to no cases in a specific area. For example, to date, we have not had a CBRN attack within our

U.S. borders. So, how do you construct an AuBA predictive model? If you have too few historical examples from which to draw or if you have missing data because there has been no attack, you use the developed AuBA Subject Matter Expert (AuBASME) methodology. This approach is very different than the typical knowledge capture of rule-based approaches for capturing expertise.

AuBASME is a true fusion of AuBA pattern classification and the advanced data gathering developed for the AuBA data collection stages. The result, unlike rule-based or knowledge-based expert systems, is that AuBASME applications can process very large numbers of combinations of antecedents that represent new, first-time occurrences. The predictive engines then convert these new constellations of antecedents into predictions of behavior, which are most likely associated with the unique, first-time occurrence in a described context.

If we want security to be more proactive, we must be able to anticipate how malicious behavior changes over time — we simply cannot just expect the past to keep repeating itself. From a network protection perspective, if the past simply repeated itself, then after 20 years of writing rules to fuel our signature detection technology, we would be ahead and the technology would just be stopping past attacks as they reoccur. This is not the case. Simply speaking, the adversary has gained the upper hand by continually presenting new attacks.

How Do You Know the Predictive Application Works?

Proving that human behavior predictive applications work is essential. Science cannot take a researcher's word that an application does what it says; you must gather quantitative data to show that actual predictions are valid and reliable. The actual validation approach that demonstrates accuracy is affected by many variables, such as the number of examples you use, the required confidence level (how much confidence do you want in your results to use them), and so on. Because many groups statistically exhibit low numbers of attacks, you use a special form of cross-validation called leaving-one-out, abbreviated as L-1 here. L-1 allows you to make optimal use of every example available.

L-1 is the validation method used by the AuBA AutoAnalyzer tool when it constructs a predictive engine. The method consists of repeatedly training a pattern classifier on all examples but one and then testing the trained classifier on the one withheld case. The process is repeated until every case has served as a withheld case for testing. Accuracy is the average accuracy across all training-test sets. For example, if you had 70 examples of terrorist behaviors (35 terrorist attacks and 35 non-attack), you would have exactly 70 training-test sets. Each training set would have 69 examples and 1 test example. Each of the 70 sets has a different test case, so that at the end of the process every case has served in both the training set and the test set. The average accuracy across all of the training-test sets provides a statistical accuracy estimate that is highly similar to an accuracy rate using many more cases. Our experience is that we want to see an average accuracy of 80 percent to 85 percent true-positive and true-negative rates with L-1 validation before we move to testing the application in the real world.

Given that you follow methodological steps as described, you can move toward a more predictive stance. By being able to better anticipate malicious tactics, you can determine how best to use existing limited security resources to provide improved protection.

Advantages of AuBA #8: Automating Behavioral and Computer Sciences to Ensure Success

AuBA is a true automated fusion of the behavioral and computer sciences. There were a number of reasons for automating this new technology. Among the reasons were the following:

- After decades of work to extend applied behavior analysis to the world of predicting malicious behavior on a global scale, as opposed to a local clinical scale, we discovered that the manual extensions and refinements were valid and reliable but time-consuming.

- Because of added features to identify global antecedents and to narrow these to actual predictors of malicious and non-malicious behavior, there was increased probability of error because of the complexity of the process.

- The prediction of adversarial behavior on a global scale proved to be extremely challenging and required the invention of new technology to achieve automation.

- Automation would be required to decrease the development of a predictive model to a fraction of the time it took to develop a manual model using the new methodology.

The end result has been the invention of two tools, ThemeMate and AutoAnalyzer, that would:

- Decrease the model development time that would include best practices validation methods to reduce the need for advanced staff skilled in validation and statistical methods by automating all pattern classification procedures and routines.

- Decrease the error that could be introduced by manual, time-consuming methods that included the automation of all key antecedent extraction from text, adding AuBASME when data was missing or sparse, automatic construction and population of the data array from days with 20 percent error to 1/2 second with no error, automatic reduction of antecedents to the most predictive set, and automated best practices cross-validation.

- Achieve three patents on new hybrid tools and methods to conduct automated prediction of malicious behavior in a valid and repeatable manner.

- Reduce model development time to a 1/400th the time required to conduct adversarial modeling, and construct cyber applications that could conduct 70 to 100 million assessments per day in real time on a network to protect against cyber threat.

- Be tested across cyber, terrorism, and many other adversarial application areas with success.

The automation makes AuBA a viable approach to construct predictive models quickly (within one day). The end result of a valid approach to prediction combined with the reduction of error means that we have the beginning of a valid, more proactive approach to security. Given that AuBA can work across languages and can automatically find antecedents in a manner that has been shown to be more effective than human extraction and that the predictive models have been validated across many different adversarial domains, it makes the approach a necessary tool for those seeking to anticipate future behavior of the adversary. That we have developed models from scratch, from text to a validated predictive engine within the context of a one-hour briefing, underscores the power of the approach. It did take many years to develop the hybrid technology, but now it is ready for use.

In Summary

Behavior analysis works as well with groups as with individuals. Common ideas, motivations, lifestyles, targeting, and distaste tie groups together for the same enemy. The commonalities of a group works to make the group behavior more consistent and more resistant to change where the individual adversary has more latitude to express unique targeting behavior and may be more changeable over time.

Predictive methods presented in this book have a strong scientific and quantifiable foundation and have been validated across a number of different adversarial conditions. State-of-the-art validation has been used for the AuBA methods to develop predictive models from historical cases and for situations where there is sparse or missing data or no actual historical precedent.

Applying a Predictive Methodology: From Principles to Practice

To this point, the book has presented an introduction to the many facets of predicting malicious behavior. We have covered individual and group modeling, as well as examples of individual and group malicious behavior. Although some of the high points of modeling malicious behavior have been introduced, this chapter will provide more detail. Two basic approaches will be described: a manual approach and full AuBA, which is primarily automated. The manual approach does incorporate the use of tools, particularly in using software for pattern classification, but because of the extent of AuBA's automation, AuBA allows for very rapid modeling. However, both approaches lead to the development of predictive software we call *engines*. Engines, when placed within software applications, can make predictive decisions within 50 microseconds, or 20,000 predictive decisions per second, on an ongoing basis. The accuracy and speed of these predictive engines provide the capability to achieve the paradigm shift needed to achieve a more proactive security stance. In this chapter, I will provide another level of detail as to how we can accurately predict malicious behavior in real time.

Construction of Predictive Models

Chapter 8 listed the basic steps required to move from defining malicious behavior to predicting it to developing an actual predictive engine. The process was developed over repeated development trials and by using different topics until results were consistent, repeatable, and proven valid. To simplify predictive behavioral modeling a bit more, we can divide the process into key areas. These areas are:

- The problem to solve
- Gathering and formatting input data
- Model development and data processing
- Validation and testing

As opposed to the steps in modeling presented in the previous chapter, these key areas provide an overview of considerations to keep in the forefront as steps are followed. In this section these four guiding areas will be briefly presented and then followed by more detail in the remainder of the chapter.

The Problem to Solve

It is essential to clearly define the malicious behavior that will be the focus of the behavioral model to be constructed. The definition is critical because it should guide all the other processes. From selection of articles describing past behavior or the selection of subject matter experts (SMEs) to contribute their knowledge to replace missing or sparse data, selection should not be taken lightly. Articles and SMEs must be right on target with the topic. Articles must be complete and from reputable sources, and to put it bluntly, you need to use SMEs for which there is general agreement on their deep level of expertise, not ones who are self-defined SMEs.

DEFINITION A *subject matter expert* (SME) is a person who is considered by others as an expert in a specific domain of interest or study and who can describe all major points of that domain, as well as the finer facts and nuances underlying the topic.

A definition does not have to be complex. It can be as simple, such as *The purpose of the predictive model is to provide a warning when terrorist group X will attack.* However, that simple definition reduces what is called *engineering creep*; that is, the focus of the application drifting to do something other than what is needed.

Gathering and Formatting Input Data

To begin the modeling process, it is essential to collect examples of past behaviors. These past accounts of behaviors should include the contexts under which such behaviors occurred. For example, any one example of behavior should have within the text what environmental context occurred before the behavior of interest and what consequences followed. Newspaper articles of past events are important. Journalists are trained to focus on the who, what, where, when, and how of an event. These elements work to form the context of a specific behavior within which we will find antecedents and consequences.

It probably goes without saying, but news articles are about past behavior. However, they contain the information necessary to predict future behavior. Again, contrary to popular belief, the prediction of future behavior does not simply focus on past behavior; rather, the prediction of behavior focuses on the antecedent and consequence associations of past behavior. Behavior occurs within a context, and if that or a highly similar context occurs in the future, we tend to see the occurrence of behavior associated with that context. For this, past news articles are perfect for antecedent and consequence extraction surrounding behaviors of interest.

Historical Events

If there are sufficient news articles or similar text documents describing past events that fit the definition of the model to be constructed, then conduct searches using such services as Google News, Nexis, Reuters, and so on. Factual articles are needed much more than opinion pieces, op-eds, or speculative articles. Facts are needed, including:

- **Who** was involved
- **What** behavior occurred
- **Where** the event took place (specifically)
- **When** the event took place (ensure local time and date)
- **How** the event unfolded

These characteristics of news articles will form a corpus of text from which behaviors and precursor conditions may be extracted, as well as consequences of the malicious behavior.

AuBASME

If data is sparse or is simply missing and you are attempting to add subject matter expertise according to guidelines for use of AuBA methodology, it is essential that real SMEs be incorporated. How can we tell a real SME from a self-appointed SME? It is not as difficult as it might seem.

First, scrutinize qualifications. If the intent is to use behavioral science SMEs, do *not* use SMEs describing themselves as behavior experts but use those who have qualifications in other unrelated fields. Likewise, if computer science experts are needed, make sure their qualifications are in computer science.

Second, scrutinize experience. Make sure their experience has been in the very specific area you need based on the definition of the model you want to construct. For example, looking back at our definition, ensure that the content domain expert is truly an expert in the terrorist group targeted for the model. Remember, in very rare cases, there are SME crossovers, meaning that the person may have one of two specialties by training and a second by experience. In this case, the presence of publications in peer-reviewed journals, exceptional performance or lifetime achievement awards, and special recognition from peers in the field for which expertise is claimed are clues to support the presence of real expertise.

Model Development and Data Processing

As I have noted earlier in the book, one of the discoveries that we have made is that there are many similarities between the prediction of malicious behavior and dynamic prediction in the physical sciences like weather. This is an important analogy. We do not expect weather prediction to be an easy process whereby we merely run a simple computer routine and receive a prediction that will be accurate repeatedly over time. Therefore, we should not expect to run a simple computer routine to obtain accurate predictions of malicious behavior over time. Both sciences require a disciplined approach with validated steps. Only if steps are followed are reproducible results are likely to be obtained.

The prediction of malicious behavior is not simply the result of applying a specific statistical technique to past data. Why? Statistics, generally speaking, are very good at describing the nuances among independent variables (the predictors) and dependent variables (what is to be predicted) for past data. If human behavior actually was nothing more than behavior of the past being repeated in the future, then this approach would be excellent for predicting malicious behavior. However, it doesn't work that way. Human behavior is characterized by alterations, variations, and an actual intent to escape normal, boring patterns. Since statistical approaches, regardless of method, cannot correctly predict this future alteration and variation and merely project the past into the future, they cannot be reliable.

The difference between AuBA methods developed and presented in this text and the basic statistical approach is the operant psychology and antecedent-behavior-consequence foundations of human behavior that have been demonstrated in many hundreds of thousands of clinical and research articles generated internationally over the past 70 years. The patented methods presented in this text started with this basic scientific foundation of human behavior and are expanded to include predictive methods, like those applied to malicious behavior for specific security applications.

NOTE Prediction of human behavior must begin with the basic understanding of human behavior — not statistics.

The methods presented here have included the foundations of applied behavior analysis and operant psychology. These were then expanded to move the foundation more toward a predictive methodology. These new extensions have been extensively validated and are now part of behavior analysis methodology. By following the steps presented, particularly with AuBA automated features, these additions are included in the data processing. In short, if you wish to construct a prediction application for malicious behavior, the steps provided should be followed closely.

Validation and Testing

Validation and testing are important parts of the process to establish a predictive application. There are many books and research articles describing validation of pattern classification applications. There is much agreement across these texts, and I would refer you to any texts describing Leaving-One-Out (L-1) cross-validation for small-n applications for more information on this sort of validation. This is the best descriptor of the validation approach used for small-n behavior analysis applications. Small-n simply means a small number of examples of behaviors or actual events. What is small? If we have two categories to predict, such as attack or no attack, we want a minimum of 30 examples in each category. When we work with a number of cases this small, it is called a small-n application. Of course, larger numbers are preferred. But, we would not hope that terrorist groups have more attacks to have larger numbers!

CROSS-REFERENCE See Chapter 8 for a brief description of L-1 validation methodology.

The reason we use small-n validation methods is that we have discovered that by far the vast majority of applications needed for determining what may be an adversary's next behavior is based on modeling a very small number of historical cases. Therefore, only a small number (n) of cases are available. This is one of the primary reasons why we may add subject matter expertise. However, if we do happen to have large-n, then the technology handles that equally as well.

What Is Needed: The Behavioral Methodologies

Behavioral psychologists, like me, place weight on how the person or group interacts with the environment. This interaction is in the form of antecedents that precede the behavior of interest and the consequences resulting from that behavior. However, it is extremely difficult to "get inside the head" of another person. In fact, how many of us actually even know ourselves? By identifying antecedents that are repeatedly associated with specific behaviors in the past, we can expect similar behavior in the future under the same or similar conditions. If the behavior occurs in the presence of the antecedents and the consequences of the behavior are favorable to the perpetrator (success), then the behavior is likely to occur again. If consequences are not desirable, then the behavior is less likely to occur. Therefore, our first objective is to identify the relevant antecedents and consequences associated with each previous occasion of the behavior of interest occurring in the past.

A second major feature of the approaches presented here is predictive analytics. Applied behavior analysis and operant psychology are not really used as predictive methodologies. For the most part, applied behavior analysis studies involve establishing a baseline of inappropriate behavior to use as a measure to compare with the effects of an intervention. If the inappropriate behavior decreases as compared to the baseline, then we can assume that the drop may have been a result of the intervention. However, if we remove the intervention and the behavior returns to baseline levels, we are more confident that the intervention was the cause of the change in behavior. However, to convince ourselves, we would add the intervention one more time. If the inappropriate behavior decreased during the second intervention, then we can assume that the intervention worked. This addition and removal of intervention is called an *ABAB design*, where *A* = baseline and *B* = intervention.

There are many different within-subject designs that go far beyond the scope of this book. *Within-subject* basically means that all data are generated by a single person. Because applied behavior analysis has a clinically based and educationally based foundation, the focus is often on developing a baseline of a single individual's behavior to alter, and then applying an intervention. However, after this first step, repeated baseline and intervention is required to ensure that the effect observed when the first intervention was applied after baseline is not the result of something else occurring just by chance at the same time. There are also alternative designs that may be used to accomplish the same purpose. Those interested may want to search for "multiple baseline design" or "alternating treatment design" to explore clinical experimental design alternatives to the ABAB design. However, the point here is that the basic use of applied behavior analysis (and related disciplines) is intervention to either decrease the incidence of inappropriate (or maladaptive) behavior or increase the incidence of appropriate (or adaptive) behavior. AuBA, although based on the basic behavioral foundations of behavioral psychology, required a multitude of additions, inventions, and enhancements to develop the current predictive methodology presented in this book.

The AuBA predictive analytics process has features that exceed typical statistical approaches. However, I contend that most statistical approaches could be useful if combined with the behavioral foundations presented — this is the nature of the patented AuBA process. The AuBA behaviorally based methodology differs from other approaches because it fuses pattern classification of computer science with behavioral foundations associated with behavioral psychology. Again, it is not the statistical approach that is responsible for accurate forward prediction of malicious behavior. It is the patented manner in which AuBA integrates pattern classification with antecedents, behavior, and consequences.

Using the Manual Approach

Prior to AuBA, I developed a manual approach that was effective in predicting malicious behavior. The advantage of developing the manual approach first was that each aspect of the modeling process could be investigated in great detail. R&D, if done properly, is not a straight track from beginning to end. Instead, it is more like a back-road trip from point A to point B where the path is not clear and the driver must feel his way based on success or non-success at a multitude of unscheduled waypoints. All scientists will recognize this analogy. As reported by many sources, Thomas Edison used more than 6,000 different substances for a filament until he tried carbon and made the lightbulb as we know it a successful invention.

The manual process is time-consuming but provides predictive models that are accurate, have been validated, and can be replicated. Science must consist of these criteria. If effects cannot be replicated, then an application is a failure.

The predictive modeling steps provided in Chapter 8 may be completed manually or with automation provided by SAIC's AuBA tools. Although the manual method achieves similar results to the automated process of AuBA, the automated methodology allows modeling at a rate of 400 times faster than the manual method and eliminates many sources of error. Both manual and automated methods have acceptable accuracy; however, AuBA achieves higher accuracy. The higher accuracy demonstrates that automation is not just for speed; it also reduces human error.

In the clinical setting, I used a *Behavior Analysis Form*, or BAF, to capture examples of the behavior of interest (an example follows). The form was divided into three columns: Antecedents, Behaviors, and Consequences. The clinician or analyst would use the form to capture information regarding a targeted inappropriate behavior. At the same time, all potential antecedents would be captured in the Antecedents column (for example, location, time of day, others in the vicinity, activities occurring, and so on) and all consequences occurring after the behavior were captured in the Consequences column (for example, client was reprimanded, others left, client was ignored, and so on).

Example BAF

ANTECEDENTS	BEHAVIORS	CONSEQUENCES
Location	Aggressive behavior: hitting, kicking	Client was reprimanded
Time of day		Others left
Others in the vicinity		Client was ignored
Activities occurring		

I used the BAF recording approach in the world's largest institution for the developmentally disabled in the early 1970s (Lincoln State School in Lincoln, Illinois) to develop a new treatment to prevent fatalities due to a severe eating disorder and to stop extremely aggressive behavior leading to serious harm and injury to others in a special program run for the most dangerous of the over 5,000 residents. An example of the latter is the case of Beth — who would sneak up on others and attack by biting and, occasionally, severing body parts. In both cases, treatment solutions were discovered as a direct result of BAF recordings. The behavior was completely gone after treatment.

These cases are tough ones, and solutions are not immediately apparent. The reader is referred to Chapter 20 to review such a case. Beth was a severe biter in an institutionalized setting. The principles of behavior analysis were used to solve this case.

The manual approaches were developed over many years using populations such as those with severe and profound mental retardation (as previously mentioned) and took place in mental-health-related settings. The common thread across all settings was aggressive and dangerous behavior in situations where typical psychological assessment and often direct contact was not possible. Settings contributing to the manual method included clinical treatment development at the following locations:

- Evansville State Hospital (Evansville, Indiana)
- Lincoln State School (Lincoln, Illinois)
- Florida State Hospital (Fort Lauderdale, Florida)
- Sunland Center at Miami (Miami, Florida)
- Mental health day treatment and residential/locked settings at the Florida Mental Health Institute, University of South Florida (Tampa, Florida)

For all these varied locations and treatment domains, I either directed treatment development or served as the primary researcher. These settings are mentioned highlight the fact that methods were developed from direct clinical observation and not simply conceptualized from an academic base. These settings were real, behaviors were dangerous, and we had to develop methods that worked.

Later, working for the U.S. government, I found it was apparent that it would not be possible to meet face-to-face with threatening adversaries. In many cases, these adversaries simply were unknown. Therefore, developing threat models that were valid and replicable from a scientific perspective required variations of the BAF and led to new methodology to predict and influence malicious behavior.

The manual methods presented have been refined through experience with extremely dangerous populations. In the U.S. government positions, threat was palpable, and the developments leading to automated behavior analysis methodology as it developed provided improved insight into adversarial behaviors and what to anticipate. This early influence of the clinical BAF has been incorporated into a modern-day fusion of computer and behavioral sciences. My clinical experience was absolutely essential to the early development of what is now accurate malicious behavior predictive capability.

Using Tools to Assist the Manual Approach

Computer tools are still useful in the manual behavior analysis methodology. Although these tools are not nearly as sophisticated as AuBA development and enhancements that automatically emulate the human reading and antecedent extraction process, the manual methods benefit greatly from such tools as Excel, artificial neural networks, pattern classification, and statistical packages.

For example, once the antecedents in text accounts of past behavior are identified and isolated, they are placed in a data array. The array has extracted antecedent candidates across the top as columns, and examples of behavior (incidents) as rows. *Antecedent candidates* are extracted precursors that are events and situations that occurred before the behaviors of concern. Later in the AuBA process, these "candidates" are automatically reduced to the most predictive set of antecedent variables. These data arrays can be very big. For example, if 200 antecedents have been extracted and there are 50 examples (rows), the array will comprise 50 rows by 200 columns, which equals 10,000 cells. If each cell has a 1, which represents the presence of that antecedent for that example, or a 0, which represents an absence of that antecedent for that example, then it is very clear that a spreadsheet is useful for the manual method. See Chapters 8, 14, and 15 for a more thorough description and examples of the data array.

The data array lends itself very well to correlations, descriptive statistics, or more advanced statistics. For correlations or descriptive statistics the reader would be wise to attach the Analysis Toolpak that comes with Excel but is not installed automatically. It is there! It is on the disk that comes with Microsoft Office, or it is already on the hard drive; you simply need to click on the Toolpak to have it show up as an option. In the walkthrough, we will show why Excel and the Toolpak are such important tools for the manual method. Refer to Chapter 15 for a description of the correlational aspects of the data array and a visual representation.

For more advanced techniques (although not needed for most applications), I recommend an IBM product, SPSS, previously known as the Statistical Package for the Social Sciences. SPSS presents a solid set of statistical tools. Others include MatLab and SAS, though I am partial to SPSS.

Excel

If you are not familiar with Excel, it is the Windows Office spreadsheet application that comes with the Microsoft Office products suite. Until recently, there were limits on the number of rows and columns you could insert/use. Occasionally, these limits would cause a problem if a particularly large set of antecedents and behaviors was being used. However, with the recent upgrades, you are not likely to approach the row and column limits. Excel can now handle up to 1,000,000 rows and 16,000 columns. If you made a data array with 1/4 inch cells, that would be a worksheet 3.95 miles long and over a football field wide (333 feet) with 16 billion cells — that should fit any data needs you might have, although we have exceeded it once! Please see `http://msdn.microsoft.com/en-us/library/ff700514.aspx` for a description of Excel extensions that were made with Excel in 2010. If you purchased Microsoft Office in 2010 or later, you have the extensions in the software you purchased or that came with your PC. The extension is nothing short of amazing, as are most technological advances.

Once the antecedent and behavior examples data array has been established, it is necessary to populate the array with 1s and 0s. As described, a 1 means the antecedent is present and a 0 means an antecedent is not present for any one cell in the array. Once the array is populated there are a number of operations that can be completed on the spreadsheet to assist the malicious behavior modeling. In the manual process, populating the array with 1s and 0s is the most time-consuming part of the process. Although time-consuming, it is essential to focus so that errors are minimized during this process. Because patterns will be calculated from the data array, errors will occur in pattern classification of the array if it is not populated adequately.

You also will want to check the array for antecedents that correlate so highly that it is best to merge them. For example, if any two antecedents correlate at 0.90 or higher, this means that the 1s and 0s in any two columns are highly similar. Therefore, significant differences between the two columns are not present and both are nearly redundant in terms of information provided. I have seen as many as five or six antecedents correlate highly enough to merge them into one antecedent column. Once this step is completed, we focus on the rows in the correlation matrix that include correlations between each antecedent and each outcome. This shows how each antecedent correlates with each outcome. For example, if our outcomes are *threat* and *no threat*, we can determine with which outcome each antecedent correlates. This demonstrates "generally" how the antecedents differentiate between the two outcomes — some antecedents correlate highly with threat, and others correlate with no threat. These correlations are not sufficient to make predictive decisions — for this we need true pattern classification. However, it does provide a quick view in which direction (threat or no threat) each antecedent lends its primary strength. See Chapter 15 for a description of this step.

Statistics and Correlation

The user would do well to check the many "how-to" books on the use of Excel. Don't shy away from the *Excel for Dummies*–type books. They are excellent and can teach you both the basic and the advanced features in a very short time. For example, they cover the use of the Analysis Toolpak, as well as pivot tables and graphing. The graphing package of Excel is more than suitable and includes line graphs, bar charts, stock charts, scatter plots, pie charts, and so on. As I mentioned previously, I am something of a student of the stock market and find the Analysis Toolpak and the advanced statistical features to be very useful. Often, people purchase expensive statistical and graphing packages when the Excel package that comes with Microsoft Office will fit all your needs. Excel is more than adequate to conduct initial behavior analysis.

However, it is important to remember that statistics, as useful as they may be, simply cannot be relied on as the primary method to predict malicious behavior. For example, anomaly detection as a cyber-based approach to detecting malicious activity relies on establishing a statistical characterization of a network as a baseline. Then, statistical deviations from this baseline are designated as malicious. Although, deviations are non-normal by definition, this does not equate to malicious activity; it simply says that flagged activity is sufficiently different from the baseline. It should be obvious that flagged activity consists of two basic types: non-normal malicious and non-normal non-malicious. To date, anomaly detection has not demonstrated the capability to differentiate between the two; hence, the result is an inordinate number of false positives (saying that activity is malicious when it is non-malicious).

Last, anomaly detection, like signature detection, is reactive because it must continually compare activity to a baseline that was established in the past. In short, whether the domain is cyber, asymmetric warfare, terrorism, or any manner of threat, statistics provide excellent baselines to which we can compare behavior in the future. But that's all they are. There are no basic behavioral foundations included in the approach, and then little can be said about how the behavior will change in the future and what precursors will foretell malicious activity. Statistics are about characterizing the behavior, and human behavior prediction is about recognizing events and situations that set the stage for malicious activity to then follow.

Automated Behavioral Modeling Tools

To develop an automated behavior analysis methodology that could reliably and accurately predict malicious behavior, it was first necessary to develop a manual method. To develop the manual method, a study was undertaken to determine how typical analysts would identify precursors. After considerable study, it was determined that most analysts identify key indicators by repetition.

For example, with the use of the BAF we would review one to two weeks of recorded antecedents, behavior, and consequences (ABCs) to determine highly similar events and situations that occurred just prior to the behavior. By listing the frequently occurring events and situations proceeding and following the behavior of interest, likely antecedents and reinforcing consequences would surface.

The exploratory process of identifying antecedents and consequences eliminates clinical biases.

WARNING When you first observe malicious behavior, you form a first impression as to causes of the behavior. This first impression should be controlled at all costs; it is seldom accurate. If you begin with the answer, then all investigation and observation that follows is geared toward confirming that initial hypothesis. This process causes many clinicians and analysts to go off track and miss basic causes.

By recording events and situations in the environment that repeatedly occur just prior to and as a consequence after the behavior of interest, you can start to significantly understand the behavior. Still, almost always, surprises occur.

This clinical process was used as a foundation to develop the manual method for adversarial malicious behavior. Instead of using the paper version of the Behavior Analysis Form (BAF), an electronic version was created. Using a database, fields were created for antecedent observations, behavior observations, and consequences. However, as adequate as the manual method is, it is time-consuming. It might take weeks to months to develop a true predictive model.

NOTE The development of the manual method made it obvious that analysts skilled in foreign languages could construct data arrays using text in their language of interest. This led to the author developing ThemeMate by emulating the cognitive process that could construct the data array by extracting antecedents in text across languages. Given that the developing AutoAnalyzer application could construct and validate a predictive engine from the ThemeMate data array, this meant that predictive models could be constructed in any language once ThemeMate was set to process that language. Validation tests revealed that predictive models could be equally as accurate using either English or Arabic only.

Automating this complicated process would be extremely involved and would have to do a number of things not yet accomplished. For example, the designed technology would have to be able to read text examples on a specific topic gathered for analysis. In the reading process, the technology would have to be able to extract antecedent events, and to be maximally useful, read text in different languages, and complete extraction for a data array across these languages.

Constructing a data array manually was very time-consuming and included populating the cells of the array; any automation would have to be capable of automatically constructing and populating the array from extracted data. This would eliminate errors in data entry and, as a result, likely increase accuracy. Finally, the pattern classification process developed over many years would have to be totally automated. Taking the data array as input, the automation would have to construct different classifiers, validate them using best practices cross-validation, provide statistical significance, show correlations, and present a report to show the effectiveness of the self-selected, best performing classifier in predicting malicious behavior. Estimates revealed that if these features could be invented, there would be an approximate savings of time in constructing predictive models by 400 times. For example, with the automation, a model could be constructed in 1 work day versus 400 work days (5 staff working for 3–4 months to complete and validate a model). Needless to say, this would be a feat.

Automated Behavior Analysis (AuBA)

To begin with the punch line, AuBA was developed and contains all of the features mentioned. To totally automate the clinical process was as difficult as anticipated. To automate all of the features and enhancements to basic applied behavior analysis and result in a truly predictive technology that could work across languages, automatically construct and populate data arrays, and automatically construct and validate pattern classifiers for prediction proved extremely difficult — but doable.

To totally duplicate and enhance the manual process of behavior analysis and extend it to the prediction of human behavior required the invention of two tools: ThemeMate and AutoAnalyzer. ThemeMate duplicates the processes involved with basic applied behavior analysis and adds considerable features, such as automated extraction of thematic antecedents, data array construction, capability to work across language, automated population of the array, and many others not associated with typical clinical processes. However, to actually predict malicious behavior, we had to develop AutoAnalyzer. By actual metrics, this is approximately 400 times faster than the manual modeling process — our initial estimate of time savings proved to be accurate. However, the manual process is still useful and may be the best way to learn how the automated process works. Because AuBA model building is so fast with the tools, the many steps required occur very quickly. By going through steps manually, one has a better understanding of all features and steps involved in the automated process.

I invented the two tools to be purposely separate since, for many applications, ThemeMate alone can be useful. This is especially the case for reports in which the writer of the report doesn't have unlimited time to read, pull out the detail, and summarize. This tool produces an output that summarizes and analyzes. For applications in which true prediction of malicious behavior is required, the output of ThemeMate can be entered into AutoAnalyzer, and result in an optimized pattern classifier. In terms of time required, we have provided briefings on AuBA for the government in which we process documents with ThemeMate and AutoAnalyzer while briefing and have a predictive model from scratch within 60 minutes, including time to present the completed model in operation. Although easy to use as tools, detailed descriptions of the operation of ThemeMate and AutoAnalyzer are best left to the patent descriptions (*Method of and Apparatus for Automated Behavior Prediction — Gary M. Jackson inventor, assigned to SAIC*).

Introducing ThemeMate as a Predictive Tool

When ThemeMate is provided with an entire document, it can summarize the document and automatically identify X number of key points. You can set the key features at any number, but it defaults to three. When compared to humans reading a document and selecting the most important points in the text and simultaneously presenting the document to ThemeMate, both methods often select the identical three (or however many) key points. However, it takes ThemeMate only about 1 minute to complete its task, and it can be in multiple languages. Because ThemeMate works by processing text with specific algorithms and not language understanding, it takes only 2 weeks to ready ThemeMate for a new language. Then ThemeMate can summarize all text and identify all antecedent themes in that new language.

If multiple documents are presented to ThemeMate, such as 200 articles on corporate espionage, then ThemeMate extracts the key points, including precursor events (antecedents), creates an association matrix (data array), and automatically populates the array with the 1s and 0s presented in the previous sections. The completion of the data array, including populating the array with 1s and 0s takes about 1–2 seconds. See Chapter 15 for additional details.

ThemeMate has the following features:

- Summarizes single or multiple documents.

- Identifies the salient features within any text.

- Creates theme components for each developed theme. If these theme components are entered into the Google search engine, Google returns the same (and many similar) documents.

- Creates a data array with antecedents as columns and behavior examples as rows to input into AutoAnalyzer.

- Populates the data array with 1s and 0s in which a 1 designates the presence of a theme (antecedent) for a specific example and a 0 designates that a theme is not present for that specific example.

- Exports the data array into Excel for correlations and statistics in the Analysis Toolpak.

- Presents useful analysis files such as primary word frequencies in the document.

- Processes and analyzes text in English and Arabic. It can have any language added within 2 weeks as measured by the time spent adding Arabic and Chinese capability.

Introducing AutoAnalyzer as a Predictive Tool

AutoAnalyzer completes the automated prediction of malicious behavior. Taking the ThemeMate data array as input, AutoAnalyzer creates numerous pattern classifiers with different configurations. Each configuration is trained automatically with the training cases provided by ThemeMate. These configurations are developed and presented based on heuristics developed for predictive applications. At the end of the training process, the performing pattern classifier with the highest accuracy is kept, while other predictive engines are discarded.

The automation removes a very burdensome task. However, there are still times when we construct, train, and optimize an artificial neural network or add a statistical engine to assist in the AuBA process. Importantly, I designed AutoAnalyzer to conduct best practices validation. It is essential for a real-world application that a pattern classifier has been tested correctly. At the end of the training and validation process, it is also important to determine how effective the classifier is in correctly predicting blind cases when presented only with the antecedents. The agreed-upon method in the scientific community is a statistical test. This type of test determines if results obtained could occur by chance or not. Typically, a level of statistical significance is set at which the calculated statistic must not exceed for results to be accepted.

A typical level of statistical significance for acceptance of research findings for publication in the behavioral and social sciences is 0.05 (5 in 100) or 0.01 (1 in 100). This means that when the statistics are calculated for our results, the level of significance must not exceed 0.05; in other words, the probability that the results were obtained by chance is not greater than 5 times in 100. AutoAnalyzer results when tested against blind cases as it learns on its own are typically 1 in 1,000,000. In other words, the probability that results were obtained by chance is no greater than 1 in 1,000,000. The statistical test that is conducted is the *Fisher's exact test*. At the completion of the training process, the optimized classifier is presented for use and an automated report details how well the classifier performs against blind cases.

Combining ThemeMate and AutoAnalyzer

To predict malicious behavior accurately, one uses a combination of ThemeMate and AutoAnalyzer. However, separately, both ThemeMate and AutoAnalyzer provide analytical products useful to intelligence analysts, intelligence officers, and strategists. The combination allows the end product of ThemeMate, the data array of antecedent by behavior examples, to serve as input to the unique and advanced behavior analytics of AutoAnalyzer. The separation of tools was by design, but the combination is greater than the sum of the parts.

The accurate prediction of malicious behavior, and any behavior for that matter, is a complex undertaking. One needs only to search for scientifically validated examples of predicting malicious behavior over time to quickly realize that they are exceedingly rare or do not exist.

ThemeMate and AutoAnalyzer tools have been used to develop the predictive engines of specific applications. For example, the current CheckMate and InMate applications for cyber threat were developed from the AuBA tools and concepts. CheckMate is an application that sits on networks to process network packet data from all users entering externally into a network. The application converts network packet activity into behavioral assessment dimensions of expertise and deception. I developed the patent for the CheckMate application to present a technology for network protection that was a departure from the two existing technologies, signature detection and anomaly detection. We offer a third technology that incorporates human behavior assessment into network protection for the first time.

CheckMate converts packet-level activity into the behavioral measures that betray threat. In creating this, I hypothesized that two dimensions were needed to signify threat on networks. First, a person must have the expertise to intervene and cause damage or commit theft. Second, the person must be deceptive to avoid detection. If the intruder possesses these two skills, then current unauthorized intrusion is successful against existing signature detection and anomaly detection applications.

However, CheckMate can determine an unusual, first-time threat and see actual attacks that are occurring or about to occur. InMate, on the other hand, is designed to detect insider threat. Instead of using expertise and deception as dimensions, InMate replaces expertise with *intent to engage in misuse*. Obviously, the insider does not need expertise to intrude into a network — he or she has a user ID and a password! So, this dimension of behavioral assessment was changed. However, regardless of whether the person is an insider or external to the network, he or she must be deceptive to avoid detection. The fact that ThemeMate and AutoAnalyzer make up AuBA and can be used to develop a multitude of predictive applications is important for initiating and supporting a paradigm shift in security.

> **NOTE** It is important to note that as a nation we did not predict the collapse of the Soviet Union, the fall of the Berlin wall, the 9/11 al-Qaeda attack, the doggedness of both the Iraqi and the Afghani wars, and a multitude of other extremely important global events. Precipitating events and situations associated with such events were present (antecedents); we simply did not possess proactive and predictive behavior technology to identify how these antecedents would lead to the collapse. AuBA was developed to fill that void.

If we examine any behavior, there are antecedents associated with that behavior. Although assuming what the antecedents are without conducting an appropriate analysis may be customary, I have never found a single scientific study to demonstrate that such speculation leads to consistent, replicable, and valid identification of precursors that can be proven to be true antecedents. However, as will be demonstrated in the walkthrough, there are consistent methods whereby suspected indicators that precede specific behavior of interest may actually be associated with the behavior.

It is important to note that the stimuli that precede behavior belong to two major classes. We have been discussing one type, antecedents associated with the occurrence of behavior. However, there are also stimuli preceding behavior that are associated with the suppression of behavior.

A traffic light serves both purposes. If you approach an intersection and the light is green, the light serves as an antecedent that assists you in the behavior of driving through the intersection. If traveling through the intersection with a green light, the consequences are safe passage through the intersection without an accident. The fact that a safe consequence occurs repeatedly when driving through an intersection with a green light reinforces the behavior.

However, if the light is red, you stop. Why? You know that if you drive through the red light, several unfavorable consequences can happen. You could have an accident with a car traveling through the intersection from the perpendicular direction because the driver is going through with a green light. You could actually die, or you could hit a pedestrian and cause a severe injury or death. The red light suppresses driving through the intersection, and the green light encourages driving through the intersection. The traffic light has what we call *stimulus control* over our behavior of driving through an intersection.

An interesting feature of this rather simple example, as real as it is, is that the same traffic light serves as an antecedent condition for all who pass through the intersection. It controls behavior of all who travel through the intersection and results in an orderly flow usually without incident.

There are an immense number of metaphorical traffic lights in our lives. We encounter them on a constant and ongoing basis. The clock on the wall or the watch on our wrist may signal when it is time to go for lunch or to go home from work. A quick glance at the alarm clock that did not go off in the morning can trigger immediate increase in activity as you struggle to make it to work on time. Although figurative, the red and green lights work to encourage and suppress behavior as we go through our day.

We go to work because of antecedent conditions. There is a time to be at work, there is a job to do that is waiting, and others expect you and may depend on you. At the same time, your boss may have irritated you, but just like a red light, arguing back is suppressed because he or she is the boss. But that same boss, if he or she praises your work, may encourage increased activity, more diligence, and higher quality.

It may be just as important to identify events and situations that precede behavior that work to suppress the behavior as it is to identify events and situations that encourage behavior to occur. Identifying suppressors can be useful in determining how to prevent malicious behavior. For example, announcing new security measures to identify insider threatening behavior may work as a suppressor for malicious behavior. Having an announcement pop up when a person logs on to the organizational e-mail each morning indicating that all e-mail and search requests will be monitored is designed to be a suppressor event. The message is clear. By logging on to the organizational site and e-mail, your actions will be tracked. The bad news is that the message is also a warning to the insider intent on exhibiting threat that he or she will have to be more discreet and covert in his or her efforts.

The AuBA process is controlled by the person who decides which documents are to be processed by ThemeMate. This is the front end. By selecting documents that describe attempts at corporate espionage, as an example, the ThemeMate and AutoAnalyzer combination will develop a human behavior predictive model that is relevant for corporate espionage. If we develop a corpus of media events in which adversarial behavior was thwarted, then we can develop a predictive engine that concentrates on suppressing behavior. The analyst has total control over the type of model that can be automatically constructed using AuBA by submitting articles that fit his or her needs. This gives the analyst a tremendous amount of flexibility in constructing the type of model that is needed.

The ThemeMate and AutoAnalyzer combination may be used to develop human behavior predictive applications that can indicate when ongoing threat behavior may be suppressed, or predict the occurrence of malicious behavior in the near future. Most important, the ThemeMate and AutoAnalyzer combination results in validated predictive engines suited to the customer's needs.

Making Sure It Works: An Introductory Example

The types of behavior analyses presented in this book have been applied to a multitude of real-world problems. To date, the technology has been used to

- Process physical sensor data of tracked movement in real time to identify malicious intent
- Convert network packet-level activity into behavior assessment measures that indicate a cyber attack is imminent
- Process internal network packet-level activity to identify real-world threat from within an organization
- Process text accounts of human behavior across different languages to build specific predictive engines

Basically, the focus has been to convert digital information to predictions of real-world behavior.

In this section, an example of the versatility of advanced behavior analysis analytics will be presented. The focus of this example is on the identification of malicious intent and behavior based on movement. The work was completed to demonstrate that the technology used for predicting malicious behavior from constructed models using text accounts of past behavior could occur with physical sensor data allowing movement of individuals to be tracked as input. My part in the overall sensor integration, tracking, and automated assessment project funded by Office of Naval Research (ONR) was to lead the design and development of the automated behavior analysis component presented in this section. The work was presented at the Institute of Electrical & Electronics Engineers, Inc. (IEEE), 2007 Conference on Advanced Video and Signal-based Surveillance (AVSS) in London, England.[1]

Even well-trained and experienced security personnel cannot be in all places at all times to evaluate the behavior of persons in an area that requires protection. If adversarial behavior is covert, or if an adversary takes standoff measures, perpetrators may not be detected until after the fact. This is especially apparent in vehicle-based bombings or suicide bombings.

If "smart" sensors can be developed where intent of the individual tracked may be determined and not just tracked movement, prevention capability may be possible. For example, in London, hundreds of thousands of cameras are in place to aid investigation when a crime is recorded. However, sensors are not capable of making intent determinations before the fact. If a crime occurs, then recordings may be reviewed to determine what happened. In the United States, the best example is speed cameras, like those used to record license plate numbers of those who go through red lights. Again, as in London, the purpose is to identify an individual who has violated the law in a purely reactive manner.

NOTE **Current physical sensors simply are not armed with predictive analytics to flag malicious behavior that is about to occur. They are used only to identify what has already happened after recordings of past events are reviewed or to capture a license plate number of an actual speeding offender or red light runner as it happens.**

Although sensors may serve as force multipliers and work tirelessly as extensions of our eyes and ears, the determination of intent requires additional, specialized processing of sensor data.

The intent analysis capability was designed, implemented, and tested as a new technology capable of predicting malicious behavior versus non-malicious behavior based on tracked movement. It was reasoned that such characteristics

---

[1] Brian Banks, Gary M. Jackson, John J. Helly, David N. Chin, T. J. Smith, A. Schmidt, Paul C. Brewer, Roger Medd, David Masters, Annetta Burger, William K. Krebs. Using behavior analysis algorithms to anticipate security threats before they impact mission critical operations. In *Proceedings of IEEE AVSS 2007*, pp. 307–12.

as direction, acceleration, speed of movement, changes on movement, time of day, and embedded patterns of known malicious behavior and normal behavior and a host of other characteristics associated with movement could all be antecedents associated with both non-malicious and malicious intent. Intent is important because it precedes actual malicious behavior and can be predictive of imminent malicious behavior.

The first step was to carefully define what the application was to accomplish. In this case, the application would process movement patterns of an individual to determine if intent was malicious (threat) or non-malicious (no threat), based on antecedent conditions and actual movement patterns of continuously tracked individuals. This form of tracking presents a digital trail as a person moves, whether the person is walking, jogging, or riding in a vehicle. (Because we are interested only in movement patterns, the form of movement doesn't matter.) Once the movement was defined, then it was necessary to develop examples of malicious and non-malicious movement so that pattern classifiers could be trained with both types of examples; this was necessary so that a classifier could learn to recognize the difference based on different antecedent conditions.

Using initial data samples of behaviors of interest and corresponding potential antecedent conditions, the automated methodology was capable of extracting the potential predictors (antecedents) from the data. These data would be used to train, optimize, and reduce precursors to the most predictive set to determine which precursor would become actual antecedents associated with movement and intent.

When completed, the pattern classifier would be capable of processing an input stream of data and returning classifier determination of threatening intent (or a prediction of specific behavior) within 50 microseconds of receiving input. These determinations could be continuous for as long as the data stream was presented to the trained pattern classifier. One of the advantages of accurately trained pattern classifiers is the speed at which they operate. The response time of 50 microseconds means that 20,000 decisions can be made per second. A security official visually scanning an area and making safety decisions works at the approximate rate of one decision every 5 seconds; the vast superiority of automated monitoring across any number of tracked individuals is apparent.

Limitations of automated determination of intent are more on the tracking front end rather than in the analytics. For example, movement can be tracked by a large variety of physical sensors. Camera views can be converted to tracks, as well as radar and other associated sensors. If sensors can convert movement of many individuals to separate tracks and each track is forwarded to a behavioral module, then intent can be determined for each person tracked in real time.

Another key feature — an application capable of converting movement into intent — can be generalized to many locations with little to no modification. This is a vast improvement over a distinct classifier/program/machine for each scenario/location. In these types of conventional approaches, sensitive areas are identified, perimeters are established, and if someone crosses a certain point, then an alarm is sounded. This leaves little time to react and is the basis for all security alarms.

For example, a house's alarm sounds if the security of the house is compromised. If someone opens a door, breaks a window, or forces entry through the back door while the house is alarmed, the alert is sounded and an alert might be transmitted to the police. This, again, is reactive. The alarm goes off as damage is occurring, rather than preventing the damage in the first place.

The behavior analysis analytical engines were developed and validated first on sample data just to determine if they worked. Development and validation testing revealed that the automated behavior analysis application was successful in detecting behavior associated with malicious intent — specifically, conducting surveillance and moving toward a restricted area — based on movement patterns.

Figure 9-1 shows a field test of the developed technology run when subject matter experts walked across the section being monitored. Their intent was either to appear as though they were acting normally, like an employee, or to initiate malicious intent. The actual application made the track red if malicious, green if non-malicious, and yellow if normal but suspicious. Because the figure is not in color, the dotted line indicates malicious intent and the dashed line is an example of non-malicious intent. The ongoing automated prediction process resulted in projections of malicious or non-malicious intent multiple times per second. On the right side of the figure, you will notice a dotted line coming from the bushes. This movement pattern was designated as malicious as soon as the person appeared from the bushes. Regardless of whether the person was an employee or a terrorist, the application recognized that he or she should not be entering from the bushes.

As a highlight of this project, the field test took place at a new site and the application had no trained knowledge of this location — the test was a surprise. The test demonstrated the robustness of a design based on movement and not location.

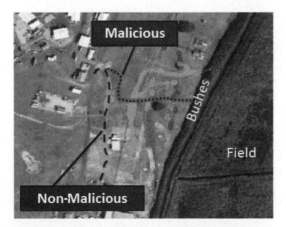

Figure 9-1: The automated behavior analysis application converting tracked movement to real-time prediction of malicious intent. Red is malicious intent; green and yellow are non-malicious intent.

The AuBA model exists as a set of reliable and valid procedures that have been demonstrated to be effective in:

- **Identifying key antecedents** (indicators) of specific threatening behaviors
- **Predicting intent** accurately in blind tests and based on developed models
- **Predicting behavior** before its occurrence in real time
- **Applying indicators** to predict various outcomes, such as tactic, direction of interest, and location of attack
- **Identifying associations** of antecedents with outcome classes to suggest intervention strategies

Once the behavioral model of intent was developed, the model was capable of processing all physical sensor and environmental variables in real time. Based on previous AuBA security-related models used for the CheckMate Intrusion Protection System, it was reasoned that this basic pattern classification methodology could be modified to provide:

- The capability to monitor, track, and assess intent across multiple sensor inputs continuously at 100 millisecond intervals for each entity on an ongoing basis.
- Visualization to depict overall intent across all sensor input and simultaneously tracked entities.
- Vulnerability and threat thresholds that may be set "on the fly." This decreases the possibility of false positives during planned events that may indicate temporary anomalous conditions.
- Automated warnings when intent exceeds vulnerability and threat thresholds.
- A well-tested validation and testing methodology that results in sequentially improved hypothesis generation. This allows planned security improvements across test bed instantiations of the presented hybrid methodology.
- An integrated capability whereby fused physical sensor and behavior analysis models may be constructed, validated, and optimized within a fraction of the time typically required by professional teams of pattern classification experts.

The automation and extension of basic applied behavior analysis as AuBA have been used in a variety of different domains with global security implications. Work in this field, such as the development of the AuBA intent classifier, has demonstrated that output from such sensors as RFID and optical, as well as others, can be processed with AuBA technology to identify antecedents of specific malicious and threatening behaviors. This is an important development because it demonstrates that it is possible to move from the reactive sensor state in which we find ourselves to a more proactive stance with analytics that can anticipate malicious behavior before it occurs.

NOTE In London, literally hundreds of thousands of cameras are located strategically around the city. Londoners are accustomed to video surveillance and appear to accept the trade-off between privacy and protection. In the United States, we now see cameras located at intersections and tunnels to capture the visual evidence and license plate number of speeding and traffic light violations. For the offenders, the first awareness that detection occurred is when they open their mail and find a picture of the car (and prominently displayed license number) with the command to mail in money to cover the fine.

When the use of such cameras was announced for the first time in the United States, there was a public outcry over privacy issues. Now, cameras are commonplace and do not appear to be of much concern. I contend that if AuBA predictive analytics were added to video surveillance to anticipate criminal behavior, then video surveillance would become a part of daily life. Malicious criminal behavior is threatening and frightening to most. The possibility of *predictive surveillance* is a concept worthy of support and development.

Testing and Use in the Real World: Implications

This is not a book on applied behavior analysis. There are many excellent texts on applied behavior analysis to be used in the classroom, institutions, and other clinical settings. For the most part, applied behavior analysis is used with individuals and uses what is called *single-subject design*, or *within-subject design*. However, this book *is* about *automated* behavior analysis (AuBA). The names are similar because I want to acknowledge the behavioral foundation that forms AuBA. There is an intentional closeness to the basic science and to the names. However, AuBA in this book is a predictive technology that has many extensions, including automation. For the most part, the discipline of applied behavior analysis is a methodology for helping people deal with problem issues; it is a discipline of influence as opposed to prediction.

AuBA has included many extensions and refinements. The following is a partial list of the extensions:

- Methods and patented technology to use applied behavior analysis to validate prediction of human behavior

- Unique pattern classification processes as applied to human behavior

- ThemeMate, as a tool to automatically read text accounts of target behaviors (in multiple languages) and summarize key features, extract antecedents, and create and populate data arrays that contain antecedents when presented with text describing past incidents

- AutoAnalyzer as a tool to automatically construct validated artificial neural network (ANN) pattern classifiers

- Incorporating statistics as part of some AuBA predictive engines

- Proven capability to identify antecedents in network packet activity, physical sensor data, virtual worlds, text, video, and statistics

- Patented behavior analytics

- Commercial applications such as CheckMate, InMate, and AuBA modeling

- Applications across government intelligence and military agencies

- Automating application of AuBA across individuals, groups, and countries

- The capability to conduct analysis and make human behavior decisions in milliseconds (as opposed to days or weeks)

Automating and extending the basic foundation has resulted in basically a new science of human behavior, a fusion of behavior and computer sciences. This fusion has had many effects on the extension of this new discipline. For example, in applied behavior analysis, an intervention is measured by a within subject design. Although there are many variants, the typical approach is to conduct the ABAB design mentioned earlier in this chapter. In addition, observation and data gathering is typically conducted with a single individual over time. Conversely, AuBA tends to use multiple examples of behavior across an individual, group, or country from text descriptions of behavior. The primary reason for this type of extraction is that the subject, or subjects, of the predictive capability is not available for observation.

Terrorists, leaders, criminals, hackers, enemy soldiers, insurgents, and those who threaten the security of the United States act covertly. This includes major terrorism efforts with state support around the world. However, we do have text accounts of past behavior in media articles, news reports, and so on. AuBA was developed to analyze, predict, and influence the behavior of adversaries that operate covertly to threaten our national security, organizations, and welfare.

To develop AuBA to be useful on a global scale as a quick reaction capability, automation is absolutely essential. Moving from manual analysis that could take weeks to assessment that occurs 20,000 times per second required innovation invention as evidenced by patents in this new area. Most significant, fusing sciences required the blending of methodologies. For example, placing behavioral methods into computer-science-based platforms means that different forms of validation are required. Unlike the typical blending of computer and behavioral sciences in which computerization assists behavioral methods, AuBA represents the addition of behavioral methods to assist computer science applications. Most attempts to predict human behavior have grown out of the mathematic and statistical world, operating as massive correlational approaches across variables. Human behavior is not statistical. Human behavior is a moment-to-moment interaction of internal motivation and drives and the environmental situations in which one finds himself or herself. AuBA brings this behavioral foundation to the computer and predictive sciences.

The world of predicting human behavior is littered with physical science skeptics, yet they will seek out a therapist or counselor in times of need. Why? Constructing applications to predict human behavior requires human behavior expertise, not statistics alone. A clear understanding of human behavior is necessary to analyze past behavior of an individual, group, or country and predict future behavior. The anticipation of human behavior is definitely not a 100 percent repetition of the past. Generally speaking, history only repeats itself with vague concepts. If the future were a perfect replica of the past, then there would be no growth.

AuBA uses small-n methods. This means that we will have a small number of examples for study. This places us in the statistical world — not understanding behavior but merely testing our application to demonstrate to the scientific community that it is valid. We confirm that it does what it is supposed to do and results are not a product of chance. When constructing an application, we use cross-validation methods, like Leaving-One-Out (L-1), that grew out of both pattern classification and computer sciences disciplines. As we continue development, testing and validation are necessary components.

Advantages of AuBA #9: Designing the Focus of an AuBA-Developed Model

An AuBA model, once constructed and validated, may be used to predict future behavior. Instead of relying on statistical associations, AuBA relies on extracting the context of each example of past behavior. The context of behavior consists of antecedent conditions and situations associated with the behavior. If the behavior occurring within past contexts is successful for the person or group, behavior is more likely to occur in the future when the same or highly similar situations or conditions exist. AuBA predicts future behavior by determining the context that currently exists to project which behavior is likely to occur within that context before it actually occurs.

Because I invented the AuBA tools to first extract contextual antecedent conditions and situations associated with historical accounts of behavior, the modeler can determine specifically the type of model that will be generated and validated simply by presenting documents that contain examples of the behavior desired to predict. For example, if we wish to determine the antecedent conditions that precede an attack from the malicious cyber group Anonymous, we would search for past accounts of attacks and collect them as a single corpus. We would also include accounts of non-attacks so that the modeling process can learn which antecedent conditions and situations may be used to differentiate between imminent attack or no attack.

AuBA automated learning works in a manner similar to the way we humans learn. If we want to study a specific topic, we obtain and read multiple accounts of past behavior. We control what we learn by selecting which documents we will read and process. For example, to learn about predicting malicious behavior and the tools and techniques to accomplish this objective, you would acquire this book and study its contents. As a result of reading it, you will know how to predict future behavior by using antecedents and consequences associated with past behavior. If we selected an electronic copy of this book and submitted it to ThemeMate as separate chapters, ThemeMate will quickly identify all key points in the book. To show this, I did just that during the writing of the book. Not surprisingly, the major concepts, or themes, that surfaced were as follows: *behavior, antecedents, consequences, cyber, individual,* and *group.*

AuBA can use structured text from databases, or it can use what is called *unstructured text.* The latter means text that has not been read to complete database fields. By collecting news media articles written about attacks perpetrated by the Anonymous group and submitting these to the AuBA predictive modeling process, we can determine the antecedents that lead to their attack behavior. In fact, Anonymous typically attacks in retaliation to some perceived assault on free speech. This is knowledge extracted from past accounts.

However, it is important to note that once you have articles selected that cover past attacks, you do not have to separate them into articles that cover targeting, timing, location, type of attack, and so forth. Once you have a corpus that covers the malicious behavior of interest and the context, ThemeMate may be directed to process the articles in such a way that different models may be constructed, with each having a very different focus. In addition, by adding different outcome columns to the array, AutoAnalyzer will find patterns among the extracted antecedents and the outcomes (for example, elevated threat vs. normal threat, DOS attack vs. phishing, and so on).

The ability to control the type of model constructed and validated by determining which articles are selected for the AuBA process helps to determine if a robust model may be constructed simply by noting the quality of the documents before the processing. For example, if you have at least 30 examples of past behavior in each category, such as attack or no attack (combined 60 examples total), there is a very good probability that you will have an accurate model.

In Summary

We have now developed manual and automated methodologies for predicting malicious behavior that have been tested and validated. Existing as a fusion of the behavioral and computer sciences, the methodologies incorporate elements of both in unique ways. As compared to signature detection or anomaly detection, the behavioral methods concentrate on predicting malicious activity based on recognizing the existence of antecedents that precede behavior as opposed to the behavior itself. This is a key characteristic of the behavioral approaches presented in this book and separates the methodologies presented from typical signature detection and anomaly detection approaches.

I provided a real-world example whereby multiple methodologies and sensors came together to demonstrate a new capability. You saw that physical sensors can do more than just sense some form of perimeter infraction. The same sensors can provide input to specially trained behavior analytic engines that can predict intent and imminent threat, thereby providing an opportunity to intervene.

CHAPTER 10

Predicting Domestic Threat

Domestic (as opposed to foreign) threat is a special case whereby malicious intent against the United States is generated and directed by a citizen. An individual who turns against his country requires very deeply seated motivation to be malicious and cause harm to his fellow citizens, especially innocent victims. A person conducting the analysis can expect to find specific incidents in the individual's past that were an insult to the person's perceived integrity, sense of what is right, and ideology, or event(s) hurting him. The malicious act is typically associated with revenge, a need to right a wrong, or, as in the case of spying for foreign governments, the added inducement of monetary gain. Basically, there are a host of complex psychological underpinnings underlying domestic threat. The fact that a perpetrator is going to damage property and/or hurt fellow citizens requires serious disenchantment.

In this chapter, we will explore domestic threat and acts perpetrated by U.S. citizens both against other citizens and against the U.S. government. Focal areas such as targeting, selection of method, and often timing of an attack are affected by past events. If we can determine how behaviors will change over time for malicious domestic acts, studying specific attacks can be used to provide the antecedent-behavior patterns to assist in predicting future malicious behavior.

Characterizing Domestic Threat

The analysis of domestic threat should include an awareness of both motivations and methods that have been common across domestic attackers in our country's history. There is not a specific personality type of an individual who attacks within country as a U.S. citizen. However, such perpetrators share certain common motivations and have used similar methods. When I first became involved in analyzing the behavior of individuals within a national security context, many of these cases were studied. Considering domestic threat as insider threat, the analysis was geared toward all forms and examples of this phenomenon with the common underlying feature of malicious intent.

Considering this type of an attack as insider threat, even if extended to include threat coming from within a country and not just from within an organization, the analysis was geared toward all forms of insider threat, including cyber. A functional analysis of insider threat revealed methods in which insider threat can be perpetrated and the motivations that fuel such behavior.

Table 10-1 displays a partial list of both motivations and methods. Any single motivation on the left side of the table can be associated with any single or combination of methods on the right side of the table. This correspondence and number of combinations that can occur between motivation and methods used to be malicious present a very large number of scenarios that are likely to happen. When one considers how motivations and methods can be intermixed and combined, it is easy to see the variety of attacks that can be generated by pairing any motivation with any method(s) even from this partial list. This analysis was used as a foundation to plan the Inmate Misuse Protection Application. It is apparent that a signature detection system would be too extensive to list rules and combinations of rules to account for all approaches that could be used. Therefore, InMate was developed to identify overall suspicious behavior that could accompany many varieties of misuse from a behavioral perspective. You can see descriptions of both the CheckMate external threat and the InMate internal threat applications in Chapters 16 and 17. However, a brief description of each application is provided here.

- **CheckMate:** A human behavior–based network intrusion protection application that is not signature detection or anomaly detection based. CheckMate was designed to assess external users coming into a network from outside of the organization. It assesses every user each 1/10 of a second with four different behavior assessment modules. These modules are AuBA-trained predictive engines capable of detecting threat in real time. The engines convert samples of packet-level activity into the degree of presence of *expertise* (E) and *deception* (D) in the samples. If E and D both exceed a set threshold, an alert designates the activity as malicious. If an option is set, the application can react by blocking the IP connection.

- **InMate:** Based on the CheckMate technology, InMate was designed to assess insiders within an organization for the presence of malicious intent based on their activities within the network. Assessment modules convert samples of packet-level activity into *intent to engage in misuse* (I) and *deception* (D). Like CheckMate behavior assessment engines, if InMate measures exceed I and D thresholds at the same time, an alert is automatically generated and forwarded to appropriate security staff to investigate. Because the person being assessed is an insider, an alert is only generated and the activity is not blocked to prevent the person from realizing that malicious activity has been discovered. This ensures that security staff can conduct a proper investigation of recognized malicious behavior.

Table 10-1: A partial list of motivations and methods associated with malicious behavior. Any method may be paired with any motivation, resulting in an extensive variety of ways one may exhibit malicious behavior.

MOTIVATION	METHOD
Disgruntled:	Cyber:
Bitter	Hacking/cracking
Passed over for promotion/recognition	Embedded messages
Revenge	Steganography
Jealousy	Denial of service
Embarrassment	Malicious code
Power	Phishing variations
Spite	Identity theft
Hate	Cyber bullying
Perception of being held back	Theft (money, secrets, valuables)
Monetary gain	Extortion
Desire to be malicious	Beating
Desire to be known as a hacker	Espionage (passing classified information)
Self-styled security tester as a cover	Sabotage
Peer pressure and need for acceptance	Physical brutality
Curiosity	Murder
Advancement in adversary organization	Stalking
Ideology	Harassment/slander

Targeting is a significant part of domestic threat. Whereas a foreign adversary has what appears to be an almost unlimited number of targets, the domestic perpetrator usually ties the targeting very closely to his or her own motivations. For example, if a person was the object of (perceived) disrespect, embarrassment, or lack of acknowledgment or did not receive the perceived deserved promotion, etc. at work, then the work site is likely to be the target. Method is strongly related to specific skill of the perpetrator. For example, if the person is skilled in steganography, then theft of proprietary material may be the method of choice, whereby the insider hides sensitive material in an image. Because the outward appearance of the image is the same and the material is hidden within the bits of the image, the image can be forwarded to an accomplice or to one's self outside the organization without suspicion and then disseminated or sold. In marked contrast, if the disgruntled person has a history of firearm use or strong interest, he or she may choose weaponized assault at the work site. There have been many examples of work-site assaults with firearms.

Security, human resource departments, and fellow employees should be concerned when there is a strong case of a disgruntled employee in the workplace. For the benefit of an obviously upset person who has perceived that he or she has been wronged and is being publicly demeaning to fellow employees as a result, it is wise to report such behavior to the immediate supervisor and the human resources department. If reported early enough, this could help to avert a disaster. It is interesting that the target may be the workplace itself, meaning that the discontent is directed indiscriminately at anyone within the work setting, not at a specific person. There are a multitude of cases in which a disgruntled employee enters the work site and simply starts shooting indiscriminately, killing anyone in the vicinity.

There are special cases in which the perpetrator takes on much more than a boss or a work site. We have had many examples in which the person decides to teach the government or the military a lesson. On November 5, 2009, Major Nidal Hasan, a U.S. Army psychiatrist, walked into a military building at Fort Hood, Texas, and opened fire, killing 13 people and wounding 29. This particular case was one of the worse shootings in our history and certainly the worst on a military base. Hasan, a Muslim who had made no secret of his distaste for the wars in Iraq and Afghanistan, was just weeks away from being deployed. There is some evidence that he viewed his deployment as one that would have him killing other Muslims.

Hasan had made many public statements against the wars in Iraq and Afghanistan and had associated with known terrorists such as Anwar al-Awlaki. It appears that al-Awlaki encouraged Hasan to act and even praised him after the shooting. This is one of those cases that seem very clear in retrospect; however, such cases still need to be behaviorally dissected to identify antecedents that may serve as warning signs in the future.

This case had elements of terrorism but appears to be more about a decorated officer developing strong disgruntlement within the Army, complicated by his Muslim associations and having to be deployed to Afghanistan. It is difficult to understand how a person could commit such an act against his fellow soldiers. However, a clearer understanding of his motivation and growing dissatisfaction along with his clear statements against the Army should have been ample warning signs.

Defining Domestic Terrorism

The reader may be surprised to discover that the term *terrorism* has no generally accepted definition. When the case of Major Nidal Hasan is analyzed, it contains many of the same elements used to brand an incident as a terrorist act. At the same time, the act appeared to be very closely associated with an imminent deployment to Afghanistan. However, Hasan's association with known al-Qaedas, partiality for extremist's views, and his symbolic targeting of the U.S. Army, appear to be very similar to known terrorist attacks. As one Israeli terrorism expert once remarked to me, "There are more definitions of terrorists and more terrorism experts than there are terrorists!" So how can we focus on domestic terrorism, or foreign terrorism, without a definition?

NOTE In 2003, the U.S. Department of State, in its annual publication, *Patterns of Global Terrorism*, defined terrorism as the "premeditated, politically motivated violence perpetrated against noncombatant targets by subnational groups or clandestine agents, usually intended to influence an audience." This is a useful document to read for those interested in terrorism and trends, and it is available for free from the U.S. Department of State website. For clarification, *noncombatants* are civilians.

The U.S. Department of State's definition works for the general public. It is a concise definition and covers 9/11 and the many foreign attacks directed against U.S. citizens over the past years. If we consider domestic terrorism, then we might alter the definition to say, "Domestic terrorism is premeditated, politically-motivated violence perpetrated against noncombatant targets (civilian citizens) within a country by a perpetrator with the same citizenship usually intended to influence an audience." As an example, the April 19, 1995, bombing of the Alfred P. Murrah federal building by U.S. citizen Timothy McVeigh fits the definition of domestic terrorism offered. I believe few government and law enforcement officials would argue with the classification of this event as domestic terrorism.

There are many definitions available, just not general agreement about which is the best one.

Differentiating Domestic from Foreign Threat

Identifying domestic threat versus foreign threat depends very strongly on the type of threat. Perhaps one of the biggest differences is how perpetrators conduct surveillance of a target. Terrorists don't just commit an act of terrorism on a whim. Typically, a great deal of financing, planning, weapons acquisition, strategy, escape planning (if it is not a suicide mission), targeting, and timing are all taken into consideration. However, surveillance is usually required prior to an actual attack. Surveillance consists of systematic or periodic observations of a target. During these observations, the presence of security and its patterns, as well as related security support such as cameras, may be noted.

NOTE Surveillance of a target is a major part of terrorist attack planning. Because of this, citizens should be aware that apparent surveillance behavior (e.g., taking pictures of the supports of a bridge) may occur before a terrorist act and report anything suspicious.

Since the 9/11 attacks, it is more difficult for foreign terrorists to move about the country to conduct surveillance. However, the disgruntled U.S. citizen harboring revenge can move around almost any public, unrestricted site without arousing suspicion. Even if the U.S. citizen with a typical American appearance and accent is taking photographs of a nonrestricted area of a military or government facility for later study and is caught, he or she can just plead ignorance as a tourist.

In the case of the domestic terrorist or individual wishing to harm other citizens, the planning of an act is typically more personal. If the individual perceives the personal need to correct a situation where he or she has been wronged, then it is possible that an act of revenge could be exhibited.

Differences

Threat can take many forms and be generated by many different sources. Usually associated with a group, such attacks as the Hezbollah vehicle-borne suicide bombing of the U.S. Marine and French military barracks in Beirut in 1983 that resulted in 241 American servicemen and 58 French soldiers being killed demonstrate the lethality of the foreign terrorist attack. The bombing of Pan Am Flight 103 leaving London Heathrow airport bound for John F. Kennedy airport in New York killed all 243 passengers, 16 crew members, and 11 people on the ground also points to the lethality of a foreign terrorist attack. Now, after 9/11, we have to add the realized threat of the event occurring within our borders with a death toll reaching almost 3,000 victims.

We know that foreign threats require planning, financing, and the ability to conduct surveillance.Even without knowing the details, we know that foreign threats require planning, financing, and the ability to conduct surveillance. The threat is typically a group threat, not an individual act. There are exceptions.

Richard Reid, the shoe bomber, and Umar Farouk Abdulmutallab, the underwear bomber, appeared to act alone, although they had ties to known terrorist groups. But, for the most part, massive attacks directed against embassies, a naval ship like the *USS Cole*, military targets, etc. require group planning and support.

Domestic terrorism is very different. Surveillance is basically undetectable because of the ease with which U.S. citizens can move around restricted sites, and the acts are more associated with only one or two actors than with a group. There are many cases that fit into domestic threat that would also fit into the definition of domestic terrorism. The following drew widespread attention and publicity:

- Theodore (Ted) Kaczynski, the Unabomber, killed 3 people and injured 23 with numerous letter bombs mailed to specific individuals for two decades. He was distressed over university treatment and airliners.

- The Oklahoma City bombing of the Alfred P. Murrah Federal building on April 19, 1995, killing 168 people, 19 of which were children, was the most devastating terrorist act on U.S. soil until 9/11. The act was jointly planned by Timothy McVeigh and Terry Nichols, but McVeigh alone drove the truck bomb to the site and abandoned it there right before it detonated. Being former military, they held a grudge against the federal assault of the Branch Davidians in Waco, Texas, and the resulting loss of life. They sought revenge against the government.

- Shortly after 9/11, anthrax in powder form was mailed in envelopes for nearly a month. Targets were offices of the U.S. Senate and news offices. Five people were killed, including U.S. postal workers handling the mail, and 17 others were infected with the anthrax. A scientist at Fort Detrick, Maryland, Dr. Bruce Ivans, was informed that he was going to be prosecuted as the perpetrator. He then committed suicide with an over-dose of Tylenol. Fort Detrick contains laboratories that contain biological agents and the strain that was used in the attacks. Although there was mounting evidence pointing to Ivans, I feel compelled to state that it was never proved that Dr. Ivans was the perpetrator. Suicide is not always an expression of guilt. It can also be the ultimate act to preserve the self. As a clinician, I know that suicide is an act to stop pain; it is not an admission of guilt. Regardless, whether the perpetrator was Ivans or someone else, the anthrax mailings resulted in the deaths of innocent victims and was an act of domestic terrorism.

- The shooting incident perpetrated by Army Major Nidal Malik Hasan mentioned earlier in this chapter is an example of a domestic terrorist act not generally labeled as such. As a Muslim extremist and a disgruntled Army major weeks away from deployment to Afghanistan, Hasan walked into a Fort Hood, Texas, soldier facility and shot and killed 13 people and wounded 30 others. He reportedly had believed he would have to kill fellow Muslims in Afghanistan and had been disgruntled with the Army for many years.

THE HYBRID: U.S. CITIZEN AS A FOREIGN AL-QAEDA TERRORIST

Anwar al-Awlaki is an example of a hybrid foreign and domestic terrorist and U.S. citizen. Born in New Mexico and educated in the United States, he earned a bachelor's degree in civil engineering and a master's degree in education and had worked on his PhD. He was proficient technically, was a bomb maker, planned several attacks against fellow Americans within the United States, and was a key al-Qaeda leader. He was a skilled orator who worked to recruit additional al-Qaeda members. In 2010 President Barack Obama authorized the killing of al-Awlaki. Just seven months after U.S. Joint Special Operations Command (JSOC) successfully planned an operation that killed Osama bin Laden in a raid on his compound in Pakistan, JSOC was successful with a September 30, 2011, drone-fired missile that killed al-Awlaki. He is the first U.S. citizen targeted in this manner. Although the act is controversial, the vast majority of the country appeared to view the killing as justified because of al-Awlaki's incessant targeting of innocent Americans in their homeland.

These examples are provided because they epitomize the more single act. Even in the case of the Oklahoma City bombing that included planning and preparation by McVeigh and Nichols, it was still McVeigh who carried out the act. Furthermore, there is not an organizational structure that supports the acts with arms, financial support, and guidance. Instead, the perpetrator does the surveillance, planning, and arms/weapons acquisition and commits the act.

NOTE U.S. Joint Special Operations Command (JSOC) successfully planned an operation that killed Osama bin Laden. Seven months later, Anwar al-Awlaki, a U.S. citizen who had turned al-Qaeda, was killed in a U.S. drone attack in Yemen.

Similarities

Although there are significant differences between foreign terrorist threat and domestic terrorist threat, there are also strong similarities. As a first similarity, the end result of both is death and destruction. Although much of the obvious support that is associated with organized foreign terrorist organizations is missing with domestic terrorism, the acts can be deadly. The fact that one or maybe two individuals play many parts in the planning and execution of their plan does not diminish how deadly domestic terrorism can be.

The Fort Hood shooting and the Oklahoma City bombing are two of the worst attacks we have experienced. The reasons for domestic attacks are often political or are associated with the need to make a statement. Ted Kaczynski wrote an extensive manifesto to describe the wrongs of others. Major Hasan attacked the very organization for which he held the grudge, and McVeigh and

Nichols, angry with the government, targeted a federal building for destruction. Similar to foreign terrorist acts, there is an underlying message to present with violence, and often the victims are just considered to be collateral damage.

Domestic and foreign terrorists show little to no regard for the innocence of victims. The Oklahoma City bombing is a prime example. The building housed a day care center, and many young children were killed. Although McVeigh later said that he did not know the center was there, it is doubtful in my opinion. One of his earlier statements of rage over the raid of the Branch Davidians was that innocent children were killed in the fire that ended the very long siege.

Targeting often carries strong similarities to precipitating events that led to the motivation to strike back. Kaczynski targeted those who caused him to feel rage. Major Hasan specifically went on base, walked into a fellow soldier building, and shot anyone who was unfortunate enough to be in his sights. Even at his execution, McVeigh said he had no regrets.

Domestic terrorism is very serious. There are many groups. It appears that the extremist groups are of the most concern. The animal rights advocates, abortion clinic haters, and so on all pose a threat. Although there are many hate crimes, crimes of violence, and just plain crime, there is a subset that fits the general definitions of domestic terrorism. As such, they share some commonalities with foreign terrorism.

The Malicious Insider: Spies, Thieves, and Sabotage

The *insider* represents a special case of threat. The insider is one of us, and we may work with him or her every day. The insider may not appear to be an extremist, and we may not feel fearful in our interactions. In comparison, if we had the opportunity to interact with the more violent domestic terrorists such as Kaczynski, McVeigh, Nichols, or Hasan, we more than likely would have picked up on the severe disgruntlement and targeted comments concerning the focus of their distaste. Kaczynski, although a recluse, made his distaste against industrial and technological development known through a 35,000-word manifesto. McVeigh, after being honorably discharged from the Army, let those around him know of his growing distaste for the federal government. The vocalization evolved into letters to the editors of newspapers. Hasan's Islamic faith created conflict that angered him; he was in communication with Anwar al-Awlaki, the al-Qaeda terrorist later killed by a Hellfire missile fired from a U.S. drone in Yemen. Hasan made his negative thoughts known via Internet postings and to those who would listen.

The types of insiders who engage in spying, theft of proprietary information, or sabotage from within is different from those who present domestic or foreign threat. Because they are inside, they have to be extremely careful and deceptive to avoid getting caught. Part of being deceptive is appearing that nothing is wrong if the task is to steal information. In this case, one does not want to be caught, so suspicious activity is to be avoided. At the same time, if an insider is not "on the take" and is simply motivated by means of being disgruntled, then he or she may be vocal and let the reasons for being disgruntled be known to those who listen. The domestic terrorist who would turn against fellow citizens must have motivation that would support acts that could harm or even kill others.

The insider who did not get the promotion believed to be deserved, or for any other such reason, may be disgruntled and let those feelings be known. Insiders who are paid to steal information may be almost undetectable. They need to be deceptive and have very good skills in theft. Raising suspicion because of negative statements could result in enough suspicion to prevent access to the information that provides them with the external compensation. The point: Insider theft is complex, and there are very different reasons why those who present insider threat do what they do. From a security perspective, we must realize these differences, what antecedent conditions lead to insider threat, and the behaviors that occur — then we have an increased chance of being proactive and preventing such occurrences.

Spies

It often takes many years to catch individual spies such as Aldrich Ames, a CIA officer, or Robert Hanssen, a key FBI counterintelligence Special Agent. Every significant intelligence agency and branch of the military has had insiders who spied for a foreign government. The fact that it may take a very long time to catch them simply shows how important it is for them to be deceptive.

Why does a person turn against his or her own country to spy and pass on secrets to a foreign government? Why does a person become a traitor? It may seem inconceivable to us that a person could betray America. Refer back to Table 10-1 to review the motivations. There are many, and this is just a small sample. But, we must realize how deep-seated and how much of a driving force these motivations are for the person who would spy or betray by committing a terrorist act against his or her own country.

> **NOTE** Robert Hanssen was extremely cautious, which made him exception-ally difficult to catch. For example, he never met a handler. Although Hanssen spied for the Russian government, they never met him, didn't know who he was, and didn't know what he looked like. There had never been a photo-graph passed, and Hanssen was cautious not to provide any information that could tie him to any other person. This was accomplished with a *dead drop*. This procedure consists of bundling desired material and leaving it in a spot that the handler knows. The spy then leaves a mark (like an X) on a nearby

tree or other location to show that the drop is loaded. The handler then later retrieves the package and leaves money. The spy then retrieves the money at a later time from the hidden spot. Those who read spy novels will recognize this procedure that is common in fiction and nonfiction.

No doubt we all have been passed over in the workplace or maybe even for a special project at school. Most of us get over what feels like neglect, knowing that there will be other times and other opportunities. However, an insider could have felt the insult so deeply as to not be able to recover. Instead, he or she starts having feelings of resentment, hate, or disgust and a growing desire to *get back* to hurt those responsible. For whatever reason, the depths of feelings harbored by the typically disgruntled insider may actually form the foundation motivation that leads to the person viewing events as they occur as additional ammunition to be disgruntled.

The growing resentment of the insider may reach the attention of the human resources department at work. We must realize that the psychological effects of harboring severe enough resentment and disgruntlement that espionage would be fueled and the person would become a traitor are likely to be noticed by others. It is difficult to hide severe resentment.

On the other hand, the spy may become a spy simply for monetary gain. There must be some form of resentment, but not enough to sell secrets. Add resentment to monetary gain, and some people will succumb to temptation. For example, if a person lives clearly outside of his or her financial means with a passed-over promotion and no other means of generating income except for maybe the lottery, then monetary gain will be more attractive.

Spies are not just individuals who decide to steal classified secrets and sell them to a foreign government. There are reasons, antecedents that set the stage, and consequences that occur that are desired associated with the actual theft behaviors. In addition to true spying for another government, corporate espionage is as real as spying for another government. It is well known that it is a legitimate and lawful practice to conduct competitive intelligence. It is the practice of one company to try to learn the competitive secrets of a competitor. For example, if two companies are in the cell phone production business, company 1 wants to know when the latest company 2 advancements will be released, and vice versa. In fact, the person who successfully learns the inside functioning of another company legitimately and passes it on for benefit to his or her own company may actually be rewarded.

However, the person who steals internal proprietary information in his or her own company and sells it to a competitor company may cause severe harm to his or her company. Depending on the company, harm could also occur to the government. For example, I am an employee of Science Applications International Corporation (SAIC). It is a Fortune 500 company and primarily a defense contractor with approximately 41,000 employees. It is a competitive business where government announcements are released frequently, indicating that the government would like to have a new capability.

The announcement, known as a broad area announcement (BAA) or request for proposal (RFP), is read by all who are interested. If a company wants to try to obtain a contract, a group of individuals within the company will prepare a proposal and submit it through the appropriate channels to the government office. Then, through a competitive process, the government reviews all submitted proposals, and awards funding to the group within a company, or the company it believes is most likely to meet the requirements of the request or announcement.

This means that companies often develop exciting new technology. These companies are often the birthplaces of new capability. There are certainly leaks as a result of competitive intelligence. The community of developers in special areas is often small, and it is not difficult to determine what company is applying or what companies have decided to partner to work together to win the award. But, this is how the process actually works. It is not the same as an employee who with full intent steals information to provide to a competitor or a foreign government. It happens often. A simple Internet search on corporate or industrial espionage will reveal many hundreds of cases. A similar search in espionage will also identify many cases of actual government spies. The organizations may be different, but the methods are highly similar and, in some cases, the same.

Sabotage

There is also a special case of the insider who is so intent on getting back at a company or organization that he or she works to harm the typical processes within that organization. This is *sabotage*. The idea may be to harm your own project to give a competitor a chance to pull ahead in a development race. It could mean that the perpetrator is highly resentful of not receiving the recognition that is perceived as deserved and wants to see the company and its employees suffer like he or she has suffered; therefore, he or she causes damage. For example, important computer files can be deleted, errors can be inserted, and demonstrations of new technology can be quietly undermined. The only limit to sabotage is the imagination of the perpetrator. This is true of any insider threat.

It is essential to realize that an insider typically does not work alone, even if he or she is the only one within an organization stealing secrets. There is often an outsider who is waiting for the information and may be willing to pay very large sums of money to acquire it. The customer may be a foreign government or a competitor. Some employees who sabotage are resentful and use this method to seek revenge. Again, in this case, the underlying motivation is the perpetrator's desire to make the organization hurt the same way the perpetrator thinks the organization hurt him or her.

NOTE In almost any case of serious theft of proprietary information, there is a customer of one form or another.

Tradecraft of Those with Malicious Intent

Insider threat, whether a spy for a foreign government or an employee selling secrets to a competitor, is rich with psychological factors and deep-seated motivations. However, a behavior analysis of past cases often shows similarities in both the actual spycraft (or tradecraft) used and the antecedents to which the insider responds.

Spies, insiders, and those who threaten us externally use tradecraft. What is *tradecraft*? Tradecraft is not limited to but includes the methods and practices that allow one to be effective in either stealing or inflicting damage while at the same time decreasing the probability of being caught by means of deceptive practices. For example, the dead drop (explained earlier) is a very effective method of exchanging material for money while at the same time using the method to ensure deception and not being recognized or identified.

How do we recognize tradecraft? There are three types of malicious tradecraft:

- Known tradecraft
- New tradecraft
- Traditional (known tradecraft but with new variations)

Known Tradecraft

There are a variety of tradecraft procedures that have been popularized in movies, television, and novels. However, practices such as *dead drops*, *brush passes*, and communicating in code are not just the acts of fiction. They are real, and they are effective ways of communicating with a handler.

There are several key points in the process of stealing proprietary or classified information at which the risk of getting caught is the highest. For example, the actual act of stealing information, getting the information out of a secure setting, and passing it to the person who is either the buyer or a representative of the buyer is especially risky. There is often a handler or a representative who is supposed to meet with the person who is stealing the information to obtain the stolen information and provide requests for specific additional information. It is risky business, as the CIA's Aldrich Ames, FBI's Robert Hanssen, and Jonathan Pollard, Naval Intelligence Command (NIC), discovered when they all were apprehended.

A former CBS television series, *Silk Stalkings*, that ran from 1991 to 1999 had the same opening scene for years, in which a leggy brunette conducted a perfectly executed brush pass. The young lady walks toward another person who is walking toward her. At the point of just passing one another she flawlessly hands off a briefcase to the other person. In a matter of a second, stolen material has been passed to a second person — this is a traditional brush pass.

The dead drop was popularized in a number of movies and television programs. A docudrama about the Robert Hanssen case (*Master Spy: The Robert Hanssen Story* by 20th Century Fox Television, 2002) highlights Hanssen placing classified material in a garbage bag and hiding it in a park in Vienna, Virginia. Hanssen *loaded* the site and placed a piece of white paper in a prominent and predetermined place so that Russian KGB handlers would know the site was loaded. They would then retrieve the information and reload with payment and any special instructions or information requests. Hanssen would then return when clear and retrieve the contents. The process would be repeated as a means to pass information back and forth without personal contact and being identified.

Perhaps the most damaging spy for a foreign government, Hanssen is serving life imprisonment in Colorado with no chance of parole.

Brush passes and dead drops are used as means to reduce the risk of being caught in the act of passing material. The key to espionage is deception and hiding. Passing material is extremely risky and is a point in the process in which spies have been caught. As mentioned, the CheckMate network protection application seeks to determine the degree of *expertise* and *deception* present in samples of network packet activity (see Chapter 11 for a detailed description). I had defined the need for both expertise and deception to be present to exhibit theft or to inflict harm by malicious individuals. In the practice of espionage, if one is to be successful, he or she must have the skill to conduct the theft and must know how to be deceptive to avoid detection.

Knowledge of behaviors requiring both expertise and deception can assist in the identification of an individual engaging in this type of theft. To steal data, whether classified or proprietary, requires a mechanism to record or actually steal the information.

> **NOTE** Of course, copying information displays a higher level of skill and is a better method of deception since the original material is left intact, making the loss of content difficult to detect.

Although the dead drop and brush pass methods have been around for a very long time, variations have surfaced that may be even more deceptive. For example, *steganography* software is available that can embed messages within an image. The image remains the same. If you place two copies of the image next to one another with one containing the embedded message or document and the other not, it is impossible to visually detect the difference in the copies. This is basically hiding key information in plain sight as part of an image. Even when looking at the image, it is not possible to detect that a message or a document is embedded within the image.

As technology has progressed, tried and true espionage methods don't disappear; newer methods and variations develop and the espionage arsenal grows. The wise security professional not only is aware of the older methods but must also keep with current technology as it continues to grow (at an astounding rate). It is important to remember that the insider is constantly reviewing new methods to help steal and to pass information.

Espionage and the stealing of proprietary information combine antecedents (presence of desired information, method of storage, promise of payment, etc. that sets the stage for theft), the actual act (stealing, hiding, and passing to a customer), and successful consequences (evading detection, receiving payment, recognition from the paying customer). These antecedents, behaviors, and consequences combined with motivation result in the loss of sensitive materials.

When early acts of insider theft are accompanied by successful consequences of evading detection and achieving monetary gain, the acts of theft are reinforced and, therefore, are likely to continue. For example, Robert Hanssen persisted in passing information to the Russians for over 20 years, all the while holding very responsible positions, including being a counterintelligence lead at the FBI.

NOTE Robert Hanssen (born 04/18/44) was an FBI Special Agent who spied against the United States for Russia and then the Soviet Union for more than 20 years. During this time, Hanssen was a devout Catholic who practiced his religion faithfully with his wife. Hanssen was a counterintelligence and Soviet Union expert with access to files of KGB spies working for the United States. Hanssen's case is considered to be one of the most damaging in U.S. history and began when he approached the Russians to offer his services by providing names of three Russians working as spies for the United States and a request for compensation. This began a career of spying until he was arrested in 2001 while at a dead drop site. He now is serving a life sentence.

Aldrich Ames (born 05/26/41) was a CIA staff member who worked in operations. While he was in Southeast Asia, it was stated that Ames had a drinking problem, ultimately resulting in him being returned to headquarters. He became a counterintelligence officer and, like Hanssen in the FBI, had access to sensitive files describing current KGB agents working for the United States in Russia and later the Soviet Union. His case was considered to be very damaging, and much of his spying work completed for the Russians overlapped with Hanssen's, although they were unaware of one another. Ames also provided the names of those spying against Russia, some of which were the same as those provided by Hanssen. These disclosures led to a number of executions by the Russians. In February 1994, Ames and his complicit wife were arrested. Ames pleaded guilty and is serving life imprisonment. His wife served five years.

Jonathon Pollard (born 08/07/54) was an intelligence analyst who began his career working for naval intelligence after being turned down for employment by the CIA. Obsessed with Israeli intelligence and recognized as exaggerating

his capabilities and qualifications across repeated interviews, Pollard managed to end up in a position of trust. His top clearances were once revoked
but were returned to him at a later date. Having met an Israeli (Aviem Sella)
who could be an accomplice, Pollard passed a large number of classified documents to the accomplice to be passed to Israel. He was discovered in 1985
and was arrested in November of that year. Pollard remains in prison, serving
a life sentence for espionage.

There are numerous accounts of past espionage conducted by U.S. citizens
against their own country. For more details, I recommend reading the account
by Katherine L. Herbig and Martin F. Wiskoff: *Espionage against the United
States by American Citizens 1947-2001*, PERSEREC, Technical Report 02-5, July,
2002. This historical account provides the detail and analysis necessary for a
deeper understanding of the phenomenon. The report is online and may be
found by searching for title and authors.

New Tradecraft

Technology today is evolving so quickly that the security professional may not
spot the latest gadget that can be used to record sensitive data and exfiltrate the
material out of the restricted setting. Currently, astounding amounts of information may be recorded on USB drives that are very small and can be carried in
and out of an organization with little chance of detection. The security officer
should be on the lookout for such small devices as earring USB drives, wristwatch cameras (sold in many malls at Christmas and can contain between 50
and 100 digital photos), and the presence of any smartphone cameras. The very
fact that a person would enter and exit a restricted setting with any of these
things would be reason enough for detaining the person and investigating his
or her activities.

Technology has made both expertise and deception easier. New products sold
in such catalogs as the Sky Mall shopper (`http://www.skymall.com/shopping/
homepage.htm?pnr=ING`) contain devices of interest that could be used to assist in
stealing proprietary or classified information. This catalog is included on most
airliners in seat pockets and free for the taking. The catalog boasts recording
devices and very small cameras. Online shopping makes it too easy. You can
find just about any type of device you desire.

Insider threat is typically dependent on very small devices; small size helps
one be deceptive and decreases the probability of getting caught. Remember
all of the great James Bond movies with Q always working on new gadgets?
Miniaturization was often a key. Bond's watch carried everything from lasers
to enough wire to scale buildings. Although fanciful at the time, one can now
purchase spy gear right off the shelf or on the Internet.

For example, a scanner can now fit in the palm of the hand and can quickly
be passed over a document several times; the associated software even stores
it as an intact document. iPads, iPods, iPod Nanos, ebook readers, and similar

devices can hold a small library. When Jonathon Pollard worked at the NIC, he removed documents slowly over time until he was caught, eventually removing enough documents to form a cube 10 feet high by 6 feet wide by 6 feet deep. That amount of storage can now be placed on a USB thumb drive.

Miniaturization provides options that didn't exist. The imagination of a disgruntled employee, combined with motivation to seek revenge, needs only to be fueled with a method. Regardless of the method chosen, it is likely to include small devices and often the Internet. Many organizations have unmonitored Internet available on all workstations. This assists greatly in many tasks. However, a hookup to the Internet makes espionage-like behavior very easy. No one can really tell what a person is doing on a workstation unless he or she is monitored properly. Simply putting all the desired documents on a hard drive and storing them in a directory make sending them over the Internet as easy as pressing a keyboard key.

Security officials should ensure that they remain technically astute and current. By being aware of new devices on the market, they can determine how these devices may be used maliciously and then be on the lookout for that type of behavior.

Traditional-New Method Hybrids

A third category of tradecraft is a combination of historical tradecraft with new advances in technology. Adversaries are intelligent and creative. It is a new information age, and the former methods of such approaches as a dead drop or brush pass are no longer necessary. The basic concepts remain viable, but the methods will likely continue to be updated by the technical savvy insider.

NOTE In June 2010, the FBI arrested U.S. Army intelligence analyst Bradley Manning for classified material leaks to WikiLeaks (`http://wikileaks. org/`), a site devoted to disseminating leaked documents. Having reportedly passed 250,000 classified documents, including embarrassing videos of U.S.-led attacks, Manning was motivated by disagreement with war practices. Videos of actual attacks had not been released before this, and it revealed the violent side of war. Electronic files can now be passed faster than traditional methods, and attribution is harder than ever to establish. Take a look at the DVD and the demonstration of the AuBA ThemeMate tool. The example provided includes news articles on this case and shows how the tools may be used for both modeling and investigative purposes.

The best offense is a good defense. The prepared network security officer must be familiar with new technology that can be used to enhance success in stealing restricted information and traditional methods.

The Digital and Network Equivalents of Traditional Spycraft

In the 1980s, portable computerization was born. Prior to this, computer centers housed large, heavy computers, and specialists operated these machines and performed distinct jobs. A typical computer in the days of keypunch cards would be located at a data center and could be 5 feet high, 2 feet wide, and 5 or 6 feet long. One job may have taken many long boxes of cards to complete. Using a keypunch machine, you, or a keypunch expert, would transfer data and instructions onto the cards, take the cards to the data center, and wait to have the job run. If you made a single mistake on a card, the card would have to be retyped. You might take your job into a busy computer center on a Monday morning and come back on Wednesday to pick up the results. For example, if a research study had been completed and an analysis was needed, then the data would be entered into keypunch cards and stacked in such a way that the statistical analysis requested could be completed. Once completed, the output of the analysis would be printed on paper that was connected and individual sheets would have to be separated at perforations that separated the sheets. This way, one continuous stream of paper would be printed for what was called a "job." To give an idea, my dissertation took approximately 400 cards for data and provided a printout that was approximately an inch high.

NOTE   There were businesses that would actually keypunch for these computer specialists, since it was very easy to make a keypunch error. The keypunch used a typical keyboard punching actual holes in a card. Therefore, the process of completing an accurate job may have occurred for repeated runs until it was apparent that the many thousands of holes across the many hundreds of keypunch cards were accurate. In other words, if there were errors in the keypunch cards, the output would not report an analysis. Therefore, errors would have to be located on a specific card so that it could be retyped and then inserted back into the correct sequence in the card deck.

During this time period, with portable computing not available, tradecraft conducted by spies had been the same for decades and actually centuries. Such techniques as the two examples of dead drops and brush passes were used the same way with very slight variation. The documented cases and movies depicting spycraft used by traitors such as Aldrich Ames and Robert Hanssen show the use of these methods to escape detection. However, when portable computers, networks to tie them together, and the Internet to create a global connectivity came on the scene, the world changed in ways that are still difficult to describe accurately because of all the implications. For tradecraft associated with malicious behavior, the possibilities were now limitless. You could use your imagination to find technologically superior methods to hide information and copy it from a network, and you could send it anywhere in the world that had connectivity in seconds. Most important, tracing back from the victim to your machine as a perpetrator was almost impossible and still is exceedingly difficult.

NOTE The design for the Internet and the manner in which networks operate was a brilliant design. When initially designed by Advanced Research Projects Agency (ARPA) pioneers (the earlier DARPA without the *D*), the design was to allow for communication to continue even if part of the network was destroyed in a nuclear war or as a result of some other calamity. Imagine a hairnet. You can start at one point on a hairnet and get to any other point by tracing a different path. Snip one thread between any two knots, and you can still go from the same beginning to the same endpoint with many different paths. This is how it all works. Therefore, there are so many *knots* (nodes in the real world) that trying to re-create the path back even if not damaged is almost impossible today.

The design of network communication, the Internet, and intranets has carried with it tremendous capability to be deceptive. This may not have been the intention, but it is certainly threatening.

NOTE I contend that most hacking and adversary cyber threat would go away almost overnight if we simply perfected the capability to trace back from a cyber attack to the actual computer used for the malicious behavior. This capability should be receiving increased funding today for serious and capable researchers.

Today's spy can conduct acts of espionage from home or work and transfer information to the hands of a foreign government in seconds. For this reason, security has to change at a faster rate. We simply must be more proactive and put improved methods of detection into place. We cannot afford another situation where an insider like Manning can steal and leak 250,000 sensitive and classified documents.

The Digital Dead Drop

It is well known that terrorists now communicate with what could be labeled as *digital dead drops*. Of course, the primary use of a dead drop is that both sides can exchange information without meeting. However, it also keeps communication very private and detection exceedingly difficult. In a U.S. Senate review of terrorist communication on the Internet,[1] Frank Cilluffo, Director of George Washington University's Homeland Security Policy Institute, describes the practice of using the Internet dead drop.

---

[1] Martha L. Arias, "INTERNET LAW — Terrorism on the Internet: Another Border to Protect One Country's Sovereignty," *iBLS: Internet Business Law Services*, May 2007: www.ibls.com/internet_law_news_portal_view.aspx?s=latestnews&id=1765

Mr. Cilluffo testified on the Institute's Internet-Facilitated Radicalization study and said, "We have created this global village — the Internet — without a police department." In presenting the institute's study, Mr. Cilluffo revealed that terrorists use, among others, hard-to-intercept communications like "dead drop." Dead drop communications are drafted e-mails stored in accounts where adepts access them and read their rebel message. No e-mail is sent; thus, no interception may be accomplished.

Just for clarity, if a terrorist is communicating with another terrorist or if an insider is communicating with an outsider to receive stolen sensitive information, one person may create a draft of a message on an e-mail site and leave it as a draft. The other person who wishes to retrieve it may enter the site, use the same user ID and password, recall the draft, read it, and then delete it. Then the process can be repeated in the opposite direction. Drafts are just drafts and kept for the writer to edit.

> **NOTE**   When e-mail hit the scene, it did so with a figurative explosion. It was introduced, and then it was pervasive. The reason for its success is the ease with which communication can occur. It is a revolution in worldwide communication. With variations such as texting and tweeting, it continues to expand.

The Digital Brush Pass

The traditional brush pass is no longer necessary. It may make great drama for a movie or TV series, but the digital age has intervened, and now the digital brush pass is easier with far less probability of detection.

It is easy to see how detection can be complicated — from extremely difficult to nearly impossible, if the process occurs in real time — when a draft is left and immediately picked up by a receiver then deleted, just like spies exchanging a briefcase as they pass.

Digital communication is still growing on a daily basis, providing millions of possible ways to exchange information. This hiding in clear view, known as *security through obscurity*, has made the job of law enforcement and intelligence more difficult. New methods are needed and are surfacing now. For example, programs exist that allow one to monitor all tweets for specific content.

Perpetrators tend to forget that the group imagination and genius behind the development of the Internet and network communication are still present — it is the same imaginative thought and genius behind the development of new security methods. This switch to a new proactive stance is absolutely necessary and has already started. CheckMate and InMate network protection applications are excellent examples of this new technology. Constantly looking behind the scenes in network activity, the applications are assessing the suspiciousness and threat projecting from human behavior leading to malicious activity, instead of the activity itself.

Digital Cutouts

In the world of insider threat tradecraft, a *cutout* is a person or method that is an intermediary between the person stealing information and the person receiving it. The cutout is unlikely to know the identity of the sender or receiver or know the content of the material passed. The advantage is he or she is simply a middle man passing the information and cannot help in any investigation if caught because he or she knows nothing of significance.

Digital drop-off sites can serve as a form of cutout. Intermediates may provide additional protection by receiving encrypted files or steganographically embedded messages.

NOTE It has been reported that steganography is used to embed love notes between high school students in images. When received, the software extracts the message from the image. If the note is intercepted, the teacher sees only an image of the Grand Canyon in the student's assigned report. The student might even receive bonus points for going the extra mile to support the assignment with images! If this is high-school-level capability, then we need to be more aware of how adversaries may operate within the cyber world.

Recognizing Deception: Nothing Is as It Seems

I have emphasized deception and expertise as attributes of malicious intent throughout this book. That is because malicious intent and malicious behavior are always associated with both these attributes. Malicious behavior does not just occur randomly. For example, phishing attacks have exploded onto the cyber world scene. A phishing attack is typically an e-mail message that has false content but is designed deceptively to be a real e-mail, usually of importance. There is usually a link or attachment in the message. The malicious intent behind the e-mail is to design the message in such a way that recipients will click on the link or attachment. When you click — and many will — malware will be immediately inserted onto your hard drive or memory. The malicious program may simply wait for any user IDs and passwords and send them back to the adversary. Now the adversary has access to the network, using your user ID and password.

NOTE Recently, I received an e-mail with the subject, "You have exceeded your mail account size." This type of message is not unusual; many people receive them at work because companies often have a limit on mailbox sizes. The e-mail went on to say that more space would be provided if I clicked the available link. Fortunately, I realized that this was a phishing e-mail and did not click the link — malware avoided! It is unusual for companies to provide a link to allow staff to automatically increase mailbox sizes. This typically requires a request to increase the size with justification. Therefore, a link on the e-mail was very suspicious. A search of current malware showed that this new approach was a recent phishing attack.

Expertise and deception are greater than ever because of the rapidly growing technology to assist the malicious user. It simply is not difficult to learn techniques to assist a U.S. citizen in targeting other U.S. citizens or U.S. targets.

Advantages of AuBA #10: Moving from Reactive to Proactive

One of the major advantages of AuBA is that behavioral models that result from the methodology provide the capability to predict future malicious behavior/events. This is a very important difference from other approaches, such as signature detection. Both approaches use past events to derive a predictive model (in the case of AuBA) or signatures (in the case of signature detection). The typical process with signature detection is to study past attacks and to forensically determine the characteristics of those attacks. Once characteristics have been defined, these are placed into rules. Most often, these rules are placed into an if-then type of format. This means that if X happens, then Y is a result. This allows us to look for the signatures in the future. If rules in a signature detection system fire, then we know that attack is occurring again. The problem is that we are being reactive. The attack must occur so that we can react.

AuBA predictive modeling is very different. Although we may use the AuBA tools to process the same text that describes historical events, we concentrate on extracting the antecedents to past attacks instead of just the behavior. By focusing on associating precursor events with types of behavior that follows, we can project what type of behavior will occur in the future when a specific set of antecedent conditions is present. This ability to predict significant adversarial behavior prior to its occurrence removes us from a reactive stance, in which all we can do is forensic in nature to describe the attack we just experienced, to a proactive stance, through which mitigation may be considered should the projected behavior occur.

Moving from rules to identify known attacks to predicting malicious behavior that may not have occurred yet, as well as projecting known attack behaviors prior to their occurrence, works within network applications and more traditional adversarial behavior such as terrorism.

The automated tools associated with AuBA do much more than we as humans when we process past incidents or events. Although we do tend to look for indicators associated with past behavior, we simply cannot find as many antecedents (precursors), nor are they of the quality of the ones found with the AuBA tools. Furthermore, through the AuBA modeling process, the identified antecedents are reduced to the most predictive set, removing much of the guesswork as to which ones are effective and the trial-and-error analysis that is typically used to develop a model.

Moving from a reactive stance to a proactive stance is one of the hallmarks of a future vision for security. We need lead time with a warning that a specific type or class of attack is coming. Then we can better act to protect people and property, as opposed to simply describing the damage.

In Summary

Domestic threat is particularly disturbing because it consists of U.S. citizens turning against their country and fellow citizens. Some of our country's most serious terrorist attacks within our own borders have been at the hands of U.S. citizens. Army Major Hasan, Timothy McVeigh, and the senior al-Qaeda leader, Anwar al-Awlaki, are infamous for their actions. Reviewing threat in the cyber world indicates that severe levels of threat and actual acts of damage or theft are coming from within. Although most insider threat cases would probably be best labeled as crime, semantics can change quickly to fit the category of domestic terrorism. Because of global interconnectedness with many varieties of group attacks, it is difficult to have sharp definitions of terrorism that differentiate between domestic and foreign terrorism.

Many of the extremist incidents, including abortion clinic bombings and shootings, animal rights activists acts, etc. could logically be labeled as domestic terrorist acts because of the associated messages attached to influence others. Whether attacks are conventional with bombings, shootings, or cyber, our national infrastructure, business, and organizations are facing daily threat from domestic terrorism. We desperately need a paradigm shift in security that will allow us to be more accurate with predictive analytics to determine when attacks are going to occur so that intervention rather than response can occur. In my opinion, we are just starting to turn the corner from reactive to proactive. This is a very good sign, but there is much work to do. As stated, I believe strongly that resources should be focused on the automated identification of perpetrators through improved traceback methods within the cyber world. If perpetrators can be identified, there would be a likely dramatic drop in threat and actual attacks — particularly state-sponsored events.

CHAPTER 11

Computer Networks: Protection from External Threat

The Sophos Security Threat Report for 2011 states that it processes new malware introduced every 0.9 seconds, 24 hours a day, seven days a week, all year. That is just under one per second. This is an astounding number by any measure. The implications are enormous. First, it means that current security products are not successful. By any stretch of the imagination, we are not stopping malware if it is being introduced once per second on a continuous basis — not even close — and this is just the number processed by Sophos, a security firm specializing in network attacks.

This chapter looks deeply at the current network protection available against external threat. The following chapter focuses on internal threat. Although current product approaches attempt to protect against threat with either signature detection or anomaly detection, the approach in this book divides the threat into external and internal. Why? The motivation of an external attacker and an insider is entirely different. Rather than focusing on products, I focus on the malicious human behavior that results in attacks. This chapter will peel away the layers of current network protection methods against external threat. At the same time, I will explain why we need a paradigm shift in security. Current technology is not working well. However, we cannot design new technology unless we understand the strengths and weaknesses of current technology.

As I discussed earlier in the book, currently there are two technology approaches to network protection:

- Signature detection
- Anomaly detection

CROSS-REFERENCE As you know by now, I have introduced a third technology that is more predictive and proactive. However, this chapter focuses on existing technology. See Chapters 16 and 17 for CheckMate and InMate descriptions.

Let's first conceptually explore signature detection and anomaly detection. This type of view reveals both the strengths and the weaknesses of both approaches. For completeness, I will not limit the discussion to network protection alone. For example, signature detection is also a primary way of attempting to anticipate terrorism, insurgence, and other forms of adversarial behavior that affect our country and our national infrastructure. First we will explore the predominant approach: signature detection. Second, we will explore anomaly detection, which even after the many years it has been present is still experimental. The reason why this approach remains primarily experimental will be provided.

Protecting Against Known Attacks: Signature Detection

Every network attack and every other form of adversary attack has characteristics. The behavior that results in the attack can be described with these characteristics. Signature detection is labeled as such because of the similarity of these attack characteristics to our signatures — they are all unique, just like fingerprints. Like written signatures that define who we are, attackers define themselves because they tend to repeat behavior because it has been successful. If a behavior had failed as a consequence, we would likely not see the behavior again. As has been stated, human behavior repeats if followed by successful consequences (and likely to even increase in frequency of occurrence) and decreases or stops if followed by undesirable consequences. Given that a signature is a unique characterization, then signature detection is the process of identifying a unique signature.

As law enforcement officers know, a burglar, serial rapist, murderer, arsonist, and all other forms of criminals tend to have signatures if repeated. Chapter 1 highlighted the behaviors of Theodore Bundy and Jeffrey Dahmer, two of the most notorious serial murderers in our country's history. Both engaged in murders of young people: Bundy killed young women, and Dahmer killed young men.

The selection of the targets, the approach to the targets, the brutal murders, and the sexual behavior after the murders all represented stylized behavior that was repeatable — their signatures. The behaviors were repeated because they were successful, until both men were eventually caught. I had some training at the FBI academy when in the U.S. Secret Service and know that in some crimes, clues to where a perpetrator actually lives may be part of the crime scene. This is because humans form patterns of behavior very quickly, and these patterns can be described as signatures.

To those who doubt the speed with which humans pattern their behavior, please note the next time you are at a conference. All walk in at the beginning of the conference and take a seat. After that first break I predict with at least 95 percent accuracy that the returning audience sits in the exact seat. I have actually been told, when I took a different seat after the first break, that I was in someone else's seat! Criminals do the same thing with their modus operandi (method of operation). A criminal may be specialized as a driver, a safecracker, a second-story man, a bomber, and so on. All are signatures.

The degree to which signature detection does work is a product of humans repeating their behavior over time. Instead of planning a unique attack for every site, a network attacker tends to use the same technique across multiple sites. This repeated attack across different sites means that, if we can characterize the attack, we can place a software set of rules in place on a network to identify that attack if it occurs again. It is a reactive approach — the attack has to occur before we can study it, understand it, convert it to rules, and add those rules to our network intrusion detection application such as Snort to wait for the next occurrence of the attack.

Signature detection as a method is very effective in detecting those repeating attacks that have been characterized with rules and added to the network intrusion protection application. However, there are many problems associated with this approach. These problems are:

- Signature detection is reactive — the attack has to occur first, be studied forensically, and then characterized with rules; in the meantime, serious damage can continue with that attack.

- New attacks can slip by existing signatures because new attacks do not have characterizations and, therefore, no rules to catch the new attack.

- The forensic process to study an attack can be costly and time-consuming and occur as a series of iterations until the set of new rules works effectively.

- It is relatively easy for a hacker to modify a known attack to slip by the protective signature detection application.

- A zero-day attack, which is a new attack focused on a specific vulnerability within the network, operating system, or so forth, is not detected by signature detection and can cause considerable damage because of the focused vulnerability attack before a signature can be developed to protect against it.

■ The signature detection methodology is neither predictive nor proactive.

■ Unless the attack is pervasive and well publicized, the fix may be developed by one organization only and not shared with others, leaving the majority of networks unprotected.

There are many other features of signature detection that result in only partial effectiveness at best. It is effective for what it does, but it is not effective enough. If we add the indisputable fact that signature detection is the primary method in use today, it is clear why we have a problem, and why we desperately need a paradigm shift resulting in new technology.

Turning to adversary warfare that is not network based, terrorists are intelligent and have received training on how to avoid detection. This is not a secret — it should be obvious. Of course, much depends on the organization. Hezbollah does repeat many of the same acts, either as terrorist attacks or as acts of insurgency. But, as we have observed, al-Qaeda switches behavior often. We have observed attacks against embassies, the naval ship *USS Cole*, the World Trade Center, and the Pentagon. There is no real signature to speak of with this group. Therefore, looking for attack signatures with al-Qaeda is fruitless. However, the group does respond to the same antecedent conditions and that has remained the same since its introduction, and predicting responses to antecedent conditions is the basis for AuBA.

Interestingly enough, the predictive accuracy of human behavior is not based on studying the behavior! Many make this mistake. Correlational approaches that associate different behaviors to find patterns are simply missing the fact that behaviors are associated with precursor antecedent and consequence conditions and situations. As someone once said, "Computers don't attack computers, people do." If we look at people, we must look for antecedents, behavior, motivations, and consequences. Studying behavior alone and correlating behaviors may lead to baselines (normal rates of behaving) but not accurate prediction.

Network Signature Detection

Computer network signature detection depends on waiting until a network is attacked so that the attack can be isolated, studied, and characterized as rules in order to identify future attempts to attack with the same approach. It is important to realize that very detailed work is required to identify one serious attack and to characterize it in a set of rules so that an application may include the characterized signature. For example, it took over five months of dedicated work among many network security professionals to isolate the basic functioning of the Conficker worm, which is a severely destructive worm that has infected many millions of computers worldwide.

Given the assault that results in new variations of malware and each second of each day and the five months it took to identify all the features of the self-propagating Conficker worm, it should be obvious why signature detection cannot possibly be adequate. Yet, it is our number one approach! Reactive as it is, signature detection is absolutely necessary. We do not seek a technology to replace signature detection; we seek a technology to augment signature detection. This is why AuBA applications have been developed.

Terrorism Signature Detection: A Comparison

Reviewing other forms of signature detection can inform the process of reviewing and modifying network signature detection. Terrorism signature detection is highly similar to network intrusion detection. Both are reactive; we must wait until an attack occurs to study that attack and characterize it with rules. There simply is not a way for reactive applications to become proactive — by definition. As an example, Richard Reid, the shoe bomber who struck shortly after 9/11, placed explosives in his shoe and attempted to light the fuse in flight. If he had succeeded, many hundreds of lives would have been lost. As a result of Reid's act, we reactively studied the example, and we have been taking our shoes off at the airport security gates since that time.

Terrorists, depending on the group and its modus operandi, plan attacks based on their motivation and the antecedents that set the stage for attack behavior. However, even though the basic ingredients exist for accurate prediction, we ignore the basic human behavior foundations and, after the fact, study the attack. Having been a CIA intelligence officer, I have always been amazed how you can feel a sense of being proactive by studying the past. We analyze past attack behavior and create signatures, and then look to the future. Surprising to most, the future does not unfold as calculated — usually future behavior occurs differently from the signatures that were created. For example, the al-Qaeda attack on the *USS Cole* can be studied in detail, as well as former al-Qaeda attacks on embassies. We can create signatures based on those attacks, but they would not lead us to the infamous 9/11 attacks on the World Trade Center and the Pentagon.

Signature detection does not predict future behavior — it simply defines the past. If al-Qaeda had attacked another U.S. naval ship, then perhaps the detailed study of the *USS Cole* would have been more useful. Predicting future behavior requires that we predict the who, what, when, where, and how of the next attack. Behavior in the past does not repeat perfectly for the future. Adversaries not only have skills and expertise to carry out serious and devastating attacks against our country and its citizens but also work to be deceptive. Repetition of behavior invites detection, and with detection comes the possibility of being apprehended. Deception works as a shield. Deception includes variation, obscurity, and misdirection. It means that with any form of adversary behavior, new attack behavior is not likely to occur in the same ways it did in the past.

To continue the basic traffic light example I have already used in this book, in the United States, the green light is predictive of our driving through the intersection, and the red is predictive of vehicles stopping. The red, yellow, and green antecedents, and the stimulus control exerted over traffic by these colors, remain stable over time. This stability of antecedent to behavior associations allows for accurate prediction. We cannot predict how I might go through that intersection — I can walk, jog, drive a car, or ride a bicycle or a motorcycle. Therefore, limiting prediction to only the study of the behavior is ultimately incomplete and non-predictive.

Studying signatures is necessary, for with study comes an increased understanding of tactics and protection against attack should the same behavior occur again. However, we should never expect prediction to spontaneously emerge from signature detection. If we do, then valuable time and resources may be lost while we observe attacks occurring again in different forms that simply were not anticipated. Prediction of human behavior requires accurate methodologies. I have found no shortcuts in the almost 30 years of analyzing adversary behavior and malicious intent.

Identifying Criminal Signatures

Motivations, targeting, and actual behaviors are very different across hackers, terrorists, and criminals. Like three surgeons with different specialties using the same model scalpel, the person using the behavioral methodology in this book can work effectively across very different types of malicious behavior. The method of signature detection is entirely different across the three areas. Unlike AuBA (which uses a methodology to identify materials to construct a model and the automated tools to apply consistency), the concept of signature detection across terrorism, network hacking, and criminal behavior fits at the conceptual level only. If we observe network-based malicious activity emanating from terrorist groups, criminals, or hackers, then there are more commonalities based on network constraints.

The following are examples of signature-based approaches and how they differ. The first is a small sample of a Snort rule for network protection that it is formatted for a computer process.

```
alert tcp any any -> 10.0.0.5 80 ( msg:"web request"; )
```

Thanks to Erin M. Britz, SAIC network intrusion detection specialist.

NOTE Snort rules comprise two main parts, the rule header and the rule body. The rule header starts with the action (`log` or `alert`), the protocol (`ip`, `tcp`, `udp`, `icmp`, or `any`), and then an IP and port combination you would find in a firewall rule with a direction modifier (`->` or `<>`). The rule body has several functions that aid in the identification of malicious traffic and facilities for notification.

The other two sample signature-based rules are more text-based and are used to guide analysis. First is a sample of a phrase that would be in a signature profile for Ted Bundy, the infamous serial killer:

Victim selection is focused on young (range=12–26, mean=19), attractive females with long hair, typically parted down the middle…

The following is a sample excerpt from a signature profile of al-Qaeda:

Al-Qaeda's motivations are based on fatwas and released statements from Osama bin Laden. Stated enemies of focus are: the United States, Israel, and Western allies. The group is motivated by the desire to rid foreign lands of U.S./ally occupation. Because all members fully embrace this basic tenet, activities of their enemies take on a special emphasis and interest…

These examples are provided to show that signature-based approaches are predominant in security. Signature detection is not owned by network intrusion detection. It is a pervasive approach in security that says, "Let's learn the signatures of adversaries so that we can detect when dangerous, malicious behaviors occur in the future." Although detection is important, it simply is not enough for the following reasons:

- Malicious human behavior is rife with variety not defined by signatures.
- Signatures describe past attacks and have limited utility for anticipating future attacks.
- Network intrusion detection signatures defined and written as rules are primarily for the more common threat — the advanced adversary is more likely to use new deceptive methods to intrude that do not have signatures.
- The focus of signature detection is on describing the actual malicious activity of concern, which means we are going to be detecting malicious activity when it is in progress, leaving little to no time to prevent the attack.

There are many criminal signatures, and law enforcement staffs are well aware of the most common. For the most part, criminal activity occurs with a focus on deception to avoid being caught. For example, criminal acts are often conducted at a time when there are few people around to provide eyewitness accounts. However, cameras are becoming available. If camera shots are expected, then a criminal may wear a mask to avoid detection. If breaking into a home, the back door or a window is highly likely as opposed to forcing entry through the front door. Computer technology and network connectivity has changed the world of criminal activity. One can now sit at home and surveil a site by live webcams. For example, I can now observe the Annapolis, Maryland, harbor to determine if there is room for my sailboat from anywhere in the world via the Internet. The webcam is located on the adjacent Marriott hotel. Amazingly, I can pan, tilt, and zoom the camera remotely from 10,000 miles away at no cost.

Not only has technology made surveillance of a site for criminal action easier with little to no chance of getting caught, it has created new categories of crime as well. Identity theft is on the rise. Credit card numbers are being stolen at an alarming rate. The introduction of phishing attacks, where a legitimate-looking e-mail lures victims to respond, and variants (for example, spear phishing, pharming, and so on) have allowed easy access to many organizations' private accounts. Spear phishing is even harder to ignore. Spear phishing attacks can be convincing since they are constructed to appear as coming from the organization's human resources department, a note from the CEO, or an announcement of an award. There is typically a request for personal information, or a link or download that requires the user to click on a spot in the e-mail. Of course, as soon as this spot is clicked, malware such as a Trojan horse is automatically inserted onto the user's hard drive to capture the user's ID and password. Now the adversary has total access to the network using the user's ID and password.

I receive and send a very high number of e-mails daily. This results in regularly exceeding my mailbox limit. When this occurs, I must empty the mailbox of some of the e-mails to reduce the overall size. The process of cleaning the mailbox includes finding e-mails with large attachments and removing them from the mailbox, therefore reducing the size. While writing this chapter I received a spear phishing attack. The e-mail had on the subject line: *Your mailbox limit has been exceeded*. This is the same message I always receive. The e-mail read the same. However, there were three additions:

- There was a link with a statement saying that there was a new feature, and if I clicked on the link I would be granted more space.

- There were unusual misspellings in the e-mail.

- For once, the e-mail had been cleaned that same day, so there was plenty of space.

This spear phishing attack was clever. I anticipate that these types of attacks can be so convincing that almost all employees of an organization will be a victim at one time or another.

Criminal activity is an immense problem because of all the potential types of criminal attacks or theft and the astronomical number of attack variants. The variety makes it very difficult to stop the variants. We do not expect to see criminal activity go away. It is a reality, and it is with us each day. Terrorism is now the same. It is here, and it is not going to go away. Hacking is here to stay, as well.

If we are going to develop improved criminal activity signatures, then again behavior analysis foundations will be required to identify better the antecedent conditions and situations associated with the criminal activity. However, at the end, we will still have signatures, and they will be reactive.

Identifying Unknown and First-Time Attacks

Signature detection, by definition, identifies signatures of known attacks. That is its designed purpose. However, we are flooded with unknown and zero-day attacks on an ongoing basis that slip past signature detection applications. Some believe that signature detection can simply be expanded by adding variants of existing rules that would catch some new attacks and some zero-day attacks. There is a reason why this is not a fruitful direction — it would take an inordinate amount of time to write enough variants for all existing rules to be effective enough to catch new attacks with regularity. A paradigm shift to catch new and zero-day attacks is not likely to incorporate this approach. This is the primary reason why I invented the CheckMate/InMate technology. As mentioned, a detailed description of the technology will be presented in later chapters. However, suffice it to say, the AuBA technology was developed specifically to identify attacks not caught by signature detection. By using both AuBA and signature detection methods together, the probability of identification of a wider range of attacks is greater.

Why can't we just write new signatures for attacks that have not occurred yet? CheckMate has the concept of *future signatures*, which is the ability of CheckMate to detect literally many trillions of combinations of detected behaviors not in the pattern classification process used to train the assessment modules.

Why can't signature detection handle billions of combinations of packet variables to detect new attacks? First, signature detection consists of a very specific set of rules written to detect specific known attacks. The process of identifying the values of variables and even what variables to use can be extremely time-consuming. The 5-month process it took to develop rules to protect against the Conficker worm is a testament to the difficulties that can be associated with signature detection. The specificity of developed rules underscores the low probability of anticipating new attacks and then to develop rules to protect against those attacks. They can't be studied and translated into rules because they do not yet exist.

Second, the concept of *combinatorial explosion* works against signature detection when it comes to anticipating new attacks. For example, the patented CheckMate technology has 2^{600} combinations of the 600 behavior monitors that may automatically be converted to measures of *expertise* and *deception* every 100 milliseconds. If both behavioral dimensions exceed a preset threshold, then empirical research and validation has demonstrated that imminent threat is present. Signature detection, on the other hand, uses a variety of specific packet-level variables in specific sets of rules. There may be thousands of signatures, which may sound like a large number until we determine just how large all possible combinations can be. For example, if only 16 variables are used, there are 65,536 possible combinations of these 16 variables. If we add just 4 more variables and look at all possible combinations, we have jumped to 1,048,576 combinations. The number explodes with each new variable.

> **DEFINITION** *Combinatorial explosion* **"occurs when a huge number of possible combinations are created by increasing the number of entities which can be combined — forcing us to consider a constrained set of possibilities when we consider related problems. (Arbib) It occurs when a small increase in the number of elements that can be combined increase the number of combinations to be computed so fast that it quickly reaches computational limits (see bremermann's limit). E.g., the number of possible coalitions (partitions of unlike individuals into like parts) among 3 individuals is 5, among 5 individuals it is 52, among 10 individuals it is 115,975 and among 20 individuals it is 51,724,156,235,572, etc. (Krippendorff)."**

www.websters-online-dictionary.org

At this juncture, adding just one additional variable doubles the combinations to 2,097,152. Figure 11-1 shows the progression of the number of combinations by consistently adding an additional variable. Notice in the figure that when we reach just 30 variables, we have exceeded 1 billion possible combinations.

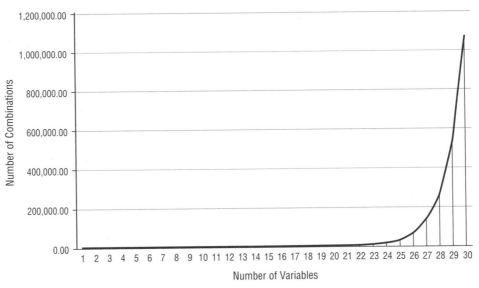

Figure 11-1: Combinatorial explosion of 30 variables

Given the number of variables that may be used to write signature detection rules, the number of possible combinations of variables present that would signify an attack is astronomical. If we used only 29 variables and spent only 10 minutes reviewing each combination, it would take 22,381 years to go through each combination. Given these numbers, it is not possible to process and review all possible combinations to prepare signature variations that would likely be a threat in the future. On the other hand, the new CheckMate technology can process any of the possible 2,600 possible combinations of behavior-based monitors and provide an accurate assessment of *expertise* and *deception*. This assessment takes 50 microseconds to occur, or 20,000 assessments per second. If a unique combination is presented to CheckMate or InMate, then assessment occurs automatically and in real time.

This capability, as compared to signature detection, allows the CheckMate and InMate technology the capability to detect new attacks without training on the pattern or without a signature having to be written. Figure 11-2 depicts a test of CheckMate against two leading signature detection products. The independent testing is proprietary, so the testing company must remain nameless. For the two leading products, in fairness, just as we change names in clinical examples, we will call one Product 1 and the other Product 2.

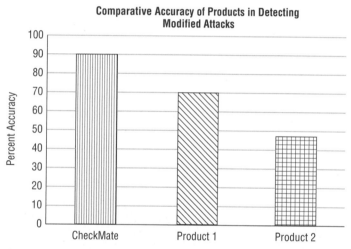

Figure 11-2: A comparison of CheckMate with two leading signature detection products after attacks were changed using hacker evasion tactics to avoid detection

The testing company presented network attacks that all three products (CheckMate, Product 1, and Product 2) could detect at 100 percent accuracy. The company then used hacker evasion tactics to alter the attacks. This was essentially a rapid way of creating new attacks based on significant variations. However, it is important to note that because attacks were used that could be detected initially, it should be possible for the *new* attacks to contain remnants of detectable attacks.

As can be seen in the figure, CheckMate detected 90 percent of the *new* attacks, while Product 2 detected 78 percent, and Product 1 detected only 48 percent. Although not a clean test of truly new attacks or zero-day attacks, the comparison conducted by an independent testing laboratory revealed that CheckMate caught significantly more attacks when past attacks were modified to defeat detection. Considering CheckMate can perform in this manner across 2^{600} different combinations of its behavior-based monitors, the new technology certainly is ready to augment signature detection.

A new, proactive paradigm shift is going to require a new form of technology that can detect new attacks or attacks that represent variations of those that can be detected. CheckMate is a move in that direction, using human behavior assessment to augment current approaches, such as signature detection.

Identifying Anomalies

The term "anomaly" does not quite mean the same across network intrusion protection, terrorism, and criminal activity. In terms of network intrusion, anomaly refers to a significant deviation from an established norm, or baseline. In criminal activity and terrorism, it tends to mean that something unusual or different has occurred that is a variant from what was expected. It is more math related in the former, and more observation oriented in the latter. Here is an example of criminal activity: I was working with a customs officer on a case some years ago, and an officer recounted the incident. At the time, he was looking at Canadian border crossings. He noticed a person driving a vehicle very carefully and at an exact speed. The person was clean shaven and immaculately dressed. At the same time, the car was perfectly clean. There just was nothing wrong with the car, the driver, or the behavior. Typically, drivers were tired and had been driving for long periods of time, cars were dirty from the trips, and drivers were speeding or going too slowly, and so forth.

However, the behavior of the driver was an anomaly. The officer knew that a person guilty of something would go out of the way to appear normal. The speeder, once spotting the radar gun, typically drives the exact speed limit, tries to act nonchalant, and is the perfect citizen. The agent stopped the car and, while inspecting the trunk, found false side panels behind which were many plastic wrapped containers of cocaine. From the perspective of an adversary, part of deception is to appear to be part of background normal baseline behavior. From the perspective of law enforcement, an agent looks for the person who is exhibiting normal baseline activity too perfectly. Even in true baseline activity, humans simply are not perfect.

In another case, which I witnessed, a group of teenagers was hanging out at the side of a convenience store at closing time. A police car pulled up, and two of the boys immediately turned and started walking quickly away. The police immediately followed the two who took off around the corner. An experienced officer knows to look for anomalies. In the case of the customs officer, he stopped the car, did an examination, and behind the trunk panels found a significant amount of cocaine that was being transported into the United States from

Canada. In the case of the teenagers, they had recently committed a robbery and were afraid of being recognized, but it was too late.

Network anomaly detection is very different from signature detection. Basically, the two-step process consists of establishing a baseline of normal network activity, and flagging significant deviations from the baseline, called a norm (for *normal*). The conceptual assumption is similar to the use of anomaly in criminal activity and terrorism — that is, deviations from the norm may be indicative of activity that could be harmful in some way. However, unlike criminal activity and terrorism, the process of establishing a norm is more formalized and not just based on experience.

Network Anomaly Detection

Network anomaly detection developed over time as an alternative or augmentation to signature detection. Anomaly was developed out of need to circumvent many of the problems associated with signature detection. Perhaps the major impetus was that signature detection cannot detect unknown, new, or zero-day attacks, unless the unique attack has remnants of known past attacks associated with it. As has already been stated, this is a serious and significant flaw in the approach. As new attacks mount every day, new technology is sorely needed as part of the paradigm shift.

Anomaly detection, however, has many flaws in its own right. In fact, in comparison to signature detection, anomaly detection has even more basic flaws in its current form. However, I believe many of these flaws could be corrected, making anomaly detection much more of a future tool in the cyber arsenal. So, what are the advantages and disadvantages?

Advantages of Anomaly Detection

The basic assumption of anomaly detection is that if there is a baseline of normal network activity, then a significant deviation could be indicative of malicious activity. Therefore, the overwhelming advantage is that anomaly detection has the distinct *possibility* of flagging a new attack or a zero-day attack in progress.

Disadvantages of Anomaly Detection

Unfortunately, anomaly detection has many more disadvantages than advantages, which is why the method has not been serious competition for signature detection as the primary approach in use today. The disadvantages are:

- The baseline, or norm, must be established for each separate network — it does not generalize well to other networks because of the unique characteristics of each network.
- The norming process can take weeks to months.

- Networks are under constant attack or scanning; therefore, it is not possible to baseline a network in a totally normal state.

- A normed network includes malicious behavior; therefore, that malicious behavior has been determined to be normal and will not be flagged in the future.

- Human behavior is noted by variation and anomalies that are considered to be totally normal — current anomaly detection cannot differentiate between *anomaly malicious* and *anomaly non-malicious* (most anomalies are normal).

- Anomaly detection is noted often by extraordinarily high false-positive rates (calling activity threatening when it is non-malicious).

- Using a combination of anomaly detection and signature detection by anything other than a dedicated, expert staff can result in very high false positives because of anomaly detection and very high false negatives (calling malicious activity non-malicious) because of signature detection — the overall effect is to have an error-ridden approach.

I suggest that AuBA approaches like CheckMate and InMate could not only be used as new approaches in their own right but also process flagged anomalies as a three-step process. Currently, anomaly detection consists, first, of establishing a norm and, second, of flagging deviations from the norm. If we put the technologies together, we may find that the whole is greater than the sum of its parts. I believe that the combination of anomaly detection and AuBA approaches offer advantages that circumvent many of the disadvantages currently presented by anomaly detection.

NOTE Currently, existing signature detection and anomaly detection methodologies are antiquated and must be cast out or updated for the paradigm shift, because current forms are not providing the protection that we need.

NOTE During 2011, I attended a number of conferences and workshops dealing with technology in network protection. Some of the best researchers in anomaly detection were in attendance and presented. With all due respect, AuBA was the only new approach presented. Small changes in signature detection or anomaly detection were noted, but certainly far less than what is needed. I have not seen an approach that is viable to attach to anomaly detection to differentiate between anomaly malicious and anomaly non-malicious of all anomaly flagged activities.

Methods of Detection

Highlighting two serious problems with anomaly detection that work in tandem to decrease effectiveness is the fact that we don't have a normal, non-malicious network to baseline and the fact that normal human behavior is rife with variation and anomalies.

NOTE All new malicious attacks are anomalous, but not all anomalous behavior is malicious.

Given these problems, if we are going to use anomaly detection, we must determine deviations from the norm to flag network activity to examine for malicious activity clues. It is fair to say that anomaly detection still exists within the research laboratory with one step in the real world — for example, Cisco now offers anomaly-detection-based products. The approach still has much potential if the problems can be solved.

The focus on determining deviations from the norm and differentiating malicious from non-malicious is not going to be solved with statistics, machine learning, neural networks, or advanced algorithms. Currently, the approach is to find a proper mathematical technique for determining an anomaly. It is not a matter of selecting the correct statistical or automated clustering approach; however, the problem is that no one is yet including human behavior and methods of determining malicious intent. Differentiating malicious anomalies from non-malicious cannot be done purely mathematically.

No doubt statistical methods, advanced math, artificial neural networks, clustering, and so forth are all important and probably could all be used. However, if we are not looking at the appropriate data, then advancements in number generation will not bring improvements in the high false-positive rates.

My prediction is that once we alter the overall way that anomaly detection works and add human behavior dimensions of intent, anomaly detection will move out of the laboratory and be used as a serious proactive network protection tool. It also does not matter whether we are focusing on external threat to a network or internal threat — it will take a whole new approach to anomaly detection that will include human behavior before we see significant decreases in overall false-positive rates.

Anticipating Anomalies

Currently, signature detection and anomaly detection do not have the demonstrated capability to anticipate anomalies before they occur. If so, the methods would have true predictive capability. Signature detection is likely to remain reactive in the future. Anomaly detection, on the other hand, may not be able to anticipate anomalies before they happen, but it is capable of detecting deviations from a normal baseline, which could include new attacks. I anticipate that anomaly detection as an approach will be improved in the next few years to include improvements in the capability to differentiate between malicious anomaly and non-malicious anomaly. It is also my belief based on many years of research in this area that the advancement is likely to occur when anomaly detection incorporates human behavior assessment, and not just a reliance on network norming.

Terrorism

Perhaps one of the best examples I have observed of anomaly detection that was especially meaningful occurred on April 12, 1988. A New Jersey state trooper noticed what he called "suspicious behavior" of a person at a rest stop in New Jersey. He detained the male based on the suspicion and as part of the process examined the trunk of the car. He found three fire extinguisher bombs filled with explosives and nails. The person was Yu Kikumura, a member of the Japanese Red Army, a known terrorist organization. Kikumura had been arrested just a few years earlier in Amsterdam for carrying an explosive device. The trooper, in this case, noticed anomalies. I have always hoped the trooper received a commendation for his work in this situation.

Terrorist groups differ widely in the degree to which they repeat attack preparation and attack behavior. For some groups, attacks vary little over time (Hezbollah), and others exhibit truly unique behavior each time (al-Qaeda). When observing terrorism, you will find that some groups are more likely to exhibit anomalies than other groups. Knowing this is a first step to anticipating anomalies before they occur. However, it is also highly likely that an anomaly exhibited by a group that is usually consistent and repeatable will be more relevant.

A behavior analysis perspective would ensure that an anomaly that was meaningful would be studied in detail to determine the antecedent conditions that were associated with the anomaly, as well as the consequences of the new behavior. If the consequences were successful for the individual or group, we would expect to see the behavior again under the same or similar circumstances. If the consequences were not successful, we would not likely observe the behavior again.

Although AuBA would not include the use of methodology to anticipate anomalies, it is possible. The reason is that the direct use of AuBA, instead of signature or anomaly approaches, leads to accurate anticipation of adversary behavior. Even if we could predict that an anomaly will occur, anticipating anomalies still does not tell us whether the discovered anomaly will be malicious or non-malicious, or which of the more than 1 billion combinations of variables, based on combinatorial explosion, will be associated with the new anomaly.

It is clear that a paradigm shift in security is complex. We are receiving attacks across terrorism, network, and criminal areas at an increased rate, and the severity is increasing with the number of attacks. We need to develop new technology — but it is not easy.

Terrorist behavior is a product of malicious intent and motivational doctrine that guides the targeting and actions of the group. The antecedents and consequence of past attacks provide guidance as to the types of conditions leading to an attack. A coherent approach like AuBA includes all components and for this reason has been shown to be predictive. This type of analysis needs to be completed on major adversarial groups facing us today. The result may ultimately be improved protection against external terrorist threat.

Networks

Network technology and protocols are in flux. Not only is protection complex, we are also seeing encryption and IPv6 surfacing. IPv6 is a new Internet protocol to make up for IPv4 IP address length restrictions. As a result, our AuBA team has incorporated an IPv6 module and can continue assessment even with encrypted content.

Signature detection capability has been far exceeded. It has to be used because new technology has not yet surfaced, but it cannot keep up with the malicious intent that is coming in waves. I am reminded of Custer's last stand. General George Custer stood and fought valiantly with his men, but there were no reinforcements on the way. We know how it ended. We are at least five years past a critical need for new technology, and it is still not in sight (unless AuBA approaches and follow-on research moves us in the direction of human assessment).

Anomaly detection shows little additional reason for optimism at this point. It has been on the scene for many years, and researchers are still attempting to differentiate malicious from non-malicious network activity by studying new statistical and clustering like algorithms. Earlier in this book, I quoted Albert Einstein's definition of insanity: *Doing the same thing over and over again and expecting different results*. This explains anomaly detection. We keep trying to differentiate between anomaly malicious and anomaly non-malicious activity by using different algorithms or statistical approaches. This particular problem is not likely to be solved with a specific statistical technique. The inability to differentiate between non-threatening and threatening anomalies is due to the failure of current approaches to go beyond the activities to the intent of the individual. The next chapter highlights one of my methods used to process digital information to extract person and psychological variables.

NOTE There are actually two categories of insider threat that I label: Insider Threat with Intent and Insider Threat without Intent. The first category is what we typically think of when we think of Insider Threat — that is, the person inside an organization who wishes either to cause damage to the organization or to steal proprietary or classified secrets. The second category is the person who is an innocent victim of an external attack, such as phishing, whereby he or she innocently responds to an e-mail designed to look legitimate by an attacker. The response results in malicious software being installed to use the innocent victim's access to navigate through the organization's network to cause damage or to steal proprietary or classified secrets. The effect is the same, but the methods are entirely different.

Criminal Behavior

Criminal behavior can be different. Often it is the result of an individual act, although it can be a group action. Criminal action is often the result of a need on the part of the criminal(s) to engage in theft. Cyber crime, or computer crime, can emanate from a variety of sources internationally. Basically, computer and networks are exploited for the purpose of monetary gain or to inflict harm/damage. There are two basic ways in which one person or group can hurt others. They can apply or present something harmful to others, or they can remove something desirable. Some examples of applying something harmful are shutting down a network with a denial-of-service attack; discrediting a person, group, or organization; defacing a website; and harassing, bullying, or stalking others, to name a few. The second category can consist of such behaviors as stealing personal information and selling it, using stolen identities to acquire money or credit, committing corporate espionage or government espionage, or engaging in many other forms of theft.

Both general categories of criminal behavior can be very harmful. Bullying has become a serious problem — we have seen preteens and teens actually take their own lives as a means to end the pain. Many individuals have lost significant amounts of money to online fraud, and we have witnessed state-sponsored groups support sophisticated attacks against the United States. China, in particular, has been singled out by the U.S. Department of State as a cyber adversary who actively targets the United States.

In developing strategies to protect against external threat to our networks from criminals, the motivations driving the acts are important to understand. Targeting characteristics become antecedents for attacks from specific individuals or groups. For example, attacks can take the form of harassment by such *wannabe* groups as LulzSec, who boast of taking down the CIA website and harassing other security/intelligence services such as the Israeli Mossad. On the other end of the harm continuum, WikiLeaks, formed by Australian Julian Assange, is a controversial site that publishes classified, private, and restricted information. There have been over a million documents stolen and published via WikiLeaks. One Army private, Bradley Manning, has been accused of passing as many as 100,000 to 250,000 Department of State classified documents to WikiLeaks.

Threat of criminal theft and damage can come from both external and internal sources. The topic of internal threat is dealt with in the following chapter.

Using Behavior Analysis to Identify New, First-Time Attacks

The patented CheckMate technology was designed to anticipate all possible combinations of the 600 behavioral monitors that process samples of network packets of all who enter a network. Every 1/10 of a second, all are assessed with multiple behavior assessment modules. The network packet activity is converted to the degree of expertise and deception present. The 2,600 possible combinations mean that the assessment technology can detect an attack that is associated with the behavior monitors used. As opposed to signatures, monitors were designed to capture activities in which all must engage.

The advanced analytics behind the monitoring determine malicious from non-malicious combinations. Validated by independent testers, the technology has been shown to detect known and unknown attacks without signatures and without anomaly detection. Because the 600 monitors were designed to cover a full range of activities, the application sits in wait for a unique first-time presentation of activities occurring together that have not been previously recognized as an attack. It is capable of identifying the new attack in as little as 1/10 of a second, allowing CheckMate to block the connection as an intervention to decrease or stop damage. Anticipation of new attacks is built into the application because of this capability. Because the advanced analytics do not need to be trained to recognize new attacks, CheckMate sets ready with anticipation and predictive capability.

Forensics: Studying and Defining the Past

Marcus Ranum, security specialist, has defined network forensics as "the capture, recording, and analysis of network events in order to discover the source of security attacks or other problem incidents" (www.ranum.com).

It is exceedingly difficult to conduct a forensic examination of past attacks to characterize exactly what happened, the nature of the attack, and how to recognize it. Isolating an attack can be difficult, and the sheer volume of generated traffic on a network is often like searching for a needle in a haystack. Forensics should be a key component of a security paradigm shift. We desperately need much improved automated methods of identifying malicious attack behavior as both human behavior and network behavior. The methodology should be capable of operating in real time. Current tools are useful but need improvements in technology.

The science of forensics is the study and analysis of past events. By studying past network attacks, much can be learned about the structure. This is important to characterize not only a specific attack but classes of attacks as well. When a class is defined, then variations may be better understood. This allows for a far improved approach to characterizing attack variations that are likely but not yet occurring naturally. Given that technology can assist greatly in identifying classes of attacks, the construction of new behavior monitors in AuBA anticipatory network protection technology can occur, leading to improved real-time identification of new attacks.

Is the Past the Best Predictor of Future Behavior?

The past is a predictor of future behavior, but there are better approaches. If we analyze past network behavior and determine that of 1,000 attacks per week, 5 percent are denial-of-service attacks directed against that network, we could say with limited success that if we have 1,000 attacks within the next week, approximately 50 will be denial-of-service attacks. If we gather such data on a weekly basis for 6 months and then calculate the base rates, we will have more accurate data and increased confidence in our projections. However, this is simply baseline projection and does not specify when a denial-of-service attack will occur.

Likewise, typical statistical correlation — a step up from baseline projections — does not imply causation. When large amounts of data are analyzed and subjected to massive correlations to drill down deeper than baseline projections, chance correlations can occur. For example, if we found a very large positive correlation of 0.90 between denial-of-service attacks on a network and the Baltimore Orioles winning a baseball game, we would not assume causation, nor would we assume a logical connection. We must take care in studying the past and use statistical approaches with care. Statistics and mathematical algorithms will provide data, not interpretations. Care must be taken to use analytical approaches with past behavior to project behavior in the future. As I have pointed out, AuBA has been successful in predicting future behavior by identifying the antecedents associated with past behavior as opposed to the behavior itself. Antecedents remain stable over time, while behavior changes constantly.

Updating How to Use Past Information

Behavior analysis stresses the use of preceding antecedents conditions that set the stage for behavior to occur and consequences of behavior that determine the future probability of the occurrence of the behavior. In short, if we have identified antecedent conditions that have been repeatedly associated with past behavior, and the behavior led to desirable consequences for the person exhibiting the behavior, then we have the basic ingredients for prediction of future behavior. This premise has been validated numerous times by my AuBA teams. There is more to it, but the basic premise modifies how we analyze past events. Instead of analyzing only behavioral information, we must include all three components: antecedents, behavior, and consequences.

There is an old saying: *The best predictor of future behavior is past behavior.* This old saying may now be updated based on empirical work across many different domains, many of which are malicious behavior based. My updated phrase is this: *The best predictors of future behavior are the patterns existing between past behavior and that behavior's associated antecedents and consequences.* By using the methods to identify patterns existing among precursor antecedents and following consequences of behavior using the methods of AuBA, it is possible to accurately predict future behavior with confidence. These concepts form the basis for a change in security approaches.

Advantages of AuBA #11: Network Intrusion — Converting Digital Information to Human Behavior Assessment

CheckMate and InMate are AuBA-derived applications. Both products contain multiple predictive engines developed with AuBA methodology. Because of this, the applications have the following unique properties:

- They are capable of converting samples of network packets into behavior assessment measures of the degree of expertise and deception (CheckMate) and degree of intent to engage in misuse and deception (InMate) present at any given time for every IP/user on a network.

- The absence of signature and anomaly detection allows these AuBA network protection applications to base threat decisions on the presence of actual human behavior, as opposed to descriptions of past attacks.

- Human behavior–based decisions based on true threat allow CheckMate and InMate to identify threat associated with new attacks and with the reoccurrence of past attacks.

- The automation of the hybrid behavior assessment and computer sciences applications allows for rapid assessment in which a complete assessment can be conducted in 50 microseconds, or 20,000 behavior assessments per second.

- The AuBA applications have two major features that appear to be unique. Because of their strong behavioral (versus statistical) foundation, the applications (1) can identify new attacks that do not have predefined signatures and are not just anomalies and (2) can predict malicious behavior before it actually occurs, giving time for mitigation.

Other AuBA applications demonstrate that digital data from physical sensors and unstructured and structured text may be used for input into the model-building process. When data is scarce or actually missing, the AuBASME process, whereby subject matter expertise may be used in a specialized manner to conduct AuBA predictive engines, can be used.

AuBA methods and developed applications have demonstrated that it is possible to convert digital information into actual predictive engines capable of predicting future human behavior. Such work has been divided into two distinct areas: (1) the development of AuBA tools that may be used to develop unique predictive applications and (2) applications in various domains that conduct automated behavior assessments of human behavior across cyber and asymmetric warfare areas of interest.

In Summary

External and internal threats are very different forms of threat. Both types of threats respond differently to antecedent conditions that make up targeting, as well as timing, of attacks. Furthermore, the motivation of the individuals and groups threatening our national security and infrastructure externally are entirely different than the motivations of those who attack us internally.

Signature detection is the mainstay method used for network protection against external attack today. Anomaly detection remains part experimental and part real. Anomaly detection is still not able to differentiate between malicious and non-malicious activities, which results in reluctance to use it as a mainstay approach. Both approaches have a few advantages and many disadvantages. This equates to a severe lack of protection against new and zero-day attacks. I am presenting a human behavior predictive methodology as a third technology that may be capable of fixing current disadvantages of signature detection and anomaly detection.

CHAPTER 12

Computer Networks: Protection from Internal Threat

Internal threat is associated with those who work from inside an organization and conduct theft of classified or proprietary information or inflict harm to the organization. The insider has motivations that tend more toward the psychological, as compared to the person presenting external threat. If we consider an employee or contractor who is working inside an organization or within the government, then that person has to be motivated in one or a combination of ways. These motivations usually include:

- Opportunity for monetary gain
- Disgruntled—some event occurred to *hurt* the perpetrator who now seeks revenge
- Lack of advancement at a self-perceived rate
- What I call the *James Bond syndrome,* in which the person is delusional and wants to be a real spy
- Ideology
- Seeks recognition from anyone, even an adversary

There is a second type of threat from the insider; however, it is really a form of external threat. I refer to true insider threat as *insider threat with intent*. This means that true insider threat is an internal person who desires either to inflict harm or to take away property, including intellectual property or classified material. The second category, *insider threat without intent*, is a form of external threat in which the external attacker uses an internal person as an unwitting accomplice. The classic example is a phishing attack. With this form of attack, although there are many variations, the external attacker sends an e-mail and the internal person reads it. It could be about a discount, the mailbox being full, a free trip, or so on. However, if the internal person responds to the e-mail, then malware will be installed automatically. This small program may collect the user's ID and password. This is forwarded back to the external attacker. Now the attacker has access.

The second category is not true insider threat in that the internal person does not have the intent to cause damage or engage in theft. The internal person, in this case, is simply manipulated as a means to gain access by an external attacker. This book is about malicious intent, and this chapter focuses on internal persons who have malicious intent. The inside person who is used without knowledge can literally be any employee of the company—he or she does not pose a threat based on intent.

The determination of psychological characteristics is very challenging. In this chapter, I will briefly describe InMate, an automated behavior analysis (AuBA) application designed to convert packet-level activity to measures of the *intent to engage in internal misuse* and *deception*, as well as the conversion of digital information to psychological characteristics that may inform the insider solution. Advances in psychological assessment from digital information are occurring, thanks to government funding. This is a pioneering area, and AuBA is at the forefront, as will be demonstrated.

NOTE Two AuBA network applications are referred to in this book: CheckMate and InMate. CheckMate was designed as a behavior assessment application that is neither signature based nor anomaly detection based. Instead, CheckMate converts sequential samples of packet-level activity by IP to the degree of expertise (E) and deception (D) that exists in each sample. If both E and D exceed a threshold at the same time, malicious intent is present. InMate, a sister product, was derived from CheckMate but focuses on internal threat. Instead of converting packet-level activity to E and D, InMate converts activity to expertise (E) and intent (I) to engage in misuse. Like CheckMate E and D measures, if both I and D exceed thresholds at the same time, malicious intent is present. Both represent a new human behavior–based technology, as opposed to network behavior.

Defining the Insider

What is an insider, and what is insider threat? An insider is someone who is usually an employee, contractor, intern, or any other person who has staff-like access of any organization. This definition includes the government. Government employees are insiders because they have access to their agency's internal network by means of a user ID and a password. A hacker must worry about gaining access to networks, but an insider already has access.

Through empirical research, the AuBA application CheckMate was developed to convert samples of network activity to measures of *expertise* and *deception*. Expertise is the level of skill that an external person requires to gain access or cause damage. Deception is the ability to hide so that detection is more difficult to unlikely. For an insider, it was clear that deception must remain. However, because the insider has access to a network, *expertise* was replaced with the *intent to engage in misuse*. Threat is the intent to cause harm, or impending harm. Together, insider threat basically means that we have those with inside access who have the intent either to engage in theft of sensitive material or to inflict harm on hardware, software, or people.

The Significance of Insider Threat

Insider threat is a significant problem. The studies comparing external and internal threat reveal statistics that favor one or the other as the most significant problem. Basically, you can choose the study that makes your case. I see these discrepancies as simply meaning that levels of external and internal threat are basically equivalent. For this reason, one would expect some variation in reporting the more significant or serious of the two. For the sake of simplicity, let's just consider external and internal threat to be basically equivalent.

However, given the equivalency of external and internal threat, it is interesting that the vast majority of products have been geared toward protection from external threat. There are only a handful of applications guarding against insider threat. Certainly, given the differences in motivation and how motivation affects targeting and behavior, applications constructed for external threat are not that relevant for insider threat.

Based on the need to assess underlying motivation and the fact that the insider is motivated by more psychological factors, the AuBA specialty of converting digital information to person characteristics is especially warranted. To show the extremes of converting digital information to real-world person characteristics, I led a multidisciplinary team as the Principal investigator on an Air Force Research Laboratory (AFRL) exploratory project. Virtual-world (VW) games are growing at an extremely fast rate with hundreds of millions of people interacting via virtual worlds. The premise of the funded contract for SAIC was to determine if real-world characteristics of persons operating their avatar in a VW game could be predicted from observations and measurements of the avatars in the VW only (Phase 1) and to see how well results generalize to new VWs in Phase 2.

Specifically, the task was to make observations of avatars in Second Life, a VW social game, and predict real-world (RW) gender, approximate age, general level of education, ideology, leadership potential, ability to follow, and ability to follow beliefs of those persons operating the avatars to AFRL's minimum accuracy requirements for each dependent variable. The Second Life game consists of a world of avatars operated by persons in the real world. Being very lifelike, avatars can dance, walk, run, and even fly. They can visit stores, homes, dance floors, and so forth and can communicate by the RW person talking over the microphone or by typing on the keyboard. One can visit many different locations and engage in many different activities within Second Life. To show the versatility, you can even attend a meeting with other avatars in a meeting room, or meet another avatar in an office.

To establish ground truth, we had 100 participants come to our SAIC laboratory and complete the Dunwoody Authoritarianism Scale (DAS), the NEO Form-s (a 60-item, self-administered personality assessment form), and a demographics form (gender, age, education, and so forth). On the VW side, we developed the Virtual World Behavior Analysis Form (VW-BAF) that measures avatar behavior, completed the NEO Form-R (observer version), and captured chat log data of VW sessions conducted by the participants. The fact that Psychological Assessment Resources (PAR) in Lutz, Florida, produces a self-rating form of the NEO and an observer form allowed us to rate the avatar on the observer form and to have the participant rate himself or herself on the self-administered form.

NOTE The NEO is one of the most popular, five-factor personality assessment instruments in use today. Based on the five-factor model, the NEO subscales provide a rich degree of information about a person's personality structure.

We selected VW variables to use as predictors based on VW and behavioral knowledge and the RW variables we wished to predict. We then used AuBA pattern classification and discriminant analysis as trained analytical engines to predict real-world characteristics from avatar behavior. Figure 12-1 shows the results of the discriminant analysis. The figure shows the minimum accuracy required for each dependent variable as the dark vertical bar, as does the vertical line crossing the graph. The lighter vertical bar for each dependent variable shows the actual predictive accuracy obtained. The methodology developed resulted in accurate predictions of RW person characteristics that met or exceeded all accuracy criteria for Phase 1 with 100 participants. Preliminary results of Phase 2 conducted on two new games (*Aion* and *Guild Wars*) with 116 additional participants reveal that higher accuracy has been obtained, showing that methods used generalize to new games. The project revealed that accurate predictors of RW person characteristics could be identified in the VW. Once identified, the VW predictors can be used to determine characteristics of those who operate the avatars without any knowledge of the real-world person.

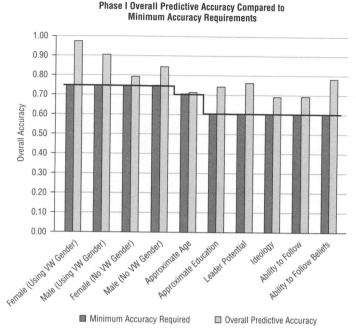

Figure 12-1: The accuracy of SAIC quantitative prediction of real-world characteristics using virtual world behavioral and psychological predictors

Although we have had many applications that predict future behavior accurately with variables (antecedents) extracted from text (for example, reports, open source media articles), this was a first-time attempt to predict (classify) psychological characteristics, as well as other person attributes, from observations of avatar behavior.

Discovering Malicious Intent: Insider Motivations

To the extent possible, it is important to be able to identify underlying factors that motivate insider attempts to engage in theft or inflict harm or damage. Motivation is the fuel that energizes and focuses behavior. Individuals do not just commit theft or inflict damage randomly or spontaneously. There are always reasons. This does not mean that the reasons are rational, but to the perpetrator, they make sense. Spies for foreign governments like Aldrich Ames (CIA) and Robert Hanssen (FBI) had their reasons for providing the Soviets with classified information from their respective agencies. Traitors always have reasons; they may have even given it considerable thought before crossing over to the other side. We may not agree with the reasons, but the more we understand about them, about what turns a person to be sympathetic to the adversary, the more we are able to develop detection measures.

For example, a disgruntled employee may act out and come to the attention of the human resources department. This type of employee could become derogatory toward the person or persons he or she blames, could turn to increased drinking, or could start coming to work late, missing work days, or otherwise appearing to be depressed. We have all seen fellow employees going through stress. All handle issues differently, and not all who experience severe stress or disgruntlement will present insider threat. For the most part, the vast majority of individuals work through issues without becoming an increased threat in any way. However, for that small percentage, clear indicators of disgruntlement on the job for whatever reason should be a flag that is raised.

Several forms of internal motivation issues may appear as a possible threat but do not tend to lead to threat:

- Personal problems (for example, separation, divorce, death in immediate family, and so on)
- Disappointment in not being promoted
- Lack of recognition
- Not being asked to serve on critical teams
- Not being asked to participate in key planning meetings
- Not being asked for opinions about future direction
- Not receiving a perceived deserved job title

Personal crisis may show up as distractibility and not being able to focus on the job. However, actions tend to be directed toward the source of the perceived problem. Therefore, the person experiencing personal problems not associated with the workplace is not likely to be a threat to the workplace. If similar behavior is the result of lack of promotions, or lack of perceived advancement, then we can expect some form of dissatisfaction and disgruntlement. Responses can range from simple derogatory statements directed toward the perceived source of the problem in private to actual theft and damage to get back at the organization.

The internal motivator of monetary gain is different and much more difficult to detect. If it is a classified environment, then the need to be discreet is very high. The insider who is contemplating receiving payment for classified information (or proprietary information if in a corporate setting) knows that being caught will have very serious consequences. The fear of being discovered can suppress the typical disgruntlement statements usually observed.

Ideology changes are also difficult to detect. People change over time, and the person who eventually becomes a serious threat may have been fine when recruited and interviewed for the organization. Bradley Manning, a U.S. Army Private, developed issues over hiding his homosexuality, and started to have problems with fellow soldiers and with superior officers. He became opposed to the war and hit a female officer in the face, all before he allegedly started sending 100,000 to 250,000 documents and a small number of select videos to WikiLeaks for distribution. In another example, Army Major Nidal Hasan became aggressive over time, opposed the war, and did not wish to be deployed. He became increasingly upset with the Army until he walked into a center for soldiers at Fort Hood, Texas, and started shooting. He had been in contact with Anwar al-Awlaki, a top al-Qaeda leader who was later killed by a drone missile on September 30, 2011. Over the years, Hasan had grown more disgruntled and made frequent statements against the Army. In addition, his allegiance to Muslim extremist views grew in strength. The shooting occurred just several weeks before his deployment to Afghanistan. He had gone from a soldier with distinction to one of the worst mass murderers by handgun. Hasan killed 13 and wounded 32.

These cases and others like it (the Oklahoma City bombing) are presented throughout this book as examples of insiders who changed significantly over time. Whether we are looking at insider threat on networks or with conventional guns and bombs, we have to realize that in cases like these we did not miss detecting a person when recruited, tested, interviewed, and hired — we missed the perpetrators because they changed over time and became disgruntled. We simply failed to detect them because continued assessment needs to be more frequent and based more on behavior assessment and monitoring.

I have talked about people and motivations prior to networks because it is the motivations of the insider that creates insider threat. If we monitor packets only, then we are missing motivation — we are just looking for signatures. Humans are extremely creative. The attacks or theft can change, but the motivations remain stable.

Acting on Malicious Intent: Insider Behaviors

The inner world of our thoughts is private unless we choose to let our thoughts be known. When a disgruntled employee vocalizes his or her contempt, there is a conscious decision to let others know of his or her disdain. This step is the first in acting on motivations that might be getting out of sync with others. Many ignore this stage, or look away, because these statements are only words. Major Hasan reportedly verbalized his discontent and made his Muslim extremist views known at an increasing rate over time. Internal motivation and verbalization, however, can quickly become intent and then action.

Considering internal motivation by itself is not enough. As has been presented, there are still antecedents and consequences that are associated with the eventual insider behavior that is a threat, should it surface. First the source of discontent can become a target. In other words, in a scenario where a person is disgruntled because a promotion was missed, a raise did not come, or a bonus did not occur, the supervisor and upper-level management can become a focus. Basically, it is possible that the source of the discontent becomes antecedents to malicious behavior.

It is also possible that the attack or theft behavior and perceived consequence of *righting a wrong* or simply *revenge* can go far beyond the significance of any event or situation that resulted in the discontent. Bradley Manning has been accused of forwarding 100,000 to 250,000 classified and restricted documents to WikiLeaks for publication. Even though he was angry at being placed back at Private, releasing more than 100,000 documents seems to be a drastic response. In the other examples, Hasan shot and killed 13 soldiers and wounded 32 others, and Timothy McVeigh killed 168 people and wounded 800 others. The discontent can grow out of proportion to the significance of events and situations causing disgruntlement. It does tend to demonstrate the degree of discontent that can develop within the person as a motivator. In many of these cases, it is apparent that there were reports of discontent and even violent or aggressive behavior prior to the occurrence of the infamous acts.

After serious study of both those who commit external threat and those who commit internal threat, it is clear that any act that is threatening will have specific characteristics. First, as mentioned in the introduction of this chapter, it is surprising that there are only two classes of behavior that can occur with either external threat or internal threat. The person can either remove something of value (theft) or inflict harm or damage. This realization is exceedingly important because it can limit our search for specific harmful behaviors. A network insider threat perspective breaks this down a little further with the realization that the perpetrator can either use the network as a vehicle for theft or damage, or the network can actually be the target.

Insider Methods of Operations

Given the motivation, the insider has to consider just how to conduct theft or inflict damage. This consideration is important because he or she is inside, and the potential for discovery and detection is considerably lower as a result. Therefore, as I have pointed out, the insider must hide his or her actions. Deception is the key. The insider does not need expertise to break in. Access is not a problem, because he or she has a user ID and a password. In the AuBA application InMate, continuous collections of packet-level activity are converted to the degree of deception and intent to engage in misuse. This second category of behavioral assessment replaced the category expertise as used in CheckMate (again because one does not need expertise to gain access as an insider).

The combination of motivation and attempts to be deceptive with intent to cause damage or engage in theft is very serious. Given attempts to be deceptive and intent to engage in misuse as actual behaviors on a network, we have learned that we can infer or assume motivation to engage in theft or to inflict harm/damage.

Observing Bradley Manning's actions, we saw his attempt to be deceptive in his taking Lady Gaga CDs to record classified documents while feigning listening to Lady Gaga. Later, he would upload the documents to WikiLeaks for distribution. This deception was effective enough to totally escape detection. The attempt to pass a single classified document to someone not authorized to view the document reveals the intent to engage in inappropriate if not illegal behavior. However, in the case of Bradley Manning, he is accused of passing 100,000 to 250,000 documents about Department of State secrets to WikiLeaks. Whether they were disseminated is a second issue, though, and unfortunately, these were. The intent, motivation, and behavior exhibited by Manning was clear from the time he inserted a Lady Gaga CD into a PC to capture classified information. The violation of trust placed in him to protect classified documents meant that disgruntlement and underlying motivation was very strong.

By using the concepts of deception and intent to engage in misuse as guiding principles, we can determine more easily what needs to be monitored. The insider who is a threat cannot get around deception — it is an inevitable component of being malicious, because one does not wish to be identified or apprehended. If the objective is theft of data, restricted or classified information, personal information, credit card numbers, identities, or any other form of useful information to be removed from inside an organization, then first the offender has to have a plan to gather and remove such data in a successfully deceptive manner. This need limits the methods used to those that can be hidden. Although one can be creative, there are constraints to being deceptive.

Hiding information for removal can occur in a limited number of ways. These common methods are:

- **Obscurity:** A primary method can be what is called *hiding in plain sight*. Bradley Manning copied classified information onto a CD that was seen as a Lady Gaga recording. To complete the deception, he would hum as if accompanying the music. There are many ways to obscure data or information in plain sight. Steganography software may be used to embed documents in other documents, such as images. When hidden, it is not possible with the human eye to detect any change in the image. Then the person simply "removes" or passes the neutral images out of the organization. There are many creative variations of this principle. Security needs to look past what is being brought in and what leaves an organization. A CD, even if stamped with popular music groups, is a recording medium.

- **Miniaturization of physical transfer and transport:** We have all seen the old spy movies where classified and sensitive information was passed by means of microfilm. Miniature cameras were hidden, documents exposed on film, and images sent in clear sight in envelopes or other forms of mail, in rings, or in just about any other way. The size was the deception. Today, you don't need to have special devices constructed by "Q" from the James Bond 007 movies; you can simply purchase online spy cameras, miniature recording devices, and special miniature electronic storage devices. There are wristwatch cameras with up to 4 GB storage; electronic storage in earrings, bracelets, and necklaces with USB connection; and so on. It should be commonplace for security to continually search for such devices on the Internet just as a perpetrator would and log these images, so that these devices can be identified if they appear in a restricted setting. There is not a justifiable reason for wearing storage devices disguised as jewelry in any classified or proprietary setting. Miniaturization is here, and security must be aware of all devices.

- **Images (pictures):** The use of steganography is so widespread that it has been reported to be used by high school students to pass love notes. Software is simple to download, and documents can be hidden in an image and passed to another person. This is a tough one to detect or prevent. However, if an insider is continually passing images that appear to be mundane to an outsider, and that outsider does not reciprocate, this should raise a flag. In a regular work setting, although prohibited, employees do use the Internet for private use. Most organizations turn their head if it is minor communication and does not detract from work. However, it usually flows both ways — not one.

- **Immediate electronic transfer:** Technology has taken us all by storm. In less than 20 years we have seen an explosion of technology, from the first real PCs with gigantic external storage devices to the Internet to flash drives to current-day marvels. Storage devices are now very small and can be easily hidden. However, given the presence of access to the Internet in many organizations, one can easily transfer large documents from the organization to an external location anywhere in the world in seconds. The days of surreptitious removal of documents a few at a time by hiding them in a coat or briefcase are gone. It is now electronic copying of electronic information onto high-capacity electronic storage and transfer via Internet to a share site, as attachments to e-mail or as embedded in other unclassified files. On a share site, large volumes may be passed in seconds and sent to practically anywhere in the world.

COMPARISON OF JONATHON POLLARD, NAVAL INTELLIGENCE COMMAND ANALYST WHO SPIED FOR ISRAEL, AND BRADLEY MANNING, U.S. ARMY PRIVATE WHO PASSED CLASSIFIED DOCUMENTS TO WIKILEAKS

From 1984 to when convicted of being a spy for Israel in 1987, Jonathon Pollard provided classified documents from NIC to Israel. The classified information covered a wide range of topics. According to journalist Ronald Kessler, the volume of classified paper passed could be stacked in a cube 10 feet by 6 feet by 6 feet. This is 360 cubic feet of paper. If stacked vertically, it would be a stack of paper 60 feet higher than a football field is long. Another way to compare it is that this is a medium-sized U-Haul truck. Carrying this many documents out of the NIC is a formidable task, which had to occur in small amounts over time.

Twenty years later, Bradley Manning, a disgruntled U.S. Army Specialist who had been demoted to Private, has been accused of removing and passing 100,000 to 250,000 Department of State classified documents to WikiLeaks. Manning did not have to collect paper — he could carry larger amounts of information out at a time on his CD and send the documents to WikiLeaks at a push of a computer button.

Identifying the Amateur Threat

When we assess the possibility of having insider threat, we need to be aware that such threat can range from rank amateurs to the extreme — someone planted in the organization as a professional by a third party. The differences in the ability to conduct theft or inflict harm/damage by the professional motivated by monetary gain and the amateur fueled by being passed over for a promotion are immense. How can we identify these differences? It is actually relatively easy. We will detect the amateur fairly quickly, but detecting the professional is going to be exceedingly difficult.

The typical person who may become disgruntled may not be technically sophisticated. In addition, a number of disgruntled individuals let their source of unhappiness shine through daily tasks and interactions. They may let their disgruntlement be known either openly or as a failure to hide it. Being hurt or being angry may be difficult to conceal. Although insider access is easy through user IDs and passwords, the professional will likely use advanced techniques to gather sensitive data. He or she may use specialized and miniaturized devices, store information on difficult to detect storage devices, or use steganography to hide internal documents in whitespace offered by mundane documents. It is not an emotional issue for the professional thief; it is a matter of money. Therefore, there is no anger or disappointment to hide, making him or her more difficult to detect by overt behavior.

Because an insider has access, InMate uses *intent to engage in misuse* as a replacement for the expertise dimension, as used for assessment of external threat in the CheckMate application. However, the assumption is that insider threat is represented by a person who has malicious intent. There can be an insider who is used without his or her knowledge as the victim of a phishing attack initiated by an attacker external to the organization. In this case, it is not true insider threat, but a special case of external threat using an insider without malicious intent. Therefore, CheckMate has a phishing-assessment engine to detect this special case by focusing on the actual phishing attack instead of the unwitting internal staff member. InMate focuses on the insider with malicious intent.

Again, if we look at it as *deception* and *intent to engage in misuse,* then we must realize that hiding is not easy. Deception requires a set of skills. The amateur that is not astute is likely to make mistakes. For example, it is amateurish to consider conducting malicious behavior when no one else is around. This might manifest itself in coming in very early or staying very late and transferring files to an outsider recipient or to the self on a different e-mail address. The amateur who is sending e-mails with attachments to himself or herself to a private address is not a good sign. This is just a mechanism to get documents out of the organization, without much thought. The underlying view is that no one will notice.

The amateur may also encrypt restricted documents and send them out to an outside address or to self under a different address — again, not a smart way to evade detection, if we are astute enough to be looking for such behavior. Hiding documents through steganography or some other means such as downloading to a USB storage device and carrying it out makes more sense. These are the differences between the amateur who is disgruntled and the professional who knows techniques or who is being coached by a smart outsider. I feel the responsibility not to describe in extreme detail how material can leave an organization for rather obvious reasons. However, security must be aware and actively search for not just smart methods of removing material but the amateurish ways as well.

In our country's history we have seen the Aldrich Ames and Robert Hanssen methods of professional spying, which have resulted in extreme loss of classified material that has even cost lives. On the other hand, we have many cases of amateurish attempts on the part of non-professionals such as William Kampiles and Sharon Scranage. Just briefly, these amateurish, real insider threats will be presented to show that even the uninitiated and non-professionals can be very dangerous.

William Kampiles was a CIA clerk who was apparently not happy with his low status. Not receiving the recognition he sorely wanted as a real James-Bond-type of spy, he stole a classified spy satellite manual and, after resigning, sold it to a foreign government. He then approached the CIA again to see if he could be hired as a double agent. Perhaps Kampiles had seen too many spy movies. Obviously, the CIA was not amused to discover what he had done. The result: He was arrested and convicted of espionage. I would submit this one to the Darwin awards (the award given to people who would not pass a survival-of-the-fittest test). This act, which occurred with very limited thought, was brainless, and it highlights the fact that some employees simply need recognition. I call this the *James Bond syndrome*. There are a few within the government who want others to see them in the 007 state they delusionally see themselves. Kampiles was one; he didn't care where the recognition came from, and he was caught, spending his delusional days in prison.

Sharon Scranage was a CIA employee in the mid-1980s who was stationed in Ghana. She met many people in Ghana, but one caught her fancy. Michael Agbotui Soussoudis, a Ghanaian intelligence officer, who actually targeted Scranage and approached her romantically. To Scranage, Soussoudis was too attractive to avoid. As part of the relationship, no doubt professionally orchestrated, Scranage gave up the identities of CIA officers, a violation of very strict policy. After she failed a required polygraph examination, it was clear that she had revealed these sensitive identities. Convicted, she spent years in jail. Again, an example of a very amateurish response. However, it is essential to note that key sensitive information can come from amateurs and the uninitiated, as well as professional quality spies.

Identifying the Professional Threat

The professional threat today comes from skilled individuals capable of intruding into networks with a high probability of not being discovered until a significant period of time has passed. In 2009, China initiated a sophisticated, organized attack against Google and more than 30 other organizations. Labeled Operation Aurora, it is possible the attack was in place for up to six months to a year before being discovered. Existing as an advanced persistent threat (APT) attack, the intrusions revealed just how sophisticated APT can be as directed against the United States. The apparent objective of the intrusions was to explore proprietary information and, perhaps, actually change code. Google announced the attack on January 12, 2010, and Hillary Clinton, U.S. Secretary of State, denounced the attack, requesting that China answer for the attacks. The U.S. Congress indicated the same week that the attacks directed against major U.S. companies would be investigated.

A professional-type attack can be exceptionally sophisticated. For example, since the Chinese did not have access as an insider, using APT they could stand at the ready until acquiring user ID and password access. Once the access was acquired, they could enter, peruse code, and even change it. This is a precise example of external threat using an unwitting insider, versus insider threat perpetrated by an insider with malicious intent.

APT is perhaps one of the most threatening types of attack or forms of theft on networks today. The name itself is explanatory. As used by China, for example, significant multiple sources can be brought to attack a single or small number of sources. As contrasted with hacking where hackers can use favorite and repeated techniques to attack multiple sites until successful, APT is singularly focused on specific selected target sites. Going back to our only two basic forms of malice of inflicting harm/damage or theft, APT can use either class of malicious activity.

One way to think of APT is to think of it as a group of specialists with well-furnished and maintained resources working together toward a common and well-coordinated goal. It is persistent against a target because the resources are such that the attempt can be relentless until success is achieved. Attackers may have the best resources on hand, and the numbers working in unison can be sufficient to keep a 24/7 operation going. The objective can be either inflicting harm or obtaining knowledge of proprietary information. Operation Aurora is an example of how sophisticated and advanced the cyber threat from APT can be.

Perhaps one of the more telling features of APT is the expertise that exists to enter the network of a specific target, gather information required, and retrieve that information without being detected. This moving back and forth without being discovered via existing signature detection or anomaly detection methodologies represents very serious threat. To move through the detection barrier, the APT operational team must first be experts in network intrusion. Knowing current technology makes it easier to avoid detection. After making it through barriers undetected, the APT team must know how to navigate to find what it wants.

If we take China as an example, China has a policy of focusing on becoming a technological leader worldwide. APT may very well be a result of a shortcut mentality. That is, to get to the top from a technology perspective, don't reinvent the wheel — steal it. The need to move to the top technologically means that China is willing to invest in cyber theft and to be persistent in cyber theft targeting until technology requirements are filled.

Long suspected and accused of spying against U.S. corporate technology and attempts to enter government-protected sites, China has become a strong focal point of interest as a cyber villain. On October 4, 2011, members of Congress called on the president of the United States to focus on Chinese cyber attacks.

There has been increasing talk in the media that the United States could counter with a military response. However, as the media reports, there are cyber offensive efforts within the United States, as well as defensive elements. In short, we are seeing the development of what could be termed cyber warfare. At this point we tend to see the skirmishes that predate actual battles. By focusing APT toward specific U.S. sites, the adversary can determine the extent and effectiveness of U.S. cyber defenses, determine how best to invade specific sites without being detected, and extract required technological knowledge.

This degree of sophisticated theft and intelligence gathering calls for the paradigm shift required within the U.S.-based cyber policies. As pointed out, we need new, more effective technology. If adversaries are adopting APT successfully against the United States (and they are), then it is past time that cyber defensive measures push past the reactive nature of signature detection and tame the very high false-positive error rates of anomaly detection.

Deception: The Primary Core of the Malicious Insider

Deception is the hallmark of the malicious person regardless of how he or she chooses to be malicious. Whether the method of choice is terrorism, warfare, insurgency, espionage, corporate theft, sabotage, network attacks, or APT, one of the major characteristics is that the person or group does not want to be detected in planning the act, executing it, or escaping. Although a small percentage of malicious adversaries may claim an act after the fact to ensure they receive credit, the time just prior to an act, the act itself, and the time immediately after the act are wrapped in deception.

Deception is especially present in the case of an insider. First, the insider does not want to be detected at any time. The insider is able to gather data that is required by remaining an insider. Keeping someone employed within a target organization can be the gift that keeps on giving. Perhaps the prime example of insider deception was Robert Hanssen, the FBI Special Agent who spied for the Soviet Union/Russia for 22 uninterrupted years. Hanssen was a master of deception. He used all the tradecraft that would keep him hidden. He would not meet with his handlers so that there would not be a risk of the adversary giving up his name. He hid in plain sight. He was in charge of various counterintelligence and counterespionage activities at the FBI. Perhaps the epitome of deception in our country's history of espionage is that fact that Hanssen was tasked to find the mole, which, of course, was Hanssen.

Hanssen was able to work his way through many files and was on top of extremely sensitive and classified information — much like the fox guarding the henhouse. His ability to be deceptive and to remain in place gave him a steady flow of Russian-desired information that he could pass on.

Behavior of an Insider Network Thief

Being an insider intent on stealing and passing along privileged information requires four steps:

1. Gaining access
2. Locating and stealing (copying) information
3. Storing it in a form that can be transferred
4. Passing the information to an outside recipient who likely pays for the information

One can be deceptive in many ways with many variations. In network attacks and theft, one needs to be deceptive to not be detected while engaging in malicious activity. Because of being an insider, the perpetrator would be wise to not use his or her own user ID and password. This is why we all should be careful when we log on to the work network — make sure no one is looking over your shoulder when you go online. Be aware of your surroundings when you log in. The malicious insider can watch from afar and over the course of days determine your password from watching your fingers on the keyboard. The user ID will be in a format that all know — it is the password that is needed. The smart insider will pick a security-oblivious employee and stand and talk with a cup of coffee just as the person is entering the user ID and password. If he or she is lucky, it can be obtained in one pass. If not, then time is on his or her side. Persistence can pay off.

Now that the insider has stolen a password, it is important to use it when the person is not there. This could be while the person is at lunch, is on a smoke break (a smoker is a great target for this reason), has taken a day off, and so forth. Over time, sensitive sites within the company's intranet can be accessed, and sensitive files downloaded to a USB drive. As we know, today's USB storage devices hold a tremendous amount of material. The USB can be identical to the one that is used within full view of everyone when working. Then when it is time to load the USB storage device, it can be replaced with the one that will go home with the perpetrator. At home, the files can be transferred via non-company e-mail to the recipient.

There are many variations of this theme. The exact method may be based on the quality of the security team and apparatus. In some companies, the information stolen may go straight to the USB storage device to avoid placing material on the hard drive. In a security-lax company, the perpetrator may simply e-mail the files to a recipient via company e-mail. Security is the key here. If security practices are known, then the perpetrator will use means not covered by security.

An entire book could be written on the insider who steals information by using the network as an accomplice. In the new electronic age, we have made it easier to work with much greater efficiency. However, this ease of working has enabled the insider with malicious intent to steal, transport, and sell classified and proprietary information.

Current Trends in Insider Threat Protection

There is a renewed interest in insider threat protection in the wake of the Bradley Manning incident. After the arrest of Manning came the full realization that he had allegedly passed 100,000 to 250,000 documents to WikiLeaks. After the embarrassment that ensued when documents were released, insider threat has taken on even more importance. This renewed interest has led to a current trend in insider threat protection. The vast majority of network protection applications/products are designed for external threat. To be effective, because of the widely different motivations that motivate the insider as compared to the external hacker, new approaches are required. Insider threat protection cannot be as simple as turning an external threat detection device inward — not if we want the application to be truly effective.

We also must extend our definition of insider threat. To paraphrase a colleague, Dr. Eric B. Cole, a highly respected network security expert, APT may be a new form of external-insider threat. I support this view strongly. The smart state-supported adversary using APT via phishing and spear phishing attacks to gain inside access to a target network is a new threat. Once inside, the adversary can act like an insider and, in fact, can have the identical access. For this reason, we at SAIC have added a phishing module to the CheckMate application that works to detect the external attacker entering a network with a phishing attack. Again, APT using phishing is a special form of threat I call *insider threat without intent*, which is really a special form of external threat.

As a smart module, CheckMate is constantly monitoring for new threat approaches and variations that APT can pose. This is the new trend. Phishing attacks and its variants are extremely successful. In private discussions with numerous security experts, all seem to agree that with a smart spear phishing attack, it is possible to get employees of an organization to click on the required link or download the attachment offered that inadvertently installs an application that will capture passwords and send them to the adversary.

Protection against insider threat will require smart and new approaches. Variations of anomaly detection may have a renewed role here, if the high false-positive error rates can be solved. New human behavior–focused applications such as CheckMate and InMate show promise in monitoring human malicious behavior and intent, and not just network behavior and activities. AuBA will have a stronger role given the predictive nature of the approach and proven capability to identify malicious intent.

A Lack of Proactive Capability

Current network protection is overwhelmingly reactive. We need anticipatory applications that can determine whether malicious intent is present and that an attack is imminent. This would allow automated and protective intervention before theft or damage could occur. Part of the reason for a lack of proactive capability is that current applications are based on the monitoring of network activity. As pointed out at the beginning of this chapter, it is possible to indirectly determine human intent and even psychological characteristics. AuBA applications convert digital information into threat measures and monitors for malicious intent in real time. We now have known state-supported intrusion activities by countries like China focusing on our agencies and technologically gifted commercial organizations. We are well beyond the ankle biters these days. We have very serious threat at our doorsteps, but we are using the same general protection that we had 15–20 years ago. It is time for a radical change in technology.

Signature Detection and Rules

A paradigm shift in network protection is going to have to be proactive instead of reactive. Reactive response is the severe downfall of signature detection. Whether the intent of a signature detection application is to protect a network from external or internal attack, successful applications in the future will have to be able to detect new attacks and variations of old attacks that pass through signature detection applications. Given the presence of APT and the known intrusion capability of such state-supported operations as the ones perpetrated by the Chinese, signature detection simply cannot serve as the lead approach in the way it does today.

The paradigm shift called for in this book must be proactive and predictive. We cannot get ahead of the game by describing an attack after it occurs and then building rules to look for that specific attack, all while attacks keep increasing in severity and frequency.

Anomaly Detection: False Positives Waiting to Happen

Can anomaly detection be part of the future as we begin to design new technology that will be predictive and proactive? The short answer is a qualified yes. Anomaly can flag unusual activity. It is plagued with very high false-positive rates because it can't differentiate between malicious and non-malicious anomalies.

However, I believe that if AuBA applications process anomaly flagged activity, then intent may be determined, thereby providing a mechanism to provide the differentiation required. At least anomaly detection does not rely on dissecting past attacks to build rules to catch the same attacks in the future. Anomaly detection has the potential to be proactive — it just needs fixed.

Taken together, signature and anomaly detections technologies are not keeping up with the rapidly mounting threat to date. The inadequacy is so great at this juncture it is not even possible to challenge this statement rationally. Our country and its infrastructure are under attack, and we even know that a portion of this is state supported. We *must* have a paradigm shift in security that means new technology is on the way — we need reinforcements!

Establishing the Need for a Paradigm Shift to Proactive Capabilities

A feature of a new proactive approach is that the technology must be predictive. We must be able to have improved technology that can anticipate and detect malicious intent. The following section describes the characteristics we need. It is the top 10 features of a new technology that would prepare us for security to successfully counter today's world of rapidly mounting external and insider threat. It is my firm belief that it takes absorbing Chapters 1–11 of this book to fully understand why the following top 10 features are presented at this point.

The Top 10 Features of a Paradigm Shift in Network Security

A paradigm shift in security to move from a reactive to a proactive stance will require new technology that will have the following features:

- The ability to determine and differentiate between malicious and non-malicious intent in real time
- The ability to predict imminent malicious behavior
- The ability to detect new attacks, variations of known serious attacks, and zero-day attacks
- Automated forensics that can rapidly find and dissect new attacks to inform new predictive technology
- The ability to automatically determine and characterize *future signatures* — that is, new attacks that are highly likely but that have not yet occurred
- A new signature detection methodology that is automatically loaded and updated with *future signatures*, so that the technology can move from reactive to proactive

- A new anomaly detection that can differentiate accurately between malicious anomalies and non-malicious anomalies

- The ability to accurately trace back an attack or attempt to attack to the actual perpetrator computer

- The ability to identify an attacker with *behaviorprints* — unique behavior patterns associated only with an attacker regardless of network activity

- Incorporate behavioral science to protect against external and internal threat based on behavioral and motivational differences between the two classes of threat

DEFINITION A *behaviorprint* is an AuBA-coined term that means there is a unique pattern of activity that can assist in the identification of a specific IP or person as determined by CheckMate or InMate. For example, CheckMate converts 100 millisecond samples of packet activity into the degree of expertise (E) and deception (D) present in that sample. By processing sequential E/D samples, it is possible to characterize typical activity of a returning attacker by behavior patterns of E and D across time without signatures or anomaly detection. Continued research is being conducted to determine if this is useful in detecting a coordinated attack or multiple attacks simultaneously from the same attacker.

AuBA, CheckMate, and InMate

I have worked diligently to demonstrate how behavioral sciences can be incorporated in network security and in asymmetric warfare. Automated behavior analysis (AuBA) and associated tools may be used to construct specific security applications such as CheckMate and InMate. Both applications work in real time and assess and monitor every user on a network every 100 milliseconds across multiple behavioral assessment modules. These modules are capable of converting continuous samples of packet-level activity into the degree of *expertise* and *deception* present in each sample. InMate converts packet-level activity and other types of insider behavior to measures of *deception and intent to engage in misuse*.

Much has been learned in the development of these new human behavior–based tools and applications. Most important, the new technology provides the capability to drill down beyond network activity to underlying human behavior and intent. From the perspective of terrorist and global threat, AuBA has been determined to be predictive in independent tests. In short, the technology serves as a start to a road map for a paradigm shift that is required to meet growing threat on global and network bases.

Advantages of AuBA #12: Powerful Predictive Analysis Engines That Fit on a Laptop

In the development of AuBA, a key consideration was to keep the analytics small as compared to advanced statistical approaches requiring a supercomputer to conduct the analysis. Currently, *big data* is a name given to the state in which data come in so fast and grow so large in databases that manual methods are too difficult to use to extract meaningful knowledge. It is somewhat intuitive that if we are to make sense of complex human behavior, we would need big data and supercomputers. In 2011, two humans competed against Watson, an IBM computerization program to play *Jeopardy!* on television. The two players were the best players in the history of *Jeopardy!* The computer won. However, it was a parallel processing system comprising 90 servers operating with 4 terabytes of stored material. This approach, and others like it, tends to use smart software combined with brute force to try to mimic what humans can do — hence, a computer that can play *Jeopardy!*

Many attempts have been made to mimic human intelligence through the accumulation of knowledge. The Watson application was one of the more public because it played *Jeopardy!* across 3 days pitted against the two best players in the game's history. Douglas Lenat's Cyc application has been in progress since 1984. This application, using machine-learning methodology, was designed to capture human knowledge in rules. It has been an interesting exercise that has resulted in query approaches and methods to access stored data with at least similarities to Watson.

AuBA automation has taken a totally different approach. Prediction of behavior does not require a supercomputer, but it does require pattern classification. By focusing on the actual antecedent-behavior-consequence associations of past events, patterns extracted even with small-n cases (about 30 cases per category to predict) may be strong enough to make accurate predictions of future behavior. By incorporating artificial neural network technology, we can construct predictive engines that learn by example and can be placed in a variety of different applications. These applications can then replicate human-like decision making. Instead of storing knowledge about many past behaviors, AuBA extracts specific patterns that exist between antecedents and behaviors extracted from past examples that were successful (followed by desirable consequences). These patterns are represented in a neural network using our training methodology. After validation, the neural network contains the structure of how to make the decision and, if provided with input, will provide an immediate predictive output.

The speed to arrive at a predictive decision given input is 50 microseconds, or 20,000 decisions per second. Because the AuBA predictive engine has learned the structure of making predictive decisions based on patterns of antecedents, it does not have to contain stored examples of past behavior. In other words, unlike Watson or Cyc, AuBA is not accessing a database or sets of rules that contain past examples of past behavior or facts to derive a decision. The AuBA predictive engine can process unique combinations of variables defined as input that were not trained and provide an accurate prediction based on the patterns of how the person or group modeled behaviors under various conditions. The capability to derive decisions without accessing factual storage makes the AuBA predictive engines not only fast but also very small. For example, many hundreds of predictive engines can be placed on a typical laptop, and many may be placed on a handheld computer.

The size makes smart AuBA applications possible on limited and cost-effective hardware with a requirement only for a typical Java or any other appropriate programming-language-based interface and reporting mechanism.

In Summary

Insider threat is driven by different motivators that affect how an insider reacts to antecedent conditions and potential consequences of planned behavior of adversaries. Internal and external threats on networks and typical terrorist and other adversarial threats on a global basis require different approaches. Insider threat is also divided further into *insider threat with intent* and *insider threat without intent*. The former is what we usually think of when we think of insider threat. It is represented by an insider who has malicious intent either to cause damage or to conduct theft. The latter is a special case of external threat, where an external attacker uses an insider without his or her knowledge to gain access by using the insider's stolen credentials.

This chapter makes the case that current technologies are simply inadequate as evidenced by the inability to counter current network threats or anticipate 9/11 types of attacks within our country. It is past time for a new approach to security and past time to incorporate improved methods of analyzing the human behind attacks and not just network packet activity or studying past global events. I have provided my view of the features of what would be new technologies to counter current and projected threat such as APT and global threat to our national infrastructure.

CHAPTER 13

Predicting Global Threat

Today's world is interconnected in ways we could have only dreamed about just one or two decades ago. The European market drops and our stock market drops hours later. There is a rebellion in Libya and we are joining NATO forces to intervene. China wants to increase its global status so it intrudes into networks to steal technology shortcuts. The advent of the Internet connects us to the point that we can communicate with almost anyone worldwide in seconds, and CNN is on the spot as we watch coups unfold and battles wage in Iraq and Afghanistan. In short, we are now a globally connected community of diverse individuals, ideas, and cultures with events observed worldwide as they occur.

The interconnectedness we now have has been a boon to communication; however, in a global economic slump, we cannot say it has been good for business. Perhaps this will change as we learn how to better use the networks that connect us all. In the meantime, the global network has created new means by which espionage, cyber attacks, and proprietary and classified information theft can occur in seconds. At the same time, perpetrators are afforded anonymity as they commit these attacks. Threat today can come from any direction globally. Whether it is a group of al-Qaeda terrorists hijacking airliners, the Chinese invading networks to steal technology, or the potential for a massive biological agent attack, the United States and its allies are facing new global threats.

Enhanced interconnectedness by means of technological advances has enhanced the capability of not only cyber attackers but traditional terrorist attackers as well. Reconnaissance, the military activity of gathering useful information about an adversary for tactical planning, can be conducted to a great extent by means of the Internet. By sitting stationary with a laptop connected to the Internet, one can gather key information about a target and even access web cams to visually observe many potential target areas in real time, including being able to operate the camera remotely. Communication among adversary members can be immediate, and remote detonation of explosives by wireless devices is well known. In short, technology that connects us all is a double-edged sword.

This chapter explores the nuances of how technology has made our world smaller and more dangerous, and how technology can assist conventional terrorism through new types of weapons and reconnaissance and surveillance.

Understanding State-Sponsored Threat

Less than a century ago, natural barriers helped to protect countries around the world. Often, when there was war, it was between neighboring countries — other countries were just too far away. Technology changed that. We are able to move about the world more easily and transport war materials and troops. The result? Two world wars, the creation of missiles that can carry nuclear weapons to another country within minutes to hours over great distances, satellites that can see all locations on Earth, and the advent of the Internet and network communications. We are now globally interconnected with instant communication.

Technological advances have increased to the point where global threat has increased significantly.

- Adversaries can move about the world easily, either by flight for traditional attack methods or electronically for almost instant communication or to present an avenue for cyber attack. Terror is portable, as we discovered on September 11, 2001. Natural barriers such as distance or vast oceans are no longer obstacles.

- Pervasive threats can confront multiple countries simultaneously. There is advanced persistent threat (APT) from state-supported operations with cyber experts that can move in and out of networks worldwide on an ongoing, ever-present basis; and there are weapons of concern, such as chemical, biological, radiological, and even nuclear (CBRN) weapons that, if released, would have global implications.

In this section, global threat is seen as well-supported and maintained persistent threat with state support.

In the past, terrorism was more local. We could label this as *local* or *regional* terrorism. For example, Hezbollah (for the most part, although there were some exceptions) maintained a struggle within Lebanon and Israel. Hamas focused on Israel, as did the Palestinian Islamic Jihad (PIJ). Now, we have al-Qaeda exporting terror on a global basis. The recent killing of U.S. citizen Anwar al-Awlaki, the al-Qaeda leader for the Yemen region, underscored how the al-Qaeda organization had gone global. Al-Awlaki was killed in a U.S. drone missile strike in Yemen. His active terrorist presence in Yemen is just one example of how al-Qaeda has spread its influence across the globe. Refer to Chapter 17 for more detail on al-Awlaki.

We also have cyber attacks directed against the United States and its allies across the world. Cyber attacks on a worldwide basis are not necessarily attacks to cause damage but can also include theft of classified or proprietary materials. The cyber attacker's network activities travel near the speed of light through networks worldwide and can intrude into our networks or the networks of our allies at will. These worldwide attacks, whether cyber based or in traditional terrorist attack form in which a group can strike anywhere, can be labeled *global terrorism*. In this case, targets may be anywhere in the world, and groups may spread their base of operations and influence across the globe.

NOTE It is beyond the scope of this book to describe the many intrusions into U.S. networks. Proprietary and classified information has been lost, although it may be difficult to identify the perpetrator with confidence. For example, it has been difficult to determine the extent to which Chinese offensive operations have been successful. The state support of an offensive operation with regimentation is like focusing the sun's rays to a single hot point with a magnifying glass. A focused operation that includes advanced cyber skills and that is persistent can lead to very successful intrusions, given our country's reactive, cyber-defensive posture.

It is clear that sophisticated phishing and spear phishing attacks work, and they work well. Given the skill to develop such attacks, it is almost impossible for the uninitiated to not click on the real-looking link, not provide the personal information, or not download the attachment, particularly if it is a spear phishing attack and the e-mail appears to be coming from the CEO or human resources department. Of course, it is a fake e-mail, and malware is inserted as soon as the link is clicked.

Organized State Support

State support can have a very strong effect on all aspects of a state-supported adversarial group. We tend to think of such support as money. However, support can include actual guidance on activities, targeting, timing, and, of course, financial support. At the time of writing this chapter, a plot to assassinate the Saudi Arabian ambassador to the United States on American soil was uncovered. All open media information led to the Iranian intelligence arranging for the assassination by contracting with a Mexican drug cartel to conduct the actual assassination. It should be said that Iran is officially denying the accusation. However, the U.S. Department of Justice had enough evidence to charge two individuals in preparing to carry out the act. One of the two individuals is a member of Iranian intelligence. It appears that a $100,000 installment on a total price tag of $1.5 million had already occurred.

In this example, the state support was beneficial in two ways. First, the reported price tag of $1.5 million is expensive — Iran has the money. Second, the death of the ambassador would accomplish political objectives for Iran. Had the assassination occurred on American soil, it could have driven a wedge between Saudi Arabia and the United States, which would be beneficial to Iran.

State support of terrorism, criminal acts, or cyber warfare serves many purposes. The objectives to be accomplished for the supporting state may vary across state-supported events and countries providing the support. However, it is not likely that a state supports a terrorist group to just exhibit general malicious activity and mayhem — there are likely specific objectives for the group to accomplish in exchange for the support.

In the example of the alleged contracted assassination of the Saudi Arabian ambassador, a behavior analysis using the antecedents, behavior, and consequences components would point to the consequences of a successful assassination as a motivation for Iranian support of terrorism. The perceived embarrassment for the United States and subsequent tension between the United States and Saudi Arabia would be motivation to fuel the support of a terrorist act. Antecedents would be associated with the announced timing of a visit of the ambassador. An announcement of such a visit would set the stage for planning, targeting, and executing the assassination behavior itself. Because of the incident, even if foiled, we can assume that a motivator for Iran is the creation of embarrassment and tension between the United States and Saudi Arabia.

Of particular note with this example is the elaborate means to achieve deception. As I have pointed out, there are two basic ingredients for any malicious act. First, the perpetrator must have the skill to carry out the planned behavior. Second, because those who commit malicious activity do not want to be caught, deception has to play a major role. In this case, deception was so much of a need that Iran tried to use a Mexican drug cartel as the perpetrator. It was clear the cartel had the expertise, and it was clear that if the act was traced back, it would likely go to the third-party perpetrator, not Iran. This likely is why the price tag for the planned assassination was so high. It would not cost $1.5 million to complete the act. However, the cartel would absorb the risk as the perpetrator, and the $1.5 million was likely negotiated to pay for the risk associated with being the actual perpetrator, not just to cover costs of carrying out the act.

Foreign State-Supported Terrorist Attacks

It has not been unusual for nations to covertly provide support to terrorist organizations. Using an existing terror organization and network is cheaper and easier than hiring and training their own special forces. Placing a layer of insulation between the government and the target, making the relationship difficult to trace back to the source, is one special benefit of this relationship.

Russia

There are ample examples of state-supported terrorism. For example, Russia has been a suspected supporter of global terrorism. In al-Qaeda's and Osama bin Laden's calls for jihad, terrorists have expressed that Israel should be targeted because of the adversarial relationship between Israel and the Palestinians, and that the United States should be targeted for its support of Israel. The use of asymmetric warfare, where there is an imbalance of forces, provides an excellent opportunity to affect tensions among nations with little effort and at a relatively small cost. The Russian approach has historically been to support Islamic extremists in their efforts to discredit the United States and Israel. As early as 2008, then U.S. Vice President Richard Cheney began strong criticism of Russia for providing arms to Syria and Iran, knowing that arms would go to Iranian-supported Hezbollah and terrorist organizations within Iraq.[1]

Pakistan

It is difficult for a country to play both sides — at some point, the apparent two-faced nature of the country will be more apparent. It appears that Pakistan, who has cooperated in the past with the United States on counterterrorism activities, also has aided and abetted terrorists.

It is now clear that Pakistan has been a strong supporter of terrorism and likely participated strongly in providing protection for Osama bin Laden during his time hiding in Pakistan. Ramzi Yousef, the first World Trade Center bombing mastermind, and Mir Aimal Kasi, the CIA killer who walked down the line of cars shooting passengers as they waited to turn in to the CIA, were both captured in Islamabad, Pakistan. This presents some concern because of the need for support when one is in hiding, especially if recognizable. The logistics required for successful hiding makes it very difficult to not be detected. The person hiding needs food, human contact, resources to pay for a place to hide, a means to escape, and the ability to continue acquiring new resources. Within the United States, when prisoners escape, it is not at all unusual that they are captured within days because of the lack of resources to hide successfully.

In the case of Osama bin Laden, it is safe to say he was likely one of the most recognizable individuals in the world, if not the most recognizable. Tremendous resources were spent trying to find him. He would need extensive security, resources for all who supported his hiding, food, water, the ability to communicate, and simple contact with others. The compound where he lived was large and had an external wall that was higher than any neighbors' walls. More important, the compound was within sight of Pakistan's military training compound.

---

[1] Cheney Accuses Russia of Supporting Terrorism, *The National*, September, 2008.

According to Secretary of Defense Leon Panetta, it seems clear that the fact that Osama bin Laden was hiding in a very expensive compound, with walls higher than any other neighbor and less than one mile from the Pakistani military training academy, reveals Pakistan's likely complicity in hiding him and keeping his location secret.[2]

Libya

Libya has also been a known supporter of terrorism for many years, supporting such groups and organizations as the Palestine Liberation Organization (PLO) when it was considered to be an overt and active terrorist organization by the United States and Israel, the Palestine Front for the Liberation of Palestine (PFLP), and the Moro National Liberation Front (MNLF) among many others in the past.

It has not been unusual for countries to covertly provide support to terrorist organizations that can do the state's bidding. It is much like the United States using Special Forces. Many countries simply use an existing terrorist organization and network. It is cheaper and more difficult to trace back to the source of the support. It also places a layer between the supporter and the target.

As mentioned, for decades some countries have supported terrorism to achieve objectives. To quote William Shakespeare, "All the world's a stage." Terrorism has become global and is played out on a world's stage. One of the primary reasons is support from nation-states. For the most part, the terrorist acts supported have been conventional. Of course, it is not likely that the world, or the media for that matter, will miss a major bombing of a market, bus, marine barracks, or airliner, or a major assassination. Cyberwarfare and cyber theft are very different, as you will see in the following section.

DEFINITION In their book *Cyber War: The Next Threat to National Security and What to Do About It* (HarperCollins Publishers, 2010), Richard A. Clarke and Robert K. Knake define *cyberwarfare* as "actions by a nation-state to penetrate another nation's computers or networks for the purposes of causing damage or disruption."

I would modify this definition to read: "Cyberwarfare consists of unauthorized actions by a nation-state to penetrate another nation's computers or networks for the purposes of causing damage, disruption, *or the theft of classified, restricted, or proprietary information or materials.*"

---

[2] Pakistan knew bin Laden hideout: Panetta, *New English Review,* January 28, 2012; Panetta on Pakistan's role in hiding bin Laden (0:52), Video, Washington Post Video Archive, washingtonpost.com, January 28, 2012.

Foreign State-Supported Cyber Attacks

The United States has been the recipient of massive numbers of cyber attacks. Targets have been the U.S. government and corporate America for the most part. There have been many perpetrators, but the Chinese and Russian attacks have been the most serious to date. Countries like North Korea have exhibited attacks, but they haven't been as sophisticated.

> **NOTE** The significant rise in attacks has resulted in increased concern and official response from the United States. During 2011, the United States officially stepped up public criticism of China and the cyber exploits directed against the United States. At that time, the Secretary of State, Hillary Clinton, began targeted statements directed to China leadership to halt cyber exploits.
>
> Normally, hackers work as individuals. Each hacker tends to pick different targets and uses favorite techniques, leading to various levels of effectiveness depending on skill. However, the Chinese have taken the concepts of militarization, cyberwarfare, intense discipline, and regimentation to create cyber operations that work in a coordinated and effective manner.

State-supported cyber attacks are occurring at an alarming rate and are of global proportions. In May 2011, the Obama administration proposed the creation of international computer standards to start gaining multi-national cooperation to counter cyber threat and to levy penalties for those countries not cooperating. At about the same time there was a congressional call for considering cyber attacks to be an act of war. As part of the call for action, it was suggested that continued cyber attacks could be met with a U.S. military response. This call for action underscores the government concern over APT.

A behavior analysis would explain the continued increase in cyber attacks as a function of the successful consequences of the attack behavior. Typical consequences have included:

- Theft of classified and proprietary information
- Cyber attacks completed without direct discovery of the perpetrators
- Ability to check U.S. cyber defenses across different sites
- Ability to determine the effectiveness of U.S. intrusion detection and network protection
- Training of cyber attack teams
- Repeated returns on investment

The cyber attacks, for the most part, have been successful. The basic tenet of applied behavior analysis is that behaviors that are followed by successful consequences are reinforced and either maintained or increased in frequency. Likely antecedent conditions for state-supported cyber attacks would likely include stated requirements from the state to the hacker teams.

The state support underlying APT is necessary to make sure the effort is as advanced as possible and that top cyber talent is retained and in the numbers required to be persistent. Because of state support, we can assume discipline, accountability, stated objectives, and evaluation of performance are all working together to support continuous improvement. The coordinated group effort is why APT is such a threat to the United States. Individuals simply can't sustain the persistence to be labeled as APT, although there are very skilled and advanced individuals who pose a very serious threat.

Describing and Identifying Future Global Threat

Identifying future global threat requires much more than cataloging past threats and simply playing them forward. Intelligence, as valuable as it is, is an approach that relies on gathering tips or clues that may be synthesized by experts to determine that an event is about to take place. Perhaps there is an informant, or perhaps a member of a group has been apprehended and has provided detailed information as to plans. In law enforcement, it can simply be good detective work in which motive is established, targeting is understood, and a criminal operates in a pattern that makes catching the person in the act possible. However, true prediction of future behavior using modeling approaches is different. The intent is to construct a model of the adversary so that the model may reveal how the modeled individual or group would respond.

The modeling approach has its share of critics and skeptics. Many just say outright that it is not possible to predict future behavior in a valid (accurate) and reliable (consistent) manner. Although there are many voices of this general view, Nassim Nicholas Taleb, in his book *The Black Swan: The Impact of the Highly Improbable* (Random House, 2007), expresses the view very well, especially as it relates to the attempt to predict rare events. His premise is that an extremely rare event, a *black swan*, cannot be predicted and that such an event may be oversimplified in retrospect after it occurs. As we know, a swan is white in color, so a black swan is an example of a rare event. Why is this view a falacy in my opinion? Because future rare events can be predicted. This does not mean that if we ask a series of specific questions as to what is going to happen, they can all be answered accurately — but in some cases, we can predict.

As shown in Chapter 14, there are times when we predict future events. As a reminder, sampling and polling are methods that may be used for very specific types of prediction. Although it seemed inconceivable to many, the national polls as a method predicted that the first African American would be elected President of the United States in the 2008 election — this had never happened in our country's history. The prediction was accurate, and President Obama accurately represents a rare event.

What the writer of *The Black Swan* is forgetting is that we predict behavior constantly — we all do. We could not even cross the street if we could not predict a safe time to cross. With AuBA behavioral modeling, we take the entire context into consideration; using this method, we can predict some events in the future.

I fear that the view that we cannot predict future behavior is one of the reasons why we are so dependent on signature detection methods — that is, describing attacks after they happen so that if they ever occur again, we will recognize them. This has been the primary method used for network protection. It is also a primary method used to look for conventional terrorist attacks. Adversaries have learned to present new attacks on an ongoing basis. In this way, signature detection is constantly defeated because it can only recognize past described attacks. AuBA was designed to predict future behavior, including variants not occurring in the past.

Why is it so important to be able to accurately anticipate, or predict, future rare events, or any human behavior events for that matter? One of the best answers I have is that we are faced with a growing threat of a chemical, biological, radiological, or nuclear (CBRN) weapon released within the United States by a terrorist organization. I have lost some hours of sleep over this mounting threat. We must remember that CBRN threat is not new, and these weapons have been used — often extensively. Prior to looking at suitable technology that can help in this area, let's review why there is potential for the use of a weapon of mass destruction in the United States. Following are a number of examples, but note that these are presented only as a sample.

> **NOTE** In short, weapons of mass destruction exist, they have been used, and we know the threat of one being released in the United States is increasing daily.

Chemical (using chemical agents such as gasses as weapons)

On March 20, 1995, Aum Shinrikyo, a Japanese terrorist group/cult, released sarin gas in a coordinated attack in the Tokyo subway system. Five members each released the poisonous gas in different areas of the subway. Although 13 people died as a result and many were injured, if the method of spreading the gas had been better, many more would have died.

On March 16, 1998, Iraqi military purposely and repeatedly dropped poisonous gas bombs from multiple military planes in a variety of passes over the town of Halabja within Kurdistan in Iraq. The attack, which included conventional attacks near the end of the assault, resulted in estimates of deaths of up to 5,000 victims, with estimates of wounded being twice as high. Different types of gas bombs were used.

Throughout history, poisons have been used to kill others. In World War I, poisonous gas was used extensively. The types of gases included mustard, tear, phosgene, bromide, and chlorine, as well as limited amounts of other gasses. It has been estimated that the actual number of deaths attributed to gas ranges from 3 to 4 percent of all World War I deaths. As the use of gas escalated across forces over time, most countries developed and used gas during World War I. Methods of delivery included simply releasing the gas on the ground and explosive dispersal devices, such as in artillery shells or as canisters fired from mortars.

Currently, it is estimated that Russia and the United States maintain the largest stockpiles of weaponized chemicals, with each country storing many thousands of tons. Scores of countries store such weapons. Of course, theft or black market transactions must be of concern.

Biological (the use of living organisms, such as viruses, toxins, and bacteria, as the fatalistic core of the attack)

In 1993, Aum Shinrikyo also tried a biological weapon comprising anthrax, but because it used the wrong strain of anthrax, the attack did not result in fatalities. The bothersome part of this group and others is the interest in using a chemical or biological attack to effect enormous losses and the desire to get it right.

On September 18, 2001, the first of a number of envelopes containing live anthrax was sent to media and political figures. It had been only one week since the infamous al-Qaeda 9/11 attacks on the United States. The letters were addressed to members of Congress and the media. Five individuals died and 17 were infected as a result of the letters. After a lengthy investigation, the FBI had determined that Dr. Bruce Ivins, a microbiologist with a history of working with biological weapons and specifically anthrax, was responsible for the attacks. Knowing that he was likely to be charged, Dr. Ivins committed suicide with an overdose of Tylenol on July 29, 2008. Although all has been questioned, the FBI has reported that it has closed the case, pointing to the extensive evidence gathered on Dr. Ivins that indicates that he is the perpetrator.

Radiological (a conventional explosive packed with radioactive material that is dispersed on detonation — not a nuclear bomb)

The use of radiological material packed into a conventional explosive is called a *dirty bomb*. This type of explosive is not a nuclear bomb because it lacks the nuclear detonation. A nuclear bomb, when exploded, results in massive damage and death, the typical mushroom cloud, and is the most powerful weapon ever developed. A dirty bomb, however, is still a very serious weapon. It is a double threat. First, we have the effects of the explosion itself. Second, the explosion disperses radioactive material that settles on anything that it touches. These extremely small radioactive particles can be breathed in, and fear of radiation sickness in the vicinity of the explosion is justified. The long-term effects can be devastating. Aside from the damage of the explosion, the radioactive contamination would render a location inhabitable until cleaned. Decontamination, or cleaning, could take an inordinately long time at great expense. Although we have not yet witnessed a dirty bomb detonation, there have been a number of aborted attempts.[3]

---

[3] Jonathon Medalia, CRS Report for Congress, *Terrorist "Dirty Bombs": A Brief Primer*, 2004.

In June 2002, Jose Padilla was arrested as an enemy combatant as he entered the United States from Pakistan. According to authorities, he was planning to detonate a dirty bomb in Chicago, Illinois. Although a U.S. citizen, born in Brooklyn, New York, Padilla had associated with al-Qaeda and was reportedly tasked to construct and detonate a dirty bomb in the United States. Having been investigated prior to arrival, he was arrested as a threat as he re-entered the United States.[4]

Nuclear (the acquisition and detonation of a nuclear weapon by terrorists in the United States)

The gravest of all possible weapons of mass destruction is perhaps the true nuclear weapon. According to Rolf-Mowatt Larssen, a former CIA intelligence officer, there are three things that keep him up at night:

▪ Pakistan puts "loose nukes" in the hands of terrorists.

▪ North Korea supplies terrorists with nuclear bombs.

▪ Al-Qaeda launches nuclear attack.

However, he goes on to state that he believes the odds are stacked against such terrorist groups as al-Qaeda obtaining such a weapon. However, if this rare event would occur, it would have devastating consequences in the form of death and destruction and the panic a detonation would cause.[5] Although we tend to think of a nuclear bomb as a large and very heavy bomb, nuclear warheads are in existence that fit in artillery, and there are a number of sources that report missing *suitcase bombs*. A suitcase bomb is a nuclear bomb small enough to fit in a suitcase. Reports of missing suitcase bombs are associated with Russia-developed suitcase weapons.[6]

Adnan Gulshair el-Shukrijumah has been of strong interest to the FBI with a $5 million reward leading to his arrest. Being dubbed a nuclear whiz kid, he is believed to have been handpicked by Osama bin Laden to lead the simultaneous nuclear explosions in at least three U.S. cities. He remains elusive and is still considered to be an extreme threat to the United States.[7]

There is no doubt that CBRN weapons exist and in enormous quantities. It also must be realized that a person with little more than basic knowledge in chemistry can produce immense quantities of poisonous gas — and with basic biological knowledge can grow bacteria or viruses within a basic laboratory. With a little more knowledge, strains may be developed that have no current treatment.

---

[4] Jose Padilla, *New York Times*, February 8, 2012.

[5] Stephen Mulvey, Could Terrorists Get Hold of a Nuclear Bomb, BBC News, April 12, 2010.

[6] Alexel Yablokov, Comments on Russia's Atomic Suitcase Bombs: Do "Backpack" Nuclear Weapons Exist?

[7] Murray Weiss, Larry Celona, and Briggite Williams-James, Feds Target Nuke Phantom, *New York Post*, June 4, 2007.

Radioactive materials may be stolen from a variety of common locations, or likely purchased, and then there are missing nuclear weapons. To underscore the concern, according to the International Atomic Energy Agency (IAEA):

> *From January 1993 to December 2011, a total of 2164 incidents were reported to the ITDB by participating States and some non-participating States.*
>
> *Of the 2164 confirmed incidents,*[8] *399 involved unauthorized possession and related criminal activities. Incidents included in this category involved illegal possession, movement or attempts to illegally trade in or use nuclear material or radioactive sources. Sixteen incidents in this category involved high enriched uranium (HEU) or plutonium. There were 588 incidents reported that involved the theft or loss of nuclear or other radioactive material and a total of 1124 cases involving other unauthorized activities, including the unauthorized disposal of radioactive materials or discovery of uncontrolled sources.*[9]

Because of the severity of CBRN threat, we must endeavor to continue to develop the most effective human behavior prediction methods and tools that science can create. We often think of weapons as countermeasures for weapons. However, the development and deployment of predictive methods that allow time for mitigation is not only a laudable goal but also a necessary one.

Although there are views, such as the one expressed in *The Black Swan*, that we cannot predict rare events and that we may oversimplify in retrospect, the potential for a terrorist-driven CBRN attack within the United States cannot be ignored. In short, the many dedicated analysts and officers within the government cannot walk away from such potential activities, even if rare. It has been my objective for three decades to present a technology that can accurately predict human behavior and that can process the volumes of global events being reported — continually seeking out antecedents that may be associated with such attacks, and identifying the antecedent conditions that would set the stage for such an attack — so that mitigation can occur prior to the event moving from potential to reality.

There are two specific situations where typical statistical approaches struggle:

- Emerging threat from an individual or group that has committed very few acts

- A serious adversary that poses threat but there is no data because a specific type of attack has not yet occurred, even though it is possible

---

[8] An incident may be categorized in more than one group — for example, the theft and subsequent attempted sale of a radioactive source. Accordingly, the sum of the incidents in the groups can differ from the total number of incidents. In 69 cases, the reported information was not sufficient to determine the category of incident.

[9] IAEA Illicit Trafficking Database, www-ns.iaea.org/security/itdb.asp

Of course, regardless of how many past examples there are that may be studied to predict future malicious behavior, there are very few examples of success that are valid and reliable.

NOTE *Validity* **is a measure of the accuracy of a model. Does it measure what it is supposed to measure, and does it predict what it should predict?** *Reliability* **is the degree to which the predictions are consistent when the same variables are presented.**

AuBA has been determined to be valid and accurate in anticipating future malicious behavior. To describe fully how this technology may be applied to such threat as CBRN, including events that have not yet happened, the following AuBA brief is presented.

A Review of the AuBA Modeling Methods

Predictive modeling for malicious behavior is very different from conducting very large, statistically based predictive studies. In the behavioral and social sciences, there are hundreds of thousands of articles dealing with large numbers. Just as an example comprising the many examples rolled into one, we can look at college grade point averages (GPAs). We can predict college GPA with a fair degree of accuracy. A typical study would be to collect data such as high school GPA, high school teacher recommendations for college, parent recommendations, and extracurricular activities. These data would be collected perhaps on 1,000 female and 1,000 male high school students selected at random across 10 high schools, with some high schools selected that are in the city and some from the suburbs. Using the high school data as predictors (independent variables), statistical methods are used to predict the dependent variable (college GPA). It is important to have a very high number to ensure a representative sample of high school students that would be like a small microcosm of all high school students in the country. The purpose of the statistical method is to determine what college GPA is associated with specific values of the predictor variables.

AuBA was not developed for this type of prediction. Statistical methods work fine when the numbers are there. Unfortunately, it seems that we often design studies to meet the needs of a favorite statistical method, as opposed to designing a study to measure the phenomenon in question. As mentioned, there are fields in which the numbers are not there. For example, if it appears after several highly similar murders in a region that there may be an emerging serial murderer, traditional statistics are not going to be useful with three cases. Nevertheless, the approach is not to wait until there are many so that an analysis can be conducted. This is precisely why profiling approaches were developed. In profiling, similar characteristics are gathered to give clues as to what to expect next. The problem is that unless there are enough cases, it may be difficult to draw conclusions. If the first three individuals murdered all had different color hair and were different in age, then numbers are going to be needed here also.

When I developed AuBA, it was based on the smallest number of cases that could be used and still use statistical principles. The forerunner of AuBA, applied behavior analysis, often concentrates research on one subject at a time. However, to meet basic statistical needs, 30 cases are needed in each category being predicted (predicting attack vs. no attack would require 30 examples in each category). This is the minimum and requires special statistics (nonparametric) and special validation methods, as described in the following section. If these minimum numbers are present, we have a chance to complete typical AuBA modeling. This is AuBA method #1 in the next section. If data is totally missing or sparse, then we use method #2, or AuBASME, the combination of AuBA and subject matter expertise. Methods are provided in more detail in Chapter 9.

The reason we use AuBA is that the emphasis is on antecedents to the behaviors as the predictors and the behavior as the classes to predict. This is very different from approaches that focus only on the behavior.

AuBA Methodology

AuBA modeling occurs in two basic ways. The first method consists of collecting articles about past events to build a corpus of documents. This corpus will consist of news articles about the who, where, when, what, and how (journalistic questions that form the basis of any good news article) of specific examples of a specific type of behavior of interest. For example, if we want to model corporate espionage, we gather news articles about past examples of corporate espionage. There are many hundreds of such examples and even databases that have catalogued such articles. My team and I were funded by a DARPA Small Business Innovation Research (SBIR) contract to specifically model corporate espionage using this method.

Once relevant articles are collected, they are processed with ThemeMate, an AuBA tool. ThemeMate extracts antecedents to the past events and constructs a data array with antecedent themes as columns and past examples as rows. ThemeMate populates the cells in the array with 1s and 0s, using 1s to indicate that the theme is present and 0 to indicate the theme is not present.

The data array is then presented to AutoAnalyzer, the second AuBA tool. AutoAnalyzer constructs a number of different classifiers and validates the best model using Leaving-One-Out (L-1) cross-validation.

CROSS-REFERENCE You can learn more about the detail of constructing an AuBA model and the Leaving-One-Out method (L-1) of validation in Chapters 8 and 9. The AuBA tools walkthrough in the accompanying DVD shows how these tools work.

Leaving-One-Out validation (L-1) is best for models constructed from a small number of cases. Basically, the L-1 method trains on all cases except one, which is withheld for testing. When trained, the antecedents for the test case are presented to the trained model to get the predictive answer. Then the process is repeated by putting that withheld case back in for training while a second different case is withheld for testing, and all cases but that one are used in training from scratch again and then tested on the one withheld case. This process is completed until all cases have been in both the training and the test sets. This process allows the construction of what is called a *confusion matrix* in the fields of pattern classification and artificial intelligence. Such a matrix presents:

- True positive (event is an *X* and the model accurately predicts *X*)
- True negative (event is *Not X* and the model accurately predicts *Not X*)
- False positive (event is *Not X* but the model incorrectly predicts an *X*)
- False negative (event is an *X* but the model incorrectly predicts *Not X*)

The first two are hits (calculation of the two categories of accurate predictions), and the last two are errors (calculation of the two categories of error).

> **NOTE** In conducting a confusion matrix, we typically see overall accuracy (average of true positive and true negative) rates of 80 percent or greater and overall error (average of false positive and false negative) of 20 percent or less.

A Fisher's exact statistical significance test is also completed; results must be less than 0.01 to be accepted (less than 1 chance in 100 that results could have occurred by chance). Typical AuBA modeling results are less than 0.0001, or less than 1 chance in 10,000.

> **NOTE** There are literally hundreds of sources for both L-1 and Fisher's exact. A Google search on either term will retrieve much more detail in these areas.

Automated Behavior Analysis Using Subject Matter Experts (AuBASME)

The second method is used when there are no past data, data are missing, or data are just scarce. When data are missing or just not available, we can substitute subject matter expertise (SME). However, to be effective, we must ensure that the experts are true specialists in the area being modeled.

The difference between AuBA and AuBASME is that antecedents, behavior, and consequences are extracted from text accounts of past behaviors with AuBA, whereas these components are generated by experts, or SMEs, with AuBASME. In those situations that we must face, such as the threat of a chemical, biological, radiological, or nuclear weapon released in the United

States, there are no past text accounts of the behaviors that would support the release of such a weapon. Therefore, we cannot model these types of threats with past incidents. Although there are no past data to learn from, we can't just walk away and say these serious topics cannot be studied. Given the presence of true experts in a specific domain of interest, experts may be interviewed in such a way that a clear enough understanding of potential behaviors may be extracted from their specific knowledge of the threat and those who could be perpetrators. Using AuBASME, we work with SMEs to generate separate highly likely scenarios. Each scenario consists of the behavior of concern, such as the release of a biological weapon in Washington, D.C., the likely antecedents that would set the stage of that behavior to occur, and the likely consequences of such an act. After the most likely scenarios with their antecedents and consequence are generated, the multiple examples are then submitted to the typical AuBA modeling process to generate the AuBA data array that is used for predictive analysis.

In the past, artificial intelligence consisted of extracting knowledge from experts to form a knowledge base. This process typically occurs by interviewing experts to determine how they make decisions and what information is required to make the decisions. Then the *knowledge engineer* creates rules that describe the decisions. Each rule includes the types of information necessary to make the decision. This information is then placed in a knowledge base. Rules are typically in an if-then format, meaning that we can describe such decisions as follows: If X and Y occur, then decision A should happen. By creating many multiple rules, the attempt is to capture the specific knowledge that experts use to make their decisions in the form of rules. In this way, a computer may use similar decision making. In some cases, these developed rule sets can be placed within an application and can make decisions when queried.

Throughout this book, you will see that it is possible to construct a predictive model using AuBA methodology. We would not expect to get every forecast 100 percent accurate; however, one of the major features of an AuBA model is that we can try many different scenarios by looking at different antecedents and their consequences. We must remember that if we have done our homework and we have an accurate model, we can test numerous scenarios composed of different combinations of antecedents of the model to determine how the modeled individual, group, or country would respond under the context described by the given set of antecedents. This presents the possibility that if we could structure conditions in such a way that a given set of antecedents can be present at approximately the same time (within days), then we would expect to see the behavior that the model predicts. Therefore, we have an influence model, as well as a predictive model. By altering antecedents as tested with the model, we can alter the target's behavior — at least more accurately than guessing how the target individual or group would react under various conditions.

An Example of the Use of the AuBASME Methodology for CBRN

Because we must be concerned with the preparation for rare events or those events that have not happened but could, in 2008, the Department of Defense gathered a group of experts from around the country to present different methodologies that could be used in this most difficult of analytical tasks. The effort was to generate white papers on how the methods could be used and then demonstrate use in an actual exercise. A report was generated that consisted of white papers prepared by the experts on how to apply methodologies to the problem of anticipating events that would be rare but could have dire consequences. The collection of white papers was assimilated into a single document titled *Topical Strategic Multi-layer Assessment (SMA) Multi-agency/Multidisciplinary White Papers in Support of Counter-Terrorism and Counter-WMD. Subtitle: Anticipating Rare Events: Can Acts of Terror, Use of Weapons of Mass Destruction or Other High Profile Acts Be Anticipated?* and published by the Department of Defense in November 2008. This first-of-a-kind report may be retrieved from the Department of Homeland Security Digital Library at `https://www.hsdl.org/?abstract&did=233523`.

This report contains my article on the use of the AuBASME methodology to predict a CBRN event that has no historical precedence. That work will be presented here as an example of the AuBASME methodology.

I was invited to participate with a group of other professionals to use our individual approaches in focusing on the anticipation of rare events. The purpose of the entire work was to explore the scientific possibilities of anticipating rare events that can affect national security. The term *rare event* was described in the foreword of the monograph describing the extensive document in the following way:

> So what distinguishes a rare event in the context of national security? The easy response is to describe them as unlikely actions of high consequence and for which there is a sparse historical record from which to develop predictive patterns or indications.

My work, titled "The Accurate Anticipation of Rare Human-Driven Events: An ABA/SME Hybrid," was described in the document as follows:

> Having presented empirically based approaches to forecasting and the evaluation of the environmental factors from which they arise, we turn our attention next to the use of applied behavior-based methodology to support anticipation/forecasting. The author of this article (4.6) is Gary Jackson. Key to his argument is the assumption that if antecedents and consequences associated with repeated occurrences of behavior can be identified, then the occurrence of that behavior in the future may be anticipated when the same or highly similar constellations of antecedents and likely consequences are present. In the absence of adequate history, Jackson has developed a hybrid approach of behavioral data combined with subject matter expert (SME) generated scenarios. A neural network pattern classification engine is trained and used to generate hypotheses given real world injects.

The underlying assumption that formed the foundation of my work is depicted in Figure 13-1, and by this point in the book, it should look familiar to you.

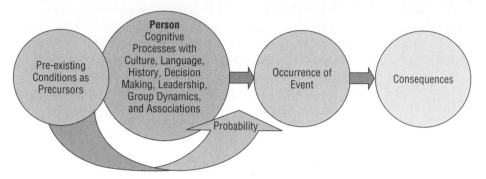

Figure 13-1: The underlying AuBA behavioral modeling foundation

The purpose of the exercise was to determine if AuBASME methodology could be used to accurately forecast an example incident of biological terrorism in the United States when there was not supportive, historical data. Figure 13-2 depicts the methodology we used for this exercise and application.

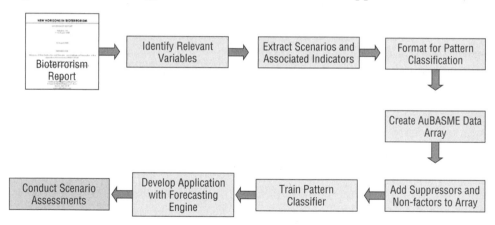

Figure 13-2: The AuBASME methodology

Once an AuBASME model was developed, my colleague and I would receive 100 sample pieces of intelligence to use as input; however, to make it more challenging, a certain percentage of the information provided would be purposeful disinformation. Therefore, prior to making a forecast, we needed to divide the legitimate intelligence from the illegitimate intelligence. All other SMEs participating were treated the same way. They received the identical legitimate information and disinformation to make their individual judgments.

We used the AuBA ThemeMate application to process all of the sample intelligence reports to differentiate accurate reports from highly similar reports that were generated by experts skilled in disinformation. Experts at the Pacific

Northwest National Laboratories (PNNL) then processed the data processed by ThemeMate and checked out the accuracy rate of determining legitimate versus non-legitimate (disinformation). After its study was completed, PNNL confirmed that the behavioral methodology used to differentiate legitimate from non-legitimate data was 80 percent accurate. So, given that we could then use only the information judged legitimate in making our forecast, our probability of accuracy increased. The steps used to construct the model were as follows:

1. Record all relevant information from three teams of multidisciplinary government professionals in areas of biological agents, terrorist attacks, CBRN threat as the team described highly likely scenarios, possible antecedent indicators, consequences, potential biological agents, perpetrators, areas of current operations, and likely global targeting.

2. Format all data for ThemeMate and run the application processing all data to form a data array with predictive themes as columns and example scenarios as rows.

3. Identify and reduce potential indicators to 170 antecedents associated with highly likely scenarios.

4. Submit the completed data arrays to AutoAnalyzer to construct and validate four pattern classifiers to forecast perpetrator, biological agent used, target, and area of current operation.

5. Using the developed ThemeMate process to identify legitimate from non-legitimate (disinformation), process the designated legitimate intelligence reports for the presence and absence of the 170 antecedents.

6. Present the vector of 1s (antecedents present) and 0s (antecedents missing) to the trained pattern classifiers to make forecasts across the four areas.

7. Process the four pattern classifiers with results giving the presentation of a vector of events and situations (antecedents) of the past week — the results are the forecast.

The results of the exercise were that the AuBA application projected the four categories accurately based on what a second expert panel determined would be a real event across (1) perpetrator, (2) current base of operation, (3) target, and (4) specific biological agent. This same AuBASME methodology was used to construct CheckMate and InMate.

Understanding the Role of Network Forensics

Forensic science is related to the study of an event to gather evidence suitable for legal prosecution. When we hear the abbreviated term, *forensics*, we tend to think of crime shows on television such as the CBS program *CSI* (*Crime Scene Investigation*), in which evidence is discovered and pieced together to prosecute a perpetrator of a crime such as murder. However, the term *forensics* has taken on a much broader meaning. Being associated with the study of a past event to discover the who and what of the event, the term is used across many fields of study in different ways. For the purpose of this book, we use the term *forensics* to mean *network forensics*. Although there are many uses of the *forensics* term, *network forensics* can be defined as *"the capture and inspection of packets passing through a selected node in the network. Packets can be inspected on the fly or stored on disk for later analysis."*[10]

Forensics is extremely important to ferret out the specific network activities underlying a specific attack. The goal of forensics is to identify attack features. Once these are identified, rules can be written to detect the hacker's signature if the attack should reoccur, or to recognize the signature on other networks as part of their signature detection.

A forensics analyst has a difficult job. If a hacker is highly skilled, it is possible that a system may have been compromised without detection. Once a breach is detected, there may be mountains of material to process. Because a truly talented hacker may use unique and inventive attack behavior (which may be why the attack evaded the front-end signature detection), the specific packet-level attack attributes can be very difficult to identify and summarize.

Because actual attack types may vary with the same hacker, the AuBA approach is to focus on the actual behavior of the hacker, as opposed to just packet-level activity. See the section "The Behaviorprint" for details of how a behaviorprint may be identified.

The forensics analyst must follow a prescribed methodology. There are preset steps, or stages, involved in analyzing an attack. It is very much like detective work. Isolating elements to identify an attack can be not only difficult but also very time-consuming, because attacks can be obfuscated by being surrounded by other activities. The following are typical steps followed in network forensics:[11]

- **Collection:** Identifying, labeling, recording, and acquiring data from the possible sources of relevant data while following procedures that preserve the integrity of the data.

- **Examination:** Forensically processing collected data using a combination of automated and manual methods, and assessing and extracting data of particular interest while preserving the integrity of the data.

- **Analysis:** Analyzing the results of the examination, using legally justifiable methods and techniques, to derive useful information that addresses the questions that were the impetus for performing the collection and examination.

---

[10] pcmag.com

[11] *Guide to Integrating Forensic Techniques into Incident Response*, National Institute of Standards and Technology, NIST Special Publication 800-86. August, 2006.

- **Reporting:** Reporting the results of the analysis, which may include describing the actions used, explaining how tools and procedures were selected, determining which other actions need to be performed (for example, conducting a forensic examination of additional data sources, securing identified vulnerabilities, improving existing security controls), and providing recommendations for improvements to policies, procedures, tools, and other aspects of the forensic process.

Once an attack has been identified, attributes of the attack have to be identified from a quagmire of network traffic. Copying relevant attack traffic in such a way that it can be fully documented as an attack is very important. Fully describing an attack by analyzing features can assist greatly in defining a class of attacks. Looking at common features across attacks of the same type can provide some idea of how an attack type can change or be altered over time.

Other Forensic Science Approaches Compared to Network Forensics

In conventional areas such as terrorism or criminal conduct, forensics is not quite as complex. Network forensics is complicated by the extreme volume of network traffic that must be processed and analyzed to focus on a specific hacker attack. In non-network forensics such as terrorist attacks (bombings, assaults, hijackings, and so on), we can study text-based reports of past incidents and use a tool such as AuBA's ThemeMate to determine antecedents of past attack behavior. Once antecedents are determined, the developed model may be used to indicate when attack behavior may be imminent. In comparison, forensics of cyber crime and network intrusion is very difficult. It can take weeks and even months to isolate and identify an attack, as well as saving it, producing adequate documentation, and preparing new signatures to identify the attack in the future. In network forensics, specific attributes of an attack are identified and placed into rules that can then be placed into a signature detection application like Snort to identify the attack in the future.

Using Past Events to Predict Future Events

Although we don't expect to see full duplication between past events and future events, there are very strong similarities. There are many reasons for this consistency across time. As we have learned from AuBA, humans pattern their behavior very quickly, and behavior that is successful is likely to be repeated under highly similar antecedent conditions. This is one of the hallmarks of applied behavior analysis. Second, adversaries usually receive some form of training. Individuals do not stray far from how they were trained. Therefore, adversarial behavior maintains some consistency across time.

If the antecedents were completely different in each case, humans would appear to be acting out of randomness. However, we are creatures of habit. We tend to go through the same routines day after day. The key to accurate prediction is the identification of the antecedents associated with the behavior of interest. If data is missing, or we are looking at rare events, we can augment with SME knowledge, as described in the AuBASME process earlier in this chapter and in Chapter 9.

One reason why we can predict changing behavior to some extent by extracting antecedents from past accounts of behavior is the use of the neural network pattern classifiers. Thanks to this form of classification, the neural network will provide an output whenever a new input is provided, even if the input has not been in the training set. An artificial neural network learns by example. When we arrange data into a training set, we are providing examples. Each example has a set of 1s and 0s to represent the presence (1) or absence (0) of each antecedent, and the outcome is also designated by 1s and 0s. For the outcome, as an example, if we are going to anticipate threat or no threat, we would have two columns, one for each category. If an example is one of threat, then the threat column receives a 1 and the no threat column receives a 0 for that example. If we have 16 antecedents and 100 examples to present to the neural network for training (learning), this would represent 100 different combinations of the 16 antecedents, as we don't want repeats.

Because there are 65,536 combinations of 16, the neural network is not trained on 65,536 examples. Therefore, once trained, if one of the combinations not present in the 100-example training set is presented, the neural network still projects either threat or no threat. We have found that if the neural network is trained properly, there is a very high probability that when the neural network is presented with the combinations not used in the training set, it is very often correct.

FOLLOW THE MOTIVATIONS

As part of an AuBA analysis, we can discover specifically what causes a group to respond with terrorist behavior. For example, if Hezbollah continually attacks Israel, then we can infer that important antecedent conditions for Hezbollah behavior are actions by Israel and the Israeli military. For example, an Israeli military attack on a Hezbollah stronghold will serve as an antecedent condition that leads to a Hezbollah attack against an Israeli target. Similarly, an important antecedent for Israeli behavior is the behavior of Hezbollah. The Hezbollah attack against Israel then serves as an antecedent condition for an Israeli attack against Hezbollah. This back-and-forth nature in which the behavior of Group A serves as an antecedent for the adversarial behavior of Group B and vice versa describes the continued adversarial behavior we have observed between Israel and Hezbollah over the past decade.

Determining State Support of Terrorist Activities

Just as with studying individual behavior, by studying past accounts of state behavior and by identifying associated antecedents, we are capturing the antecedents that form the context for associated state behavior occurring shortly after the presence of the antecedents. When a state is directly guiding and supporting an attack group (guidance), the use of terrorism is like any weapon used by the state. However, an attack group may be completing an act at the request of the supporting nation-state but not be directly supported or claimed (no guidance). Analysis of any past relevant state behavior, particularly as associated with attacks by a group suspected to be supported by the state, may provide clues concerning support of terrorism by that state. For example, if there are frequent occasions in which the state provides criticism concerning another state and shortly after each criticism a terrorist act occurs within the criticized state, then we may reach a point where these associations are not likely to be chance or a series of unlikely coincidences. This is true whether the support is direct or indirect.

As an example of how associations of events and antecedent conditions can lead to cause and effect, I will provide a real example from my neighborhood. If there was a break-in in your neighborhood every 2 or 3 months over the past year, and each time, regardless of where in the neighborhood that break-in occurred, you noticed the same red car parked in front of your house, and you had never seen the car at any other time, how many times would it take before you become suspicious and get the license plate number or call the police? In other words, the first time you saw the car would likely not mean much; the second time could be a coincidence; the third time you would likely call the police — and maybe you could have helped to prevent additional break-ins. The number of observations certainly do not prove who the culprit is, but it does not take many observations before the suspicious behavior can lead to a police investigation that could obtain the evidence to support the determination that passengers of the red car are, in fact, the perpetrators.

> **NOTE** Once we have identified the antecedent conditions associated with behavior, we can often infer the motivation behind events in the future. This is important because we want to understand why and under what conditions the behavior occurs.

Gathering Evidence of State-Supported Malicious Behavior

Given a functional AuBA model, the predictability establishes a connection between antecedents and the following behavior. That is, if we develop a training set for the neural network that includes repeated examples of antecedents that just precede behavior of interest, then the way in which we train will validate the model by testing each case blindly using the L-1 method. Once we complete the L-1 training, which includes each case being predicted and tested blindly, we calculate a Fisher's exact statistical test. Because this gives us the probability that our test results could have been achieved by chance, if the results indicate a Fisher's result of 0.001, we know that there is no less than 1 in a 1,000 chance that results could have been obtained by chance. In other words, if our model is predictive using the validation method used and the Fisher's exact is very low, then the associations are likely to be real; otherwise, the model would not be predictive. Given the AuBA modeling methodology described, most models we develop range in accuracy from 80 percent to 90+ percent overall accuracy on real-world tests.

Once a terrorist behavior occurs (and if it is in the service of state-supported antecedent conditions), we may have a clearer idea as to how a state responds to environmental and global occurrences, as well as its underlying motivations. Does it mean that an incident like the one discussed earlier involving Iran and the Mexican drug cartel can be predicted? The answer is that we do not know until we try.

Although we may not be able to predict a specific target, that doesn't mean that we can't predict when the next terrorist act will happen. There may be certain parts of a prediction that we can do accurately, even if it isn't all the potential aspects of an impending terrorist act. Skeptics often view the prediction of human behavior as a single event and, as such, present the case that prediction of human behavior is not possible. For example, although al-Qaeda has exhibited many different terrorist acts, 9/11 is often looked at as a single event and quickly followed with the fact that no one predicted it. This is different from determining the accuracy rate over many different attacks or other forms of behavior.

Prediction of future adversarial behavior is complex. Until we construct and validate a viable model, we will not know the extent to which prediction can occur. However, based on my experience with AuBA modeling, it is safe to say that some key aspect (who, what, when, where, or why) can be predicted. We may be able to predict targeting, the timing of the next attack, the location, or the actual type of attack, any and all of which are valuable pieces of information, but maybe not all with equal accuracy. In behavioral modeling we can then use verification and testing tools to have an excellent idea of the accuracy of the model and how antecedents are tied to different types of behavior.

The Behaviorprint

AuBA technology allows for a feature that I have labeled *behaviorprint*. This is a very interesting feature. We all have unique fingerprints, just like we have unique DNA. Given that our fingerprints are in a database, and we have a set of fingerprints to compare to the fingerprints in the database, our fingerprints are unique enough that the analytical software can find a match in the database if we provide a copy of our fingerprints. *Voilà*, a match is found, and we have our identity attached to the fingerprints presented.

AuBA technology as presented in CheckMate (external network threat) converts packet-level activity in continuous 100 millisecond samples into levels of *expertise* and *deception* present in each sample. The hypothesis in the beginning was that if expertise and deception measures both go high at the same time over a critical threshold, then the person is exhibiting malicious intent prior to theft or damage.

Figure 13-3 shows an expertise/deception (E/D) panel with CheckMate. Although CheckMate and InMate are totally self-tending, an administrator can call up an E/D panel and view the behavior of any IP on the measurement panel as behavior continues. In the figure, expertise is on the vertical axis (up and down), and deception is on the horizontal axis on the bottom. Therefore, an E and D measure is seen as a single dot (for example, E of 7 and D of 7 would be plotted as 7,7). Every 100 milliseconds (10 times a second), there is an assessment that is plotted. If the same plot occurs repeatedly (for example, 7,7; 7,7; 7,7), then the points are just superimposed on one another.

By crossing the E and D dimensions, we have quadrants. The upper-right quadrant is high E and high D, which means a plot in that quadrant shows malicious intent. The lower-left quadrant shows low E and low D, or lack of malicious intent. Basically, as behavior occurs on the network, it is converted to E/D measures, and we can see that malicious intent is occurring as plotted points move to the upper right.

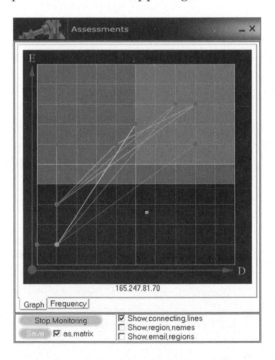

Figure 13-3: The AuBA CheckMate application expertise/deception panel for tracking malicious intent. This example shows a characteristic behaviorprint with malicious intent moving into the upper-right critical region.

From Fingerprints to Behaviorprints

In developing CheckMate, I noticed that individuals tend to operate up to their highest level of expertise and deception, regardless of the activity. In using a vulnerability generator, an automated tool that hackers can use to help devise attacks, the application would produce a signature as shown in Figure 13-3. Even if the vulnerability generator were doing something different each time, the same E/D pattern occurred, a pattern, as I indicated in the previous section, I call a *behaviorprint*. This pattern is important because the implication is that if you come into the network, you could be recognized by an E/D pattern, not as a signature of a specific type of attack, as used in signature detection.

This raised the possibility of a behaviorprint. We are all familiar with the concept of fingerprints — we are all unique, and our fingerprints reflect that by being unique as well. A CheckMate or InMate behaviorprint is a unique pattern of behavior on the E/D (CheckMate) or I/D (InMate) panels.

I observed a well-known ethical cyber hacker operate as he would when testing network defenses. He had a swivel chair and a number of PCs. Each PC had a different IP (address). He would simply move from PC to PC, attacking the same test site while coming from different IPs. He also bounced the connection to different servers to make it appear as though he was coming from different locations. To the site being attacked, he was five different people coming from five different countries. This is the type of expertise and deception we have to be concerned about with global threat. However, it appears that CheckMate has the potential to identify the perpetrator as the same person, because five different E/D panels would show a highly similar E/D pattern of activity. This feature is not possible with signature detection and anomaly detection. The behaviorprint may provide a mechanism to identify a coordinated attack in which several attackers use the same approach coming from different locations simultaneously. If the CheckMate option is set to block traffic, the IP connection is severed before damage can occur.

Modeling as a Form of Proof

Our AuBA teams have learned much from applying our automated tools to the process of developing models across many different adversarial domains from a global threat perspective. We have modeled nation-state threat, criminals, terrorists, terrorist attacks, insurgency, tracking and locating, threat from sensor tracks of movement, and so on. As part of the process the patented methodology has been refined to the point that if we collect a corpus of text-based accounts of past adversarial behaviors or if we use SMEs when data is sparse or missing, the automated tools will result in a viable model.

For accuracy, we expect to find 80 percent overall accuracy in our cross-validation methodology called Leaving-One-Out (L-1). As mentioned previously in this chapter, L-1 in computer science basically means that we train our neural network pattern classifiers on all sample cases but one. Once the classifier is trained, we test the one blind test. This way, the classifier does not have knowledge of that one case, so it becomes a fair test. We then put that case back and remove another case and repeat the training. Again once the classifier is trained with all cases but the one, the withheld case is tested. The process is repeated until all cases are tested blindly. Once the cases are validated, we turn the model to the real world and enter antecedents that have just occurred to derive a prediction.

During this process we have learned that we will arrive at a predictive model unless something is wrong with the data. We can use modeling to determine the accuracy of the presented data for the model.

Moving from Detection to Protection: A Major Leap

Global threat is growing quickly. We now have APT, with such countries as China launching serious attacks and stealing classified information and proprietary data. 9/11 has taught us that terrorists can strike within our country's border with devastating effects. Crime is real, and we still confront crime in every city in our country. Crime has also grown to global proportions. Still, from cyber and other adversarial warfare perspectives, we continue to maintain a more reactive stance. When we look at current approaches, we see they are heavily influenced by signature detection. As mentioned, anomaly detection is still coming onto the scene but is also is experimental because of the propensity to present very high false-positive rates. AuBA modeling is moving more toward a proactive, predictive approach.

Skepticism has led to a lack of imagination and willingness to explore true behavioral-based prediction methodologies. One of the primary findings of the more than 500-page 9/11 commission report was that our lack of preparedness was a lack of imagination. We simply did not see it coming. We also missed the fall of the Soviet Union and the Berlin Wall and the longevity of the Iraq and Afghanistan wars. We simply need to start moving strong support to predictive work, or we will remain in the past.

History is about the past; intelligence should be about the future. However, we can't become predictive if we remain reactive. Signature detection as a concept is sound; it just is not enough. It is past time to bring the behavioral sciences to bear as we continue to fuse methods with the computer and network sciences. Ironically, we have brought communication on a global basis to the speed of light, yet our methods are used to study the past.

Behavioral science is about the future. Behavioral science has a strong role to play looking forward — whether is it clinical and we study behavior so that we know how to alter it for the better in the future, educational so that we can grant knowledge to the youth to better prepare them for tomorrow, counseling so that we can help others cope better in the future, experimental so that we can identify variables that are associated with future behavior, or industrial so that we can improve workplaces to foster greater job satisfaction. Accurate prediction does not spontaneously evolve from technology, and it does not surface from statistical correlation. There is a science of human behavior, and we need to fuse it with the computer sciences, network protection, counterterrorism, counterintelligence, and counterespionage.

Detection is recognizing the known only. The world is changing quickly, and we need to identify new malicious behavior. Adversaries are capable, and their motivation will continue to drive their behavior toward anti-U.S. behaviors. We must learn how to make better use of predictive methods that already exist, and begin to consider skepticism just to be an opposing view, not a suppressor for the development of protective technology that we need for our nation's infrastructure. It is too easy to be a naysayer.

Advantages of AuBA #13: The AuBA Behaviorprint and How It Compares to Signatures

Signature detection is the cornerstone of network intrusion detection almost universally. When a new form of intrusion occurs, specialists in network intrusion detection study the characteristics of the method used and write signatures that will detect the attack should it occur again. These signatures are added to the signature repository of existing signature detection products/applications. Signature detection is very good at detecting known intrusion attempts, but is very weak at detecting new or zero-day attacks, unless the intrusion attempt has elements of known signatures included. Signatures are written based on the network behavior of the malicious activity.

AuBA focuses on human behavior as opposed to network behavior. As part of the AuBA capability, the focus is on converting digital information to human behavior assessment. For example, the CheckMate application converts typical network packet activity (network behavior) to the determination of the degree of expertise represented by the network activity and the degree of deception that is present. These two human assessment measures are calculated every 1/10 of a second and tracked for as long as the individual is in the network. All those in the network are assessed at this rate. If both expertise and deception go above a determined threshold at the same time, then it has been determined that malicious intent is present and an intrusion is likely to occur or is imminent. In this way, instead of seeking to identify known signatures, CheckMate can identify the attacker by behavior, even if new intrusion tactics are used. In other words, actual threatening intent is identified.

Because of the expertise and deception tracking across time, a pattern of activity is established. Instead of an attack signature, this track represents the degree of expertise and deception of the person across time. In our tests, even if an individual changes activity each time he or she enters a network, the degree of expertise and deception remains stable enough to generate a pattern whereby a return to the network might be noted. This is especially useful if several attackers work together and coordinate a common attack. The probability that their behavior is similar is high because of similar expertise and deception patterns.

These differences place CheckMate into a proactive and predictive mode, as opposed to the reactive stance of signature detection. This is a significant advantage in that protective measures can occur for some new or zero-day attacks. The addition of human behavior assessment can work with existing signature detection approaches to provide stronger protection that combines elements of both. CheckMate is demonstrating true human behavior assessment for external threat to a network, and InMate is demonstrating the utility of human assessment for internal threat.

In Summary

This chapter has focused on escalating global threat and the need to meet it with predictive technology that actually exists. Views and books, such as *The Black Swan*, can be informative and part of a healthy scientific debate; however, there is little to no science behind proclamations that rare events or human behavior cannot be predicted. We scientists who have worked for decades to develop proactive and predictive technology have science, validation, third-party validation, and data. It is time to pit this science against the naysayers who don't have data, only opinions. There is room for both, and the debate can be healthy. However, in the meantime, we have a national infrastructure that is being attacked on a daily basis. We are losing proprietary and classified information on a daily basis. Our network protection technology is inadequate. We may be facing another 9/11. Our water supplies, power grid, and innocent citizens' lives could be at stake. Let's keep skepticism where it belongs — it is nothing more than an opinion. At the same time, let's look at the science of predicting human behavior, make it better, and construct the applications we need to have a paradigm shift in security.

AuBA methodology, tools, and applications are starts in the right direction. Technology must become more proactive and predictive to better anticipate adversary behavior directed at us. With accurate prediction, prevention becomes a true capability.

Part

III

Applying Tools and Methods

In This Part

Predictive Capability in Software: Tools for a New Approach

Conducting an analysis of human behavior, whether the focus is an individual or a group, is very difficult. There are many types of analyses, ranging from the qualitative reading and processing of reports while using intuitive ability to characterize the focus to the very empirical and quantitative approaches that present objective results. An excellent analogy is investing in the stock market, the epitome of human behavior prediction. Methods range from superstition and guessing to advanced proprietary algorithms that invest and sell automatically.

There are a number of reasons why analysis of human behavior from a manual perspective has become so difficult. Some of the primary reasons are:

- The amount of global information to process in most cases is voluminous and in some cases comes in at a fire-hose rate.

- Because anyone can post anything on the Internet, there is a significant amount of false or misleading information embedded with accurate information.

- In contrast, in some cases with covert attackers, the type of information needed for complete analysis is scarce or simply missing.

- Humans have biases and often form an opinion too early, which moves their analysis toward seeking information to support their biases.

- The idea of history repeating itself is an antiquated and uninformed concept — future behavior is not a replication of past behavior.

- Human behavior does, however, occur in response to antecedents and consequences of past behavior. (These patterns must be understood if future behavior is to be anticipated accurately.)

- Humans often believe their personal insight is correct; however, I have not seen a single empirical study to show that human insight can accurately predict behavior of an individual or group on a consistent basis over time.

In this chapter, it will be demonstrated why tools are needed if we are going to anticipate future behavior. Biologists use a microscope, astronomers use a telescope, and tax accountants use a calculator and tax software; using supportive tools does not take away from the person doing an analysis — tools add value.

Fusing Computer and Behavioral Sciences

It is my contention that the accurate anticipation of future human behavior requires expertise, a solid methodology that is followed religiously, and tools to assist in gathering data for analysis. In the development of AuBA, I fused computer sciences with behavior sciences. This hybrid automates what was developed as a manual method and is 400 times faster. The automated features reduce error and increase accuracy.

We have all been surrounded by others and have witnessed examples and varieties of human behavior in our lifetimes. Interactions have been countless, and we have all been people watchers at one point or another. This lifetime of observation has led many of us to believe that we have special insight into the causes of and reasons for behavior. However, formal training in the social and behavior sciences encourage the development of specialized knowledge, analysis skills, and understanding of behavior. Often research findings are counterintuitive, and the inner motivations of another person are extremely difficult to ascertain, even for the highly trained. It is difficult to know ourselves fully, let alone to know another person simply from observations.

Trusting our impressions or intuition is much like standing at a roulette wheel. You bet on red because you just know that red will come up, or you pull the level on the slot machine because something told you this slot machine was the one. We are wrong often. Our first impressions can be proven wrong, and the stereotypes we apply are unfair. We need behavior science so that we know not to trust first impressions and intuitive feelings about others.

The study of human behavior has taught us much. First, adversarial behavior is often not very understandable. Ted Bundy brutally killed over 30 very young women. We still do not know fully what motivated Bundy, Jeffrey Dahmer, Adolf Hitler, and any number of others who exhibited extreme malicious behavior. However, though we may not understand it, by the nature of the manner in which behavior responds to the environment, we can predict it with some success.

Behavior is not just a product of inner thoughts; it is a function of the complex inner workings of an individual and the environment. It is this interaction that is observable, and it is the environmental antecedents to which the individual responds that makes predictability possible. Social and behavioral sciences have given us a foundation that allows us to at least study human behavior adequately, as nonintuitive as that behavior may be.

There are many skeptics who flatly refuse to acknowledge that human behavior is predictable because of the difficulties in predicting human behavior. However, to start this chapter, I mention two areas that are irrefutable evidence that we can predict human behavior.

Sampling and Presidential Polls

I have made a career of analyzing and predicting human behavior across clinical, academic, research, intelligence, and military domains. Over my career, it has always been amazing to me how closely presidential polls predict the voting behavior of an entire country of voters. A poll uses the power of sampling to make a prediction about a population.

NOTE *"Sampling* is a process used in statistical analysis in which a predetermined number of observations will be taken from a larger population. The methodology used to sample from a larger population will depend on the type of analysis being performed, but will include simple random sampling, systematic sampling and observational sampling. The sample should be a representation of the general population."
`investopedia.com`

By asking people in this very small sample who they will vote for, the pollsters obtain percentages that serve as a prediction of the actual vote of the entire population. The accuracy is usually within 1 to 2 percentage points. This is prediction of human behavior on a grand scale.

Figure 14-1 displays the Gallup Poll final survey results for the past three elections and the actual results after the vote with the percentage error. At the bottom of the last column is the average deviation, or error, over the past three elections, which is 1.46 percentage points. Considering that the poll results are published prior to the election and a typical Gallup poll consists of only 1,000 people, the similarity between Gallup Poll results and presidential election results is a testament to careful sampling.

NOTE I encourage you to follow this link (`http://www.gallup.com /poll/9442/election-polls-accuracy-record-presidential- elections.aspx`) to the Gallup site to see the results of all presidential elections since the 1936 Roosevelt-Landon election. It is irrefutable that the

difference between predicted voting behavior and actual voting behavior
for all candidates since 1936 presents a mean difference of 2.11 percentage
points. The Gallup Poll survey results may be an example of one of the largest
predictions made repeatedly over many years with a high degree of accuracy
and completed only every 4 years with results open to review.

Year	Candidates	Final Gallup Survey Projection %	Actual Election Result %	Difference in Projected and Actual %
2008	Obama	55	53	2
	McCain	44	46	2
2004	Bush	49	50.7	1.7
	Kerry	49	48.3	0.7
	Bush	48	47.9	0.1
2000	Gore	46	48.4	2.4
	Nader	4	2.7	1.3

Mean Difference = 1.46%

Figure 14-1: Presidential Gallup Poll accuracy in the last three elections.

The 2008 election resulted in 129,391,711 votes among the U.S. population.
This is 129,391 times the size of a typical-sized Gallup sample. Yet, the prediction of national voting behavior of a collection over 129 million Americans was
within 2 percentage points.

High-Speed Automated Stock Market Prediction

High Frequency Trading (HFT) is a process of monitoring and making buy and
sell decisions for stocks automatically at blinding speed. It is called *high frequency*
because it is far faster than humans can operate. The speed and accuracy of
this type of trading is a distinct advantage, and many billions of dollars worth
of transactions occur daily. Of course, the algorithms and methodologies are
highly proprietary and will not see the light of day.

What makes HFT predictive?

- First, it processes extreme amounts of precursor data rapidly.

- Second, it projects if a stock will rise or fall in the very near future.

- Third, it puts solid money behind the prediction, perhaps the ultimate
  faith that a capitalist can have in a prediction.

It is not gambling. It is a science of human behavior being practiced by the rich
to be richer. It is a science of predicting white swans, black swans, geese, ducks,
apples, and oranges. As pointed out in Chapter 13, a black swan is a metaphor
for a rare event (although I do not agree with the premise; see Nassim Nicholas

Taleb's *The Black Swan: The Impact of the Highly Improbable*, Random House, 2007). On a separate topic, there is little consistency across stocks — basically, apples and oranges. The key to predictors is those indicators that reflect aggregated behavior. For example, the price of gold or a barrel of oil reflects the buying and selling behavior of all on any given moment throughout the day. The end result is the prediction of percent gain, or how the aggregate behavior will affect the closing price for the day. Stock prices are complex and based on all who deal with that stock. For every transaction, there is someone selling and someone buying. You can't have one without the other. When buying outweighs selling, the stock raises in values. When selling outweighs the attempt to buy, then the value drops. However, it gets exceedingly complex when you finally realize that a transaction does both — someone buys and someone sells. This is not an endeavor for the weak at heart. It is a roller coaster, and without the proper form of analysis, you may as well be throwing dice in Las Vegas. Analysis can give you the edge. Why is HFT so important? It is a fascinating example of predicting massive human behavior and intent moving at high speeds. Major buy and sell decisions occur so quickly that traders can actually monitor (changes in intraday volume) and price changes in real time. This is capitalistic human behavior at a high level and a "game that is played by the big boys," as they say. HFT now likely accounts for the majority of trades per minute, hour, and day.

This is new territory. The upside is that many billions of dollars of profit are being taken in by those who use this predictive approach. However, there is a downside. On May 6, 2010, this high-speed trading caused what is now called a *flash crash* in the stock market. During this high-speed crash of 1,000 points, panic moved at the same high speed as the trading and quickly affected the much slower humans. Though the recovery occurred fairly quickly, it was enough of a scare that there are measures now to stop such a crash from happening again — for example, putting a halt to all trading for the rest of the day.

Would HFT not exist and be growing at an accelerating rate if it did not reach profit margins that cannot be exceeded by manual buying and selling? Are there black swans (rare events) here? Yes, but the systems are performing admirably as evidenced by their growth. Again, this is prediction of human behavior. It is very *specific* buying and selling of stocks behavior, on a massive scale, but it is prediction, and it works. It is a fact that HFT is growing because of its effectiveness at predicting a movement of specific stocks in the right direction to obtain massive profits.

It is time for skeptics to realize that prediction of human behavior is not only possible but driving the stock market. There are advantages and there are disadvantages to HFT. However, it is real, it works, and it is being adopted at a rapid rate. The human cannot compete with the speed of the automation. Automation and algorithms are driving this phenomenon, and the best and the brightest are being hired to pursue this new form of executing the profit motive. Let's just say that the predictive systems work, and we all need to accept the inevitability of the capability to predict human behavior on a massive scale.

AuBA Prediction of Terrorism

I invented the AuBA process and tools, and it was fully developed by several teams I have led over the years. This application has resulted in hard-core prediction of adversarial behavior. A test for the government was developed some years ago to show the validity of the methodology and tools to predict four categories of behavior of a specific adversarial group (attack/no attack, military/civilian target, general location, and general approach). The predictions were to be made weekly and forwarded to the government agency, with a third, independent agency calculating accuracy. Predictions were to occur weekly for 24 weeks, and accuracy would be determined at the end by the third-party agency. Data used to develop predictive models was typical, open source news media articles of past events of the group.

The AuBA team completed the work, and the automated components of the application made the weekly predictions. The predictions were then forwarded weekly to the funding organization. They were then sent to a third-party organization of subject matter experts to determine if weekly predictions were accurate.

The results at the end of the 24 weekly predictions across all four categories were 85 percent accuracy on attack/no attack and almost 90 percent accuracy on the other categories if attack occurred. Most impressive, there were seven weeks of no attacks, and the AuBA application predicted that six of the seven weeks would not have an attack.

The application has many other examples, particularly as it relates to AuBA. However, my contention is that we now know that prediction of human behavior not only is possible but is in practice. I also believe that these examples are irrefutable. Non-acceptance would have to be based on pure bias and not healthy scientific skepticism. The latter is needed; the former is a liability that prevents a science of human behavior prediction from moving forward.

We are being attacked mercilessly on a daily basis in the cyber world and we are engaging in a continuing war on terrorism. Our national infrastructure is at risk. Our defenses are clearly reactive, and we need to be proactive. The technology of human behavior prediction is there. However, human biases are preventing its full exploration and inclusion for something as important as new proactive protection for our national infrastructure. This is why we need a security paradigm shift.

Using the Computer's Speed and Memory to Our Benefit

HFT (in the preceding section) was listed as an example for a specific purpose. HFT is automation at its best. The days of a Sherlock Holmes–type of approach used by an analyst (reading reports and newspapers, assessing the current situation, then divining what is going to happen next by intuition) are long gone — or they should be! There simply is no scientific evidence that this approach is valid. This is not to diminish any work by analysts. As a former intelligence officer, I have tremendous respect for analysts. They perform many invaluable assessments, and most are extremely talented. They just should not rely on intuition alone to foretell what is going to happen next. If tools are used, and used appropriately, the outcome is often very different from intuition — fortunately! Basically, it is more accurate. There is nothing as inaccurate as intuition. Nostradamus and Sherlock Holmes have no place in modern-day determinations of adversarial threat.

Why do we need a computer to help us, and how can this increase the accuracy of our predictions? Humans are exceptionally good at using the synthesis of information to derive unique ways of viewing situations in ways that a computer cannot yet do. But, humans cannot compete when it comes to memory and speed of processing data. First, computers have perfect memory. Human memory is affected by bias, fatigue, and external influences. The computer, on the other hand, has perfect memory and can make associations among data points many thousands times faster, far beyond what human cognitive processing can accomplish.

As an example, the AuBA CheckMate cyber threat application described in this book can make 20,000 assessments a second and accurately determine new threat when it sees it. The human brain can handle maybe five or six different variables at one time, but CheckMate processes 435 separate variables at a time, in addition to processing the 2^{435} possible combinations of variables, and provides an accurate human behavior assessment. This is an astounding number of combinations that exceeds the number of atoms in the universe, and CheckMate can make these calculations 10 times a second. However, speed and perfect memory are only tools. The human analyst has the capability to process the actual results and make sense of the reports across many assessments. The human is essential for overall synthesis.

The need for the human analyst in making decisions from synthesizing multiple automated reports is very similar to the need for astronauts. Automated robot-like excursions into space can report back sensor data, but the automated systems cannot write poetry or descriptions of what has been sensed that provides the gestalt of findings. This needs the human element. However, the human elements need the data. If done correctly, the combination is certainly greater than the sum of the parts.

The computer's superior speed and memory mean nothing unless the information being processed is suitable. In addition to suitable data we need a methodology that makes analysis standardized, reliable, and valid. I contend that if we are processing examples of human behavior, we need a foundation from which principles of human behavior can be derived. Using AuBA, we process antecedents and consequences associated with multiple examples of behaviors of interest. In this way, we can store all possible antecedent candidates simply because they occur temporally before the behavior and all candidates for consequences because they occur after the behavior.

NOTE We begin the process of identifying antecedents and consequences by simply noting events and situations occurring before the behavior (antecedent candidates) and after (consequence candidates). Clearly, many events are occurring just before and after the behavior simply by chance. Of the candidates, those that repeat across multiple occurrences of the behavior will be the true antecedents and consequences, whereas those that are associated purely by chance and do not repeat across behaviors are dropped.

As I have alluded to throughout the book, the following definitions apply to this type of data analysis:

- **Antecedent:** An antecedent is any event or situation that occurs before a behavior that is logically related to the behavior.
- **Behavior:** A behavior is any action exhibited by an individual or group selected for analysis or prediction.
- **Consequence:** A consequence is any event or situation that follows a behavior that is logically related to the behavior.

If a database of antecedents, behaviors, and consequence candidates is collected, then it is possible to begin the analysis that leads to prediction (see the prediction walkthrough in Chapter 20 and on the DVD). The process is simply not possible without using the speed and memory advantages of the computer.

REFERENCE Refer to Chapter 7 to see how the principles of antecedents and consequences work together for behavior to occur.

Applying Simple Tools to Gain Advanced Results

A tool is a device to assist and augment a typically manual task or process. Computer tools in analysis of human behavior are intended to assist with the manual process of analyzing human behavior. Speed and power of processing can be extremely useful in analysis of human behavior for a number of reasons. First, in a new world of massive communications, we must take advantage of the speed of a computer to allow us to process the fire hose of information available on a moment-to-moment basis. Second, the storage capability of a modern-day PC allows us to collect a library of documents for analysis on a single computer hard drive.

Given that we collect the correct corpus of documents on a topic of interest, and given that we have a methodology like AuBA with the automated tools, then we can analyze the behaviors of interest with associated antecedents and consequences to build predictive models. However, there are a variety of less sophisticated tools that can assist in the beginning of an analysis.

In the introduction to this chapter, I provided a number of reasons why conducting manual analysis of human behavior has become so challenging. These reasons were derived from my decades of analysis working with many talented individuals who analyze malicious adversarial behavior, including clinical cases. To seriously conduct analysis of human behavior on a global scale requires tools. When one conducts analysis, one must collect multiple examples of any behavior that is being studied. A single example could be anomalous and not representative of the individual or group being studied. As with presidential election polling, analyzing malicious behavior requires a significant sample. The more representative that sample is of the population, the more accurate analysis will become. This is a function of data and not the skill of the analyst.

For example, imagine that we are studying a criminal gang who has had 500 criminal infractions over the past 20 years. We would want a small sample made up of representative types of behaviors. If the group engages primarily in breaking and entering, armed robbery, and ATM theft, we would want to make sure we started with the most recent examples and work back until we have our sample. Then we have to follow a step that may not seem intuitive. We must have a matched number of examples of non-criminal behavior from the same group, to the extent that we can.

For example, consider a biker gang that attends a bike rally each year. Perhaps they made the news for making a contribution to a fellow biker who was killed in an accident or so forth. The reason for completing a set of non-malicious examples (we call these *nons*) is that pattern classification works by differentiating among different classes of behavior. We have found out that predictive accuracy increases when we train our pattern classifiers with different antecedents associated with different classes of behavior. In other words, AuBA technology works by identifying the antecedents associated with malicious threat versus no malicious theat. Each time we enter antecedents that are present for a given time period, the pattern classifier's job is to determine if threat or no threat is associated with this particular set of antecedents. More than likely antecedents of both classes are present. This is why a trained and tuned pattern classifier is required to make the very fine judgments to accurately select the correct class, which is the prediction of the behavior to follow.

Why do we need a PC and software? There are a number of reasons (some of which I've touched on already in this chapter):

- Because of the need to process and analyze multiple examples of behavior, adequate storage of the entire documents, or raw data, is required that is 100 percent reliable. PC storage is reliable.

- PC storage keeps all documents and different steps of analysis secure while allowing rapid access to a specific document out of many or any specific components of an analysis being completed.

- PC hard drives today hold an astounding amount of information. A drive can hold all raw data, analyses, reports, and PowerPoint presentations and still have the majority of hard drive space left over.

NOTE Microsoft Office products are all useful in analysis — Microsoft Word for document and summary creation, Microsoft Access as a database, Excel for a spreadsheet and data analysis (see below), and PowerPoint for presentation of results.

- The Internet is essential — you can search for just about any topic and find multiple examples of almost any malicious behavior to analyze. Once found, the articles can be downloaded to a directory on the PC's hard drive as a single repository.

- A paperless analysis is efficient and effective with all components stored and preserved for as long as necessary.

TIP You must back up all information on the PC hard drive to an external hard drive daily, and you should make a habit of saving your work every few minutes as you work. It is extremely disheartening to lose either raw data that you cannot go back to or components of an analysis. It happens. And it doesn't matter how good you think your PC may be or how much you paid for it — electronic components can fail. Simply purchase an external hard drive for backups when you purchase a computer, or go to a store that sells computer products and purchase a backup drive.

Excel and the Analysis ToolPak: Methods and Examples

Although detail will be provided in the walkthrough in Chapter 20 and in the accompanying DVD, the use of the Excel and the Analysis ToolPak is so much a part of analysis that I have given it a preview here. The Excel spreadsheet is a perfect product to create and analyze a data array for a behavioral analysis. A data array is essential because in that structure you can have columns serve as antecedents and rows serve as the examples of behavior. If a "1" is in an intersecting cell, it means that the antecedent for that column is present for the behavior example in that row. If a "0" is present in an intersecting cell, then that means that that the antecedent is not present for the example of behavior in that row.

For example, in my hometown, a local convenience store has had its ATM stolen twice in the past few years. Thieves drive up to the store after hours, break through the front window, wrap a chain around the ATM, hook the chain to a pickup truck, and haul it out of the store. In a second location, they break into the ATM with a blowtorch and remove a considerable amount of cash. To demonstrate the methodology I am talking about, I have collected a series of news articles describing similar ATM attacks to conduct a behavior analysis that could identify predictive antecedents to such attacks. After searching, it was clear that ATMs are a target and have been violated a variety of different ways. Being a mini-bank, an ATM can hold as much as $20,000 when loaded, but typically it holds somewhat less. Given their presence in a variety of non-secure locations such as convenience stores, ATMs are likely targets for smash and grabs.

Figure 14-2 depicts a portion of a data array that was created by cutting and pasting the association matrix automatically produced by ThemeMate, an AuBA tool, to Excel. Excel can also be used to produce such an array manually. The resulting data array has common conceptual themes that were extracted across all documents as columns. Each row is an example of behavior. Themes are antecedents to the behaviors. In other words, events or situational variables preceding the occurrence of the behavior are logically related to the behavior. The rows are created by naming all documents for a specific example of behavior with the same identifier name. Whether created as an association matrix by ThemeMate or created manually, the data array always has the same basic arrangement. Data arrays can be very large because the default for ThemeMate is to find and describe as many as 250 themes and can be extended to a maximum of 500 themes.

NOTE Manually, humans tend to find far fewer themes to use as antecedents — hence, one of the advantages of the ThemeMate automation is the identification of more themes, or antecedents.

In Figure 14-2, the different examples of ATM thefts are represented by the rows. Across the top, a portion of the themes, or antecedent conditions, are shown for illustration purposes. For example, the first theme (T1) is time of day the incident occurred; T2 is time as A.M. or P.M.; T3 is whether it was light or dark at the time of the incident; T4 is the typical day of the week the ATM

Incident	T1	T2	T3	T4	T5	T6	T7	T8	T9	T10	T11	T12	T13	T14	T15	T16	T17	T18
BEx001	1	1	1	1	1	1	1	1	1	1	1	1	1	1	1	1	1	1
BEx002	1	1	1	0	0	1											0	0
BEx003	1	1	0	1	0	1											0	0
BEx004	1	1	1	1	1	1											0	0
BEx005	1	1	1	1	1	1											0	1
BEx006	1	1	1	1	1	1											1	1
BEx007	1	1	1	1	1	1											0	1
BEx008	1	1	1	1	1	1											0	1
BEx009	1	1	1	1	1	1	1	1	1	1	1	1	1	0	0	1	1	1
BEx010	1	1	1	1	1	1	1	1	1	1	1	1	1	1	1	0	0	1
BEx011	1	1	1	1	1	1	1	1	1	1	1	1	1	1	1	1	1	1
BEx012	1								1	1	1	1	1	1	1	1	0	1
BEx013	1	1							1	1	1	1	1	1	1	1	1	1
BEx014	0	0							0	0	0	0	0	0	0	0	0	0
BEx015	0	0							1	0	0	0	0	0	0	0	0	0
BEx016	0	0							0	0	0	0	0	0	0	0	1	0
BEx017	0	0	0	0	0	0	0	0	0	0	0	0	0	0	0	0	0	0
BEx018	0	0	0	0	0	0	0	0	0	0	0	0	0	0	0	0	0	0
BEx019	0	0	0	0	0	0	0	0	0	0	0	0	0	0	0	0	0	0
BEx020	0	0	0	0	0	0	0	0	0	0	0	0	0	0	0	0	0	0
BEx021	0	0	0	0	0	0	0	0	0	0	0	0	0	0	0	0	0	0
BEx022	0	0	0	0	0	0	0	0	0	0	0	0	0	0	0	0	0	0
BEx023	0	0	0	0	0	0	0	0	0	0	0	0	0	0	0	0	0	0

Callout:
T1 = Time of Day (24 Hours)
T2 = AM or PM
T3 = Light/Dark
T4 = ATM Cash Loading Schedule (Day of Week)
T5 = ATM Cash Loading Schedule (Time of Day - 24 Hours)

Callout:
Independent examples of the desired behavior to model.

Figure 14-2: The antecedent by behavior examples data array.

is loaded; and T5 is the time of day the ATM is typically loaded. A data array is very versatile, with each column representing an antecedent condition or situation. For example, the first antecedent theme (T1) might be an ATM in a convenience store, T2 might be an ATM in Y location, and so on. We also can organize by time. T10 might be noon to 3:00 P.M., and T11 might be 3:01 P.M. to 6:00 P.M. Basically, we can incorporate any event or situation that is identified by ThemeMate or by manual means by making the event and variations columns in the array. Each row is an actual example. In this case, an actual smash and grab robbery. To illustrate, if the first example (row 1) was a break-in at a convenience store at 4:00 P.M., T1 and T11 would have a 1 under that column for row 1. In short, this array allows us to capture and represent both antecedent conditions for each example. Once the array is completed with 1s and 0s, we are ready for pattern classification.

An analysis of the antecedent conditions can be enhanced by correlating all antecedents against all other antecedents. This shows how specific themes group together for specific types of behavior. In addition, a behavior-consequences analysis can be completed, resulting in a separate array. In Excel, the Analysis ToolPak, which you can add to Excel through the "Add In" feature on the toolbar, includes a variety of statistical methods that may be applied to the data in the spreadsheet. For example, correlations, ANOVA, moving averages, descriptive statistics, and other methods are included with the Excel Analysis Toolpak.

The Pearson Product Moment Correlation, the type of correlation available in Excel, can be very useful for correlating the themes in the data array. Figure 14-3 shows the correlations of all antecedent themes in the ATM example against one another. The inset shows a magnified portion of the left top corner of the array.

	T1	T2	T3	T4	T5	T6	T7	T8
T1	1.000							
T2	0.719	1.000						
T3	0.686	0.960	1.000					
T4	0.820	0.734	0.696	1.000				
T5	0.654	0.921	0.959	0.739	1.000			
T6	0.764	0.960	0.917	0.775	0.375	1.000		
T7	0.654	0.921	0.959	0.659	0.875	0.875	1.000	
T8	0.733	0.921	0.959	0.739	0.915	0.959	0.915	1.000
T9	0.565	0.759	0.797	0.656	0.338	0.797	0.755	0.838
T10	0.654	0.838	0.875	0.739	0.315	0.875	0.830	0.915
T11	0.621	0.882	0.918	0.703	0.358	0.833	0.958	0.871
T12	0.702	0.882	0.918	0.784	0.358	0.918	0.871	0.958
T13	0.702	0.882	0.918	0.703	0.371	0.918	0.958	0.958
T14	0.541	0.797	0.833	0.621	0.371	0.748	0.784	0.734
T15	0.589	0.757	0.791	0.667	0.327	0.791	0.739	0.827
T16	0.507	0.757	0.791	0.583	0.327	0.704	0.739	0.739

Figure 14-3: The correlated data array.

Correlations range from -1.00 to 1.00. A correlation near 1.00 shows that both variables are very closely associated and move in the same direction (as one increases, so does the other). A 0.0 correlation shows the absence of any association between the two variables. High correlations near -1.00 show a very high association between the two variables but in the opposite direction (if one increases the other decreases).

Using conditional formatting in Excel, I issued a command to highlight all correlations in the array above .90 — a high positive correlation showing a strong association between antecedents. The shaded areas show these strong correlations. For example, Theme T2 shows a strong positive correlation between T2 (the T2 column) and themes T3, T5, T6, T7, and T8. Looking back at Figure 14-2 you can see that T2 is A.M. or P.M. and T3 is light or dark, so you would expect a high correlation here. However, conducting this first stage of analysis often reveals surprises that are non-intuitive and important to include in behavioral modeling.

In the DVD walkthrough examples, this stage, as well as others leading to accurate prediction, is explained. However, at this stage in the explanation, all you need to know is that such tools as Excel are invaluable in the behavior modeling process.

NOTE Although AuBA's ThemeMate and AutoAnalyzer, when used together, automate the behavioral modeling process, I always conduct the types of analyses shown here to gain understanding of the complex human behavior analyzed. Often, the analyses show elements of a specific class of behavior that has been unknown, resulting in true discovery that often is not intuitive. ThemeMate analysis resulting in the data array and in the detailed list of themes demonstrates key features to past behavior that are relevant for anticipating future behavior. When conducting an analysis, customers want to know much more than a specific prediction. They want to know how we know what will happen next, the antecedents that are associated with malicious behavior, and the antecedents not associated with malicious behavior. Because the presence of specific antecedents has an influence on the behavior of the person or group we are modeling, we can study the antecedents to determine, or we can affect their occurrence either by suppressing the occurrence of some or by encouraging the occurrence of others. The result is behavior change.

Advanced Tools: SPSS, SAS, and Other Statistical Packages

Based on the skills of the person conducting the analysis of behavior, advanced tools can be very effective for drilling down to a deep understanding of the behavioral phenomenon in question. If you have done the foundation work carefully and have not taken shortcuts, the data will be of high quality, meaning that follow-up analysis will be of high quality.

You have to be extremely careful in using advanced tools. Typically, you enter data and they give a result — it is that simple. It is up to you to know if you are using the tools properly. I cannot stress enough that if you are using a specific statistical technique, read the background information on the technique to ensure you are using data properly and are not violating assumptions for the use of the technique. Like any tool, these techniques are useful in the hands of a skilled user. A gun can be an excellent tool for protection, but you can also shoot yourself in the foot!

I recently observed a presentation where the person presenting had used Bayesian analysis to prove his point. However, it was clear that the data used for the presentation had actually violated all three assumptions for the use of Bayes. Unfortunately, the presenter's case was made and accepted. This was an example of unethical presentation of results. It is the presenter's responsibility to ensure proper use of the data and proper interpretation.

NOTE *Bayesian analysis*, which can be very powerful, has three basic assumptions that must be met: the variables must be mutually exclusive (for example, on or off); collectively exhaustive (for example, colors of the flag are red, white, and blue); and probabilities must add to 1.0 (for example, 0.25 + 0.25 + 0.50 = 1.00).

There are a variety of statistical software packages that can be used to conduct advanced analysis. It is not within the scope of this book to delve deeply into statistics, nor is it really necessary for accurate prediction of human behavior. However, additional analysis is sometimes required based on the specific needs of a task.

NOTE Good statistical packages are not cheap, and the statistics that come in the Microsoft Analysis ToolPak (discussed in the previous section) are sufficient for most needs. If deep analysis is needed, I recommend SPSS, formerly called the *Statistical Package for the Social Sciences* before it was acquired by IBM, and SAS. Both packages have been in use for decades. SPSS has long been a mainstay for behavioral scientists, and SAS has a long history in business applications.

For example, I often use discriminant analysis and logistic regression to assist in analyzing variables in specific applications. Discriminant analysis is particularly useful in conducting a stepwise discriminant analysis to reduce a set of predictors to the most useful and predictive set of variables.

Currently, there are a variety of efforts to predict human behavior from pure statistical methods. These approaches collect examples of behavior and conduct massive correlations to find patterns that they hope will assist in predicting future behavior. As I have mentioned throughout this book, developing accurate applications to predict behavior from simply observing and analyzing behavior is not likely to be fruitful. Behavior occurs in response to environmental antecedents, and these associations must be identified and used to predict future behavior. This is not a function of a statistical method.

As pointed out in the patented automated method of human behavior prediction for AuBA, any number of statistical methods may be used. Although I have tried almost every statistical method as a pattern classification approach, I am partial to artificial neural networks, in general, and the back propagation network (BPN) specifically. The neural network, when used properly, is a very powerful pattern classification approach.

DEFINITION *Bias* is the inability of a person to analyze human behavior on an impartial basis because of interfering preconceived notions, ideas, or external influences.

Human Bias: The Enemy to Accuracy and Analysis

One of the many reasons for developing AuBA was to automate behavioral modeling to predict and influence human behavior with minimal to no bias. Bias is one of the primary reasons why prediction does not logically flow from studying behavior. The typical approach of studying documents and then using intuition to study and interpret behavior produces so much error that accurate prediction is simply not likely to occur reliably over time. Humans are simply subject to bias, and it is extremely difficult to rid oneself of such bias in conducting analysis.

Because methods of predicting human behavior have not been standardized, those who attempt to present future scenarios often infer inner motivations of a target of study as a means to anticipate future behavior. This is exceedingly difficult. A person may not fully understand his or her internal motivation. Many individuals seek out therapists or counselors to help them understand why they are like they are. Determining the motivation of another individual or a group of individuals is fraught with error. If the person or group being studied lives in another part of the world, then cultural nuances may actually make it implausible for us to understand them. If we are analyzing suicide bombings, we may have a difficult time understanding how a person can walk into a market crowded with people and detonate a bomb.

Traditional methods used in science may actually contribute to bias. As part of the typical scientific methodology, we state our hypothesis, place it in the form of a null hypothesis (no difference), and then conduct experiments to disprove the "no difference" hypothesis, leaving our alternative hypothesis as the reason for the phenomenon under question. To disprove the null hypothesis, we submit the data collected across different experimental conditions and see if the results are statistically significant. The statistics used must indicate that the probability of accepting a false hypothesis is less than 5 chances in a 100, or less than 0.05. In many cases, a probability of less than 1 in a 100 is preferable ($p < 0.01$). If these levels are not achieved, then results will not be published by a typical peer-reviewed journal.

There are many problems with this approach, as it contains much room for judgment, manipulation of data, and faulty interpretation of results obtained. The subjective features of what is believed to be an objective scientific method means that we may have accepted many tenets of human behavior that simply may not be true.

This may seem to be a harsh indictment. It is not. It is simply a view that acknowledges the degree to which bias can invade the prevailing scientific approach used today to result in published research, which is not the same thing as published truth.

An Example of Biased but Publishable Bad Research

An example is necessary for clarity. Disclaimer: This is a hypothetical example and has no resemblance to any known researchers or actual research known to me. If it bears resemblance to any available research, it is clearly unintentional.

Say a researcher in the social and behavioral sciences believes that when a person exhibits injury and becomes incapacitated on a busy street in a major city such as Manhattan, that passersby may do just that, simply pass by without offering assistance, but some may stop and try to help. The researcher believes strongly that a primary reason that a person may pass by and not offer assistance is the fear that litigation can occur if he or she does something wrong in the act of trying to be a Good Samaritan.

The researcher is becoming known in the area of altruistic behavior and decides to conduct an experiment to validate his views. The researcher states the following null hypothesis: *The fear of legal action for making a mistake after having offered assistance to someone who has become incapacitated on a public street in a major city is* not *a reason for passing by the incapacitated person.*

An experiment is then devised whereby an accomplice would simply fall on the sidewalk near Broadway in Manhattan and fake being incapacitated. Then those who enter the scene would be interviewed after either passing by or stopping to offer assistance. There would be two groups: (1) those who stop to offer assistance, and (2) those who pass by without offering assistance. In an interview, although a number of questions would be asked, the primary question the researcher would consider would be:

> Did you fear legal action resulting from stopping (for those who stopped)?
>
> or
>
> Did you consider legal action as a reason for not stopping (for those who passed by)?

The researcher would complete the study when 100 people have passed by and 100 people have stopped to offer assistance.

The researcher would then conduct a statistical significance test on the results of the primary question. Consider if the researcher found that there is a statistically significant difference between the two groups of subjects. More individuals answered yes to the question if they passed by than answered yes to the question if they stopped to offer assistance. He or she would then prepare a research article describing the results, with fear of litigation being the primary difference between the groups. He or she finds a statistically significant difference of 0.02. Therefore, he or she would report the findings as $p < 0.05$ (less than 5 chances in 100). The researcher's conclusion would be that people passing by a person in need of assistance do so primarily out of fear of legal action should they do something wrong.

From my time as a reviewer of a refereed journal in psychology, I estimate it would take me about five (single-spaced) pages to offer a review of this study. It is logically appealing, but it is a very bad study. Bias enters in and basically ruins the study. Any reader who is a competent researcher will see the problems. However, I believe that there would be a referred journal that would publish these results if they were written in such a way to obscure the weaknesses.

The overwhelming problem is that the researcher did not diligently attempt to discover the difference in the two groups. Instead he asked the one question that would confirm his beliefs — that is, whether fear of litigation was the reason for stopping or not. In short, bias ruined this hypothetical study, and a careful writer could get it published.

How could the researcher have minimized bias to improve this study? The major weakness: It is very clear that the researcher had already decided why people would simply pass by, and it is even stated in the hypothesis — that is, fear of legal action. The study was actually designed with this bias interfering from beginning to end. Instead, if passersby were stopped and simply asked why they did not stop, as opposed to asking if they feared legal action, many other answers could have surfaced, and the study would not only be more interesting but more accurate as well, For example, having worked in emergency rooms as a PhD student, I have seen many cases when the ambulance would pick up a person and deliver him or her to the hospital. The driver would mention that the person was on the street and no one helped. The reason he or she gave was that most people just simply don't know what to do. Occasionally someone would stop and try to help but would cause more damage than good. The desire to help was there, but the knowledge and skill were missing.

The example I have presented to show bias did at least try to follow convention within the scientific community. It missed the mark, but there was a hypothesis, a study (of sorts), and results that were written and presented to peers. This process does not happen within the government, in the reality of working against adversaries.

NOTE When I left the academic community and went to work for the government in 1985, I joked that I left the "publish or perish" culture for a "publish *and* perish" culture! We don't publish much — classified issues discourage publication.

There is a vast difference between work for academia and operational government work. In the latter, there is not a requirement for hypothesis, statistical significance testing, or publication. The focus isn't publication — the focus is solving real-world problems that can threaten our nation's security and infrastructure. Having been firmly entrenched in both environments, I admit that the government setting is far more challenging, is far more demanding, and may be far more rewarding.

In government work, we are often presented with such a low number of historical cases to study that a statistician would run in the other direction; therefore, special methods designed for small-n (small number of cases) have to be used to do the job. We do not have the luxury to turn down a task to analyze a group with few past examples to study. This is where AuBA is most useful. AuBA was developed as a small-n application, meaning it was constructed to require fewer cases than we would see in academia while still maintaining scientific integrity, testing for statistical significance, and resulting in careful interpretation of results due to automation.

NOTE The three primary reasons for the development of AuBA were:

- **To reduce the time it takes to model human behavior accurately (400 times faster)**
- **To reduce error in the modeling process by eliminating the vast majority of the reasons for bias entering the modeling and analysis process**
- **To present a technology for accurately predicting human behavior**

Identifying Bias

Perhaps one of the major types of bias to guard against is predicting a conclusion prior to analyzing the problem. As an example, consider the growing concern over China's blatant and persistent attempts to obtain technological advancements from the United States by means of cyber theft. The advanced persistent threat is real and is beginning to be viewed as war. Members of the U.S. Congress have stated that we are under attack, and the United States has officially accused China of the activity with the request to stop. As we continue to process packet-level activity and continue development of the CheckMate intrusion protection system, we have to resist the view that all attack behavior is China-based. Knowing that China is proficient in the use of phishing attacks, we may start seeking out phishing attacks, which we will likely find. However, this bias may lead us to focus solely on China, specifically on phishing attacks from China. This single-mindedness could lead us to miss new attack behavior and sources.

Recency can also be a very big problem in analysis. If we look at a specific adversarial group that engages in a full range of behavior, we tend to be influenced by the more recent events. If a terrorist group engages in remote bombings, suicide bombings, and assault but the three most recent attacks have been assaults, we have a tendency to view that group as relying primarily on assault. However, baseline frequency of the three types of behaviors might indicate that assault makes up only 25 percent of its attack behavior. This bias can affect which documents we select to process and analyze, placing undo focus on assault and skewing our results.

We may also be influenced externally. For example, I once worked with a subject matter expertise (SME) panel of experts with seven members. The panel was composed of six peers and a supervisor. It was fascinating to watch the subtle control the supervisor had on the expert opinions of the other six. For the most part, the peers would actually modify opinions to seek the approval of the supervisor. It was such a powerful influence that the supervisor was asked to be "too busy" to participate as a member of the panel. Not surprisingly, the SME panel began to work very well as a team once the supervisor left.

External influence can be a problem when a team is asked to study a specific problem area to provide an assessment. If the tasker lets the team know what result is expected, even if only subtly, the report may tend to move that direction. Although we all prefer seeing ourselves as independent thinkers, we are all influenced one way or another.

Sometimes, we may be influenced by data. This is a very serious problem. Earlier in this chapter I mentioned the presentation I recently attended in which a Bayesian analysis was used to present a specific assessment. The analysis violated all three assumptions that one must have to use this method, yet it was used and led to faulty interpretation. We may be led down the wrong path because of the use of disinformation. Bad data can lead to bad analysis, and lack of skill in using tools can lead to bad results. As they say, "garbage in, garbage out" (GIGO).

PENNY STOCKS

There are those who actually rely on our biases to make a profit, purposely spreading disinformation to lead those analyzing data in the wrong direction. As I mentioned earlier, I like to observe the stock market as a major human behavior challenge. Some individuals try what are called penny stock investments. These stocks literally can cost only pennies per share.

Deception is extremely rampant in this area of the stock market. If you gather data on specific stocks and determine patterns to know when to buy and sell, you have to be aware that false information is placed on the Internet to get you to buy.

If enough people respond to the false information and actually purchase many shares of a poor-performing stock, the people placing the false information on the Internet may see the price of their stock go up and sell their stock so that they can realize a profit. Then, the stock falls back and may even drop further. It is then too late for the buyers to see a profit, and they may hang on to the stock out of desperation as it continues to move down in value. The person or group spreading misinformation, using the biases of those who work within the over-the-counter market to manipulate the system, has made a profit at the average holder's expense.

NOTE There are many forms of bias, and we all are subject to influence. Perhaps the worse bias of all is the perception that we are independent thinkers and cannot be influenced!

Removing Bias via Automation

Automation can be a very powerful shield to protect against bias. Given that we collect the appropriate documents or open source news articles describing past events (so that we are free of selection bias), AuBA takes it from there, and we avoid almost all forms of bias from that point. This is perhaps one of the most important reasons why AuBA can lead to accurate prediction of adversarial malicious behavior. To the extent of my knowledge, AuBA is the only truly automated approach to behavioral modeling for the purpose of predicting or influencing adversarial behavior. Once presented with a set of text documents, the AuBA process completes extraction and analysis in a completely non-biased manner.

At each stage of analysis where automation can be applied, some form of bias is eliminated. The analyst who relies on reading and interpreting all documents on his or her own with no analysis is providing an open door to all forms of bias — and many forms of these biases may not be recognized by him or her. We all have ultimate faith in our own abilities. No one can believe in our abilities like we can! In fact, we are often surprised that all others do not really recognize just how good we are! This is how bias occurs. We readily accept our intuition — we do not argue with our own perceptions and decisions. However, as will be shown in the following section, full automation from beginning to end protects us from ourselves and removes the vast majority of bias from the analytical process.

Automating Behavioral Principles: Applying AuBA

Automated behavior analysis (AuBA) is based on a foundation of applied behavior analysis. The latter is a field in psychology that focuses on how the environment influences behavior and is primarily clinically based, existing to help others change their maladaptive or inappropriate behavior for the better. In the clinical walkthrough I presented in Chapter 9, I provide an actual case in which the methods I developed for applied behavior analysis led to new clinical treatments. However, applied behavior analysis (unlike AuBA) was designed not to be predictive but rather to be an approach to influencing behavior. Certainly, applied behavior analysis has not been used to focus on adversarial behavior on a global scale, or on cyber threat, terrorism, insurgency, and so on, as AuBA has. When I developed AuBA, I based it on the foundation of applied behavior analysis; however, AuBA had to be extended on many fronts.

First, because applied behavior analysis is a more clinical approach and is used to help modify (not predict) behavior, a predictive methodology had to be invented that was accurate and reliable. In addition, applied behavior analysis, for the most part, is used with people who are constrained within an environment. For example, it is used in classrooms, institutions, prisons, the home, the workplace, and so on, where antecedents to behavior are primarily within that constrained environment. In contrast, I developed AuBA to work on a global basis where antecedents to adversary behavior could be present anywhere in the world, including a host of political, social, and cultural nuances. Applied behavior analysis has not been used with adversaries that target the U.S. infrastructure, except for my many years of work extending it to terrorism, insurgency, conventional war, asymmetric warfare, tracking and locating, and cyber threat, including external and internal threat.

Although AuBA is now very different from applied behavior analysis, I want to give credit where credit is due. The antecedent-behavior-consequence sequence is real, and it works. That is why AuBA uses that very basic formulation that was constructed on the backs of many thousands of researchers working to help people modify their maladaptive behavior or to improve education as a foundation. AuBA is different and it is automated, but applied behavior analysis was the mother of AuBA. Perhaps this is an example of the offspring exceeding the capabilities of the parent, particularly when it comes to the patented automation of the prediction of human behavior.

Fortunately, the automation has proven to be objective and to remove the vast majority of subjective bias, external influence, and costs associated with bad data.

Capturing Cultural Nuances

Because AuBA includes ThemeMate as a tool, text in native language can be processed to extract antecedents that are more likely to be culturally sensitive. To date, ThemeMate has been constructed to automatically extract antecedents associated with behavior from English and Arabic text. The capability to do the same in Chinese is almost completed. At the time of the publication of this book, all three will be available. Best estimates are that it takes two weeks to prepare ThemeMate to process a new language. In one study funded by the Defense Advanced Research Projects Agency (DARPA), AuBA was used to build an Arabic-language model and an English model using the identical past examples of behavior. The difference is that one model used Arabic news sources in native language and the other used English news articles covering the same incidents. The cross-validation Leaving-One-Out tests results for both models were identical, although antecedents were different (with some overlap). The differences could be attributed to cultural differences.

Given that ThemeMate can process native language text, it is possible to provide a body of information to ThemeMate that includes the text that the adversary uses to keep up with world events. This is a distinct advantage. For example, news releases and articles released from a foreign news source in the native language is not a barrier. In fact, it is an advantage because cultural perspectives captured by native language reporters or writers can provide more local or regional antecedents not captured by Western reporters in English. One of the advantages is that this tool can process both English and Arabic simultaneously. It is much like a multilingual analyst reading Arabic and English accounts of past incidents to extract predictors — except that ThemeMate on the average finds 5 to 10 times as many potential antecedents. The bottom line is that AuBA can capture and use cultural characteristics.

Moving from Theory to Practice: A Necessary Transition

The incorporation of behavioral science into the effort to protect our national infrastructure has not been a top priority over the years. However, moving from a current, primarily reactive stance of security to a new approach that would be proactive requires knowledge of human motivations of adversaries and patterns of behavior that can lead to anticipating their actions in the future. It is true that when you look at a cyber security, the term *behavior* is currently used; however, it is used as a shorthand term for *network behavior*, not the human behavior behind the scenes that is driving network attacks. There has been a blatant ignoring of behavioral science, perhaps not in all respects but certainly in enough areas that it is safe to say that behavioral science is not being considered a part of our future protection.

Computer science and engineering are naïve to the understanding of human behavior, but we read much about predictive analytics surfacing out of the fields of computer science and mathematics. To me this is like saying we are going to understand the proliferation of biological viruses throughout the world without using biologists and specialists in viruses — that computer science can simply understand biological phenomena through statistical correlation. This is absurd, as is the concept that physical sciences can understand and predict human behavior simply from correlating examples of human behavior.

As has already been explained, the prediction of human behavior depends heavily on antecedents and consequences of behavior in the environments and has little to do with just studying or correlating behaviors. A paradigm shift from reactive signature detection approaches to anticipating attacks before they occur based on identifying precursors to attacks is within our reach. AuBA has approached this complex area and has shown that:

- Human behavior is predictable.
- Determining human intent is possible from digital information.
- Cyber threat and adversary behavior can be identified without signatures.
- New malicious behavior not identified by signatures can be identified.
- A successful fusion of the behavioral and computer sciences to anticipate behavior that has not yet occurred is possible.

If we review the textbooks, we are not likely to see any recipes for automatically predicting human behavior. This is why AuBA is a patented approach. It is new, and it is unique. Behavior theory indicates that behavior occurs in response to the environment. We have now demonstrated this to be the case. Regardless of the complex inner motivation that drives an individual or a group, behavior occurs in response to specific precursor antecedents and is encouraged to occur again or to diminish in the future based on whether successful or unsuccessful consequences follow.

AuBA has demonstrated real-time prediction of human behavior and the identification of first-time behaviors across numerous adversary and malicious domains. The automation has removed the opportunity for many different forms of bias to be present to decrease effectiveness. The automated tools approach has allowed AuBA behavioral modeling to occur in a fraction of the time that the manual method takes. Both work, and as much work has gone into validation as it has into development so that others may replicate results where necessary.

AuBA extends the behavioral psychology found in current textbooks. This book is an attempt to push the envelope and move behavioral psychology clearly into the prediction of adversary behavior on a global scale. By recognizing that human behavior can be predicted, we may be able to start incorporating new behavioral technology that can assist in moving from a reactive stance to a new, proactive security stance.

Advantages of AuBA #14: Incorporating Key Technological Advances

During the development of AuBA over the past 30 years, it was abundantly clear that the prediction of human behavior on a reliable and accurate basis is difficult, at best. Over the course of this time, I continually tried other approaches in comparison to the AuBA methodology I was developing. Some approaches came close, only to drop when applying the consistency criterion. Some worked once but failed on a second and third attempt. AuBA, on the other hand, has consistently resulted in effective behavioral models that predict malicious behavior accurately across time. At the same time, I was able to add technology as it improved.

The first attempts to automate key components met with some success, but the technology available at the time required improvement. For example, early spreadsheets were difficult to use and had many space limitations. Pattern-classification software was not very advanced, had memory restrictions, and was DOS based. The disk operating system (DOS) was a forerunner of the now universal Windows operating system. If you are young enough not to be familiar with DOS, you did not miss much. Even early Windows was buggy. Today, AuBA incorporates fast PCs and excellent operating systems. Because of the advances in hardware technology, with almost unlimited storage and very fast random access memory (RAM), or temporary memory, AuBA tools work extremely fast.

The ThemeMate application that processes text to identify antecedents, present them in report form and constructs and populates (completes) an elaborate data array for advanced pattern classification; the embedded artificial neural network engine in AutoAnalyzer; and many additional features would not have been possible just 25 to 30 years ago. The technological developments of the past few decades combined with the discovery of how to accurately predict human behavior across time to form a true marriage between the behavioral and the computer sciences.

AuBA incorporates best practices reliability and validation methodologies from both sciences. One of the problems in development was that the behavioral and computer sciences use different terminology. Therefore, AutoAnalyzer incorporates the accuracy metrics of pattern classification areas most notably found in the computer sciences and the statistical significance test found in the behavioral sciences. I believe that both are important when used together. The accuracy metrics can tell us precisely how accurate the predictions are, and the Fisher's exact statistical significance test tells us by how much our results exceed what would be expected by chance. In short, the advanced analytical AuBA that is presented in this book would not be possible without the combined contributions of both sciences.

We continue to make improvements in AuBA to ensure that we incorporate technical advances as they occur. We find that such tools as Microsoft Excel and IBM's SPSS are useful tools to conduct analyses to support the AuBA technology. As stated in the patent, we find that any number of pattern classification approaches may be used as a plug-in for the analysis engines. Again, it is not the pattern classification that results in the accurate predictive capability but simply a necessary component. Because we have discovered that very specific methodology is required to reduce antecedent candidates to the smaller set of truly predictive antecedents and because during the training of pattern classification training must be stopped at a certain point in the process to obtain accurate prediction and generalization, we have incorporated these features into the AuBA predictive tools.

The end result is a strong behavioral foundation represented within advanced computerization, resulting in assessment engines that can make a predictive assessment within 50 microseconds of receiving input. This means that 20,000 predictions per second may be made by one assessment engine. If more predictions are needed, we simply add more assessment engines. Although it took decades to arrive at this point, we have moved from a very significant clinical approach still in heavy use today that could take weeks and many observations to understand and influence behavior to true behavior assessments occurring almost instantaneously. We have learned to construct accurate behavior prediction engines from physical sensor outputs, text accounts of past behavior, and behavior embedded in network packets. The next decade will be very exciting and will be the decade of application.

In Summary

In the introduction to this chapter, I provided six reasons as to why manual analysis of human behavior has become difficult. We now have the software and tools to respond to each of these points.

- **The amount of global information to process in most cases is voluminous and in some cases comes in at a fire-hose rate**. Automation (such as that provided in AuBA) and tools, if used properly, can allow for high-speed modeling that, once constructed, can keep pace with rapid flows of information. (For example, CheckMate can make behavioral assessments at the rate of 20,000 per second.)

- **Because anyone can post anything on the Internet, there is a significant amount of false or misleading information embedded with accurate information.** The AuBA ThemeMate process identifies themes by finding similarities across multiple documents. For this reason, inaccuracies that occur randomly across documents are not likely to be included in themes identified by repeated instances. Furthermore, there is a very small probability that an accurate prediction engine will result from inaccurate information given the Leaving-One-Out validation method used in AutoAnalyzer. This latter process is a check on the veracity of the information. The Fisher's exact statistical test provides a calculation that gives the probability that results obtained by the validation process could have been obtained by chance. If the calculation is less than 0.05 or 0.1, we can assume a pattern classifier that is accurate and meaningful.

- **In contrast, in some cases with covert attackers, the type of information needed for complete analysis is scarce or simply missing.** AuBASME methodology can augment scarce and missing data with subject matter expertise (SME) to result in predictive engines where data is especially thin. (See Chapter 13 for more on this topic.)

- **Humans have biases and often form an opinion too early, which moves their analysis toward seeking information to support their biases.** The use of AuBA replaces many opportunities for human bias with automated functions. The reduction of such opportunities results in increased accuracy.

- **The idea of history repeating itself is an antiquated and uninformed concept — future behavior is not a replication of past behavior.** AuBA has demonstrated that the underlying concept of antecedents-behavior-consequences accompanied by other AuBA enhancements demonstrates that future behavior is a product of past antecedent-behavior associations and not just past behaviors.

- **Human behavior does, however, occur in response to antecedents and consequences of past behavior. (These patterns must be understood if future behavior is to be anticipated accurately.)** This has been thoroughly demonstrated with AuBA. We have developed validated predictive engines that can make accurate decisions when presented with unique combinations of antecedents not in the set of cases used to train the pattern classifier engines.

- **Humans often believe their personal insight is correct; however, I have not seen a single empirical study to show that human insight can accurately predict behavior of an individual or group on a consistent basis over time.** AuBA and its results, in contrast, have been independently validated to be predictive across multiple domains.

AuBA has moved into rapid model development and rapid predictive assessments. The speed with which AuBA assessment engines can make decisions is essential in today's rapidly moving and interconnected world.

CHAPTER 15

Predictive Behavioral Modeling: Automated Tools of the Trade

Throughout this book, I have mentioned automated behavior analysis (AuBA) and its associated tools: ThemeMate and AutoAnalyzer. Using these two tools properly with an adequate text corpus describing past incidents enables the construction of behavioral models that can predict future behavior in a valid and reliable manner. Although I developed a manual process first, AuBA tools can result in the construction of a predictive model 400 times faster than the manual process. Even the manual process had to have some components constructed in software, such as the pattern classification component. However, as it exists today, AuBA has many features that require automation to be totally effective. For example, the ThemeMate tool that processes text examples of past events and identifies antecedents and creates the data array of advanced pattern classification does not exist in the manual method. AutoAnalyzer, which automatically constructs and validates the predictive engine, is exclusive to AuBA and is not in the manual method.

Because of the AuBA components, the ability to identify relevant antecedents in past text examples has increased significantly. In the past, using the manual method, we would tend to identify fewer than 100 antecedent candidates. We limit ThemeMate at 500. In addition to the many new features that AuBA has over our manual process and the automation is a reduction of bias. As the previous chapter discussed, the automation of the modeling features eliminates most forms of bias, which results in increased accuracy.

AuBA automation has been validated across a wide variety of threat conditions and environments. For example, some of the threat areas have included terrorism, malicious intent identified from movement patterns, predicting characteristics of human behavior from avatar measurement in virtual world games, external attacks coming into a computer network, and insider threat within an organization. The AuBA tools have demonstrated real-time prediction with unprecedented accuracy, as well as the ability to identify key patterns existing among precursor antecedents and subsequent behavior. Because of the maturity of applied behavior analysis as a science of behavior change, the development and validation of AuBA tools and methods to date, and the decades of experience of the AuBA developers, the application of AuBA allows for rapid prototyping.

This chapter focuses on the tools and how to use them. It is not a walkthrough of method — that comes later in the book. Instead, this chapter is an introduction to the tools and their many features.

Automated Behavior Analysis (AuBA)

To summarize AuBA, the automated process can be used to construct predictive models from text-based reports of past behaviors. The text can be structured as in a database or spreadsheet or unstructured in the form of separate electronic free text. For example, by processing multiple reports of conflict behaviors and events and situations preceding such behaviors and non-conflict behaviors and precursor events and situations, the process automatically extracts predictors of each class of behaviors. Once this content is submitted to the pattern classification and validation process, a predictive model is developed that returns predicted conflict versus no conflict when presented with the presence or absence of the identified antecedents present at any one time. Once the predictive engine is trained, the validated pattern classifiers are capable of generalization. In other words, if the antecedents present at a given time do not exactly match a representation of antecedents used for training the classifier, the predictive engine is likely to still predict the correct outcome.

A trained and validated AuBA predictive engine may lead to the accurate anticipation of the who, what, when, where, and how of specific behaviors. In short, once environmental antecedents working as a constellation of factors leading to specific outcomes are identified through the proper behavior analysis and pattern classification processes, then the presence of similar antecedent groupings in the future as processed through the trained pattern classifier can lead to the accurate anticipation of similar impending behavior. Part of the AuBA methodology includes knowledge about how a specific behavioral area may be divided into separate predictive engines. It is not unusual for an AuBA predictive application to include different predictive engines that can combine to form a single decision, or prediction.

To conduct an AuBA modeling project, you can use a manual process or an automated process that uses ThemeMate and AutoAnalyzer predictive modeling tools. The automated modeling process is approximately 400 times faster than the manual process. The following sections introduce the tools in initial detail.

ThemeMate

ThemeMate is a statistically based application used to extract predictors from text describing details of past behaviors of interest. The application has been validated to identify conceptual precursor themes (antecedents) and summarize text in both English and Arabic, although it is possible to prepare ThemeMate to process text in any language. It takes our staff 1–2 weeks to prepare ThemeMate for a new language. When text is processed, significant conceptual themes are produced with each listed theme hyperlinked to all sentences across all of the documents that are relevant to that theme. These themes become the antecedents.

Multiple documents may be combined to provide overall themes across documents. Documents can be processed across time to provide shifts and trends, and single documents may be compared to determine similarities and differences. As a final product, the ThemeMate application produces a data array of all extracted antecedents by behavior example. This data array is then presented to AutoAnalyzer for automated pattern classification.

ThemeMate replaces a manual process that was developed to be a first step in constructing predictive human behavior models. This first step usually consists of an analyst collecting and reading through many text accounts of an individual's or group's past behaviors, or examples of past events of a specific type (for example, serial murders, cyber theft, and so forth), and identifying what some call *pre-incident indicators*. However, the concept of an antecedent is far more sophisticated than the concept of a pre-incident indicator.

Searching for pre-incident indicators tends to be a search looking for causes of the behavior to occur, often on a one-to-one basis. There is not a concept of behavioral foundations or a basis for how antecedent conditions are associated with behavior, which is then maintained, increased, or decreased by consequences — as with AuBA. These differences are reflected in AuBA software. The advanced pattern classification used with AuBA is required to handle the very complex interactions between antecedents, behaviors, and consequences. The use of pre-incident indicators involves finding events and then expecting the behavior to occur sometime after simply because it occurs. AuBA captures antecedents that suppress behavior and can also set the stage for behavior to occur. In addition, I know of no scientific studies to show that the use of pre-incident indicators results in accurate prediction of human behavior. Although there are many other differences, the focus here is on AuBA.

If we submit the same articles used for pre-incident indicator searches to ThemeMate, the application will automatically find the significant variables that are common across all of the documents. For example, if we wanted to build a predictive model of cyber threat phishing attacks, we would collect many news articles of past phishing features or examples of the actual e-mails that included the phishing attacks. When compared to humans trained to identify antecedent candidates in text (not yet validated to be predictive antecedents), Theme-Mate can identify similar themes that humans find, except it finds many more and completes the entire process in just a few minutes. The combination of ThemeMate and AutoAnalyzer allows the entire antecedent-behavior-consequence behavior foundation to work in such a way that accurate prediction can occur.

The software application has numerous features; the following are representative of the most significant.

- ThemeMate's underlying technology is language independent. To date, it has been validated to be effective in identifying key predictive themes in both English and Arabic. It takes approximately two weeks to validate the application for a new language and make adjustments to processing. Currently, work is being completed on processing Chinese text.

- Using ThemeMate across languages allows a translator to concentrate on the extracted key themes that comprise the most significant antecedent candidates contained within the text instead of the whole document, thereby reducing significantly the amount of time required to translate documents to obtain meaning.

- ThemeMate works as a front end to AutoAnalyzer. Given the correct structuring of text, you can move from ThemeMate analysis directly to AutoAnalyzer, which produces a self-validating, predictive model. The combination of these two applications working in concert can provide unique automated behavioral modeling that results in the construction of predictive engines.

- ThemeMate provides a rapid hyperlinking of all sentences that relate to a constructed theme, thereby providing justification for the construction of any given theme.

- ThemeMate can analyze single or multiple documents. By presenting multiple documents, ThemeMate presents overall themes across all presented documents as a single corpus.

- Hyperlinked analyses of several documents conducted individually allows for a rapid comparison of different documents' similarities and differences.

- ThemeMate can be directed through a *focused search* feature to develop themes in a very specific area to the exclusion of others; therefore, a single general collection of documents may be used to identify antecedents to specific behaviors.

- ThemeMate produces keywords associated with a specific theme that may be used as a search string for Internet searches (for example, with Google) that brings back the same and highly similar documents to enhance the foundation corpus being used for analysis.

- ThemeMate contains options to allow you to customize the theme extraction process to meet specific needs. The user can indicate which words to ignore, eliminating the need to construct specific sentence and word parsers. The user can choose to ignore numerals or include them as part of the analysis. The user can analyze one sentence to extract key search terms or analyze multiple sets of large documents simultaneously.

- ThemeMate also offers a number of specific tools within the application. For example, ThemeMate can operate for the sole purpose of presenting search terms, compressing documents, locating key sentences, and comparing different sets of documents for similarities and differences.

The next few sections take a look at some of these features in more detail.

Human Interaction with AuBA Automated Features

I designed ThemeMate after studying in detail the process by which humans process documents manually and identify antecedents, behavior, and consequences. The application duplicates this cognitive process, which makes it different from data mining and machine learning methods, which are based on computer science methodology. ThemeMate was designed from a human factors and task analysis process, not from a computer science perspective. Instead, the design came from how humans process documents, and then computer science features were selected that matched the human cognitive process. The automated features duplicate the cognitive steps we go through when we read documents and identify significant points to highlight with a yellow highlighter or summarize with significant note-taking.

From an automation perspective, ThemeMate can identify many more themes across a collection of documents than humans, and can construct a data array useful for advanced analytics in approximately 1/2 second. When the manual process was first developed as a forerunner to automation, it would take 2–3 days to complete the array and populate it because of human error. It is time-consuming because it requires two staff completing the data array independently and then comparing notes to identify the discrepancies. After this step, they would have to argue the discrepancies and agree on an entry for each cell in the array. If two humans do not try to achieve agreement, then a very large number of errors is introduced. Given that the criterion of agreement is 80 percent, if two people can achieve 80 percent agreement across all the cells, one typically is allowed to complete the process because it is not realistic to expect two observers to always be available. It is important to note that because ThemeMate does verification of each statement that goes with each theme, it is 100 percent accurate in completing the array.

Unlike humans, a computer is very fast, has perfect memory, and does not make mistakes. Therefore, the analytical process can be completed in a fraction of the time it would take to assemble a manual array. The speed is especially useful so that a collection of documents can be processed, themes extracted, and a data array constructed and populated — all within a few minutes.

As I previously discussed in Chapter 14, automation also means bias is not possible during all the steps that do not require human intervention. Because the human elements have been removed from the front end and back end of the modeling process, human error is almost eliminated. However, it must be stated that the ThemeMate and automated modeling process should not occur without human oversight. We do not have the technology today to duplicate the entire human synthesis capability. By overseeing what documents are presented to ThemeMate, the staff member has total control.

Document selection is the first step where the person has control of what ThemeMate will process. The second human step is when ThemeMate has produced the themes and has constructed and populated the data array. It is important to review the product at this point. ThemeMate could have produced a small number of themes that I call *duhs*. In other words, the identified themes are reviewed and out of 250 there may be a few that elicit a *duh* from the user. For example, say that of all the useful antecedent themes, one theme is that bombs are associated with explosives. The appropriate response would be *duh*! The theme can then be dropped from the array by simply deleting that column.

Of course, the vast majority of themes is more significant, such as one noting as a possible antecedent that U.S. Forces move into a local region inhabited by *X* terrorist group members. Need I say more? This act, especially in combination with other acts contrary to the motivation of specific terrorist groups, may very well be a predictive feature associated with a terrorist or insurgent response. There is no value judgment here. It is simply fact. Such a U.S. action, especially when combined with other similar actions, may set the stage for a terrorist or insurgent response.

The point here is that human oversight of the automated response is essential.

NOTE   ThemeMate is a tool. ThemeMate is to the analyst as a microscope is to the pathologist or a telescope is to the astronomer. There is no substitute for human synthesis, and there is no substitute for automated theme extraction that can identify themes not possible to identify manually. However, both must work together to foster a precise methodology that will result in accurate prediction of future behavior of an adversary.

Language Independence

ThemeMate's capability to construct a truly predictive behavioral model using the native language of an adversary is very important. If antecedents are those events and situations that precede the behavior of interest, then we have to know that the adversary would be aware that the antecedents occurred if those antecedents are to have an effect on the adversary's behavior. This is logical and is a very strong testament to using open source information available in the same region in which the adversary is at the time. Whether we are targeting a domestic serial murderer or an adversary hiding in another country, we want to use open source information that the adversary is likely to know. Given that ThemeMate can process documents in foreign languages, identify themes, and construct the data array that leads to predictive engines in that language means:

- We can be relatively certain the adversary would be aware of the event or activity.

- ThemeMate will extract antecedents with cultural nuances that would likely not be present in Western accounts.

In the past, when comparisons have been made between models constructed with English accounts of incidents and models constructed from Arabic text accounts of the exact same incidents, antecedents overlap, but many are different — although overall predictive results are similar.

Still, if we had our choice of a model constructed with Western accounts versus regional accounts in the native language, we would obviously select the latter. Why? Because AuBA models are not just useful for prediction. They are also useful for influence. We must remember that the more clinical field of applied behavior analysis is an influence approach. The purpose is to assist others in altering their behavior in school, prison, the workplace, their home, or myriad other settings. It is not a predictive approach.

AuBA was developed to extend this science to include accurate prediction through the many features that have been added. This is why AuBA has a basic foundation resemblance to applied behavior analysis — both emphasize antecedents, behavior, and consequences. So, applied behavior analysis is useful for influence, whereas AuBA is useful for both influence and prediction. Even if developing models in Western press language and native regional language may result in equally effective predictive models, if our goal is a way to influence behavior, we definitely want regional antecedents identified that if altered could result in a change of behavior. Regional, native language text is simply more likely to provide antecedents that are culturally based than Western text accounts of the same incidents.

As indicated, it takes approximately 1–2 weeks of work to prepare ThemeMate to process and extract antecedents and to construct a data array in a new language.

Using ThemeMate in this way saves the need for a translator to read all text to try to find relevant themes. Instead, ThemeMate can find the relevant themes, and then the translator can translate just those themes. This is a tremendous savings of a translator's time.

This feature means one of two things (or both):

1. A translator can work with many more times the amount of text because he or she is translating only key text that has been pulled from a very large corpus by ThemeMate.

2. A translator can complete the translation required for model building in one example in a fraction of the time it takes to translate an entire corpus before the analysis starts.

My best estimate of savings for a single model constructed in a foreign language because of the automation is that it will take only 1/100 of the time required for the translator to process the entire corpus processed by ThemeMate. This means that a translator involved in the modeling process can handle 100 times more foreign language text in the same amount of time (and can likely work on many models simultaneously) or can translate language required for a single model in 1/100 of the time, thereby accelerating model construction in a foreign language by 100. This equates to the use of a translator for 5 hours instead of 500 hours.

The statement that ThemeMate is language independent is very literal. Essentially this means that because of the manner in which ThemeMate has been constructed, with a small amount of work ThemeMate can process foreign language documents such as news articles of past events in an identical manner as it does in English. Of course, any type of text document may be used. In other words, there is not a decrement in performance because the corpus is in a foreign language. Because ThemeMate is statistical, the language of the text used doesn't really matter. The emulation of the human cognitive process that ThemeMate performs is the same regardless of the language. This is an important and distinguishing feature.

Other ThemeMate Features, Including Cross-Language

There are a variety of other features that are particularly significant when it comes to the software's abilities, whether in foreign languages or in English. ThemeMate has the capability, called *compression*, whereby the application processes a document and identifies the most important feature(s) in the text. This was conceptualized and designed into the software to quickly return the essence of the text to the user and to result in a significant savings in time. Any savings in time at this stage means an analyst can apply more time to synthesis and essential report writing.

> **NOTE** I submitted the Old Testament, which is very wordy, to ThemeMate. In less than 30 minutes, ThemeMate returned the most important and frequently occurring theme. It is a *begat* concept with many variations. It is important to note that this result is based on actual concepts returned, which we label as *themes* — it is not a word frequency analysis. For those who are familiar with the text, you'll recognize a large part of the Old Testament is a compendium of who begat whom. If we ask for more than the most important feature, themes of vengeance by God surface. As we ask for more themes in order of significance, we can see a smart summary.
>
> Some of those who are familiar with ThemeMate and who have a historical bent have suggested processing such texts as Adolph Hitler's *Mein Kampf* or Karl Marx's *The Communist Manifesto* to derive themes and the most important elements in the text. Of course, the same process can occur with current documents in real time.

You may be asking, "If an application does not understand language, how can it possibly identify the most important features of a documents or across documents?" By the nature of how ThemeMate processes documents, it identifies key themes present in those documents. These themes are concepts. A concept is a general idea derived or inferred from specific instances or occurrences. When ThemeMate processes text, it seeks out and constructs concepts based on the specific occurrence within the text that points to each unique concept (theme). The manner in which the process identifies the most important features is proprietary; however, when we compare it to humans in a head-to-head comparison, ThemeMate tends to identify the same most important features as does the human who studies the same texts. However, it is a distinct advantage that ThemeMate can do this form of extraction and identification in any language.

This is an especially important feature with foreign text. By processing a document or set of documents in foreign text, the results of the compression feature is the x most important sentences or phrases (the x number is set by the user with a default at the three most important). Then a translator needs only to translate this small amount of text instead of the entire corpus.

If you are working under strong time constraints, this is an important feature in that you can identify key features in a document or set of documents very quickly. I have used this feature plus the data array component to prepare reports concerning behavior very quickly. In one situation, I was called in on a weekend to process data and to determine if a real threat was present. By using ThemeMate I prepared a report in one day that turned out to be accurate. Without ThemeMate, it would have taken more than the entire weekend. In such situations, the tool is invaluable and adds to confidence in results and reporting.

Text Summarization: Automated CliffsNotes?

Text summarization is another important feature of ThemeMate. By using the compression feature for each section only, you can derive the most important sentences or phrase(s) for that section. By placing the derived sentences and phrases in order, then you can compress the entire document into a fraction of the space, retaining most of the meaning — hence the name *compression*.

Compression was completed for the 511-page 9/11 commission report, and the document was compressed to 10 pages while maintaining most of the main features as a summary, resulting in an automated 50-to-1 compression. In other words each 50 pages was compressed to 1 page while maintaining the significance of the text. Again, think of this applied to situations involving text in foreign languages and consider the time saved when translation need occur on only 1/50 of the text.

This is not the same as extracting key themes used for predictive modeling. However, you might often have the need to summarize text, and we have found that the process of what we call compression is no less effective than a manual approach used to summarize a large document.

Identifying Predictive Indicators (Antecedents)

Chapter 20 will present a walkthrough of the manual method of AuBA. Although I call it manual, it has automated features such as pattern classification to result in the predictive engine. However, the process of identifying antecedents from text is manual. By going through the manual process, it gives a better appreciation for the process of identifying antecedent candidates that can lead to the reduction to actual predictive antecedents.

As I have discussed earlier in the book, in the development of AuBA, the manual method was developed first to work out the procedure so that ideas for automation could be developed. It was somewhat of a surprise that I found that when the advantages of computer sciences could be added to the manual process, there were improved ways to get to the final result. Therefore, the automated process is a more refined and more sophisticated way to derive final antecedents. However, the manual method is very effective.

When the manual method was developed, we were using databases to store antecedent and consequence candidates that occurred in association with the behavior of interest. The database record was separated into four primary sections:

- Basic information about the event (time, day of week, and so on)

- Type of behavior (phishing, spear phishing, denial of service, and so on)

- Antecedent candidates (any event or situation that occurred before the behavior)

■ Consequences (successful penetration of a network, non-successful penetration of a network, and so on)

Each candidate was allotted 80 characters, or one line per candidate. The process, again covered in Chapter 20, resulted in processing lines of text to derive key antecedent candidates occurring across common types of events.

ThemeMate uses a different process whereby textual associations are discovered by words within a sentence and not by whole sentences. In the manual method, seeking conceptual similarity across sentences actually worked well, but the granularity is not nearly as great as when ThemeMate works at the word level. Basically, once automation was made complete and ThemeMate was designed to work at the word level, many additional features were made possible.

Constructing Data Arrays for Predictive Analysis

It is essential to remove any events from the analysis that led to unsuccessful consequences. Humans do not tend to repeat behaviors that lead to failure. However, you must be careful in determining what a failure is. For example, one terrorist group may be reinforced for getting apprehended because it leads to media coverage, which may be the goal. You might think that blowing yourself up would be a failure of sorts, but for a suicide bomber it is a resounding success. If in a coordinated assault one of five terrorists is killed, but many targets are killed in the process, the act may have been a success. Success or lack of success must be considered from the adversary's perspective.

To serve as a bridge between extracted antecedent candidates and examples of past behaviors, we need a data array. We have found that such an array works best when we have extracted antecedent candidates as columns in a spreadsheet and examples of behavior as rows. Again this type of array may be completed by hand, but as I have mentioned, that can be very time-consuming. One of the primary features of ThemeMate is that when it completes its extraction of candidates, it automatically constructs the data array, which takes approximately a half second. In a busy work environment or when there are multiple analyses to complete, this feature is extremely valuable as an extreme time-saver. In addition, it is error free, which is not the case when the array is constructed by hand. There are just too many opportunities for error in the manual process, even if we put in safeguards. This is an ideal example of where automation can increase accuracy by decreasing errors and bias.

To complete the process for entry into AutoAnalyzer, we simply add the outcomes as final columns to the array. For example, if the purpose of the process is to predict which one of two tactics will likely occur next, we simply create a "1" in the intersecting cell of the tactic and the row of the example that include that tactic. For example, in Figure 15-1 an abbreviated data array is shown that has 23 antecedent candidate columns and past incidents as rows. I have added the outcomes we desire to predict, which are Threat 1 tactic (Thrt1 column) or Threat 2 tactic (Thrt2 column).

Incident	T1	T2	T3	T4	T5	T6	T7	T8	T9	T10	T11	T12	T13	T14	T15	T16	T17	T18	T19	T20	T21	T22	Thrt1	Thrt2
12111	1	1	1	1	1	1	1	1	1	1	0	1	1	1	0	1	1	1	1	0	0	0	1	0
12211	1	1	1	0	0	1	1	0	0	0	0	0	1	0	0	0	0	0	0	1	0	0	1	0
12411	0	1	1	1	1	1	1	0	1	1	0	1	1	0	0	1	1	1	1	0	0	0	0	0
12711	1	1	0	1	0	1	0	1	0	0	1	0	0	0	0	0	0	0	0	0	0	0	1	0
13011	1	1	1	1	1	1	0	0	1	1	0	1	0	1	1	1	0	0	0	0	0	0	0	1
13011b	0	0	0	0	0	0	0	1	1	1	0	0	0	0	0	0	0	0	1	0	0	0	1	0
13111	1	1	1	1	1	1	1	1	1	1	0	1	1	1	0	1	0	1	1	0	0	0	1	0
20211	0	0	0	0	0	0	0	0	0	0	0	0	0	0	0	0	0	0	0	0	0	0	0	0
20311	0	1	1	1	1	1	1	0	1	1	1	1	1	1	1	1	1	1	1	0	0	0	0	1
22811	1	1	1	1	1	1	1	0	1	1	0	1	1	1	0	0	0	1	1	1	1	1	1	0
30911	0	0	0	0	0	0	0	0	0	0	0	0	0	0	0	0	1	0	0	1	1	1	0	0
31411	1	0	0	0	1	0	0	0	0	0	0	0	0	0	0	0	0	0	0	1	1	1	0	0
32211	1	1	1	1	1	1	1	0	1	1	0	1	1	1	0	1	0	1	1	0	0	0	1	0
41411	0	0	0	0	0	0	0	0	0	0	0	0	0	0	0	0	0	0	1	0	0	0	0	0
41811	0	0	0	0	0	0	0	0	0	0	0	0	0	0	0	0	0	0	0	1	0	0	0	0
42411	0	0	1	0	0	0	0	0	1	0	1	0	0	0	1	0	0	0	1	1	0	0	0	1
43111	1	1	0	1	1	1	1	1	1	1	0	1	1	1	0	1	1	1	1	0	0	0	1	0
51411	0	0	0	0	0	0	0	1	0	0	0	0	0	0	0	0	0	0	0	0	0	0	1	0
51511	0	1	0	1	1	1	1	1	1	1	0	1	1	1	0	0	1	1	1	1	1	1	1	0
52911	1	1	1	1	1	1	1	1	1	1	0	1	1	0	0	1	1	1	1	0	0	0	1	0
60511	0	0	0	0	0	0	0	0	0	0	0	0	0	0	0	0	1	0	1	0	0	0	0	0
61611	0	0	0	0	0	0	0	0	0	0	0	0	0	0	0	0	0	0	0	0	0	0	0	0
63011	1	1	1	1	1	1	1	1	1	1	0	1	1	1	0	0	0	1	1	0	0	0	1	0
70211	0	0	1	0	0	0	0	0	0	0	1	0	0	0	1	0	1	0	1	1	0	1	0	1
71911	0	0	1	0	0	0	0	0	0	0	0	0	0	0	1	0	0	0	0	0	0	0	0	1
80111	0	0	0	0	0	0	0	0	0	0	1	0	0	0	0	0	0	0	0	0	0	0	0	1
81211	1	1	1	1	1	1	1	0	1	1	0	1	1	1	0	1	1	0	0	0	0	0	0	0
81311	0	0	1	0	0	0	0	0	0	0	1	0	0	0	0	0	0	0	0	0	0	0	0	1
81411	0	0	0	1	0	0	0	1	0	0	0	0	0	0	0	0	0	1	0	1	0	0	1	0
90111	0	1	1	0	1	0	1	0	0	0	0	0	1	0	1	0	1	0	0	0	0	0	0	0
91511	0	0	0	0	0	0	0	0	1	0	0	0	0	1	0	0	0	0	0	1	1	0	0	0
101011	0	0	1	0	0	0	0	0	0	0	1	0	0	0	1	0	0	0	0	0	0	0	0	1
101411	0	0	0	0	0	0	0	0	0	0	1	0	0	0	1	0	0	0	0	0	0	0	0	1
101411b	1	1	1	1	1	1	1	0	1	1	0	1	1	1	0	1	1	0	0	0	0	0	0	0
101411c	1	0	0	1	0	0	0	0	0	0	0	0	0	0	0	0	1	0	0	1	1	1	1	0
110111	0	0	1	0	0	0	0	0	0	0	1	0	0	0	1	0	0	1	0	0	0	0	0	1
110311	1	0	1	0	0	0	0	0	0	0	0	0	0	0	1	0	1	0	0	1	1	1	0	1
110311b	0	0	0	0	0	0	0	0	0	0	0	0	0	0	0	0	1	0	0	1	1	1	0	0

Figure 15-1: A data array depicting antecedent candidates by behavior example with threat tactic outcomes added at the far right.

In the example, the highlighted two columns on the far right are the outcome columns. ThemeMate identifies the antecedent candidates, creates the data array, and populates it automatically with the 1s and 0s discussed. However, we must add the outcome columns *because ThemeMate cannot divine what we would like to predict — that is up to us*. These two outcomes will become the variables that will be predicted. For example, if we are trying to predict threat or no threat, we would add two columns — one for threat and one for no threat. Then we simply place a 1 in the appropriate cell for a specific behavior example that is in a specific row, and a 0 in the remaining cell on that row. Therefore, for each example of behavior (row) there will be two outcome columns — one with a 1 and one with a 0. The behavior examples have the date of occurrence as the identification rows. If more than one incident occurs on one day, the second is labeled as the date plus "b" and the third for the same day is labeled as "c." Using dates is important in that we can sort by date and detect trends over time.

If we have more than two outcomes, we simply add more outcome columns (for example, if theft, we could have theft in the A.M., theft in the P.M., and no theft). The key is that the one relevant column receives a 1 in the cell that coincides with any row in which the outcome in the example for that row receives a 1, and all others receive a 0 for that row. When we have completed this process, we have all that is required for pattern classification.

However, it should be mentioned that although this is possible manually, and we have done it, there are difficulties with the manual approach. The following lists several issues:

- It is very time-consuming unless there are a very small number of examples; the array just gets too big.

- Error in placing all the 1s and 0s into the array is not only possible but highly probable.

- The manual process is based on identifying candidates whereby precursor events are found, listed as they are identified, and tallied with multiple occurrences across the documents. However, we know that the automation contained within AuBA (that is, ThemeMate) can find many more antecedent candidates, meaning that the array will be richer and completed automatically with no errors.

- The manual approach to determining if an event or situation is an antecedent candidate relies on judgment and, unfortunately, bias. This makes it very difficult for two arrays completed by two observers to be the same.

The concept of using the data array to translate real-world antecedent events and situations (columns) that are associated with past behaviors (rows) is sound. It is only the completion of the array that is difficult. ThemeMate automation in AuBA solves all the listed problems associated with the manual approach.

In Figure 15-1 you can see the addition of the outcome columns. If we submit this entire array to Excel for correlations (again, this will be demonstrated in the DVD walkthrough), we now have the outcome columns attached. The correlation matrix compares each antecedent theme to every other antecedent theme. This is important for two reasons:

- For antecedent themes correlating at a high number, such as 0.90 or higher, we are likely to merge them into one column.

- The bottom rows now show the two outcome columns we had added and how each theme correlates with each of the antecedent themes (Figure 15-2).

The correlation of outcomes with each antecedent theme provides some insight into which antecedents favor which outcome. This is useful for synthesis of results and eventual report writing. However, because correlations of antecedent themes with outcomes are linear in our array, with the array correlations showing how a single antecedent theme is correlated with each outcome and is not affected by its neighboring antecedents, it is not a true picture of how pattern classification actually works. The Excel matrix just gives us an idea of what is associated with what. In reality, the pattern classification process is nonlinear, and during the training of the pattern classifier, all the antecedent themes for an example (all the 1s in a row) are taken into consideration at one time. This is a method that is many times more powerful than a strict linear approach. Human behavior and its association with antecedent events and situations are basically nonlinear. The AuBA neural network, and in some cases other computational algorithms, is designed to work in a nonlinear manner, which is the reason I chose these approaches for AuBA.

The advantage of the designation of outcomes attached to the data array is very important, as Figure 15-2 depicts. Figure 15-2 shows the results on the Pearson Product Moment Correlation of the data array in Figure 15-1. The difference in correlating the data array produced by ThemeMate and shown in Figure 15-2 and the one in Figure 15-1 is the addition of the outcome classes (Threat Tactic 1 and Threat Tactic 2). The last two rows in the figure are the outcome classes, which represent the correlation of each antecedent candidate with each outcome. By adding these outcome classes, we can see how each of the extracted antecedent candidates correlates with the two outcomes.

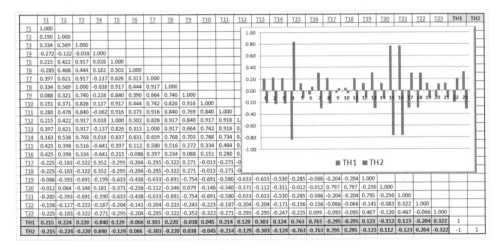

	T1	T2	T3	T4	T5	T6	T7	T8	T9	T10	T11	T12	T13	T14	T15	T16	T17	T18	T19	T20	T21	T22	T23	TH1	TH2
T1	1.000																								
T2	0.190	1.000																							
T3	0.334	0.569	1.000																						
T4	-0.272	-0.122	-0.038	1.000																					
T5	0.215	0.422	0.917	0.038	1.000																				
T6	-0.285	0.468	0.444	0.182	0.502	1.000																			
T7	0.397	0.621	0.917	-0.137	0.826	0.313	1.000																		
T8	0.334	0.569	1.000	-0.038	0.917	0.444	0.917	1.000																	
T9	0.088	0.321	0.740	0.238	0.840	0.390	0.664	0.740	1.000																
T10	0.151	0.371	0.826	0.137	0.917	0.444	0.742	0.826	0.916	1.000															
T11	0.280	0.478	0.840	-0.062	0.916	0.373	0.916	0.840	0.769	0.840	1.000														
T12	0.215	0.422	0.917	0.038	1.000	0.502	0.826	0.917	0.840	0.917	0.916	1.000													
T13	0.397	0.621	0.917	-0.137	0.826	0.313	1.000	0.917	0.664	0.742	0.916	0.826	1.000												
T14	0.163	0.538	0.768	0.016	0.837	0.631	0.659	0.768	0.703	0.768	0.734														
T15	0.425	0.398	0.516	-0.641	0.397	0.112	0.580	0.516	0.272	0.334	0.464														
T16	0.425	0.398	0.334	-0.641	0.215	-0.086	0.397	0.334	0.088	0.151	0.280														
T17	-0.225	-0.183	-0.322	0.352	-0.295	-0.204	-0.295	-0.322	0.271	-0.013	-0.271														
T18	-0.225	-0.183	-0.322	0.352	-0.295	-0.204	-0.295	-0.322	0.271	-0.013	-0.271														
T19	-0.086	-0.393	-0.691	-0.199	-0.633	-0.438	-0.633	-0.691	-0.754	-0.691	-0.580	-0.633	-0.633	-0.530	-0.285	-0.086	-0.204	-0.204	1.000						
T20	-0.012	0.064	-0.146	0.181	-0.371	-0.256	-0.112	-0.146	0.079	-0.146	-0.340	-0.371	-0.112	-0.311	-0.012	-0.012	0.797	0.797	-0.256	1.000					
T21	-0.285	-0.393	-0.691	-0.390	-0.633	-0.438	-0.633	-0.691	-0.754	-0.691	-0.580	-0.633	-0.633	-0.530	-0.285	-0.086	-0.204	-0.204	0.795	-0.256	1.000				
T22	-0.156	-0.127	-0.223	-0.187	-0.204	-0.141	-0.204	-0.223	-0.243	-0.223	-0.187	-0.204	-0.204	-0.171	-0.156	-0.066	-0.066	-0.066	-0.141	-0.083	0.322	1.000			
T23	-0.225	-0.183	-0.322	-0.271	-0.295	-0.204	-0.295	-0.322	-0.352	-0.322	-0.271	-0.295	-0.295	-0.247	-0.225	0.099	-0.095	-0.095	0.467	-0.120	0.467	-0.066	1.000		
TH1	0.215	0.224	0.220	-0.840	0.129	-0.066	0.303	0.220	-0.038	0.045	0.214	0.129	0.303	0.124	0.763	0.763	-0.295	-0.295	0.123	-0.112	0.123	-0.204	0.322	1	
TH2	-0.215	-0.224	-0.220	0.840	-0.129	0.066	-0.303	-0.220	0.038	-0.045	-0.214	-0.129	-0.303	-0.124	-0.763	-0.763	0.295	0.295	-0.123	0.112	-0.123	0.204	-0.322	-1	1

Figure 15-2: The data array with outcomes added. The inset shows the correlations of antecedent candidates with the outcomes (Threat Tactic 1 and Threat Tactic 2).

NOTE As a reminder, correlations represent from -1.00 through 0.0 to +1.0. A high positive correlation approaching 1.00 indicates that as one variable increases the second increases, 0.0 shows no relationship at all, and -1.0 shows that as one variable increases the other decreases.

For example, if the behaviors of interest targeted for identification include security breaches, identified patterns underlying the associations among identified antecedents and the selected threat/intent outcomes (the latter two columns of the data array) may lead to the accurate anticipation of the when, where, how, and what of future occurrences of adversary behavior. Once environmental antecedents are identified through proper pattern classification, then the presence of similar antecedent groupings in the future as processed through the trained pattern classifier can lead to the accurate anticipation of similar impending malicious behavior.

To make the correlation matrix clear, and as a simple example, if we have 10 themes and 2 outcomes, then we might label the 10 antecedent themes as T1, T2, . . . T10. This leaves two columns for our threat/no threat outcomes we want to predict. Again, we must add these since no technology can tell what we want to predict!

A correlation matrix takes each of these 12 variables (10 antecedent themes and 2 outcome classes) and compares each variable against all other variables. In Figure 15-2, notice that the rows are now labeled the same as the columns. This is because each will be compared against all other variables. In this way, the last two columns become the last two rows. The advantage is that you can look at threat and no threat and by going across the matrix determine to what degree each antecedent theme correlates with the two last rows, or outcomes.

Again, to be clear, the ThemeMate data array has antecedents and outcomes as columns by each behavior example as rows. The correlation matrix has all variables correlated against all other variables. For this reason, notice the diagonal line in Figure 15-2 — it goes from the upper left to the lower right. This diagonal line has all 1.00 correlations. This is because it represents a variable correlated with itself. This should obviously be a 100 percent correlation, or 1.00. If we don't have this, then something is wrong with the correlation matrix.

In Figure 15-2, as I indicated previously, we are interested in the last two rows, which represent the correlation of each antecedent candidate with each outcome (Threat Tactic 1 and Threat Tactic 2, or TH1 and TH2). The inset in the upper-right corner shows the result of using the graph capability in Excel to produce a bar chart of the data in the final two rows. As can be seen, the inset shows the major correlations among the antecedent candidates and the outcomes. As you can see, antecedent 4 (T4) correlates highly with the second threat tactic (TH2) and antecedent 15 (T15) and antecedent 17 (T17) are correlated with Threat Tactic 1 (TH1). The correlations assist us in determining which antecedents are associated with different outcomes.

The advantage of the correlation matrix that includes the outcome classes is that we get a picture of what antecedent candidates are more closely associated with the two outcomes to be predicted. It should be stated that AuBA does not make decisions based on correlation — the pattern classification analytics are far more complicated. However, the correlational step does provide a picture of significant relationships.

The difference between Figures 15-1 and 15-2 is that Figure 15-1 was generated by ThemeMate automatically, and we have just added the two outcome classes of threat and no threat. I might add that this step is very easy if we label our text examples beginning with a *T* for threat and an *NT* for no threat. Then we simply label each row in the outcome class to match whether that row is threat or no threat. Figure 15-2 was generated by Excel simply by going to the data analysis section of Excel, clicking on Correlation, and then highlighting the ThemeMate data array. Then by designating where you want the correlation matrix to go (same work sheet by location or another work sheet), Excel generates the correlation matrix you see in Figure 15-2, but without the outcome classes that we must add because only we know what we want to predict.

Human behavior is more accurately presented (and predicted) in a multilinear manner with a constellation of factors having a combined effect, as opposed to seeing how one candidate at a time is associated with the outcomes. However, in many situations linear and multilinear approaches are highly similar. Therefore, the correlational depiction can provide insight into the effect of key antecedent candidates on outcomes. I have prepared significant reports based simply on the correlational associations. However, I must add that if the goal is prediction of human behavior, simple correlations will not get you there. To obtain at least 80 percent accuracy across true negatives and true positives consistently across time (for example, weekly), then the multidimensional pattern classifier is required. To get technical for a moment, the hyperdimensional qualities of an artificial neural network are ideal to capture the complexities required to predict behavior accurately and consistently. *Hyperdimensional* means that all the input variables (antecedents) are taken into consideration at one time in many more dimensions than the three that we understand. I refer the reader to the many texts available on hyperdimensional space and neural networks simply by searching on the terms. I will say it is absolutely necessary for prediction as we are discussing in this book. The mathematical details of hyperdimensional feature space as used in AuBA go well beyond the scope of this book. However, for those interested, many books, journal articles, and reports are available for what we call a *deep dive*.

WARNING You must be careful to not infer causation because there is a high correlation. For example, there is a well-known very high negative correlation between the number of mules in a state and the number of PhDs! In other words, the more mules, the less PhDs, and the more PhDs, the fewer mules. Obviously, one does not cause the other, and there are intervening variables that likely account for this finding. For example, a state that is primarily rural would not have as many opportunities for PhDs but would have more need for mules. A high correlation also does not mean that there is no causation. We just can't determine causation from a correlation alone.

AutoAnalyzer

The AuBA analytical process to produce predictive models occurs in sequential steps. Following the presentation of initial text describing samples of behaviors of interest, which includes descriptions of events and situations occurring prior to and after the behaviors of interest, the automated process progresses through the following steps with limited to no human assistance:

1. Extract key precursor antecedent thematic concepts associated with key outcome behaviors (for example, threat) from text examples of past events/behaviors.

2. Construct and populate a data array that includes all potential predictors.

3. Prepare validation and pattern classification training and test data sets.

4. Reduce antecedents to the most predictive set.

5. Construct pattern classifiers.

6. Conduct a best practices, Leaving-One-Out validation of each pattern classifier.

7. Optimize all pattern classifiers by identifying the most effective pattern classification configuration and reduce antecedent candidates to the most predictive set of antecedents.

8. Present the highest accuracy classifier as defined by highest true-positive and true-negative accuracy rates and the lowest Fisher's exact test of statistical significance.

9. Use predictive engine(s) for real-world and real-time prediction of malicious behavior.

ThemeMate completes the first two steps, and AutoAnalyzer completes the remainder of the steps described.

AutoAnalyzer is an application that offers the first automated approach to applied behavior analysis modeling, including multiple extensions and additions of AuBA. By presenting the data array constructed and populated by ThemeMate to AutoAnalyzer, the application automatically:

1. Constructs a gradient descent pattern classifier

2. Reduces extracted predictors to the optimal set

3. Optimizes the pattern classifiers for maximum predictive performance

4. Validates the pattern classifier by testing against blind examples using Leaving-One-Out cross-validation methodology

5. Produces overall validation accuracy

6. Repeats the pattern classification process by constructing and validating additional classifiers with different configurations

7. Presents the highest accuracy model for real-time predictive use

8. Presents a report of accuracy and statistical significance achieved by the best model

Ultimately, by entering the presence or absence of the extracted antecedents for a given time to the trained classifier, the result is an immediate prediction or classification.

It is also important to note that the constructed model is an *emulation* of the intended target's behavior under different antecedent conditions. This is different from a simulation that attempts to describe how a target might operate by observation of a simulated target. The emulation is viewed as a substitute for determining how a target will operate under different conditions when the target is not present for us to determine and observe how it would operate. For this reason, if we provided the most recent antecedent conditions present to the model, we derive a prediction of what the target will do next. However, because the model is a representation of the target individual or group, we can enter different variations of antecedents and see what would happen under these different conditions. We can do "what ifs" for possible influence considerations. In other words, we can ask ourselves, "If we can make the following environment have the following conditions, how would the target respond?" and the trained classifier can give us a prediction for that given set of conditions (antecedents) we are testing.

Remember what I said earlier in the chapter — whereas applied behavior analysis is focused on changing behavior, AuBA is about both changing behavior and predicting behavior. In my opinion, AuBA has a distinct advantage in terms of application to security because it focuses on both influence and prediction. We can predict, and we can then determine how best to alter the environment to result in a change of the adversary's behavior, as opposed to simply looking at how we can influence behavior — even on a global basis.

AUTOANALYZER AND NEURAL NETWORKS

There are hundreds of types of neural networks and variants; however, the back propagation network (BPN) is a workhorse of artificial neural networks and is one of the neural networks AutoAnalyzer relies on to work. It is less esoteric than other exotic neural networks. Dr. Charles Butler, a neural network expert who is now deceased, in his study of neural network applications for two decades, stated to me that the results of his study show that the BPN is responsible for 85 percent of all successful neural network applications. A BPN is an example of supervised learning. This means that the BPN is given an example of inputs and the right outputs. Each time it is presented with a case, it has to predict the output. The real answer is then compared and error is determined, and this is fed back to the network. As the BPN iterates through the data set many times, error drops until the BPN converges to a specific point.

When trained, it then can process a set of inputs extremely fast, as this chapter has pointed out.

Over the course of working with BPNs, as well as other pattern classification approaches, we have developed algorithms that stop a BPN from training precisely at the time where it is likely to be the most predictive. This and other heuristics are embedded in AutoAnalyzer so that when it runs, it optimizes the final predictive engine to achieve maximal predictive performance.

Using the Advantages of Speed, Accuracy, and Lack of Bias

When ThemeMate processes a text corpus that contains reports of past malicious behavior or security threats or when an AutoAnalyzer-constructed pattern classifier produces a prediction based on the antecedents you fed it, you have excellent examples of the powerful combination of computer speed, accuracy, and lack of human cognitive bias AuBA provides — and how we can leverage those features to our benefit.

Speed

From a speed perspective, ThemeMate processes 100 documents in 1–2 minutes. During that time, conceptual themes are identified and placed in a number of different output files, including a file that contains all themes with all of the sentences that contain a theme placed under each individual theme. A person conducting analysis can quickly see the themes extracted and then see all of the sentences across all of the documents that belong to that theme. Of course, the all-important data array is produced at the same time.

Once a pattern classifier is constructed and validated, it can be extracted and placed into an application with an appropriate interface for inputting data and for providing a report. The AutoAnalyzer-constructed pattern classifier can produce an output within 50 microseconds of receiving input. This rate of speed can allow 20,000 decisions per second, or 72 million decisions per hour with validated accuracy and high confidence levels. This significant decrease in development time allows for more rapid adjustments and refinements of predictive models so that actual predictive applications may be readied for use for a given conflict.

Accuracy

Because theme extraction and data array creation depends on computer science, and a theme can be checked for its presence in every sentence across all documents, ThemeMate is 100 percent accurate in determining if a theme is present for any of the examples provided. A computer, even a PC, is amazingly fast at comparing themes to each sentence in a document to determine the presence or absence of each theme within each sentence of all documents combined. The result is a completed and accurate data array with all themes as columns and all behavior examples as rows with 1s and 0s populating all cells to determine the presence or absence of each theme for each behavior example.

Bias

As I discuss more thoroughly in Chapter 14, there are many opportunities for human bias to enter into any analytical process. The fact that ThemeMate can process documents and extract themes that are relevant for each behavior example presented prevents the typical process of humans trying to do this. When humans do this step, preconceived notions, fatigue, typos, and mistakes all occur. As a result, a manually constructed data array may be 80 percent accurate — our calculation for optimally manually constructed data arrays. ThemeMate data arrays are 100 percent accurate with no bias, no fatigue, and no typos. ThemeMate checks every sentence of the entire corpus for each constructed theme and then populates the entire data array with the presence (1) or absence (0) of each theme for each example in each row.

WHAT IF DIFFERENT WORDS ARE USED IN THE TEXT THAT MEAN THE SAME THING?

This is a common question. Because ThemeMate processes in a unique manner and does not use language understanding, it is possible that antecedent themes could be formed with synonyms. For example, if one theme focused on a "battle" within Afghanistan and another theme focused on a "fight" within Afghanistan, with both pointing to U.S. forces and Afghani terrorists, then it would appear that we should have one theme, not two. There are two answers to this important question: (1) Often we find that what appears to be a synonym actually has a different meaning in different contexts, so separate themes are justified, and (2) using a correlation matrix, such as the one depicted in Figure 15-2, we correlate all themes against one another. If the meaning is that same, these two themes will correlate very highly — from 0.90 to 1.00. We then merge any two or more antecedents that correlate at this high level, because the meaning is the same. As an estimate, each time we construct a model, we will typically find two sets of two themes to merge and about the same number to leave separate. We see both ways of handling this issue frequently. This means that 98 percent of the themes remain as were automatically constructed.

When we realize that automated construction of the array and automated completion of all cells with presence or absence 1s and 0s is error free, we decrease error rates from 20 percent to 0 percent. This is significant and one of the reasons why we see the accuracy we do. As an example, if we have a data array with 250 themes across 100 example incidents, an "association matrix" in which all themes extracted by each behavior example provided would result in 250 x 100, or 25,000 cells that would have to be completed manually. This would take many days, and the 80 percent human error we estimate would mean that 5,000 cells of the 25,000 available would be in error if completed manually. Contrast this to 1/2 second to complete with ThemeMate at 100 percent accuracy. There is no human who can beat this! Because the AuBA tools can process data rapidly and without error or bias, our confidence can increase significantly when using the automated tools as compared to manual methods.

SCIENTIFICALLY BUILDING PREDICTIVE ADVERSARY BEHAVIORAL MODELS

Constructing AuBA models, first of all, is a scientific process. If modeling is not a scientific process, it is not likely to work well. Behavioral modeling requires discipline, lack of bias, and a solid methodology. More important, it means not continuing to tweak a model by looking at the results and modifying the data until the model performs well with that data set. This is a scientific egregious error! This is called *overfitting* and introduces serious bias. Although the current model may work on the data set used because of the tweaking to make it fit, it will not likely work in the real world on new data. The latter point is very important. Without a solid validation methodology to follow, our tendency is to keep trying variations until the model looks accurate. This is a scientific egregious error! When building a model that is truly predictive, there can be no knowledge of the test set. The test set needs to be saved until it is time for a final test. Then, because the model has no knowledge of the final test, it is a fair assessment of the true accuracy of the model before trying it in the real world.

As I have mentioned, before trying the trained model on a final test set, it should be evaluated with a cross-validation methodology such as Leaving-One-Out (described in Chapter 13). This ensures that as we manipulate a model, it is always being tested on a case that is unknown to the training. However, to protect against what is called overtraining, we still need the independent final validation test set aside until we are finished. Then we test against this set.

Conducting Behavioral Modeling: Integrating ThemeMate and AutoAnalyzer

By now you should have a sense of how the combination of ThemeMate and AutoAnalyzer provides the capability to conduct rapid predictive modeling with reduced error and minimal bias. Table 15-1 presents features and benefits of using true AuBA modeling by using these two unique tools together.

Table 15-1: AuBA Tools — Features and Benefits

FEATURES	BENEFITS
The proven track record of AuBA tools (ThemeMate and AutoAnalyzer) across numerous malicious behavior and adversarial domains.	Because of existing software and the unique AuBA modeling expertise as outlined in this book, AuBA predictive models may be extended to new domains with full confidence.
Proven track record of automated extraction of salient features required for predicting human behavior in the future.	The validated automation minimizes bias that serves to threaten predictive accuracy that requires objective treatment of data.
ThemeMate and AutoAnalyzer have been used to construct predictive models across languages with equal effectiveness (for example, English and Arabic). It takes two weeks to prepare AuBA for a new language.	Processing news articles in the native language ensures the extraction of culturally sensitive antecedents of which the adversary is likely to be aware.
AuBA may be used for both the prediction and the influence of malicious behavior.	The basic applied behavior analysis foundation is for modifying behavior. AuBA has extended this to prediction. The same predictive engine can be used for either or both.
AuBA has a very strong scientific foundation across both the behavioral and the computer sciences and has been effective across many adversarial domains.	Because of the strong scientific and behavioral base, AuBA may be used to develop predictive models relating to cyber crime, asymmetric warfare, conventional warfare, criminal activity, and other forms of malicious behavior and intent for which current security solutions have no proven predictive capability.
AuBA automation removes the need for exceptionally qualified behavioral psychologists and computer scientists to be directly on hand and consulted.	Almost any individual or team may use AuBA automation to develop highly effective and exacting models.

Although when integrated ThemeMate and AutoAnalyzer duplicate and extend the manual method of constructing predictive models, both tools are very useful in their own right. The data array produced and populated by ThemeMate can be used for a variety of different statistical approaches. Given that the tools can process a corpus of hundreds of documents in minutes and can produce an array with potential predictor variables within minutes, you can save days of analyst work in any number of contexts. AutoAnalyzer can take a data array of any type of data if formulated properly and automatically generate a predictive engine.

I have used ThemeMate often to process a broad area announcement (BAA) or a request for proposal (RFP) to determine the most important areas to focus on in a proposal. BAAs and RFPs are written documents that the federal government releases to the public to outline the type of work it is requesting for funding. Contracting organizations, whether small or Fortune 500 companies, build much of their revenue from winning awards from the proposals they submit in response to the BAAs and RFPs. My teams and I have been awarded funds based on a ThemeMate analysis of the announcements. In processing one of these types of documents, ThemeMate returns the most important themes in the document. This includes awards to improve AuBA. In this way, the technology has paid its own way.

There are many other non-malicious avenues for AuBA. Basically, if human behavior is the focus, then AuBA is relevant. We recently started a relationship with a company that provides treatment for disorders. As a demonstration, we processed progress records with ThemeMate to extract antecedents associated with later progress in treatment and lack of progress in treatment. We then constructed the predictive engine and tested blind cases. The application achieved more than 85 percent accuracy in identifying those who would be successful in treatment and those who would not. Because much of treatment success depends on the compliance of the person being treated and not just the treatment regimen, such an application could identify those predicted to be unsuccessful in treatment so that early intervention could occur to ensure success. This approach is likely to be able to better use limited resources and place intervention where it is most needed.

It is interesting that my beginnings were in the clinical area. I moved to malicious behavior on a global level, and now we are moving back to a clinical arena with much improved technology while continuing on our path of predicting malicious behavior.

Advantages of AuBA #15: What Is the AuBA Predictive Engine?

Once checked, the ThemeMate data array referred to in this chapter is processed by AutoAnalyzer. Although the processing in AutoAnalyzer develops best practices pattern classifiers with different configurations, trains each one using validation methodology, reduces the antecedent candidates to the most predictive set, and presents the highest performing classifier for use, it is important to note that the process is managed by automated heuristics that have taken decades to develop. In the past when my teams and I developed the pattern classifiers manually, we had to discover the optimal settings, how best to train, when to stop the training to ensure prediction and not overtraining, and how best to validate the process, it was a time-consuming undertaking. When we automated AuBA, we constructed this oversight knowledge into instructions that manage the pattern classification construction so that an expert is not needed to construct accurate and validated models. Furthermore, the entire process is orders of magnitude faster than the manual process.

Part of the discovery of how best to predict future behavior was the need for a multidimensional classifier that operates in hyperdimensional feature space. This is a fancy way of saying that the AuBA process treats the presence and absence of all antecedents as a complex combination, not just any one antecedent or any simple linear sum. This is required because, not surprisingly, human behavior and prediction is exceedingly complex. Dynamic systems in science, such as weather, have hyperdimensional features that can even lead to chaotic behavior of the system when trying to predict. In short, we had to have the right type of predictive engine that could best maximize the predictive power embedded in the data array created by ThemeMate. To properly predict human behavior, the entire contexts within which past behaviors occurred would have to be handled within the classifier.

This need for multidimensionality called for artificial neural networks as a possible approach. I had first explored many different statistical approaches, and all worked to some extent, but none produced high enough accuracy consistently. It was clear that the back propagation network (BPN) would fit the requirements for a suitable classifier methodology. There are hundreds of types of neural networks and variants; however, the BPN is a workhorse of artificial neural networks. It is less esoteric than other exotic neural networks. According to Dr. Charles Butler, a neural network expert who is now deceased, in his study of neural network applications for two decades, the BPN is responsible for 85 percent of all successful neural network applications.

A BPN is an example of supervised learning. The BPN is given an example of inputs and the right outputs. Each time it is presented with a case, it has to predict the output. The real answer is then compared and error is determined, and this is fed back to the network, where internal hidden layer weights are adjusted. As the BPN iterates through the data set many times, error drops until the BPN converges to a specific point. When trained, it then can process a set of inputs extremely fast — 50 microseconds, or 1/20,000 of a second — on a typical PC.

Occasionally, we use a different, more traditional engine that has been trained and validated in a similar manner. For example, logistical regression and discriminant analysis have served well in specialized situations. The key here is that although we use advanced pattern classification, the predictive power of AuBA is embedded in both the front-end ThemeMate process and the back-end pattern classification. Either one alone does not produce the pattern recognition accuracy and consistency required for ongoing confidence in prediction — the whole is certainly greater than the sum of its parts.

In Summary

You can perform AuBA in two ways: One has more manual features with some automation, and the other uses ThemeMate and AutoAnalyzer to add almost total automation. Both are demonstrated with examples on the accompanying DVD. AuBA can be used for both prediction and influence. ThemeMate can process text regardless of language and identify key antecedent candidate themes that can be validated and reduced with AutoAnalyzer to a set of true antecedent predictors. ThemeMate can also summarize text to find the most salient points. The data array produced by ThemeMate can be created and populated in less than one second. If the data array is forwarded to AutoAnalyzer, it can develop a predictive engine that is validated using best practices pattern classification cross-validation methodology. The end of the ThemeMate–AutoAnalyzer process is a predictive/influence engine. The next chapter will provide more detail to the modeling process and cover some of the applications developed from the AuBA tools.

CHAPTER 16

Developing AuBA Applications

The previous chapter focused on AuBA tools such as ThemeMate and AutoAnalyzer. Whether we use an automated assist for the manual method or use the tools to fully automate the process, predictive engines will be the result. I call them *predictive engines* because, much like a car, they are the engines that provide the power to make the vehicle go. In a predictive application there are a number of features that support the predictive engine. For example, we need a graphical user interface (GUI) that allows us to interact with the predictive engine, a method for entering input data, and a reporting feature that provides output and interpretation. Of course, there are also standard features such as Save, Save As, Print, Delete, and so on.

There is a distinction between AuBA tools and AuBA applications. The tools are used to construct and validate a predictive engine — the heart of all AuBA applications. The application is a finished set of features that is user-friendly and allows us to use all the features. As an example, the AuBA tools described throughout this book are used to develop the predictive engines for a variety of applications. CheckMate is an application that protects networks from external hacking attacks. It contains a number of predictive engines, each serving a different predictive purpose.

Modeling from text accounts for any methodology consists of a typical manual process of reviewing all relevant documents to extract clues, associations, and the preparation of data for some form of statistical analysis.

It is probably fair to say that in some organizations it is possible to obtain as many different types of analyses and reports as there are analysts, if all were assigned the same topic. For the most part, there is no single, standardized analytical process.

One reason for the lack of standardization is that experts do not agree on a single best approach. My intent is to present a standard, automated methodology that results in the accurate prediction and influence of malicious behavior. This chapter provides more details about how to use AuBA tools and applications that have stemmed from the use of these tools to construct predictive and influence applications. The examples provided in this chapter should give you ideas about how to construct predictive models, the types of features available, and the utility of each application.

Modeling from Text Accounts of Past Behavior

Using ThemeMate to process a corpus (collection) of documents identifies themes that can serve as antecedents. Of course, other uses of the tool have been described in past chapters, but the focus here is on extraction of antecedent predictors.

As an example, we developed a cyber threat model from open source text (news reports). The reports consisted of actual cyber attacks. Using news articles and written reports of past attacks, as well as reports on vulnerabilities, we collected a corpus of documents. This collection was submitted to ThemeMate to process. By using settings in ThemeMate, which the walkthrough on the DVD that accompanies this book will demonstrate, we can provide guidance to ThemeMate in terms of how it operates. We can instruct it to parse content and place it in phrases and sentences or to process content line by line. Although the approach taken does not result in dramatic differences, there are differences in the construction of antecedent themes. On occasions, subtle differences in the construction of themes are useful when we are comparing one method to another.

Because it is difficult to conceptualize what this process looks like, Figure 16-1 shows the first theme that was constructed by processing the corpus for the open source cyber model. When ThemeMate runs, it identifies themes and labels each theme with a two-word pair. Although the process of constructing themes is much more complex, we have found that labeling each theme with a simple word pair containing part of the correlating feature helps us to quickly grasp the theme's content. For example, ThemeMate identified a common theme across all documents dealing with *remote attackers*. This particular run was made with sentence parsing off just to get a quick idea of content. There were, in fact, over 100 themes identified. So, the first run we keep simple just to see the first themes.

T1 Theme # 1 (occurring 16222 cumulative times)

remote-attackers

and 7 on Windows Server 2008 allows remote attackers to execute arbitrary
remote attackers to execute arbitrary SQL commands via the txtName
allow remote attackers to upload files to arbitrary directories via
Communication Manager 3.1.x, allow remote attackers to obtain (1)
Pro 0.0.7 allows remote attackers to execute arbitrary PHP code by
remote attackers to execute arbitrary SQL commands via the id_document
versions, allow remote attackers to execute arbitrary code via long
Links 1.3 and earlier allows remote attackers to execute arbitrary SQL
versions, allows remote attackers to execute arbitrary code via a DivX
6.3 before SP2 allow remote attackers to execute arbitrary code via a
Ghostscript 8.64, and probably earlier versions, allows remote attackers
allows remote attackers to include and execute arbitrary files via a ..
remote attackers to execute arbitrary SQL commands via the
media files, which allows remote attackers to execute arbitrary code via a
SP3; allows remote attackers to execute arbitrary code via a crafted Word
an unspecified string, which allows remote attackers to execute arbitrary
the Excel spreadsheet file format, which allows remote attackers to
allows remote attackers to execute arbitrary code via a crafted Word 97
document, which allows remote attackers to execute arbitrary code via
allows remote attackers to execute arbitrary code via a web page that
and SP1, and 7 on Windows Server 2008 allows remote attackers to execute
Gateway (IAG) before 3.7 SP2, allow remote attackers to execute arbitrary
allows remote attackers to cause a denial of service (application crash)

Figure 16-1: A display of the first theme identified by ThemeMate for the open source cyber application (over 100 such themes were identified).

ThemeMate also creates a file called *theme components* when it runs. If we click on the theme components for T1 (Theme 1 — Remote Attackers), the unique words are automatically submitted to a search engine of choice, and highly similar documents and often the original document are returned from that search. Figure 16-2 shows the results of this automated search. As you can see, the content returned provides additional information that we can then use to build our corpus further.

The key to using ThemeMate is to know the content of the historical documents you are going to provide, so that you can provide the detailed set for analysis. If you provide general news articles on terrorism, then antecedents and behavior will be extracted about general terrorism. If you provide only documents describing past al-Qaeda attacks, then an al-Qaeda model will be constructed.

ThemeMate identified 100 themes like the one depicted in Figure 16-1. Given that each theme's components through automated search results in the identification of many more similar documents (Figure 16-2), you can see that the tool is very interactive. If you are accustomed to having to work with many documents daily, then ThemeMate provides many features to summarize, expand, and identify themes and to present an association matrix that you can export to Excel and to AutoAnalyzer for predictive modeling.

Figure 16-2: An automated search using the theme components feature of ThemeMate and using the unique words extracted during the formation of the remote attackers theme (T1).

Modeling Adversaries and Adversarial Groups

On occasion, it is possible to model a malicious group even if the group may not be identified. Identification of a group is not entirely necessary to predict future malicious behavior. For example, for the open source cyber application mentioned above, past articles describing cyber attacks were collected. Although the perpetrator was not identified, it was clear that perpetrators were state supported. However, the articles of past events were clear about the what, where, when, and how of the attacks. That means a corpus collected on the past attacks, when processed by ThemeMate, would yield antecedents that could be associated with past attacks at the data array stage.

As mentioned, the data array includes the extracted antecedent candidate themes as columns and examples of attacks as rows. Each row is a specific instance of malicious behavior. It is preferable to obtain multiple articles of the same incident. Although ThemeMate can be used to process a single document that will result in summarization, themes embedded in the document, and key statements in the text, the association matrix that becomes the data array for AutoAnalyzer is not formed from a single document. We must have multiple documents because ThemeMate builds the array, or matrix, from themes gathered across documents.

> **NOTE** I have on a number of occasions used a single book as a corpus. If you divide the book into chapters as separate text files, then you can submit the separate files and obtain the array even though the book was initially one document.

Ideally, the adversary is known, we have many articles describing past incidents, and we can develop a clear model. Knowing the adversary does help us to consider motivation. Although the modeling process is not affected, motivation and detailed knowledge of the adversary assists us in developing the predictive reports that provide results.

Extracting Significant Data from Past News Articles

There are several features that we might use when running ThemeMate to help extract antecedent candidates. First, because ThemeMate can extract on a statistical basis and can work across languages, it is possible that the first time we process a corpus we may extract some themes that are not useful and are just artifacts of the body of news articles. For example, a theme could be extracted because each page says *copyright* at the bottom. Therefore, we often run it once to see what words may be associated with themes that are not useful. Once completed, we can then place the word *copyright* into what is called the ignore-words file. Then when we run ThemeMate the second time, the word is removed from analysis and does not occur as part of a theme.

Occasionally, we extract news articles from specific sources that include advertisements and much non-related material, particularly on web searches of documents. It may be worth the time to actually separate out the actual text of the articles so as not to have confusing material be part of the extraction process. A utility is provided that turns any Microsoft Office product into text so that ThemeMate can process it correctly (for example, Excel, Power Point, Access, and so on).

A question often arises about how we ensure the accuracy of the information used to construct our models. (For example, information extracted from the Internet can be notoriously inaccurate, depending on where it is obtained.) There are three basic answers:

1. Select articles from reputable sources only, such as reputable news sources (they check the accuracy of the information they publish), government reports, scientific journals, commissioned reports, and authoritative monographs and books. Stay away from blogs, opinion pieces, and obviously slanted or biased material.

2. Select multiple text examples of the same event. We have used as many as 10 articles per event. This ensures that antecedent themes will be identified on the most frequent variables.

   Note that even the time of an event can be wrong. For example, we have had multiple examples in which we have collected multiple articles describing an event in another part of the world. One article reports the event occurring in local Washington, D.C., time where the article was written, whereas other articles provided the time of the incident in their local times. These times differ, which can lead to erroneous antecedents. We have found the best way to guard against faulty information across many hundreds of potential antecedents is simply to provide multiple examples of reports per incident. The outliers simply do not result in antecedent themes.

3. Do not use material authored by those with obvious extremist views. We need objective analyses of past events and situations.

Testing Your Model

Once the predictive engines are developed, they should be validated, or tested, in four basic ways:

- Using cross-validation, such as Leaving-One-Out (L-1) for small data sets.
- Dividing data into two sets — one to use for developing a model and one for the end when it appears a model is ready to test for the first time.
- Testing against new attack behavior. Can it catch new attacks, or modified attacks?
- Testing in the field under real conditions but as a test only — this gives time to tweak if necessary.

These methods are not methods of choice in which one selects a method. If the application is a small-n application, then all methods should be used, in sequence. If the application is based on a very large number of case examples used to train the pattern classifier, then L-1 may be skipped in lieu of using the second method. However, it is exceedingly important to always test the classifier with cases never used in pattern classification training. The key to a usable and accurate application is not just the development of the application — it is the testing. I have seen applications presented in which the testing was simply substandard. The first question you should ask when seeing a new application is, "May I see the validation and testing data?" If the application builder cannot provide it, you don't want the application.

Testing is absolutely necessary, and it must be conducted in a non-biased manner. To the extent possible, use an independent group of testers. If one who assisted in the development ends up testing the application, it is too easy to make excuses for the performance, and misses might not be counted, giving a false determination of performance and accuracy. For more on this, see the section "Testing and Validation for CheckMate" later in this chapter.

When thoroughly tested in the field, errors are manageable, and there is satisfaction with both the performance and accuracy. Then true production can start.

Using Your Model to Predict

An AuBA model has been constructed either from historical text accounts of past behavior or from subject matter expert (SME)-generated scenarios for the AuBASME methodology. In both cases, we develop a user interface for the front end where the user clicks off the relevant antecedents for a given time and clicks on "run," and a predictive report is presented. Because of the artificial neural network predictive engine and how it has been trained, the identification of current antecedents can be slightly forgiving. For example, an antecedent that may not actually be present could be entered with others by mistake, or conversely, we may have neglected to add one that was there but was missed based on incomplete identification of the constellation of antecedents covering the current situation. However, I emphasize that the discrepancy must be only *slight*. In other words, we can't do an incomplete job of searching to determine which antecedents are present and absent to enter into the application. If we miss an antecedent or add one that wasn't truly there, the classifier will probably still provide an accurate answer. However, if we do a quick review of a global situation and check off the presence of antecedents to enter into the application and miss several antecedents, we are likely to obtain faulty results. This is not the fault of the application. AuBA applications are trained to predict the behavior that will occur under different contexts. This means that the context must be described as accurately as possible by checking which antecedents are present and which are absent. Basically, if we miss too many antecedents that are present or add several that are not truly present, we have described a totally different context than the one that is present. Therefore, the predictive application will provide a prediction of the behavior that will occur under this "different" context.

Current and past work of the AuBA teams has focused on the automated determination of the presence and absence of antecedents, like CheckMate and InMate applications. These two predictive applications are different in many ways from the AuBA applications in which typical asymmetric warfare is the focus. CheckMate and InMate automatically process network traffic with over 500 behavior/activity monitors; each capable of outputting a "1" if the antecedent in present and a "0" otherwise. This is done for all monitors so that a large vector is presented to the different pattern classification engines to convert network packet-level activity to behavior assessment measures. As a reminder, CheckMate converts packet-level activity in sequential, 1/10 of a second samples of packets to the degree of expertise (E) and deception (D) present. We have discovered that if high E and high D are present at the same time, then malicious intent is present and an attack is imminent. InMate uses the intent to engage in misuse (I) in place of expertise — the insider already has access and doesn't need expertise to "break in." However, InMate also uses deception (D). In this case, if I and D go high at the same time, the insider malicious intent is present.

As it turns out, it is far easier to monitor for specific and occasionally simple behaviors composed of network packets in 100 millisecond intervals compared to finding antecedents in text. Text is exceedingly complex. However, we are approaching 80 percent accuracy. In our continued development, if we reach 90 percent in identifying an antecedent in text when it is available, we can use the "slightly off" capability to achieve the vector that, when presented to the pattern classifier, will return an accurate prediction. If this is accomplished for world media, then news media could be monitored on an automated basis — the world's current situation processed automatically by the trained predictive engines.

Constructing Open Source Cyber Threat Models

While developing a cyber-based application that does not rely on the analysis of network packet activity like CheckMate and InMate (see later in this chapter), we noticed that open source news had been reporting on foreign threat and actual attacks on U.S.-based networks. This was particularly relevant because many of the reports described the typical what, when, where, and how (and sometimes who) of the attacks that we look for to extract antecedents and detailed accounts of behavior.

After collecting numerous examples of separate incidents, we developed a single corpus with all of the examples. Once we were satisfied that we had a very good representative sample of these foreign attacks that could be labeled as advanced persistent threat, or APT, we converted from different formats to a .txt format, so that we could process with ThemeMate. To balance the attack articles, we also located many articles that were cyber focused but not attack behavior, for example, articles describing how China was adding military cyber departments that would focus on defense.

We also had a threat category for output and a non-threat category. By renaming each article as the date preceded by a T for Threat or NT for Non-Threat, we had the raw data needed for ThemeMate. For example, if an incident occurred on September 20, 2011, and it was a threat example, the ID for that article was T092011. The Threat and Non-Threat designation is important for a reason I will describe shortly.

Figure 16-3 shows the resulting report superimposed on the items that are essentially the antecedents that have been validated to be predictive of *Cyber Threat* and *No Cyber Threat*. There are two basic ways in which input data can be presented to a completed AuBA application:

- In applications such as CheckMate and InMate, a detector determines if an antecedent is present or absent automatically and passes 1 (present) or 0 (absent), along with all other antecedents, to the pattern classifier.

- We construct a user interface that lists the antecedents to an application as a computer screen checklist with a checkbox for each antecedent. The user assesses the environment by reading the newspaper and maybe watching the latest television news reports, and checks with the cursor those antecedents that are present at that time. Behind the scenes, the check boxes are assigned a 1 and the unchecked boxes remain a defaulted 0. This string, when finished, is passed to the pattern classifier for processing as the context.

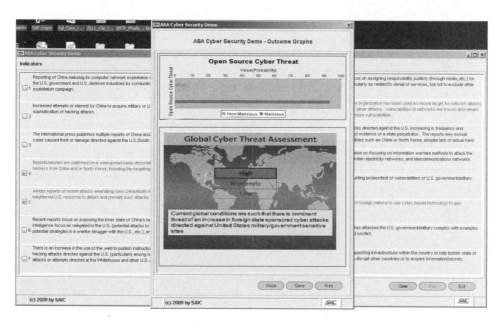

Figure 16-3: A screenshot of the open source model being used. The antecedents have been selected, and the superimposed screen shows the results (antecedents are obscured for security purposes).

Once selected, *Run* is clicked and the report is generated. It should be noted that for security purposes, the actual antecedents are purposely obscured. Figure 16-4 shows an enlargement of the actual report.

The report shows that, given the situation described with the selection of current antecedents on the input screen, the AuBA Open Source Cyber application projects an imminent increase in cyber threat will be directed against U.S. military/government sites. The report is fairly typical for AuBA whereby results are presented graphically and with a text-based interpretation. For example, the bar graph at the top provides the normalized probability of threat and no threat. As you can see, there is a 93 percent probability of an increase in threat and a 7 percent probability of less threat. Both threat and no threat are presented as probabilities to show the strength of both projections. For example, if threat won but was 51 percent, and no threat was 49 percent, our interpretation would have to be different. In that case, given the probability of a 1 percent error, the projection would have been matched for both although threat won as a projection.

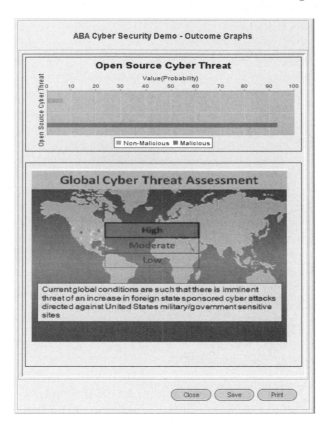

Figure 16-4: The open source cyber report.

Of equal importance to prediction of threat or no threat is the possibility of using the application developed for influence. The same application is used for both prediction and influence. The difference is that with prediction we select antecedents that are currently present, while with influence we can query the application with different constellations of antecedents to determine what will happen under these different scenarios. For example, if we query a number of different scenarios and find that some show high No Threat, then if we alter the environment to ensure that these antecedent conditions occur, we may see a decrease in threat. The basic applied behavior analysis discipline that formed the initial foundation for the automated and expanded version in this book is a more clinical approach, designed to alter behavior by changing the environment. It is a well-tested principle that we can change the behavior of others by altering the antecedents and consequences conditions associated with past behavior. This approach has been known as applied behavior analysis, behavior modification, behavioral psychology, and operant psychology, as well as other terms.

Modeling from Sensor Output

Physical sensor output is another form of antecedent. Sensor output represents a different form of data, though the behavioral features serving as a foundation to malicious intent and malicious behavior remain the same. For example, if motion is detected on the perimeter of a secure installation, it may be an antecedent to a break-in attempt. However, it could also be an innocent intrusion into the perimeter by a security guard. It is important to remove the antecedent conditions from the actual intent or the behavior.

This differentiation is perhaps the major problem with anomaly detection as an approach. Trained on normal situations, any significant departure from this *norm* is flagged as an intrusion. However, the simple fact that an anomaly occurs does not point to malicious behavior. As seen with the security guard example, the intrusion may have been caused by an innocent and harmless behavior. In an airport security line, an anomalous condition may be a reason to stop an individual for questioning, but it does not mean that the person is engaged in malicious activity.

Given that AuBA separates antecedents from behavior and also considers consequences in developing a security model, the resultant model is much more discriminating than an anomaly detection approach. Furthermore, the AuBA model is not looking for signatures. Signature detection simply cannot anticipate all of the potential security abuses, and it is reactive — the behavior for which a signature was written must occur before the detection occurs. It is simply a reactive approach, much like a home burglar alarm. In the case of the latter example, when the home alarm goes off, the intrusion has already happened.

When we consider physical sensors as devices that simply generate antecedents, then we can rely on a predictive engine to make a determination of malicious versus non-malicious behavior or intent. The advantage is that the sensor may be providing information on precursors to malicious behavior before it actually happens. A classic example is that surveillance and reconnaissance typically occur prior to an actual malicious act. It is indeed rare for a break-in to occur without the perpetrator checking out the situation first. In fact, reconnaissance to gather information may occur on repeated occasions prior to an actual more malicious act. In this case surveillance and reconnaissance are forms of antecedents that precede an actual malicious activity.

Predicting Malicious Behavior from Sensor Tracking of Movement

In Chapter 9 an AuBA application was presented that converted sensor tracked movement to intent (malicious and non-malicious). Figure 9-1 shows the results of a field test of this capability. There is an important feature to tracking movement to determine intent that should be noted. Typically, antecedents and consequences are external to the individual or group. By identifying these external factors as associated with movement, we can predict intent based on movement patterns. However, during the course of constructing this application we discovered that the patterns of movement themselves serve as antecedents that can be predictive.

In other words, early patterns of movement can serve as a glimpse as to what major movement patterns are coming. If one walks off a trail and moves slowly into the bushes and begins skulking around while circling a restricted area, it would seem logical that malicious intent is building. Perhaps surveillance is starting to occur. We can assume that specific types of malicious behavior will follow because we know that reconnaissance and surveillance activities often serve as antecedents to a real attack, assault, or theft. Also speed of movement, acceleration patterns, and high-frequency pausing can all be meaningful.

Another discovery that we had is that sensors are not perfect, nor is the production of tracks. For example, a sensor might be getting a "skip" off a building as someone walks through the sensor field.

Figure 16-5 is a reproduction of Figure 9-1 to save you from flipping back and forth.

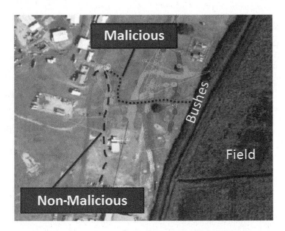

Figure 16-5: A field test of the AuBA application to convert sensor tracked movement into malicious and non-malicious intent.

Notice that on the field test screen shot there is movement as indicated with small circles that are attached and move in a set direction. Also notice there are some fine lines on the left that jump from the circles to a building and back.

These fine lines are sensor skip and are not to be interpreted as movement. To get around the problem of skips, we trained our pattern classifiers with skips. The pattern classifier was basically instructed with training examples to ignore skips. This was necessary because a predictive engine is so fast that it could provide a faulty output if it classified a skip as actual behavior.

There is a key point here. When using ThemeMate and AutoAnalyzer we almost always get some surprises. When using AuBASME we also get surprises. We find new information that we must consider and use because we often work with behaviors that have not been modeled. The discovery of new information makes the development very interesting.

For example, after 9/11, I collected a large corpus of articles about the attack. When I submitted the articles to ThemeMate, a number of very interesting themes surfaced. One of the more surprising findings that surfaced in pieces across a number of documents was information on the architect of the World Trade Center, Minoru Yamasaki. When I conducted a second search by using Yamasaki's name as part of a queried search, a theme popped up associating the Japanese-American famed architect with the bin Laden family and Saudi royalty. Osama bin Laden's family was known as construction giants and worked closely with Minoru Yamasaki. He had designed Islamic features into the World Trade Center. Needless to say, I would not have likely found these associations that were existing as separate pieces in text across multiple documents. ThemeMate is to the analysts what a microscope is to a biologist or a telescope is to an astronomer. We simply can see better if we use the right tools.

PREDICTIVE MODELING APPLIED TO NETWORK PACKETS

"You can perform financial fraud online. You can steal trade secrets online. You can blackmail and extort online. You can trespass online. You can stalk online. You can vandalize someone's property online. You can commit libel online. You can rob a bank online. You can frame someone online. You can engage in character assassination online. You can commit hate crimes online. You can sexually harass someone online. You can molest children online. You can ruin someone else's credit online. You can disrupt commerce online. You can pillage and plunder online. You can incite to riot online. You could even start a war online."

Richard Power, *Tangled Web: Tales of Digital Crime from the Shadows of Cyberspace*, Que Corporation, 2000, pp. 3–4

The severity and frequency of cyber attacks directed against government, private, and public sectors are increasing at an alarming rate. Meanwhile, current intrusion detection and protection methodologies struggle to provide effective countermeasures. The proliferation of hacker intrusion knowledge via the Internet, conferences and publications, and personal intercommunication contribute greatly to the escalation in severity and frequency of network intrusions.

Even the unsophisticated hacker who does his or her homework and downloads easily accessible hacking instructions or scripts can inflict serious and costly damage. The inadequacies of current signature-based and anomaly detection methodologies in preventing serious misuse, combined with the inordinate amount of highly skilled and costly staff required to operate and maintain these types of systems, dictate the need for a new and effective technology.

In short, we desperately need new technology to augment the current methodologies. Emphasizing human malicious intent with a focus on human behavior is required. Observing network activity/behavior is essential; the focus just simply does not serve to stop the high frequency of attacks and thefts we are experiencing today. For this reason, we have developed a new technological approach using the foundations of AuBA.

CheckMate and InMate: Implementing Behavior-Based Network Protection

As a new technology, two AuBA network cyber applications have been developed using the AuBASME technology described in this book. Currently, and for the past 10 to 15 years, there have been two approaches applied to network intrusion: signature detection and anomaly detection (see Chapters 11 and 12 for more detail). Signature detection is a mature approach in use today. However, it is outdated, and it is reactive. Basically, when an attack occurs, the attack is studied and rules are written to recognize it in the future. For example, it took a reported 5 months to fully characterize the infamous Conficker worm so that it could be detected. New and zero-day attacks may take an inordinate amount of time to identify, characterize, and then prepare in signature form, unless the attack is simple.

If you research such attacks as the Conficker worm, you will find that it takes a massive effort among many groups to characterize these sorts of attacks. It took over five months to characterize the Conficker worm and its many variants, and the attack is still there. Over the years, network attacks have become more sophisticated, and they morph over time, introducing many different variants. These variations pose severe problems for writing reactive signatures. Now that it is under some semblance of control, we simply wait for more serious attacks so that we can study and write rules. This technology is all we have for the most part, and this underscores the need for more proactive technology to be developed and put into place to protect networks.

Anomaly detection is still experimental to a great degree. It is a very good idea, but it has not evolved to the point where it can differentiate *anomaly malicious* from *anomaly non-malicious*. Although both approaches have been around for two decades, advancement has been minimal. In the meantime, the expertise and the deceptive practices of adversaries have grown by leaps and bounds. The result is that a single network may be attacked successfully every day, if not every hour.

The current attack focus, for the most part, is not to shut down networks. The current focus is to steal information, and there is much to steal. From theft of credit card numbers to identities to very sensitive classified and proprietary information — it is all going out the door, and in many cases we don't even know it until it is gone.

As I have discussed in earlier chapters of the book, the AuBA applications of CheckMate and InMate are attempts to introduce a new technology for network protection. Unlike signature detection and not anomaly detection, the technology is based on true human behavior assessment that focuses on discovering the intent of any individual in a network at any one time. The assessment engines are exceedingly fast, likely being the most rapid behavior assessment applications in existence.

One of the many challenges in designing and developing the CheckMate and InMate technologies was to develop a methodology that could assess antecedents and give a true human behavior assessment within 100 milliseconds (10 times per second). This assessment speed is contrasted with the many days, if not weeks, it takes to manually conduct a typical behavioral assessment.

Basically, CheckMate was designed to protect against external threat — those who enter a network from the outside and who are not insiders (for example, employees, contractors, interns, and so on). On the other hand, InMate was designed to review network activity of the insider only. The reason for separating the two applications is that antecedents and motivations for external individuals and for internal individuals are very different.

Perhaps the most important feature of the patented technology is the capability to identify new and zero-day attacks. A new attack is one that has not been observed before. A zero-day attack is a new activity that has not been identified in the past but is designed to exploit a discovered vulnerability. Because there is no time to prepare (zero-day), the attack can be particularly damaging, given the presence of the identified vulnerability. See Chapters 5 and 12 for a more detailed description of detection methodologies.

To conduct behavioral assessment, the technology must convert packet-level activity into measures within a behavioral domain. This process occurs within 50 microseconds, allowing the predictive engine to process thousands of individuals per second. As with all AuBA applications, the current status of the environment is determined by indicating the presence or absence of antecedents validated for the specific application.

CheckMate Network Intrusion Protection System

The hypothesis that formed the foundation for CheckMate was created after lengthy study of malicious activity on networks. As described elsewhere in this book, if one is to be malicious in a successful manner, then he or she must have the skill (expertise (E)) and must engage in some form of deception to avoid detection (D). Therefore, the initial hypothesis for CheckMate was this: *If we monitor packet-level activity in 100 millisecond intervals in real time and through repeated assessments convert the packet-level activity to the degree of expertise and deception present in all samples, then malicious intent is present and malicious behavior is imminent if E and D both exceed empirically determined threat thresholds.*

Figure 16-6 shows the basic conceptualization. As you can see, the expertise and deception dimensions are on separate axes. This creates four regions: High Expertise/High Deception, Low Expertise/Low Deception, High Expertise/Low Deception, and Low Expertise/High Deception. The lowest threat is in the bottom left corner and the highest threat is in the upper right. Each 100 milliseconds each IP/User receives an assessment, which is plotted on the figure. Although CheckMate is totally self-tending, the administrator may call up this plot for any IP/User. As hypothesized, assessed E/D points are plotted so that patterns of activity may be analyzed.

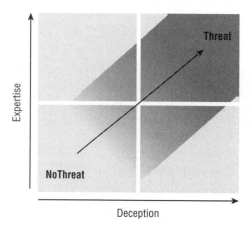

Figure 16-6: The conceptual description of how CheckMate determines the presence of malicious intent without signatures. If activity reached the upper right (high E and high D), then malicious intent is present.

The CheckMate technology collects packets for a 100 millisecond sample and then processes this packet-level activity as a two-stage process. First CheckMate processes the sample for the presence or absence of over 500 behaviors/activities. If a behavior is present, then a "1" in inserted into the vector at the appropriate location. If a behavior is absent, then a "0" is entered. The resulting vector of 1s and 0s serves as the input to the pattern classification assessment stage that converts constellations of antecedents to the measure of E/D for that vector.

The 100 millisecond samples are continuous. Consistent with AuBA applications, there are a number of separate assessment modules with each module presenting its own E/D determination (for example, there is an SMTP mail module, a new phishing assessment module, a cross port monitor [not designating any port], and an IPv6 module). For each 100 millisecond interval the presence or absence vector provides input to all assessment modules simultaneously, and the results are fused into one final E/D assessment.

All IP/Users are assessed each 100 milliseconds and monitored as an entire group (see Chapter 17). Empirically, a critical region and tracking region have been identified. In the screenshots of CheckMate and InMate shown in the next section (Figure 16-7), the shaded section in the far right is formed from E/D ratings that indicate imminent malicious activity if behavior falls in that region. The larger shaded area is a tracking region. This region is not as serious as the critical region, but indicates the behavior is suspicious enough to track and watch.

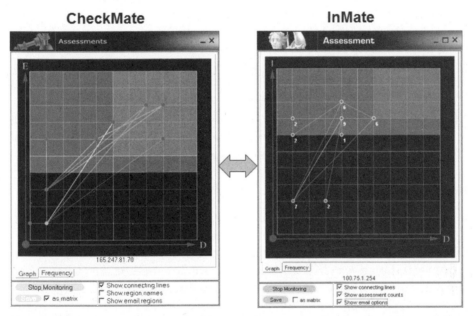

Figure 16-7: The 2D plots for CheckMate and InMate. Notice the dimensions of E/D with CheckMate and I/D with InMate.

InMate Misuse Detection System

Insiders (employees, contractors, interns, and so on) have different motivations for malicious intent. A missed promotion, perceptions that there are those who are preventing advancement, desire to hurt a company, and simple monetary gain from selling proprietary or classified information to an adversary or competitor are all motivators for the insider who has malicious intent. For this reason, insiders do not want to get caught — continued theft can hurt a company or organization severely, and if not detected the activity can continue indefinitely. For example, Robert Hanssen, an FBI Special Agent working within the areas of counterintelligence and counterespionage, had excellent access to the most sensitive information within the bureau. However, by practicing extreme deception with top-level spy tradecraft expertise, he sold classified information to the Soviet Union/Russia for over two decades. It is difficult to determine the total damage he caused, but it may have been the most damaging to date.

CheckMate, as described, depends on two behavioral dimensions: expertise and deception. For InMate it is clear that an insider does not need expertise to access a network by hacking — he or she has a user ID and password. However, like Hanssen, if the person has malicious intent, then deception must occur to avoid detection. For this reason the behavioral dimension of expertise was changed to *intent to engage in misuse* (I). Therefore, we have I and D with InMate and E and D with CheckMate. Figure 16-7 shows both the CheckMate and the InMate screens used to report activity in real time.

The InMate technology was based on the same behavior assessment methodology, but with different behavior dimensions for assessment and different behaviors to monitor on the front end of the assessment process. This front end, like CheckMate, processes a 100 millisecond sample of packets to convert to I and D. The vector that results from the 100 millisecond sample also serves as the input to the pattern classification assessment engines. Details of the actual process remain proprietary and restricted because of the need to protect the security of the CheckMate and the InMate applications.

Testing and Validation for CheckMate

As an example of testing and validation for all applications listed in this chapter, the following will be described for CheckMate, which is typical testing strategy for AuBA applications. First, during the pattern classification process, best practices cross-validation was used, in particular the L-1 method. For CheckMate and InMate we used two SMEs (Eric and Bob). Eric and Bob were trained in the assessment of threat using E and D measures and in the InMate I and D measures. Once trained, we presented unusual combinations of the front-end behavior monitors to Eric and Bob and requested they provide E/D ratings for each set of unique combinations that represented new activity. These combinations were not in the pattern classification training set.

At the same time, we independently submitted the combinations to the trained CheckMate predictive engines. Eric and Bob had to agree on their E and D ratings for each set of behavior monitors. Figure 16-8 shows the results of this test. In the figure, each column of numbers at the bottom represent which behavior monitors formed each test. For each combination two lines are plotted. The line with the squares is the E (first square) and D (second square). These squares are connected showing the E/D rating by the SMEs. The lines with the circles at the end are the E and D ratings (first circle and second circle) connected by a line and are the ratings provided by the automated pattern classification process.

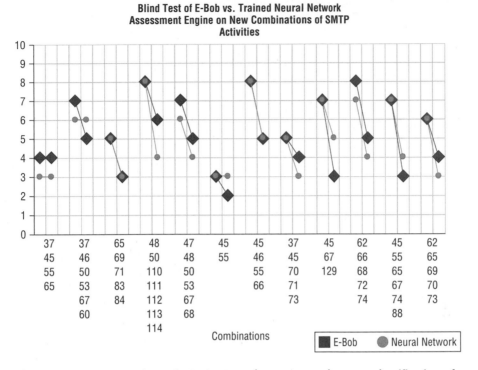

Figure 16-8: A comparison of two SMEs to the automated pattern classification of CheckMate to determine expertise and deception for unknown combinations of behavior monitors in CheckMate.

By comparing the two lines for each combination, we can determine how close the CheckMate engine comes to Eric's and Bob's (E-Bob) ratings. As you can see, the two lines are close to being the same. This essentially means that the CheckMate engines perform in a manner that is consistent with two world-class SMEs. However, a trained engine can be duplicated in as many applications as we need, is many times faster (50 microseconds versus minutes), can operate in real time, and can exceed the 6–10 monitor limit that can be processed at one time by the SMEs.

The second test was conducted by an independent testing company. The test consisted of identifying attacks that CheckMate and two of the leading products could all catch at 100 percent accuracy (name of testing company and products withheld on purpose). The independent team then used hacker evasion tactics to change the attacks. Once changed, the new attacks were sent back to the network so that a determination could be made concerning how each product performed in detecting *new* attacks. As you can see in Figure 16-9, CheckMate caught more of the new attacks. The results confirmed CheckMate's ability to detect new attacks without signatures or without anomaly detection.

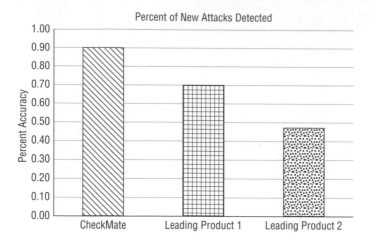

Figure 16-9: An independent, third-party comparison of CheckMate with two leading products in detecting new attacks created with hacker evasion attacks.

Advantages of AuBA #16: Extending Our Analytical Brains

As mentioned previously, AuBA tools are to an analyst what a microscope is to a biologist or a telescope is to an astronomer. However, ThemeMate works to enhance what we can "see" cognitively, whereas the microsope and telescope extend only what we see with our eyes. The ability to read hundreds of documents or volumes of sensor data and network packet data requires talent, acquired skill, and patience. Humans tend to find patterns, even if those patterns are meaningless. For example, the constellations are a result of our ancestors looking at the night sky of shining stars, seeing patterns in these stars, and imagining pictures. These pictures were given names, and we ended up with constellations. Finding patterns is essential work. Detectives read many reports, view photographs, and conduct many interviews. They need to find patterns after a crime has been committed to identify clues that can lead to the reconstruction of the crime to help in identifying a perpetrator. We have a natural tendency to find patterns.

Although we tend to find patterns in what we see and hear, we have to realize that what we recognize as patterns may be our interpretations of the truth, as opposed to the truth itself. We tend to project our own histories and biases into what we are observing. This tendency is so strong that the entire field of psychological projective testing was based on projecting our thoughts, beliefs, and even personality into what we observe. For example, almost everyone has heard of the Rorschach test — commonly known as the "inkblot test." Hermann Rorschach developed the test in the early 1920s. Basically, the test comprises a number of cards with free-form designs on the cards. It is a psychological assessment device. It is used because when people are asked to describe what they see in the inkblots, the responses are widely different. These responses, according to theory, provide some insight into the inner person. The inkblot cards are standardized, meaning all people see the same cards. The number of interpretations equals the number of persons being tested. This is also why many eyewitness accounts are unreliable. Three eyewitnesses of a crime may report three different views of what a perpetrator looked like and exactly what happened.

We also project our views and biases into analytical work. If three analysts are provided with a large set of documents with the task to read all the text and provide a summary, we tend to see three different summaries. Individual histories and biases are very powerful reasons why we tend to report on data as we see it from our own perspectives.

Working with many analysts across many different topics, I have seen self-guided interpretation of the same data occur almost as a matter of practice. Because humans are notoriously bad at deriving the same analysis from the same data, we often conduct inter-rater reliability studies to determine the degree to which analysts agree. Often, disappointedly, we do not obtain high levels of agreement between observers. Therefore, we have to develop operational definitions to guide the observations just so that we can help analysts focus on the same nuances and obtain agreement. Then, different analysts can report the same results — the problem is that we have guided observation for the sake of obtaining reliability. This we need, but we have suppressed the many different interpretations and clues for the sake of agreement on a few guided observations.

ThemeMate was developed to circumvent the preceding issues. As ThemeMate processes text that describes past behavior, it identifies themes objectively, summarizes these themes, creates a data array, populates it, and presents a variety of detailed reports about the past events. If we repeat the process with a second run of ThemeMate with the exact same documents, we obtain precisely the same reports — word for word. Because ThemeMate is not given operational definitions to guide the discovery of clues and associations, it is free to conduct true discovery. This discovery is invaluable. The tool also has neither the limitations of attention span nor the limited ability to handle more than two or three concepts at once, as we humans do. For these reasons, we obtain highly accurate and reliable observations that far exceed what we can discover, count, and associate to obtain complex patterns. Invariably, we obtain information that is a surprise. Just as ThemeMate discovered the association between the World Trade Center architect and Osama bin Laden's family, we receive information that gives us a deeper understanding of the individual or group we are analyzing.

Like the microscope and telescope, ThemeMate enables us to see more, understand better, and assemble pieces of information in new ways to help us synthesize results to better anticipate future behavior. Once we process the

ThemeMate end product data array with AutoAnalyzer to construct the predictive pattern classifier, we can obtain true prediction of future behavior. If we study the results of ThemeMate and not just use it to provide a data array for AutoAnalyzer to process, we will understand the adversary at a deeper level and have an improved context with which to understand the predictions when they are made.

In Summary

AuBA tools and AuBA applications cover a wide variety of topical areas dealing with malicious behavior. The purpose of this chapter was to describe a few applications while providing more detail on the model construction process. The models used covered both the construction of models from historical accounts in text (open source cyber threat) and the applications using the AuBASME approach (CheckMate and InMate). Other AuBA applications are presented in different places within this book.

It is important to note that the AuBA tools are versatile and can be used in an interactive process to ensure adequate data. Although ThemeMate has many different features, one feature was highlighted in particular that focused on using specific themes that have been developed to conduct searches via a search engine to bring back additional similar documents to enrich a developing model.

All developed AuBA applications and predictive engines must be tested and validated to ensure they are likely to work before we try them in the field. Where possible, third-party, or independent, testing is recommended.

Perhaps the most important key, critics aside, is that future malicious behavior may be predicted. Whether we are focusing on an individual, groups, or countries, all entities respond to external antecedents and consequences. Through the tools presented we can capture these relevant external variables, and through proper pattern classification we can predict future occurrences of behavior.

CHAPTER 17

Mastering AuBA Tools for Real-World Use

This chapter emphasizes the usability of automated behavior analysis (AuBA) tools and applications matched with basic knowledge of behavior principles and techniques. Because decades of work have gone into refining tools, features, and applications, much has been learned about the prediction of malicious behavior. Any good research and development (R&D) effort will feed back results of tests to the development process to make adjustments as required to achieve maximal performance and accuracy. From an R&D perspective, these lessons learned and the feedback from test results to the development process have resulted in continual improvements in both the unique technology supporting prediction of malicious behavior and the tools/applications themselves. Using customer feedback and input, we can make adjustments to interfaces and outcome reporting to best meet customer needs.

AuBA has been a two-part approach whereby first we needed to demonstrate that prediction of future malicious behavior can be accurate (valid) and reliable and second we needed to automate the process. Because of the focus on automation, the points requiring human manual manipulation have been reduced to a minimum, including validation. The automation means that the analytical team can spend its time on more important endeavors such as giving briefings, preparing reports, and gathering appropriate materials for analysis.

As I have noted in previous chapters, one of the primary reasons for introducing automation to the behavioral modeling approach was to reduce opportunities for the insertion of human cognitive bias. This is a very important feature. The manual process that leads to the development of AuBA tools is effective; however, there are certainly additional errors when compared to fully automated AuBA. Although these errors can be detected and fixed, it is a time-consuming process that simply adds to an already lengthy process. For this reason, we now use automation extensively.

Predicting the Unpredictable: Identifying Future Malicious Behavior

AuBA efforts over the past decades have demonstrated that the concepts of applied behavior analysis when extended, refined, and automated enable the AuBA process to predict malicious behavior accurately. Not only have the key concepts of antecedents, behavior, consequences as used for influence and behavior change and been validated across hundreds of thousands of research and treatment articles internationally for applied behavior analysis, but the AuBA advances demonstrate that these basic principles may be extended to prediction of behavior on a global basis. Although applied behavior analysis is *primarily* a method used to alter behavior to help others usually within constrained environments, AuBA, as described in this book, has extended the basic behavioral-change science firmly into prediction of malicious behavior and into global environments.

Antecedent determination within a constrained environment like a classroom or the home limits potential antecedents to a much smaller number as compared to AuBA as applied to focal areas such as international terrorism or network threat. In the latter examples, antecedents must be identified from an immense number of variables.

Applying AuBA to Future Threat

There are a number of trends in malicious behavior on a global scale that have been identified by AuBA. If we project these current global threat trends into the future, there are several significant points that surface. Among the trends that we can expect to occur in the future are the following:

- Continued and increased severity of foreign terrorist threat directed at Americans worldwide

- Increase in the number of U.S. citizens who seek to assist foreign terrorist groups targeting U.S. interests, either by leaving the country or by working covertly as a group member inside U.S. borders

- Given the present level of discord at the executive and congressional levels within the U.S. government, increased frustration resulting in the spawning of rogue extremist/militia attacks from highly disgruntled U.S. citizens

- Increased state-supported cyber penetration into sensitive U.S. government, military, and private/commercial proprietary technologies with the primary consideration being theft not disruption

- Continued and more advanced malicious code insertion into U.S. networks that represents ongoing morphing of attacks to evade signature detection

- Increased risk of significant and debilitating damage to such national infrastructure entities as economic sites, the water supply, and the power grid within the United States (separate from increased probability of theft)

To me, these are clear trends. Troop removal from Iraq removes Iraq as a location to attack Americans. However, it is not likely that the need and motivation to attack Americans will decrease once troops have vacated Iraq. Therefore, it is likely that there will be an increase in foreign attacks directed at Americans anywhere in the world and an increase in the need to perpetrate attacks within the borders of the United States.

Americans have learned to report anything or anybody who looks suspicious. Several actual incidents have been foiled by concerned citizens reporting suspicious activity. For example, on May 1, 2010, in New York City, a T-shirt vendor noticed smoke coming from a vehicle parked on a street with the motor running and lights on but no one inside. He alerted a mounted policeman who alerted authorities. Authorities discovered an ignited propane bomb that just had not exploded yet. The attempted bombing was foiled before explosion, damage, and injuries could occur.

However, increased diligence encourages new levels of malicious creativity. For example, terrorists are likely to rely more on disgruntled and sympathetic U.S. citizen assistance. This means that U.S. citizens who are focused on being an Islamic extremist or believe in other forms of extremism are likely targets to be approached for assistance. Likewise, the request to assist may flow from the disgruntled citizen to the foreign terrorist group. The disgruntled American can move freely throughout the country, explore networks, learn security holes, and ultimately be either an enabler of foreign terrorism or the actual perpetrator on U.S. soil.

Current U.S. Citizen Trends to Aid Terrorism

There are three primary means by which a U.S. citizen may become a traitor in the name of terrorism:

- Leave the country and join a foreign terrorist group
- Stay within the country as a type of citizen-based insider
- Plan and execute terrorist attacks within the country independently as a form of domestic terrorism

Leaving the Country

Perhaps the single best example of a U.S. citizen rising to the highest level of a foreign terrorist group was Anwar al-Awlaki. As a U.S. citizen, he rose to near the top of al-Qaeda and commanded operations in the Arabian Peninsula. Al-Awlaki encouraged others to engage in terrorist attacks within the United States. The underwear bomber, Umar Farouk Abdulmutallab, who attempted to blow up a U.S. airliner on Christmas day in 2009, was in repeated contact with al-Awlaki, and U.S. Army Major Nidal Malik Hasan (see the "Remaining Inside the United States as a Foreign Agent" section next) was in repeated contact seeking and receiving encouragement and praise.

On September 30, 2011, al-Awlaki was killed by an American drone strike in Yemen, bringing to an end the extreme al-Qaeda threat posed by this U.S. citizen traitor. In the same strike, Samir Khan, another U.S. citizen, was also killed. Khan, born in New York and then moving with family to South Carolina, came to al-Qaeda's attention through his increasingly persistent anti-American blogging. In 2009 he left his family and moved to Yemen, pronouncing that he was proud to be a traitor. Two weeks after the strike that killed al-Awlaki and Samir Khan, al-Awlaki's 16-year-old son, Abdulrahman al-Awlaki, a U.S. citizen born in Denver, Colorado, was killed in another American drone strike in Yemen. Adam Yahiye Gadahn, another U.S. citizen, remains with al-Qaeda today. Trading in his Christian upbringing for Islam, Gadahn moved to Pakistan, married an Afghani, and rose to lead communications for bin Laden. He has been active since 2004.

Remaining Inside the United States as a Foreign Agent

Al-Awlaki had also encouraged U.S. Army Major Nidal Malik Hasan, the Fort Hood shooter, to commit the horrific assault on fellow U.S. soldiers, killing 13 and wounding 29. Major Hasan had been espousing increasingly Islamic militant leanings and was scheduled to be deployed to Afghanistan in 3 weeks. He walked into a soldier center at Fort Hood, Texas, and started shooting at random victims. In probably the worst such military assault on a base by a soldier in our history, Hasan was wounded and paralyzed. With ties to al-Awlaki, it is clear that Hassan was, at a minimum, an al-Qaeda sympathizer. It is logical that al-Awlaki's encouragement had an effect on Hasan's deserting his country and his military service with one single devastating act.

Acting on Their Own

On November 1, 2011, the FBI arrested four men in Georgia for plotting to perpetrate a number of different types of attacks, including explosives, assassinations, and chemical attacks. The ages of the four men were 65, 67, 68, and 73. Claiming to be motivated by the U.S. Constitution, these citizens stated that some must die when the Constitution must be protected. Their plan included the use of the highly toxic chemical ricin, a poison they planned to release from a car near Atlanta, and a "bucket list" of government employees, politicians, corporate leaders, and members of the media who would have to be killed to make things right. With shades of Timothy McVeigh's Oklahoma City bombing incident, the self-named *Covert Group* had decided that to be patriots, they would have to use violence. They perceived past government actions were perceived as motivation for their planning, meaning that specific government entities (offices, agencies, staff, politicians, and even media personnel) were antecedents for targeting.

Unfortunately, there have been a number of planned incidents with U.S. citizen involvement. The border that clearly separated foreign and domestic terrorism in the past has become blurred in more recent years. The interconnected world of communications has made it simple for a disgruntled U.S. citizen to approach a foreign adversary to offer assistance. By using the Internet from one's home, it is possible to become a bona fide foreign terrorist group member. This is a new and little recognized trend, and one that requires strong vigilance. Samir Khan, the U.S. citizen who was killed in the same drone attack in Yemen that killed al-Awlaki, basically recruited himself for al-Qaeda by being persistent with his anti-American and pro-Islamic blogging. In this sense, the Internet makes U.S. borders meaningless. There are no borders on the Internet, and as some U.S. citizens have demonstrated, there are no boundaries either.

Increased vigilance of U.S. citizens within our borders is a powerful new weapon against foreign conventional terrorism. Reporting of suspicious activity has resulted in law enforcement foiling a number of apparent terrorist acts. The increased vigilance has made it more difficult for the 9/11 type of operation. However, it has not made it impossible. The vigilance needs to continue.

Terrorists have proven time and again that if one avenue is blocked, they simply move to a new avenue. For example, if our internal vigilance makes it more difficult to operate within U.S. borders, then there are other avenues to explore. It would appear that terrorist groups such as al-Qaeda have not had difficulty being approached by U.S. citizens who offer their assistance. The damage caused by the U.S. deserters al-Awlaki, Gadahn, and Khan, as examples, is difficult to measure. It appears highly likely that there will be continued citizen desertion.

At the time of writing this book, the country appears to be in the midst of growing frustration. Perhaps this is best exemplified by the Occupy Wall Street protest that began on September 17, 2011, that was started by Adbusters, a Canadian group. Adbusters is primarily anti-capitalist. Very quickly, New York City dwellers joined the protest and made Zuccotti Park their temporary home, complete with delivered meals by local restaurateurs and tents (see Figure 17-1). The basic premise for protesting was ambiguous, at best. However, the slogan, which has become their calling card, was "We are the 99 percent." This slogan refers to the division between the top 1 percent of the country who maintain the wealth, and the other 99 percent who don't. This slogan adds weight to the notion that the movement was at its core protesting corporate greed.

Figure 17-1: Typical tent city for the rapidly expanding Occupy Wall Street protest highlighting disparities between the richest 1 percent and the remainder of Americans (99 percent)

© Peter Kim | Dreamstime.com

A current snapshot shows that the partisan politics are not working well and often are at a stalemate. The inability of the legislative and executive branches to achieve agreement on any real substantive issues has resulted in mounting frustration. The Tea Party movement, spawned from the Republican Party, represents a new conservatism. The forces at play are likely to energize fringe extremists within the United States.

The current atmosphere can be viewed as a massive set of antecedents that precede malicious behavior. As the Occupy Wall Street movement grew to an enlarged effort in over 2,000 cities worldwide within just 6 weeks, it was clear that there was much dissatisfaction. Unrest itself can serve as antecedents to more serious malicious behavior.

One of the advantages of AuBA is that the tools can be used to construct models that include shifts resulting from changing conditions. By collecting top news articles each day over time, you can identify general trends in the antecedent-behavior-consequence modeling. To ensure that a model developed in the midst of changing conditions can accurately anticipate future behavior of the modeled entity, you can use the AuBASME methodology to include additional scenarios that may not have occurred yet in the model. In addition, periodically we will want to add recent data to keep the assessment engine tuned and up-to-date. Once completed, the model can deal with antecedents that tend to lead to mainstay behaviors and the AuBASME additions, including new antecedents to AuBASME-generated scenarios that have not occurred but that are likely to occur. Thus, a hybrid model is developed that can lead to valid and reliable anticipation of malicious behavior of a modeled adversary.

Because change is occurring quickly, it is essential that model building occur quickly. Often we use AuBA to process new, incoming information by producing rapid models just to determine what degree of change is occurring and the trend of the change. In my opinion, this is not possible with a straight correlational approach, which is the prevailing approach used at the time of writing this book.

There is also a strong likelihood that the same disgruntlement that fueled Occupy Wall Street and the public reaction to some of the government paralysis that we have observed is likely to fuel an increased probability of domestic threat. The enemy within is a formidable adversary. Having complete access and looking and acting like everyone else in an organization makes insiders extremely difficult to detect. However, automated assessment of insider behaviors is lacking in bias and other concerns that could suppress valid information. In addition, automation is much faster and far more sensitive than manual human behavior assessment. This allows for rapid modeling. By developing a model of top world events on a daily basis, and then comparing models by querying antecedents, you can obtain an accurate prediction of new, or emergent, adversary behavior, even if the behavior is from within our own borders and organizations.

Cyber Attacks

Cyber attacks directed against the United States represent a totally different form of attack or theft than those discussed thus far in this chapter. Cyber attacks directed against key U.S. assets and resources are already very successful. However, it is very clear that the sophistication of the attacks has increased in expertise and deception. Advanced persistent threat (APT) and the very advanced recent variations of phishing pose a new type of problem for the United States. Instead of an attack being directed against a network or operating system, the new attacks simply use the employee of an organization as an unwitting accomplice as a means to gain access.

Related to social engineering from the perspective that access information might be gathered by the telephone (whereby an employee is tricked into giving up a user ID and password), malicious phishing e-mail attacks are so good and look so real that they are difficult to prevent. Given the apparent authenticity of a well-planned phishing attack, it is difficult to imagine a certain fraction of employees not responding, thereby taking a step toward giving up access.

The sheer number of scans and reconnaissance activities that a major network experiences on a day-to-day basis is astronomical. The only way to deal with the high volume of malicious activity is to either formally or informally list categories of attacks and draw a line. If the attack falls above the line, we will endeavor to characterize it, but if it falls below the line, we ignore it. This is not a good strategy. Because of the increase in volume and seriousness of attacks, as well as the prevalence of new or modified forms of attacks, there is danger that the line will become raised to such a degree that damaging attacks start getting through simply because the resources are not available to launch sufficient countermeasures.

These are reasons why we need a paradigm shift in security. Total network protection is so far behind attacks that we basically continue to chase past attacks to characterize the attacks with rules. If it were a perfect world and adversaries did not change over time, grow, or use their creativity, then the current signature detection methods would eventually work. However, it is certainly not a perfect world, and adversaries change every day within the cyber world. This means we will continue to be flooded with (1) the same attacks as used in the past, (2) new attacks created by modifying past attacks, (3) new attacks representing new classes of attacks (for example, new phishing variants), and (4) zero-day attacks that have not been observed before that target specific vulnerabilities.

To get ahead of the game, it is logical that we need technology to quickly anticipate a serious attack by identifying antecedents that are associated with new classes of attack behavior. It is important to realize that new attacks are not going to yet have the characterizations that describe the new activity as a whole. Currently, our SAIC team is expanding our CheckMate characterization to include automated characterization of new attacks.

AuBA has a strong role to play in the current changing world. Because of their track record in asymmetric warfare areas, within the cyber world, and in anticipating future attacks, the methods are truly proactive and predictive. Because of the future-leaning design, AuBA applications have human assessment engines that are:

- **Proactive:** Assessment engines are trained in such a way that if new combinations of input occur, then the assessment engines can still provide accurate assessment of threat. Assessment engines are always ready to anticipate future threat should it occur.

- **Predictive:** Assessment engines have been validated to predict future occurrences of targeted behavior over time.

Applying AuBA to Network Security

Current cyber security from a software/hardware/network perspective focuses primarily on signature detection. As emphasized in this book, anomaly detection is a second basic approach, but it is not entirely accepted because of its inability to determine flagged non-malicious from flagged malicious activity. It simply flags activity as sufficiently different than the established norm for that network. The most-recent trend is to focus on policy. By policy, I mean the formal guidelines prepared by an organization that determine how a network will function. These guidelines can be extensive and will determine access for everyone inside. They may also determine who from outside the organization will have access to what and could even determine who does not gain access.

There is also a new approach that is not a new methodology but an approach that has some advantages. *Threat intelligence* has surfaced more recently and is really a way to collect threat information on attacks and share it across multiple networks simultaneously. This reduces the need for each staff across participating networks to do the entire discovery, know the latest threats, and conduct the usual network protection activities in isolation. The threat intelligence approach is more efficient and can maximize efforts for protection to the extent that current technology can do its part.

CheckMate: Protecting Networks from External Threat

Incoming external threat to networks is a complex mix of methods, motivations, activities, and an enormous multitude of approaches either to inflict damage or to engage in theft of restricted information. Current defensive methodologies do not attempt to view beyond incoming packets to try to determine characteristics of the individual or the scripts written by individuals. Instead, the defensive process begins when the packets hit the network. The signature experts have beforehand created rules to determine if packets coming into a network have specific characteristics that should be flagged. In other words, does the stream of packets contain activities that would be caught by pre-existing rules? If so, the activity will be flagged by the signature detection component.

This is an effective approach, but with each day as attacks morph, new attacks occur, and we see ever-increasing APT, and signature detection is becoming less effective. The problem with this approach is the inordinately high false negatives (actual attacks that slip by since there are no signatures to catch them). A false negative is more serious than a false positive because it means that malicious intent is now within the network from an external source.

Of course, if we can apply anomaly detection — after the software has been trained on the normal activity of the network, it can flag activity coming in that is significantly different from the norm. However, then we have the opposite problem: inordinately high false positives (calling an IP and activity as threatening when it is not). At the time I was writing this book, this problem has not been solved and without introducing additional pattern classification technology is not likely to be solved. There are many problems with the anomaly detection approach. Anomaly detection requires norming the software on activity within the network when it is considered normal. Today's onslaught of scans, surveillance, and network attacks is not likely to leave a network in a normal state for training. Therefore, when we train anomaly detection, we are training as normal whatever is happening within the network at the time of training. Therefore, if attacks are present during training, the method has learned to label them as normal and will not flag them in the future. It will, however, flag activity that is sufficiently different from the norm to result in a warning.

Objectively analyzing the effectiveness of these two approaches and given the degree of successful intrusions into our most sensitive networks on a daily basis, we must conclude that current approaches simply are not providing a sufficient defense against intrusion into our networks. In many cases, we don't identify serious malicious activity until a system has already been compromised. In other words, the newest emerging approach is to wait until compromised, identify the cause, characterize it, and then track it down. This approach is basically admitting defeat and moves us from protecting a network to continually trying to clean it from the malware that simply keeps coming.

Human Behavior, NOT Network Behavior

It is essential that true knowledge of human behavior, malicious intent, and the conditions under which malicious human behavior can circumvent current technologies be interjected into network protection. For the most part, when we currently read about behavior analysis of network behavior, the intent is not to focus on *human* behavior; the focus is on the behavior of the *network*. This can be very misleading. To be proactive and predictive, we need technology based on identifying characteristics of the human who is behind the packets at this juncture.

If we focus on network behavior, we are focusing on the very small number of rules that exist to identify specific packet-related activities that could cause harm. Given that we are tracking the presence or absence of specific combinations of network activity to define network activity that should be flagged, we are talking about an astronomical number of malicious combinations of network packet activity. There are thousands of activities to monitor. This equates to a number that is extremely high, one that far exceeds human capability to place into rules for true protection.

Because rules are extremely specific and static, it is not difficult to understand how 10,000 rules cannot detect combinations of activities that are new, or zero-day, and could number into the trillions of potential combinations that have the potential to form a new attack. In fact, even identifying and characterizing all forms of current intrusions as rules is not possible. The number is just too overwhelming. However, it is easy to see that if we simply rely on writing signatures after we have been attacked and compromised, then we are simply always going to be in a catch-up (reactive) mode.

Automated Human Behavior Assessment from Packets

The CheckMate tool approaches the problem from a different perspective. First, there are steps in the development process that used subject matter expert (SME) input to help in determining *expertise* (E) and *deception* (D) ratings for specific types of human behavior, as well as simple activities. When CheckMate analyses the behavior of an IP, it automatically collects all packets from an IP for 100 milliseconds and then, based on the activity/behaviors detected, converts the result of the monitoring to measures of E and D.

NOTE We have found this process to be very effective in that the AuBA pattern classification methodology, when compared to human SMEs, essentially provides the same E/D ratings — with the exception that if many combinations of monitored behaviors occur at the same time, the human cannot determine ratings accurately. CheckMate can handle any number of combinations of monitored human behaviors, as well as typical network activities, and provide an E/D assessment within 50 microseconds. Even if only a few combinations of monitored behaviors occur at the same time, it can take the SME many minutes to characterize an attack just for one entity. In comparison, if it takes the SME 5 minutes to characterize an attack, it is possible for CheckMate to have conducted 6 million assessments in that time. If there are 100 individuals within the network during this period of time, each will have received 3,000 E/D assessments during the 5 minute period that the SME has been busy conducting a single assessment.

Human behavior analysis is conducted by using multiple observations to help provide a picture of characteristics of the individual. These samples of collections of behavior help to determine overall characteristics of the individual. Some approaches base analysis on deep or detailed analysis of each packet. In contrast, CheckMate backs off and gathers activity for 100 milliseconds to get a macro view. This view can tell us something about the individual, which is a very different approach. For example, if we looked at all the pores in the body one at a time with a microscope, it will not give us a photograph of the individual. CheckMate tries to determine behavioral snapshots of the person behind the packets by determining the degree of *expertise* being exhibited and the degree to which he or she is trying to be *deceptive* in each sequential 100 millisecond interval. Although these are samples of behavior, the samples are continuous and never stop for as long as the person is in the network.

Instead of identifying attacks comprising many activities, CheckMate was based on a concept that is very similar to the Periodic Table of Elements. This table used by chemists, physicists, and other physical scientists contains the 103 common elements that when combined in different patterns include all known substances in the universe. (There are 15 additional elements that occur in very rare form and hardly last long enough to even measure.)

For example, in the table shown in Figure 17-2, if we combine hydrogen atoms (H) and oxygen (O) in the ratio of 2 hydrogen atoms to 1 oxygen atom, we have the common H_2O molecule, or water. If we add an additional oxygen atom to get H_2O_2, then we have hydrogen peroxide. The combinations can have very dramatic differences. Hydrogen by itself can be extremely explosive and was the gas that filled the famous *Hindenburg* blimp, which exploded on landing in New Jersey on May 6, 1937. The disaster killed 37 people and was a vivid example of the explosive nature of hydrogen. However, if instead of hydrogen by itself if we add 1 oxygen atom to 2 hydrogen atoms, we obtain the familiar H_2O molecule — we have water that may be used to extinguish the fire.

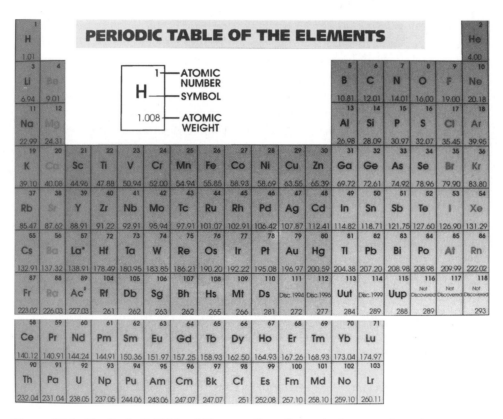

Figure 17-2: The Periodic Table of Elements lists all atomic elements that when combined into different patterns account for all physical substances in the universe.

© Joseph Helfenberger | Dreamstime.com

Like the different combinations of the elements in Periodic Table of Elements to define different substances, CheckMate monitors 521 different behavioral primary elements. They are the smallest behavior elements. To pay homage to physics and chemistry and the periodic table of elements, we call these elements *atomic elements*. One of the basic ideas underlying CheckMate is that the determination of which combinations define malicious activity versus non-malicious activity occurs at the pattern-classification stage. Therefore, no attempt is made to define a signature of any type of attack nor is an attempt made to define normal. Instead, if expertise and deception both exceed a critical threshold at one time, then we know the combination of monitored activity equates to threat, even if the combination represents a new form of attack not before observed. However, because the methodology detects threat based on the degree of presence of expertise and deception, known attacks can also be identified without signatures. The technology goes beyond packets to determine behavioral measures of the intent behind the packet level activity.

Proactive, Predictive, and Protective

The AuBA CheckMate and InMate (discussed later in this chapter) network protection tools share three common major characteristics that separate the technology from other approaches such as signature and anomaly detection. These applications are:

1. Proactive
2. Predictive
3. Protective

The following sections describe each of these characteristics.

Proactive

As has been highlighted throughout this book, the primary reason we are not keeping up with current levels and sophistication of cyber insults to our networks is that the leading technology is reactive only. By definition, signature detection cannot become proactive in its current form. Because the technology is reactive, the best we can hope for is that attacks can be identified and characterized rapidly, signatures written, and signatures distributed to all relevant sites so that the known attack may be prevented in the future. However, we must remember that it took multiple teams 5 months to identify all aspects and to characterize the Conficker worm. This is an eternity in network speed. Furthermore, even with a new signature in place, if the attack is modified by using any available number of hacker evasion tactics, the attack has an excellent chance of not being caught because it will miss the signatures designed to catch its predecessor.

For technology to be truly proactive, it is necessary for it to anticipate threat. Thought must have been given to the design so that it can conform to anticipated needs of the future. For example, it is clear that phishing attacks and variants of phishing are highly likely, and increases in insider threat will be a strong part of future malicious behavior on networks. CheckMate has a new phishing module that is extensive and extendable, and InMate is prepared to identify new insider threat attacks that have not been previously observed. (InMate is discussed in more detail later in the chapter.) Furthermore, although we still have not witnessed an extensive use of IPv6, CheckMate already has a tested IPv6 module ready to be initiated on appropriate installations. IPv6 will replace the current IPv4 Internet protocol that is rapidly running out of IP address space. To be proactive is to be ahead of the mounting threat.

Predictive

There appear to be two scientific camps when it comes to the ability to predict human behavior accurately and reliably. The first camp firmly believes that the prediction of future human behavior is not possible. The second camp believes it not only is possible but may be working diligently within the area. The first camp often makes comparisons to the physical sciences, which it claims is more lawful. I often point out that within the physical sciences such focal areas as earthquakes, weather, hurricane tracks, tornados, tsunamis, volcanoes, amount of snowfall, and so forth are extremely difficult for the physical sciences to predict. However, to some extent, progress is being made in prediction in some of these areas. Comparing these areas to the prediction of human behavior using the procedures and technology composing AuBA reveals AuBA to have superior predictive capabilities to the current methods of prediction in these specific dynamic physical science areas.

One of the reasons why many doubt the ability of science to predict human behavior accurately is the perception that the human brain and inner workings of cognition, personality, motivations, and drives are just too complex and varied to allow for accurate prediction. This has always been surprising to me. As pointed out continually in this book, we do not accomplish predicting behavior by studying behavior any more than the physicist predicts a future hurricane path by studying the most recent hurricane in excruciating detail. The AuBA approach of antecedent-behavior-consequence has its companion in the physical sciences. To predict the path of a hurricane, the weather SME studies the environmental conditions that precede the path. Such variables as temperature, water temperature, barometric pressure, longitude, latitude, and so forth allow models to use many complex variables preceding and external to the hurricane itself to predict its path.

In the many AuBA briefings I have provided to many varied audiences, it is always interesting to see the reaction when someone realizes for the first time that prediction of human behavior is not about studying the inner workings of the complex human organism but rather about the preceding environmental variables that the complex human responds to and the consequences of the behavior.

AuBA has been constructed with the use of tools that were developed to focus on the preceding antecedents and following consequences. It is my opinion that AuBA has been predictive of malicious behavior because of the:

- Reduction of bias due to automation and an accurate overall behavioral science foundation that identifies the antecedent-behavior associations

- The effect of consequences of past behavior
- The specific pattern classification approach developed to use antecedents as input and behaviors or threat as output

Having worked with many clinical populations across many different settings in the past, it was clear to me that formal diagnosis of mental impairment, personality testing, and clinical interview results in extremely unreliable variables to use to try to predict future behavior. It was not until the antecedent-behavior-consequence methodology was incorporated that accurate prediction started occurring. (However, it should be stated that if the goal is influence and not prediction, then these other more clinical variables are very useful.)

Protective

To protect is to shield from harm. The purpose of intrusion detection is to provide a capability to shield networks from damage or theft. However, the current use of detection tools appears to be slipping more toward forensics. That is, the goal seems to focus on the study and identification of what happened as opposed to form a better shield to protect against the malicious event. This is one of the primary reasons why we need a paradigm shift in this area. To help prevent cyber damage and cyber theft and to offer a shield against APT, we must have a technology infusion that can accurately anticipate an attack before it occurs, recognize a new form of attack, and be able to stop an attack early enough to limit or prevent damage.

CheckMate and InMate offer new approaches that fit these criteria. The basis of the technology is that direct signatures of past attacks are not sought. Instead, the technology can detect significant malicious intent of the activity entering a network regardless of the activity itself. Because true intent can be identified by the technology, whether the attack is live and driven by a human at a keyboard or in the form of scripted attacks constructed by a human, we can convert such activity to behavioral measures that can betray the underlying intent of the activity.

Both CheckMate and InMate have an option that is available to block the IP if the E/D or *intent/deception* (I/D) move into the critical region for a set number of times. In other words, if one is in the network and CheckMate determines that E and D have exceeded a threshold at the same time, the connection is severed and the user is suddenly disconnected from the network. The repeated occurrences are to ensure confidence that the IP should be blocked, because if it is a new form of attack, there will be no characterization. I do not imply that these two applications are the only answer; however, I do propose that the underlying concepts will be necessary to incorporate with any technology if we are going to truly protect our networks from damage or theft.

NOTE The most important principle for the future is that network technology must be capable of identifying the intent of the individuals behind the packets and not just detect specific characterizations of packets as known attacks.

Automated, Real-Time Malicious Behavior Assessment

The volume of threat activity entering our networks today is unparalleled, as is the degree of foreign state support for approaching the United States as a source of key technologies to steal. We simply no longer have the time or the luxury to wait until we have been compromised to study what happened and then to write rules to protect against a specific attack in the future. True, we must have it, but we need to augment with the new technology.

It is also imperative that new technology be automated to the point that identification of intent can initiate a course of action in a measure of milliseconds. CheckMate and InMate make threat decisions every 100 milliseconds for all IPs (or an employee designator for InMate) operating within a network. This is 10 assessments per second per entity monitored. This can be faster if need be, but it seems sufficient. One of the keys is that once a decision of threat has been made (E/D or I/D exceeds critical thresholds), then a course of action is initiated immediately to prevent damage.

NOTE It is time to augment signature detection and anomaly detection with behavioral intent detection.

InMate: Identifying Insider Threat

Threat posed by insiders on networks within an organization at a minimum equals the threat presented by those external to an organization. However, the vast majority of software and hardware approaches to network protection have focused on protecting networks only from external threat. Given the paucity of products developed and deployed to protect networks from insiders such as employees, contractors, interns, visitors, visiting staff, and so on, the problem is exacerbated by the reactive nature of the few existing products. That is, the protection that does exist is based primarily on the identification of attacks already occurring. In other words, signature detection is a tool to protect against the past, not the future. Furthermore, signatures prepared to protect against attack are based on intricacies of network-based behavior and not on the behavior of humans perpetrating the attack. The result is a typically very high rate of false negatives, whereby new attacks simply pass right through reactive signature protection barriers.

As was the case in external threat approaches, for internal threat to counteract the reactive nature of the signature detection approach, anomaly detection methods have been developed to norm the behavior of a network for insiders and, once the technology is trained, to compare all network activity to the norm to flag deviations from this norm. Unfortunately, the technology has not been shown to be particularly useful because of the inordinately high false-positive rates associated with the inherent inability of the method to differentiate between deviations that are non-malicious and those deviations that are truly malicious. Clearly, a radical paradigm shift is needed. As external and internal threat increase on an almost daily rate, we are still applying ever-faster applications that are based on decade-old technologies, at best. We are losing the fight. As we examine methods used to combat external threat and internal threat, the descriptions sound almost identical. The reason for this is that the focus began first with external threat, and the very same methods were basically refocused for the insider.

To counter the inherent inability of signature detection to anticipate new attacks and the inability of anomaly detection to differentiate "malicious" from "non-malicious" deviations from a network-specific norm, a new technology is needed that is:

- Proactive and capable of anticipating new attacks not previously identified (attackers continually change attack behavior to bypass signature detection)

- A human behavior–based methodology capable of anticipating classes of malicious intent and how intent fuels internal attack behaviors

- A real-time human behavior assessment paradigm that can identify malicious intent that precedes an attack in real time so that immediate mitigation and courses of action can be implemented to prevent damage

The InMate application is capable of providing real-time behavioral assessment of internal network users for the purpose of identifying those individuals who possess malicious intent to engage in network misuse. True human behavior assessment occurs by means of two neural network–based assessment engines that convert network activity of an inside user into validated behavioral measures of *intent* (I) and *deception* (D). InMate represents a new behavioral assessment technology for internal network misuse identification.

DEFINITION *Intent* **is defined as the assessed intent to engage in misuse.** *Deception* **is defined as the attempt to use methods that would make it more difficult to identify an inside user engaging in misuse.**

Currently, InMate collects network activity of each inside user and conducts multiple assessments per second for the duration the inside user is logged onto the network. Real-time assessment is accomplished by means of SMTP and cross port assessment modules. The results of assessment modules are aggregated to produce a determination of assessed activity as legitimate, suspicious, or critical from an insider threat perspective.

InMate represents the first real-time *human* behavioral assessment technology to detect insider network misuse. InMate accomplishes this by converting internal network activity to behavioral dimensions of *intent* and *deception*. Currently, InMate can assess 1,000 inside users simultaneously. Assessments result in dual ratings along the stated behavioral dimensions. These ratings represent the degree of threat or suspiciousness represented by the employee's network behavior. Each inside user receives individual assessments.

This human behavior–based, anticipatory, paradigm-shift technology exists at SAIC and is known fully as the InMate Network Misuse Detection System. It is an extension of AuBA and CheckMate Intrusion Protection System technologies.

Psychological and behavioral assessment consists of rating behaviors on single dimensions and then combining the individual measures to form a single profile. InMate incorporates this principle by creating a two-dimensional grid that creates four quadrants (low intent – low deception, low intent – high deception, high intent – low deception, and high intent – high deception). Low intent – low deception is in the lower-left quadrant, and high intent – high deception is in the upper-right quadrant. The output of an assessment is a scaled rating for intent and a scaled rating for deception.

Like CheckMate, InMate incorporates artificial neural network assessment engines. These pattern classifiers convert detected network activity into ratings of intent and deception behavioral measures in real time. The assessment engines are trained to provide dual assessment ratings for any combination of detected activities. Unlike rule-based signature detection systems using a few thousand signatures at best, InMate is capable of providing assessments for 2^{100} combinations of monitored behaviors/activities. This capability allows InMate to detect unknown forms of activities if dimensional ratings indicate suspicious or critical behavior. Two tunable regions determine separate suspicious and critical regions. If an inside user's activities result in ratings that fall within the suspicious region, that employee's activity and assessment results will be tracked and associated by assessment interval. If an employee's activities result in ratings that fall within the critical region, the inside user will be tracked and is considered to be engaging in serious internal network misuse. Monitoring staff may choose to be alerted when an employee's activities result in ratings falling within either or both regions.

Blind validation tests indicate that the neural network–based InMate assessment engines perform in an almost identical manner as nationally recognized network intrusion experts who have been trained in providing activity-specific intent and deception ratings. The InMate prototype exists as a self-tending, rack-mountable appliance. Typically, within 45 minutes of placing InMate in a rack, the application may be configured and be totally operational with no additional tuning required. Because of the unique behavioral assessment technology, the incidence of false positives is minimized, while the true positive identification rate is enhanced, particularly for unique forms of internal misuse.

Advantages of AuBA #17: Versatility

This book focuses on the prediction of malicious behavior. However, AuBA works equally as well for predicting non-malicious behavior. The same principles, techniques, and tools work with appropriate behavior. All human behavior responds to antecedents and following consequences. Currently, our AuBA team is working on a number of projects that emphasize appropriate behavior. For example, we are in a proprietary relationship with a company that emphasizes treatment. We have used AuBA to process treatment notes to extract antecedents associated with future success in treatment and non-success in treatment. Initial validation indicates that such prediction can reach a minimum of 85 percent true-positive and true-negative accuracy. This is significant in that identifying early those who could be a treatment risk in the behavioral areas can ensure early intervention to assist in treatment success. If we know who might not benefit, then we can develop methods to better continue the effects of treatment over time.

Applied behavior analysis focuses on more clinical areas, as well as education and socially relevant issues. It is important to note that the automation underlying AuBA may be used in very similar areas. If reports of behavior are in text form, ThemeMate can be used to identify the antecedent candidates associated with behaviors that interfere with appropriate behavior so that they may be suppressed. If text reports are not available, the AuBASME methodology can be used to create a data array for an individual or a group, with antecedent candidates as columns and examples of behaviors or projected scenarios as rows. Then the data array can be submitted to AutoAnalyzer to construct and validate the predictive engine.

Although the method is identical, if constructing behavior models of non-malicious behavior, the purpose will certainly be different. The modeling of non-malicious behavior occurs so that we can study the model to determine how best to influence the behavior of the individual or group by altering antecedents and see how behavior would likely change. In this case, we can learn to alter the environmental context to obtain the behavior desired and reinforce it when it does occur. In this way, the focus moves more away from prediction to one of influence. We encourage the presence of appropriate behavior and discourage the presence of inappropriate behavior. In this manner, AuBA becomes an automated assistant to those areas suited for traditional applied behavior analysis.

In Summary

The mastery of AuBA tools may be viewed in two ways: the mechanical operation of the tools and applications and the use of the AuBA methodologies to increase understanding of future malicious behavior. Because of the automation described in this book, predictive models can be developed rapidly and applied to new applications. However, in developing predictive human behavior models, you learn much about the behavior being studied. First, you learn that prediction comes from identified antecedent-behavior associations that are strengthened or weakened by successful or unsuccessful consequences, respectively. Because of the focus on the true variables that affect future behavior, you can determine trends that may be projected into the future, as well as more precise behaviors.

There are clear trends occurring currently. Network intrusions will increase, insider threat will worsen, and U.S. citizen involvement with foreign terrorist groups will continue to increase.

We can no longer afford to rely only on reactive approaches to fight malicious behavior. The heightened awareness of U.S. citizens to report anything suspicious has led to foiled terrorist events. Although not a sophisticated approach, it has already proven its value. It is, in fact, proactive and should be a forerunner to how we pursue new technology to protect our country's infrastructure. New technology must be capable of anticipating attacks to ensure time to initiate courses of action to prevent damage or theft.

AuBA represents a behaviorally based, proactive, and predictive set of technologies to be used with existing technologies. Mastering the methodologies of AuBA, the tools, and the applications represents a step in the direction of a new paradigm shift in security and network protection.

CHAPTER 18

Analyzing Future Malicious Behavior

This is an important chapter. The preceding chapters provide the foundation for understanding the nuances underlying accurate prediction of future malicious behavior. This chapter will introduce the concepts to better understand the contexts within which future behavior occurs and not just prediction of specific behavior. Because we have been conditioned to focus only on behavior, if we do consider prediction of future adversarial behavior, then we tend to think:

- **What** malicious behavior will occur next?
- **When** will the next malicious behavior occur?
- **Where** will the next malicious behavior occur?
- **Who** will be the focus, or victim, of the malicious behavior?
- **How** will the next malicious behavior occur?

These are exceedingly important questions. Why? Because if we can predict the future occurrence of malicious behavior accurately, then we can prevent that actual occurrence. Doing so seems to be the ultimate goal. If we afford ourselves the luxury of accepting the notion that we can predict future behavior, we are obviously going to focus on what actual behaviors will be predicted.

However, because automated behavior analysis (AuBA) methodology results in the prediction of future behavior by requiring the antecedent-behavior-consequence

sequence, we can also add a number of other features to predicting future behavior, such as:

- To what events and situations will the target respond in the future?
- What are the projected characteristics of a target in the future?
- What are the projected effects of the terrorist events that will serve to reinforce the terrorist act?
- What events and situations would suppress the terrorist act?

These questions consider more than behavior — they consider the context within which future behavior will occur. This is important! Methods that correlate behaviors, emphasize statistical analyses of behaviors, or simply focus on past behaviors cannot achieve accurate prediction of future behavior consistently, reliably, and confidently across time. AuBA, because of the many extensions of applied behavior analysis to a global context, predicts future behavior by predicting the context under which the behavior will occur, not just the behavior itself.

This chapter delves deeply into analyzing antecedent and consequence elements of an adversary's behavior that are likely to occur in the future and will interact to result in a behavioral event. The more detailed the elements that can be predicted, the more logical and encompassing the description of behavior to occur will be. Much like pieces of a jigsaw puzzle, individual elements such as antecedents, behaviors, consequences, suppressors, motivations, drives, and so on all come together to form a single picture of a future behavioral event.

This chapter focuses on how we can use AuBA to predict individual components of future events and how we combine those components to form a complex snapshot of future behavior.

The Necessity of Context in Predicting Future Behavior

AuBA is not just a set of tools, methodologies, and follow-on applications. It is a method by which we can view malicious behavior from a perspective that exceeds the behavior itself. It is a method that forces us to consider the context under which behavior occurs. Without understanding the context, we are not going to be able to predict the behavior. By this point in the book it should be obvious why. As we know, behavior does not occur in a vacuum. Whether it is past behavior, current behavior, or future behavior, or whether it is the behavior of a mentally disabled individual or the behavior of a stellar scientist, or world leader, human behavior occurs in response to antecedents, and its future occurrence under these conditions depends on the consequences. If consequences were beneficial to the person, then the behavior is likely to occur again in the future under the same or highly similar antecedents. If the behavior is followed by undesirable consequences, then the behavior under that same or highly similar antecedent in the future is less likely to occur.

DEFINITION *Context* means

1. **The parts of a discourse that surround a word or passage and can throw light on its meaning**

2. **The interrelated conditions in which something exists or occurs: environment, setting <the historical context of the war>**

Merriam-Webster Dictionary (m-w.com)

The overall approach of correlating behaviors and perhaps a selected variable such as time is that the predictive value of contextual information is totally ignored. Human behavior is context-dependent and, therefore, so is AuBA. The process of thoroughly processing text on a sentence-by-sentence basis with ThemeMate ensures that we are focusing on not only the behavior described by the document but the preceding events and situations and what follows as well. The antecedents and consequences of the underlying A-B-C sequence provide the context that supports the behavior in question. It is logical that if we collect common antecedents and consequences across many examples of behavior of different types (for example, assault, bombing, kidnapping, and so forth) then each category of behavior will have its own antecedents and consequences. Given the presence of a set of antecedents in the future, it is likely that the behavior more closely associated with that set of antecedents in the past would be the one to surface.

The prediction of future malicious behavior is a direct function of how effectively we have studied the antecedent-behavior-consequence sequences of past behaviors of the type on which we are focusing. Once we have the typical antecedents that were present in the past that preceded a specific behavior consistently, then we can, with some confidence, assume that the behavior will occur in the future under the same or highly similar antecedent and consequence conditions.

Conceptually, this information is embedded throughout our conceptual steps to predictive behavioral modeling:

1. Collect a corpus of past text articles describing a malicious behavior (for example, cyber attack) or class of behaviors of interest (terrorist attack: assault, suicide bombing, stand-off improvised explosive device [IED], and kidnapping).

2. Collect a corpus of non-malicious behaviors of the same entity to add to the overall corpus.

3. Using the manual antecedent identification method or the AuBA ThemeMate tool, identify common antecedent candidates across all corpus documents for those behaviors considered to be successful for that entity.

4. Create a data array with antecedent candidates as columns and examples of separate behaviors as rows and populate the array with presence (1) or absence of a candidate (0) for each example for each cell in the array.

5. Reduce the number of antecedent candidates to actual antecedents by selecting only those antecedent candidate themes that correlate with outcome classes that have been added and merge candidates that correlate at 0.90 or higher together.

6. Add output columns (the outcomes to predict, such as threat (1) and no threat (0)).

7. Submit to pattern classification (AutoAnalyzer recommended because of complexities).

8. Use the trained classifier to process current presence or absence of all antecedents occurring "today" that survive the reduction and merge process. The outcome class that achieves the highest score (threat/no threat) is the prediction.

As you can see by reviewing these basic steps in the predictive process, antecedents and consequences considerations, particularly antecedents, are a component throughout the entire process. Context for past behaviors are essentially antecedent and consequence events and situations. As the old saying goes, *When in Rome, do what the Romans do.* This saying, which has been around so long we consider it cliché, reveals the basic theme that our behavior is a function of the environment in which we find ourselves. In my words, our behavior at any one time is a function of the environmental context. We need only to observe others and ourselves when in an elevator versus a party. Our behavior suddenly changes from all standing forward and not communicating to all facing one another in animation that is often excessive. For this reason, knowing the context can allow us to predict behavior within the context.

Who among us can't predict the behavior of individuals the next time we go on an elevator or the next time we attend a party? Even then, there are divisions. For example, if we predict behavior within the context of a party at work versus a party on a Saturday night at a friend's home, would we expect differences?

NOTE In actual practice, there are many nuances not covered under the scope of this book simply because of space. For example, the back propagation neural network (BPN) has many settings, such as the type of learning rule, and technical features, such as transfer function momentum and convergence criteria. There are also training criteria, such as when to stop the classifier from learning, and the specific validation methods to use. Chapter 20 and the accompanying DVD provide many of the nuances required for accurate prediction of future behavior.

Analyzing the Individual and the Group

When we have made the decision or we have been tasked to develop a predictive model for either an individual or a group, we need to consider several key points. For most points, the overall conceptual steps remain the same, but there are minor differences, more nuances than major dissimilarities, between group and individual modeling.

> **WARNING** I have discovered over many years of predictive modeling that shortcuts, even minor ones, can decrease the amount of accuracy achieved by the final model. Usually the types of models constructed are for a worthy cause or are significant for any number of reasons. Therefore, we want every percentage point of accuracy that we can obtain. To achieve the highest accuracy possible, then full attention must be made to every detail of the modeling process. No step can be missed, and no step can be shortened. Altering sound methodology will always have an effect on the functioning of the completed model.

How are individuals and groups different? As a general rule, a group's behavior tends to have more variety, behaviors occur under very different conditions, and behavior is more stable than the behavior of an individual. Because of peer pressure, group guidelines, group culture, and ongoing pressure to look like and act like the group, group members face many more constraints than the individual acting alone. For example, such groups as al-Qaeda, Hezbollah, and Hamas all exhibit a variety of types of terrorist activities under a wide variety of conditions. In marked contrast, Ted Kaczynski, the Unabomber, or Ted Bundy, one of our country's worst serial killers, exhibited very similar behaviors repeatedly across incidents. Each bombing by Kaczynski and each murder of yet another attractive, young woman by Bundy was more noted by their similarities over time than by their differences. For this reason, historical examples may appear to be highly similar for the individual and more different for examples of malicious group behaviors.

How does knowing the subtle differences between predictive modeling of individuals and groups help us? We know that it is always important to gather documents on a number of multiple malicious behaviors, but with groups who exhibit a wide variety of type of behaviors, we need to ensure that we have multiple examples for each types of behavior (for example, suicide bombing, vehicle-borne IED, IED planted in roads, assault, kidnapping, and so on). If we are modeling a serial murderer, then the multiple murders are likely to have many similarities. We know that each type of behavior has its own set of antecedents. Therefore, a wide variety of behavior requires many documents for each type of behavior to ensure that the descriptions include sufficient preceding antecedent candidates so we can identify true predictive antecedents for each type of malicious behavior.

We want to ensure to have multiple documents for each incident, as well. Multiple documents per incident allow us to corroborate information. For example, if we collected six different articles describing the exact same bombing and five indicated the incident occurred at 2:00 in the afternoon on a specific date and one indicated the incident occurred at 3:00 in the afternoon, then we can discount the 3:00 time. If that article had been the only one used for modeling, an incorrect time would have been included in the modeling process.

Therefore, adequate modeling requires many past examples of malicious behavior and many examples from different sources of each incident. In my experience, it has not been unusual to include 50 to 100 different incidents with five to six articles from different sources for each incident. This equates to a total corpus size of 250 to 500 articles just for the descriptions of malicious behavior. Of course, as mentioned in several places in this book, we also want examples of non-malicious behavior from the individual or group. This helps the process of identifying antecedents that tend to predict malicious from non-malicious behavior.

As you might infer from the preceding paragraphs, prior to actual analysis steps, you need to engage in two key steps:

1. Gathering background information
2. Searching and selecting documents for the corpus to be used

These steps are discussed next. Once these considerations have been made for either the individual or the group to be modeled, then actual analysis may begin.

Gathering Background Information

When we conduct predictive AuBA modeling of an entity (that is, an individual or a group), gaining a basic understanding of who the adversary is and how the adversary has operated in the past is very important. We need to do this before searching for and selecting textual articles for analysis. For example, if the entity is a terrorist group, then many terrorist groups actually publish what they wish the world to know about them, as well as their goals and their objectives. In short, they are going to tell us the general guidelines of how they will operate in the future and who they are going to target. These desired communications with the outside world are very important because they divulge the motivation that drives the group. A classic example is the past videotapes provided by Osama bin Laden and the corresponding translated transcripts. These communiques focused on the basic anti-Israeli, pro-Palestinian themes and the continued anti-American thrust of expelling Americans and their occupation from foreign lands. They provide key clues to identifying such al-Qaeda antecedents as perceived American occupation of foreign lands.

I am often asked, "If adversaries know how this works, can't they just provide false information?" The answer is, yes they could. But then they would not be providing the message they want to communicate. However, to guard against deliberate misinformation (disinformation), we collect multiple examples of text describing a single behavioral event from many different sources. For example, a significant event is often covered by multiple journalists. Of course, journalists are trained to provide the who, what, where, when, and why of an event. Therefore, multiple reports of the same event provide sets of facts that may be compared. When processed with ThemeMate, or if analyzed manually, the facts that agree are used. In addition, AuBA works by gathering information about the context that was present before and during the behavior. Because of the process of identifying antecedent candidates that occur across multiple examples of behavior and the reduction to a final set of antecedents that are strongly associated with the behavior, it is difficult to "guess" which antecedents are used in a predictive analysis.

Last, if the documents processed are communiqués or other forms of self-generated documents and designed to provide specific doctrine, then care should be taken to focus on stated likes and dislikes as potential antecedents. Individuals occasionally provide key documents that allow us to analyze goals and objectives that can translate to targeting antecedents. As a classic example, Ted Kaczynski, the Unabomber, insisted that his lengthy 35,000 word manifesto be published. This document was so important to him that he promised to halt all bombing on a permanent basis if it were published by a major entity. Regardless of the literary value, significance from a philosophical perspective, typos, inconsistencies, or errors, the modeler is simply concerned with extracting the motivation that drives the entity. Not all adversaries prepare documents to be released that describe why the entity was formed and operates, but many do. These are invaluable. Kaczynski's focus on pushing for revolution against the technological-industrial complex in his manifesto mirrored his focus on targeting those associated with technology with his bombs.

Although self-generated documents would appear to be very important, they are important only if antecedents of past events can be extracted. Long diatribes describing the adversary's biases may actually be misleading.

AuBA is basically controlled by the information used to form the basic corpus from which all analysis is derived. In the absence of a corpus in those situations where we use AuBASME, then the subject matter experts (SMEs) selected take on prime importance. Just as important as selecting the proper background documents that provide a glimpse of the target's motivation, the selection of true SMEs is imperative. In identifying SMEs, one piece of solid advice is to seek out SMEs who are considered experts by other knowledgeable individuals, as opposed to a self-described expert in the domain. Once the SME is identified, begin with an interview to simply assess background of the target. Let the SME answer why the group exists, why the group was formed, if there are designated targets, and what the primary goals and objectives of the target are.

The background gathered before any aspect of analysis is important for many reasons. First, excellent predictive results can lose all credibility when results are presented that include basic errors when describing the perpetrator. Such errors can result in total loss of credibility, negating all subsequent results presented. There is no substitute for the modeler or analyst knowing the domain and target under study. This does not mean that predictive analysis comes from this basic understanding, but the accurate background is essential just to have credible interchanges with others on the topic at hand.

Selecting Documents for the Basic Corpus

Perhaps the primary reason for conducting background work on the target of the analysis to occur is to guide how one searches for and selects documents describing past behaviors. It is exceedingly rare to have documents that describe all significant past events of a group, unless the group is new or emerging. Therefore, we rely on samples. Sampling can be a critical component of the document selection process. To construct the basic corpus of documents, we want to select a sample that contains full descriptions of past incidents. What is a full description? Given that we *must* extract antecedents and consequences from context, and not just a description of the behavior, a full description of a past event will include answers to the typical journalistic questions of who, what, where, when, and how. I continually encounter articles that simply describe the past behavior. Ironically, these are not as useful as typical open source news articles prepared by writers who capture as much of the context surrounding the behavior as possible.

Once we have determined the types of documents we require to conduct a predictive analysis, we must then identify the individual articles, search for articles describing the examples, and collect the articles as a single corpus. In this section, I described the importance of studying self-generated documents, videos, communiquees, and statements of grievances generated by an adversarial group or from a perpetrator. These documents are important because they can help provide focus about what antecedents may be relevant versus other antecedents that may not be as relevant.

If there is a match between an extracted antecedent, or set of antecedents, and a statement generated by a group describing why it exists, then this set of antecedent conditions should be viewed as particularly relevant. As an example, statements generated from al-Qaeda over time have consistently included reference to the United States occupying foreign lands. If antecedents extracted from past examples of al-Qaeda adversarial behavior include movement into foreign land or increases in what would be perceived as increases in occupation, then we have a match among antecedents in those instances in which we support allies with troops on the ground.

However, in many cases, we do not have internally generated declarations of purpose. We then must rely on past textual descriptions we use for predictive modeling to also be used as a corpus from which we can infer internal drives, motivation, and general focus.

Determining Inner Dynamics from External Data

Inferring inner dynamics of an adversary from external observations of examples of past behaviors and the contexts associated with these examples is a complex undertaking. This topic could very well be a single focus of a book in its own right. It is a very important topic because an accurate description of the drives and motivation of an adversary, whether that adversary is an individual or a group, enables a better synthesis of why antecedents and consequences of past behavior are actually associated with that behavior.

Rather than attempting to provide a description of such a complex topic within one small section of one book, I believe it may be best to provide a few examples to show the logical relevancy that ties knowledge on internal drives with external and observable antecedents, behaviors, and consequences. I have described two individuals in this chapter who had exhibited serious levels of malicious behavior. Both individuals engaged in behaviors that killed fellow citizens. In the case of Ted Kaczynski, the Unabomber, he insisted on and had published his lengthy manifesto. This document provides exceptional insight into the inner drives and motivation of this person. There are definite matches in the statements made and the targeting observed. On the other hand, Ted Bundy, one of our worst and most brutal serial killers, did not generate any type of similar document to give clues about the inner dynamics that drove him.

In the case of Bundy, an analysis of the past murders provides clues to the inner workings of Bundy as an individual. All of the murdered victims were young and female, were described as attractive, parted their hair down the middle, had long hair, were brutally killed typically with blunt force, were sexually abused at death, and were sexually abused after death. Simultaneously with the murders across time, Bundy worked diligently to appear to have a normal life. He was social, liked by women, went to law school, and had fans, including wedding proposals while on death row from the very type of individuals he actually had murdered in the past. Extracting such characteristics allows us to piece together an internal dynamic of a person obsessed with females who fit a specific profile and a seemingly uncontrollable desire to engage in acts that would end their lives in a violent and sexual manner. The internal obsession would match with external antecedents when an unfortunate attractive female with long hair, parted down the middle, and of the right age would come into his path within an environment where he could gain control.

From the perspective of the unfortunate victims, they were simply at the wrong place at the wrong time. From the perspective of Bundy and his obsessions, they happened to be in the right place at the right time, and the murder pattern would be initiated yet once again. Understanding Bundy's apparent internal obsession and combining it with antecedents to his murders, it was clear that college campuses would fulfill a location in which the probability of his finding a young female who would fit his "profile" would be highest. This would be the pool from which he could select. His fascination and association with colleges and college campuses were an apparent fusion of potential pool, antecedents, successful consequences, and misdirected motivation and violent sexual obsessions.

Analyzing Bundy's past murders is obviously easier because of the after-the-fact availability of the many articles written about the murders and the contexts under which each murder occurred. But, what if the target of the analysis is an apparent serial murderer who has not been apprehended and there is no real movement toward identification? This is why inferring internal states from observable behaviors and the contexts under which they occur can be so important. By identifying antecedent candidates and apparent successful consequences of past acts from the perpetrator's perspective, we can begin to develop a picture of internal states that may be driving the person. These internal states combined with apparent environmental antecedents can assist in providing insight into who the person might be, how targeting occurs, and high probability targets in the future.

Anticipating Adversarial Individual and Group Transition

The process of analyzing malicious behavior of organized groups and individuals is usually focused on what the adversary will do next. This objective really needs no elaboration. From a security perspective, the primary method by which we can move from a primarily reactive approach to security to a true predictive approach is to accurately anticipate what the adversary will do next. To the extent that we can also predict elements of the context within which a behavioral event will occur, so much the better. However, because AuBA is based on identifying cultural consideration, contextual elements, and precursor antecedents, there are other significant types of analyses that can occur. For example, being able to determine that an adversary is either in transition or just ready to start a transition can be extremely valuable from a security perspective. Knowing how an adversary can change and when allows us to better prepare proactively, instead of waiting until after the malicious behavior has occurred.

Because of the methodology underlying AuBA, we process accounts of past attacks by identifying antecedents associated with past attacks that led to success from the adversary's perspective. If we order past attacks in sequence and analyze the antecedents that have been associated with the past behaviors, we will basically observe that antecedents are stable over time. Furthermore, with a stable adversary, the behaviors will be highly similar across this sequential time-based analysis.

To determine if a shift is occurring, the corpus can be modified by processing only the most recent malicious behaviors for the current year as compared to the malicious behaviors that occurred in the previous year. For example, if we analyze the behaviors of the past year and compare them to the behaviors of two years ago, we can determine if antecedents associated with behaviors occurring in the past year are the same as the antecedents associated with behaviors of two years ago. If the adversary is stable, then AuBA-determined antecedent-behavior associations will be the same for the past two one-year periods. If we observe changes in the antecedent-behavior associations in the most recent year as compared to the one-year period beginning two years ago, then a shift is occurring.

This approach is more powerful than just noting that the malicious behaviors are changing. Noting different antecedent-behavior associations across the two-year period provides a context for the change. We can say with some confidence that behaviors are changing and the change can be tracked to how the adversary is responding to different environmental situations and events.

What to Do When Data Is Missing

It is not unusual during the modeling process to discover that some data may be missing, or at a minimum sparse in one area or another. For example, once we begin the antecedent candidate theme extraction across all documents and construct the data array with threaded outcome classes (for example, in a cyber application on phishing: No Phishing, Spear Phishing, Other Phishing) we might find that spear phishing has very few themes associated with it. We could, of course, convert the model to Phishing versus No Phishing. However, if one of our objectives is to differentiate other forms of phishing from spear phishing, we are going to have to take additional steps to ensure that the spear phishing class is represented.

Basically, to address this issue we have to enrich the corpus with additional spear phishing examples. We can:

- Search for additional examples, add to the corpus, and redo the antecedent candidate theme extraction
- Use ThemeMate to help us find additional relevant articles to add to the corpus
- Augment the data array with SME knowledge using the AuBASME methodology

First, it is relatively easy to return to our search engine of choice and identify additional relevant articles, in this case on spear phishing. If we had basically found all that appeared to be relevant using the same search engine the first time, we would try a new search engine. Regardless of the search engine used, all of the relevant material on the Internet on a specific topic cannot be identified with a single search engine. I will almost always repeat the same search with different search engines initially just to determine if a few additional articles may be identified for the initial corpus (and to ensure we are not searching again later). Once the additional articles are identified, we simply add them to the corpus and begin again. However, this time, we are likely to not have sparseness as related to the Spear Phishing class of behavior.

If we are using ThemeMate to automate the theme extraction process, ThemeMate forms what we call *theme components* for each theme that was extracted. For example, let's say that Theme 22 (T22) was related to spear phishing. Because we need additional spear phishing examples, we can go to the Theme Components section and click on T22, and ThemeMate automatically conducts a web search using these word components associated with spear phishing. The result is a return of highly similar articles. We add these articles to the corpus and repeat the theme extraction process. However, we could have conducted this step as part of building the initial corpus and have avoided this particular fix.

A third way to add to the corpus, particularly when it appears that additional information simply is not available, is to augment the data array with additional examples and themes identified through the AuBASME process. We can actually merge the data array constructed with the corpus of past events and the data array constructed via AuBASME. Once we have added our additional information, then we can move to constructing our final model.

AuBASME: A New Method for Using Subject Matter Expertise

AuBASME is a combination of AuBA predictive technology and the augmentation of the predictive process by subject matter expertise (SME) when data are sparse or missing or simply when there are no historical examples from which data can be extracted. The use of subject matter expertise is not new. Akin to signature detection, typical extraction of knowledge from a SME or a panel of SMEs has usually consisted of interviewing experts to see either how they view the world or if they can describe specific steps they engage in to make decisions. Once interviews occur, the extracted knowledge is placed in a *knowledge base*, and the usual if-then rules are generated to emulate all the facets of decision-making that the SME(s) goes through to process incoming information to derive specific decisions or courses of action. If done properly, this rule-based approach can be useful in that it can react faster than the experts, who might not be available in a crisis, and can be duplicated in multiple sites, which is not possible for unique experts. This approach is known as an *expert rule-based system* and is considered to be a form of artificial intelligence. However, it is important to realize that the AuBASME methodology is very different.

I was involved in a specific application in the past in which the task was to emulate how a very unique person in the government made decisions. She was ready for retirement and much would be lost with her absence. After a year of interviews and careful rule generation, my colleagues and I generated over 13,000 rules to capture her decision-making process. It worked — sort of. There were problems. Rule-generation (signature detection) was very rigid. If-then rules of classic artificial intelligence did capture very clear conditions. However, human decision-making also includes *educational guesses*, and rule-generation fails miserably at educational guesses.

It was at that time that I decided that if we are to capture the knowledge and true decision-making of experts, then a different paradigm would be required. Over the years in developing AuBA, it was clear that the neural network–based pattern classifiers were making judgments. Even when all antecedents were selected from past examples of behaviors, it was clear that when unusual combinations of antecedents were presented to the trained classifiers, these classifiers were *forced* to provide a prediction. In a number of detailed validation studies across asymmetric warfare and cyber applications, it was clear that the AuBA classifiers made educated guesses and when doing so were more often right than not even though the actual examples were not in the training set during pattern classification.

This work led to the development of AuBASME, a true hybrid between AuBA and the capture of expert knowledge. The process is very different from typical artificial intelligence (AI) generation of knowledge bases that are processed with rigid if-then rules. Instead, expert knowledge is captured much like we capture past examples of adversarial behavior to submit to the AuBA methodology to result in human behavior predictive models. In short, AuBASME is a drastic departure from typical AI approaches to decision-making.

AuBASME and Prediction

Instead of interviewing a SME or panel of SMEs to determine how they make decisions, AuBASME is a methodology that requires SMEs to generate highly likely scenarios that could happen in areas for which there are no data. These highly probable scenarios are described as behaviors as if they had actually happened. Then, once these behaviors have been identified, the SME is taken through an exercise to identify the likely antecedents that would have been associated with these behaviors (even if they had never occurred). Surprisingly, if real SMEs are identified, this is not as difficult as I anticipated. In a similar manner, likely desired consequences for the perpetrator are not difficult to generate.

The manual-based AuBA process is based on completing the same process duplicated in the automated components of AuBA. The sequential steps are a true fusion of the behavioral and computer sciences. AuBASME is a true hybrid between the manual approach to AuBA and the fully automated versions. Figure 18-1 depicts the basic sequential steps used when automated components are broken out to its basic clinical steps. Typical AuBA using text-based accounts of past behavior found in news articles, reports, and so forth is based on constructing a corpus of articles that contain many examples of the behavior to be modeled. Because the AuBASME process is used when there are no data, missing data, or very sparse data, there are no textual accounts of past behavior. In essence, the SME panel becomes the generator of scenarios that are highly likely to occur in the future. However, the AuBASME process forces the SMEs to generate each scenario in much the same form as a news article. That is, each scenario must include answers to the typical who, what, when, where, and what of the scenario. This is in marked contrast to the typical AI process to construct expert knowledge bases to then fuel if-then-type captures of SME knowledge. In AuBASME the focus is on the scenarios.

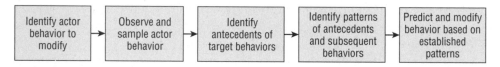

Figure 18-1: The sequence of steps followed in AuBA whether fully automated or partially automated.

If more than one SME is used (and there should always be more than one, if possible), there can occasionally be disagreement. It is important to use the Delphi method in these cases. The Delphi method requires experts to converge on any answer given to ensure that agreement is present for every decision as to whether antecedents are present or not. In our modified approach, I have had experts answer the same question independently. We then compare answers and require convergence to a common answer. I refer readers to an excellent article on the Delphi method: *The Delphi Method: Techniques and Applications*, edited by Harold A. Linstone and Murray Turoff, 2002, `http://is.njit.edu/pubs/delphibook/delphibook.pdf`.

Because the scenarios are generated and treated like a media report, there are two basic ways to proceed.

- The first is for the SMEs to generate a report much like a journalist would of each scenario in text to construct the SME corpus.

- The second way is for the modeler to focus on the elaboration of descriptions of any antecedents and consequences generated by the SMEs for each scenario.

Both appear to work equally well. In the former approach, the text-based corpus is submitted to ThemeMate for typical extraction and automated creation of the data array to be used for the following predictive method. In the latter approach, the modeler goes straight from antecedent and consequence elaborations to construction of the data array and then populates the array.

I have found that top SMEs tend to think in terms of what is likely to happen next and constantly observe events to validate what they had envisioned. Although this is a private process that is not usually shared with others, it is a process that improves with time. It does allow for private Monday morning quarterbacking, with adjustments over time. If totally honest, most will admit that the track record is not that great, which keeps SMEs humble. Humans just are not good at predicting future events and behavior. However, SMEs contain the knowledge to do so; it just needs to be processed by a methodology such as AuBASME so that validated predictive components can be added. The marriage of SME knowledge and AuBA predictive capability allows us to move into areas where there simply have not been past events to analyze. These can include chemical, biological, radiological, and nuclear scenarios; threat to water supply; and power grid threat, among others.

The AuBASME methodology moves us away from conjecture and speculation to actual processing of highly likely antecedents that would be associated with events should they occur and likely consequences that would follow that would reinforce the malicious acts. How often have we seen an expert on CNN or FOX news interviewed and project what will happen? I actually follow some of these to see what happens. Many times the expert is wrong. In fact, the true expert on newscasts learns quickly to frame such projections in such general terms that he or she covers both sides of a projection so that there will be some element of being correct regardless of what happens. However, this *art* is difficult to master. If one is too careful to frame the report in such a way that there will always be some elements of correctness, then the statement itself becomes meaningless and the attempt transparent. In many political debates we can see this effort as a pure art form with the question in many cases simply not being answered.

Achieving accurate prediction of behavior when there have not been past examples of the behavior to analyze depends on adding analytical methodology to SME knowledge. There are many reasons why humans do not predict well. The issues of cognitive bias, pressure to form one projection or another is always present, and faulty logic all interplay to make us notoriously bad at anticipating future events accurately. However, in my opinion, the primary reason is that there has not been an attempt to identify likely antecedents to which an adversary would respond and the consequences that would fuel a future act. For this reason, when we start with the raw ingredients, SME knowledge, and add AuBASME methodology to generate highly likely behavioral scenarios and the highly likely associated antecedents and consequences, we have moved from speculation to analytical anticipation of future events. As events do unfold, we actually have a model that can be tweaked to become even more accurate in the future. We can add or subtract actual antecedents, and we can better determine the actual consequences that may have entered into the adversaries' reasons for committing a malicious act.

Analyzing Threat on a Global Level

I have emphasized that although AuBA pays homage to applied behavior analysis, we have made many extensions to applied behavior analysis and invention of technology to achieve accurate prediction on a global basis in AuBA. Perhaps the number one extension beyond the obvious automation and move to accurate prediction is the realization that dealing with potential antecedents on a global basis is very different from identifying *local* antecedents. Applied behavior analysis, for the most part, occurs within environments such as classrooms, mental health treatment facilities, facilities for the developmentally disabled, and prisons, and if we stretch applied behavior analysis to include behavioral psychology treatments such as behavior therapy, cognitive behavior therapy, and so on, then we can include private treatment settings, the home, and a variety of other constrained environments. Furthermore, there have been many very creative applications as applied to speeding, littering, and other socially related problem areas. However, even in these latter less-constrained environments, antecedents associated with the actual behaviors under study are still very local (within eyesight, hearing range, and so on).

The advantage of applying the antecedent-behavior-consequence sequence and components for each example of behavior to be studied is that context is captured and becomes the centerpiece of predictive capability. Behavior simply does not just occur on its own; all behavior is generated by humans within a context. This context is external to us and provides the reason for behavior to be emitted. The context can be separated into preceding events and situations (antecedents) and events and situations that follow the behavior (consequences). When we take AuBA and move to a global stage and we select behaviors to add to our corpus for analysis, we find we have a host of antecedent candidates that have occurred prior to the actual behavior, far more than occur in the more local and constrained instances applied behavior analysis generally deals with. This is one of the most daunting considerations when identifying antecedents that appear to have an influence on the actual occurrence of the malicious behavior under study.

First, we must consider as candidates those events and situations that appear to be logically related to the behavior and, most important, related to the motivation and inner principles of the adversary that drive the occurrence of the behavior in the presence of antecedent conditions. I have found three primary ways to achieve relevancy among antecedent conditions and following behavior: frequency, judgment, and correlations.

- The first and most important is **frequency**. If an antecedent is truly associated with a specific type of behavior, then that antecedent will occur repeatedly across different instances of the behavior occurring. If we are analyzing different types of cyber attack, for example, then there should be common antecedents associated with phishing versus denial of service versus no attack. If the identical events and situations occurred across all three outcomes to be predicted, then they are not of value. Antecedents that set the stage for an adversary to act in a specific manner would be associated primarily with one type of behavior to the exclusion of other behaviors.

  In AuBA, antecedent candidates are the events and situations that occur repeatedly across examples of specific types of behavior. Obviously, antecedent candidates that do not repeat are excluded during this process, leaving only antecedent candidates that are associated by relevancy.

- The second method is **judgment**. Although we can use the fully automated version of AuBA methodology, we still want to add review at the antecedent candidate selection stage. For example, if ThemeMate has been used to process the corpus of documents we have selected, a data array will be one of the products of the process. This array will have the extracted candidates as columns and the identification of each example of behavior used as rows. However, the extracted list of themes should be reviewed to ensure that themes extracted by frequency do not include themes that hit the frequency criterion but do not appear to be relevant. As an example, if the documents we selected for analysis just happen to mention SANS (a network security institute) and CERT (Community Emergency Response Team) in the body of the articles and two themes surfaced on the basis of frequency with one SANS-based and one CERT-based, we would want to excise these columns from the data array based on non-relevancy.

- As a third method, we submit the entire array to **correlations**, meaning that each extracted theme is correlated with every other theme. This sounds like a massive task, but if the array is opened in Excel and the correlation feature of the Analysis ToolPak is used, the entire correlation process takes less than one minute to set up and run (see the walkthrough on the accompanying DVD to see how to do this). Figure 18-2 shows a small correlation matrix generated by Excel from a ThemeMate generated data array. Those themes that correlate at a minimum of 0.9 or 0.95 (to be more conservative) should be merged. From a predictive perspective, such a high correlation between any two themes indicates that both are providing essentially the same information. Merging is accomplished by simple vector addition. The high correlation occurs because the 1s and 0s in the columns are highly similar. If they were identical, then the correlation would be 1.00, which is what the correlation matrix shows when a theme is correlated with itself.

When we apply all three approaches, we will have a final data array that is ready for the pattern classification stage. The only step left is to remove themes that do not correlate well with outcome classes, which is described in the accompanying DVD. From the completed data array stage on, the process is identical whether we are completing a clinical case within a constrained environment or a complex cyber or terrorist attack on a global stage. It is in the early stage of antecedent candidate extraction and creation of the final data array that the global nature of our model has the most impact.

	t1	t2	t3	t4	t5	t6	t7	t8	t9	t10	t11	t12
t1	1.00											
t2	-0.22	1.00										
t3	-0.05	-0.52	1.00									
t4	0.12	0.58	-0.90	1.00								
t5	-0.16	-0.16	0.31	-0.28	1.00							
t6	0.33	-0.29	0.27	-0.51	-0.10	1.00						
t7	-0.15	0.91	-0.46	0.51	-0.14	-0.26	1.00					
t8	0.94	-0.18	-0.18	0.20	-0.06	-0.10	-0.14	1.00				
t9	-0.23	0.14	0.26									
t10	-0.35	-0.07							1.00			
t11	-0.16	0.35	-0.18						-0.12	1.00		
t12	-0.23	0.14	-0.26	0.29	-0.08	-0.15	0.18	-0.08	-0.12	-0.18	0.69	1.00

(Annotations within figure: "Perfect correlations of 1.00 for a theme when correlated with itself"; "Correlations this high between two themes indicate they should be merged")

Figure 18-2: An Excel-generated correlation matrix of data within a ThemeMate-generated data array

Incorporating Multiple Models

Unless the predictive model is focused on a simple yes/no prediction of an adversary's behavior such as attack/no attack or threat/no threat, then it will be necessary to have multiple models operating in concert to provide an overall predictive assessment. During the early development of the AuBA methodology it was very clear that prediction of complex individual or group malicious behavior would have to be based on dividing a predictive problem into component behaviors. For example, in areas such as the prediction of asymmetric threat as with terrorism, predicting a terrorist event could include the following questions:

- Will the adversary attack or not attack?
- If attack, where would the general location of the attack occur?
- If attack, what would be the general modus operandi?
- If attack, would the target be civilian or military?

These are complex questions that cannot be answered with one single model. Each question represents different aspects of behavior of an adversary requiring overlapping and different antecedent conditions and situations serving to set the stage for different combinations of these components to occur. For example, we could have: Attack, within Jerusalem, suicide bombing as a general approach, and a military target. On the other hand, we could have: No attack predicted, or a variation such as Attack, not within Jerusalem proper, roadside assault, and civilian target. It is clear that as the complexity of the problem grows, prediction of terrorist behavior takes a complexity of modeling, as well.

It was also clear that a specific type of prediction, such as military or civilian target, would lead to the identification of antecedents that were unique to one class or the other. In this way, through pattern classification, the identification of antecedents in the current environment would more likely be associated with either a military or a civilian target, given that it had been determined that there would be an attack. Therefore, AuBA also consists of how we break up a complex predictive problem into component parts. Each part receives its own predictive model. When used, all models are run simultaneously by inputting which antecedents are present versus which antecedents are not present.

We communicate the presence and absence of the set antecedents by means of a simple vector of 1s and 0s. This vector is created behind the scenes from a user interface that lists each antecedent with its own checkbox. By clicking on all the boxes that correspond to the antecedents that are present at any given time and then clicking on Run, a vector is created of 1s and 0s. If there are 20 indicators on the user interface and the user clicks on antecedents 3, 10, and 16, a vector is created and forwarded to the trained neural network as input. This vector will be all 0s, except for 3, 10, and 16, which will be 1s. After due consideration has been given to all antecedents, the vector of 1s and 0s is forwarded to the pattern classification engines with each engine using whatever antecedents have been designated for each engine. These 1s and 0s are then processed by the trained and validated predictive engines and each engine provides its output. The overall assessment of what is likely to happen is a product of all outputs combined to form an overall assessment of likely occurrences for the next event, should one be predicted to occur.

There can be many advantages to dividing a complex set of predictions into individual predictive engines, the results of which are combined to make the ultimate prediction. For example, over time it may become apparent that targeting is changing for the group that has been modeled. Now, instead of civilian or military as targets, a third category has surfaced that includes local government representatives. Therefore, by including more recent articles into the corpus used to develop the model, we can retrain the targeting predictive engine, retest and revalidate the model, and then add it to the application as a replacement for the former targeting predictive engine.

THERE IS ALWAYS A NEED FOR HUMAN EXPERTISE

We can't and don't want to automate everything. To date, the division of a complex predictive problem into its component parts still requires domain expertise. We still need human experts to define the parts of the problem. However, I highly recommend that domain expertise be present in some form anyway if serious predictive problems posed by known adversaries are going to be tackled. Because of the importance of behavior models, humans should supervise the process to ensure that all works well.

Interpreting Results of Multiple Models

AuBA, as shown in previous chapters, includes a reporting function once the application has been developed. Tremendous care must be taken when we get to the application stage to ensure that the interface to the application and the reporting be what is beneficial to the customer. One of the basic mistakes made by modelers is that they think they know what is best for the customer. Care should be taken to determine the type of user-friendly interface the customer would like to have, and even more care taken in designing an interpretive output of all models when combined.

Multiple predictive models are combined within AuBA to present the total prediction of the next event. Interpretive reporting is used in much the same way as automated interpretation is used in computerized psychological assessment. That is, the end result of a predictive model is how results will be represented to users. Certainly, a well-prepared interpretation of results is better than simply providing the output of multiple predictive engines. Typical AuBA applications present several views of results. Textual descriptions provide an interpretation with text being based on different output values. Graphical representation is provided to give a view about how different output values compare to one another. The textual description of the details of the next behavior is also important.

CheckMate is a prime example of multiple predictive assessment engines working simultaneously with fused results as opposed to individual results being presented. CheckMate, a network tool to detect external threat to a network, converts samples of network activity by an IP/user into the degree of expertise (E) and deception (D) present in each sample. Assessments are made by multiple predictive engines with results fused into one E and D assessment. The application provides multiple views that are important for different purposes. First, as shown earlier in this book (Figure 13-3 if you want to go back to take a look), the individual E/D panel that may be reviewed in real time depicts the E/D values plotted on a 2D panel. The viewer can watch the ongoing assessment that betrays threat if E/D exceeds critical region threshold. This is significant if one wishes to track 1 of 1,000 individuals being assessed every 1/10 of a second.

Another entirely different view is provided that displays all individuals within the network at one time. This view, as shown in Figure 18-3, allows monitoring of all individuals at any one time. The panel displays E/D ratings by IP. One can sort the IPs by the highest E/D scores. The composite score is an algorithm that converts the E and D plot seen in the individual panel to a single score. The higher the score, the more threatening the behavior being predicted.

It is possible to depict results in many different ways. The key is to ensure maximum utility and to describe as much information as possible with the visual aids that computing allows.

Figure 18-3: The CheckMate monitoring screen: Multiple IPs/users can be monitored simultaneously for the combined E/D assessments.

Anticipating Events

The primary purpose of AuBA predictive engines is to predict future behavior. However, because AuBA predicts future behavior based on predicting the future context that results in specific types of behavior, the projection of context is very useful. This allows us to predict location, timing variables, group approach, type of event, and basically any contextual elements required for an application. To build in a new contextual element, we simply need to repeat the modeling process to identify the antecedents associated with that aspect of the behavior and then add it to the application as an additional predictive engine. Once it is integrated into the application, we then modify the reporting structure to include the new contextual element.

The overall result of all predictive engines working together allows us to truly anticipate future events. The accurate anticipation of events allows us to think more proactively about courses of action that can take place once accurate anticipation is presented. This allows for the capability to have a course of action in place prior to the malicious behavior actually occurring. Then, when the behavior occurs, there is an immediate protective response. CheckMate, for example, has the capability to sever the connection of an IP to the network. If CheckMate determines that E/D activity is exceeding the critical region, and the blocking option is on, then the IP connection will be severed with the idea being that actual damage that would be caused by an imminent attack is mitigated or prevented. Thus, accurate anticipation allows for a shift in security practice.

Rather than preparing signatures to catch a known attack, CheckMate can *catch* a new attack and predict the threat associated with that new activity and react before the attack is fully manifested in the network. Accurate anticipation of future malicious behavior as events is key to moving from a reactive to a more proactive security posture.

Implications for Security

The role of security is to protect and to prevent. Currently, the security approach we are taking can be typified by a house burglar alarm. We know by experience that a break-in is likely to happen through a door or window. Therefore, if we alarm all doors and windows and add motion detectors and perhaps glass breakage detectors within the house, it is likely that we can alert the occupants of the house, as well as the police, if an intruder has gained access. The key here is that the security system is set to detect once the intrusion has occurred. The only concept of prevention here is that a potential intruder may determine that a security system is present and move on to another location. This does provide a level of protection, even if alerts occur once an intruder is within the actual location.

To become truly proactive and predictive, security would change from detection once an intruder is present to alerting when it appears that an intrusion is imminent. The alert would occur prior to the actual breakage of the glass or prior to an intruder forcing open a locked door. To initiate this feature with our home security alarm example, moving to a more proactive stance could mean the addition of a perimeter security detector that sets an alarm off if a potential intruder approaches within 20 feet of a door or window of house at 2:00 A.M. The inherent prediction implied by the detection apparatus is that an individual tripping a perimeter alarm at 2:00 A.M. would intrude if not prevented.

We need to implement predictive security so that alerts can occur earlier than they do now. Whether they apply to network security or security that protects against asymmetric threat such as terrorism, we need true predictive applications that can determine that malicious behavior is imminent, so we can then react prior to the attack actually occurring. This is a dramatic change in security posture. No doubt protective measures that would include predictive features would be quickly adopted. It is our job to demonstrate through AuBA applications that such predictive capability exists is accurate and that we can have confidence in the anticipation of future behavior that is presented.

Advantages of AuBA #18: Automated Characterization of Network Attacks

One of the major problems facing us today with cyber attacks is the continued reliance on signature detection as a primary approach in our cyber arsenal. The problem may be not so much the approach but the time it takes to generate signatures. Although this time can be very fast for simple attacks, it can range up to an inordinately long time if the attack is sophisticated and continues to morph as it occurs, and hackers continue to invade with new attacks altogether. A large part of this time is spent trying to characterize the attack. Once the attack is understood and characterized, then signatures may be written to identify the attack in the future. It has often been said that if the signatures could be written with enough variation, perhaps more new attacks could be detected. This is one of those areas that is far more complex in practice than it sounds. Because the number of attributes of a cyber attack is very large, the number of combinations of these attributes makes writing signatures to cover distinct types of attacks nearly impossible. For example, there are a billion combinations of just 29 attributes. As this number goes up, the total number of combinations grows exponentially (refer to Chapter 11, Figure 11-1).

Basically, the number of possible variations makes writing generalizable signatures very difficult, if not impossible. In our AuBA work we are exploring the possibility of automatically characterizing an attack. Because AuBA emphasizes antecedent conditions associated with malicious human behavior, we believe we can identify the antecedent conditions that lead to classes of attacks, as opposed to very specific attacks. The AuBA behavior-based framework places more emphasis on antecedents associated with imminent attack, not just the attributes of the attack itself. This is a major departure that makes CheckMate and InMate, as well as other AuBA applications described in this book, proactive instead of reactive. Because of the ability to identify antecedent conditions automatically, it is possible for our cyber-based applications to be used to help provide specifics concerning *attack states*. Given that certain situations and events precede attack behavior, antecedents associated with malicious activity can be much broader than specific attacks. This is a distinct advantage. Given the high number of behaviors monitored by CheckMate, attack states may be automatically described by the behavioral attributes associated with any given attack - even new attacks. We already have automated characterization as an approach, and it looks promising.

In Summary

AuBA represents a unique and patented approach to predicting future behavior. The focus may be counterintuitive because the prediction of future behavior is not based on analyses of past behaviors per se. Rather, prediction of future behavior is based on identifying the contextual elements of past behavior that when projected forward will result in specific behavior. Context of past behaviors is captured by identifying preceding antecedent events and situations and consequences that follow past accounts of behavior. The basic premise that has been validated across numerous examples of malicious behavior in very different domains is that behavior occurs in the presence of specific contextual antecedents. If we identify the antecedents associated with malicious behavior, as well as antecedents associated with non-malicious behavior, then we can expect the same behavior to occur in the future when the same or highly similar antecedents occur. This provides us with the capability to predict specific behavior in the future.

The fact that AuBA includes the identification of the context associated with specific types of behavior allows AuBA predictions to be rich with detail. Rather than simply predicting that a bombing or serious cyber attack will occur, we can also anticipate such contextual elements as time, general location, and targeting. Accurate anticipation of malicious behavior as events provides a foundation from which a new security posture can surface. This paradigm shift moves security from a more reactive stance to a more proactive and predictive stance. Increased capability to anticipate threat and the associated contextual details can result in decreased damage from cyber attack and conventional asymmetric warfare such as terrorism and can also result in decreases in loss of proprietary and sensitive data from our networks. The use of accurate predictive methods will allow us to have courses of action in place at the time that predicted malicious behavior is expected to occur.

Part

IV

Predicting Malicious Behavior: Tools and Methods to Support a Paradigm Shift in Security

In This Part

AuBA Future Extensions Today

This book focuses on the tools and methodologies to accurately predict future malicious behavior. This specific chapter focuses on how technology can move into the future and specifically why we need such technology. It is not enough to have technology that can predict future behavior if we don't incorporate such technology into a new security framework. To move from complacency that embraces current reactive security practices to a more proactive approach that anticipates threat will require current security practices to embrace forward-looking technologies that are human behavior–based.

It is not unusual for practice to follow technological developments. This is particularly true for security practices. It is time to at least alert security specialists that we do have technology that can anticipate everything from advanced cyber threat to conventional asymmetric threat such as terrorism. It is time to not rely simply on signature detection or after-the-fact forensics to see what caused the compromise or damage. We need a new proactive security stance that can anticipate malicious behavior accurately and respond by having a course of action in place waiting when the attack comes. This chapter provides the background to suggest that the capability to be proactive is here now.

Predicting New Adversary Threat with Enhanced Accuracy

One of the primary problems with signature detection today is that once signatures have become apparent and we know there is a signature, we just need to work around it through hacker evasion tactics, new attacks, and zero-day attacks. The seriousness of the situation we find ourselves in simply shows current approaches are not sufficient, even if they are part of the solution. If we all admit that signature detection is an important part of the solution, given the onslaught of successful intrusions, inflicted damage, lost identities, lost passwords, and the constant outflow of proprietary and restricted information out of our networks to adversaries, we have to admit it is not sufficient in and of itself to provide adequate protection. This is not opinion; it is simply fact. We are in a cyber war, and we are being schooled. Rhetoric and threats against adversaries are not working. Advanced persistent threat (APT) is there, and it continues as part of a shameless and bold attack against our resources as a country every minute of every day.

How do we get ahead of the tremendous amount of realized threat coming our way on a continual basis? We could stop using networks. Yes, if we want to keep proprietary, sensitive, and classified information safe, keep it off networks. If it's on a network, keep it all on a network with absolutely no outside connection. Why do we persist in making it available? There is no rule that says we must treat sensitive technological information that other countries want to steal in such a way that we make it vulnerable so that we can pass it to and fro as e-mail attachments. Is our love for e-mail and efficient transfer of files across the Internet that great? So first, our new proactive security paradigm could include getting off networks that have public interfaces and connections. In some cases this restriction is important and warranted and should be part of a new security paradigm shift. The concept is very simple — if we can't protect it, stop access.

However, if we want to keep sensitive information with network access because it enhances the way we work, then we must have new network protection and defense technology. Admittedly, signature detection is important but it is not nearly enough. In my opinion, unless we can accurately determine the intent of individuals within our networks, then they shouldn't be in the networks. If we don't know anything other than an IP address, why would we assume all is okay, and why would we wait until we are compromised to determine distrust?

We have technology that determines intent on an ongoing basis. The CheckMate technology constantly determines the underlying themes of intent by assessing the degree of expertise (E) and deception (D) present every 100 milliseconds for all IPs in a network at one time on a 24/7 basis. This technology determines malicious intent even before an attack actually occurs. The AuBA application predicts imminent threat. If threat is detected, we need to block the connection before damage occurs. Current technology in widespread use cannot do this.

We have only four options:

- If we insist on placing sensitive, proprietary, or classified information on networks that we clearly cannot protect, then such information should have much stronger policy restrictions, with some information available on intranets only.

- If specific information would cause serious damage if released, leaked, or stolen, then there should be no avenue from this information to the outside world — the ingenuity of the adversary cannot be underestimated.

- Develop and implement true traceback capability that identifies the perpetrator of an attack.

- Develop a new security policy based on new technology that can determine intent before damage is attempted and implement countermeasures to prevent the attack.

There really are no other options. Perhaps the best approach for the near future is to do all four — that is, provide the funding to support the removal of access to sensitive information on networks that can be compromised until such time as new technology can show total protection, develop new traceback capability, compartmentalize data that could be seriously damaging if available, and implement such proactive and predictive technologies such as AuBA-related applications.

CROSS-REFERENCE Refer back to Chapters 4 and 5 for more detailed coverage of security-related concerns.

Defining Future Signatures: The Department of Pre-crime?

The 2002 movie *Minority Report*, starring Tom Cruise and Colin Farrell and directed by Steven Spielberg, is based on the book of the same title by Phillip K. Dick. The premise of the movie is that police in the mid-21st century arrest criminals before a crime is committed. Determining that the intent to commit a crime is present and the crime is imminent, the police swoop in and arrest the criminal, preventing the actual commission of the crime. It is certainly an intriguing movie for sci-fi fans. Although the methods are movie-made, the concept is admirable. If we are going to be effective in true prevention of adversary attacks, then we basically have to have pre-crime methods that can anticipate an attack before it occurs so that the actual attack or at least the damage from the attack can be prevented.

Given that we develop new technology to protect against the significant losses and damage we are encountering and not just take all access to significant data and information away from a network, it is apparent that we must move to being proactive and being able to anticipate threat of attack before the actual attack occurs. It is that simple. We either develop or implement technology that can predict that an attack is about to occur so that courses of action can prevent damage or loss of information, or we remove access to sensitive information and dictate that access is not available.

A new AuBA area I am investigating is one I call *future signatures*. This new capability extends beyond the current AuBA capability to predict future malicious behavior. How can we have a future signature? Signatures are rules by which we currently describe a known attack in such a way that the signature(s) can detect the same attack if it returns. How do we determine what signatures will be needed in the future before an attack actually occurs?

Based on the dependency we obviously have with signature detection — we persist with it even if it is ineffective — the future needs to include signature detection, albeit much improved. To move from reactive to proactive, a signature would have to be written for a serious attack that has not yet occurred. Then, a collection of serious *future signatures* could be in place waiting for new attacks that have been predefined. This means that AuBA might be used to define highly probable attacks that have not occurred, and then in signature formats those defined attacks could be added to existing signature detection technology that is already in place, saving the costs associated with changing hardware and software. For network protection, AuBA applications such as CheckMate and InMate would still provide added protection against unknown attacks and attack variations that would pass by existing signature detection. This is not science fiction — this is possible, both in network protection and in conventional asymmetric warfare such as terrorism or insurgency, as well as criminal acts.

The advantage is that the approach can move existing signature detection from being only reactive to actually being proactive. So, how do we use AuBA to produce future signatures of serious attacks that have not yet occurred? The process is this (avoiding proprietary detail, of course): We can interrogate our existing CheckMate and InMate assessment engines that can detect unknown attacks to identify highly probable behavior monitor combinations that are associated with critical region threat versus those combinations not associated with threat. This can provide new information and attack configurations that have not occurred, but it could be extremely damaging if and when they do occur. This takes very powerful computer resources. However, the end result is automatically generated rules that define highly probably and serious attacks. These rules are future signatures that can then be loaded into existing signature detection applications, creating proactive signature detection — a new concept.

So, although AuBA predictive applications represent new technology, we can also use the same technology to support and augment existing technology. Therefore, new proactive protection for networks can include CheckMate, InMate, and future signatures. This tri-fold approach is a significant departure from current reactive approaches.

Converting Reactive Technology to Proactive Protection

There are two existing approaches to network protection. One is well accepted and a mainstay of current protection approaches: signature detection. The second still has a foot in the research area, because it is a good idea, but it is flawed: anomaly detection. The following is how AuBA proactive and predictive technology can enhance existing signature detection and anomaly detection technologies. Although AuBA network protection technologies represent a new proactive, predictive approach, it also can enhance and augment current network protection methods.

The following shows how AuBA can effectively move signature detection from reactive to proactive, and how the technology can remove the singular flaw (exceedingly high false positives) that has kept anomaly detection in the realm of just a good idea. It should be added that the following potential solutions are the result of exhausting empirical work, not just speculation. The use of AuBA to augment and improve existing signature detection and anomaly detection has been investigated scientifically with results providing the confidence to offer the following suggestions to move both existing inadequate technologies to more adequate protection.

Augmenting Signature Detection with AuBA

Like it or not, we are heavily invested in the current technology being used to protect our networks. Unfortunately, effectiveness is limited and is diminishing as APT increases in sophistication and effectiveness. Developing new technology to increase protection does not mean that existing hardware and software need to be replaced. It is much like having a basic home security system with front and back door sensors. Subsequently, we can then add window, glass breakage, and external perimeter motion detectors. We now have full protection achieved by augmenting the existing, basic security system. This is directly analogous to our current plight with network protection. The basic technology is in place, but the protection is not complete. We simply are not prepared for new attacks, zero-day attacks, hacker evasion tactics, morphing malware, and new highly deceptive and highly skilled ingenuity of the adversary — current signature detection does not cover these areas.

Using the concept of augmenting current, basic protection technology, we have to move away from real-world reactive approaches. Such approaches include:

- Chasing causes of why we were compromised
- Relying on forensics to define how the damage occurred
- Relying solely on writing rules to protect against the attack that already resulted in damage or loss of sensitive information

It is much like clinical work. I have observed many examples of working with extremely disturbed and mentally ill individuals who receive a technical diagnosis. The diagnosis is simply a label — it is not treatment. Discovering how we were compromised is a label. It doesn't fix the damage. If we dissect a terrorist attack after the fact, we may end up with an elaborate description of what happened, but property damage and loss of life are not altered. This is not to say that forensics and other after-the-fact reactive approaches are not necessary — they may be a part of the solution, but we must stop thinking of after-the-fact activity as *the* solution.

The concept of *future signatures*, as previously discussed in this chapter, represents a method to convert an existing reactive technology to a proactive technology.

Augmenting Anomaly Detection with AuBA

Anomaly detection is a very interesting idea, although hopelessly flawed in its present form. Anomaly detection basically says that if we analyze a network and establish *norms* (baselines), any departure from the norm would be anomalous and therefore should be flagged as threatening. Here is the flaw that cannot be eradicated given current approaches. If we analyze a network to determine the norm, our first problem is that all networks are constantly scanned by external entities to determine if the network can be compromised. Therefore, there is not a state in which the network is *normal* for learning. However, if we somehow get past this very serious problem, it is very time-consuming to determine a norm of a network. If scanning and reconnaissance activities are occurring during norming, then these patterns will be considered "normal," and if they occur again, then they will be passed as normal. This is very serious if an approach such as APT has resulted in a compromise and sensitive data is being extracted and sent to the adversary. None of this activity will be flagged as anomalous — by definition, anomaly detection learns all on the network as normal behavior during the learning process. This is serious flaw number 1.

Serious flaw number 2 is that if all is normed and the technology catches activity that is significantly different from the norm, then the activity is flagged as suspicious. However, human behavior is rife with variation, alterations, and constant change. Significant difference from the norm does not mean that alterations are necessarily malicious. Significant differences from the established norm can fit into two categories:

- Anomalous threatening
- Anomalous non-threatening (just normal variation)

Current anomaly detection cannot tell the difference between anomalous bad and anomalous good. This is a major problem that cannot be fixed statistically.

I have been invited to several advanced technology workshops presented by the U.S. government that have featured the best and the brightest researchers and developers. At the workshops anomaly detection was presented as the new hope because it was possible that new activity that could be threatening might be detected as anomalous. However, the bottom line still was that anomaly detection simply cannot differentiate between anomalous bad and anomalous good. Why? Because if we are going to differentiate between anomalous behavior that is malicious from anomalous but innocuous behavior, then we must focus on human behavior behind the activity and not just network behavior. We must be able to ascertain the intent behind the activity that is being monitored if we are going to break down anomalies in a true threat versus no threat manner. In short, the ability to determine human intent is a key to future success in network security. AuBA is moving rapidly in this direction, having already been validated to identify malicious intent from non-malicious intent both in network security and in identifying intent from movement patterns (see Chapter 9, the section titled "Making Sure It Works: An Introductory Example").

How can AuBA help? If we use existing anomaly detection to flag an IP on a network that is anomalous, then that activity by that IP can be processed by CheckMate (if external) and InMate (if interval). The AuBA-based technology can then take the anomalous activity and determine malicious intent based on the conversion of packet-level activity to measures of *expertise* and *deception*, if external, and *intent to engage in misuse* and *deception* if internal activity. In short, pure anomaly detection flags those IPs that are significantly different from the norm. By passing this anomalous activity through CheckMate and InMate, the inability of anomaly detection to differentiate between normal and non-normal behavior is solved by follow-on advanced behavior prediction AuBA analytics. This solves the inordinately high false positives associated with anomaly detection (calling activity as threatening when it is not threatening). AuBA technology can process anomaly flagged IPs doing something out of the norm and determine if the flagged activity is anomalous bad versus anomalous good.

AuBA presents two ways to augment existing signature detection and anomaly detection. First, clearly, both approaches are not sufficient to stop the current onslaught of serious cyber attacks, or we would not be having the serious damage and losses we are experiencing every single day. We can add future signatures to current signature detection and move a reactive signature approach to a more proactive approach by providing signatures of serious attacks that have not yet occurred. But, we will be ready when they do occur. Second, AuBA applications can process IPs that anomaly detection indicates are different from the norm and increase the probability of true positives (calling malicious intent accurately) and true negatives (calling non-malicious intent accurately). This automatically drops false positives (error: calling non-malicious activity malicious) and false negatives (error: calling malicious activity non-malicious).

The Elements of Proactive Security

Network security has not kept pace with network threat. The primary approach of signature detection remains a reactive approach and is destined to remain the same by definition. It has been the primary approach for network protection for decades. During this period of time, the adversary who works to intrude into our networks either to inflict damage or to steal restricted information has grown by leaps and bounds in sophistication. This rapid growth in sophistication now includes APT, and adversaries enjoy the support of foreign state resources. The adversary is capable of generating activity that simply passes by current signatures.

My analogy of our current situation is the BP Deepwater Horizon oil spill in 2010 that occurred as a result of an explosion that killed 11 men and injured 17. The explosion resulted in the largest underwater oil gusher in history. It was a very frustrating time, and environmental/economic fears were at a maximum. Cameras caught the tremendous flow of oil escaping unabated into the Gulf of Mexico every second of every day (Figure 19-1). Environmental and economic concerns were at a maximum as coastal economies were wrecked. Any attempts to cap the gusher were unsuccessful. All who watched had a feeling of hopelessness and were powerless to stop it. Fortunately, almost 3 months later, the gusher was finally capped.

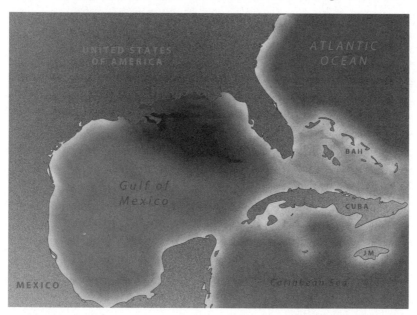

Figure 19-1: The BP underwater oil gusher in the Gulf of Mexico that went unchecked for almost 3 months. It is a strong analogy to unchecked advanced persistent threat directed against our networks today.

© Keith Bruce | Dreamstime.com

The current network flow of threat is much like the BP oil gusher. The threat is persistent; it simply does not stop. Our current signature detection technology is powerless to stop it. The difference is that the great oil gusher was capped, much to the relief of all who had to watch it and who had been powerless to do anything. From a network perspective, the gusher of threat continues unabated, and it is even getting stronger. It is not capped.

When we face this gushing network threat at current line speeds armed with only reactive technology, the feeling of hopelessness is ever-present. Our best defense is our amazingly talented network protection teams who work tirelessly to protect our networks. However, when advanced attacks such as sophisticated phishing attacks are sent our way and the unaware employee is tricked into responding to an important e-mail, it is too late. The damage has been done. The adversary may now have internal access. Given that current signature detection cannot anticipate new threatening activity and is restricted to a reactive approach of using signatures of past attacks, it is clear our protection is not forward-leaning. Unfortunately, for the reasons provided just prior to this section, anomaly detection cannot move us into the future because of high false-positive and false-negative rates (unless we add AuBA-related technology or some other form of proactive technology that has not yet surfaced). In a way, anomaly detection is an anomaly in and of itself. It has high false positives because it flags non-malicious activity different from the trained norm as suspicious, and high false negatives when malicious activity is present during the training of the anomaly detection system — it simply learns that this activity is normal and misses it in the future.

The AuBA automated modeling tools described on the accompanying DVD (ThemeMate and AutoAnalyzer) are used to develop predictive engines that may be placed into applications designed to meet specific anticipatory needs. Specific applications, such as CheckMate and InMate, that protect networks from external and internal threat, respectively, are representative of how proactive, predictive technology can be used to augment current network protection technology. AuBA is a third technology that can augment both signature detection and anomaly detection.

A Behavioral Science–Based Paradigm Shift

A *paradigm* within science is a shared, common view among scientists. We can extend this traditional use of the term to other areas. For example, World War I and World War II were typical of a paradigm of warfare. For the most part, an enemy used extensive air, naval, and ground forces; powerful weapons; strategies; and massive manpower pitted against the same on the adversarial side. Then, the world encountered examples of asymmetric warfare known as terrorism. More like the fighting tactics of our minutemen of the Revolutionary War, the strategies employed by terrorism demonstrated that a very small force using the element of surprise could accomplish extensive damage. The Japanese massive, more conventional attack on Pearl Harbor on December 7,

1941, as compared to the 19-man, September 11, 2001, al-Qaeda attack within our borders 60 years later show marked contrast. Terrorism has forced a paradigm shift in how we combat adversaries. In World War II, a B-29 Superfortress dropped the first of two atomic bombs on Japan, ending World War II. Sixty years later, we now see small, robotic drones that have conducted surgical strikes, killing such terrorists as Anwar al-Awlaki.

Asymmetric warfare such as terrorism has its analogue in network security. Hackers, for the most part, represent asymmetric tactics in that a single person working within the protection of distance and under a cloak of anonymity can be in a foreign country such as China and attack a network in Washington, D.C. Such asymmetric strategies on networks have evolved to include advanced persistent threat (APT) supported by vast foreign state support. The APT is serious and underscores the cyber war in which we, as a country, are now engaged. Yet, our network protection strategy has remained the same since the inception of the Internet and networks over the past 20 to 30 years. There is an obvious lack of a paradigm shift in network security to match the paradigm shift we clearly recognize that has surfaced in the fight against terrorism. We are using the same basic signature-based approaches to fight cyber threat that we always have.

Figure 19-2 depicts my conceptualization of rising cyber threat, including rapidly progressing foreign state–supported APT, as compared to the decreasing effectiveness of signature detection to counter this mounting threat. On April 8, 2010, a significant number of worldwide Internet traffic was hijacked by China and routed through that country for 18 minutes. During that time, almost anything could have occurred with that traffic. China initiated APT continual attacks directed against U.S. sites in successful theft of restricted information that could give it an edge in what is now a new technology race. At the time I wrote this chapter, it appears that our country has had the first national infrastructure attack. Traced to Russia, a hacking attack against a Springfield, Illinois, water supply pump caused the pump to fail. This is a serious incident. A water pump that supplies fresh water must first be primed with water so that the pump immediately starts pumping water. If not primed properly, the pump will simply try to pump air and will burn up in the process. This is what happened. Keep in mind this is an attack from a foreign entity that destroyed a pump essential to a fresh water supply. This is exceedingly important because this attack demonstrates not only our vulnerability, but also success for an adversary. As we know in behavior analysis, behavior followed by success increases the probability that the behavior will occur in the future when the same or highly similar antecedent conditions occur.

Congress has stated emphatically that we are under attack — we are at war in cyber space. Only the very ill-informed could deny the seriousness with which we are suffering continual assault, damage, and theft.

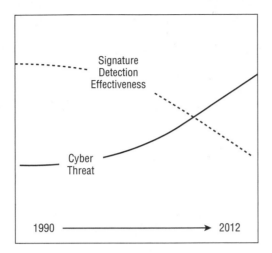

Figure 19-2: My conceptualization of the increasing threat to our networks as compared to the relative decrease in effectiveness of signature detection that has remained stable for decades.

Why is signature detection failing and why can't anomaly detection be rid of the inextricably associated high false positive rates? Why do we not have effective methodologies that are a step ahead of threat that are truly proactive and predictive so that countermeasures can stop the current onslaught of malicious behavior being directed at our country and infrastructure? Could we actually see a double-threat attack where there is a conventional terrorist attack like 9/11 and at the same time a coordinated attack against communications and networks that would prevent adequate and coordinated first responder emergency response?

I posit that the primary reason for lack of readiness today is that we look only at network activity that is presented on a minute-to-minute basis. The key is not network behavior/activity. The key is that we are not using existing technology such as AuBA to determine the intent of the incoming activity to our networks. We have technology to go beyond the actual network activity being exhibited to assess the actual intent behind of the attacker. Is the intent malicious or non-malicious? If we can determine the intent behind the network activity, then we will have a much better justification for blocking activity with malicious intent before it can actually cause damage or result in successful theft of sensitive and restricted information.

I have worked to invent technology that can determine human characteristics from the digital information presented. In other words, unless we fuse the behavioral sciences with the computer and network protection sciences, we are not likely to be able to anticipate the actual intent behind specific network activity that we observe. Network activity that is assessed by signature detection and anomaly detection is not true behavioral assessment of the individual or individuals behind the attacks. AuBA applications look a level deeper. For example, with CheckMate, the degree of human expertise and deception that is present directly relates to the perpetrator and not to network activity. If we can assess malicious versus non-malicious intent of the actual individual or individuals behind the network activity, then we have an enhanced capability to detect threat earlier and react accordingly.

In short, we must incorporate behavioral science. We must know something about the intent of the attacker if we are going to be proactive and not just wait until our systems are compromised to determine that there was a real threat. At that point, it is simply too late. The behavioral science that underlies AuBA allows us to determine malicious intent of the IP, not just the network activity. Being a true fusion of the advanced computer and behavioral sciences as applied to network security indicates that this unique and patented fusion of the sciences has much to offer, as backed up by external and third-party validation.

We have learned through such AuBA applications as CheckMate and InMate that determining malicious intent provides a proactive and predictive approach that moves us away from reactive signature detection. Does this mean that new technology emphasizing behavioral science replaces existing technologies? No! It simply means that we have new behavioral science approaches that go beyond network activity assessments to determine true intent of the incoming activity, which is far better than just looking at network activity from a signature perspective.

AuBA is a true fusion of the computer and behavioral sciences with the goal of predicting malicious behavior accurately. The advantage of this new approach as applied to network security is that the focus is on precursors (antecedents to attack). This is the context that precedes an attack. Given that we can accurately determine these preceding antecedent conditions, then we can be proactive and predictive. Accurate determination of pre-existing conditions that precede an attack through a determination of malicious intent means that we can get ahead of attacks and present countermeasures. For example, if CheckMate determines that expertise and deception are mounting and exceed a critical region, then the IP can be blocked before the actual attack is implemented by the adversary. Using the behaviorprint feature (see Chapter 13), behavior is also tracked, meaning that if the IP changes, the adversary can be identified by behavior patterns exhibited.

In a similar way, if we are addressing terrorism, then we can anticipate a terrorist attack by recognizing the antecedents that precede an attack. If we identify antecedents that have been validated to be associated with terrorist attacks and such antecedents are identified, then we can have time to react, instead of waiting for attacks to occur and then react.

In summary, we must include behavioral science in current network security and asymmetric warfare threats. Threat to our national welfare is generated by humans. Human behavior can be both understood and anticipated. As we say, *machines don't attack networks, people do*. We have technology to identify the intent behind digital and network activity. Unless we use this knowledge and expertise, we will be forever locked into waiting until an attack occurs before we intervene. The addition of the behavioral sciences to provide insight into malicious intent is absolutely necessary if we are going to be more proactive.

Why We Need a New Approach to Security

Using the term *security* in a broad sense, we need to improve upon our methods to protect not only ourselves and our welfare but our national infrastructure as well. How we anticipate threat includes intelligence and the analysis and synthesis of global data on a moment-to-moment basis. This book has focused on malicious behavior associated with asymmetric warfare such as terrorism and cyber threat and, to a slightly lesser degree, criminal behavior. When we observe the past on a global basis, we have repeatedly failed to anticipate serious and significant global events ahead of time. The following section highlights a sample of the big human events in history that we have failed to accurately anticipate. This is exceedingly important because without accurate anticipation of threat and the contexts leading to such threat with all implications therein, there cannot be adequate, focused security.

The failure to anticipate major events on a global basis has created a type of status quo in security methods. Although we have seen improvement and have had more recent success in a war against terrorism because of improved methods, we still need vast improvement in predictive methods. Given that we develop and implement proactive and predictive technologies as related to malicious human behavior, shifts in how we approach security will follow.

We, as a country, even given our vast intelligence and military capabilities, have experienced a failure in anticipation of major, global events. We have been surprised a number of times. In retrospect, events are typically clearer; however, even in retrospect we must wonder at times how we missed some events. I maintain that such events essentially can be subdivided to get to the heart of the failure. This failure is a product of the inability to predict human behavior.

Fall of the Soviet Union

As 1991 ended, the Soviet Union disintegrated, to the surprise of the world. After the United States and the Soviet Union had been locked in an intense cold war for the past 45 years, December 1991 signaled the end, almost overnight. During that month, the Soviet Union splintered into 15 separate countries. This was a time of dramatic changes. Just 2 years before, the Berlin wall had fallen, resulting in the reunification of Germany. The Soviet Union was number one on our intelligence and military radar for decades. Second in nuclear power, the Soviet Union had many conflicts with the United States. The Cuban missile crisis in October 1962 had resulted in a Cuba, Soviet Union, and United States conflict that brought us right to the brink of nuclear war. The space race was intense. Intelligence moved to space with satellite reconnaissance. Open conflict between the U.S.S.R. and the United States was observed in the United Nations, on television, and in the press.

In December 1987, I was present at the White House when President Ronald Reagan met with Russian Secretary-General Mikhail Gorbachev, accompanied by wives Nancy Reagan and Raisa Gorbachev, respectively. I remember well the excitement and palpable tension in the air as the leaders and wives came together for remarks. Security was high on both sides, and the event was a microcosm that underscored the tension between the two countries on a global basis.

However, almost overnight in December 1991 the world went from two superpowers to one. We truly missed the fall of the Soviet Union. Perhaps because this was the strongest and most significant conflict between superpowers in history, one that brought us to the brink of nuclear war, we simply failed to anticipate this most significant event.

September 11, 2001 (9/11)

Much has been written about the surprise 9/11 attack that killed almost 3,000 innocent people at the World Trade Center, at the Pentagon, and in a citizen-terrorist struggle that downed a third airliner in a rural field in Pennsylvania. The event was a surprise attack within our own borders that may have actually exceeded the Pearl Harbor attack in a number of ways. It took 353 aircraft, 6 aircraft carriers, and support craft to attack Pearl Harbor. The death toll was approximately 2,400. The 9/11 attack occurred with just 19 terrorist perpetrators who hijacked 4 airliners with no more than box cutters as weapons. At the end of the attack, nearly 3,000 innocent victims were killed, and we are still recovering from the physical destruction 11 years later. 9/11 was the epitome of surprise. The resulting damage and loss of life was immense and unified our country to ensure that no such event ever occurs again. However, we totally missed anticipation of this event — even after official reporting had noted that there were foreign individuals taking flying lessons with little interest in how to land.

Fall of Our Economic Foundation and the Bailout

For 5 days in October 1987, the U.S. stock market plummeted. The Dow Jones Industrial Average lost 31 percent of its value. And this example is a sample only. The loss in confidence of the U.S. economy has been part of a growing crisis that now includes Europe approaching a financial meltdown. Now that countries are totally interdependent on a global basis, we can observe the European and Asian markets and watch the same up or down trend occur hours later within the United States. The stock market, perhaps the most challenging and largest example of massive human behavior changing on a second-by-second basis, is extremely difficult to accurately anticipate.

We have missed predicting massive down days. High performance computing works on individual stocks, but we continually miss major drops in the market. The U.S. bailout of financial institutions has been a major form of frustration and is a prime example of being reactive as opposed to proactive. This is such a major problem that almost all efforts are reactive based on the need to contain the problem. On August 5, 2011, the problem became so serious that for the first time in history Standard & Poor's dropped the credit rating for our country from the top possible at an AAA rating to AA+.

These are just examples. There are many more, such as the bombing of the USS *Cole*, embassy bombings, and many elements of the continued crises in the Middle East.

This is not to say that we don't have predictive technology. It is my contention that technology such as AuBA, as well as other technologies, could come together to give us an enhanced capability to anticipate not only events such as the ones described but more subtle, significant events as well. We are missing the elephant in the room. If we miss significant events, then developing new and improved security to meet emerging threats will be extremely difficult. With a proactive and predictive capability to anticipate threats before they occur, security resources and practices may be focused much more efficiently and consist of improved courses of action to serve as successful countermeasures for specific types of threat.

Current Status

As a result of the 9/11 al-Qaeda attack within our country, the President of the United States and Congress established the 9/11 Commission, composed of five Republicans and five Democrats. Established under The National Commission on Terrorist Attacks Upon the United States (Public Law 107-306, November 27, 2002), the Commission's stated singular purpose was to investigate facts and circumstances relating to the terrorist attacks of September 11, 2001. Within the resulting 586-page 9/11 commission report, there is a very powerful statement that sums up the situation prior to the attack: "We believe the 9/11 attack revealed four kinds of failure: imagination, policy, capabilities, and management."

If we look at threat to U.S. citizens today and, for the sake of argument only, exclude domestic criminal activity, we are facing asymmetric threat from terrorism and cyber threat. To give credit where credit is due, and to solve which administration did what, it is safe to say that the day after 9/11 a paradigm shift started within the Bush administration. It was clear that our internal resources had to be coordinated to a much greater degree, and that conventional warfare could only be a part of the future — covert actions against specific al-Qaeda operatives and supporters would have to happen. For example, a new view of fighting terrorism as a warfare tactic would require conventional warfare in such countries as Iraq and Afghanistan.

Terrorists basically rushed to these locations to engage in actions directed at U.S. occupation of these countries. Whether we agree or not in these conflicts, the adversaries were easier to find because they came to U.S. and allied forces, and many are now gone as a result.

Then, enter the Obama administration. There were now improved methods of battling specific terrorists with improved intelligence and military capability designed for asymmetric warfare. For example, the use of armed drones has been effective. In 2011 alone, Anwar al-Awlaki, a U.S.-born individual who betrayed his country to become an al-Qaeda leader in Yemen, and another U.S.-born traitor betraying the United States for al-Qaeda membership, Samir Khan, were both killed by drone-fired Hellfire missiles in the same strike.

The new infrastructure for a new type of war was initiated by President Bush and his administration, and President Obama used the tools and pulled the trigger. In the same year, through U.S. efforts, a joint U.S. Special Forces and CIA operation killed Osama bin Laden, burying him at sea shortly after the killing. Revenge for the many lost lives and immense damage during the 9/11 attack was complete to a certain extent — and it took a coordinated effort of both administrations and changes within intelligence and the military to get there. Furthermore, it appears that a NATO strike with a drone played a key role in forcing the situation that resulted in the capture of Libyan leader Muammar Gaddafi, resulting in his death shortly thereafter. There is little doubt of Gaddafi's complicity in supporting terrorism directed against the United States over the past years.

A paradigm shift in how we conducted efforts to stop terrorism did occur after 9/11. The shift also resulted in technology advances that assist the soldier on the ground and new forms of surgical weapons like the drone. Looking back at the findings of the 9/11 commission report, the paradigm shift directly affected all four areas of criticism:

- **Imagination:** New advances and expansion of tools and weaponry occurred that were more directly applicable to asymmetric warfare and not just to conventional warfare expansion, and they were implemented with success.

- **Policy:** The overall policy directing a war on terrorism took on a whole new importance. In the past, terrorist rendition was less of a priority, although it was present. Such terrorists as Ramzi Yousef (the original World Trade Center bombing mastermind) and Mir Aimal Kansi (the CIA killer) were tracked and captured by means of a more on-the-ground rendition policy at the time. Kansi was later executed in November 2002 after criminal proceedings, and Yousef will remain in prison for his life with no chance of parole. More recently, policy has changed to coordinated intelligence and more likely drone attacks. There is a much greater cooperation across agencies and military as part of a policy shift. For example, as media report, the operation to kill Osama bin Laden was reported to be a CIA-led team of U.S. Navy Seals.

- **Capabilities:** In many ways, 9/11 was a wake-up call indicating that a small number of foreign terrorists could operate within our borders to perpetrate a coordinated attack killing almost 3,000 people and bringing unparalleled destruction to the World Trade Center and the Pentagon. The resulting war on terrorism was initiated with renewed vigor and with a strong national desire to ensure that such an event would never occur again. The nation's shift from a more pre-9/11 reactive approach to a proactive and more offensive approach took the war to Afghanistan and the Taliban, as well as to Iraq.

  Technology has improved and is more focused toward the smaller terrorist target. Predators armed with missiles have proven their worth. The unparalleled cooperation across intelligence and military efforts is paying off. Improvements in analytical capability have also proven to create an improved situational awareness. In my opinion, we have terrorism contained. We can't say we have won. We will see incidents now and again. We would never expect to see crime eliminated; it is not realistic. Terrorism is with us now, much like crime. But with the right tools and continued cooperation, we will continue in building our effective proactive stance.

- **Management:** Paradigm shifts don't occur overnight. From my experience with rendition, counterterrorism, and direct support on a global basis, it is clear that Presidents George H. W. Bush, Bill Clinton, George W. Bush, and Barack Obama should be united to take pride in together leading one of the more important military and intelligence paradigm shifts in this country. This shift has led to the decimation of terrorists such as Mir Aimal Kansi, Ramzi Yousef, Osama bin Laden, Anwar al-Awlaki, and senior al-Qaeda leadership and the eradication of those foreign leaders such as Saddam Hussein and Muammar Gaddafi who supported death and destruction of not only U.S. citizens but their own people as well. We live in a safer world because of the leadership efforts of these presidents, all contributing to the overall effect. A paradigm shift is cumulative, and we are at the point where we have made significant gains against the adversary.

There have been strides against terrorism. However, there is still much room for improvement. The continued move to predictive capability in which we can better anticipate the occurrence of terrorist acts with improved courses of action is still a very strong need.

Unfortunately, the world of cyber interdependencies and how we protect our networks has not seen a parallel paradigm shift. For the most part, it is security practices and technology as usual. It is apparent that when we experience an attack within our borders the magnitude of a 9/11 al-Qaeda attack, we *must* defend ourselves. Death and destruction the magnitude of that infamous day cannot be ignored. Such an action will result in a reaction, and we have reacted. Cyber war is different. We don't see death and destruction. There are not destroyed buildings, and no one has died. The devastating effects of cyber attacks are so much more difficult to determine. However, the damage is real and truly devastating. We cannot be complacent.

Current technologies being applied today across such fields as network security, physical security, law enforcement, tactical military strategy, and intelligence for the most part are reactive. At best, reactive approaches typically consist of analyzing past malicious activity of an adversary, statistically determining base rates of different tactics, and simply projecting these base rates forward. For example, if 100 terrorist incidents from a specific group are selected at random and 80 were assaults, 10 were suicide bombings, and 10 were roadside bombings, then given that the group exhibits another attack, there is a 0.80 probability of assault, 0.10 probability of suicide bombing, and 0.10 probability of roadside bombing.

However, true AuBA prediction of malicious behavior would likely predict *what* is going to happen next (including the possibility of no attack at all), and *where*, *when*, and likely *who* from a generic perspective (for example, military or civilian). This is very different from simply projecting base rates forward. Projecting base rates simply says that certain tactics are more likely than others to occur sometime in the future. But, from a behavior analysis perspective, we know that each of the 100 past incidents was a product of specific precursor antecedent conditions. The base rate was simply a count of different types of events. In short, the use of base rates can be descriptive of a group, but does not represent true forward prediction of actual malicious human behavior.

As I have stressed throughout this book, accurate prediction of malicious human behavior is not derived from simply studying or counting past behavior. Instead, and as the basis for AuBA, accurate prediction of future malicious behavior is based on projecting past antecedents, behavior, and consequences (context) forward. When the same or highly similar antecedents associated with a suicide bombing occur in the future, then the same or highly similar malicious behavior is highly likely to occur.

Given that we have not experienced a much needed paradigm shift within the cyber world, Table 19-1 shows a comparison of current network protection deficiencies and how AuBA predictive technology relates to the specific deficiencies.

Table 19-1: A Comparison of Current Security Deficiencies versus Potential AuBA Fixes

CURRENT DEFICIENCY	AuBA TECHNOLOGY FIX
Lack of reliable technology to detect new attacks with low errors	Apply technology that identifies malicious intent and predicts new human malicious behavior
Lack of technology that can detect malicious activity early enough to prevent damage or theft	Utilize new technology that is capable of identifying antecedents to imminent attack so that countermeasures can immediately be used to prevent damage or theft

CURRENT DEFICIENCY	AuBA TECHNOLOGY FIX
Lack of capability to identify attempts to engage in coordinated attacks from multiple sources simultaneously with different activities	Incorporate AuBA concept of behaviorprints
Lack of capability to trace back malicious activity to the actual server with no errors	No known technology can now do this — needs to be developed as a high priority
Lack of capability to identify a return attacker regardless of the activity presented and IP address changes	Incorporate AuBA concept of behaviorprints
Current lack of technology to augment or convert existing technology from reactive to proactive	Apply new technologies that are proven in the laboratory and field tests (such as AuBA, CheckMate, InMate, future signatures, behaviorprints) and implement

Advantages of AuBA #19: AuBA in the Future

As we near the end of the book, you probably have a good idea about how AuBA works and, perhaps, application areas. Now that you have a basic understanding, I would like to emphasize the future of AuBA. Where is it going? What types of applications are likely to be developed? What new features are expected to surface? The following are some of the highlights:

- AuBA will continue to be used to improve network protection from external threat, with a renewed focus on insider threat.

- The behaviorprint concept will continue to provide a form of behavior-metrics, as opposed to biometrics, for authentication and to determine the nature of an attacker.

- The future signatures concept will continue to grow to the point where we can automatically determine antecedents to a multitude of attacks that we have not seen before.

- We now have constructed and validated models using database text, unstructured text, network packets, and physical sensor output. This will be expanded to process images to extract key features for behavior monitoring and prediction.

- Our developed predictive engines are very small, with current applications working on a laptop. In the near future, AuBA applications will move to handheld applications for portability.

- We currently link multiple trained neural network engines together to form a complex answer. We plan to construct large nets of assessment engines with links to solve multiple and complex predictive requirements.

- We will continue in our quest to make AuBA even more user-friendly.

- We will emphasize areas of interest that continue to make us stretch development to meet customer needs.

Although we have had many successes with AuBA, the technology is still young. We hope to work with researchers to extend the technology to a host of other areas.

In Summary

AuBA represents a third technology that can augment both signature detection and anomaly detection within the area of network intrusion security. It also has direct relevance in a similar way to other forms of asymmetric warfare such as terrorism. In the past two to three decades, we have witnessed a paradigm shift in the war against terrorism. Any paradigm shift brings with it debate, skepticism, and detractors — change is not easy because it bucks the status quo. However, the events of 9/11 escalated this paradigm shift as our nation wanted to see that justice prevailed after this devastating attack. The year 2011 was the year of the small drone moving slowly while following identified terrorists to release surgically aimed missiles at adversaries. These adversaries were working to plan additional attacks against U.S. citizens. There have been a number of effective strikes.

The year 2011 was also the year that Osama bin Laden was killed in a joint CIA–U.S. Navy on-the-ground assault on bin Laden's compound. The mounting successes point to the still evolving paradigm shift in this area. There is still a great need for additional improvement, and the addition of AuBA as a means to anticipate attack is warranted.

On the cyber side, there has not been any attempt to establish a needed paradigm shift. We are using the same signature detection approach to intrusion detections as we have for the past decades, even as sophistication of attacks has increased significantly and foreign state support of attacks against the United States is having its effect. This chapter has shown how AuBA as an approach and resultant network protection applications can make a difference. In the next chapter, I will show how to use AuBA to make a difference.

CHAPTER 20

How to Predict Malicious Behavior: A Walkthrough

Behavioral psychology as a discipline is international and is based on many hundreds of thousands of research and treatment articles. These publications range from those with a very strong operant psychology and experimental foundation to very applied projects in clinical and social settings, businesses, schools, facilities, and so on. This book is based on the fusion of principles found across behavioral psychology and applied behavior analysis in general and, specifically, the computer sciences.

Automated behavior analysis (AuBA) exists as a patented set of tools and methods to extend behavioral principles to actual prediction of human behavior. For the purposes of this book, the focus is on using the tools and methods to predict future malicious behavior. This chapter focuses on my progression of the initial clinical approaches to total automation of behavioral modeling suitable for prediction of malicious behavior on a global basis. I recommend using this walkthrough chapter in conjunction with Chapters 7–9, which provide detail on behavior principles and how to apply them in behavior modeling.

A Manual Walkthrough of AuBA Principles

The evolution of AuBA from applied behavior analysis began when I developed new treatment approaches for such difficult and challenging clinical problems as life-threatening rumination in developmentally disabled institutionalized individuals and challenging mental health–related problems, such as tardive dyskinesia, a disorder caused by psychotropic medications that manifests itself as uncontrollable tongue thrusting and facial grimacing. These applied clinical techniques resulted in a number of publications showing treatment success with difficult populations, including how to use behavioral principles to alter the treatment environment to result in behavioral change with those diagnosed with mental illness.

How does this work tie in to predicting behavior on a global basis? It is a good question that takes some explanation. First, the work with many of the groups described did not lend itself to typical psychological assessment methods. Many individuals treated had conditions so severe that communication was not possible. Likewise, traditional psychological assessment requiring clients to complete assessment instruments by answering items was not possible either. This left one approach — AuBA. This approach is based on observation. We can define behaviors, count their occurrence, provide an intervention, and determine if the behavior increases or decreases as a result. Chapter 7 describes this approach in more detail.

> **WARNING**   Although I have omitted many graphic details in the section "A Clinical Case Example," if the reader is squeamish and does not have a strong stomach, it is highly recommended that this section be skipped.

A Clinical Case Example

There are many case examples, but I will provide a sample of examples simply to demonstrate the tremendous power that environmental antecedents and consequences have over behavior.

I was director of a special program at the Lincoln State School in Lincoln, Illinois, in the 1970s. At the time, it was the world's largest facility for the developmentally disabled, with over 5,000 residents. The behavior problems presented, in some cases, were considered to be intractable. The program I directed was one that took the facility's, and in some cases the state's, most dangerous and aggressive residents. One resident was committed at 5 years of age for strangling and killing his 3-year-old younger sister. He had been restrained for 40 years, had been subjected to a prefrontal lobotomy (brain surgery in which the frontal lobe was disconnected from the rest of the brain), and was on unparalleled doses of psychotropic medication — yet his aggressive behavior was not altered. He would attempt to attack others over 100 times per day. We were successful in reducing his attacks to once a day with using behavioral methods presented in this book.

Beth was a very special case. Out of all the cases, hers is presented to show how behavioral principles can alter behavior. Beth was admitted to my project when she bit off the nose of another resident. This was not a rare occurrence, and Beth would consume the parts removed before intervention could occur. Beth was blind, severely developmentally disabled, and a walking, biting machine. In addition, she was extremely disruptive and could flip a hospital bed on her own when extremely upset. She was extremely strong. One common characteristic of the extremely dangerous is that when they are upset, the adrenalin flows and the degree of strength they possess is truly amazing.

Beth's primary tactic was to walk barefooted, sneak up behind a person, and when making contact immediately bite, causing serious damage before the victim realized that attack had even taken place.

I began using a behavior analysis form (BAF), which was an improved version of an earlier form started by David M. Congdon, a psychologist at that facility. The form was designed to record each specific inappropriate behavior and any potential antecedent conditions occurring before the behavior, such as location, persons in the vicinity, time of the event, and so forth. The form was also designed to record any events or situations that followed the behavior; in other words, the consequences. Therefore, each page of the form was divided into three columns: antecedents, behavior, and consequences. This new form placed the columns in sequence to make it easier to record.

Although staff always intervened to the best of their abilities and tried to ensure that no one was injured, we placed an emphasis on recording inappropriate behaviors on a 24/7 basis. The recordings were faithfully completed by all staff members on each occasion of aggressive behavior. After one to two weeks of recordings, it was possible to process all of the recorded entries to look for common antecedents that could be prompting the behavior to occur and the consequences that were maintaining it.

Before a sample entry is provided for you to solve, one more fact needs to be added. When Beth was admitted to my special project, I asked for volunteers from the facility to assist with her. Often, it is possible to find dedicated volunteers who have a special affinity for a resident in such severe settings. As might be imagined, there was not an overwhelming response. However, Susan volunteered. She had worked with Beth on a continuous basis for the previous 2 years. She was the only employee who could approach Beth, and Beth responded very warmly in her presence, so I accepted the employee as a new staff member, along with Beth as a patient. It was decided that because of her personal situation, she would work the second shift: 3:00 P.M. to 11:00 P.M., one of the quieter shifts.

Susan worked with Beth well and seemed happy to be in this very difficult and challenging program. After two weeks of recording inappropriate behavior, I took all of the BAFs and began to look for common antecedents and common consequences. There were over 100 entries of severe aggressive behavior, with many resulting in injuries regardless of the staff's best attempts to prevent injury. As I processed these entries, some patterns came to light immediately. The clue to this problem is in the following bullets. See if you can solve this problem as you read through it. Keep in mind that this behavior had persisted for many years.

- By processing the antecedent entries, I found it was apparent that the extreme aggressive behavior occurred during the evening, rarely late at night or during the day.

- The aggressive behavior almost never occurred on the weekends.

- The vast majority of the entries were made by Susan, the staff member who had volunteered to come with Beth.

Table 20-1 contains typical entries provided by Susan with an emphasis on events and situations preceding the dangerous behavior (antecedent conditions) and what happened following the behavior (reinforcing consequences).

Please note that many detailed items are deleted for clarity purposes so that we can focus on key, primary events. Most of the entries were the same as the ones shown here in the table. All the information needed to solve this behavioral problem is present. Can you solve it?

Table 20-1: Excerpts of Approximately 100 Antecedents, Behavior, and Consequences Recorded Regarding Beth on the Behavior Analysis Form

ANTECEDENTS	BEHAVIOR	CONSEQUENCES
Date: **Time**: 7:35 P.M. **Location**: Main Dayroom **People in Vicinity**: John, Jim, Alice, and Beth **Activities**: John - napping, Jim - watching TV, Alice - playing with puppets, me - (Susan) had just entered the Dayroom	Beth became highly agitated, was sitting next to John, reached over and grabbed John's arm, and before I could stop her, she bit John on the arm.	I immediately hugged Beth to calm her down and gave her a piece of candy to distract her. Emergency Services was called to treat John's bite. All residents became upset, requiring additional staff. Recorder: Susan Smith
Date: **Time**: 10:16 P.M. **Location**: Dorm **People in Vicinity**: Beth, Mary, Alicia, and me (Susan) **Activities**: Mary and Alicia - preparing for bed, Beth - being resistant to preparing for bedtime	I (Susan) saw Beth approaching Alicia quietly from behind and grasp Alicia's arm.	Fearing that Beth was going to bite Alicia, I rushed in, put my arm around Beth to calm her down, removed her grasp on Alicia's arm, and gave Beth a piece of candy to distract her, which usually works. Recorder: Susan Smith

This is actually an amazing example of the power of the environment over subsequent behavior. Whether the person, or persons, being analyzed is a developmentally delayed resident in a treatment facility, part of a couple having marital problems, a world leader, or in a terrorist group, all humans emit behavior in response to events and situations within their environment. If we can discover the common antecedents and consequences associated with a specific type of behavior, then we can assume the same or highly similar behavior will occur in the future when the same or highly similar conditions are present.

In the case of Beth, given that there was a multitude of BAF entries similar to the two provided in Table 20-1, all you need to solve Beth's problem is in this table. This is what was happening, and fortunately Susan had volunteered to work with Beth.

The Clinical Analysis and Solution

When behavior occurs only during the evening in a facility, this is typically a shift schedule for staff. Given the vast majority of entries was made by Susan, who was there only for second shift and not on the weekends, it was clear that the behaviors occurred in the presence of Susan. Virtually no one wanted to interact with Beth, and people avoided her; Susan was the only means for Beth to receive hugs and candy. When it was apparent that Susan was present, the stage was set for severe aggressive behavior. Beth knew that her source of contact (hugs) and candy had now entered her living space. How would Beth receive the hugs and candy if Susan was present? Bite someone or become extremely aggressive! As a result, Susan would run over and give her hugs and candy to calm her down. Susan, with the best intentions, had actually inadvertently trained Beth to be aggressive over time by providing hugs and candy only when she was extremely aggressive.

We treated this behavior successfully by first explaining to Susan what was happening. She had no idea and actually wept when she understood that her best intentions had been causing the problem. We actually scheduled Susan to come in at different times of the day. When she came in she would immediately go to Beth and give her attention by catching her *being good*. If Beth started to become upset or aggressive, Susan would leave the room immediately. In other words, we changed hugs and candy to times when Beth was not aggressive and aggressive behavior would result in the loss of Susan. To make a long story short, the behavior totally disappeared over the next two treatment months, and after about six months Beth was transferred to a halfway house for community experiences. She was a totally different person. The environment had actually caused the problem. I might mention that if we could not have solved the problem, the next step was that the medical section had determined that all of her teeth would be pulled simply to protect other people.

Notice that if our objective was to predict behavior, we could have predicted Beth's imminent aggressive and dangerous behavior by watching for the primary antecedent — that is, the presence of Susan. This was my first realization that a treatment process used to alter a person's behavior could result in accurate prediction. Simply stated, the prediction of behavior was based on identifying the antecedent conditions that led to the behavior. Second, it was the consequence that maintained that behavior.

The basic clinical process used for Beth led to a number of successful treatments for seemingly intractable problems. The process developed followed these steps:

1. Define the problem behavior to influence/alter.

2. Complete observations and complete a BAF entry on each occasion of inappropriate behavior.

3. After collecting a significant number of BAF entries, analyze the content. Analysis consists of identifying the common events and situations that occurred prior to the behavior in the antecedent column of the BAF and common consequences as a result of the behavior.

4. Identify the antecedent and consequence events and situations that repeat across different examples of the behavior. These indicate which antecedents set the stage for the behavior to occur (for example, the presence of Susan the employee) and what consequences are maintaining the behavior and encouraging it to reoccur.

The clinical case example demonstrates just how local antecedents and consequences can be. In the case of Beth, the malicious behavior was totally a function of whatever clinical setting she was in at the time — that is, the building, the rooms in that building, the other individuals, the time of day, the presence of one staff member, and the common events and situations occurring within that environment. This was the world of influence for Beth; therefore, it was important to discover the antecedents and consequences influencing the occurrence and maintenance of Beth's very disruptive behavior in that environment.

Further Clinical Examples

We discovered many other examples of successful treatment, as well as many other examples of what was previously thought to be organic problems being rather a product of the institutionalized environment. Colleagues like Charles Antonelli and I worked so that entire cottages housing many scores of residents were reconstructed to provide environments that supported appropriate, adaptive behaviors as opposed to maladaptive and malicious behaviors. Treatments for attention-related disorders, life-threatening rumination resulting in the deaths of 4 percent of profoundly retarded individuals, and severely aggressive and self-injurious behavior were developed and published. You can refer to the following as examples of this type of work:

Jackson, G. M., & Eberly, D. A. (1982). Facilitation of performance on an arithmetic task as a result of application of a biofeedback procedure to suppress alpha wave activity. *Biofeedback and Self-Regulation*, 7(2), 211–221.

Using EEG biofeedback at a teaching machine and automated measures of non-attention and distractibility, we established antecedent conditions with a green light and audible counter. The light would come on only if alpha wave activity occurred — brain wave activity associated with a relaxed and even meditative state that is incompatible with attention to a task. The developmentally disabled individuals were simply told to keep the light on while working arithmetic tasks, and at the end of sessions, the number on the counter could be used to purchase items in the laboratory store. Results revealed that performance increased to the level of same-age peers who were not developmentally disabled when the light and counter conditions were present. Residents were capable of suppressing their own brain wave activity that competed with paying attention to the task.

Jackson, G. M. (1979). The use of visual orientation feedback to facilitate attention and task performance. *Mental Retardation*, 17(6), 281–284.

Similar to the EEG study, an adult resident at a work task within a workshop had a small green light placed in front of him and was instructed that when the green light was on, he would earn privileges. The green light was on when he was performing adequately at his task and turned off when he was distracted. Results indicated a dramatic improvement in on-task behavior when the green light condition was used.

Jackson, G. M., Johnson, C. R., Ackron, G. S., & Crowley, R. (1975). Food satiation as a procedure to decelerate vomiting. *American Journal of Mental Deficiency*, 80(2), 223–227.

It has been estimated that 4 percent of the profoundly developmentally disabled die from rumination. Rumination is the process of expelling and re-consuming food. With this population it occurs to such a severe degree that nutritional value from food is not maintained and the person loses so much weight that he or she dies from complicating health factors. Rumination had been treated for centuries, but this study discovered the environmental cause — not enough food at mealtime and no access to food at other times. The result is that the individuals in this lowest functioning group produce food the only way they can, by forcing up food that was swallowed, and then reconsuming it — and the cycle repeats. The frequency of this behavior can reach many times per minute. The treatment involves providing food to the point of satiation and a food supplement one hour after meals. The problem ceases immediately — the person gains weight and typically levels off at a more normal weight eventually with an absence of the problem.

Jackson, G. M., Schonfeld, L. I., & Griffith, K. (1984). A comparison of two behavioral treatments in decreasing the orofacial movement of tardive dyskinesia. *Biofeedback and Self-Regulation*, 8(4), 547–553.

Jackson, G. M., & Schonfeld, L. I. (1982). Comparisons of visual feedback, instructional prompts, and discreet, discrete prompting in the treatment of orofacial tardive dyskinesia. *International Journal of Behavioral Geriatrics*, 1(2), 35–46.

Orofacial tardive dyskinesia is a muscle control problem considered to be involuntary and irreversible and caused as a side effect of prolonged use of antipsychotic drugs. The problem exists as a tongue-chewing movement and can include strong thrusts of the tongue out of the mouth on a rapid basis. This work demonstrated that different behavior-based methods could be used to establish antecedents for sufferers that would prompt the suppression of the facial movements. When the prompting device was used to provide an audible alert through a noninvasive earphone, it was discovered that the movement could be suppressed. Over time the interval of time between audible alerts could be lengthened to the point that the suppressive behavior could be maintained without the prompts.

Jackson, G. M., & Patterson, R. L. (1982). Single case behavioral treatment. In R. L. Patterson, L. W. Dupree, D. A. Eberly, G. M. Jackson, M. J. O'Sullivan, L. A. Penner, & C. D. Kelly, *Overcoming deficits of aging*: *A behavioral approach*. New York: Plenum Press.

Jackson, G. M., & Patterson, R. L. (1982). Behavioral principles and techniques. In R. L. Patterson, L. W. Dupree, D. A. Eberly, G. M. Jackson, M. J. O'Sullivan, L. A. Penner, & C. D. Kelly, *Overcoming deficits of aging*: *A behavioral approach*. New York: Plenum Press.

Patterson, R. L., & Jackson, G. M. (1980). Behavior modification with the elderly. In M. Hersen, R. M. Eisler, & P. Miller (Eds.), *Progress in behavior modification*. Vol. 9. New York: Academic Press.

Patterson, R. L. & Jackson, G. M. (1981). Behavior approaches to gerontology. In L. Michelson, M. Hersen, & S. Turner (Eds.), *Future perspectives in behavior therapy*. New York: Plenum Press.

Using the concept of structuring an entire set of environments to influence behavior for the better, my colleagues and I structured an entire facility for a totally different clinical group — the aging with mental illness–related issues. The structuring of the clinical environment was an approach to alter environmental antecedents and consequences to encourage behaviors typically considered to be on irreversible declines with the elderly. Again, the work resulted in a book with behavioral treatment specifics that outlines the effectiveness of this approach.

These studies demonstrated that the environment in a facility for the elderly with mental illness–related problems could be structured in such a way as to strongly influence client's behavior. The use of behavior principles and the presentation of the behavior analysis form for this group were highlighted. We discovered and refined many treatments within this mental health research facility (Florida Mental Health Institute) associated with the University of South Florida–Tampa.

Moving Beyond the Clinical Setting to Expanded Environments: Automated Assist

The effects of behaviorally based methods applied in a multitude of treatment approaches across scores of different treatment domains internationally and documented in many hundreds of thousands of scientifically based clinical publications are irrefutable. Altering antecedents and consequences associated with human behavior results in planned behavioral change. This is the strong foundation of AuBA for prediction of future behavior.

Although the publications in the previous section are only samples of the work completed, they are listed to demonstrate the power of environmental antecedents on maladaptive, malicious, and inappropriate behavior. The foundation that began the development of automated behavior analysis was the demonstrated power of behavioral psychology approaches within relatively constrained environments. Beginning with influence as the major objective following variations of the steps provided in the earlier section of this chapter "The Clinical Analysis and Solution," my work progressed to prediction of malicious intent and behavior.

There would be many obstacles and challenges in extending forward-leaning, behavioral-based treatment development that had as its primary goal the influence and change of behavior to the proven capability of new methods to predict future behavior. In short, the methods of treatment are related to, but do not lead to, actual validated prediction capability. Second, the treatment environments, although very different, are all constrained. Developing expanded methods of influence to include prediction of future behavior on the basis of expanded environments, including on a global basis, required new methods and procedures.

What are expanded environments? For the most part, typical clinical approaches comprise environments like schools, treatment facilities, prisons, businesses, or organizations bounded by *bricks and mortar*. For rather obvious reasons, treatment approaches that work in a clinical setting do not extend well to cyber space, global variables found worldwide, political contexts, perceived U.S. occupation of foreign lands, and economic variables operating within and across countries worldwide. The expansive contexts worldwide support fluctuating values of gold and oil, and stock markets. I have maintained that all expanded areas are a product of human behavior, just as areas in clinical settings are. The scope of the problems to analyze, the potential for relevant antecedents and consequences that affect target behaviors, and the methods and tools all must operate with expanded technology.

It is clear that after focusing on the development of the methods and tools for these expanded environments specifically as they relate to asymmetric warfare such as terrorism, network hacking, criminal behavior, and so on that behavioral principles are very much relevant — they just have to be used in an expanded mode.

How do we move from antecedent and consequence identification and behavior influence in clinical and constrained environments to prediction of asymmetric and criminal behavior in expanded environments? The following are the steps required:

1. Given that direct observation is not possible, gather select documents such as past news articles describing past events in which the types of behavior you need to predict are described along with the who, what, where, when, and how of each event.

2. Using a database divided into antecedent and consequence candidate sections along with description of the actual behavior of interest (an electronic version of the manual BAF), sort by the behavior type and identify common antecedents and consequences associated with each type of behavior.

3. Create a data array with extracted antecedents (columns) by specific behavior examples (rows) and populate the data array with a 1 in a cell that means that the antecedent in that column is present for the example on that row. If the antecedent is not present for that example, then the cell is populated with a 0.

4. At the end of each array, add output columns, which are the behavior types to predict — enter a 1 in the outcome class that occurred for the example in that row, or 0 if that outcome did not occur for the example for that row. For example, if there are two outcome classes, like threat and no threat, then one would receive a 1 and one would receive a 0.

5. Subject the completed data array to pattern classification (see the accompanying DVD), and validate prediction using k-fold cross-validation.

6. Once validated, the pattern classifier may be used for prediction by entering a vector of all antecedents present at one time with a series of 1s and 0s in which a 1 indicates that specific antecedent is present now and a 0 indicates that specific antecedent is not present. For example, if 40 antecedents had been extracted and are being used in the model, then a series of 40 1s and 0s would be used as input, and the classifier's output that is the highest numerically (threat or no threat) is the prediction.

Full Automation of the Prediction of Human Behavior: Automated Behavior Analysis

To this point in the chapter, two approaches have been presented:

1. A proven clinical method based on direct observation of individuals by recording examples of behavior to influence using the BAF

2. An extending of the clinical examples to prediction of human behavior on an extended environments basis that can include asymmetric warfare examples such as terrorism, criminal behavior, and cyber threat using automated assists from computer science such as pattern classification

Although the second method moved away from clinical examples to significant threat facing security across a wide variety of threat domains, and although automated assists were developed to aid prediction, the process was still time-consuming.

In many discussions with analysts across commercial and government military and intelligence settings, including my experience as a Research Psychologist within the U.S. Secret Service and as an Intelligence Officer within the CIA, my insistence on finalizing methods and tools that capture the cognitive processes of trained prediction specialists working with the new methods described was imperative.

Beginning with the clinical cases represented by Beth, the path to automated prediction of malicious behavior was clear — by combining the best of outside-the-envelope behavioral science with the best of advanced computer science pattern classification/artificial neural networks, it has been possible to automate the entire predictive process.

My analogy for building this complex automation was the television set. When a viewer turns on the television and the magic of the electronic waves being transmitted are converted to televised programs, the viewer doesn't ask how the television works. The results are real, accurate, and reliable, and the television is accepted as a tool of current-day communication. Similarly, automated behavior analysis (AuBA) had to be so effective in automating this new fusion of behavioral and computer sciences that when the process was used to develop sophisticated models, the effectiveness would be realized and recognized.

It is not easy to describe all of the inner workings of the technology. This book is the first attempt to do so. However, there is a difference in my chosen analogy and AuBA. When we turn on the television set, it is rare indeed that it malfunctions. The TV is a miracle of modern technology. It works, and it works well every time. It brings the world and current events to our eyes and ears as they unfold. We see wars in real time. We see terrorist attacks in real time, and we all watched as the 9/11 attack brought down the World Trade Center buildings as they actually collapsed. With such perfection of technology, we do not need to understand how the TV works — just keep the programs coming uninterrupted!

However, the prediction of human behavior can never be as reliable as turning on the TV and receiving exactly the presentation requested. Human behavior is adaptive and exceedingly complex. Once antecedents are identified that influence the occurrence of behavior and once the consequences are identified that maintain the behavior, then we can speak of the probabilities of occurrence of future behavior, but not certainty. In many AuBA applications, we tend to achieve prediction in the 80–90 percent true positive and 80-90 percent true negative ranges. These are impressive accuracy rates, but not 100 percent. However, as I have noted earlier in this book, they far exceed the physical sciences capability to predict such dynamic (complex and ever-changing) physical phenomena such as tsunamis, volcanic eruptions, earthquakes, weather, hurricane paths, and tornados. In fact, many of these phenomena remain essentially unpredictable.

Moving from a coin flip, or a 50–50 chance of predicting future events, to 80–90 percent is significant improvement, and this is an increase that can be relied on to serve as a foundation for a security paradigm shift. It is an accuracy rate that can move us from a reactive approach in which we wait for an attack to occur before we react to a new approach that can reliably anticipate an attack. Accurate anticipation allows us to have in place adequate countermeasures to prevent the effects of an attack, whether conventional or cyber based.

The automation component of true AuBA allows us to construct predictive models that result in predictive engines that can process input variables and produce a predictive output within 50 microseconds. To show the continued progression from clinical analysis, to automated assist of asymmetric examples within expanded and global environments, to AuBA full automation, the following steps are now possible and are the basis for the first patent on the tools and methods for the automation of the prediction of human behavior.

1. Collect multiple documents for each example behavior to be predicted across multiple incidents.

2. Submit the unstructured corpus (all documents) to the AuBA ThemeMate tool that will process all documents and automatically extract antecedent candidates emulating exactly the human cognitive process used to identify relevant antecedents except in more detail (more antecedents) and orders of magnitude faster.

3. Once antecedent candidates are automatically extracted, ThemeMate constructs and populates the data array that has antecedents as columns and examples of behavior as rows and populates the 1s and 0s across all cells in the array in approximately 1/2 second.

4. The data array is then presented to the second AuBA tool, AutoAnalyzer, which automatically constructs and optimizes a specialized artificial neural network pattern classifier that is validated using best practices cross-validation methodology (k-fold, Leaving-One-Out).

5. As part of the validation process, the number of antecedent candidates is reduced to the most predictive set, or the true antecedents. This reduction can be significant and can convert 200+ candidates to 30 or 40 actual antecedents.

6. Once validated, the predictive engine can be removed and placed into a predictive application or the predictive engine can be used within AutoAnalyzer. In either case, one enters the actual presence or absence of antecedents that remained as part of the validation process, and the predictive engine returns that actual prediction.

7. To be used for influence determination, any possible combination of antecedents can be entered to determine "what ifs," or what the modeled entity is likely to do under that set of presented antecedents.

If you compare the clinical, automated-assist, and AuBA steps, the progression in technology is apparent. True, fully automated AuBA is a more complex set of methods and requires automated tools that had to be developed to achieve the quality of prediction necessary. The ThemeMate tool can process documents in any language once it has been set for that language, and the automated identification exceeds human extraction in both detail and speed.

Table 20-2 shows a comparison of all three methods that are all relevant for their specific purposes. The progression of technology is apparent.

Table 20-2: A Comparison of the Different Methods, Ranging from Clinical Analysis to Current AuBA

FEATURE	CLINICAL METHOD	AUBA AUTO-ASSIST	FULLY AUTOMATED AUBA
Observation	Direct observation with a BAF entry completed for each example of behavior to change.	Collect documents such as news articles describing each example of behavior to predict in detail, including context. Place in database records as electronic BAF.	Collect documents such as news articles *in any language* describing each example of behavior to predict in detail, including context.
Identify and extract relevant antecedent candidates	Using BAF forms, read across all forms and manually select common events and situations that precede behaviors to change.	Use manual sorting process to identify relevant antecedents from database.	Use AuBA ThemeMate to process all documents at once to identify and extract all relevant antecedents.
Construct data array	NA	Use manual method of creating data array with antecedent candidates as columns and examples of behavior as rows. Add outcomes to predict as additional columns and populate with 1s and 0s.	ThemeMate automatically completes data array and populates the array with 1s and 0s with no errors and adds additional output columns.
Develop and validate predictive engine	Assumes that extracted common antecedents across case examples will be part of modification within a constrained environment to change behavior.	Submit completed data array to pattern classification by creating Leaving-One-Out training and test files for neural network and optimize.	Submit completed data array to AutoAnalyzer that automatically creates an optimized pattern classifier and automatically validates to achieve highest probability of behavior prediction.

The progression of AuBA does not mean that the current automated tools and methods replace past methods. Rather, AuBA is used for different purposes. For example, if the AuBASME process is used whereby examples of past events are replaced by subject matter expertise–developed scenarios with highly likely antecedents, then the AuBA Auto-Assist method is preferable. In this case, the data array is manually developed, and ThemeMate is not used to process past documents describing malicious behavior. In some cases, particularly if the target for the analysis is an individual, elements of applied behavior analysis are used along with AuBA. Currently, because of the work over the past decades with malicious behavior on a global basis, I believe that we now have a number of tools in our arsenal. We can now determine characteristics of people behind digital information they have created. However, if rapid and accurate predictive modeling is required, then fully automated AuBA is the way to go.

Walking Through the AuBA Methodology

This section walks you through the AuBA methodology and use of the automated tools to enhance the modeling process. To summarize capabilities of the software before the walkthrough is presented, I ask you to consider the following key points:

- Early applied behavior analysis model in operant psychology demonstrated that behavior occurs in response to environmental antecedents and is maintained by consequences of the behavior.

- Early psychology model was not capable of validated prediction or application to asymmetric and operational environments.

- The patented AuBA technology presents prediction, influence, pattern classification, and automated analysis within operational environments.

- AuBA is the only automation and extension of applied behavior analysis.

- Current AuBA tools have automated much of the day-to-day data extraction and modeling tasks, pointing analysts to salient features of a problem and leaving time for analysts to conduct more advanced analysis and synthesis of findings.

- AuBA technology has now been developed to use text, network packets, and physical sensor data as input into predictive applications.

Figure 20-1 depicts the AuBA process, both in words and pictorially, to show the flow of major steps. Although there are many nuances to each step in the process, the sequences are now straightforward: Text as input ➤ ThemeMate ➤ Data Array ➤ AutoAnalyzer ➤ Prediction and Influence. For the walkthrough presented here, we will follow these major steps, providing some of the nuances required to model correctly. In the accompanying DVD, the use of the tools and the outputs will be shown in video clips with voiceover to describe the process in more detail.

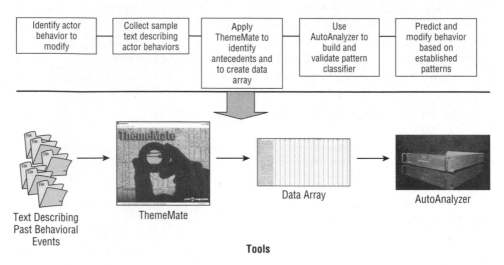

Figure 20-1: The AuBA methodology as a process

Text as Input

One of the key advantages of AuBA is that direct observation required in applied behavior analysis has been replaced by textual accounts of a target's past behaviors of interest. This was a result not of preference but more of necessity. Those who exhibit malicious behavior targeting our country simply are not available for observation. Osama bin Laden is perhaps the best example. He was not observed for over 10 years. However, we had many accounts of al-Qaeda behavior in described media articles and a number of declarations, statements, speeches, and published fatwas (declarations of war). The text produced by the target, summaries of past attacks, and news articles describing past behaviors can be combined into a common text corpus to be processed with the AuBA tools.

I want to stress that the AuBA process is not a statistical process — it is behavioral. Typically if we were conducting a statistical approach, we would want the documents selected to be representative of the base rate of the malicious behavior being modeled. For example, if we had selected a malicious group that had engaged in 80 percent assault and 20 percent bombings, then we would want examples randomly selected in a similar proportion to be representative. AuBA does not work that way, nor does accurate prediction.

AuBA is based on identifying the antecedents associated with specific types of behavior. Therefore, if we were modeling assault and bombing, we would want equal numbers of both examples. Matching the base rate of occurrence of both types of incidents is meaningless when we are trying to identify the antecedents. If we simply used the base rates, we would say that there is an 80 percent probability that the next incident will be an assault. AuBA, instead, would look at three classes of behavior and would want documents equally distributed across all three. Although we have talked about assault and bombing, we have to have examples of behavior of the group that are non-attack related. This allows AuBA to predict whether an assault, bombing, or non-attack is going to be imminent based on the nature of the antecedents that are present at any one time.

> **NOTE** We call the non-attack examples *nons*.

The antecedent-behavior connection is far superior to looking only at the behavior. Given that so much data exists within the world of behavioral psychology to demonstrate the power of precursor antecedents on following behavior and the power of consequences to maintain or decrease the probability of occurrence of future behavior, we know we are on solid ground using this approach for AuBA. However, unless we also add nons, we cannot accurately predict if it is time for an attack or non-attack.

For obvious reasons, it is important to select text examples of past malicious and non-malicious behaviors. This is almost always possible to accomplish. You might ask, "How do I find nons when I am modeling an aggressive adversary having the goal of killing Americans?" Though terrorist groups typically see themselves as in a war with us as the enemy, they do still engage in other behaviors that are not focused on attacking the United States. For example, Hezbollah is known for constructing schools and engaging in other similar projects even while they also attack Israeli and U.S. targets with a true vengeance. Usually, finding nons is not an issue.

Furthermore, for ThemeMate to process the corpus of documents collected, articles must be in separate files with unique names. We typically use the data of the behavior as the incident number. If there is more than one incident in one day, as in the 9/11 attack, then the names of the files might be 091101a (World Trade Center), 091101b (Pentagon), and 091101c (Pennsylvania). It is also useful to include other articles on the same incident within the same file. For example, 10 articles on the World Trade Center for the 9/11 attack would all be attached and placed in the same 091101a file. This allows for a more robust extraction of data.

Last, all documents must be in plain text format. If documents collected are in different formats such as `.pdf` or `.doc`, it is easy to open the document and save as `.txt` format. Therefore, a description of the World Trade Center attack might be in a document format (`.doc`), and when it is opened and saved as text, a copy is made that will be `091101a.txt`. To put multiple text documents in the same file, just copy and paste each article at the end of the other examples within the same file. We actually use a utility that can covert essentially any Microsoft format to a text format. There are many such utilities available.

The selection of articles to present to ThemeMate is the most important point where we can manage the modeling process. Determining the types of articles is very important. If there are many articles available and many possible outcomes (assault, hijacking, roadside bombing, suicide bombing, and kidnapping), it might be wise to have two predictive engines. The first simply predicts attack or non-attack, and the second predicts the specific type of attack and is used only if the first engine predicts attack.

NOTE I am establishing a website (`pre-threat.com`) to share detailed information should users wish to ask questions while in the process of using any form of AuBA modeling presented in this book.

Processing the Text Corpus of Your Choice with ThemeMate

The accompanying DVD will demonstrate how to use the ThemeMate application in video clips in the process of conducting an actual analysis and creation of the essential data array. In this section, I describe a key component of ThemeMate, the Tools menu. For example, if you want a data array that is necessary for actual prediction of malicious behavior, you must fulfill two requirements:

1. You must have multiple documents in the corpus and not just one document for summarization.

2. You must select the Statistics option from the Tools menu, as shown in Figure 20-2.

The ThemeMate product interface panel is focused on providing users a rapid means by which to analyze text documents, and the initial processing scenario starts with the selection of a feature from the Tools drop-down menu on the window menu toolbar. Tools available include the following:

■ **Theme Index:** This feature tool produces extracted key themes as antecedent candidates. Each extracted theme is hyperlinked to all sentences contributing to a theme. These sentences are placed under the theme to show the evidence for the creation of that theme.

Figure 20-3 depicts a single theme from more than 100 extracted themes. Each extracted theme is characterized by a single word-pair. Every sentence placed under that theme contains that word-pair. Although the automated process to place a sentence under a theme is far more sophisticated than the process to create a theme containing a word-pair, we use that single pair just as a shorthand index term. This particular processing of a cyber-attack-based corpus of 150 separate documents took 2 minutes to run and produced over 100 antecedent candidates and created the data array for predictive analysis in less than 1/2 second. In the past, using AuBA automated assist, this entire process would have taken weeks. It would take about 2–3 days just to create the data array.

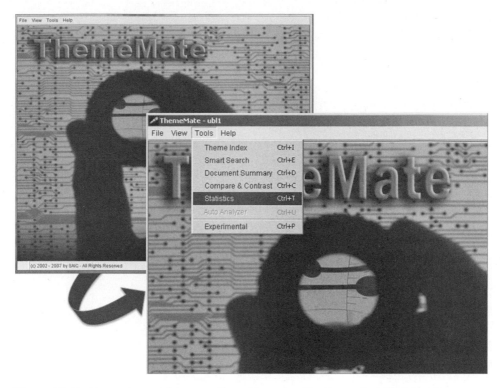

Figure 20-2: To produce a data array for pattern classification, select Statistics from the Tools drop-down menu.

- **Theme Components:** This feature produces theme-based keyword search terms for use with existing Internet search engines. Every extracted theme produces a key set of terms that, if clicked, will result in an automated Internet search. The same or highly similar documents will be identified. This can be especially useful in interactively building a larger and more robust corpus or in searching for analytical clues.

- **Document Summary:** This tool provides summarization of original text. It returns the most important sentences in a single document or across all documents if multiple documents are processed. When compared to humans who have been asked to identify the most important sentences in a document, ThemeMate identification and human identification of the most important sentences in a corpus are often identical. This feature works equally well with English or Arabic.

NOTE Given that it takes just two weeks to prepare ThemeMate for a new language, the fact that it can return the most important sentences can save extensive amounts of translation time — the translator can just translate the *important* information returned, and not a whole corpus to determine what is important.

T1 Theme # 1 (occurring 16222 cumulative times)
remote-attackers

	and 7 on Windows Server 2008 allows remote attackers to execute arbitrary
	remote attackers to execute arbitrary SQL commands via the txtName
	allow remote attackers to upload files to arbitrary directories via
	Communication Manager 3.1.x, allow remote attackers to obtain (1)
	Pro 0.0.7 allows remote attackers to execute arbitrary PHP code by
	remote attackers to execute arbitrary SQL commands via the id_document
	versions, allow remote attackers to execute arbitrary code via long
	Links 1.3 and earlier allows remote attackers to execute arbitrary SQL
	versions, allows remote attackers to execute arbitrary code via a DivX
	6.3 before SP2 allow remote attackers to execute arbitrary code via a
	Ghostscript 8.64, and probably earlier versions, allows remote attackers
	allows remote attackers to include and execute arbitrary files via a ..
	remote attackers to execute arbitrary SQL commands via the
	media files, which allows remote attackers to execute arbitrary code via a
	SP3; allows remote attackers to execute arbitrary code via a crafted Word
	an unspecified string, which allows remote attackers to execute arbitrary
	the Excel spreadsheet file format, which allows remote attackers to
	allows remote attackers to execute arbitrary code via a crafted Word 97
	document, which allows remote attackers to execute arbitrary code via
	allows remote attackers to execute arbitrary code via a web page that
	and SP1, and 7 on Windows Server 2008 allows remote attackers to execute
	Gateway (IAG) before 3.7 SP2, allow remote attackers to execute arbitrary
	allows remote attackers to cause a denial of service (application crash)

Figure 20-3: A sample theme of more than 100 extracted by ThemeMate after processing a large corpus of text articles describing recent cyber attacks against networks

- **Compare and Contrast:** This feature provides side-by-side Theme Index reports for either two different documents or two separate sets of documents for the purpose of rapid identification of similarities and differences. This is particularly useful to determine if key themes have shifted in a location over time. This change detection can be useful for sentiment analysis, detection of new trends over time, and key changes in antecedents that affect malicious behavior. For example, if you want to identify trends across time for a specific location, such as Israel, then documents for week 1 can be compared to documents in week 2. The extracted themes would be similar if little change occurred, and should be very different if change is occurring across the two-week period.

- **Statistics:** This feature provides a numerical output data array that has extracted themes (antecedents) as columns and examples of behaviors in files as rows. The array may be used for detailed analyses conducted with such commercial off-the-shelf applications as SPSS, SAS, and AuBA AutoAnalyzer.

- **Focused Search:** This may be one of ThemeMate's key features. ThemeMate can process a corpus of text documents in two ways: in a non-constrained manner to identify all relevant predictive antecedent theme candidates across all of the documents or to identify key themes of a very specific type of predictive model. For example, in the case of the former, we would have a data array that contains all relevant themes across the corpus. However, if we entered the following words in the focused search section, we would obtain only themes relevant to phishing attacks: phish, phishing, spear phishing. In this way, we can create many predictive models ranging from a general predictive model to highly specialized models.

Once you have completed the ThemeMate process, you can pare it down from antecedent candidates to the most likely predictive antecedents (this will be demonstrated in the accompanying DVD). Once you have the finalized data array, you submit the array to the second AuBA tool — AutoAnalyzer.

Generating a Predictive Engine with AutoAnalyzer

If you review Figure 20-1, the AuBA process, you can see that the completed data array generated by ThemeMate can be submitted to AutoAnalyzer. This application, AutoAnalyzer, is 100 percent automated. Simply submit the data array and click on start. The process is initiated, and at the end you will be presented with a predictive engine that may be used for optimized prediction of future behavior.

As an automated pattern classification model generator, AutoAnalyzer processes the data array prepared by ThemeMate and reduces the set of antecedent candidates to the most relevant events and situations serving as antecedent predictors for defined outcomes. The application then constructs back propagation network (BPN) pattern classifiers and validates each model using the best practices Leaving-One-Out (L-1) method of cross-validation or other form of k-fold validation if the number of cases is large. All weighting is accomplished automatically during the pattern classification construction process.

For each developed model, the true positive, true negative, false positive, and false negative rates are presented. In addition, a Fisher's exact statistical significance test is automatically calculated on the blind testing results. The Fisher's exact test presents the probability that results obtained could have occurred by chance. Therefore, the lower the Fisher's exact statistic, the more confident we can be in the results. This process is completed for the model that demonstrates the highest accuracy rate, lowest error rate, and best Fisher's exact statistic with the end result of this best model being presented for use.

The tested and reduced antecedent themes may be used for prediction by entering a vector of 1s and 0s representing which antecedents are present and absent for a given day, respectively, or various vectors with different combinations of antecedents may be presented to determine likely behavior under a range of conditions. Developed models have been validated across terrorist groups, specific behavior of an individual terrorist; chemical, biological, radiological, and nuclear (CBRN) threat; corporate espionage; and network hacker behavior, tracking, and locating.

ThemeMate results, including the data array, are offered as different user-selected reports. The reports are detailed, presenting the end result of analysis. AutoAnalyzer presents results with a graph that shows the accuracy of the presented model when tested on blind cases. Figure 20-4 depicts one example (more are shown on the DVD). In this screen shot, AutoAnalyzer presents the result of the Leaving-One-Out validation process — in other words, how good the model is at predicting the outcomes of blind cases when presented with the antecedents that are present at a given time. The ThemeMate and AutoAnalyzer combination provides precise feedback to the user on the functioning of the newly developed model.

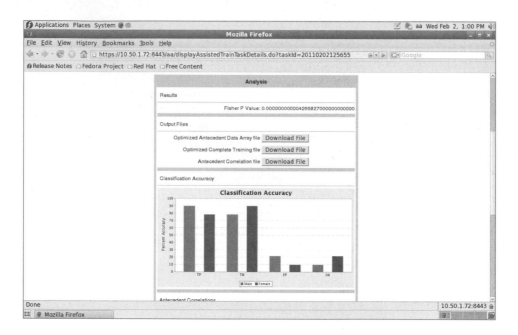

Figure 20-4: The AutoAnalyzer output showing the accuracy rates for the automatically generated optimized model as tested on blind cases

The figure shows the true postive and true negative accuracy rates and the corresponding false positive and false negative error rates. This particular model was used to predict gender by using antecedents observed in a virtual world (see Chapter 12). The true positive (a specific real-world gender was predicted from avatar observation only and the gender was correct) is that gender was predicted and the actual gender matched, and the true negative was that the application predicted that the gender was not a specific gender and it was not that gender. These are hits and represent correct calls. As you can see, the accuracy rates are in the 80–90 percent range. One way to think of the false positive and false negative rates is that each is 1 – the appropriate complementary accuracy rate. For example, a false positive is 1 – true negative, and a false negative is 1 – true positive. Therefore, the true positive + false negative rates must add to 1.0, and the true negative + false positive rates must add to 1.0.

Also, notice the Fisher's exact significance test result. Remember the lower the better, and it must be less than 0.05, or less than 5 chances in 100 that the results could have been achieved by chance. See how low the Fisher's exact significance test result is here.

THE INTERNAL WORKING OF AUTOANALYZER

An artificial neural network, specifically a back propagation network (BPN), under the control of a computer instructions program that automates the flow of data and files, processes the data from the ThemeMate-produced data array. This process uses the antecedent candidates (themes) as indicators and the outcomes to predict as output. By using Leaving-One-Out cross-validation, the program can determine the predictive accuracy of the best performing BPN in predicting blind cases. It is important to note that any form of pattern classification may provide acceptable results. However, in my extensive experience comparing methods at this stage, the BPN appears to provide the best accuracy results consistently across all applications.

Results of the neural training/testing are then used to reduce the original antecedent set to the most predictive antecedents to achieve the highest predictive accuracy. The optimization process configures different neural network parameters as the BPNs train using the provided sample data set. The training is based on extracting the best patterns existing between the input and the output by training on all cases but one and testing the derived network against the indicators of the unknown case. Then the process repeats by replacing the test case and extracting a new unknown for repeated training and a single unknown test. Once all cases have been trained and tested, overall accuracy against blind tests is calculated and the entire process is repeated with a new neural network configuration. The overall accuracy results are sorted by highest accuracy. The configuration resulting in the highest accuracy is the BPN determined to be the configuration most suitable for prediction.

By creating a vector of any given time in which an antecedent is present (1) or absent (0) for each antecedent in the model, and then by submitting that vector to the trained BPN, you will get an end result that is the output of the BPN — which is the prediction.

Continued

THE INTERNAL WORKING OF AUTOANALYZER (*continued*)

The BPN is a very impressive pattern classifier. If we overtrain it on facial features, then we would have a biometric application that could possibly recognize a face in the crowd. This overtraining, although suitable for exact match facial recognition, is not suitable for prediction of future behavior. Why? Because we are not seeking exact matches of antecedents as they have been related to past behaviors. Human behavior does not repeat itself exactly; it does not always look the same (whereas a person's face more or less does). The key to prediction of human behavior is a methodology that works by projecting highly similar behavior that has occurred in highly similar antecedents and consequences in the past. Human behavior is rife with variation, but within limits.

Over the course of 25 years, I have learned heuristics that inform the learning process of the BPN to stop it from learning before it is overtrained. Instead, the halting of the learning process results in a BPN that is optimized for prediction of human behavior. These heuristics are embedded in AutoAnalyzer and act by controlling the BPN learning process to stop it at the optimal moment for accurate prediction.

Once the AutoAnalyzer process is completed, we have a predictive engine that has been completed 400 times faster than the former automated-assist method, and represents accurate prediction of malicious behavior.

Advantages of AuBA #20: Final Thoughts

This is the last chapter of *Predicting Malicious Behavior: Tools and Techniques for Ensuring Global Security*. I have attempted to demonstrate that future malicious behavior in the areas of cyber threat, terrorism, criminal behavior, and other forms of severe malicious behavior is not only possible but a reality. The technology is currently here to conduct a paradigm shift in such areas as cyber threat with such AuBA applications as CheckMate and InMate. Simultaneously, the AuBA constructs, methods, and tools such as ThemeMate and AutoAnalyzer provide a new approach to developing predictive engines that can be placed with applications. I have presented methods for extracting key antecedents and consequences from historical cases or as an alternative method, the extraction of key data from subject matter expertise to present predictive models.

The book has presented a very powerful concept — that is, the reliable prediction of future behavior over time cannot result from simply studying behavior, regardless of the sophistication of statistical methods applied. The prediction of future behavior is the result of identifying the precursor antecedents that set the stage for the behavior to occur and the consequences of the behavior that determine if behavior will increase or decrease in the future. Furthermore, if we wish to predict behavior in the future, then we must use pattern classification to identify the complex interaction of antecedents and subsequent behavior.

Several methods of developing predictive engines were presented, all based on AuBA concepts. If we use all available advanced AuBA tools (ThemeMate and AutoAnalyzer), we can then develop optimized predictive models 400 times faster, with fewer errors, and that, for the most part, remove bias, as compared to manual or automated-assist methods presented.

Most important, when we realize that malicious behavior can best be determined by identifying preceding antecedents and successful consequences, then we can better anticipate adversary malicious behavior, even without constructing full AuBA predictive models. AuBA is a way of viewing malicious behavior in the world that confronts us on a daily basis. By following the processes, concepts, and methods in this book, you will gain far better insight into the darker side of life — and what its next move might be.

Many malicious behaviors are not the result of organic problems. They simply exist because antecedent conditions set the stage for their occurrence and then successful consequences that follow simply strengthen the occurrence of the behavior under those conditions. Therefore, when those conditions occur again in the future, we can expect the behavior to occur yet again. If we wish to influence behavior, we can test what would happen if we enter a set of different antecedent conditions to the model and see how the targeted entity would react. If we can make those antecedents happen, then we are likely to see the behavior occur.

In Summary

This chapter completes the written part of this book. However, I strongly recommend viewing the accompanying DVD. This DVD will show actual examples of using the tools to construct a predictive model. Furthermore, the DVD will show sample AuBA products working. If you have read this book in its entirety, then you will be armed with new concepts, methods, and perhaps even tools to analyze and predict malicious behavior. If you have questions about the book, presented methodology, applications, or tools, as well as behavioral approaches to predict malicious behavior, you can visit my website: `prethreat.com`. I will maintain the site in support of this book to support dialogue about the book, to answer questions, and to highlight advancements with AuBA tools and applications as they occur and are released.

We now have an approach that can support a paradigm shift in security. Security should not be reactive, although that will always be necessary. Instead, it should be reactive *and* proactive. There will always be those occasions that we simply could not predict and security response is a necessity. However, the concepts and methods presented in this book demonstrate that it is now possible to predict malicious behavior before it occurs so that we can have countermeasures in place when it occurs.

What's on the DVD?

This appendix provides you with information on the contents of the DVD that accompanies this book. For the latest and greatest information, please refer to the ReadMe file located at the root of the DVD. Here is what you will find:

- System Requirements
- Using the DVD
- What's on the DVD

If you are reading this in an electronic format, please go to `http://booksupport.wiley.com` for access to the additional content.

System Requirements

You can watch the videos on this DVD from any computer with a compatible DVD-ROM drive, but if you want to use the software discussed in this book, your computer will need to meet the following requirements:

- The DVD contains information on both AuBA tools and sample applications. The purpose of the DVD is to demonstrate the use of the tools in constructing predictive models and a sample of applications to provide the look and feel of AuBA applications. Although the DVD contains no code, the AuBA tools are available through SAIC. The ThemeMate and

AutoAnalyzer tools operate on a Windows-based operating system and typical tabletop PC or laptop.

- PC running Windows 98 or later
- An Internet connection with an Internet browser such as Internet Explorer and the Google search engine
- A DVD-ROM drive

Note: Videos on the DVD are viewable only from within the interface.

Using the DVD

To access the content from the DVD, follow these steps.

1. Insert the DVD into your computer's DVD-ROM drive. The license agreement appears.

   Note: The interface won't launch if you have autorun disabled. In that case, click Start ➤ Run (For Windows Vista, Start ➤ All Programs ➤ Accessories ➤ Run). In the dialog box that appears, type D:\Start.exe. (Replace D with the proper letter if your DVD drive uses a different letter. If you don't know the letter, see how your DVD drive is listed under My Computer.) Click OK.

2. Read through the license agreement, and then click the Accept button if you want to use the DVD.

   The DVD interface appears. The interface allows you to run the content with just a click of a button (or two).

What's on the DVD

This DVD is a practical *how-to* DVD that shows you through instructional videos how the automated behavior analysis (AuBA) tools work and how you can use them. The DVD for the book is divided into two sections:

1. Details in the use of the AuBA tools, ThemeMate and AutoAnalyzer
2. Demonstrations of CheckMate and InMate, two cyber-based, network protection tools designed to protect networks from external and internal threat, respectively, that were constructed using AuBA

By watching the videos on this instructional DVD, you will be presented with the details of how to conduct AuBA predictive modeling for the prediction of human behavior and with a walkthrough of new technology for network protection that is not signature based or anomaly based. These two applications convert packet-level activity in real time to assessments of human behavior threat and presence of malicious intent.

Customer Care

If you have trouble with the DVD, please call the Wiley Product Technical Support phone number at (800) 762-2974. Outside the United States, call 1(317) 572-3994. You can also contact Wiley Product Technical Support at `http://support.wiley.com`. John Wiley & Sons will provide technical support only for installation and other general quality control items. For technical support on the applications themselves, consult the program's vendor or author.

To place additional orders or to request information about other Wiley products, please call (877) 762-2974.

Index

John Wiley & Sons, Inc. End-User License Agreement